Business Ethics in Canada

SECOND EDITION

EDITED BY

Deborah C. Poff & Wilfrid J. Waluchow

Prentice-Hall Canada Inc., Scarborough, Ontario

To Alex and Gail
with love and appreciation

Canadian Cataloguing in Publication Data

Main entry under title:
  Business ethics in Canada

2nd ed.
Includes bibliographical references and index.
ISBN 0-13-092396-6

1. Business ethics. 2. Business ethics – Case studies.
I. Poff, Deborah C. (Deborah Charmaine), 1950–
II. Waluchow, Wilfred J., 1953–

HF5387.B88 1991   174'.4'0971   C90-095736-0

© 1991 Prentice-Hall Canada Inc., Scarborough, Ontario

Prentice-Hall, Inc., *Englewood Cliffs*, *New Jersey*
Prentice-Hall International, Inc., *London*
Prentice-Hall of Australia, Pty., Ltd., *Sydney*
Prentice-Hall of India Pvt., Ltd., *New Delhi*
Prentice-Hall of Japan, Inc., *Tokyo*
Prentice-Hall of Southeast Asia (Pte.) Ltd., *Singapore*
Editora Prentice-Hall do Brasil Ltda., *Rio de Janeiro*
Prentice-Hall Hispanoamericana, S.A., *Mexico*

ISBN 0-13-092396-6

Production Editor: Amy Lui-Ma
Copy Editors: Catherine Leatherdale   Mary Beth Leatherdale
Production Coordinator: Anna Orodi
Cover Design: Greg Dorosh
Typesetting: Colborne, Cox and Burns

98 97 96   RRD 10 9 8 7 6 5 4

Printed and bound in the United States of America by RR Donnelley
and Sons

Contents

Acknowledgements

We would like to take this opportunity to thank Reidel Publishing Company. As with the first edition of this text, they have generously waived all reprint fees of the articles which first appeared in the Journal of Business Ethics. We would also like to thank the staff of the Institute for the Study of Women, Mount St. Vincent University for their hard work over the past year, especially Susan Marsh who worked on the much improved index in this edition.

Deborah C. Poff
Wilfrid J. Waluchow

I would further like to thank my husband, Alex Michalos, for his love and support.
D.C.P.

INTRODUCTION

Ethical Theory in Business

WILFRID J. WALUCHOW

MORAL PHILOSOPHY

Contrary to a popular slogan, the phrase "business ethics" is not a contradiction in terms. Decision-making in business has and always will have a moral dimension, just as it does in medicine, government, the professions, and life in general. It is possible to conduct business in an ethical manner, and so questions concerning the ethics of business — i.e. business ethics — are significant. The interests of business people and moral philosophers do converge.

If the interests of business people and moral philosophers or "ethicists" converge, then what are their respective roles? Moral philosophers are not moral experts, capable of providing ready-made answers when difficult or intransigent moral conflicts arise in business. Rather, they perform more modest tasks: clarifying the terms of moral debate; scrutinizing distinctions to see if they stand up to rational examination; assessing the validity and cogency of arguments; and examining the fit between moral principles and moral practice.

Moral philosophers also will defend their own moral theories and convictions, particularly when they detect unwarranted, dogmatic beliefs in business practice or the theories proposed by other moral philosophers. But a student unaccustomed to the ways of the moral philosopher might find his or her arguments a trifle strange. The moral philosopher often will seek to defend or justify the obvious — e.g. that it is morally wrong to deceive a client intentionally about the dangerous defects hidden in one's product, or that it is wrong knowingly to dump deadly toxins into a community's water supply. At other times, the moral philosopher will offer arguments which question the obvious. He might even try to defend a position that seems patently false to many or most people — e.g. that it

1

is morally questionable to use one's good looks to attract customers, or that wining and dining clients is morally wrong.

The moral philosopher's chief motivation for defending *or* questioning the obvious is expressed in a maxim propounded by the ancient Greek philosopher Socrates: *the unexamined life is not worth living*. Socrates and other moral philosophers want to know *why* we should believe the things we do, even those things we firmly and passionately believe to be true. Many of our moral beliefs just seem right to us. We've never had occasion to question them or to ask ourselves why we hold them. If pushed to articulate the *grounds* or *bases* of our moral beliefs, we often are unable to provide them, and if we do manage to come up with something, we often find that our grounds do not stand up well to critical scrutiny.

For example, it may seem obvious that sales people should not intentionally withhold information that is relevant to a customer's decision whether to buy a product. We might offer this general principle, *P*, as an obvious grounding for certain of our moral judgments, e.g. that it is wrong to deceive customers intentionally about the dangerous defects in one's product. If I know that the chemicals I am about to sell, while otherwise safe, are highly unstable and liable to explode under normal conditions of transport, then I do my customer, and perhaps other innocent bystanders, a serious injustice if I conceal this information.

But now ask whether principle *P* stands up to rational scrutiny. A relevant piece of information in almost any sales situation is the availability of less expensive alternatives offered by the competition, information customers obviously would like to know, and that sales people are often in a position to provide. If we accept principle *P* and require that sales people divulge any and all information relevant to their customers' decisions we thereby require that sales people tell their customers about the lower prices offered down the road, do we not? Doesn't the unacceptability of this requirement show that principle *P* must be rejected or at least modified in some way? If so, what might the alternative be? It is here that the moral philosopher might be of some help. Moral philosophers should be viewed as partners with people in business in worrying through troublesome moral questions which arise in the practice of business.

The family of activities pursued by the moral philosopher is prompted largely by a desire for clarity of thought and integrity of action. But moral philosophy is not the moral conscience of business and the related professions. Moral philosophers are not out to criticize for moral failure — except perhaps when blind dogma rules moral practice, where the lives we lead remain largely unexamined. To raise or consider moral questions surrounding business practice is not to imply that there is something inherently immoral or unethical about business, although some will defend this view, nor is it to question the integrity of people in business. It is merely to seek the clarity and understanding which philosophical reflection often brings. The student of moral philosophy must be prepared to approach the subject with a willingness to challenge the obvious, and to consider seriously both the questionable and the strange.

Morality versus Ethics

Moral persons are equally distributed in all walks of life, including business. Morality is always of relevance in business. Business people agonize over what is the right thing to do in difficult cases, whether the issue is insider trading, or padding an expense account. Those who disagree with others or are generally perplexed do not necessarily have any less moral integrity. No one can claim to be a moral expert. Ethics or ethical theory is another matter. Ethics, as opposed to morality, is the systematic, critical study of the basic underlying principles and concepts utilized in thinking about moral life. Ethics, so understood, is something the average person concerns herself with infrequently, if ever. But this is not true of moral philosophers or "ethicists." They are primarily concerned with ethical theory, and as a result have acquired a certain level of expertise in the field. They have developed concepts, theories, and techniques of argument that can be of use to non-philosophers in finding their way through the tangled moral issues to which the practice of business often gives rise. In later sections, we will consider the ethical theories of some of the most influential moral philosophers of Western civilization, but first should look at the nature and role of ethical theories in general.

LEVELS OF MORAL RESPONSE

Put to an opponent of bribery in international business, the question "Why do you think it's wrong to bribe a foreign official to secure a contract for your company?" can trigger one of three different types of responses.

The expressive level

At the most basic level, the answer to this question is likely to be "because bribery is repugnant" or "I hate that kind of underhandedness." These responses are unanalyzed expressions or feelings which, in themselves, do not constitute any kind of justification or reason for the position taken. This is not to deny that feelings are relevant to morality or that moral convictions are often accompanied by strong emotions. It is simply to say that the mere fact one feels a certain way about an action or practice is not an adequate justification for a moral pronouncement on the practice.

The pre-reflective level

At the next level of response, justification is offered by reference to values, rules, and principles — i.e. norms — accepted uncritically, most often in the form of what we will call a "conventional" norm. Such a standard may be expressed in a legal injunction, in one of society's conventionally accepted values, in a church pronouncement, or in a professional or corporate code of ethics. It is a defining feature of this level of response that such conventional norms are uncritically accepted and acted upon. We don't stop to think *why* we should act or base our judgments upon the conventional norms or why they are good standards to adopt. While any behaviour ensuing from conventional norms may be classified as conventionally moral or ethical, it is a species of externally directed behaviour, the blind following of standards set by somebody else. Assuming the norms are good ones, this is not necessarily bad. Sometimes conventional norms are capable of reasoned defence; they can be fully justified morally. Sometimes there is good moral reason to follow conventional rules because they *are* accepted conventionally, since conventional norms can help to foster common understandings, and serve to ground others' expectations concerning how we will conduct ourselves. Sometimes it is crucial to know that other people will be playing by the same rules we are. Imagine, for example, what it would be like if there were no conventionally accepted rules governing the making of promises. We would never be certain whether a promise had been made, or whether its author considered it at all binding.

It is a serious mistake, however, to think that morality is exhausted by conventional norms or that moral justification ends with the invocation of a conventional rule. The norms must always be subject to critical moral scrutiny. Perhaps there are much better rules which we should try to persuade others to adopt, or perhaps existing conventions are morally objectionable. That X is generally accepted as morally right never in itself entails that X *is* morally right. Slavery was at one time widely accepted as morally correct. Slavery nonetheless was, and always will be, morally wrong.

The reflective level

At this level of response, our moral judgments are not based entirely on conventional norms blindly accepted but on principles, rules, and values to which we ourselves consciously subscribe and with regard to which we, as rational moral agents, are prepared to offer reasoned moral defence. It is possible, of course, that the norms to which we subscribe at the reflective level are norms conventionally accepted as well. They might, for instance, be norms that have found their way into a professional code by which one is expected to abide. But at the reflective level of moral response, we are prepared to consider for ourselves whether they are justified, or whether other, perhaps wholly novel, norms are those by which people should lead their lives.

At the reflective level, one's opposition to bribery might take the following form: "I oppose bribing foreign officials because it provides the company offering the bribe an unfair advantage over its competitors." Here a *reason* is given — a *basis* or *ground* for the moral judgment is provided. The complexity and sophistication of a response at this level invites competing judgments with plausible bases. One can imagine, as a reply to the above, the following retort: "Bribery may be wrong in theory. But if everyone is doing it, and it's the only way to do business in countries with corrupt officials, then the company deciding not to offer a bribe suffers an unfair *dis*advantage. On top of all that, a manager who, on principle, declines to offer a bribe and thereby loses a lucrative contract, violates the fiduciary responsibility she has to earn the highest profits she can for her shareholders." As this example illustrates, ethics at the reflective level admits of few easy answers!

Of the three levels considered, the reflective level is the one at which most of the discussion in this book takes place, despite grounds for misgivings about the possibilities for full resolution of moral controversies at this level. Reflection does not guarantee agreement. As will be evident throughout this book, moral reflection often yields "a" defensible position but not "the only" defensible position. People not only feel differently at the expressive level, and favour different conventional rules at the pre-reflective level, but also reach different conclusions at the reflective level. It is important to stress, once again, that there are no moral experts, and that at each level, including the reflective one, we often are met with genuine dilemmas and competing bases for moral belief. Arriving at unassailable moral judgments is difficult, and some think impossible, not only because there are different levels of approach to morality but also because people approach moral questions from very different perspectives.

A VARIETY OF APPROACHES

The different approaches moral agents take to moral questions may be illustrated by distinguishing between three ways the term "know" can be used.

Sometimes the claim to know amounts to nothing more than a claim to *feel* sure or certain, a subjective, psychological criterion. While emotionally reassuring, a feeling of certainty is not a reliable mark of *bona fide* moral judgments. Others with different, even opposing, moral views may feel just as strongly that they are right. One who claims to know, and tries to add as a warrant that she feels certain about what she believes, offers no warrant at all. Her certainty is no more a warrant than the certainty with which many people at one time believed slavery to be morally justified.

Second, the claim to know may be a claim that the position held is the one for which the best reasoned justification seems possible. The requirement of reasoned defence is acknowledged here, as well as the possibility that the position held may not be the only defensible one. Such a claim recognizes that rational people of good will and integrity may reasonably disagree about moral matters, and that no one can declare, with absolute certainty, he has the one right answer.

The third use of "know" is much stronger than the second, and, according to many moral philosophers, is quite unwarranted. It is equivalent to: "I know my view is the right one, and anyone who disagrees with me suffers from moral blindness or misunderstanding." Leaving aside the question whether, in moral life, there are ever uniquely correct solutions to moral issues, the degree of self-assurance underlying the above claim amounts to audacity and arrogance. Even a commitment to the notion there is a "final truth" in ethics should be accompanied by the acknowledgement that in practice we must operate in humility, with only partial knowledge and approximations to the truth.

Misgivings about the ethical enterprise may go even deeper than the foregoing comments suggest. There are profound philosophical disputes about the status of ethics itself — about whether moral judgments are in the end capable of full justification. Three of the more extreme difficulties are as follows.

The issue of verification   The problem of verification in the context of moral judgments may be illustrated by reference to the following scenario. Apple Mary is sitting in the downtown Hamilton market selling her produce. Suddenly, a suspicious-looking character furtively slips in behind her and clubs her. As she falls to the ground, her assailant scoops up her purse and vanishes.

Imagine two witnesses commenting as follows:

A. Did you see that?

B. I did.

A. What a dreadful thing to happen in downtown Hamilton.

B. I agree.

A. What that man did was terribly wrong.

B. I didn't see anything wrong.

A. How can you possibly say that?

B. Easily. Let's go over what happened carefully.

A. Let's do that.

B. I saw Apple Mary sitting at her stall. I saw a man creep up behind her. I saw him lift a club and bring it down on her head. I saw Mary slump to the ground and her assailant take off with her purse. I didn't *see* any wrong.

The clue to the dispute between A and B is to be found in the ambiguity of the word "see." Of course, B is correct if by "see" we mean physical seeing. We do not see the wrong in the way we see arms raised, clubs wielded, and purses snatched. Moral seeing is more like "seeing that" (making a judgment) than seeing with our eyes. We see that assault is wrong. We see that stealing is wrong. Moral insights are expressed in the form of judgments which are not verifiable empirically in the way observational statements are. Rather, they are substantiated by reference to principles, rules, or values which serve as their grounds or warrants. According to the first ethical theory we will examine, as well as one version of the second, we justify our actions in terms of the following schemata:

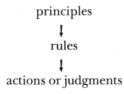

$$\text{principles}$$
$$\downarrow$$
$$\text{rules}$$
$$\downarrow$$
$$\text{actions or judgments}$$

The contemplated action, or a moral judgment concerning it, falls under a rule, and the rule, in turn, conforms to a higher-order principle. By contrast, the third theory we will consider involves identifying principles specifying "*prima facie* duties," and in situations of conflicting *prima facie* duties, determining which takes precedence. But more on this later. The point to be stressed at this stage is that we do not *see* moral properties in the way we see the club hit Apple Mary. Moral judgments are not open to empirical verification — indeed they cannot be substantiated by way of a universally agreed-upon routine or procedure. There are numerous competing theories on how our moral judgments are to be substantiated. Most, but not all, may be mapped onto the above schemata.

A plurality of ethical systems   The plurality of the approaches to the justification of moral judgments may be a cause for dismay. It is one thing to be made aware that the morality of our actions is not open to empirical verification; it is quite another to learn that different ethical theories prescribe quite different routines to be utilized in moral reasoning. It would certainly be simpler if there were only one theory and one routine. The only problems then remaining would be problems of casuistry (i.e. application of rules or principles to particular cases). But we have yet to discover an ethical theory upon which all reasonable people agree, and, as we have already seen, there are those who believe that no such theory will ever be found. As the understanding we have of ourselves and the world around us increases, we should expect our ethical theories to change and progress. The best we can do at present is to engage in the pursuit of a defensible ethical theory, and to try to learn as much as we can from those who have done so in the past. There is much to be learned from the theorists whose views will be outlined below.

The limits of justification   If one were to adopt, for example, a Kantian or rule-utilitarian position, the prescribed routine for justifying moral judgments would be more or less clear. It might be difficult to tell precisely what the theory requires of us in a particular case, but how to go about trying to answer that question would be reasonably clear. For Kant, as we shall see, an action is morally obligatory if it conforms to a rule, and the rule, in turn, conforms to a principle Kant calls the Categorical Imperative. For a rule-utilitarian, there is an analogous procedure. Our actions must conform to a rule, and the rule must conform not to Kant's Categorical Imperative but to the "principle of utility." For fully committed utilitarians or Kantians, justification is limited to judgments made within the prescribed framework. They inquire: "Does the action in question conform to the rule, and the rule to the (appropriate) principle?" If the answer is affirmative, the morality of the action is settled, and they know what the theory prescribes as the right thing to do.

It is possible, of course, for a rule-utilitarian to raise questions about Kant's Categorical Imperative, or for a Kantian to challenge the principle of utility. This would involve raising questions concerning the validity of the frameworks themselves. In such cases, what we have is a *philosophical* dispute, the kind of dispute that is a primary concern of ethical theorists. Utilitarians and Kantians will marshal philosophical arguments that challenge the validity of the others' ethical theory. They will do so even when it is clear what the opposing frameworks require of us in particular cases, and even when the different frameworks prescribe exactly the same actions. The two theorists may agree on what we should do, but disagree about why we should do it, since the philosopher is concerned to understand *why* we should do certain things and refrain from others.

External philosophical questions concerning the validity of ethical frameworks are best dealt with in books devoted exclusively to ethical theory. This is not such a book. In what follows, we will outline three competing frameworks, and only briefly mention some of the many external, philosophical questions that have been raised about them. Some students will likely feel a strong affinity for one of the three theories discussed in a later section, but most will find something of value in each one. This is not surprising. Each of the theories to be examined reflects currents of thought that have dominated western culture in recent centuries. For those strongly inclined to think that one of the theories represents the truth of the matter, the old adage should be borne in mind: "Those who live in glass houses should not throw stones." External challenges to other systems should be seasoned with a measure of caution and humility, and the recognition that questions of morality and ethics are ones upon which reasonable people of good will and integrity often reasonably disagree.

Given these profound difficulties with the ethical enterprise, the student may wonder why we should bother at all with an introduction to ethical theory. Why not just get on with an analysis of the various specific moral issues arising in the practice of business, issues like affirmative action or manipulative advertising? One response is that we are not warranted in dropping ethical theory altogether simply because it has difficulties. Quantum physics is fraught with theoretical difficulties too, but it would be silly to give it up entirely because of this. Another response is that there are valuable lessons to be learned from the way in which some of the greatest thinkers within our cultural history have seriously and systematically approached ethical issues. These are thinkers whose formulations have been extremely influential, and whose theories provide the frameworks within which current ethical disputes are argued. One cannot get too far in modern moral debate without encountering some appeal to the concept of utility, or to the value of individual autonomy. These two concepts are the cornerstones of the theories of Mill and Kant, respectively.

SOME BASIC CONCEPTS

Before examining the theories of Kant, Mill, and Ross, we should look at some basic terminology employed by ethical theorists. This terminology will be introduced by way of noting several distinctions.

First, we should distinguish between *judgments of obligation* and *judgments of value*. Judgments of obligation concern what we ought to do. In expressing such judgments, we use sentences like: "You *ought* to have told the truth to your client"; "Your *duty* was to protect the financial interests of your shareholders"; "You were under an *obligation* to honour your contract"; "It wasn't *right* to run that kind of advertisement"; "He had a *right* to that property." All of these judgments have to do directly with our conduct, with how we should behave.

Judgments of value, by contrast, are not directly related to action. These are judgments not about the right thing to do but about what is *good* or has *value*. For instance, the judgment that freedom is a good thing for human beings to enjoy, or that pleasure is the only thing of intrinsic worth are judgments of value. They don't tell us what it is right to do, as do judgments of obligation.

According to some ethical theories, a judgment of obligation is dependent on, and follows directly from, a judgment of value. If an ethical theory does hold that judgments of obligation are dependent in this way, then it is what philosophers call a *teleological* or *consequentialist theory of obligation*. A teleological theory of obligation posits one and only one fundamental obligation, and that is to maximize the good consequences and minimize the bad consequences of our actions. Insofar as we need to know, on such theories, which consequences are good in order to maximize them and which are bad in order to minimize them, it is easy to see why a teleological theory of obligation presupposes a *theory of value*. Such a theory will provide us with the basis for justifying our judgments of value and, ultimately, our judgments of obligation.

The duty to maximize the good and minimize the bad consequences of our actions is the only *fundamental* duty on a teleological theory of obligation. On such a theory, then, any other obligations such as the obligation to honour our contracts or to tell the truth, are secondary, and derivable from this one primary obligation. Mill's utilitarianism, as we shall see, is a teleological theory of obligation. In his view, all questions concerning what we ought to do should be decided ultimately on the principle of utility, which requires that we maximize what is intrinsically good, namely, happiness or pleasure, and minimize what is intrinsically bad, unhappiness or pain.

In contrast to teleological theories of obligation are non-teleological or *deontological theories of obligation*. Deontological theories of obligation essentially deny what teleological theories assert. They deny that we have one and only one fundamental duty to maximize the good and minimize the bad consequences of our actions. Basically, this denial can take two forms. First, a theory may suggest that the good and bad consequences of our actions have no bearing whatsoever on whether they are morally right or wrong. Such a strong deontological theory of obligation can operate independently of any theory of value. We needn't know, as we do with teleological theories of obligation, what the good is, if we are to know what we ought to do; our obligation does not in any way involve the maximization of good consequences, and so we needn't have a theory of value to tell us what that is. Kant, as we shall see, appears to have held a strong deontological theory. Kant is notorious for suggesting that the rightness or wrongness of our actions is totally independent of whether or not they maximize good consequences. According to Kant, a judgment of obligation, like the judgment that vendors must tell their customers the truth about dangers inherent to the products they sell, is in no way justified in terms of consequences. It is justified if and only if it meets the Categorical Imperative test, which ignores consequences altogether.

A deontological theory of obligation need not, however, follow Kant's lead and claim that the consequences of our actions are completely irrelevant to their rightness or wrongness. There is a second kind of deontological theory which makes the weaker, negative claim that good and bad consequences are not always the only factors of moral importance, and that we have other basic obligations in addition to our duty to maximize the good and minimize the bad consequences of our actions. According to Ross, for example, the principle of beneficence, which requires promoting the good of others in our actions, is only one of a number of basic principles defining our moral obligations. Others include the obligation to be grateful for benefits given, and the duty to be fair to other people. In Ross's view, we sometimes have a duty to be grateful even when neglecting this duty would on that occasion lead to the best consequences overall. There are some actions, e.g. displays of gratitude, which are right, regardless of their consequences. There are other actions, e.g. instances of unfairness, which are sometimes wrong, even when they lead to good consequences.

Unlike Kant and Mill, then, Ross suggests that we have many fundamental obligations. The duty to be grateful and the duty to be fair are not based on any ultimate principle of obligation. This clearly separates Ross from Kant and Mill. We frequently have a duty to be fair, Mill would urge, but this is because being fair normally maximizes the balance of good over bad consequences. Ross will have none of this. For him, the duty to be fair is as important as the duty to maximize good consequences, and our many basic obligations cannot be reduced to any of the others. Ross's theory of obligation, insofar as it is not based on a single, fundamental principle defining a single, fundamental obligation, is a *pluralist theory of obligation*. A pluralist theory of obligation, put simply, is one that does not posit a single, fundamental obligation upon which all other obligations are based. A *monistic theory of obligation*, by contrast, does posit one such obligation. A utilitarian will be happy to talk of obligations to tell the truth or to be fair to others in our dealings with them. She will simply add that we have these obligations because fairness and truth-telling usually lead, in the end and all things considered, to the best consequences. Hence her theory is monistic. So too is Kant's.

To recapitulate, teleological theories of obligations are all logically dependent on theories of value. Some deontological theories of obligation are also dependent on a theory of value, while others are not. Strong deontological theories such as Kant's exclude as irrelevant questions about the good or bad consequences of our actions (i.e. the value or disvalue to be realized in them). They therefore have no need of a theory of value. But most deontological theories do have such a need, since most deontological theories are pluralistic, like Ross's, and include principles which direct us, but not exclusively, to the good and bad consequences of our actions.

Turning to theories of value, we find that these too may be categorized as either monistic or pluralistic. A *monistic theory of value*, as one might expect, posits one and only one thing, or characteristic of things, as being of value for its own sake. In other words, it posits only one thing or characteristic as *intrinsically valuable*. Hedonism is one influential type of monistic theory of value. On this view, pleasure is the only thing that is valuable for its own sake. Anything else we value, say money or friendship, is valuable only *instrumentally*, as a means to the pleasure it brings. Classical utilitarianism of the form espoused by Mill and his teacher Jeremy Bentham is hedonistic. But classical utilitarianism needn't be hedonistic. Utilitarians who agree on a theory of obligation may divide on their theories of value. G.E. Moore, for instance, was like Mill a utilitarian. But unlike Mill, Moore espoused a *pluralistic theory of value*, which saw pleasure as only one of many things of intrinsic value; knowledge and aesthetic experience were other things worthy of pursuit for their own sakes.[1]

If a person holds a pluralistic theory of value, then he is faced with a difficulty similar to one with which defenders of pluralistic theories of obligation must grapple: what to do in situations where two or more values conflict or cannot be pursued together. If both freedom from manipulation and pleasure are intrinsically valuable, then we may have to choose somehow between allowing advertisers to manipulate us with their entertaining ads and prohibiting such activities entirely. But is it possible to compare these very different values? Is comparing freedom from manipulation with pleasure, so as to see which is of greater value or importance in the circumstances, something that can be done rationally? Is an attempt to compare the two things a bit like trying to compare apples with oranges? If, on the other hand, we adopt a monistic theory of value, we may seem to rid ourselves of such problems. We only have to compare, say, one pleasure with the next. But there are serious difficulties even here. How does one compare one person's pleasure with that of another person, especially if those persons are as different as Wayne Gretzky and Pierre Trudeau? Monistic theories of value face another difficulty of some importance. According to many people, there are numerous things in the world ultimately, irreducibly valuable. Friendship, for example, seems to be compromised if its value is reduced to the pleasure it brings. As will be seen, the attempt to place "value" on human lives and welfare, an integral part of cost-benefit analysis, is fraught with such difficulties. Some of these difficulties will be explored later in discussions of worker health and safety and the impact of business activities on the environment.

THREE ETHICAL THEORIES

A brief survey of three major types of ethical theory follows. The contributions of Kant and Mill have dominated western moral thought since the scientific revolution, so their theories must be included. Kant strove to establish ethics as a purely *rational* enterprise. Mill believed that an objective standard of right and wrong could be discovered using the methods of the empirical sciences; that is, since the rightness of our actions depends on the pleasure and pain they produce, we ought to be able to estimate their rightness by empirical observation, measurements, and induction. Mill's utilitarianism is an ancestor of modern theories of cost-benefit analysis. Between them, Kant and Mill uncover the respective roles of intention and consequences in shaping our moral responses. One cannot get very far in a discussion of ethics without paying deference to the Kantian notions of autonomy and universalizability or the injunction to treat human beings as ends in themselves and not merely as means, or without paying deference to Mill's emphasis on protecting and promoting human happiness or well-being.

W.D. Ross's reaction to Kant and Mill is an invaluable contribution to ethics. In certain crucial respects, it seems to reflect more accurately the ordinary thinking and practice of moral agents rather than the more systematic reflections of professional moral philosophers. This quality is particularly evident in Ross's opposition to Kant's and Mill's reductionism in moral theory. While acknowledging the powerful contributions of Kant and Mill to ethical theory, Ross was unwilling to subscribe to a monistic theory of obligation, and resisted elevating either the Categorical Imperative or the principle of utility to the status of a foundational first principle from which all other moral principles, rules, and judgments follow. In coming to grips with the moral issues considered in this text, it will be difficult to escape making reference to Ross's notion of *prima facie* duty.

Utilitarianism

Utilitarianism is a monistic, teleological theory of obligation which, owing to its teleological nature, rests on a theory of value. A utilitarian's theory of value can, of course, be either monistic or pluralistic. We shall largely ignore the different theories of value espoused by utilitarians, and concentrate instead on their theories of obligation.

Essentially, there are two different kinds of utilitarianism, *act* and *rule*. Act utilitarianism (AU) defines the rightness or wrongness of individual actions in terms of the good or bad consequences realized by those actions. In other words, AU defines the rightness or wrongness of an action in terms of its "utility" and "disutility." The term utility stands for whatever it is that is intrinsically valuable on the utilitarian's theory of value, disutility for whatever is intrinsically bad. According to John Stuart Mill, "actions are right in proportion as they tend to promote happiness; wrong as they tend to produce the reverse of happiness."[2] For him, "utility" means happiness, and "disutility" unhappiness. Mill went on to identify happiness with pleasure and unhappiness with pain. Hence, Mill may be characterized as a *hedonistic* utilitarian, one on whose theory of value pleasure is the only thing of intrinsic worth. But a utilitarian needn't make this identification, nor need he define utility in terms of happiness. Some utilitarians think it best to define utility in terms of the satisfaction of our actual preferences, while others would have us look to satisfy preferences we would have were we fully informed and rational. Regardless of the theory of value with which it is associated, however, AU always makes the following claim:

> AU: An act is right if and only if there is no other action I could have done instead which either (a) would have produced a greater balance of utility over disutility; or (b) would have produced a smaller balance of disutility over utility.

We must add (b) to account for those unfortunate situations where whatever we do, we seem to cause more disutility than utility — where we're damned if we do and damned if we don't. In short, AU tells us to act always so as to bring about the best consequences we can, and sometimes that means trying to make the best of a bad situation.

AU was made famous in the modern era by Mill and Bentham, at a time when many people thought that some individuals simply count more than others, that members of the aristocracy, the Church, or a particular race were in some sense more worthy or superior than others, and were therefore deserving of special consideration or privilege. The utilitarians were part of a social revolution which would have none of this. In the famous words of Bentham, "each is to count for one, none to count for more than one." In other words, according to utilitarians, *all* those affected by my actions should count *equally* in my deliberations concerning my moral obligations. The equal happiness of the King is to count equally with the equal happiness of the milk man. Mill put this important point this way:

> I must again repeat what the assailants of utilitarianism seldom have the justice to acknowledge, that the happiness which forms the utilitarian standard of what is right in conduct is *not* the agent's own happiness but that of all concerned. As between others, utilitarianism requires him to be as *strictly impartial as a disinterested benevolent spectator.*[3]

Thus, built into AU is a commitment to equality and impartiality. We are to be concerned equally and impartially with the happiness or welfare, i.e. utility, of all those, including ourselves, who might be affected by our actions. On these grounds alone, AU is a very appealing theory. What could be better than to be sure that I always maximize not my own happiness or that of my friends but the happiness of all those people affected by my actions, whoever they might be? What more could morality require?

Despite its inherently desirable features, many philosophers have come to find serious difficulties with AU, leading some utilitarians to opt for an alternative form of the theory. One of the more serious difficulties revolves around *special duties* and *special relationships*. These include duties of loyalty, of fidelity, and familial obligations, resting in part on the special relationships which arise out of family ties and require some degree of partiality and special concern towards family members. It would be wrong, some think, to be impartial between friends and family, on the one hand, and perfect strangers on the other.

Let's centre on promises as an illustration of the difficulties facing AU. Suppose I am the executive director of a non-profit association like the Heart Foundation. I have made a firm agreement with the booking agent at the Holiday Inn to hold the Foundation's yearly convention at his hotel. The agent is an old business acquaintance with whom the Foundation has dealt for years and who has always treated me fairly, courteously, and efficiently. He has even given the Foundation the odd special break now and then. Several months later, however, I discover that the recently opened Walnut Inn is willing to give me a much better deal than my friend at the Holiday Inn. The Foundation will be way ahead even after we pay the standard cancellation fees to the Holiday Inn. It is also clear that Holiday Inn will lose big if we pull out. The cancellation fees will not be nearly enough to compensate for the arrangements they have made and the bookings they have lost because they were holding their facilities for us. Despite this, I add up the utilities and disutilities involved for all affected, and correctly conclude that overall utility would be maximized if my friend and the Holiday Inn were left holding the bag, despite the special relationship we have developed over the years and despite the commitment I have made. Indeed, as a good act utilitarian, I consider it my moral obligation to maximize utility, even at the expense of harming some individuals and violating the trust that has been placed in me.

Many think examples like this one show that AU takes promises, commitments, special relationships of trust, and so on, far too lightly. Indeed, some think AU makes such factors totally irrelevant, since AU is a monistic theory of obligation which posits one and only one obligation — to maximize utility. Future consequences are all that count. Past commitments are irrelevant. A defender of AU, on the other hand, will likely reply that the critic has simply failed to consider all of the relevant consequences. Of crucial importance here is not simply the fact that a much better deal can be arranged with the Walnut Inn but also the fact that going with the new hotel will destroy a valuable relationship which, in the long run, would add significantly to the future utility I can bring about in my role as executive director. Who knows whether Walnut Inn will give me the same deal in the future? Probably they won't. Who knows whether the Holiday Inn will be willing to make the same concessions they have in the past if I desert them now? Surely they will not. All of these long-range, indirect consequences of breaking the agreement, when put into the balance, tip the scales in favour of keeping the initial agreement with Holiday Inn. Those who think, say its defenders, that AU takes special relationships and commitments far too lightly have simply ignored all the long-range, indirect effects of doing so.

So the defender of AU has a fairly forceful reply to such counter-examples to this theory of obligation. We should always be sure to ask, when a critic provides such an example: Have all the relevant consequences, long-range and indirect as well as immediate and direct, been accounted for? More often than not they haven't been, whether we're talking about breaking hotel bookings, lying to a close friend about her prospects for promotion, or padding an expense account.

Philosophers are fairly industrious when it comes to thinking up counter-examples to ethical theories. Having met with replies like the one outlined above, they alter counter-examples to get rid of those convenient indirect, long-range effects upon which the defence is based. Some have dreamt up the *Desert Island Promise Case*, a version of which follows.

Suppose you and a friend are alone on a deserted island. Your friend is dying and asks you to see to it when you are rescued that the elder of his two sons receives the huge sum of money your friend has secretly stashed away. You now are the only other person who knows of its existence. You solemnly promise to fulfil your friend's last request, and he passes away secure in the knowledge that his last wish is in good hands. Upon rescue, you are faced with a dilemma. The elder son turns out to be a lazy playboy who squanders to no good end — and with no pleasure — whatever money he has. Even when he has lots of money to spend, he still ends up being miserable and causing misery to other people. Your friend's younger son, however, is an aspiring researcher in dermatology. He is on the brink of uncovering a solution to the heartache of psoriasis, but will fail unless he receives financial backing. All his grants have been denied unjustly, and he has been left in desperation. As a good act utilitarian, you reason that utility would obviously be maximized if your solemn word to your dying friend were broken and you gave the money to the younger son. Think of all the utility that would be realized, all the suffering that would be alleviated! Compare this with the very little utility and considerable disutility that would result were you to give the money to the elder son.

Notice that in this case all the indirect, long-range consequences to which appeal was made in the hotel-booking case are absent. No one will know that the promise is being broken, and there are no valuable, utility-enhancing relationships in jeopardy. Your friend is dead. There seems little doubt in this case that the promise should be broken according to AU, as a moral obligation. But surely, the opponent will argue, this cannot be so. Solemn promises to dying friends, regardless of the good consequences which might be realized by breaking them, *must* be kept, except perhaps where impending disaster would result from keeping them. That AU seems to give no weight at all to such promises shows that it is a faulty theory of obligation. Solemn promises should weigh heavily — and independently of good consequences. Hence AU cannot be an adequate theory.

So promises and other special commitments pose difficulties for AU. Free riders do, too. Suppose there is a temporary but serious energy shortage in your community. All private homes and businesses have been requested to conserve electricity and gas. Private homes are to keep their thermostats no higher than 15 degrees Celsius, and all businesses are temporarily to cut production by one half. Everyone's chipping in this way will avoid a serious overload that would prove disastrous. Being a good act utilitarian, and knowing the tendencies of your neighbours, you reason as follows: "I know that everyone else will pay scrupulous attention to the government's request, so the potential disaster will be averted regardless of what I do. It will make no difference whatsoever if I run my production lines at two thirds capacity. The little bit of extra electricity we use will have no negative effect at all. Of course, if everyone ran at two thirds, then disaster would result. But I know this isn't going to happen, and so the point is irrelevant. As for my employees, they will see a reduction, and assume that the cut was to one half, so no one will know but me. Using two thirds, then, will in no way prove harmful, but it will make a considerable amount of difference to my balance sheet! The extra production will enable the company to show a much higher profit this year. All things considered, then, it is morally permissible, indeed, my moral obligation, to run at two thirds. This is what AU tells me I should do."

Imagine the moral outrage that would result were your acting on this line of reasoning to become common knowledge. You would be labelled a "free rider," one who rides freely while others shoulder the burdens necessary for all to prosper. Your actions would be thought most unfair to all those who had willingly sacrificed their best interests for the good of everyone concerned; all this despite your efforts to maximize the utility of your actions.

In response to these (and similar) sorts of objections, some utilitarians have developed an alternative to AU. Consider further what would be said if your free riding came to light. The likely response would be: "Sure, no one is harmed if you use the extra electricity. But imagine what would happen if everyone did what you are doing. Imagine if that became the norm. Disaster would result!" The request "Imagine what would happen if everybody did that" has great probative force for many people. If not everyone could do what I propose to do without serious harm resulting, then many are prepared to say that it would be wrong for anyone to do it, and hence wrong for me to do it. In response to the force of this intuition, some utilitarians have developed a very different variety of theory called *rule utilitarianism* (RU). On this version, the rightness or wrongness of an action is not to be judged by its consequences but rather by the consequences of everyone's adopting a *general rule* under which the action falls.

As an introduction to RU, consider a case outlined by John Rawls in his paper "Two Concepts of Rules."[4] Rawls asks you to imagine that you are a sheriff in the deep American south. A white woman has been raped, and although the identity of the rapist is unknown, it is clear that the offender was black. The predominantly white and racially bigoted community is extremely agitated over the incident and great social unrest is threatening. Riots are about to break out, and many people will be killed. If you were able to identify and arrest the rapist, the unrest undoubtedly would subside; but unfortunately you have no leads, other than the fact that the rapist was black. It occurs to you that you don't really need the actual culprit to calm things down. Why not simply concoct a case against some black man or other who has no alibi, and have him arrested? The crowd will be placated, and although one man, possibly or even likely innocent, will suffer, many innocent lives will be saved.

Rawls uses this example to illustrate an apparent weakness in AU, and how RU allows one to overcome it. The consequences of framing the (possibly) innocent black are far better (or less bad) in terms of utility than allowing the riot to occur. Hence AU seems to require the frame, an action which is clearly unjust. (Of course, the defender of AU has several tricks up her sleeve at this point. She can once again appeal to the possible indirect effects of the frame. Suppose the lie came to light. Terrible social paranoia and unrest would result; people would no longer trust the judicial system and would wonder constantly whether they might be the next person to be framed. Indirect consequences such as these, the defender of AU will argue, clearly outweigh any short-term, direct benefits.) But Rawls suggests that we consider a different question than the one AU would have us ask. We are to consider whether a *general rule* which permits the framing of innnocent persons could possibly figure in a moral code, general acceptance of which would result in the maximization of utility. If it could not, which is surely the case, then the proposed frame is impermissible. Since no such general rule could find its way into an acceptable moral code, largely for the reasons mentioned above, an action in accordance with that rule would be morally wrong. Hence, it would be morally wrong on RU to frame the possibly (likely) innocent black, even if the consequences of that particular action would be better than those of the alternatives.

We are morally required, on RU, not to perform actions which individually would maximize utility. Rather, we are to perform actions that accord with a set of rules general observance of which by everyone would maximize utility. Actions are judged according to whether they conform with acceptable rules; only the rules themselves are judged in terms of utility.

> RU: An act is morally right if it conforms with a set of rules general observance of which by everybody would maximize utility.

One extremely important difference between RU and AU is worth stressing. It is quite possible, on RU, to be required to perform an action which does not, on that particular occasion, maximize utility. Observance of the best set of general rules does not always, on each individual occasion, lead to the best consequences; it *generally* does, but there are exceptions. The defender of RU seems willing to live with this for the sake of overall, long-term utility gains, and the ability to deal with desert-island promises, free riders, and so on.

RU is not without its difficulties, of course. For example, some utilitarians claim that RU really does violate the spirit of utilitarianism, and amounts to "rule worship."[5] If the ideal behind utilitarianism is the maximization of utility, then should we not be able to deviate from the generally acceptable rules when doing so will serve to maximize utility? If the defender of RU allows exceptions to be made in such cases, then he runs the risk of collapsing his RU into AU. The rules would no longer hold any special weight or authority in our moral decisions. We would end up following the rules when it is best to do so and depart from them when that seems best.[6] In each case we seem led to do what AU requires, namely, maximize the utility of our individual actions. If, on the other hand, the defender of RU holds fast and says we must *never* deviate from rules which generally advance utility but sometimes do not, then the charge of rule worship comes back to plague the utilitarian.

A second problem facing RU can be summed up in an example. Suppose it were true that the best set of rules for the circumstances of our society would place an obligation on first-born children to provide for their elderly parents. I, the younger of two daughters, reason that I therefore have no obligation whatsoever to provide for my elderly parents, even though I know that my elder sister is unwilling to provide more than the 50% she thinks we each ought to provide. My parents end up living a life of abject poverty on only 50% of what they need to sustain themselves. Something seems clearly wrong here. Our obligations, it would seem, cannot be entirely a function of an *ideal code* which may never in fact be followed by anyone except me. We seem to require, in an acceptable moral theory, some recognition of how other people in fact are behaving, what rules they in fact are following. The rules they are following may be perfectly acceptable but not ideal, in which case I should perhaps follow them, too. This precept is as true in the business world as elsewhere. Financial ruin would be the result were an idealistic business person to act according to an ideal code, general observance of which would maximize utility, when no one else was prepared to do so. Perhaps here the excuse "But no one else is willing to do it" has some purchase.

There are significant differences between AU and RU, and neither theory is free from difficulty. AU requires that we always seek, on each particular occasion, to maximize utility. It has difficulties with, among other things, free riders, desert-island promises, and sheriffs tempted by good consequences to commit injustice. RU tells us to perform actions that conform to a set of rules, general observance of which would lead to the best consequences overall. This theory seems to provide solutions to many of the problems plaguing AU but it does so only at the expense of introducing new puzzles of its own. It must somehow provide a bridge between the best ideal code and the actual beliefs, practices, and accepted rules of one's society, all the while steering a course between rule worship and a straightforward reduction to AU.

Deontological ethics — Immanuel Kant

Kant, like Mill, proposes a monistic theory of obligation. Unlike Mill's theory, however, Kant's theory is thoroughly non-consequentialist. It denies that the consequences of our actions are what determine their rightness or wrongness:

> An action done from duty has its moral worth, *not in the purpose* [the consequences] to be attained by it, but in the maxim in accordance with which it is decided upon; it depends, therefore, not on the realization of the object of the action, but solely on the *principle of volition* [the maxim] in accordance with which, irrespective of all objects of the faculty of desire [i.e. pleasure, happiness, preferences] the action has been performed.[7]

In this remark, we see that Kant's ethical theory includes a deontological theory of obligation. The morality of an action is determined not by its consequences but by the maxim, the general principle, to which it conforms. Its moral worth lies not in the happiness or pleasure it produces but in the *kind* of action it is. Let's try to see a bit more clearly what all this means.

A key notion in Kant's theory is that of a maxim. By maxim, Kant means a general rule or principle which specifies what it is a person conceives of oneself as doing and the reason for doing it. For example, suppose I decide to tell a lie in order to avoid serious financial loss. The maxim of my action could be expressed in the following way: "Whenever I am able to avoid serious financial loss by lying, I shall do so." This maxim makes plain that I conceive of myself as lying, and that my reason is the avoidance of financial loss. It makes plain that I consider the avoidance of such a loss a *sufficient reason* to lie. Were I to act on my maxim, in effect I would be expressing my commitment to a general rule whose scope extends beyond the particular situation in which I find myself. In supposing that the avoidance of serious financial loss is a sufficient reason in this situation to lie, I seem to commit myself to holding that in any other situation just like it, i.e. any other case in which a lie would serve to avoid a serious financial loss, I should tell a lie. This *generalizability of reasons* and maxims can be illustrated through an example involving a non-moral judgment.

Suppose you and I are baseball fans. I say to you: "The Toronto Blue Jays are a good baseball team because their team batting average is about .260 and the average ERA among their starting pitchers is under 3.50."

You reply: "What is your opinion of the Montreal Expos?"

I say: "They're a lousy team."

You reply: "But their team batting average is also about .260 and the average ERA among their starters is 3.4."

I am stuck here in a logical inconsistency. I must either modify my earlier assessment of the Blue Jays — say that they too are a lousy team — or admit that the Expos are also a good team. By citing my reasons for judging the Blue Jays a good ball team, I commit myself to a general maxim that *any* baseball team with a team batting average of over .260 and whose starting rotation has an ERA of below 3.50 is a good baseball team. If I don't like the implications of that general maxim, i.e. I still think the Expos are a bad ball team, then I must either reject or modify the maxim. Perhaps I'll add that, in addition to a team batting average of over .260 and an ERA among starting pitchers of under 3.5, a good baseball team must have several "clutch" players. I would add this if I thought that the absence of clutch players explains why the Expos, unlike the Blue Jays, are not a good team. Of course, I could make this alteration only if I thought the Blue Jays did have at least a few clutch players.

So, my maxim that whenever I can avoid serious financial loss by lying I will, insofar as it expresses a general reason, applies to other situations similar to the one in which I initially act upon it. But this isn't the full extent of my commitment. If avoiding serious financial loss is a sufficient reason for *my* telling a lie, then it must also be a sufficient reason for *anyone else* who finds himself in a situation just like mine. According to Kant, and virtually all moral philosophers, acting upon a maxim commits me, as a rational moral agent, to a *universal* moral rule governing all persons in situations just like mine (in the relevant respects). I must be prepared to accept that a sufficient reason for me is a sufficient reason for anyone else in precisely my situation. If I think some other person in a position to avoid serious financial loss by lying should *not* tell the lie, then I must either retract my earlier maxim or specify some relevant difference between our situations, as I did when I tried to show that the Expos are a bad baseball team despite their strong team batting average and pitching staff.

Acting for reasons, that is, acting rationally, (which, according to Kant, is required if we are to be moral) commits me to universal rules or maxims which I must be prepared to accept. Kant expresses this point in terms of my capacity to will that my personal maxim should become a universal law. According to the first formulation of the Categorical Imperative, the fundamental principle of obligation in Kant's monistic system, "I ought never to act except in such a way *that I can also will that my maxim should become a universal law.*"[8] Later he writes: "*Act as if the maxim of your action were to become through your will a universal law of nature.*"[9] Immoral maxims and the immoral actions based upon them can never, under any conceivable circumstances, pass Kant's Categorical Imperative test, not because the consequences of general observance of an immoral maxim would be undesirable in terms of utility but rather because the state of affairs in which the maxim is observed as a universal law is *logically impossible* or *inconceivable.*

Some states of affairs simply cannot exist, in the strongest sense of "cannot." The state of affairs in which I am, at one and the same time, Robbie's father *and* Robbie's son is logically impossible. It cannot exist. Were I for some strange reason to will that this state of affairs exist, my will, Kant would say, *would contradict itself*. It would be willing inconsistent, contradictory things, that I am Robbie's father and son at one and the same time. Now consider a case actually discussed by Kant, and of obvious relevance to business where promises play an essential role. Suppose that a man

> finds himself driven to borrowing money because of need. He well knows that he will not be able to pay it back; but he sees too that he will get no loan unless he gives a firm promise to pay it back within a fixed time. He is inclined to make such a promise; but he has still enough conscience to ask 'Is it not unlawful and contrary to duty to get out of difficulties in this way?' Supposing, however, he did resolve to do so, the maxim of his action would run thus: 'Whenever I believe myself short of money, I will borrow money and promise to pay it back, though I know that this will never be done.' Now this principle of self-love or personal advantage is perhaps quite compatible with my own entire future welfare; only there remains the question 'Is it right?' I therefore transform the demand of self-

love into a universal law and frame my question thus: 'How would things stand if my maxim became a universal law?' I then see straight away that this maxim can never rank as a universal law of nature and be self-consistent, but must necessarily contradict itself. For the universality of a law that every one believing himself to be in need can make any promise he pleases with the intention not to keep it would make promising, and the very purpose of promising, itself impossible, since no one would believe he was being promised anything, but would laugh at utterances of this kind as empty shams.[10]

It is important to be clear about what exactly Kant is saying in this passage. He is not objecting to insincere promises on the grounds that they will cause others to lose confidence in us and thereby jeopardize the good consequences of future promises, nor is he arguing that false promises contribute to a general mistrust of promises and the eventual collapse of a valuable social practice. These *consequentialist* considerations to deontologist Kant are totally irrelevant to questions of moral obligation. Kant's point is a very different one. He is suggesting that a state of affairs in which everyone in need makes false promises is incoherent. There is a contradiction because, on the one hand, everyone in need *would* borrow on false promises. They would be following the maxim "as a law of nature," with the same regularity as the planets observe Kepler's laws of planetary motion. Yet, on the other hand, in this very same state of affairs, no one *could* borrow on a false promise, because if such promises were always insincere, no one would be stupid enough to lend any money. Promising requires trust on the part of the promisee, but in the state of affairs contemplated there just couldn't be any, and so promises of the sort in question would simply be impossible. Hence any attempt to will, as a universal law of nature, the maxim "Whenever I believe myself short of money, I will borrow money and promise to pay it back, though I know that this will never be done," lands us in contradiction. "I . . . see straight away that this maxim can never rank as a universal law of nature and be self-consistent, but must necessarily contradict itself."[11]

With Kant, then, we have a moral test of our actions that does not lie in an assessment of their consequences; nor does the test lie in weighing the consequences of adopting a general rule which licences those actions. Rather, the test considers the logical coherence of the universalized maxim upon which I personally propose to act. Whether this test successfully accounts for all of our moral obligations is questionable. Is there anything incoherent in the state of affairs in which everyone kills her neighbour if he persists in playing his stereo at ear-piercing levels? Such a state of affairs might be highly undesirable, but it seems perfectly possible or conceivable. Yet killing off annoying neighbours hardly seems the right thing to do.

Kant provided two further formulations of his Categorical Imperative. The additional formulations bring to light two important principles which most people find highly appealing and which may prove helpful in dealing with many of the problems discussed in this text.

According to Kant, if I act only on maxims that could serve as universal laws, I will never treat people as *mere means to my ends*. The Categorical Imperative requires that I "Act in such a way that [I] always treat humanity, whether in [my] own person or in the person of any other, never simply as a means, but always at the same time as an end."[12] In more colloquial terms, we should never just *use* people. The emphasis here is on the *intrinsic worth* and *dignity* of rational creatures: I treat rational beings as ends in themselves if I respect in them the same value I discover in myself, namely, my freedom to determine myself to action and to act for reasons I judge for myself. As Kant observes, there can be nothing more dreadful to a rational creature than that his actions should be subject to the will of another. I treat others as mere things rather than as persons, subject them to my will in the way I do a tool, if I fail to respect their dignity. This principle has an important role to play in assessing, for example, manipulative advertising, employment equity, or a worker's "right" to choose safe or hazardous working conditions.

Kant's third formulation of the Categorical Imperative seems closely tied to the second. In effect, it spells out what in rational agents gives them their dignity and worth. It requires that we treat others as *autonomous* agents, capable of self-directed, rational action. The capacity to rise above the compelling forces of desire, self-interest, and physical necessity, to act freely on the basis of *reasons*, is what gives rational beings their dignity and worth. To treat a person as an end in herself, then, is to respect her autonomy and freedom. As noted, it rules out various kinds of manipulative practices and paternalistic behaviours. In a case involving asbestos poisoning (discussed later in Part Four, Reading 14), company doctors neglected to tell workers the alarming results of their medical tests. This action was rationalized on the grounds that nothing could be done to curb the disease anyway, and so the workers were better off not knowing. Such paternalistic conduct clearly violates Kant's Categorical Imperative. It fails to respect the autonomy and dignity of the asbestos workers. This conduct might have been fully justified by AU, although whether in the long run such deceptions serve to maximize utility is certainly an arguable point.

Kant provides a clear alternative to the monistic, teleological theory of obligation propounded by the act and rule utilitarians. Kant's theory is clearly deontological and, at the very least, monistic in its intent, since he attempts to ground all our obligations on one fundamental principle: the Categorical Imperative. Kant puts forward three formulations of this principle, although it is difficult to see how they are exactly equivalent. In any event, we may view Kant as requiring that we ask the following three questions:

1. Would I be unable to consistently will, as a universal law, the personal maxim upon which I propose to act?
2. Would my action treat some rational agent (including possibly myself, in which case I would be guilty of self-degradation) as a mere means?
3. Would my action violate the autonomy of some rational agent, possibly myself?

Should any of these three questions be answered in the affirmative then Kant would hold that my moral obligation is to refrain from acting on my personal maxim.

Pluralism — W.D. Ross

Ross's theory of obligation arose mainly out of his dissatisfaction with utilitarian theories. While Ross's main target was G.E. Moore, his criticisms are relevant to utilitarianism in general, particularly AU. According to Ross, utilitarianism in all of its guises grossly oversimplifies the moral relationships in which we stand to other people. Utilitarianism is, in the end, concerned exclusively with the overall consequences of our actions (the maximization of utility), or the rules under which we perform our actions. In Ross's view, morality does indeed require this kind of concern, but not exclusively. Ross believes utilitarians err in thinking that consequences are all that matter, in thinking that "the only morally significant relationship in which my neighbours stand to me is that of being possible beneficiaries [or victims] of my action."[13] In other words, utilitarianism errs in being a monistic, teleological theory of obligation. Ross proposes instead a pluralistic theory of obligation that recognizes several irreducible moral relationships and principles. In addition to their role as possible beneficiaries of my actions, my fellow human beings "may also stand to me in the relation of promisee to promiser, creditor to debtor, of wife to husband, of child to parent, of friend to friend, of fellow countryman to fellow countryman, and the like."[14] "The like" no doubt includes the relation of sales person to customer, employer to employee, and manufacturer to consumer, relationships that are integral to business life, and which are ignored at the cost of moral confusion.

In Ross's view, utilitarianism not only oversimplifies the moral relationships in which we stand to others but also distorts the whole basis of morality by being thoroughly teleological in orientation. On utilitarian theories, we must always be *forward-looking* to the future consequences of our actions or rules. But sometimes, Ross proposes, morality requires that we look *backwards* to what has occurred in the past. There is significance, for example, in the sheer fact that a promise has been made, a promise which has moral force independently of any future good consequences there might be in its being kept. This moral force explains why we should normally keep promises made to dying friends even if utility would be maximized were we to break them. A promise itself, in virtue of the kind of action it is, has a moral force that is totally independent of its consequences. Teleological theories, because they ignore such features and are entirely forward-looking, distort morality. Promises, contracts, agreements, loyalty, friendship, and so on, all have moral force; all can give rise to obligations independently of good or bad consequences.

Ross provides us, then, with a pluralistic, deontological theory of obligation. In this theory we find a number of fundamental principles, only some of which are consequentialist in orientation. According to Ross, each of these principles specifies a *prima facie* duty or obligation. These are duties we must fulfil *unless* we are also, in the circumstances, subject to another, competing *prima facie* duty of greater weight. We have a *prima facie* duty to tell the truth, which means that we must always tell the truth unless a more stringent duty applies to us and requires a falsehood. An example from Kant illustrates this feature nicely.

Kant is notorious for arguing that the Categorical Imperative establishes an *unconditional* duty always to tell the truth. He has us consider a case where a murderer comes to our door asking for the whereabouts of his intended victim. Should we tell him the truth, that the victim is seeking refuge in our house, the latter will be murdered. Both AU and RU would undoubtedly license a lie under such extraordinary circumstances, but according to Kant the Categorical Imperative does not. The duty to tell the truth is *unconditional*, despite the consequences of its observance. "To be truthful (honest) in all declarations . . . is a sacred and absolutely commanding decree of reason, limited by no expediency."[15] According to Ross's theory, though, Kant's case is clearly one where our *prima facie* duty to be truthful is overridden or outweighed by more stringent duties to our friend.

Ross's list of *prima facie* duties provides a helpful classification of the various duties and morally significant relationships recognized in our everyday moral thinking. There are:

1. Duties resting on previous actions of our own. These include:
   (a) duties of *fidelity* arising from explicit or implicit promises;
   (b) duties of *reparation*, resting on previous wrongful acts of ours and requiring that we compensate, as best we can, the victims of our wrongful conduct.
2. Duties resting on the services of others; duties of *gratitude* which require that we return favour for favour.
3. Duties involving the *fair* distribution of goods; duties of *justice* which require fair sharing of goods to be distributed.
4. Duties to improve the condition of others; duties of *beneficence* (which in part form the basis of utilitarian theories of obligation).
5. Duties to improve our own condition; duties of *self-improvement*.
6. Duties not to injure others; duties of *non-maleficence*.[16]

Ross's list of duties may not be exhaustive, and, no doubt, many would quarrel with some of the duties he has included. For instance, it might be questioned whether duties of self-improvement belong on a list of *moral* duties. It is plausible to suppose that moral duties arise only in our relationships with other people, that the demands of morality govern *interpersonal* relationships only. Allowing one's talents to lie unused or allowing one's health to deteriorate may be imprudent or foolish, but is it immoral? Perhaps it is if others, say our children, are depending on us. But in this case, it's not a moral duty of self-improvement that is violated but rather duties such as the duties of beneficence and non-maleficence. Another questionable candidate is the duty to be grateful. If someone does me a favour, is it true that I am *required*, as a matter of *duty*, to be grateful? Is gratitude something that can be subject to duty, or rather, is it something that must be freely given, given not out of a sense of duty but out of genuine, heartfelt gratitude? If a favour is done with the sense that something is owing as a result, then perhaps it is not really a favour at all but an investment.

In any case, the intention here is not to take issue with Ross's list — only to suggest that its contents are perhaps open to question. This leads to a point of some significance. According to Ross, that we have the *prima facie* duties he mentions is simply *self-evident* to any rational human being who thinks seriously about the requirements of morality. The existence of these duties, and the validity of the principles which describe them, are known through *moral intuition*. To say that a principle is self-evident and known through intuition is to say that its truth is evident to an attentive mind, that it neither needs supporting evidence nor needs to be deduced from other propositions, but stands alone as something obviously true. In this instance, it stands alone as something whose truth is known directly through moral intuition.

This feature of Ross's theory is very controversial among philosophers, who are generally suspicious of "self-evident principles" and "intuition." In the case of morality, the apparent obviousness of some principles, and the certainty with which many believe them, seem better explained by things such as uniform moral upbringing and common experiences. And then there is the problem of disagreement. If a principle truly is self-evident, then shouldn't everyone agree on its validity? Yet this is seldom, if ever, the case with moral principles, including those on Ross's list. One who asserts that his claims are self-evident has little to say to us if we wish to disagree with him. He can ask that we think again, but he cannot undertake to *prove* his claims to us. If his claims truly are self-evident and known through intuition, they are in need of no proof — and more importantly, none can be given. So if, after careful reflection, you continue to disagree with some of the principles on Ross's list, he has little recourse but to accuse you of moral blindness. He must view you as equivalent to a person who cannot see the difference between red and blue; your moral blindness is on a par with his colour blindness. One might ask whether this is a satisfactory response to serious moral disagreements among reasonable people of good will and integrity.

Ross believes that his self-evident principles articulate *prima facie* moral obligations. These obligations hold unless overridden in individual cases by a more stringent or weightier duty. As for how we are to determine which of two or more *prima facie* duties has greater weight in a given case, Ross provides no answer except to say that we must use our best judgment, and fails to tell us the considerations upon which our judgments are to be based. Ross is fully aware that in most cases of conflicting obligations it is far from clear which duty is more stringent. Reasonable people of moral integrity will disagree. We therefore seem left with a serious gap in the theory and must either accept that in cases of conflict there just is no one right thing to do, that the best we can do is fulfil one of our conflicting duties and violate the other; or we must continue to look for a *criterion* in terms of which conflicts can be resolved.

It is at this point that the utilitarian will be more than happy to offer assistance. In his view, Ross has isolated the basis for a set of rules which are indeed important in everyday moral thinking. According to the defender of AU, these Rossian rules are useful *guidelines* or *rules of thumb* we are well advised in most cases to follow. If we follow them regularly, our actions will in the long run end up maximizing utility. The act of promising usually does maximize utility, as does a display of gratitude. But in those cases in which a conflict between the rules arises, or where an applicable rule seems inappropriate for good utilitarian reasons, we must resort directly to the AU criterion and decide which action will maximize utility. As for the proponent of RU, she will likely claim that Ross's rules will almost certainly figure in the set of rules general observance of which within a modern society will maximize utility. The proponent of RU is also likely to claim that, in cases in which the rules conflict, direct recourse must be made to the principle of utility, and that should follow the rule which, in the circumstances, will lead to the maximization of utility. Of course, Ross must reject the utilitarian's offer of rescue. Were he to follow the utilitarian's lead, he would in effect be adopting the principle of utility as defining a single, ultimate obligation, and this would be to deny Ross's central claim that each of his *prima facie* duties is equally important and irreducible. However, without a means of adjudicating among conflicting *prima facie* duties, Ross leaves us short just where we need guidance the most.

THE LANGUAGE OF RIGHTS

An introduction to the basic theories and concepts of ethics would be radically incomplete without some mention of "rights." At one time, it was quite natural to express moral requirements using concepts such as "ought," "duty," and "obligation." The three ethical theories just discussed were presented by their authors using these terms and concepts. Today, however, our moral vocabulary is dominated by the notion of rights. Instead of saying "You *ought* not to have done that," a modern person is more apt to remark "You had no *right* to do that." But rights come in a variety of forms. In order to facilitate discussion of the moral issues raised in this book, a brief analysis of these differences follows. The conceptual map sketched is largely derivative from the theory proposed early in this century by the American legal scholar Wesley Hohfeld, and from the more recent account developed by the contemporary moral philosopher Joel Feinberg.[17]

Hohfeld attempted to explicate the various normative relationships expressible in the vocabulary of rights by arranging certain basic concepts in pairs of opposites and correlatives. He thought that the best way to explain a group of related concepts is to outline the logical relationships which hold among them: pairs of correlatives must always exist together and opposites cannot exist in the same person in relation to the same subject matter. For example, duty and privilege are opposites, so if I have a duty to help you, I cannot also have the privilege of not helping you. Hohfeld formally defined the notions "correlative" and "opposite" as follows:

> A and B are *correlatives* if and only if the presence of the one in an individual X implies the existence of at least one other person Y in which the other is present.
>
> A and B are *opposites* if and only if the presence of the one in an individual X implies the absence in himself, X, of the other.

The correlatives are right/duty and privilege/no right. The opposites are right/no right and privilege/duty.

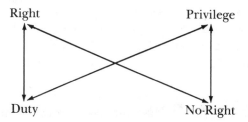

In the above diagram, the correlatives are connected by vertical arrows, the opposites by diagonal arrows.

Claim-rights

Strictly speaking, Hohfeld thought, a right is an *enforceable claim* to someone else's action or non-action. If one has a right to something, then one can demand it as one's due, as that to which one is entitled. The other person, or group of persons, has a correlative duty or obligation to respect your claim. For instance, I have a right not to be assaulted by you. This entails that you are under an obligation of non-action — a duty not to assault me. This kind of right, a claim against other people, is what Hohfeld calls a *claim-right*. A claim-right is always paired with a corresponding duty or obligation, which applies to at least one other person. Violation of my claim-right is always the violation by someone else of his or her duty towards me.

Claim-rights come in a variety of different forms. Joel Feinberg distinguishes between:

(a) *in personam* and *in rem* rights;
(b) positive and negative rights; and
(c) passive and active rights.

In personam rights are said to hold against one or more determinate, specifiable persons. These are determinate persons who are under the corresponding or correlative obligations. For example, if Miriam owes Beth a weekend at Kennebunkport, then there is a specific person, Miriam, against whom Beth enjoys her claim-right. Other examples are rights under contract, rights of landlords to rent payments from their tenants, the right against one's employer to a safe and healthy working environment, the right to equitable compensation for one's services, and so on. Many of the duties on Ross's list of *prima facie* duties could easily be expressed in terms of the correlative claim-rights. Paired with a Rossian duty of fidelity, for example, would be a claim-right against a person with whom one has made a contract to the honouring of the agreement. That person has a duty to perform his/her end of the deal; you have a correlative claim-right to his/her performance.

In rem rights, on the other hand, are said to hold not against some specifiable, namable person or group of persons, but against "the world at large." For instance, my right not to be assaulted holds not against any particular person or group of persons but against anyone and everyone who might be in a position to commit such an offence against me. All other such persons have a correlative duty not to assault me. This latter, correlative duty, would no doubt fall under Ross's duties of non-maleficence.

A positive right is a right to someone else's positive action. A negative right, on the other hand, is a right to another person's non-action or forbearance. If I have a positive right to something, then this means that there is at least one other person who has an obligation to *do* something, usually something for my benefit. By contrast, I have a negative right when there is at least one other person who has a duty to refrain from doing something that affects me in some, usually undesirable, way. Depending on what it is that the other person(s) must refrain from doing, my negative right can be either passive or active.

Active rights are negative rights to go about one's own business free from the interference of others. Paired with active claim-rights are duties of non-interference. Business people who complain that government should "get off their backs" are usually asserting active claim-rights not to be interfered with or hindered in their commercial ventures. Corresponding to such rights, they argue, is a duty on the part of government to allow business people a certain degree of freedom and autonomy. As we shall see in Part One of this text, the free-market libertarianism of Milton Friedman is fundamentally based on the assertion of negative, active rights to non-interference.

Passive negative rights are rights not to have certain things done to us. We might, for convenience, call them "security rights." Obvious examples are the right not to be killed and the right not to be assaulted. We might add here the right not to be inflicted with disease and injury by negligent or reckless employers. Those who assert a right against hostile corporate takeovers presumably have in mind a negative, passive right not to be adversely affected by the activities of corporate raiders. Passive rights are not rights against interference with one's own activities; they are not rights to do things without interference. Rather, they are rights not to have certain unwanted or harmful things done to us.

It is worth noting that, typically, active rights of non-interference can be protected only at the expense of other people's passive security rights. The active right of a manufacturer to pursue a livelihood within the capitalist system often competes with the passive, *in personam*, security rights of workers. It also competes with the passive, *in rem* rights of the community or world at large not to have its environment fouled by industrial activities. In general, a key problem of moral, legal, and political philosophy is how to balance active freedom rights against passive security rights. Different theories will place differing emphases on the competing rights. The same is true in the area of business ethics. A free-market capitalist like Friedman will place greater weight on active freedom rights, while environmentalists, workers' rights activists, and critics of the capitalist system typically will place far greater weight on passive security rights. Sometimes they will go so far as to assert *positive* rights to assistance from employers and government. The resolution of such conflicts is as difficult as the resolution of conflicts among Ross's *prima facie* duties.

To recapitulate, claim rights can be either *in personam* or *in rem*, positive or negative, and if they are negative, they can be either passive or active. Always correlated with any one of these rights is a duty or obligation on the part of at least one other individual. Such rights are claims against others who are under duty to respect them.

Liberties or privileges

According to Hohfeld, some of the situations in which people assert rights do not involve claims against others who are under correlative obligations. Rather, they involve what Hohfeld calls "privileges" or "liberties." My having a privilege does not entail that others are under obligation towards me. Rather, it entails only the *absence of duty* on my part. Hence, the opposite of privilege is duty. If I enjoy the privilege of doing something, then I am free or at liberty to do it (or not do it) and do no wrong should I exercise my privilege. In short, a privilege is "freedom from duty." An example from law might help to clarify the nature of privileges.

In most legal systems, there is a standing duty to provide the court with whatever information it requests. However, most jurisdictions also recognize a right — a privilege — against self-incrimination. In this special area — i.e. evidence which may implicate them in a crime — citizens are at liberty to decline the court's request. Here they enjoy an absence of duty. But if I have no *claim-right* against self-incrimination, only a privilege, then a sharp lawyer who somehow gets me to incriminate myself has in no way violated my rights. Were my right a claim-right against her, then the lawyer would be under a corresponding duty or obligation to respect a claim I would have against her. But with privileges, there are no such corresponding duties — only the absence of duty on my part. I have a freedom to act (or not to act) but it is not a freedom which enjoys the protection afforded by corresponding duties on the part of other people to respect my freedom. There is no requirement on their part that they refrain from interfering with my actions.

Examples in business where the notion of a privilege or liberty arises are not perhaps as obvious as in law, but can be found, however, in situations in which some people are exempt from duties to which they would otherwise be held. Employees, for instance, are granted the privilege of entering the employer's premises. Some are also privileged with respect to confidential information. Access to private premises or confidential information is something from which the general public is barred. The general public is under duty to respect the confidentiality of private company records. They have *no right* to these privileged items. Those who are privileged, however, enjoy a freedom from this duty. They are exempt from the general duty to keep away or to mind their own business, which applies to the public generally.

The correlative of a privilege is what Hohfeld, finding no better term available, calls "no-right": If X has the privilege of doing A, there is no other person who has a right against him that he do or not do A. If my employer grants me the privilege of examining confidential documents for purposes of an audit, then he has no right against me that I not examine those documents. He does not enjoy against me the right he enjoys against everyone else to whom he has not granted this special privilege. These others, because of the claim-right, the enforceable claim my employer has against them, are of course under duty to "mind their own business."

It is worth stressing once again that privileges are unprotected freedoms. Contrast a situation in which you are granted the privilege of examining confidential company documents with that of a court-appointed auditor. If the auditor is granted a claim-right to examine the files, then my employer must respect that right. She has a duty to turn them over and does wrong if she fails to do so. If, by contrast, my employer, upon granting me the privilege of examining the documents, forgets to give them to me, she has in no way violated my rights. I enjoy a mere privilege, not a claim-right with which is paired a corresponding duty.

Further reflections on rights

One should be alert when encountering talk of "rights." It is important to ask whether the right being asserted is a claim-right or a privilege. These are different conceptually and have very different implications. If the right is a claim-right, then one should ask whether it is *in rem* or *in personam*. It may be particularly crucial to determine whether the right is negative or positive. Does it require only that others refrain from doing something, or does it require a positive action? This important difference figures prominently in many public debates. One famous case in which the difference proved crucial was the United States Supreme Court's decision in *Roe* v. *Wade*. The Court ruled that every woman has a right to abort a fetus within specified limits. This decision was interpreted by some to mean that the Court had recognized a positive right to abortion, which entailed aid and financial assistance from the state. A 1977 ruling, however, made it clear that, while it was unconstitutional to prevent a woman from having an elective abortion within the prescribed limits, women did not have a right to aid or financial assistance. In other words, *Roe* v. *Wade* had granted only a *negative*, not a *positive*, right to an abortion.

The difference between positive and negative rights is as vital in ethical and political theory as it is in the law. Some theories emphasize negative rights and liberties (almost) to the exclusion of positive rights. Friedman and other libertarians like Robert Nozick and Jan Narveson stress the liberty or privilege to pursue one's own interests free from any positive duties to provide for others.[18] They also give great weight to the protections afforded by negative, active claim-rights to non-interference. The free market demands such enforceable claims and is corrupted by misguided state intervention in the name of positive rights. Theories of this sort find appeal in the notion of the individual's unconstrained (but protected) freedom to pursue his own interests and projects as he sees fit and as he defines them. The fundamental purpose of morality and law, on this view, is simply the protection and enhancement of individual liberty.

Some theories are willing to assert positive rights to assistance from others. Utilitarians who wish to employ the vocabulary of rights will be prepared to affirm positive rights when their observance generally serves to maximize utility. On such a theory, we are not merely to leave people alone but are to concern ourselves with their welfare and be willing, at least sometimes, to sacrifice our own interests for theirs. As we saw earlier, the same is true on Ross's theory. In addition to the duty of non-maleficence, to which corresponds a negative right against the duty holder, Ross includes a duty of beneficence, with which will be paired a positive right to beneficent actions on the part of others.

CONCLUDING THOUGHTS

As the preceding discussion illustrates, there are numerous moral theories and different vocabularies with which to express them. The question naturally arises: How should someone interested in applying the insights of moral philosophy to actual practice respond to this somewhat perplexing situation? The strategies one could adopt in linking moral theory to practice are numerous and varied. Nevertheless, it is possible to isolate three basic patterns of response.

(a) **Make decisions on an *ad hoc*, case-by-case, basis, ignoring ethical theories altogether**.   This is neither a promising nor an inviting option. Although there is some truth in the adage that "no two cases are ever alike," it would be a serious mistake to exaggerate it. Any two cases will necessarily be unlike one another in many respects, but it fails to follow that they are unlike one another *in* *the relevant respects.* No two murders are completely similar, but they are alike in what is often the only relevant respect: a human being has been killed. If cases can often be classified as being similar in a limited number of relevant respects, and these cases are familiar and recurring ones, then the possibility arises of discovering moral rules and principles to govern them. We are able to fashion workable legal rules governing murder because there is a limited number of recurring, relevant aspects of murder cases that can be dealt with in simple, general rules. The same is often true with moral rules and principles.

If the possibility of moral rules, and ethical theories to generate them, exists, then it would be counter-productive to ignore it entirely. We would have to "start from scratch" every time we had to make a difficult moral decision, inefficient to say the least, and a hindrance to moral understanding. Understanding the world involves recognizing similarities and differences. Without moral rules, principles, and theories to generate them, we make it difficult, if not impossible, to gain moral understanding. Working with an admittedly deficient theory is better than working with no theory at all.

(b) Make a firm and irrevocable commitment to a particular ethical theory. While this option promotes single-mindedness, it has the disadvantage of creating a blind spot to the possible insights of other ethical theories. It compels one to resolve all moral quandaries within the boundaries of the theory chosen. This tack smacks of artificiality and arbitrariness — unless one is convinced one "knows the truth" with absolute certainty, an unlikely possibility for someone willing to ascend to the reflective level of moral thinking (see "Levels of Moral Response," page 3). Blindly committing oneself to an ethical theory is no better than blindly committing oneself to a conventional rule. It is to descend to the pre-reflective level where blind acceptance replaces critical reflection and the possibility of moral progress.

(c) Allow for both fixity and flexibility. The fixity is provided by acknowledging that moral conflicts need not, and perhaps should not, be resolved within a moral vacuum, and that the application of an ethical theory with which one is not entirely happy nevertheless often can shed light on the issues in dispute. At the very least, it may bring some of the important considerations into relief, where they may be more easily examined and discussed rationally. Flexibility in acknowledging that competing theories could offer insight as well may even lead us judiciously to extract rules and principles from competing systems as determined by their apparent relevance to the case in question. It may be true that sometimes Mill seems to provide a better answer than Kant, and that the tables are reversed at other times. As Ross seemed to appreciate, this is not necessarily a cause for dismay. Consider an analogous case in physics. Sometimes the wave theory provides a better account than the particle theory of the properties and behaviour of light; at other times the reverse is true. A single, unified theory would no doubt be preferable. But until such time as one becomes available, it would be imprudent to ingore the existing theories altogether, or to subscribe to one and forget about the other(s). The same is true in ethics. We must not let our failures to achieve completeness blind us to the incremental gains in knowledge that have been made. Aristotle once remarked that "precision is not to be sought alike in all discussions. We must be content, in speaking of such subjects [e.g. ethics and politics], to indicate the truth roughly and in outline."[19] We would do well, perhaps, to heed Aristotle's caution.[20]

ENDNOTES

1. See G.E. Moore, *Principia Ethica* (London: Cambridge University Press, 1903).
2. John Stuart Mill, *Utilitarianism* (New York: Bobbs Merrill, 1957), p. 10.
3. *Utilitarianism*, p. 22.
4. John Rawls, "Two Concepts of Rules," *The Philosophical Review*, Jan. 1955.
5. See J.J.C. Smart and Bernard Williams, *Utilitarianism: For and Against* (London: Cambridge University Press, 1973), p. 10.
6. See David Lyons, *The Forms and Limits of Utilitarianism* (Oxford: Oxford University Press, 1965) where it is argued that any version of RU faithful to the utilitarian credo collapses logically into AU.
7. Immanuel Kant, *Groundwork of the Metaphysics of Morals*, trans. H.J. Paton (New York: Harper & Row, 1964), pp. 67–68.
8. *Ibid.*, p. 70.
9. *Ibid.*, p. 89.
10. *Ibid.*, pp. 89–90.
11. *Ibid.*, p. 90.
12. *Ibid.*, p. 96.
13. W.D. Ross, *The Right and the Good* (Oxford: Clarendon Press, 1930), p. 21.
14. *Ibid.*, p. 13.
15. Immanuel Kant, "On a Supposed Right to Lie From Altruistic Motives" in Lewis White Beck, ed. and trans., *Critique of Practical Reason and Other Writings in Moral Philosophy* (Chicago: The University of Chicago Press, 1949), pp. 346–350.
16. *The Right and the Good*, p. 21.
17. See W. Hohfeld, *Fundamental Legal Conceptions* (New Haven: Yale University Press, 1919) and Joel Feinberg, "Duties, Rights and Claims" in *Rights, Justice and the Bounds of Liberty* (Princeton: Princeton University Press, 1980).
18. Nozick's provocative political theory is developed in his *Anarchy, State and Utopia* (Oxford: Blackwell's, 1974). For Narveson's view, see "Have We a Right to Non-Discrimination?", p. 279 ff, this text, and *The Libertarian Idea* (Philadelphia: Temple University Press, 1989).
19. Aristotle, *Nicomachean Ethics*, trans. J.L. Ackrill (New York: Humanities Press, 1973), 1094b 12, 18.
20. Some of the material in this introductory essay derives from the general introduction to ethical theory found in *Well and Good: Case Studies in Biomedical Ethics* (Peterborough: Broadview Press, 1987), co-authored by W. Waluchow and John E. Thomas. I hereby extend my thanks to John Thomas for his indirect contribution to the content of this essay.

PART ONE

What Business Does Ethics Have in Business?

INTRODUCTION

In this section, we begin with the most basic of all questions regarding business ethics, a question that must be addressed before we can begin to consider the various issues discussed in subsequent parts. The question is: What business does ethics have in business? Is it the case that business is business and ethics is ethics, and never the twain shall meet? Or does ethics in fact play a vital part in the everyday practice of business? If so, what kind of role does it play? Is there perhaps a special ethics governing the role of business person, as distinct from the ethics of people in everyday life, or is all daily conduct governed by the same standards?

These are the questions discussed by the authors in Part One. The section opens with a famous and influential essay by the economist Milton Friedman. According to Friedman, the role of ethics in business is rather limited, or at least it would be if business people were clear-headed about the roles they should play in society. Friedman is concerned to combat what he takes to be a pernicious doctrine: the social responsibility thesis. According to this thesis, at least as Friedman sees it, business people are not to be concerned exclusively with financial profit but must take a central, perhaps leading, role in protecting and improving society and the environment; their concern should lie with their fellow humans, not with profit. Friedman will have none of this. In his view, "there is one and only one social responsibility of business — to use its resources and engage in activities designed to increase its profits so long as it stays within the rules of the game,

which is to say, engages in open and free competition without deception or fraud."
The "rules of the game" of which Friedman speaks are those found in law, and in
the requirement that all business activities be conducted without outright deception or fraud. This latter requirement is based on Friedman's belief that fully
informed, free exchanges of goods are the most efficient and politically desirable
means of rationally distributing goods within society. Within these constraints,
essential for the proper working of the free market, a responsible business manager will simply pursue profits.

Friedman's view has basically three grounds. First, managers have a fiduciary
obligation (a Rossian duty of fidelity) to advance and protect the interest of those
whom they serve. The "key point is that, in his capacity as a corporate executive,
the manager is the agent of the individuals who own the corporation . . . and his
primary responsibility is to them." This is the "Loyal Agent's Argument," which
serves as the primary focus of Part Five of this text. Friedman is stressing the
importance of the special relationship existing between the business manager
and the owners (usually the stockholders) of the company he helps to manage.
According to Friedman, it would be a violation of duty were the manager to strive,
out of some misguided sense of social responsibility, to advance the welfare or
utility of society as a whole. It would be as wrong for a business manager to ignore
the special duty he owes to the owners (who enjoy correlative claim-rights against
him) as it would be for parents to ignore the special duties they owe to their
children. Recall W.D. Ross's claim that, in addition to their role as possible beneficiaries of my actions, fellow human beings "may also stand to me in the relation of
promisee to promiser, creditor or debtor, of wife to husband, of child to parent, of
friend to friend . . . and the like." "The like," Friedman would add, includes the
relation of manager to company owner(s). This special relation founds special
duties of fidelity.

Friedman's second ground lies in his belief that productive organizations
must aim directly at the maximization of profits if society is to achieve an acceptable level of consumer satisfaction. Society is in the long run better off in terms of
social utility if business people take as their primary goal the pursuit of personal
and corporate profit, says Friedman. We're all better off if companies try to make
money for themselves by producing the best products for the least money. The
invisible hand of the free market will ensure that such selfishly motivated competitive behaviour results in the overall maximization of social utility. Were business
people to aim directly at social utility instead, the free market would be corrupted.
Prices would rise along with inefficiency, and production would drop off. The
well-intentioned, but seriously misguided, efforts of business people would prove
futile, and we would all be worse off in the long run. Note the distinctly utilitarian
flavour of this argument. Its structure is quite similar to arguments fashioned by
act and rule utilitarians to show how utility is maximized by such activities as
keeping promises, honouring commitments, and paying one's own way. In all
these cases, the argument goes, utility is maximized in the long run if we refrain

from applying the principle of utility directly and instead follow practices and rules of thumb which indirectly lead to the best consequences overall.

Friedman's third ground lies in his political libertarianism, a theory that celebrates the liberty of individuals to pursue their own interests, projects, and welfare according to their own individual lights. It is a theory that stresses the value of Hohfeldian liberties and negative claim-rights and looks with suspicion upon positive rights and government efforts to protect them. Libertarianism essentially views human beings as autonomous individuals whose liberty to acquire, trade, dispose of, or otherwise use their own private property for their own purposes must be respected so long as the individual in question respects the similar liberty of others. All exchanges of private property should be made freely, openly, and honestly. In this way, no one's property will be forcefully and unjustly appropriated by others who have no right to it. Society, on this model, is a collection of individuals and the voluntary associations into which they enter for mutual gain. The notion that people should be forced to help one another is anathema to libertarians.

Friedman's political libertarianism clearly underlies his views on the proper role of government, which is to protect private property and ensure that all exchanges are unforced and voluntary, that is, freely and knowledgeably under-taken; hence the desirability of legal regulation requiring no more than that transactions be open and free from deception and fraud. Were government — or moralists — to require anything more of business people, instead of autonomous individuals freely, openly, and efficiently engaging in exchange for mutual advan-tage, we would have the unjust and inefficient appropriation of private property. We would have, to use Friedman's own words, "pure and unadulterated socialism," where the scope of government extends "to every human activity," and liberty is threatened.

So Friedman would be opposed, on grounds of political principle and utility, to laws and doctrines of social responsibility requiring such things as affirmative action in employment or employment equity. Forcing companies to spend money to aid underprivileged groups would be unjustly restricting a company's right to use its private capital to its own best advantage. It would also be playing havoc with the free market in which labour, as much as wood, steel, and computer pro-grammes, is a commodity with a certain value for which an appropriate price must be paid. This price must be determined by the free market. Analogous objections would be made to other "socially responsible" initiatives, like efforts to avoid pollution or reduce inflation.

In summary, Friedman proposes a theory that sees a threat to individual liberty, autonomy, and utility in doctrines requiring business people to assume, in their roles as business people, responsibilities other than maximization of profits within "the rules of the game."

None of the other authors whose work is represented in Part One sees a danger in such doctrines. Mulligan objects to Friedman's platform on a number of grounds. He questions the paradigm upon which Friedman's critique of the social responsibility thesis is based. Mulligan sees that efforts to be "socially responsible" are not always the product of a "Lone Ranger" executive, deciding to pursue social objectives without the consent of other stakeholders. As Mulligan explains, socially responsible actions are often the result of decisions taken in accordance with corporate policy. "Founders, board members, major stock-holders, and senior executives may all participate in defining a mission and in setting objectives based on that mission. In so doing, these people serve as "legislators" for the company." It is worth noting, perhaps, that the fundamental obligation of managers on Friedman's account is not, strictly speaking, to maximize *profits*, but to advance the *desires* of the owners. Friedman's view is that the desires of owners *usually* lie in profit maximization. Yet it is quite possible, and if Mulligan is correct, quite normal, for the owners' desires to extend beyond the bottom line. If so, then socially responsible business activities may be required by Friedman's very own premises!

Mulligan also questions, along with Michalos, Friedman's suggestion that business people are ill-equipped to predict and assess the future consequences of "socially responsible" actions and policies. Citing the ability of successful business people to make difficult decisions under less than optimal conditions of knowledge, Mulligan suggests that a business person is perhaps better off than many others in trying to evaluate the social consequences of business decisions. He "has even less cause than most moral agents to abstain from social responsibility out of a sense of the futility of knowing consequences, since he is more practiced than most in the techniques for making action decisions in the absence of certainty."

In sharp contrast to Friedman, Michalos defends the claim that business people cannot isolate themselves from their *general* moral responsibilities as moral agents. There is no special morality for business people as distinct from the morality of all persons as moral agents. On the contrary, Michalos suggests, "There can be only one kind of morality, and it is universal. Businesspeople, like everyone else, must be judged morally responsible or irresponsible in terms of this morality. There is no third option." But what does it mean to be morally responsible in business? According to Michalos, human action, and thus the action of people in business, is morally responsible "insofar as it is reasonably intended to impartially maximize human well-being" — not, it should be stressed, the well-being of owners alone. Michalos is quite clearly advocating a utilitarian theory of some kind, a monistic theory of obligation that views our sole fundamental obligation to lie in the maximization of utility (or welfare). Michalos' utilitarian theory requires that a business person consider impartially the possible impact of her activities upon all those whose utility might in some way be affected by those activities. It rejects Friedman's notion of special fiduciary relationships existing between managers and owners as grounds for the right and indeed the duty of managers to concern themselves (almost) exclusively with the commercial interests of owners. It is therefore a much wider, and potentially much more demanding conception of morally responsible action than is advocated by Friedman. In defence of his wider conception, Michalos answers fourteen different arguments which have at one time or other been advanced against the sort of conception he favours. Some of these objections are clearly Friedman's, or at least derivative from Friedman's main theses. It will be worthwhile to consider how Friedman might respond to Michalos' challenge, and whether there are other viable conceptions of morally responsible business activity in addition to the ones these two writers defend. For instance, should an acceptable theory of moral responsibility in business recognize the importance of the fiduciary duties upon which Friedman lays so much stress but insist, along with W.D. Ross, that those duties are *prima facie only*? If they are only *prima facie*, then the possibility arises of competing duties, say of non-maleficence and possibly even beneficence, which compete with and sometimes override the fiduciary duties. For those inclined, along with Michalos, towards a monistic, utilitarian conception, perhaps room must be made for Friedman's "ground rules" within the utilitarian framework, along the same lines as utilitarian accounts of the binding quality of promises and other special commitments.

Part One closes with a thoughtful piece by Sir Adrian Cadbury, chairperson of Cadbury Schweppes PLC. Sir Adrian's comments are especially pertinent given their source. Some think that pious talk of ethics is simply out of place in the real business world where managers have neither the time, nor the ability, nor the inclination to take ethics seriously. Yet as Cadbury makes plain, "Business is part of the social system and [business people] cannot isolate the economic elements of major decisions from their social consequences." If Cadbury is right, those who take this advice to heart will profit for having done so, both in terms of moral integrity *and* the bottom line.

1

The Social Responsibility of Business Is to Increase Its Profits

MILTON FRIEDMAN

When I hear businessmen speak eloquently about the "social responsibilities of business in a free-enterprise system," I am reminded of the wonderful line about the Frenchman who discovered at the age of 70 that he had been speaking prose all his life. The businessmen believe that they are defending free enterprise when they declaim that business is not concerned "merely" with profit but also with promoting desirable "social" ends; that business has a "social conscience" and takes seriously its responsibilities for providing employment, eliminating discrimination, avoiding pollution and whatever else may be the catchwords of the contemporary crop of reformers. In fact they are — or would be if they or anyone else took them seriously — preaching pure and unadulterated socialism. Businessmen who talk this way are unwitting puppets of the intellectual forces that have been undermining the basis of a free society these past decades.

The discussions of the "social responsibilities of business" are notable for their analytical looseness and lack of rigor. What does it mean to say that "business" has responsibilities? Only people can have responsibilities. A corporation is an artificial person and in this sense may have artificial responsibilities, but "business" as a whole cannot be said to have responsibilities, even in this vague sense. The first step toward clarity in examining the doctrine of the social responsibility of business is to ask precisely what it implies for whom.

Presumably, the individuals who are to be responsible are businessmen, which means individual proprietors or corporate executives. Most of the discussion of social responsibility is directed at corporations, so in what follows I shall mostly neglect the individual proprietor and speak of corporate executives.

In a free-enterprise, private-property system a corporate executive is an employee of the owners of the business. He has direct responsibility to his employers. That responsibility is to conduct the business in accordance with their desires, which generally will be to make as much money as possible while conforming to the basic rules of the society, both those embodied in law and those embodied in ethical custom. Of course, in some cases his employers may have a different objective. A group of persons might establish a corporation for an eleemosynary purpose — for example, a hospital or a school. The manager of such a corporation will not have money profit as his objective but the rendering of certain services.

In either case, the key point is that, in his capacity as a corporate executive, the manager is the agent of the individuals who own the corporation or establish the eleemosynary institution, and his primary responsibility is to them.

Needless to say, this does not mean that it is easy to judge how well he is performing his task. But at least the criterion of performance is straightforward, and the persons among whom a voluntary contractual arrangement exists are clearly defined.

Of course, the corporate executive is also a person in his own right. As a person, he may have many other responsibilities that he recognizes or assumes voluntarily — to his family, his conscience, his feelings of charity, his church, his clubs, his city, his country. He may feel impelled by these responsibilities to devote part of his income to causes he regards as worthy, to refuse to work for particular corporations, and even to leave his job, for example, to join his country's armed forces. If we wish, we may refer to some of these responsibilities as "social responsibilities." But in these respects he is acting as a principal, not an agent; he is spending his own money or time or energy, not the money of his employers or the time or energy he has contracted to devote to their purposes. If these are "social responsibilities," they are the social responsibilities of individuals, not of business.

What does it mean to say that the corporate executive has a "social responsibility" in his capacity as businessman? If this statement is not pure rhetoric, it must mean that he is to act in some way that is not in the interest of his employers. For example, that he is to refrain from increasing the price of the product in order to contribute to the social objective of preventing inflation, even though a price increase would be in the best interests of the

corporation. Or that he is to make expenditures on reducing pollution beyond the amount that is in the best interests of the corporation or that is required by law in order to contribute to the social objective of improving the environment. Or that, at the expense of corporate profits, he is to hire "hardcore" unemployed instead of better-qualified available workmen to contribute to the social objective of reducing poverty.

In each of these cases, the corporate executive would be spending someone else's money for a general social interest. Insofar as his actions in accord with his "social responsibility" reduce returns to stockholders, he is spending their money. Insofar as his actions raise the price to customers, he is spending the customers' money. Insofar as his actions lower the wages of some employees, he is spending their money.

The stockholders or the customers or the employees could separately spend their own money on the particular action if they wished to do so. The executive is exercising a distinct "social responsibility," rather than serving as an agent of the stockholders or the customers or the employees, only if he spends the money in a different way than they would have spent it.

But if he does this, he is in effect imposing taxes, on the one hand, and deciding how the tax proceeds shall be spent, on the other.

This process raises political questions on two levels: principle and consequences. On the level of political principle, the imposition of taxes and the expenditure of tax proceeds are governmental functions. We have established elaborate constitutional, parliamentary and judicial provisions to control these functions, to assure that taxes are imposed so far as possible in accordance with the preferences and desires of the public — after all, "taxation without representation" was one of the battle cries of the American Revolution. We have a system of checks and balances to separate the legislative function of imposing taxes and enacting expenditures from the executive function of collecting taxes and administering expenditure programs and from the judicial function of mediating disputes and interpreting the law.

Here the businessman — self-selected or appointed directly or indirectly by stockholders — is to be simultaneously legislator, executive and jurist. He is to decide whom to tax by how much and for what purpose, and he is to spend the proceeds — all this guided only by general exhortations from on high to restrain inflation, improve the environment, fight poverty and so on and on.

The whole justification for permitting the corporate executive to be selected by the stockholders is that the executive is an agent serving the interests of his principal. This justification disappears when the corporate executive imposes taxes and spends the proceeds for "social" purposes. He becomes in effect a public employee, a civil servant, even though he remains in name an employee of a private enterprise. On grounds of political principle, it is intolerable that such civil servants — insofar as their actions in the name of social responsibility are real and not just window-dressing — should be selected as they are now. If they are to be civil servants, then they must be selected through a political process. If they are to impose taxes and make expenditures to foster "social" objectives, then political machinery must be set up to guide the assessment of taxes and to determine through a political process the objectives to be served.

This is the basic reason why the doctrine of "social responsibility" involves the acceptance of the socialist view that political mechanisms, not market mechanisms, are the appropriate way to determine the allocation of scarce resources to alternative uses.

On the grounds of consequences, can the corporate executive in fact discharge his alleged "social responsibilities"? On the one hand, suppose he could get away with spending the stockholders' or customers' or employees' money. How is he to know how to spend it? He is told that he must contribute to fighting inflation. How is he to know what action of his will contribute to that end? He is presumably an expert in running his company — in producing a product or selling it or financing it. But nothing about his selection makes him an expert on inflation. Will his holding down the price of his product reduce inflationary pressure? Or, by leaving more

spending power in the hands of his customers, simply divert it elsewhere? Or, by forcing him to produce less because of the lower price, will it simply contribute to shortages? Even if he could answer these questions, how much cost is he justified in imposing on his stockholders, customers and employees for this social purpose? What is his appropriate share of others'?

And, whether he wants to or not, can he get away with spending his stockholders', customers' or employees' money? Will not the stockholders fire him? (Either the present ones or those who take over when his actions in the name of social responsibility have reduced the corporation's profits and the price of its stock.) His customers and his employees can desert him for other producers and employers less scrupulous in exercising their social responsibilities.

This facet of "social responsibility" doctrine is brought into sharp relief when the doctrine is used to justify wage restraint by trade unions. The conflict of interest is naked and clear when union officials are asked to subordinate the interest of their members to some more general social purpose. If the union officials try to enforce wage restraint, the consequence is likely to be wildcat strikes, rank-and-file revolts and the emergence of strong competitors for their jobs. We thus have the ironic phenomenon that union leaders — at least in the U.S. — have objected to Government interference with the market far more consistently and courageously than have business leaders.

The difficulty of exercising "social responsibility" illustrates, of course, the great virtue of private competitive enterprise — it forces people to be responsible for their own actions and makes it difficult for them to "exploit" other people for either selfish or unselfish purposes. They can do good — but only at their own expense.

Many a reader who has followed the argument this far may be tempted to remonstrate that it is all well and good to speak of government's having the responsibility to impose taxes and determine expenditures for such "social" purposes as controlling pollution or training the hardcore unemployed, but that the problems are too urgent to wait on the slow course of political processes, that the exercise of social responsibility by businessmen is a quicker and surer way to solve pressing current problems.

Aside from the question of fact — I share Adam Smith's skepticism about the benefits that can be expected from "those who affected to trade for the public good" — this argument must be rejected on grounds of principle. What it amounts to is an assertion that those who favor the taxes and expenditures in question have failed to persuade a majority of their fellow citizens to be of like mind and that they are seeking to attain by undemocratic procedures what they cannot attain by democratic procedures. In a free society, it is hard for "good" people to do "good," but that is a small price to pay for making it hard for "evil" people to do "evil," especially since one man's good is another's evil.

I have, for simplicity, concentrated on the special case of the corporate executive, except for the brief digression on trade unions. But precisely the same argument applies to the newer phenomenon of calling upon stockholders to require corporations to exercise social responsibility (the recent G.M. crusade, for example). In most of these cases, what is in effect involved is some stockholders trying to get other stockholders (or customers or employees) to contribute against their will to "social" causes favored by the activists. Insofar as they succeed, they are again imposing taxes and spending the proceeds.

The situation of the individual proprietor is somewhat different. If he acts to reduce returns of his enterprise in order to exercise his "social responsibility," he is spending his own money, not someone else's. If he wishes to spend his money on such purposes, that is his right, and I cannot see that there is any objection to his doing so. In the process, he, too, may impose costs on employees and customers. However, because he is far less likely than a large corporation or union to have monopolistic power, any such side effects will tend to be minor.

Of course, in practice the doctrine of social responsibility is frequently a cloak for actions that are justified on other grounds rather than a reason for those actions.

To illustrate, it may well be in the long-run interest of a corporation that is a major employer in a small community to devote resources to providing amenities to that community or to improving its government. That may make it easier to attract desirable employees, it may reduce the wage bill or lessen losses from pilferage and sabotage or have other worthwhile effects. Or it may be that, given the laws about the deductibility of corporate charitable contributions, the stockholders can contribute more to charities they favor by having the corporation make the gift than by doing it themselves, since they can in that way contribute an amount that would otherwise have been paid as corporate taxes.

In each of these — and many similar — cases, there is a strong temptation to rationalize these actions as an exercise of "social responsibility." In the present climate of opinion, with its widespread aversion to "capitalism," "profits," the "soulless corporation" and so on, this is one way for a corporation to generate goodwill as a by-product of expenditures that are entirely justified in its own self-interest.

It would be inconsistent of me to call on corporate executives to refrain from this hypocritical window-dressing because it harms the foundations of a free society. That would be to call on them to exercise a "social responsibility"! If our institutions, and the attitudes of the public make it in their self-interest to cloak their actions in this way, I cannot summon much indignation to denounce them. At the same time, I can express admiration for those individual proprietors or owners of closely held corporations or stockholders of more broadly held corporations who disdain such tactics as approaching fraud.

Whether blameworthy or not, the use of the cloak of social responsibility, and the nonsense spoken in its name by influential and prestigious businessmen, does clearly harm the foundations of a free society. I have been impressed time and again by the schizophrenic character of many businessmen. They are capable of being extremely far-sighted and clear-headed in matters that are internal to their businesses. They are incredibly short-sighted and muddle-headed in matters that are outside their businesses but affect the possible survival of business in general. This short-sightedness is strikingly exemplified in the calls from many businessmen for wage and price guidelines or controls or income policies. There is nothing that could do more in a brief period to destroy a market system and replace it by a centrally controlled system than effective governmental control of prices and wages.

The short-sightedness is also exemplified in speeches by businessmen on social responsibility. This may gain them kudos in the short run. But it helps to strengthen the already too prevalent view that the pursuit of profits is wicked and immoral and must be curbed and controlled by external forces. Once this view is adopted, the external forces that curb the market will not be the social consciences, however highly developed, of the pontificating executives; it will be the iron fist of Government bureaucrats. Here, as with price and wage controls, businessmen seem to me to reveal a suicidal impulse.

The political principle that underlies the market mechanism is unanimity. In an ideal free market resting on private property, no individual can coerce any other, all cooperation is voluntary, all parties to such cooperation benefit or they need not participate. There are no "social" values, no "social" responsibilities in any sense other than the shared values and responsibilities of individuals.

Society is a collection of individuals and of the various groups they voluntarily form.

The political principle that underlies the political mechanism is conformity. The individual must serve a more general social interest — whether that be determined by a church or a dictator or a majority. The individual may have a vote and a say in what is to be done, but if he is overruled, he must conform. It is appropriate for some to require others to contribute to a general social purpose whether they wish to or not.

Unfortunately, unanimity is not always feasible. There are some respects in which conformity appears unavoidable, so I do not see how one can avoid the use of the political mechanism altogether.

But the doctrine of "social responsibility" taken seriously would extend the scope of the political mechanism to every human activity. It does not differ in philosophy from the most explicitly collectivist means. That is why, in my book *Capitalism and Freedom*, I have called it a "fundamentally subversive doctrine" in a free society, and have said that in such a society, "there is one and only one social responsibility of business — to use its resources and engage in activities designed to increase its profits so long as it stays within the rules of the game, which is to say, engages in open and free competition without deception or fraud."

2

A Critique of Milton Friedman's Essay "The Social Responsibility of Business Is to Increase Its Profits"

THOMAS MULLIGAN

In his famous essay, Milton Friedman argues that people responsible for decisions and action in business should not exercise social responsibility in their capacity as company executives. Instead, they should concentrate on increasing the profits of their companies.[1]

In the course of the essay, he also argues that the doctrine of social responsibility is a socialist doctrine.

The purpose of this paper is to assess the merit of Friedman's arguments. I shall summarize his main arguments, examine some of his premises and lines of inference, and propose a counter-argument.

Friedman's argument: Corporate executives should not exercise social responsibility

Friedman argues that the exercise of social responsibility by a corporate executive is:

(a) unfair, because it constitutes taxation without representation;

(b) undemocratic, because it invests governmental power in a person who has no general mandate to govern;

(c) unwise, because there are no checks and balances in the broad range of governmental power thereby turned over to his discretion;

(d) a violation of trust, because the executive is employed by the owners "as an agent serving the interests of his principal;"

(e) futile, both because the executive is unlikely to be able to anticipate the social consequences of his actions and because, as he imposes costs on his stockholders, customers, or employees, he is likely to lose their support and thereby lose his power.

These conclusions are related.

Points (b) and (c) depend on (a), on the ground that "the imposition of taxes and the expenditure of tax proceeds are governmental functions." Point (d) also depends on (a), because it is precisely in imposing a tax on his principal that this executive fails to serve the interests of that principal. Point (e) depends, in part, on (d), since it is the executive's

From *Journal of Business Ethics* 5 (1986) 265–269. © 1986 by D. Reidel Publishing Company. Reprinted by permission.

failure to serve the interests of his principal which results in the withdrawal of that principal's support.

Point (a) is thus at the foundation of the argument. If (a) is false, then Friedman's demonstration of the subsequent conclusions almost completely collapses.

Is it true, then, that the executive who performs socially responsible action "is in effect imposing taxes . . . and deciding how the tax proceeds shall be spent"?

To make this case, Friedman argues by depicting how a company executive would perform such action.

He first introduces examples to illustrate that exercising social responsibility in business typically costs money. He mentions refraining from a price increase to help prevent inflation, reducing pollution "beyond the amount that is in the best interests of the corporation" to help improve the environment, and "at the expense of corporate profits" hiring 'hardcore' unemployed.

To establish that such costs are in effect taxes, he argues:

1. In taking such action, the executive expends "someone else's money" — the stockholders', the customers', or the employees'.
2. The money is spent "for a general social interest."
3. "Rather than serving as an agent of the stockholders or the customers or the employees . . . he spends the money in a different way than they would have spent it."

The first two premises suggest a similarity between this money and tax revenues, with respect to their sources and to the purposes for which they are used. However, an expense is not yet a tax unless it is *imposed* on the contributor, irrespective of his desire to pay. Only Friedman's third premise includes this crucial element of imposition.

This third premise reveals the essential character of the paradigm on which Friedman bases his whole case.

Friedman's paradigm

In the above examples of socially responsible action and throughout his essay, Friedman depicts the cor-

porate executive who performs such action as a sort of Lone Ranger, deciding entirely by himself what good deeds to do, when to act, how much to spend:

> Here, the businessman — self-selected or appointed directly or indirectly by the stockholders — is to be simultaneously legislator, executive and jurist. He is to decide whom to tax by how much and for what purpose.

On this paradigm, the corporate executive does not act with the counsel and participation of the other stakeholders in the business. This is the basis of Friedman's claim that the executive is *imposing* something on those other stakeholders — unfairly, undemocratically, unwisely, and in violation of a trust.

But does Friedman's paradigm accurately depict the socially responsible executive? Does it capture the essential nature of socially responsible action in business? Or has he drawn a caricature, wrongly construed it as accurate, and used it to discredit the doctrine it purportedly illustrates?

A counter-paradigm

Friedman's paradigm is valid in the sense that it is certainly possible for a corporate executive to try to exercise social responsibility without the counsel or participation of the other stakeholders in the business.

Friedman is also correct in characterizing such conduct as unfair and as likely to result in the withdrawal of the support of those other stakeholders.

Yet Friedman insists, at least with respect to the executive's employers, that the socially responsible executive "must" do it alone, must act in opposition to the interests of the other stakeholders:

> What does it mean to say that the corporate executive has a "social responsibility" in his capacity as a businessman? If this statement is not pure rhetoric, it must mean that he is to act in some way that is not in the interest of his employers.

There is no good reason why this remarkable claim must be true. The exercise of social responsibility in business suffers no diminishment in meaning or merit if the executive and his employers both understand their mutual interest to include a proactive social role and cooperate in undertaking that role.

I propose a different paradigm for the exercise of social responsibility in business — one very much in keeping with sound management practice.

A business normally defines its course and commits itself to action by conceiving a mission, then proceeding to a set of objectives, then determining quantified and time-bound goals, and then developing a full strategic plan which is implemented by appropriate top-level staffing, operating procedures, budgeted expenditures, and daily management control.

Many stakeholders in the business participate in this far-reaching process.

Founders, board members, major stockholders, and senior executives may all participate in defining a mission and in setting objectives based on that mission. In so doing, these people serve as "legislators" for the company.

Top management's translation of these broad directions into goals, strategic plans, operating procedures, budgets, and daily work direction brings middle management, first-line management and, in some companies, employee representatives into the process. This is the "executive branch" of the business.

When the time comes to judge progress and success, the board members and stockholders serve as "jurists" at the highest level, and when necessary can take decisive, sometimes dramatic, corrective measures. However, the grass-roots judgment of the court of employee opinion can also be a powerful force. More than one company has failed or faltered because it did not keep a course which inspired and held its talented people.

In sum, a business is a collaborative enterprise among the stakeholders, with some checks and balances. In general, this system allows to any one stakeholder a degree of participation commensurate with the size of his or her stake.

For a business to define a socially responsible course and commit to socially responsible action, it needs to follow no other process than the familiar one described in the preceding paragraphs.

On this paradigm, if socially responsible action is on the corporate executive's agenda, then it is there because the company's mission, objectives, and goals — developed collaboratively by the major stakeholders — gave him license to put it there and provided parameters for his program. Lone Ranger executives are no more necessary and no more welcome in a socially responsible business than in one devoted exclusively to the maximization of profit.

This paradigm conforms more accurately than Friedman's to the reality of how action programs — socially responsible ones or otherwise — are conceived and enacted in a strategically managed business. The corporate executive in this process, in contradistinction to Friedman's corporate executive, does not impose unauthorized costs, or "taxes", on anyone. On this account, he usurps no governmental function, violates no trust, and runs no special risk of losing the support of the other stakeholders.

The problem of knowing future consequences

The preceding argument addresses most of Friedman's objections to a corporate executive's attempts to exercise social responsibility.

Friedman, however, provides one objection which does not rest on his paradigm of the Lone Ranger executive. This is the objection that it is futile to attempt socially responsible action because the future social consequences of today's actions are very difficult to know.

Suppose, he writes, that the executive decides to fight inflation:

> How is he to know what action of his will contribute to that end? He is presumably an expert in running his company — in producing a product or selling it or financing it. But nothing about his selection makes him an expert on inflation. Will holding down the price of his product reduce inflationary pressure? Or, by leaving more spending power in the hands of his customers, simply divert it elsewhere? Or by forcing him to produce less because of the lower price, will it simply contribute to shortages?

The difficulty of determining the future consequences of one's intended good acts has received attention in the literature of philosophical ethics.

G.E. Moore, in his early twentieth century classic *Principia Ethica*, writes of "the hopeless task of finding duties"[2] since, to act with perfect certainty, we would need to know "all the events which will be in any way affected by our action throughout an infinite future."[3]

Human life, however, requires action in the absence of certainty, and business people in particular have a bias toward action. They do not wait for perfect foreknowledge of consequences, but instead set a decision date, gather the best information available, contemplate alternatives, assess risks, and then decide what to do.

Decisions about socially responsible actions, no less than decisions about new products or marketing campaigns, can be made using this "business-like" approach. The business person, therefore, has even less cause than most moral agents to abstain from social responsibility out of a sense of the futility of knowing consequences, since he is more practiced than most in the techniques for making action decisions in the absence of certainty.

Social responsibility and socialism

Some of Friedman's most emphatic language is devoted to his position that the advocates of social responsibility in a free-enterprise system are "preaching pure and unadultered socialism."

He asserts this view in the first and last paragraphs of the essay, and concludes:

> The doctrine of "social responsibility" . . . does not differ in philosophy from the most explicitly collectivist doctrine.

Friedman's argument for this conclusion is located roughly midway through his essay, and it too rests on his paradigm of the socially responsible executive "imposing taxes" on others and thereby assuming governmental functions:

> He becomes in effect a public employee, a civil servant. . . . It is intolerable that such civil servants . . . should be selected as they are now. If they are to be civil servants, then they must be elected through a political process. If they are to impose taxes and make expenditures to foster "social" objectives, then political machinery must be set up to make the assessment of

taxes and to determine through a political process the objectives to be served.

This is the basic reason why the doctrine of "social responsibility" involves the acceptance of the socialist view that political mechanisms, not market mechanisms, are the appropriate way to determine the allocation of scarce resources or alternative uses.

I shall raise three objections to this line of reasoning.

First, this argument rests on the paradigm which has already been called into question. If we accept the counter-paradigm proposed above as truer to the nature of a socially responsible corporate executive, then there is no basis for saying that such an individual "imposes taxes," becoming "in effect" a civil servant.

Second, it is not apparent how the propositions that, under the doctrine of social responsibility, a corporate executive is "in effect" imposing taxes and "in effect" a civil servant logically imply that this doctrine upholds the view that political mechanisms should determine the allocation of scarce resources.

To the contrary, as Friedman points out, his paradigmatic executive is not a true political entity, since he is not elected and since his program of "taxation" and social expenditure is not implemented through a political process. Paradoxically, it is Friedman who finds it "intolerable" that this agent who allocates scarce resources is not part of a political mechanism. Nowhere, however, does he show that acceptance of such a political mechanism is intrinsic to the view of his opponent, the advocate of social responsibility.

Third, in order to show that the doctrine of social responsibility is a socialist doctrine, Friedman must invoke a criterion for what constitutes socialism. As we have seen, his criterion is "acceptance of the . . . view that political mechanisms, not market mechanisms, are the appropriate way to determine the allocation of scarce resources to alternative uses."

The doctrine of social responsibility, he holds, does accept this view. Therefore the doctrine is a socialist doctrine.[4]

However, this criterion is hardly definitive of socialism. The criterion is so broad that it holds for virtually any politically totalitarian or authoritarian system — including feudal monarchies and dictatorships of the political right.

Further, depending on the nature of a resource and the degree of its scarcity, the political leadership in any system, including American democracy, is liable to assert its right to determine the allocation of that resource. Who doubts that it is appropriate for our political institutions, rather than market mechanisms, to ensure the equitable availability of breathable air and drinkable water, or to allocate food and fuel in times of war and critical shortages?

Therefore, Friedman has not provided a necessary element for his argument — a definitive criterion for what constitutes socialism.

In summary, Friedman's argument is unsound: first, because it rests on an arbitrary and suspect paradigm; second, because certain of his premises do not imply their stated conclusion; and, third, because a crucial premise, his criterion for what constitutes socialism, is not true.

Although he complains of the "analytical looseness" and "lack of rigor" of his opponents, Friedman's argument has on close examination betrayed its own instances of looseness and lack of rigor.

Conclusion

I have considered Friedman's principal objections to socially responsible action in business and argued that at the bottom of most of his objections is an inaccurate paradigm. In response, I have given an account of a more appropriate paradigm to show how business can exercise social responsibility.

Friedman is right in pointing out that exercising social responsibility costs money. If nothing else, a company incurs expense when it invests the manhours needed to contemplate the possible social consequences of alternative actions and to consider the merit or demerit of each set of consequences.

But Friedman is wrong in holding that such costs must be imposed by one business stakeholder on the others, outside of the whole collaborative process of strategic and operational business management. He presumes too much in intimating through his imagined examples that the business person who pursues a socially responsible course inevitably acts without due attention to return on investment, budgetary limitations, reasonable employee remuneration, or competitive pricing.

My purpose has been to provide a critique of the major lines of argument presented in a famous and influential essay. The thrust has been to show that Friedman misrepresents the nature of social responsibility in business and that business people *can* pursue a socially responsible course without the objectionable results claimed by Friedman. It would be another step to produce positive arguments to demonstrate why business people *should* pursue such a course. That is an undertaking for another occasion.

For now, I shall only observe that Friedman's own concluding statement contains a moral exhortation to business people. Business, he says, should engage in "open and free competition without deception or fraud." If Friedman does not recognize that even these restrained words lay open a broad range of moral obligation and social responsibility for business, which is after all one of the largest areas of human interaction in our society, then the oversight is his.

ENDNOTES

1. Milton Friedman, "The Social Responsibility of Business Is to Increase Its Profits," *New York Times Magazine*, 13 September 1970, p. 32 ff. Unless otherwise noted, all quotations are from this essay. (See this text, p. 41 ff.)

2. G.E. Moore, *Principia Ethica* (London: Cambridge University Press, 1971), p. 150.

3. *Ibid.*, p. 149.

4. In the concluding paragraph of his essay, Friedman states, "The doctrine of 'social responsibility' taken seriously would extend the scope of the political mechanism to every human activity." "Every human activity" certainly seems at least one extra step beyond the set of activities involved in "the allocation of scarce resources to alternative uses." Unfortunately, Friedman's essay contains no explication of the reasoning he used to make the transition from the language of his argument midway through the essay to the grander claim of this concluding paragraph.

3

A Reply to Thomas Mulligan's "Critique of Milton Friedman's Essay 'The Social Responsibility of Business Is to Increase Its Profits'"

BILL SHAW

Introduction

Professor Thomas Mulligan's "A Critique of Milton Friedman's Essay 'The Social Responsibility of Business Is to Increase Its Profits'"[1] is a thoughtful effort, perhaps even the 1000th such effort since 1970, purporting to discredit Friedman's influential position on the issue:

> In a free-enterprise, private-property system, a corporate executive is an employee of the owners of the business. He has direct responsibility to his employers. That responsibility is to conduct the business in accordance with their desires, which generally will be to make as much money as possible while conforming to the basic rules of the society, both those embodied in law and those embodied in ethical custom. Of course, in some cases his employers may have a different objective. A group of persons might establish a corporation for an eleemosynary purpose — for example, a hospital or a school. The manager of such a corporation will not have money profit as his objectives but the rendering of certain services.
>
> In either case, the key point is that, in his capacity as a corporate executive, the manager is the agent of the individuals who own the corporation or establish the eleemosynary institution, and his primary responsibility is to them.[2]

Mulligan lodges three principal objections against this view. The first is to Friedman's impoverished paradigm that characterizes the socially responsible executive as a Lone Ranger-type, that is, one who spends "someone else's money . . . for a general social interest . . . in a different way than they would have spent it." Mulligan's counter-paradigm reduces but does not eliminate the arbitrariness of such impositions, or "taxes," by moving corporate executives into a participative or consultative role with corporate stakeholders. These stakeholders include major stockholders, but not all the

From *Journal of Business Ethics* 7 (1988) 537–543. © by Kluwer Academic Publishers. Reprinted by permission.

stockholders, and in some cases it includes employee representatives.

Secondly, Mulligan assails Friedman's reluctance to unleash socially responsible corporate executives on such problems as inflation, unemployment, environmental protection and the like. Friedman argues that these efforts are likely to be futile, Don Quixotesque at best, and at worst, counterproductive. The special competence of business persons, Friedman insists, does not extend to problems of this magnitude. Mulligan replies that all business decisions are made under conditions of uncertainty, and since business people are practiced in these techniques, their bias towards action should override the risk implicit in the absence of perfect foreknowledge. Managers then are urged to do something even if they do it wrong. Good intentions evidently count for much despite the possibility of negative or unsatisfactory consequences.

Mulligan's third criticism revisits the Lone Ranger paradigm, but it chiefly turns upon Friedman's lack of precision in defining socialism, in distinguishing it from other political systems (including democracies) that also allocate resources, and in explaining why he believes that social responsibility necessarily implies socialism. While Friedman's definition of socialism may well be an embarassment to political theorists, he is not nearly so far off the mark as is Professor Mulligan who concludes that participative and/or consultative management is a full and satisfactory reply to the allegation that socially responsible executives are "in effect" civil servants.

In brief, Professor Mulligan has presented an interesting and thought-provoking counter-thesis to Friedman's narrow and somewhat flawed vision. One cannot but notice however that Friedman scarcely concerns himself with a defense of his highly-regarded position, a position articulated even more blatantly eight years prior to his social responsibility essay. In a free economy, he wrote,

> . . . there is one and only one social responsibility of business — to use its resources and engage in activities designed to increase its profits so long as it stays within the rules of the game, which is to say, engages in open and free competition, without deception or fraud.

Few trends could so thoroughly undermine the very foundations of our free society as the acceptance by corporate officials of a social responsibility other than to make as much money for their stockholders as possible. This is a fundamentally subversive doctrine. If businessmen do have a social responsibility other than making maximum profits for stockholders, how are they to know what it is? Can self-selected private individuals decide what the social interest is? Can they decide how great a burden they are justified in placing on themselves or their stockholders to serve that social interest? Is it tolerable that these public functions of taxation, expenditure, and control be exercised by the people who happen at the moment to be in charge of particular enterprises, chosen for those posts by strictly private groups? If businessmen are civil servants rather than the employees of their stockholders then in a democracy they will, sooner or later, be chosen by the public techniques of election and appointment.[3]

There are very good reasons why Friedman has not rushed into print with rebuttals and I think that chief among these reasons is that he is not under any penetrating intellectual threat, or at least he is under no attack here that goes to the heart of his position. The fact that he does not perfectly defend his view is his own business and not a matter that will concern me now. For purposes of this essay I will simply observe that Friedman's concerns about the worth of "social responsibility" are legitimate concerns given the political/economic structure of the nation. Mulligan's critique, and that of many who have gone before him, is unsatisfactory because it contents itself with surface skirmishes. *Friedman will not be dislodged until it can be shown that the social and political institutions of this nation, that is, the mechanisms for determining how power and control over economic resources are distributed, are inadequate to promote the common good and social justice.* The reason this is so is that these institutions determine the nature and limits of the role of corporate managers and, in turn, their moral responsibilities. Hence, Friedman's vision, however imperfect, is coherent and it bristles with potential. That is a lot. It is as much as we are entitled to expect of one person. Now it is past time to quit chipping away at Friedman, to acknowledge the power of his worldview and its depth, and to be at least as clear as Friedman in advancing one's reasons in support of an alternative view.

Paradigms lost

Professor Mulligan's counter-paradigm is a distinct advance over Friedman's concept of socially responsible executives at war with profit maximizing shareholders. In the defense of profit, Friedman makes some excellent points, but he engages in overkill as well and in the process loses a certain amount of credibility. In the first place he advances the quite common-sensical view that socially responsible managers should not waste corporate resources in the grandiose pursuit of curing inflation, unemployment, pollution. These problems are systemic in nature and their remedy will not be brought about by even the most committed and well-intentioned managers.[4] It is scarcely conceivable that the uncoordinated efforts of our top 100 or even 500 firms could have much impact in this area beyond doing what they do best — creating quality goods and services at competitive prices. These problems are not unlike the ones presented by the national debt — how much debt can our economy stand, and what are the social repercussions of reducing or expanding the debt? Policy questions of this magnitude are simply not amenable to private tinkering and, beyond that, it is not our private sector firms but our political institutions that are designed to address such matters. After all, in environmental matters, how clean is clean enough? Regarding consumer products, how safe is safe enough? These are matters that reasonable people, people of good will, can have honest differences of opinion about, and that is why only collective, democratic decisions are appropriate.

It is much the same with inflation and employment as well. These issues demand some kind of national, even international, consensus and resolve. If it is expected of corporate managers that they do their "bottom line" tasks well, and in the process bring an end to other social evils, that is being unrealistic. It puts corporate managers in an untenable position of taking responsibility in areas in which

they have no training, experience, or authority. Friedman has served us well in warning of the dangers here, and these dangers are not overcome, as Mulligan seems to believe, simply by moving the focus from Scenario-One, (the single, willful executive) to Scenario-Two (the cooperative, participative, consensus building executive). Professor Mulligan ignores the reality that even consensus builders leave hard core dissenters in their wake, and does not address the moral insensitivity of doing so. But that is the lesser of his oversights. Even with a virtually unanimous (and virtually inconceivable) consensus, Friedman's objection on political principle is not even addressed. It misses Friedman's point to say that a supportive majority of shareholders legitimates a particular behavior (scenario two) that a passive majority merely allows or fails to prohibit (scenario one). While Mulligan's paradigm is imminently more sensible than Friedman's in terms of managerial tactics, he has by no means refuted Friedman's point that systemic problems (problems on the magnitude of the national debt, inflation, employment, pollution) are the principal mission of our political institutions. On the basis then of political principle, and on the basis of consequences, i.e., certain futility, the concept of social responsibility must be rescued from Mulligan no less than from Friedman.

Friedman does something else, however, that is not worthy of the high marks he earned with the foregoing analysis. He characterized as "hypocritical" and "approaching fraud" those executives who extol the social side of business endeavors that are also profit oriented. It is true of course that the socially responsible aspect of these ventures can be touted beyond the point of credibility. Slick public relation campaigns that deceive the public into believing that altruism is the sole motive behind programs of this type would indeed be fraudulent. But it is not Friedman's intention here to belabor the obvious. In the defense of profit, capitalism, and free enterprise, which he perceived to be under fire in the late sixties and early seventies, Friedman denied to social responsibility any semblance of an ethical base while casting in purely economic terms programs that are justified on more than one level.

By monopolizing every inch of middle ground between the mean-spirited, short-term profit maximizer, and the more thoughtful long-term strategist who sees business in a social context, Friedman controls the structure and language of the debate.

Examine his illustration of a corporation, a major employer in a community, that finds its long-run interests to be linked with the expenditure of resources on community amenities. Friedman has no difficulty articulating the economic base for such a program in that it may attract desirable employees, reduce the wage bill, lessen losses from pilferage and sabotage, or have other worthwhile effects. By practically anyone else's account that project is socially responsible. Whether it was inspired initially as an economic measure, or whether community leaders induced it from corporate management as a means of revitalizing an urban shopping district, the corporate behavior itself is multifaceted. The economic base is there for management to hang its hat on, but in terms of actual dollars earned or saved (the famous "bottom line"), a satisfactory return may be greater or lesser depending on management's expectations and its measure of success for these amenities. Beyond that, one may quantify the goodwill that is traceable to community spill-over effects, or positive externalities, and plug that figure into the financial calculus as well. In the final analysis, all such corporate efforts, including, to use another of Friedman's illustrations, corporate giving, can be reduced to economic terms and evaluated on the basis of a satisfactory return to shareholders. But the language of the calculations does not make these projects any less socially responsible. Advocates of social responsibility are not supporters of corporate waste as Friedman would have one believe; neither are they so narrow as to deny legitimacy to the moral content of projects that have a multiple base that includes economic considerations.

Friedman operates on the assumption that all the consequences of corporate behavior can be monetized or quantified with some degree of accuracy, and further that by reducing the language of debate to dollar bills, and the structure of debate to

economics, that every other consideration is at best trivial, at worst "approaching fraud." It is a foolish proposition then to do battle with him on those terms. Mulligan's consultative scenario never had a chance, first, because it was insensitive to minority, unconvinced and uncooperative shareholders,[5] secondly, because it presumed that corporate officers mandated with a shareholder majority were not only empowered but also equal to the task of combating systemic evils, and, finally, because it allowed Friedman to structure the debate so that he occupied all that is credible about the concept.

In brief, it is incumbent on Professor Mulligan and those who share his view to show why our social and political institutions are inadequate to promote the common good and social justice. Christopher Stone advanced his reasons in an excellent 1975 work, *Where the Law Ends,*[6] but it is even more important to Mulligan's thesis because he goes so much further than Stone in his expectations of managerial performance. Stone was principally (though not exclusively) interested in revamping corporate structure in such a manner that its private sector functions could be performed efficiently as well as responsibly. But the basis for an expanded role for corporate executives in resolving identifiably public policy type questions — inflation, unemployment, pollution, and to the original list one might add crime, housing, poverty, racism — must be thoroughly documented. Professor Mulligan has not done that. Remember that no single corporation has caused these problems, and while it goes without saying that a firm is responsible for the wrong that it does cause, societal or system pervasive problems require a collective, democratic solution.

On those occasions where the community or social need is pronounced and demonstrable, and the corporation is capable of responding in a manner commensurate with the task, there are some widely regarded "rescue" principles that can serve to bring direction and coherence into corporate social policy.[7]

(1) *Need* — Need increases responsibility even though the need has been caused by someone else, or even by an Act of God. For example, corporate giving to

the Red Cross or local emergency relief groups in times of flood or natural disaster. The need of those injured by wrongful acts of others, e.g., battered women or abandoned children, is within the range of corporate rescue as well.

(2) *Ability* — Even though shareholders have no reason to expect pure profit maximization, they do have legitimate economic claims that cannot be ignored. The corporation's obligation to act responsibly, and within an area of competence, in the process of building a better community and a better society is offset to an extent by other valid demands made upon the corporation. Not any single corporation (nor all of them together) has the ability to cure society's systemic ills, but guided by their areas of experience and competence, corporations can participate in the process of improving the quality of life without jeopardizing or sacrificing their principal economic function, that is, producing quality goods and services at competitive prices.

(3) *Proximity* — Notice or knowledge of a social need is normally imparted by nearness or proximity. Physical or spacial proximity alone is not the key however. The obligation to respond or rescue is a product of the firm's ability, the severity of degree of need, and awareness of that need. A failure of awareness or knowledge of the need *may or may not* be excusable.

(4) *Last Resort* — The rescue operation may indeed be more appropriate for some other social institution. Milton Friedman warned that self-appointed civil servants posed a threat to our democratic institutions, and, while there is a core of truth to that proposition, there is nevertheless a range of potential projects that are worthwhile but perhaps not affordable with limited tax dollars, not priority items, or projects that the government has made "fair game" by staying away. After all, the government cannot be expected to do everything, and the resolve to address social issues does not necessarily spell sedition or self-aggrandizement. It simply amounts to doing the right thing when the job needs to be done and no one else is doing it.

Damn the torpedos

It cannot be Professor Mulligan's point that simply because corporate executives do act under conditions of uncertainty and with imperfect information (like everyone else does, by the way), that they are thereby empowered to combat inflation, and presumably all other systemic ills, with their "business-like" approach. That would be a lot like urging the Boy Scouts to target an equally out-sized and elusive foe with military precision but without a prayer of success.

The fact remains that a single firm can chip away forever at inflation, unemployment, pollution and a laundry list of other social evils without ever making its presence felt.[8] About the most certain outcome would be that "free riders," i.e., non-conforming firms in the industry, would cut into the "responsible" firm's profits. Either the government must uniformly compel particular behaviors, or induce them with appropriate incentives, or else individual firms (and coalitions or industry groups) must keep a close rein on their exuberance and their expectations. Corporate programs that are unduly ambitious, and that lose touch with their economic mission while seeking to accomplish social objectives, are likely to be counter-productive and to harm further the credibility of the social responsibility concept. It is not a matter really of being unable to see into the future. Corporate social responsibility is more a matter of targeting "do-able" projects, and of bringing wisdom, coherence, and discipline to the sensitive proposition of redistributing corporate (shareholder) wealth toward the solution of problems that the corporation did not cause.

Friedman on socialism: Preaching to the choir

Regarding Professor Mulligan's third and concluding argument, it may well be conceded that Friedman is a little "fuzzy" on his definition of socialism. But that is not the heart of the matter. Our democratically constituted policy-making institutions, moving within the limits of the U.S. Constitution, continue to fashion the rules of the economic game just as they have historically. That is scarcely a matter of contention and I do not understand Friedman to be denying this reality. On the other hand you can practically "set your clock" by Friedman's knee-jerk condemnation as (more or less) socialistic any congressional policy that makes inroads on private property by redistributing wealth from those who can afford to pay for quality housing, for example, to those who cannot. He is not an absolute blockhead on this subject, but he can be awfully tedious.

So with this general understanding of what Friedman means by socialism, take another look at Professor Mulligan's third critique. Friedman baldly labels as socialistic and subversive the particular behavior of taking shareholder wealth (someone else's money) and throwing it away on projects so preposterous in their design and objective as to be positively absurd. However, if you will recall, he did not object to community revitalization and other such achievable projects though he was narrow and begrudging in crediting any other than economic justifications.

I take this to mean, then, that when Friedman sees a redistribution of shareholder wealth towards projects he opposes, he will vocally object and label that conduct subversive and socialistic. As long as the law permits this conduct, it is obviously not subversive in a criminal sense. But is it subversive (and, I suppose, socialistic) in the sense that private sector institutions are engaging in behaviors, i.e. redistributing wealth, that he identifies with socialist governments and, in his view, anything that smacks of socialism is also subversive.

But Professor Mulligan does not "expose" Friedman, nor even really address his point, by moving from Scenario-One (Friedman's paradigm of a willful executive) to Scenario-Two (counter-paradigm of a consensus-building executive). A tax, tranfer payment, or redistribution is no less a reality whether a passive majority allows it to be imposed (scenario one), or whether one happens to be in the majority or supporting consensus (scenario two). It is still a tax, transfer payment, or a redistribution. Since Mulligan's counter-paradigm does not alter that

reality, it has no force in his attempt to topple Friedman's position. In Friedman's view, a corporate consensus (scenario two) cannot confer legitimacy on a private sector "tax." A corporation simply cannot, by majority vote or otherwise, bestow upon itself political power and authority.

Friedman can be damned for his worldview, but it is at least a rational, principled opposition he takes on corporate financed responses to national agenda items. Those problems demand national consensus solutions, he is basically insisting, and those solutions should be hammered out by publicly elected and accountable officials. Whenever he detects private sector executives doing the kind of tasks that U.S. Senators and Representatives are elected to do, he is going to call that socialism.

Let him. Let him call that socialistic and subversive as well. But more importantly, let go of Milton Friedman. He has made an important contribution and that is more than most have done. Beyond that, he has set the tone for the Corporate Social Responsibility debate for too long.

Conclusion

It is past time to ask whether corporations should be socially responsible. It is time now to spell out what those responsibilities are.

Professor Mulligan has an excellent conclusion to his piece, and writers in this area should conscientiously pursue his advice. It consists of the need to produce positive arguments to demonstrate why business people should pursue a morally and socially responsible course. Even Friedman's admonition to business people to comform to the basic rules of society embodied in law and in *ethical custom* is a potentially revolutionary mandate. In its most modest construction, it must include something like a moral minimum: truth-telling and promise-keeping, fidelity, fairness, and doing no harm. It is easy to see how these fundamental moral propositions are supportive of a market economy. Even the minimal demands of the rescue principles are reinforced by the concept of fairness — fairness to shareholders in terms of their economic expectations and fairness to victims in terms of their need.

Perhaps the concept of beneficence would supply an even stronger base for the rescue principles, but that is not the type of thing I want to pursue here. It is the type of consideration, however, that Professor Mulligan has challenged us to explore, and that course is more promising by far than another "Friedman Revisited."

ENDNOTES

1. *Journal of Business Ethics* **5** (1986), pp. 265–269.

2. Milton Friedman, "The Social Responsibility of Business Is to Increase Its Profits," *New York Times Magazine*, 13 September 1970. (See this text, p. 41 ff.)

3. Milton Friedman, *Capitalism and Freedom* (Chicago: The University of Chicago Press, 1962), p. 133.

4. A reviewer of this article suggests that unlike some systemic problems (e.g., inflation, unemployment, and pollution — issues that are always with us in one degree or another), other systemic problems (e.g., tax fraud, securities fraud) can be resolved by the socially responsible conduct of simply obeying the law. I fully concur that such problems, whether they are regarded as system pervasive or aberrational, can be dealt with on the individual or corporate level. Friedman's concept of "ethical custom" seems also to be in concurrence with the reviewer's observation as does the notion of a "moral minimum," addressed briefly in the conclusion to the paper.

5. Professor Mulligan makes the common sense point that a socially responsible manager will build a consensus for his or her programs. This is quite an advance over Friedman's view of such executives as disloyal agents and as destructive of shareholders rights. Mulligan has no apparent qualms however that minority shareholders, i.e. those who object to the programs of consensus-building and consultative-type officers, are still going to be neglected or ignored. It would appear to be the sounder case to argue that all shareholders make their investment on the supposition that some corporate activities will not be guided by short-term profit maximization but by long-term objectives that balance or trade-off economic and non-economic considerations.

6. See especially Chapter 10, "Why the Market Can't Do It," and Chapter 11, "Why the Law Can't Do It."

7. John Simon, Charles Powers and John Gunnemann, *The Ethical Investor* (New Haven: Yale University Press, 1975), pp. 22–25.

8. It should be acknowledged, however, that there are many in-house, employee related projects such as drug, alcohol, and family counseling, day care centers for employees' children, job training and higher education programs that practically everyone would characterize as socially responsible. Friedman would not use that phrase, but would likely approve of such projects insofar as they had some economic basis. These illustrations give evidence, I think, that socially responsible projects, virtual "investments" in human resources, can on some occasions reinforce the bottom line rather than intrude upon it. Projects of this nature supply the best avenue for Professor Mulligan and others to explicate the dimensions of "ethical custom" and, if anything, indict Friedman for his reluctance to ascribe a moral base to such projects.

4

Moral Responsibility in Business

or

Fourteen Unsuccessful Ways to Pass the Buck

ALEX C. MICHALOS

INTRODUCTION

In the Middle Ages, philosophic essays had a standard format. An author would begin by stating a thesis to be proved. Then arguments opposed to that thesis would be presented and systematically demolished. Following the demolition, the author would present arguments in favour of the thesis. If all went according to plan, nothing further could be done. There would be no good reasons left supporting the other side, and only good reasons left supporting the author's thesis. It's a tedious process to be sure, but effective. By the time one reaches the end, one is pretty sure of one's conclusion.

This is not the Middle Ages, so I am not going to provide that sort of analysis. Instead, I am going to undertake the first half only. My thesis is that businesspeople should be morally responsible agents *as* businesspeople. In other words, my thesis is that businesspeople ought to be morally responsi-

ble agents not merely in their role as citizens of a moral community, but in their role as people engaged in competitive enterprise. My strategy of defence will be to present apparently plausible arguments opposed to my thesis, and to show that these arguments are defective. If I am successful, you will be persuaded that, so far as we know, there are no good reasons to deny or reject my thesis. I leave it to another occasion to persuade you that there are, in addition, good reasons to accept it.

Before I get to those defective arguments, however, let me clarify some terminology.

Complementary versus Contrary Terms

The words "moral" and "ethical" in English are ambiguous insofar as they may be used merely to designate classifications or to designate evaluations. So it will be useful to eliminate this ambiguity.

This essay first appeared in the first edition of this text; an earlier version was presented at the 17th World Congress of Philosophy in Montreal, Quebec, August 1983. Most of the fourteen arguments presented here were suggested in T. Beauchamp and N. Bowie's *Ethical Theory and Business* (Prentice-Hall, 1983). The author of this essay would like to express his thanks to the editors and authors of that volume.

First, it is necessary to distinguish complementary from contrary terms. *Complementary terms* are used to divide the world, the whole world, into two mutually exclusive and exhaustive classes. For example, everything in the world is a competitor or a noncompetitor, a horse or a nonhorse, a banana or a nonbanana. Quite generally, take any word at all and then put a "non" in front of it, and you have a pair of complementary terms. Thus, whatever "moral" and "ethical" mean, one may divide the whole world into things that are moral and nonmoral, or ethical and nonethical. To say that actions are moral or nonmoral, when these words are used as complementary terms, is not necessarily to make a moral appraisal of those actions; it is, or may be, merely to classify the actions prior to a moral evaluation. To perform the latter task, one would make use of contrary terms.

Contrary terms are used to divide only a part of the world into mutually exclusive and exhaustive classes. For example, within the subset of the world known as competitors, there are winners and losers. All competitors are winners or losers. Similarly, within the subset of actions appraised from a moral point of view, there are morally good and morally bad (evil) actions. Unfortunately, in English one may use the words "moral" and "ethical" alone as abbreviations of "morally good" and "ethically good," respectively. In such cases, the words are used as contrary terms and their opposites are "morally bad" and "ethically bad," respectively, or simply "bad." Thus, in the next section when social are distinguished from moral responsibilities, it is the complementary or classificatory sense of the word "moral" that is intended. The distinction is not between morally good and bad responsibilities, but between moral responsibilities and nonmoral responsibilities.

Social versus Moral Responsibilities

In most of the literature on business ethics, people refer to social responsibilities and contrast them with other kinds of responsibilities. In virtually all cases, the phrase "social responsibilities" is used to designate what are really "moral responsibilities,"

roughly as these will be defined shortly. The issues typically discussed under the rubric of "social responsibilities" are usually not merely matters of good manners or etiquette, but of something much more serious. So, it will be useful to clarify this distinction.

Roughly speaking, one may say that human action is socially responsible insofar as it does not violate any rules of etiquette, good manners, good taste or generally accepted social practice. Examples of socially responsible behaviour include such things as thanking people for gifts received, arriving at and leaving parties at suitable times, answering letters or other messages requesting acknowledgement, and so on. Socially responsible action is necessary for human community, and in one way or another appropriate criteria of evaluation and sanctions for irresponsible action are routinely developed in all societies.

There are at least two ways to identify morally responsible action, a narrow way and a broad way. Narrowly speaking, one may say that human action is morally responsible, or simply moral, insofar as it does not violate any generally accepted moral maxims. Examples of moral maxims include such things as "One should not steal," "One should always tell the truth," and "One should avoid harming innocent people." Broadly speaking, one may say that human action is morally responsible or moral insofar as it is reasonably intended to impartially maximize human well-being. Since the actual consequences of action often involve unexpected, unintended and uncontrollable elements, one cannot require the actual maximization of well-being with every action of every agent every moment of every day. Instead, one requires a reasonable amount of attention to the likely consequences of one's action, a reasonable amount of care with one's performance and a relatively clear intention to act so as to produce a fairly specific sort of result. In particular, one should intend and try to act so that everyone affected by one's action is affected in an even-handed, unbiased, impartial or a similar way unless there are good reasons for affecting some people in different ways.

Perhaps the easiest and most morally neutral

way to understand the terms "impartial," "even-handed" and "unbiased" in the preceding sentence is probabilistically. That is, these terms should be understood as indicating that one is intending and trying to act such that every person affected by one's action has the same probability or chance of being affected in roughly the same way. More precisely, one is trying to give every affected person both an equal probability and as high a probability as possible (consistent with the former) to maximize their well-being. Since there is a generally accepted formal principle of justice that demands that similar people and similar actions should be treated in similar ways unless there are good reasons for treating them in different ways, the broad criterion of morally responsible action includes a condition of justice. Thus, on this broad account of moral action, one who acts morally must also act justly to some extent. It is not clear (to me at least) that morality and justice are entirely coextensive domains, but there is some overlap.

Clearly, what I have called the narrow and broad ways to identify morally responsible action might not define exactly the same set of actions. What's more, this might not be merely the result of a semantic disagreement or the fact that people have just never gotten around to articulating all the moral maxims they implicitly accept. On the contrary, the narrow and broad ways to identify morally responsible action might be based on significantly different views of what is required for such action. In particular, some people might believe that no one is ever morally required to try to maximize anyone's well-being. They might say that morality is essentially concerned with trying to prevent certain kinds of harm from certain kinds of people, and that while universal beneficence is praiseworthy, it cannot be morally required. In short, they might say such beneficence is appropriate for saints or those who aspire to sainthood, but it has no essential role to play in the morality of ordinary people.

There is no rule book to consult now in order to decide whether a reasonable and morally good person should adopt the narrow or broad way to identify morally responsible action. In fact, I prefer the broad way because I think a world populated by people holding such a view would be a better place to live in than a world populated by people holding the other view, all things considered. In other words, I think a world populated by people motivated by universal beneficence would be better than one motivated merely by a desire to prevent certain harms. Moreover, since morality is to some extent always a matter of aspiration rather than achievement and the latter may easily be constrained by limitations in the former, I think wisdom is on the side of taking a broad view of morally responsible action.

Moral Maxims versus Moral Theories

It will be worthwhile to draw one other fundamental distinction before proceeding to the main part of my story. I have already referred to moral maxims such as "One should tell the truth," One should not steal," and so on. In all countries around the world maxims of this kind are recommended. Students are sometimes shocked by this assertion, for they often have the mistaken belief that in some far-off places radically different maxims are accepted. Of course there are *some* contradictory moral maxims recommended in different countries, e.g., that women should or should not have to cover their faces, or that men should or should not be allowed to have more than one wife. However, that is entirely consistent with my claim that there are some universally accepted maxims. To take the simplest example just to prove my point: around the world it is universally accepted that it is morally wrong to kill innocent babies for pleasure. Such actions, including the particular motive mentioned, are always condemned. Furthermore, there are no societies in which a contradictory maxim would be recommended. That is, there are no societies (and I would be willing to bet there never have been any) in which the following maxim is part of their moral codes: "It is morally right to kill innocent babies for pleasure" or, briefly, "One ought to kill innocent babies for pleasure."

Although there is universal agreement about some moral maxims, there is no such agreement about the justification, reason or warrant for accepting these maxims. Much of moral philosophy is concerned with questions of justification. We want to explain why it is reasonable to accept some maxims and not others. As rational beings, we want to have good reasons, warrants, or justifications for accepting some maxims and rejecting others. In other words, we want our moral judgements to be well-grounded or well-supported rather than capricious, unprincipled or *ad hoc*. In short, we want to have our moral maxims derivable from moral theories. Just as any scientist wants to have generally acceptable theories to account for observable facts and law-like regularities, moral philosophers want to have generally acceptable moral theories to account for moral claims and maxims.

Moreover, just as all scientific theories are fallible and limited, so are all moral theories. In truth, there are few, if any, scientific theories that can claim the longevity of some moral theories, which also surprises some people. In particular, for better or worse, no scientific theory has lasted as long as the theory that moral maxims ought to be accepted because they are legislated by God. But longevity is beside the point here. The main point is that while there is some universal agreement about some moral maxims, there is no universal agreement about moral theories. Thus, it is obvious that whenever one is engaged in any moral controversy, it is a wise strategy to try to resolve issues at the level of moral maxims. If that is impossible and one must resort to higher-level moral theories, one is bound to encounter more problems. Again, as rational beings, we must have theories, and occasionally theoretical agreement is precisely what is required to solve some lower-level problems. But, to paraphrase a remark made by Martin Luther King Jr. concerning violence, when you resort to theories, the main issues tend to be theoretical and practical questions of right and wrong may be swept aside.

Let's now examine in detail the fourteen arguments already alluded to.

ARGUMENTS AND REPLIES

1. **Adam Smith's argument.** Whether or not the 18th century economist endorsed exactly the following argument, it is often attributed to him and is generally consistent with his views. Simply stated, the argument is that if each person would pursue his or her own interests in a fairly enlightened way, then in the long run social well-being or welfare would be maximized. Moreover, people do seem to be naturally inclined to pursue their own interests rather than anyone else's. Therefore, it is pointless for businesspeople or anyone else to concern themselves with morally responsible action. In short, if people would do what comes naturally instead of trying to perform the relatively unnatural actions recommended by moralists, the very results that the latter desire would be achieved. Clearly then, the recommendations of the moralists are at best redundant.

Reply. The trouble with this argument is that its premises are empirically incorrect. If it is true that people are naturally inclined to pursue their own interests and it is also true that such activity will naturally maximize social well-being, then why has the latter not occurred? Presumably, a world that has recessions and depressions, unemployment, poverty and inefficiencies resulting from near-monopolies is not a world in which social well-being is being maximized. Moreover, it cannot plausibly be argued that we have not waited long enough to obtain the benefits of unbridled, universal, self-interested action, because virtually all of the restraints and remedial activities introduced into allegedly free markets have only been introduced when the destructiveness of unbridled self-interested action was obvious to everyone. For example, since self-interested monopolists would try to exploit everyone else (as long as that was perceived to be in their own interests), practically everyone has been willing to introduce anti-monopoly laws *a priori* into allegedly free-enterprise systems. What's more, empirical research has repeatedly shown that the closer one comes to monopolistic domination of a market (in food, cars, fuel, etc.), the more consumers are robbed through gross inefficiencies in production and inflated prices. Again, unemployment insurance was introduced only after it became clear that the unbridled avarice of some people would keep many other people without any adequate means of support. Similarly, social insurance systems were initiated only after it became clear that many old people, single-parent mothers and children would live and die in poverty unless the state intervened for them.

Instead of arguing that we have not waited long enough to obtain the benefits of unbridled self-interested action, one might argue, following Plato nearly four hundred years before Christ, that people don't always know what is really in their own interests. Whatever their natural inclinations might be, people tend to misperceive, misrepresent and generally make mistakes when they try to look out for themselves. In fact, one might add a heavy dose of stupidity to human avarice to account for the fact that things haven't turned out as Smith predicted. That, I suppose, is a bit extravagant. It's bad enough to have a theory that leads to false predictions. To suggest that one's theory leads to false predictions because most people are too stupid to make the most of their avarice really adds insult to injury. It would be simpler and wiser to just abandon the theory altogether.

2. Agnosticism regarding ends. A second argument that might be used to argue that businesspeople should not be concerned with morally responsible action involves agnosticism regarding the appropriate ends of such action. According to this view, no one knows exactly what goals, objectives, aims or ideal ends are really desirable for all the people in any society. Therefore, it is pointless at best and possibly dangerous, at worst, to try to get businesspeople (or anyone else, for that matter) to pursue such allegedly desirable ends.

Reply. Given the great variety of human interests, abilities and resources, as well as what the economist Frank Knight called the "perversity of folks," it is indeed unlikely that there are many ideal ends that are desirable for every person in every society. Fortunately, however, it is also

irrelevant. Just as it would be silly to abandon rules of the road because some people can't tell their right hand from their left, it would be silly to abandon the pursuit of all ideals because some people can't benefit from their pursuit or realization. There are plenty of identifiable goals whose realization *would* be desirable for the vast majority of people in any society, i.e., there are plenty of socially and morally desirable goals. For example, most people would benefit from full employment, an equitable distribution of wealth and incomes, safety from environmental pollutants, the elimination of dangerous food additives and unsafe consumer durables (cars, toys, household appliances, etc.), universal and adequate health care and education, good housing and transportation, and equitable access to political power.

3. Agnosticism regarding means. Supposing it is granted that there are clearly identifiable socially and morally desirable ends to pursue, it might be argued that it is pointless and perhaps even dangerous to urge businesspeople to pursue them because no one knows exactly what any particular person, in particular circumstances, must do to achieve such ends. The road to hell is certainly paved with good intentions. Among those who believe that full employment is a desirable goal, for example, some seem to think the most efficient means of achieving this would involve government regulation only to prevent monopolies or obviously harmful activities; others think some government planning can be useful in the allocation of private resources and public resources; and some think total government control of all means of production is the best strategy. Again, according to some people, children are most likely to get an adequate education if schools are controlled by local communities, while others believe that because of the great disparities in local community resources, the best strategy involves some national intervention and contribution. Thus, in view of such controversies over the appropriate means to obtain recognized desirable ends, agnosticism is justifiable, for businesspeople as well as everyone else.

Reply. This argument proceeds from relatively reasonable premises to an unreasonable conclusion. From the facts of controversies and difficulties regarding the identification of optimal strategies to be used to pursue shared ends, it is concluded that total agnosticism is warranted. But if such agnosticism means the denial of any knowledge regarding appropriate means to obtain shared desirable ends, then the argument involves a *non sequitur*. It is plainly false that we know of no appropriate strategies to follow to try to realize our goals. In the case of the pursuit of full employment, for example, we know that it is useful in the first place for governments to obtain reliable and valid labour force statistics, including numbers of available workers by geographic region, age, sex, education, skill training and employment status. It is useful to have a thorough understanding of a nation's resource production and consumption, past, present and estimated future supplies and demands. In the third place it is useful to set relatively realistic employment targets and finally to experiment with a variety of tactics for hitting those targets. Of course, there will be controversies and difficulties in the pursuit of shared goals since all knowledge is fallible, all activities have some unintended consequences and very often the intended consequences of social engineering will not equally satisfy every affected person. Still, to grant all this is to grant nothing sufficient to warrant total agnosticism and abandonment of attempts to find optimally desirable means to obtain similar ends.

4. **Absence of right.** Roughly speaking, we may say that one has a right to something insofar as one has a special entitlement or claim to it which everyone else has a duty or obligation to recognize. Rights may be described as positive or negative, depending on whether people have a duty to provide things in someone else's interests, or merely to avoid doing some things or to prevent some things that would harm someone else, from being done. For example, in Canada, children are supposed to have a positive right to at least a primary school education, which means that adults have an obligation to provide it. All people are supposed to have a negative right to life, which means, at a mini-

mum, that all of us have a duty to avoid wantonly destroying other people's lives, or at a maximum, that all of us have a duty to prevent the wanton destruction of people's lives. Hence, in the interests of insuring that Canadians have these rights protected, we are taxed to pay for the operation of educational institutions, our systems of criminal justice punish people legally for intentionally taking people's lives, and in some instances we morally condemn people for failing to prevent such destruction.

A fourth argument leading to the conclusion that businesspeople should not be concerned with morally responsible action *as* businesspeople is based on the simple premise that businesspeople do not have a right to engage in such action. According to this view, there is nothing in the special role, expertise or character of such people that would give them such a right, and in any case few people outside the class would recognize any obligation to provide or prevent anything in the interest of protecting the alleged right.

The idea behind this argument is that businesspeople have certain roles to play and a certain kind of expertise which are relatively limited. To suppose or demand that an obligation to perform morally responsible action can or should be included in the definition of those roles, or in every sort of expertise is a mistake. Thus, for example, the business of selling shoes, insurance or cars can and should be defined without any appeal to moral responsibilities, and one may be a good shoe salesperson, insurance agent or car dealer without having anything to do with such responsibilities. On the contrary, one's responsibilities would include, say, knowledge of the different qualities of shoes, the requirements of different people for different shoe styles, the appropriate prices to pay to suppliers and to charge to consumers, and so on. These sorts of things, it would be said, cannot reasonably be expected to create rights to making moral decisions.

Reply. In response to this argument, it may be insisted that businesspeople *as* businesspeople certainly have a right to act rationally. This may be regarded as a positive right insofar as some education, training and socialization is a necessary condition of rational action, and initially someone (without specifying the particular agent) has to provide it. Indeed, it may be said that education, training and socialization must be provided precisely in the interest of protecting people's right to act rationally. Without some of the former, most human babies would not even survive to adulthood, since rational action is typically necessary for survival.

If it is granted that businesspeople have a right to act rationally, then it must be granted that they have a right to estimate all the consequences of their actions, as far as that is possible in different circumstances. Without such estimates, people could not assess the ratio of benefits achieved to costs expended. In other words, without such estimates, people couldn't determine if their actions were self-constructive or self-destructive, i.e., they couldn't assess the survival value of their actions. That ignorance, of course, should be resisted. Thus, it must be insisted that people have a right to estimate all the consequences of their actions, and that must include all the moral and immoral consequences of their actions too. Insofar as businesspeople are interested in performing rational actions, they must also have a right to perform them. Moreover, this implies a right to consider and perform morally responsible actions, since these also produce benefits and costs.

5. **Level of competence.** Supposing it is granted that businesspeople have a right to perform morally responsible actions *as* businesspeople, it might still be argued that since they will have such low levels of competence regarding moral actions, they should not be encouraged to perform them. Given a society in which most people are relatively free to choose their occupations, it is likely that people who choose the world of business or competitive enterprise probably are more interested in engaging in the activities characteristic of this world than in those of its alternatives. Similarly, those who choose careers in government service, social work or, broadly speaking, in any of the "helping professions" (such as the ministry or priesthood, teaching, lawyers working in legal aid

and public health personnel) probably are more interested in engaging in the activities characteristic of these occupations than in those of business. Clearly, the career interests of those in the helping professions are more compatible with those of moralists than the career interests of businesspeople. Moreover, it is likely that interest is usually a necessary condition of competence, since people are not likely to be or become good at doing things that they are not interested in doing. Thus, in fact the most competent people regarding morally responsible actions will probably be outside the world of business and, therefore, these are the people who should be urged to perform such actions rather than businesspeople. The latter will almost certainly botch the job.

Reply. Those who use the preceding argument incorrectly assume that competence in performing morally responsible actions is an exclusive trait which people develop at the expense of other traits. On this view, becoming a morally responsible person is analogous to developing a special skill or becoming a specialist in a particular area of knowledge. Becoming a morally responsible person, on this view, is like becoming a good dentist or historian. It is simply another kind of specialization. On this view, if, for example, *Macleans* or *Time* wanted to include reports of morally responsible actions, they would merely add another section. Besides their traditional sections on business, sports, books, international affairs, and so on, there would be a section on morality. Presumably, it would be a section reporting on who did what morally good or bad thing to whom, for what and with what interesting consequences.

If one adopts what I earlier called the narrow way to identify morally responsible actions, there is a strong tendency to think of morality in precisely this way, that is, as a specialized field with special interests, principles and practitioners. Then one is hardpressed to find good reasons for most people, who typically would not think of themselves as specialists in moral matters, to be interested in such matters. Short of striving to become some sort of new renaissance person or the local champion at *Trivial Pursuits*, there would appear to be little motivation for most people to try to keep up with the news in yet another area of specialization. Might as well leave it to those who go in for that sort of thing.

As you might have expected, the unhappy scenario just described provided one of the motivating factors for my adoption of what I called the broad way of identifying morally responsible actions. With this view of such actions, there would be no special section of *Macleans* devoted to morality because there is no such specialization. On this view, *any* action has moral significance insofar as it is appraised from a moral point of view. In other words, *any* action has moral significance insofar as it is assessed from the point of view of its being reasonably intended to impartially maximize human well-being. Thus, if, to continue my illustration, the editors of *Macleans* wanted to include reports of morally responsible actions, they would not add any new reports or any new sections. Instead, they would merely appraise the actions routinely reported in their specialized sections from a moral point of view. Competence in making such appraisals is not, therefore, an exclusive trait of moral specialists. On the contrary, since such appraisals involve the most comprehensive review of any and every human action, urging people to adopt a moral point of view is tantamount to urging them to develop a uniquely inclusive trait. It is a habit of mind, a mental set or disposition to think of all actions from the point of view of their moral impact, which is thoroughly inclusive rather than exclusive.

6. **Reduced economic efficiency.** In the interest of trying to impartially maximize human well-being, one might fail to maximize profits. In that case, one would also fail to be economically maximally efficient. Insofar as one fails to be economically maximally efficient, one is being wasteful, since inefficiency simply means there is less output per unit of input than there could be. Thus, since wastefulness is inexcusable, it should not be allowed to occur for the sake of achieving other goals.

Reply. This objection represents the tip of an iceberg involving a variety of more or less contro-versial arguments concerning an alleged trade-off between the aims of economic efficiency and morality. In the fifth volume of my *North American Social Report* (D. Reidel, 1982), I presented nearly two dozen arguments that have been used by proponents of one side or the other. For present purposes, it is enough to report two main conclusions of that analysis. First, it is of course possible to imagine situations arising in which one would be faced with a choice between economic efficiency and morality. Second, given the distribution of wealth and income in Canada (and even more in the United States), it is highly probable that such choices do not arise. Since the richest 20 per cent of Canadians own around 70 per cent of the wealth, the other 80 percent of the population has to get along on the remaining 30 per cent. Under these circumstances, it is virtually impossible for the wealthy fifth to actually use much of their wealth. In the simplest terms, one can only consume so much lobster and champagne, take so many trips, wear so many suits or dresses, live in so many houses, and even enjoy the natural beauty of one's own land, to a certain point of saturation.

Moreover, except for the very needy, few people make the maximum use of things they own. So one would expect that those who can accumulate goods at the relatively lowest personal cost would also be the most wasteful. They would have more things lying around idle and they would be least concerned with apparent waste. In short, given the current distribution of wealth and the likely uses to which that wealth can be and is put, it is highly probable that *any* activity that would tend to redistribute wealth in the direction of greater equality (in the interest of morality) would reduce waste and would, therefore, be economically efficient. Put more bluntly, I think that the current distribution of wealth in Canada creates such gross economic inefficiency that it is practically impossible to make adjustments toward greater equality in the interest of morality that would not create greater economic efficiency.

7. **Increased government control.** Ignoring my first reply to the argument concerning reduced

economic efficiency, further developments in that scenario may be elucidated. In particular, the "nonmoralists" may argue that the immediate result of excessive wastefulness will be shortages, and that excessive shortages will lead directly to increased demands for government intervention. When the government finally intervenes, it will probably be in the form of regulating production and prices, and rationing consumption. The latter combination of activities, then, will probably lead directly to so-called black markets, that is, to illegal transactions in which the unscrupulous few rip off those who may or may not be able to afford to be ripped off. Increased illegal activities, of course, tend to generate increased demands for greater law enforcement, meaning additional government bureaucracy to manage additional taxation, to pay for more salaries of more law enforcement personnel (police officers, clerks, court officials, correctional officers and institutions), and to pay for more buildings and the sophisticated technological hardware characteristic of our modern enforcement agencies. Thus, since no one in his or her right mind wants to live through this scenario, everyone should be reluctant to suffer economic inefficiency even if it requires ignoring alleged moral responsibilities. Indeed, faced with the spectre of such an outrageous scenario, many people would be inclined to describe their perceived obligations in fairly moralistic terms. That is, they would be inclined to insist that in the interests of humanity, civilization or a free society such a scenario should be resisted.

Reply. Naturally, I would welcome the move from talk about economic efficiency to talk about humanity or, more particularly, morality. It is always helpful to have agreement about relatively ultimate aims, or about that for the sake of which relatively immediate actions are being performed or recommended. However, for present purposes, it will be wise to ignore those who might accept my aims and to concentrate on those who might not.

Since, for the sake of argument (i.e., Argument #6), I have allowed the other side to assume that actions performed in the interest of morality would lead to reduced economic efficiency, it is worthwhile to remember that standard practices alleg-

edly leading to increased efficiency are notoriously inefficient. In order to avoid any misunderstanding or confusion about apparent paradoxes, one must never forget that all measures of efficiency are ratios of benefits to costs, and that there is no standard rule book to tell people exactly *how* to measure *which* benefits and costs to *whom* in *what* time period. Thus, it is easy for an employer to replace relatively expensive human labour (people, that is) with relatively cheap machines, and to increase efficiency defined as a greater benefit to cost ratio *for the employer*. On the other hand, since the very same replacement (by hypothesis) puts some people out of work, it is easy for these employees to show a decrease in efficiency defined as a smaller benefit to cost ratio *for the employee*. Hence, the fact that efficiency measures are essentially ratios with controversial numerators and denominators largely explains the apparent paradoxes involved when certain actions are claimed to be both efficient and inefficient. Without first getting some agreement about how to measure which benefits, etc., it is logically impossible to obtain generally recognized definitive answers.

In the absence of the required agreement about how to measure whose benefits, I would merely remind those who use this seventh argument that widespread poverty and unemployment are two extremely wasteful by-products of the sort of economic efficiency they are recommending. As the economists of the "small is beautiful" or "appropriate technology" view have argued, it cannot be rational to try to continually replace labour with capital when there is relatively plenty of the former and little of the latter. In more human terms, it cannot be reasonable to insist on capital accumulation for a few in the interest of a kind of "efficiency" that makes relative paupers of many others.

Consideration of waste aside, the main reply I would offer to the argument before us is that the alleged choice between a free society and a society highly controlled by government is a false dichotomy. All highly industrialized societies are characterized by high levels of functional interdependence. In such societies almost everyone is more or less dependent on many other people to maintain his or her lifestyle. Although it is possible for people to raise their own sheep, spin the wool, weave cloth, manufacture needles, design clothes, carve buttons, make clothes, etc., few people have the inclination to engage in such activities. The vast majority of people prefer a style that makes them more dependent on the productive activities of others. In highly industrialized societies, this preference has the unfortunate by-product that most people are probably even more dependent on others than they would like to be or should be for their own best interests. Indeed, the whole field of business ethics is largely a response to the realization that a system of production, distribution and consumption of goods and services is almost synonymous with a way of life.

Such a system necessarily socializes, conditions and, finally, even controls people in fundamental ways. Thus, if one were going to insist on any dichotomy, I would suggest at the risk of oversimplification, that between control by elected officials in the public interest, and control by private industrial officials in their own interests. Given the fact that people will certainly become socialized with certain kinds of expectations, aspirations and ideas about a good life, the real issue is how such a life should be defined and what strategies should be used to achieve it. It is a raw red herring to suggest that it is possible to just let everyone do whatever turns them on. That never happens. Moreover, as argued earlier, it is highly unlikely that the result of such unconditioned activity would benefit most people. Finally, granted that in fact elected officials do not always act in the interests of society as a whole and that private industrial officials do not always act in their own interests narrowly defined, this sort of dichotomized thinking is probably not particularly helpful in the long run.

8. **Loyal agent's argument.** Elsewhere I have examined this argument in considerable detail.* I will summarize that discussion here. The argument runs as follows. (1) As a loyal agent of some principal (i.e., employer), I ought to serve his or her

interest as he or she would serve them if the latter had my expertise. (2) Such a principal would serve his or her own interests in a thoroughly egoistic way. Therefore, (3) as a loyal agent of such a principal, I ought to operate in a thoroughly egoistic way in the interests of that principal. In other words, loyal agency seems not only to permit but to require that people should be selfish in the interests of their employers.

Reply. One may be regarded as operating in a thoroughly egoistic way if all one's actions are designed to optimize one's own interests and one has no inclination at all to identify the interests of anyone else with one's own. One may very well be a self-confident, self-starting, self-sustaining and self-controlled individual. These are all commendable personal characteristics. But one must be selfish, self-centered and/or self-serving. In conflict situations when there are not enough benefits to satisfy everyone, an egoist will try to see that his or her own needs are satisfied whatever happens to the needs of others. One is more interested in being first than in being nice, and one assumes that everyone else is too. One may even believe that if everyone behaved this way, the world's resources would be used in a maximally efficient way and everyone would be materially better off. But that is a secondary consideration. One's first consideration — the only prudent one — is to look out for Numero Uno, oneself.

The trouble with the loyal agent's argument is that both premises are problematic. The second premise assumes that all people are egoists; but people who try to defend their actions with this argument assume that their own actions are *not* egoistic. Their basic assumption is that they are loyal agents motivated by a desire to serve the best interests of their employers. However, if it is possible for them to have such nonegoistic motives, then it must be possible for other people to have such motives too. Hence, the very assumption required to make the argument look plausible in the first place makes the second premise look implausible. So the argument is self-defeating.

The first premise — that an employee's responsibility is to the employer alone — looks as innocuous

*See this text, p. 236 ff.

as motherhood and apple pie, and in a way it is. Its only weakness is that its limitations are not built into it. In this respect it is like most moral principles and rules of law. Short of turning every principle and rule into a self-contained treatise, it is impossible to indicate every possible exception. For example, no one should kill anyone, except *maybe* in self-defence, war, capital punishment, euthanasia or suicide. Similarly, a loyal agent ought to pursue the interests of his or her employer except. . . . In the famous Nuremberg trials, the Charter of the International Military Tribunal recognized, for instance,

> . . . that one who has committed criminal acts may not take refuge in superior orders nor in the doctrine that his crimes were acts of states. These twin principles working together have heretofore resulted in immunity for practically everyone concerned in the really great crimes against peace and mankind. Those in lower ranks are protected against liability by the orders of their superiors. The superiors were protected because their orders were called acts of the state. Under the Charter, no defence based on either of these doctrines can be entertained.

Canadian and American laws relating to loyal agency do not sanction any illegal or unethical actions. Thus, there is no doubt at all that the first premise of the loyal agent's argument cannot be regarded as a licence to break laws. No respectable court would permit it. In fact, although the courts have no special jurisdiction over moral law, they have shown no reluctance to condemn immoral acts allegedly performed in the interests of fulfilling fiduciary obligations.

9. **Materialist orientation.**

In the fifth argument above it was indicated that people whose primary interests are in business would probably have low levels of competence in performing morally responsible actions. I replied that the flaw in this argument was the assumption that competence in performing morally responsible actions was an exclusive trait or skill, and that the broad way of understanding morality which I have

adopted is more inclusive than exclusive. One might still argue that, given the materialistic orientation of businesspeople, when they try to make a broad benefit-cost analysis in the interest of morality, they are bound to spoil it. As Aristotle said a long time ago, as a person's character is, so is the world seen. People who spend most of their time evaluating things from a materialistic point of view will tend to make moral evaluations from the same point of view. So, when they try to do things in the interests of everyone impartially, they will probably not be doing the sorts of things moralists would like them to be doing. For example, from the point of view of Canadian businesspeople, the support of economic research designed to show that Adam Smith's argument (argument #1) was basically sound might be regarded as impartially benefiting everyone. Quite generally, then, such people might regard anything that reinforces their view of the world as impartially benefiting everyone. Thus, urging these people to be universally beneficent might lead to universal materialism, which most moralists would find unacceptable.

Reply. As suggested earlier, it is almost certainly an oversimplification to say that businesspeople usually have a materialistic orientation. Given the variety of businesses that people can enter, the variety and ambiguity of human motivations, and the variety of personal philosophies of life and lifestyles, it is unlikely that people in business, broadly construed, are uniformly materialistic. If there is any reliable and valid research indicating such bias, I haven't seen it. Secondly, it would be a mistake to think that all materialism is dangerous and objectionable. Some material goods do make positive contributions to the quality of life, e.g., reliable consumer durables such as cars, household appliances, dwelling units and communications hardware (telephones, radio, television). Finally, Aristotle's remark is obviously not the whole truth. As much as people's interests influence what they perceive and believe, what they perceive and believe also influences their interests. Indeed, my reading of the evidence accumulated so far indicates that perception and belief contribute more to interest than the reverse. But the literature on this subject is diverse, complicated and controversial.

10. **Need for pluralism.** In a pluralistic society like Canada, there are many perspectives from which controversial issues may be viewed. There are many important issues about which various people have unsettled opinions, and there are others about which there are solid and contradictory opinions. To expect businesspeople to have uniform and settled opinions, and to urge them to see that these are predominant is unwarranted and unwise. It is unwarranted because there is no good reason to expect businesspeople as such to be intellectually more tidy or clearheaded than the rest of the population and, therefore, it is unwise to urge these people to strive to make their views predominant over all others. Given the enormous overt and covert power of businesspeople, they might go even farther than they already have to create a one-dimensional society. The only reasonable course to follow is a pluralistic one.

Reply. This argument, too, is a red herring. To urge businesspeople to engage in morally responsible action is not to urge *only* businesspeople to engage in such action. Of course pluralism will and ought to continue, if that means that there should be a variety of perspectives from which important issues may be viewed. No one in his or her right mind would insist on silencing all voices but one, or on excluding all points of view but one. It would be as bad to have only businesspeople steering the ship of state as it would be to have only philosophers, moralists or gymnasts doing so.

The other problem with this argument is that it is self-defeating. If it is true that businesspeople are so powerful that they represent a threat to the rest of society, then morally irresponsible businesspeople would represent an even greater threat. Hence, if this argument has any value at all, it is only to reinforce the view that urges businesspeople to be morally responsible.

11. **Overload.** The world of competitive enterprise is notoriously complicated already. Compared to those in other occupations, business executives have a relatively high incidence of heart attacks and strokes. To insist that such overloaded people should take on yet another responsibility and, indeed, such a controversial and inherently complex one as moral decision-making, is to risk complete systemic failure. Quite apart from the arguable facts that the engagement of businesspeople as such in morally responsible action would be redundant and incompetent, there is no good reason to risk destroying currently reasonable business practices by overloading decision-makers.

Reply. If this argument proves anything, it proves too much. Life, after all, is complicated. So, if complexity were sufficient to eliminate the burden of attending to moral responsibilities, then all of us could take a permanent moral holiday. Clearly, however, a society in which no one attended to any moral responsibilities would have virtually nothing to recommend it as a human and humane community. In such a society, if it could even be called that, life would be "nasty, brutish and short," as the 17th century British philosopher Thomas Hobbes said. Secondly, the argument still seems to presuppose that morality is some kind of specialization which people can get into or not, as they choose. As I have indicated above, this is a mistake. The moral point of view is not another specialized perspective, but is inherent in all major decisions.

12. **Inconsistency.** Perhaps one of the most frequently heard arguments against businesspeople engaging in morally responsible action is that such action is logically inconsistent with competitive enterprise. To engage in competition in an open market is essentially to try to do better than others. The rough rule is to buy cheap and sell dear. To engage in morally responsible action is essentially to try *not* to have some come out better than others. The rule then is to buy and sell at no monetary gain. Thus, those who recommend that businesspeople as such should be morally responsible are talking literal nonsense and recommending that businesspeople should perform actions that are aimed both to make someone and no one come out better, which is absurd.

Reply. I believe the unsoundness of this argument may be demonstrated by consideration of competitive games of fair play. For example, there is apparently nothing immoral about such competitive games as chess, tennis, golf and track-and-field events, to name only a few. Rules are designed to insure that, in principle, all competitors have an equal probability of winning. Each chess player gets the same number of pieces, uses the same board, has the same time constraints and so on. Moreover, each player is free to play, or not, depending on the relative benefits and costs of playing. Hence, since chess games are thoroughly competitive and morally unobjectionable, it is logically possible for something to be so. Thus, those who think there is some logical absurdity involved in recommending that businesspeople should be moral and competitive are plainly wrong. If there is any inconsistency involved, it is certainly not a matter of logic or conceptualization.

13. The Godfather's argument.

The Godfather's argument in that excellent book and series of movies was simply that as long as a business provides goods and services demanded by some consumers and a substantial family income for producers, few people should ask anything more of it. After all, business is business, and businesspeople are not saints any more than the rest of us. Life, as the great British-American philosopher Alfred North Whitehead said, is robbery. All living things draw their sustenance from other living things. So, a Godfather-type disciple might have concluded, we are doomed to be predators. The most we can hope for is to make a reasonable living for ourselves and our families, granting always that there is an unattractive aspect to our business activities.

Reply. Dazzling — and pragmatic — as the rhetoric may sound, it's still nonsense. Granting that all living things live by consuming the corpses of other living things, it does not follow that we are all robbers, thieves or murderers. Poetic licence is not a licence to commit logical fallacies. There are important differences between, for example, chopping up vegetables for a Caesar salad and chopping up Caesar. The facts that some people may be willing to pay to have someone murdered and that

some other people are willing to perform the murder are not sufficient to justify the transaction. The person whose life is being negotiated also has an interest that ought to be protected, as do the rest of us whose lives would be at risk if such business transactions were legal.

14. Particular morality.

Finally, one might argue that the basic presupposition of this essay is a red herring, because few if any businesspeople have to be persuaded to be morally responsible. How many people in business have you ever heard saying that they should be morally irresponsible, immoral, morally bad or evil? Not many, probably. No one is born a businessperson. Most people in business were taught roughly the same moral maxims at home and in school, and most of these maxims had roughly the same origins in the Judeo-Christian religions. So most people have been socialized to be morally responsible. Businesspeople generally intend to act and are expected to act the same as everyone else. Thus, to assume that businesspeople are in need of special remedial training, encouragement or admonitions to be nice is simply to make a false assumption.

On the other hand, it is true that the moral maxims to which virtually everyone is exposed are not necessarily predominant in the world of competitive enterprise. Just as chess players and golfers agree to accept particular rules of behaviour for the sake of their games, businesspeople also adopt special rules for the sake of their work. Like chess players, then, businesspeople may be said to have particular codes of ethics in addition to and occasionally in opposition to ordinary or universal ethics. Many actions that would appear to have questionable moral status, judged by the maxims of universal morality, may be morally good judged by the maxims of the particular morality of the world of business. Therefore, instead of condemning businesspeople for acting immorally, one ought at least to appreciate their particular ethical positions and perhaps praise them for steadfastly adhering to the rules of their own game.

Reply. This apparently tolerant approach to the identification and appraisal of morally responsible action is yet another self-defeating argument. Insofar as the argument has any strength at all, it tends to undermine *all* morality. One of the basic aims and functions of morality or codes of ethics is the resolution of disputes involving conflicting interests. Moral maxims and, more importantly, the ideal of universal beneficence are designed to provide rules for settling disputes without resorting to legislated civil or criminal laws. The recognition of a supreme moral principle of action, namely, the intention to impartially maximize human well-being, is a necessary condition of morality achieving its basic aims. Without such a tie-breaking principle, a principle to adjudicate between conflicting interests or lower level maxims, appeals to morality are useless.

Thus, the concept of particular moralities is logically incoherent, for it entails maxims of action which both include and exclude a supreme principle. In other words, it posits a set of maxims which are relatively equal in status but also not relatively equal to one supreme principle. Unless the maxims of any so-called particular morality are roughly equal to those of other particular moralities, one cannot use them to claim special privileges for one's behaviour. However, granting them such equal status implies eliminating the possibility of appealing to them to resolve conflicts. If, for example, businesspeople, bandits and baseball players all have equally important ethical codes to live by, then, when there are conflicts between people in different groups, each can retreat to his or her own special code, with the result that no resolution of the conflict is possible. If one would take the additional step that some people seem to recommend, namely, that everyone should have his or her own moral code, then morality would be radically relativised and absolutely useless. Clearly, the way out of this logical and moral morass is simply to abandon the idea of particular morality. There can be only one kind of morality, and it is universal. Businesspeople, like everyone else, must be judged morally responsible or irresponsible in terms of this morality. There is no third option.

SUGGESTED FURTHER READINGS

FLEW, ANTHONY. "The Profit Motive." *Ethics* 86 (1976).

FRIEDMAN, MILTON. *Capitalism and Freedom.* Chicago: The University of Chicago Press, 1962.

GOLDMAN, ALAN. "Business Ethics: Profits, Utilities, and Moral Rights." *Philosophy and Public Affairs* Vol. 9, No. 3 (1980).

HODGES, LUTHER, and FRIEDMAN, MILTON. "Does Business Have a Social Responsibility?" *Magazine of Bank Administration*, 47 (April 1971).

LEVITT, THEODORE. "The Dangers of Social Responsibility." *Harvard Business Review* (Sept.-Oct. 1958).

NARVESON, JAN. "Justice and the Business Society" in T. Beauchamp and N. Bowie (eds.). *Ethical Theory and Business*, 2nd. ed. Englewood Cliffs, N.J.: Prentice-Hall, Inc., 1983.

PATTEN, JOHN. "The Business of Ethics and the Ethics of Business." *Journal of Business Ethics* 3 (1984).

PATTANTYUS, JOHN. "Profits and Ethics" in James Wilber (ed.). *Economic Analysis*, Proceedings of the Twelfth Conference on Value Enquiry.

5

Ethical Managers Make Their Own Rules

SIR ADRIAN CADBURY

In 1900 Queen Victoria sent a decorative tin with a bar of chocolate inside to all of her soldiers who were serving in South Africa. These tins still turn up today, often complete with their contents, a tribute to the collecting instinct. At the time, the order faced my grandfather with an ethical dilemma. He owned and ran the second-largest chocolate company in Britain, so he was trying harder and the order meant additional work for the factory. Yet he was deeply and publicly opposed to the Anglo-Boer War. He resolved the dilemma by accepting the order, but carrying it out at cost. He therefore made no profit out of what he saw as an unjust war, his employees benefited from the additional work, the soldiers received their royal present, and I am still sent the tins.

My grandfather was able to resolve the conflict between the decision best for his business and his personal code of ethics because he and his family owned the firm which bore their name. Certainly his dilemma would have been more acute if he had had to take into account the interests of outside shareholders, many of whom would no doubt have been in favor both of the war and of profiting from it. But even so, not all my grandfather's ethical dilemmas could be as straightforwardly resolved.

So strongly did my grandfather feel about the South African War that he acquired and financed the only British newspaper which opposed it. He was also against gambling, however, and so he tried to run the paper without any references to horse racing. The effect on the newspaper's circulation was such that he had to choose between his ethical beliefs. He decided, in the end, that it was more important that the paper's voice be heard as widely as possible than that gambling should thereby receive some mild encouragement. The decision was doubtless a relief to those working on the paper and to its readers.

The way my grandfather settled these two clashes of principle brings out some practical points about ethics and business decisions. In the first place, the possibility that ethical and commercial considerations will conflict has always faced those who run companies. It is not a new problem. The difference now is that a more widespread and critical interest is being taken in our decisions and in the ethical judgments which lie behind them.

Secondly, as the newspaper example demonstrates, ethical signposts do not always point in the same direction. My grandfather had to choose between opposing a war and condoning gambling. The rule that it is best to tell the truth often runs up against the rule that we should not hurt people's feelings unnecessarily. There is no simple, universal formula for solving ethical problems. We have to choose from our own codes of conduct whichever rules are appropriate to the case in hand; the outcome of those choices makes us who we are.

Lastly, while it is hard enough to resolve dilemmas when our personal rules of conduct conflict, the real difficulties arise when we have to make decisions which affect the interests of others. We can work out what weighting to give to our own rules through trial and error. But business decisions require us to do the same for others by allocating weights to all the conflicting interests which may be involved. Frequently, for example, we must balance the interests of employees against those of shareholders. But even that sounds more straightforward than it really is, because there may well be differing views among the shareholders, and the interests of past, present, and future employees are unlikely to be identical.

Eliminating ethical considerations from business decisions would simplify the management task, and Milton Friedman has urged something of the kind in arguing that the interaction between business and society should be left to the political process. "Few trends could so thoroughly undermine the very foundation of our free society," he writes in *Capitalism and Freedom*, "as the acceptance by corporate officials of a social responsibility other than to make as much money for their shareholders as possible."

But the simplicity of this approach is deceptive. Business is part of the social system and we cannot isolate the economic elements of major decisions from their social consequences. So there are no simple rules. Those who make business decisions

have to assess the economic and social consequences of their actions as best as they can and come to their conclusions on limited information and in a limited time.

As will already be apparent, I use the word ethics to mean the guidelines or rules of conduct by which we aim to live. It is, of course, foolhardy to write about ethics at all, because you lay yourself open to the charge of taking up a position of moral superiority, of failing to practice what you preach, or both. I am not in a position to preach nor am I promoting a specific code of conduct. I believe, however, that it is useful to all of us who are responsible for business decisions to acknowledge the part which ethics plays in those decisions and to encourage discussion of how best to combine commercial and ethical judgments. Most business decisions involve some degree of ethical judgment; few can be taken solely on the basis of arithmetic.

While we refer to a company as having a set of standards, that is a convenient shorthand. The people who make up the company are responsible for its conduct and it is their collective actions which determine the company's standards. The ethical standards of a company are judged by its actions, not by pious statements of intent put out in its name. This does not mean that those who head companies should not set down what they believe their companies stand for — hard though that is to do. The character of a company is a matter of importance to those in it, to those who do business with it, and to those who are considering joining it.

What matters most, however, is where we stand as individual managers and how we behave when faced with decisions which require us to combine ethical and commercial judgments. In approaching such decisions, I believe it is helpful to go through two steps. The first is to determine, as precisely as we can, what our personal rules of conduct are. This does not mean drawing up a list of virtuous notions, which will probably end up as a watered-down version of the Scriptures without their literary merit. It does mean looking back at decisions we have made and working out from there what our rules actually are. The aim is to avoid confusing ourselves and everyone else by declaring one set of principles and acting on another. Our ethics are expressed in our actions, which is why they are usually clearer to others than to ourselves.

Once we know where we stand personally we can move on to the second step, which is to think through who else will be affected by the decision and how we should weight their interest in it. Some interests will be represented by well-organized groups; others will have no one to put their case. If a factory manager is negotiating a wage claim with employee representatives, their remit is to look after the interests of those who are already employed. Yet the effect of the wage settlement on the factory's costs may well determine whether new employees are likely to be taken on. So the manager cannot ignore the interest of potential employees in the outcome of the negotiation, even though that interest is not represented at the bargaining table.

The rise of organized interest groups makes it doubly important that managers consider the arguments of everyone with a legitimate interest in a decision's outcome. Interest groups seek publicity to promote their causes and they have the advantage of being single-minded: they are against building an airport on a certain site, for example, but take no responsibility for finding a better alternative. This narrow focus gives pressure groups a debating advantage against managements, which cannot evade the responsibility for taking decisions in the same way.

In *The Hard Problems of Management*, Mark Pastin has perceptively referred to this phenomenon as the ethical superiority of the uninvolved, and there is a good deal of it about. Pressure groups are skilled at seizing the high moral ground and arguing that our judgment as managers is at best biased and at worst influenced solely by private gain because we have a direct commercial interest in the outcome of our decisions. But as managers we are also responsible for arriving at business decisions which take account of all the interests concerned; the uninvolved are not.

At times the campaign to persuade companies to divest themselves of their South African subsidiaries has exemplified this kind of ethical high-handedness. Apartheid is abhorrent politically,

socially, and morally. Those who argue that they can exert some influence on the direction of change by staying put believe this as sincerely as those who favor divestment. Yet many anti-apartheid campaigners reject the proposition that both sides have the same end in view. From their perspective it is self-evident that the only ethical course of action is for companies to wash their hands of the problems of South Africa by selling out.

Managers cannot be so self-assured. In deciding what weight to give to the arguments for and against divestment, we must consider who has what at stake in the outcome of the decision. The employees of a South African subsidiary have the most direct stake, as the decision affects their future; they are also the group whose voice is least likely to be heard outside South Africa. The shareholders have at stake any loss on divestment, against which must be balanced any gain in the value of their shares through severing the South African connection. The divestment lobby is the one group for whom the decision is costless either way.

What is clear even from this limited analysis is that there is no general answer to the question of whether companies should sell their South African subsidiaries or not. Pressure to reduce complicated issues to straightforward alternatives, one of which is right and the other wrong, is a regrettable sign of the times. But boards are rarely presented with two clearly opposed alternatives. Companies faced with the same issues will therefore properly come to different conclusions and their decisions may alter over time.

A less contentious divestment decision faced my own company when we decided to sell our foods division. Because the division was mainly a U.K. business with regional brands, it did not fit the company's strategy, which called for concentrating resources behind our confectionery and soft drinks brands internationally. But it was an attractive business in its own right and the decision to sell prompted both a management bid and external offers.

Employees working in the division strongly supported the management bid and made their views felt. In this instance, they were the best organized interest group and they had more information available to them to back their case than any of the other parties involved. What they had at stake was also very clear.

From the shareholders' point of view, the premium over asset value offered by the various bidders was a key aspect of the decision. They also had an interest in seeing the deal completed without regulatory delays and without diverting too much management attention from the ongoing business. In addition, the way in which the successful bidder would guard the brand name had to be considered, since the division would take with it products carrying the parent company's name.

In weighing the advantages and disadvantages of the various offers, the board considered all the groups, consumers among them, who would be affected by the sale. But our main task was to reconcile the interests of the employees and of the shareholders. (The more, of course, we can encourage employees to become shareholders, the closer together the interests of these two stakeholders will be brought.) The division's management upped its bid in the face of outside competition, and after due deliberation we decided to sell to the management team, believing that this choice best balanced the diverse interests at stake.

Companies whose activities are international face an additional complication in taking their decisions. They aim to work to the same standards of business conduct wherever they are and to behave as good corporate citizens of the countries in which they trade. But the two aims are not always compatible: promotion on merit may be the rule of the company and promotion by seniority the custom of the country. In addition, while the financial arithmetic on which companies base their decisions is generally accepted, what is considered ethical varies among cultures.

If what would be considered corruption in the company's home territory is an accepted business practice elsewhere, how are local managers expected to act? Companies could do business only in countries in which they feel ethically at home, provided always that their shareholders take the same view. But this approach could prove unduly restrictive, and there is also a certain arrogance in dismissing foreign codes of conduct without considering why they may be different. If companies find, for example, that they have to pay customs officers in another country just to do their job, it may be that the state is simply transferring its responsibilities to the private sector as an alternative to using taxation less efficiently to the same end.

Nevertheless, this example brings us to one of the most common ethical issues companies face — how far to go in buying business? What payments are legitimate for companies to make to win orders and, the reverse side of that coin, when do gifts to employees become bribes? I use two rules of thumb to test whether a payment is acceptable from the company's point of view: Is the payment on the face of the invoice? Would it embarrass the recipient to have the gift mentioned in the company newspaper?

The first test ensures that all payments, however unusual they may seem, are recorded and go through the books. The second is aimed at distinguishing bribes from gifts, a definition which depends on the size of the gift and the influence it is likely to have on the recipient. The value of a case of whiskey to me would be limited, because I only take it as medicine. We know ourselves whether a gift is acceptable or not and we know that others will know if they are aware of the nature of the gift.

As for payment on the face of the invoice, I have found it a useful general rule precisely because codes of conduct do vary round the world. It has legitimized some otherwise unlikely company payments, to the police in one country, for example, and to the official planning authorities in another, but all went through the books and were audited. Listing a payment on the face of the invoice may not be a sufficient ethical test, but it is a necessary one; payments outside the company's system are corrupt and corrupting.

The logic behind these rules of thumb is that openness and ethics go together and that actions are unethical if they will not stand scrutiny. Openness in arriving at decisions reflects the same logic. It gives those with an interest in a particular decision the chance to make their views known and opens to argument the basis on which the decision is finally taken. This in turn enables the decision makers to learn from experience and to improve their powers of judgment.

Openness is also, I believe, the best way to disarm outside suspicion of companies' motives and actions. Disclosure is not a panacea for improving the relations between business and society, but the willingness to operate an open system is the foundation of those relations. Business needs to be open to the views of society and open in return about its own activities; this is essential for the establishment of trust.

For the same reasons, as managers we need to be candid when making decisions about other people. Dr. Johnson reminds us that when it comes to lapidary inscriptions, "no man is upon oath." But what should be disclosed in references, in fairness to those looking for work and to those who are considering employing them?

The simplest rule would seem to be that we should write the kind of reference we would wish to read. Yet "do as you would be done by" says nothing about ethics. The actions which result from applying it could be ethical or unethical, depending on the standards of the initiator. The rule could be adapted to help managers determine their ethical standards, however, by reframing it as a question: If you did business with yourself, how ethical would you think you were?

Anonymous letters accusing an employee of doing something discreditable create another context in which candor is the wisest course. Such letters cannot by definition be answered, but they convey a message to those who receive them, however warped or unfair the message may be. I normally destroy these letters, but tell the person concerned what has been said. This conveys the disregard I attach to nameless allegation, but preserves the rule of openness. From a practical point of view, it serves as a warning if there is anything in the allegations; from an ethical point of view, the degree to which my judgment of the person may now be prejudiced is known between us.

The last aspect of ethics in business decisions I want to discuss concerns our responsibility for the level of employment; what can or should companies do about the provision of jobs? This issue is of immediate concern to European managers because unemployment is higher in Europe than it is in the United States and the net number of new jobs created has been much lower. It comes to the fore whenever companies face decisions which require a trade-off between increasing efficiency and reducing numbers employed.

If you believe, as I do, that the primary purpose of a company is to satisfy the needs of its customers and to do so profitably, the creation of jobs cannot be the company's goal as well. Satisfying customers requires companies to compete in the marketplace, and so we cannot opt out of introducing new technology, for example, to preserve jobs. To do so would be to deny consumers the benefits of progress, to shortchange the shareholders, and in the longer run to put the jobs of everyone in the company at risk. What destroys jobs certainly and permanently is the failure to be competitive.

Experience says that the introduction of new technology creates more jobs than it eliminates, in ways which cannot be forecast. It may do so, however, only after a time lag, and those displaced may not, through lack of skills, be able to take advantage of the new opportunities when they arise. Nevertheless, the company's prime responsibility to everyone who has a stake in it is to retain its competitive edge, even if this means a loss of jobs in the short run.

Where companies do have a social responsibility, however, is in how we manage that situation, how we smooth the path of technological change. Companies are responsible for the timing of such changes and we are in a position to involve those who will be affected by the way in which those changes are introduced. We also have a vital resource in our capacity to provide training, so that continuing employees can take advantage of change and those who may lose their jobs can more readily find new ones.

In the United Kingdom, an organization called Business in the Community has been established to encourage the formation of new enterprises. Companies have backed it with cash and with secondments. The secondment of able managers to worthwhile institutions is a particularly effective expression of concern, because the ability to manage is such a scarce resource. Through Business in the Community we can create jobs collectively, even if we cannot do so individually, and it is clearly in our interest to improve the economic and social climate in this way.

Throughout, I have been writing about the responsibilities of those who head companies and my emphasis has been on taking decisions, because that is what directors and managers are appointed to do. What concerns me is that too often the public pressures which are put on companies in the name of ethics encourage their boards to put off decisions or to wash their hands of problems. There may well be commercial reasons for those choices, but there are rarely ethical ones. The ethical bases on which decisions are arrived at will vary among companies, but shelving those decisions is likely to be the least ethical course.

The company which takes drastic action in order to survive is more likely to be criticized publicly than the one which fails to grasp the nettle and gradually but inexorably declines. There is always a temptation to postpone difficult decisions, but it is not in society's interests that hard choices should be evaded because of public clamor or the possibility of legal action. Companies need to be encouraged to take the decisions which face them; the responsibility for providing that encouragement rests with society as a whole.

Society sets the ethical framework within which those who run companies have to work out their own codes of conduct. Responsibility for decisions, therefore, runs both ways. Business has to take account of its responsibilities to society in coming to its decisions, but society has to accept its responsibilities for setting the standards against which those decisions are made.

SUGGESTED FURTHER READINGS

DONALDSON, THOMAS. "Constructing a Social Contract for Business." In *Corporations and Morality*. Englewood Cliffs, NJ: Prentice-Hall, 1982.

FRIEDMAN, MILTON. *Capitalism and Freedom*. Chicago: The University of Chicago Press, 1962.

GOLDMAN, ALAN. "Business Ethics: Profits, Utilities, and Moral Rights." *Philosophy and Public Affairs*, Vol. 9, No. 3, (1980).

LEVITT, THEODORE. "The Dangers of Social Responsibility." *Harvard Business Review*, (Sept/Oct 1958).

LITZINGER, WILLIAM and THOMAS SCHAEFER. "Business Ethics Bogeyman: The Perpetual Paradox." *Business Horizons*, (March/April, 1987).

NARVESON, JAN. "Justice and the Business Society." In T. Beauchamp and N. Bowie (eds.) *Ethical Theory in Business*. Englewood Cliffs, NJ: Prentice-Hall, 1983.

NUNAN, RICHARD. "The Libertarian Conception of Corporate Property: A Critique of Milton Friedman's Views on the Social Responsibility of Business." *Journal of Business Ethics* 7 (1988).

PASTIN, MARK. "Ethics and Excellence." *New Management*, (Spring, 1987).

SELDON, RICHARD, (ed.) *Capitalism and Freedom: Problems and Prospects: Proceedings of a Conference in Honor of Milton Friedman*. Charlottesville: University Press of Virginia, 1975.

SORENSON, RALPH. "Can Ethics and Profits Live Under the Same Corporate Roof?" *Financial Executive*, (March/April, 1988).

STROUP, MARGARET *ET AL*. "Doing Good, Doing Better: Two Views of Social Responsibility." *Business Horizons*, (March/April, 1987).

TRUNDLE, ROBERT. "Is There Any Ethics in Business Ethics?" *Journal of Business Ethics* 8 (1989).

PART TWO

Corporations as Moral Agents

INTRODUCTION

What precisely is a corporation? Is it merely an aggregate or collection of individual shareholders, managers and employees? Or is it something distinct unto itself? If corporations are distinct, then does it make any sense at all to conceive of them as non-human "persons" to whom one can ascribe intentions, aims, goals, responsibilities, and perhaps even rights?

These are difficult conceptual questions with which the law has grappled for many years. In a famous Canadian case, *Rex* v. *Fane Robinson Ltd.*, the question arose whether a corporation can be guilty of a criminal offence, which typically requires what lawyers call *mens rea*. That is, to commit a criminal offence, a person must not only perform an action (*actus reus*) but must (normally) do so knowingly, intentionally, or recklessly, with a "guilty mind." It is highly problematic whether a corporation is the kind of thing logically capable of acting — let alone the kind of thing that can possess a guilty mind. There is no doubt that the various people within corporations perform actions and sometimes have guilty minds, but it is highly questionable whether the same thing can be said about the corporation itself. There is something very common-sensical and appealing in the view, expressed by Viscount Haldane in *Lennard's Carrying Co.* v. *Asiatic Petroleum Co.*, that "A corporation is an abstraction [a legal fiction]. It has no mind of its own any more than it has a body of its own. . . ." This had been the view of the presiding judge in *Fane Robinson*. Judge Tweedie had dismissed criminal charges laid against Fane Robinson Ltd. on the ground that "there is no power in a corporation to commit criminal acts in which *mens rea* is a material element, even with the authorization of the shareholders or the directors." The shareholders and directors might be liable, but not the company itself, and the charge had been laid against the latter. The Alberta Court of Appeal thought otherwise. They overturned Tweedie's verdict, claiming that George Robinson and Emile Fielhaber "were the acting and directing will of Fane Robinson Ltd. . . . their culpable intention (*mens rea*) and their illegal act (*actus reus*) were the intention and the act of the company. . . ."

In the more recent English case, *Regina* v. *Andrews Weatherfoil Ltd.*, similar issues arose. The principal question before the English Court of Appeal was whether the trial judge had properly instructed the jury concerning the law of corporate liability. It is not sufficient, in establishing liability on the part of the corporation itself, to show that criminal acts were undertaken by a "responsible agent" or "high executive" or "manager." It must be shown, the Court said, that that "natural person" is in a "sufficiently responsible" position. Presumably that person must, as the court noted in *Fane Robinson*, be the "acting and directing will" of the company. If he is not, then he alone, not the company itself, is criminally liable. Nevertheless, in both *Andrews Weatherfoil* and *Fane Robinson*, there is clear acceptance of the proposition that corporations can be entities unto themselves and that these entities are capable of possessing a "guilty mind."

Legally speaking, a good deal can hinge on whether criminal actions are properly attributable to companies or only natural persons. If the company must pay the fine, then the money is likely to come from company resources. But the company's pockets will likely be much deeper than those of individual directors. If so, then directors may not be nearly so motivated to avoid illegal activities as they would be were they, not the company, the ones held accountable.

Philosophers have recently begun to ask whether moral personhood and responsibility can sensibly be ascribed to corporations. Here the question is whether a corporation is a "moral agent" capable of performing intentional actions for which moral praise and blame are appropriate. Some argue that corporations do have moral standing in much the same way as they have legal standing. Others argue that this is sheer nonsense. To speak of corporations as moral agents is to indulge in a moral fiction, just as speaking of corporations as legal persons is, for some, to subscribe to a legal fiction. Referring to a corporation as though it were itself an agent over and above the people who labour within the corporate structure is just a shorthand way of referring to a complex group of natural persons. To say that Pacific Western Airlines acquired Wardair is merely a shorthand way of saying that certain human beings within the corporate structure of PWA acted in such a way that they (and perhaps others, e.g., shareholders) assumed a controlling interest in Wardair. The corporation didn't act, only those responsible people did. On this account, it makes no sense, literally speaking, to ascribe actions, responsibilities, and rights to PWA itself, as though these were distinct from the actions, responsibilities, and rights of the human beings who collectively make up the groups we call the shareholders and directors of PWA.

Organization of the Course:

Lecture	Topics	Associated Reading for the Lecture
1.	Introduction and Analysis of 'morality' and 'moral rule'	EBPL, Introduction; EBPL, Chapter 1, parts 1.1 and 1.2
2.	A survey of historically important ethical theories	EBPL, Chapter 1, part 1.3. Follow the commentary in EBPL quite closely here.
3.	Survey of ethical theories (concluded) (starting with Rigorism); and Development of a theory of rational social morality	EBPL, Chapter 1, part 1.3 (concluded); EBPL, Chapter 2; Compare PW, Introduction (by Waluchow)
4.	Rational morality (concluded) and The Free Market	EBPL, Chapter 2; EBPL, Chapter 3
5.	The Free Market (continued) and Comparison of "Perfectly Competitive" market idea	EBPL, Chapter 3; The Perfectly Competitive Market, see Allan Buchanan, Ethics, Efficiency, and the Market (not required reading)
6.	(a) Free Market – basic ideas (concluded)	EBPL, Chapter 3; Also PW selections #1-3; Friedman, pp. 41-45; Also, commentaries by Mulligan and Shaw, pp. 46-57
	(b) The Customer: What are his or her rights, and why?	EBPL, Chapter 4; The subject of deception in particular, compare PW #48 (Michelman), pp. 513-521
7.	Consumer Rights (continued): Risk and Safety; pricing; enforcement and Advertising	EBPL, Chapter 4; EBPL, Chapter 5; PW, Part 9 (all)
8.	Advertising (continued)	EBPL, Chapter 5; PW, Part 9 (all)
9.	Advertising (concluded); Ethics for Owners and Managers; Corporations (beginning)	EBPL, Chapter 5; PW, Part 9 (all); EBPL, Chapter 6; PW, Part 5 (all)

DO ASSIGNMENT ONE HERE

10.	Corporations (continued)	EBPL, Chapter 7; PW, Part 2 (all)
11.	Employers and Employees' Rights and Duties: beginning through Fair Wages	EBPL, Chapter 8; PW, Part 4
12.	Employers and Employees' Rights and Duties (concluded); Employee Equity (beginning)	EBPL, Chapter 8; EBPL, Chapter 9; PW, Part 6
13.	Employee Equity (continued)	EBPL, Chapter 9; PW, Part 6; Philip Montague, "The Laborers in the Vineyard and Other Stories" (refer to Selected Readings section)
14.	Employee Equity (concluded) – Affirmative Action and Social Structures for Workers – "Industrial Democracy" and Unions	EBPL, Chapter 9; PW, Part 6 – #28, Hawkesworth in particular, pp. 295-307; EBPL, Chapter 10, "Trade Unions' Dilemma"
15.	The Professional (in general) and Professional Virtues	EBPL, Chapter 11; PW, Part 3
16.	The Professional (concluded) and Society and Business: Public Goods Problems	EBPL, Chapter 11; EBPL, Chapter 12; PW, Part 7

DO ASSIGNMENT TWO HERE

17.	Public Goods Problems (continued)	EBPL, Chapter 12; PW, Part 7
18.	Environmental Issues (continued)	EBPL, Chapter 12; PW, Part 7
19.	International Business	EBPL, Chapter 13; PW, Part 8
20.	Criticisms of Business Society	EBPL, Chapter 14

DO ASSIGNMENT THREE HERE

In the first of our selections, Peter French defends the "Moral Person Theory" against the kind of objections sketched in the preceding paragraph. It is French's belief that moral agency and responsibility can indeed be ascribed, quite literally, to companies who are moral agents. According to French, every corporation has a corporate internal decision structure (a CID structure) that is capable of transforming the actions of natural, biological persons, say the corporate directors, into the intentional actions of the corporation itself. These are actions *of* the corporation, performed *by* the corporation, and *for* corporate reasons. Such a transformation occurs when (a) conditions specified in the appropriate decision-making procedures are satisfied by the directors' actions, and (b) the decision is consistent with, or is an instance of, established corporate policy. Under these conditions, the decision is "corporate intentional" and thus morally accountable as the actions of a moral person — the corporation.

In assessing French's theory, it might be useful to ask the following questions. How does one determine what is really "corporate policy" and thus the company's reasons for action? What are these "corporate reasons" upon which French places so much emphasis? Do we look to what certain key people within the corporate structure *say* are the company's aims and ideals? Or do we look rather to what these people actually *do* or *bring about*? The two are not always identical. And what are we to say when the directors' understanding of company policy is different from that of the shareholders? Indeed, will we often, if ever, find substantial agreement among shareholders concerning the ideals and goals of the company? If not, does this lack of agreement undermine the suggestion that there is something called "corporate policy" and "corporate reasons for action" in terms of which human actions are transformed into the actions of a corporation?

Yet another question worth pondering is whether French has succeeded in showing that corporations are *moral agents*. It might be true that companies are things over and above the human persons who function within corporate structures, but it does not follow from this alone that they are moral agents. As a parallel, consider long-standing sports teams, which seem to have an identity over and above their individual members. It makes sense, for example, to talk of the Montreal Canadiens, a team with a certain character and tradition, which at one time included Rocket Richard, at another Guy Lafleur, and now includes Patrick Roy. The team persists through time even though its members constantly change. It would be a mistake to identify the team with any particular group of individuals who at any given moment in time constitute its membership. But it would require a great leap of logic to infer from this that the Montreal Canadiens is a moral agent.

The same may be true of corporations. Massey-Ferguson was a company that had existed for many years and whose identity, character, and traditions persisted even though the human persons who functioned within it had changed dramatically over the years. All this may be true enough and shows the good sense in suggesting that corporations are things over and above their members. But as with sports teams, the question remains: Are corporations moral agents? The answer to this question must be left to the reader, who should once again bear in mind this point: It fails to follow from the fact that *X* is *a thing in itself* that *X* is a *moral agent*.

It is here that Patricia Werhane's critique of the moral personhood thesis takes its lead. According to Werhane, the corporation is not the *kind* of entity to which one can sensibly ascribe moral agency. It may be a thing unto itself, but it is not a moral agent. As evidence for this thesis, Werhane points out that a corporation is restrained and determined by its formal structures in ways that render it incapable of moral action. She agrees with French that corporate activities are rule-governed, but submits that "these rules, as impersonal operating procedures, preclude rather than imply moral agency. And just as it is silly to ascribe moral responsibility to machines, so too, the organization, structure and goals of a corporation suggest that it does not make sense to ascribe to it moral responsibilities." The important point here is that moral responsibility requires freedom and the ability to entertain and evaluate alternative courses of action, a kind of flexibility and freedom sorely lacking within corporate structures. The very (CID) structures upon which French so heavily relies to effect his corporate transformations in fact undermine the attempt, according to Werhane. Despite all this, Werhane suggests, "a corporation might adopt moral goals . . . or might institutionalize morally appropriate behaviour as a corporate aim so that such a corporation could be labelled socially responsible." But again, this is different from moral agency: "moral agency cannot be ascribed to formal institutions."

In "Dismemberment, Divorce and Hostile Takeovers: A Comment on Corporate Moral Personhood," Rita Manning sheds a quite different light on the moral personhood debate. The burden of French's argument is to establish that "corporations can be full-fledged moral persons and have whatever privileges, rights and duties as are, in the normal course of affairs, accorded to moral persons. . . ." One right that is normally ascribed to moral persons is the right not to have one's life terminated unjustifiably. With human persons, we call this the right not to be killed, and acts which violate this right we call acts of murder. If French's argument were sound, we would seem to be committed to finding an equivalent right for companies. Yet as Manning points out, such a right is nowhere to be found. The "killing" of a company via takeover, merger, and the like is not viewed in nearly the same way as the killing of human persons. The fact that we don't equate corporate extinction with murder seems to militate against the plausibility of French's view. Or does it? At one time the killing of slaves would have been viewed as the mere disposal of property. It would have been met with the same moral indifference as is now evident in the case of "corporate killings." But killing slaves was and always will be wrong, past moral indifference notwithstanding. Perhaps the same is true in the case of corporations. Our moral indifference may, in time, be replaced by moral outrage at the unjustifiable extinction of a full-fledged moral person. Or is this pushing things a bit too far?

Harry Glasbeek no doubt thinks so. As a lawyer, he is principally concerned about the law's ascription of agency and responsibility to companies, though there is little doubt his worries both could and would be extended to the moral sphere as well. Glasbeek sees grave moral and political danger in the personhood theory: "the mythology of the corporation being an individual in its own right should be attacked." If responsibility is placed on the shoulders of companies, then we allow the real culprits to hide behind the corporate facade. We run the risk of letting "the corporate form obscure the fact that there are real people who act wrongfully" and who therefore should be held individually accountable, both legally and morally.

6

The Corporation as a Moral Person

PETER A. FRENCH

... I am interested in the sense ascriptions of moral responsibility make when their subjects are corporations. I hope to provide the foundation of a theory that allows treatment of corporations as members of the moral community, of equal standing with the traditionally acknowledged residents: biological human beings, and hence treats responsibility ascriptions as unexceptionable instances of a perfectly proper sort without having to paraphrase them. In short, corporations can be full-fledged moral persons and have whatever privileges, rights and duties as are, in the normal course of affairs, accorded to moral persons. ...

I shall define a moral person as the referent of any proper name or description that can be a non-eliminatable subject of what I shall call (and presently discuss) a responsibility ascription of the second type. The non-eliminatable nature of the subject should be stressed because responsibility and other moral predicates are neutral as regards person and person-sum predication.[1] Though we might say that, The Ox-Bow mob should be held responsible for the death of three men, a mob is an example of what I have elsewhere called an aggregate collectivity with no identity over and above that of the sum of the identities of its component membership, and hence to use "The Ox-Bow mob" as the subject of such ascriptions is to make summary reference to each member of the mob. For that reason mobs do not qualify as metaphysical or moral persons.

There are at least two significantly different types of responsibility ascriptions that should be distinguished in ordinary usage (not counting the lauditory recommendation, "He is a responsible lad.") The first type pins responsibility on someone or something, the who-dun-it or what-dun-it sense. Austin has pointed out that it is usually used when an event or action is thought by the speaker to be untoward. (Perhaps we are more interested in the failures rather than the successes that punctuate our lives.)

The second type of responsibility ascription, parasitic upon the first, involves the notion of accountability. "Having a responsibility" is interwoven with the notion "Having a liability to

Adapted from *American Philosophical Quarterly*, Vol. 16, No. 3 (July 1979). Reprinted by permission.

answer," and having such a liability or obligation seems to imply (as Anscombe has noted[2]) the existence of some sort of authority relationship either between people or between people and a deity or in some weaker versions between people and social norms. . . .

A responsibility ascription of the second type amounts to the assertion of a conjunctive proposition, the first conjunct of which identifies the subject's actions with or as the cause of an event (usually an untoward one) and the second conjunct asserts that the action in question was intended by the subject or that the event was the direct result of an intentional act of the subject. In addition to what it asserts, it implies that the subject is accountable to the speaker . . . because of the subject's relationship to the speaker (who the speaker is or what the speaker is, a member of the "moral community," a surrogate for that aggregate). The primary focus of responsibility ascriptions of the second type is on the subject's intentions rather than, though not to the exclusion of, occasions. Austin wrote: "In considering responsibility, few things are considered more important than to establish whether a man *intended* to do A, or whether he did A intentionally."[3] To be the subject of a responsibility ascription of the second type, to be a party in responsibility relationships, hence to be a moral person, the subject must be at minimum, what I shall call a Davidsonian agent.[4] If corporations are moral persons, they will be non-eliminatable Davidsonian agents.

For a corporation to be treated as a Davidsonian agent it must be the case that some things that happen, some events, are describable in a way that makes certain sentences true, sentences that say that some of the things a corporation does were intended by the corporation itself. That is not accomplished if attributing intentions to a corporation is only a shorthand way of attributing intentions to the biological persons who comprise, for example, its board of directors. If that were to turn out to be the case, then on metaphysical if not logical grounds there would be no way to distinguish between corporations and mobs. I shall argue, however, that a *Corporation's Internal Deci*-

sion Structure (its CID Structure) is the requisite redescription device that licenses the predication of corporate intentionality.

Intentionality, though a causal notion, is an intensional one and so it does not mark out a class of actions or events. Attributions of intentionality in regard to any event are referentially opaque with respect to other descriptions of that event, or, in other words, the fact that, given one description, an action was intentional does not entail that on every other description of the action it was intentional. A great deal depends upon what aspect of an event is being described. We can correctly say, e.g., "Hamlet intentionally kills the person hiding in Gertrude's room," (one of Davidson's examples), but not "Hamlet intentionally kills Polonius," although "Polonius" and "the person hiding in Gertrude's room" are co-referential. The event may be properly described as "Hamlet killed Polonius" and also as "Hamlet intentionally killed the person hiding in Gertrude's room (behind the arras)," but not as "Hamlet intentionally killed Polonius," for that was not Hamlet's intention. (He, in fact, thought he was killing the King.) The referential opacity of intentionality attributions, I shall presently argue, is congenial to the driving of a wedge between the descriptions of certain events as individual intentional actions and as corporate intentional actions.

Certain . . . actions are describable as simply the bodily movements of human beings, and sometimes those same events are redescribable in terms of their upshots, as bringing about something, e.g., (from Austin[5]) feeding penguins *by* throwing them peanuts ("by" is the most common way we connect different descriptions of the same event[6]), and sometimes those events can be redescribed as the effects of some prior cause; then they are described as done for reasons, done in order to bring about something, e.g., feeding the penguins peanuts in order to kill them. Usually what we single out as that prior cause is some desire or felt need combined with the belief that the object of the desire will be achieved by the action undertaken. (This, I think is what Aristotle meant when he maintained that acting requires desire.) Saying "Someone (*X*) did y intentionally" is to describe an event (y) as the upshot of X's having had a reason for doing it which was the cause of his doing it.

It is obvious that a corporation's doing something involves or includes human beings doing things and that the human beings who occupy various positions in a corporation usually can be described as having reasons for *their* behavior. In virtue of those descriptions they may be properly held responsible for their behavior, *ceteris paribus*. What needs to be shown is that there is sense in saying that corporations and not just the people who work in them, have reasons for doing what they do. Typically, we will be told that it is the directors, or the managers, etc., that really have the corporate reasons and desires, etc., and that although corporate actions may not be reducible without remainder, corporate intentions are always reducible to human intentions.

Every corporation has an internal decision structure. CID Structures have two elements of interest to us here: (1) an organizational or responsibility flow chart that delineates stations and levels within the corporate power structure and (2) corporate decision recognition rule(s) (usually embedded in something called "corporation policy"). The CID Structure is the personnel organization for the exercise of the corporation's power with respect to its ventures, and as such its primary function is to draw experience from various levels of the corporation into a decision-making and ratification process. When operative and properly activated, the CID Structure accomplishes a subordination and synthesis of the intentions and acts of various biological persons into a corporate decision. When viewed in another way, as already suggested, the CID Structure licenses the descriptive transformation of events, seen under another aspect as the acts of biological persons (those who occupy various stations on the organizational chart), into corporate acts, by exposing the corporate character of those events. A functioning CID Structure *incorporates* acts of biological persons. For illustrative purposes, imagine that an event E has at least two aspects, that is, can be described in two non-identical ways. One of those aspects is "Executive X's

doing y" and one is "Corporation C's doing z." The corporate act and the individual act may have different properties; indeed they have different causal ancestors though they are causally inseparable. (The causal inseparability of these acts, I hope to show, is a product of the CID Structure: X's doing y is not the cause of C's doing z nor is C's doing z the cause of X's doing y, although if X's doing y causes event F then C's doing z causes F and *vice versa*.)

Although I doubt he is aware of the metaphysical reading that can be given to this process, J.K. Galbraith rather neatly captures what I have in mind when he writes in his recent popular book on the history of economics: "From [the] interpersonal exercise of power, the interaction . . . of the participants, comes the *personality* of the corporation."[7] I take Galbraith here to be quite literally correct, but it is important to spell out how a CID Structure works this "miracle."

In philosophy in recent years we have grown accustomed to the use of games as models for understanding institutional behavior. We all have some understanding of how rules in games make certain descriptions of events possible that would not be so if those rules were non-existent. The CID Structure of a corporation is a kind of constitutive rule (or rules) analogous to the game rules with which we are familiar. The organization chart of a corporation distinguishes "players" and clarifies their rank and the interwoven lines of responsibility within the corporation. An organizational chart tells us, for example, that anyone holding the title "Executive Vice President for Finance Administration" stands in a certain relationship to anyone holding the title "Director of Internal Audit" and to anyone holding the title "Treasurer," etc. In effect it expresses, or maps, the interdependent and dependent relationships, line and staff, that are involved in determinations of corporate decisions and actions. The organizational chart provides what might be called the grammar of corporate decision-making. What I shall call internal recognition rules provide its logic.

By "recognition rule(s)" I mean what Hart, in another context, calls "conclusive affirmative indication"[8] that a decision on an act has been made or performed for corporate reasons. Recognition rules are of two sorts. Partially embedded in the organizational chart are procedural recognitors: we see that decisions are to be reached collectively at certain levels and that they are to be ratified at higher levels (or at inner circles, if one prefers that Galbraithean model). A corporate decision is recognized internally, however, not only by the procedure of its making, but by the policy it instantiates. Hence every corporation creates an image (not to be confused with its public image) or a general policy, what G.C. Buzby of the Chilton Company has called the "basic belief of the corporation,"[9] that must inform its decisions for them to be properly described as being those of that corporation. "The moment policy is side-stepped or violated, it is no longer the policy of that company."[10]

Peter Drucker has seen the importance of the basic policy recognitors in the CID Structure (though he treats matters rather differently from the way I am recommending.) Drucker writes:

> Because the corporation is an institution it must have a basic policy. For it must subordinate individual ambitions and decisions to the *needs* of the corporation's welfare and survival. That means that it must have a set of principles and a rule of conduct which limit and direct individual actions and behavior . . .[11]

Suppose, for illustrative purposes, we activate a CID Structure in a corporation, the Gulf Oil Corporation. Imagine that three executives X, Y and Z have the task of deciding whether or not Gulf Oil will join a world uranium cartel. X, Y and Z have before them an Everest of papers that have been prepared by lower-echelon executives. Some of the papers will be purely factual reports, some will be contingency plans, some will be formulations of positions developed by various departments, some will outline financial considerations, some will be legal opinions and so on. In so far as these will all have been processed through Gulf's CID Structure system, the personal reasons, if any, individual

executives may have had when writing their reports and recommendations in a specific way will have been diluted by the subordination of individual inputs to peer group input even before X, Y and Z review the matter. X, Y and Z take a vote. Their taking of a vote is authorized procedure in the Gulf CID Structure, which is to say that under these circumstances the vote of X, Y and Z can be redescribed as the corporation's making a decision: that is, the event "XYZ voting" may be redescribed to expose an aspect otherwise unrevealed, that is quite different from its other aspects e.g., from X's voting in the affirmative.

Redescriptive exposure of a procedurally corporate aspect of an event, however, is not to be confused with a description of an event that makes true a sentence that says that the corporation did something intentionally. But the CID Structure, as already suggested, also provides the grounds in its other type of recognitor for such an attribution of corporate intentionality. Simply, when the corporate act is consistent with, an instantiation or an implementation of established corporate policy, then it is proper to describe it as having been done for corporate reasons, as having been caused by a corporate desire coupled with a corporate belief and so, in other words, as corporate intentional.

An event may, under one of its aspects, be described as the conjunctive act "X did a (or as X intentionally did a) & Y did a (or as Y intentionally did a) & Z did a (or as Z intentionally did a)" (where a = voted in the affirmative on the question of Gulf Oil joining the cartel). Given the Gulf CID Structure, formulated in this instance as the conjunction of rules: when the occupants of positions A, B and C on the organizational chart unanimously vote to do something and if doing that something is consistent with, an instantiation or an implementation of general corporate policy and *ceteris paribus*, then the corporation has decided to do it for corporate reasons, the event is redescribable as "the Gulf Oil Corporation did j for corporate reasons f," (where j is "decided to join the cartel" and f is any reason (desire + belief) consistent with basic policy of Gulf Oil, e.g., increasing profits) or simply as

"Gulf Oil Corporation intentionally did *j*." This is a rather technical way of saying that in these circumstances the executives voting is, given its CID Structure, also the corporation deciding to do something, and that regardless of the personal reasons the executives have for voting as they do and even if their reasons are inconsistent with established corporate policy or even if one of them has no reason at all for voting as he does, the corporation still has reasons for joining the cartel; that is, joining is consistent with the inviolate corporate general policies as encrusted in the precedent of previous corporate actions and its statements of purpose as recorded in its certificate of incorporation, annual reports, etc.

The corporation's only method of achieving its desires or goals is the activation of the personnel who occupy its various positions. However, if *X* voted affirmatively purely for reasons of personal monetary gain (suppose he had been bribed to do so) that does not alter the fact that the corporate reason for joining the cartel was to minimize competition and hence pay higher dividends to its shareholders. Corporations have reasons because they have interests in doing those things that are likely to result in realization of their established corporate goals regardless of the transient self-interest of directors, managers, etc. If there is a difference between corporate goals and desires and those of human beings it is probably that the corporate ones are relatively stable and not very wide ranging, but that is only because corporations can do relatively fewer things than human beings, being confined in action predominately to a limited socio-economic sphere. The attribution of corporate intentionality is opaque with respect to other possible descriptions of the event in question. It is, of course, in a corporation's interest that its component membership view the corporate purposes as instrumental in the achievement of their own goals. (Financial reward is the most common way this is achieved.)

It will be objected that a corporation's policies reflect only the current goals of its directors. But that is certainly not logically necessary nor is it in practice true for most large corporations. Usually, of course, the original incorporators will have organized to further their individual interests and/or to meet goals which they shared. But even in infancy the melding of disparate interests and purposes gives rise to a corporate long-range point of view that is distinct from the intents and purposes of the collection of incorporators viewed individually. Also, corporate basic purposes and policies, as already mentioned, tend to be relatively stable when compared to those of individuals and not couched in the kind of language that would be appropriate to individual purposes. Furthermore, as histories of corporations will show, when policies are amended or altered it is usually only peripheral issues that are involved. Radical policy alteration constitutes a new corporation, a point that is captured in the incorporation laws of such states as Delaware. ("Any power which is not enumerated in the charter and the general law or which cannot be inferred from these two sources is *ultra vires* of the corporation.") Obviously underlying the objection is an uneasiness about the fact that corporate intent is dependent upon policy and purpose that is but an artifact of the socio-psychology of a group of biological persons. Corporate intent seems somehow to be a tarnished illegitimate offspring of human intent. But this objection is another form of the anthropocentric bias. By concentrating on possible descriptions of events and by acknowledging only that the possibility of describing something as an agent depends upon whether or not it can be properly described as having done something (the description of some aspect of an event) for a reason, we avoid the temptation to look for extensional criteria that would necessitate reduction to human referents.

The CID Structure licenses redescriptions of events as corporate and attributions of corporate intentionality while it does not obscure the private acts of executives, directors etc. Although *X* voted to support the joining of the cartel because he was bribed to do so, *X* did not join the cartel, Gulf Oil Corporation joined the cartel. Consequently, we may say that *X* did something for which he should be held morally responsible, yet whether or not Gulf Oil Corporation should be held morally responsible for joining the cartel is a question that turns on issues that may be unrelated to X's having accepted a bribe.

Of course, Gulf Oil Corporation cannot join the cartel unless X or somebody who occupies position A on the organizational chart votes in the affirmative. What that shows, however, is that corporations are collectivities. That should not, however, rule out the possibility of their having metaphysical status, as being Davidsonian agents, and being thereby full-fledged moral [legal] persons.

This much seems to me clear: we can describe many events in terms of certain physical movements of human beings and we also can sometimes describe those events as done for reasons by those human beings, but further we can sometimes describe those events as corporate and still further as done for corporate reasons that are qualitatively different from whatever personal reasons, if any,

component members may have for doing what they do.

Corporate agency resides in the possibility of CID Structure licensed redescription of events as corporate intentional. That may still appear to be downright mysterious, although I do not think it is, for human agency as I have suggested, resides in the possibility of description as well.

Although further elaboration is needed, I hope I have said enough to make plausible the view that we have good reasons to acknowledge the non-eliminatable agency of corporations. I have maintained that Davidsonian agency is a necessary and sufficient condition of moral personhood. I cannot further argue that position here (I have done so elsewhere). On the basis of the foregoing analysis, however, I think that grounds have been provided for holding corporations *per se* to account for what they do, for treating them as metaphysical persons *qua* moral persons.[12]

ENDNOTES

1. See Gerald Massey, "Tom, Dick, and Harry, and All The King's Men," *American Philosophical Quarterly*, Vol. 13 (1976), pp. 89–108.

2. G.E.M. Anscombe, "Modern Moral Philosophy," *Philosophy*, Vol. 33 (1958), pp. 1–19.

3. J.L. Austin, "Three Ways of Spilling Ink," in *Philosophical Papers* (Oxford: Oxford University Press, 1970), p. 273.

4. See for example Donald Davidson, "Agency," in *Agent, Action, and Reason*, edited by Binkley, Bronaugh, and Marras (Toronto: University of Toronto Press, 1971).

5. Austin, p. 275.

6. See Joel Feinberg, *Doing and Deserving* (Princeton, NJ: Princeton University Press, 1970), p. 134f.

7. John Kenneth Galbraith, *The Age of Uncertainty* (Boston: Houghton-Mifflin Co., 1971), p. 261.

8. H.L.A. Hart, *The Concept of Law* (Oxford: Clarendon Press, 1961), Ch. VI.

9. G.C. Buzby, "Politics — A Guide to What A Company Stands For," *Management Record*, Vol. 24 (1962), p. 5ff.

10. *Ibid.*

11. Peter Drucker, *Concept of Corporation* (New York: John Day Co., 1964/1972), pp. 36–37.

12. This paper owes much to discussions and comments made by J.L. Mackie, Donald Davidson and Howard K. Wettstein. An earlier version was read at a conference on "Ethics and Economics" at the University of Delaware. I also acknowledge the funding of the University of Minnesota Graduate School that supports the project of which this is a part.

7

Formal Organizations, Economic Freedom and Moral Agency

PATRICIA HOGUE WERHANE

Contemporary societal expectations place an onus of moral responsibility on the activities of economic institutions, specifically on the activities of modern business corporations. However the economist Milton Friedman claims that:

> Few trends could so thoroughly undermine the very foundations of our free society as the acceptance by corporate officials of a social responsibility other than to make as much money for their stockholders as possible.[1]

In this paper I shall make three arguments. First, I shall argue that while society tends to hold corporations morally responsible, and while one might agree that corporations should be morally accountable, corporations, as formal institutions, are so structured that such accountability is philosophically inappropriate. I shall criticize certain recent suggestions offered to make sense out of corporate moral responsibility because these suggestions either confuse corporations with other kinds of institutions, or they tend to confuse the concept of social responsibility with moral accountability.

Second, I shall claim that my conclusion that corporations are not structured as moral agents does not support Friedman's argument that in a free society the only responsibility of business is to its stockholders. This is because social responsibility and moral accountability are not interchangeable concepts, and because profit maximization and social responsibility are not contradictory corporate functions.

I shall conclude the paper by arguing that Friedman's notion of a free society involves the notion of moral accountability, and that corporate moral agency is a condition for the proper functioning of a private free enterprise system. Thus, if economic freedom and autonomy are important, corporations might wish to examine what the notion of institutional moral agency entails.

A number of contemporary philosophers have attempted to justify the argument that it is appropriate to hold corporations morally responsible. In a recent paper entitled "The Moral Responsibility of Corporations"[2] David Ozar tries to establish the claim that corporations are single individuals or are sometimes treated as individuals, and thus, like individual human beings, corporations are morally liable. To this end Ozar compares corporations to other kinds of institutions such as clubs and nations. Ozar points out that corporations, like clubs and nations, operate like single individual entities. Corporations have legal status as individuals, and each of these kinds of institutions has rules or by-laws governing their actions considered as individuals. The rule model, Ozar argues, implies agency. And because we hold human agents morally responsible, and because we hold clubs and nations morally responsible, so too we can hold other rule-governed institutions such as corporations morally responsible.

The issue Ozar's paper raises is not whether we treat corporations as individuals nor whether corporations adopt rule-governed behavior. Rather the issue centers on whether all rule-governed behavior implies moral agency so that it makes sense to say that corporations, like clubs and nations operate as *morally responsible* individuals. There are important differences between corporations and clubs and nations. These differences include structural differences in the roles of institutional rules and goals, and differences in the relationships between the institution and its members. These differences, I shall argue, preclude making the analogy that corporations, like clubs and nations, are moral individuals.

The relationship of a club or a nation to its members or citizens is different from the relationship of a corporation to its employees. The well-being of individuals, or groups of individuals, constitutes an essential part of the ends or goals for which a club or nation is constituted. Clubs and nations are, by and large, structured for their members, and many, if not all, of the rules, by-laws, constitutions, etc., of these institutions apply to their members or to the rights and conduct of their members. The modern business corporation however, is an economic institution structured primarily for the achievement of material ends external to the corporation. Corporate goals include customer satisfaction, technological advancement, market penetration, profit maximization, etc. Corporate

rules and guidelines are aimed at the efficient maximization of these goals. "Following a rule" in corporate activities usually involves maximizing corporate goal achievement as efficiently and productively as possible. Thus the corporation is a formal organization constituted to achieve impersonal ends external to the organization.

In his paper, "Morality and the Ideal of Rationality in Formal Organizations"[3] John Ladd argues that corporations are formal organizations in another sense. Corporate employees are impersonal members of corporations. Employees are one of the means through which a corporation is a success or failure, but not an end for which the corporation operates. In corporations, clubs and nations, many of the activities of their respective members are regulated by corporate policies, by-laws and constitutions. But while rules and goals of clubs and nations are structurally connected to their members or citizens, corporate aims and company guidelines are not so related to company employees. In a corporation rules function more like operating instructions than moral prescriptions, since in corporate activities disobeying a rule means not performing one's job.

In modern corporations employee rights are defined by institutions external to the corporation, e.g., unions, government agencies, and laws. But seldom are employee rights embodied in the structure of the corporation as an institutional part of its operations. In talking about actions of clubs and nations, however, the rights or absence of rights, of its members or citizens is an important issue. Corporate employee rights are an issue only insofar as these contribute to corporate success. As a club member or a citizen I have, at least in principle, a right to protest rules, goals or actions of my club or country when I think they are unjust or unfit. In a corporation, employees have no such rights. Such protests would be considered inappropriate, the employees would be accused of disrupting economic activities, and the employee likely would be fired.

One might suggest that stockholders, who are the owners of corporations, have a relationship to a corporation somewhat analogous to the relationship of a club member to a club, since one of the aims of a corporation is to maximize earnings for shareholders. However, this not the case. Because most stockholders are not corporate employees nor sit on boards of directors, most stockholders have little or no responsibility for what happens in a corporation. They are not involved in establishing corporate aims nor in realizing (or criticizing) these aims, and there is some question whether stockholders have *any* decision-making rights. In reality, stockholders are an abstract group of owners who happen to hold stock on the particular day when earnings are paid out.

Clubs and nations are so structured, then, that the club or nation is responsible to each of its members, and its members have certain rights defined by the club. Moreover, members of a club or nation are morally responsible or held responsible for the activities of that club or nation. For example, we tend to hold the German nation as a whole responsible for Nazi activities during World War II, even though many Germans were not Nazis. However it would be illogical to hold assembly-line workers at General Electric responsible for General Electric's alleged price-fixing activities in the 1960's. Thus one might ascribe moral responsibility to a club or nation, and therefore to its members, but such ascription of moral agency to a corporation is questionable in light of the largely abstract and impersonal relationships of the corporation both to its employees and its stockholders.

Thus, as Ladd argues in his paper, corporations are structured very much like machines. Corporate rules and operating procedures, like the design and structure of a machine, are set up to achieve external economic ends rather than designed in relation to, or as a consequence of member employees.[4] Each employee in a corporation, like each part in a machine, plays an important role in achieving corporate ends, but any weak or dissident employee, like any malfunctioning part, could be, and should be, replaced in order to operate at maximum corporate efficiency. Therefore, while corporate activities are rule-governed, these rules, as impersonal operating procedures, preclude rather than imply moral agency. And just as it is

silly to ascribe moral responsibilities to machines, so too, the organization, structure and goals of a corporation suggest that it does not make sense to ascribe to it moral responsibilities.

The notion of corporate responsibility might be explained in terms of social responsibility. It is often claimed that corporations have certain kinds of responsibilities to the society in which they operate. It is then claimed that we can ascribe such responsibilities to corporations despite the way in which corporations are structured as formal institutions, and that such responsibility can be defined as "moral accountability."

To make this point Kenneth Goodpaster, in his paper "Morality and Organizations",[5] suggests that the comparison of corporations to machines is too static and too narrow. Corporations operate more like organisms than machines, because corporations, like other organisms interact with society through various feedback mechanisms. Just as the environment and societal expectations trigger certain kinds of responses in other organisms, so too corporations often act or react according to the kinds of feedback they receive from society. If this model is descriptive of corporations, Goodpaster argues, then it allows a "space" in which a corporation might be expected to adopt moral goals as a response to community criticism or esteem.

The idea that formal organizations might adopt moral goals is further developed by Thomas Donaldson in his paper, "Moral Change and the Corporation."[6] Donaldson points out that even in the pursuit of economic ends corporations often react to moral restraints imposed on them by society. Moreover, Donaldson argues, it is not impossible, and indeed it is highly plausible to suggest that formal institutions such as corporations could adopt moral goals. These goals could be institutionalized within the structure of the corporation such that they became ends for which a corporation might operate. For example, a corporation could adopt a policy of hiring qualified minorities without giving up its goal of economic gains.

Both Goodpaster and Donaldson have enhanced the concept of corporation and shown that it is not impossible for a formal organization to adopt goals which we would ordinarily label as "moral." I would suggest, however, that they have not succeeded in demonstrating that corporations, like clubs, nations, and human individuals are moral agents. For while a corporation might adopt moral goals in response to societal feedback or might institutionalize morally appropriate behavior as a corporate aim so that such a corporation could be labeled socially responsible, this is different from moral agency, and moral agency cannot be ascribed to formal institutions.

To argue this point, let us consider a mythical example. One might imagine a corporation which was operated solely by robots and computers. Such an organization, let us call it Robotron, would have a charter and legal status. It would operate like other corporations. It would own property, manufacture products, conduct marketing, correspond with other corporations and with customers, replace obsolete equipment, develop new product lines, write proxy statements, answer SEC inquiries, etc. Robotron would have stockholders and pay out dividends. Only a visitor to corporate "headquarters" would learn that Robotron had no human employees. And such a corporation could be programed to respond to feedback from societal expectations such as requests for anti-pollution devices, safer products, etc. In fact one could imagine that Robotron was an organization such as CARE which institutionalizes valued moral goals as its corporate aims.

This corporation, Robotron, meets all the Donaldson-Goodpaster requirements. It lives up to societal expectations, it conforms to requests of government agencies, it institutionalizes moral goals in its operations, and from an economic point of view it operates efficiently and profitably. But Robotron, I would argue, is not morally responsible. It is not morally responsible because it is not a moral agent. And its lack of moral agency is not merely a result of its lack of human employees. Even if Robotron *did* have human employees, the relation between Robotron and its computers would be much the same as the relation between Robotron and its human employees, because the structure of Robotron as a formal organization would remain un-

altered. Decision making by non-human employees would consist of institutional decisions, and non-efficient employees, like obsolete computers, would be replaced. And the role of the human or computer employee in achieving corporate moral goals, such as those of CARE, would be the same as in achieving the production of light bulbs or airplane engines.

This last point needs elaboration. What I am suggesting is that the qualitative value of institutional goals does not necessarily determine whether or not the institution is a moral agent. CARE has highly commendable goals, and most of its employees are not robots. But CARE is a formal organization. The relationships of the institution, the structure of the institution and institutional goals to its employees are impersonal relationships. This is because the operators of any corporation, whether they are human or robots, are themselves merely operators. They are part of the institution only to achieve ends which are not their own. Their choices are important only when they affect the success of achieving corporate goals. And corporations, such as CARE, exist not for their members but for the successful pursuit of ends which have little or no relation to the employees who realize them.

Therefore one may assign corporations and other formal organizations moral goals, and these institutions may institute moral goals themselves into their corporate structure as part of their operating procedures. Such corporations are socially responsible institutions and society should commend these actions. However, even in these cases I would suggest that one cannot make the further claim that these corporations are morally responsible. Social responsibility does not necessarily imply moral agency. Corporations are not structured such that they operate as moral agents. The relationship of corporate members (employees, robots and stockholders) to corporate rules and goals and the absence of a reciprocal relationship between the corporation and its employees precludes such agency.

It is beyond the scope of this paper to explore what corporate moral agency might entail. I would suggest, however, that if it is the case that a corporation such as Robotron can operate as a socially responsible organization it is obvious that merely to alter the goals of a formal organization does not, in itself, alter the moralness of the institution as an agent. Achieving corporate moral agency would involve, in brief, internal alterations of corporate structure; that is, there would have to be a radical restructuring of the relationship of the corporation, both to its goals and even more importantly to its member employees. And the role of the individual in the organization would have to be such that the Robotron analogy will not hold.

Corporations have been operating as highly successful economic institutions for some years. The fact that they are not structured as morally responsible agents might not be offensive to them. Such institutions never made that claim nor thought that moral agency was necessary for economic success. Why, then, might the question of moral agency be important to a business corporation? In what follows I shall develop the claim that moral agency is necessary for economic freedom and autonomy. Applying this to formal institutions, if corporations wish to operate freely without social or governmental constraints and if this form of operation actually enhances the economic life of the community as some economists suggest, then corporations might wish to take the idea of moral agency seriously.

Milton Friedman argues that economic freedom is a necessary condition for political freedom. By economic freedom Friedman has in mind a society consisting of autonomous privately owned economic enterprises each pursuing its own ends and freely competing with each other in the marketplace. In this society government would have little or no role in economic activities and political power and economic success would be separate. In such a society, Friedman suggests, economic freedom, and thus political freedom prevails.[7] It is this concept of economic freedom that prompts Friedman to claim that profit maximization and social responsibility are incompatible corporate goals. Friedman's picture of ideal free enterprise is incomplete on two grounds. First, as I suggested earlier, social responsibility is not incompatible with the operations of formal organizations. Thus a corporation might be

socially responsible, it might adopt moral goals as part of its corporate aims, and be highly profitable as well. Second, Friedman does not consider corporate *moral* responsibility an issue at all, because, I think, Friedman would agree that moral agency does not apply to formal economic institutions. However a difficulty arises because there is an inconsistency in Friedman's concept of a corporation as a *free autonomous* institution to whom the notion of moral agency does not apply. This inconsistency is best illustrated by re-examining the computer corporation, Robotron.

Suppose Robotron began manufacturing toxic substances injurious to the health of anyone who came in contact with the substance. Societal mechanisms would interfere with Robotron's program and alter its manufacturing techniques to prohibit further manufacture of these toxic substances. No one would accuse Robotron of moral irresponsibility; it just happened to manufacture socially unacceptable substances. Nor would we accuse society of interfering with the rights and freedoms of Robotron since, as a formal organization made up of nonhumans, Robotron has no rights or freedoms. Any formal organization which operates impersonally is, in principle, in the same position as Robotron. Because it neither understands the concept of moral responsibility nor acts as a moral agent, such an institution cannot expect to be treated as a free autonomous agent. And society should feel no moral compunction in enforcing its demands on such an institution.

It would appear, then, that if the concept of economic freedom makes sense, and if as Friedman suggests, such freedom is necessary for political freedom, the notion of moral agency as applied to economic institutions is very important. Corporations cannot expect to operate freely *and* nonmorally. Freedom and moral agency go together, and it is inconsistent to demand one without accepting the consequences of the other.

I am not arguing that all corporations should restructure themselves as moral agents. Nor am I agreeing (or disagreeing) with Friedman's claim that economic freedom is a condition for political freedom. But I am pointing out that freedom and autonomy imply moral agency, and moral agency does not apply to corporations as formal organizations. Therefore corporations cannot expect to be treated as free autonomous enterprises. Thus if economic freedom is a value, and if corporations wish to operate without societal constraints, then they need to examine what might be involved in reconstituting themselves as morally accountable institutions.

ENDNOTES

1. Milton Friedman, *Capitalism and Freedom* (Chicago: The University of Chicago Press, 1962), p. 133.

2. David Ozar, "The Moral Responsibility of Corporations," in Thomas Donaldson and Patricia H. Werhane, eds. *Ethical Issues in Business: A Philosophical Approach*, (Englewood Cliffs, NJ: Prentice-Hall, Inc., 1979.)

3. John Ladd, "Morality and the Ideal of Rationality in Formal Organizations," *Monist*, 54 (1970), pp. 488–516.

4. Ladd, p. 400.

5. Kenneth Goodpaster, "Morality and Organizations," paper originally presented at the Pacific Division Meetings, American Philosophical Association, 1978; Donaldson and Werhane, 1979.

6. Thomas Donaldson, "Moral Change and the Corporation," *Proceedings of the Bentley College Second National Conference on Business Ethics*, 1979.

7. Friedman, pp. 1–6.

8

Dismemberment, Divorce and Hostile Takeovers: A Comment on Corporate Moral Personhood

RITA C. MANNING

When ATT agreed to settle with the SEC by allowing itself to be dismembered, some cheered, some booed, but most thought that the victory or defeat was, in some sense, a moral one. When Bendix and Martin Marieta slugged it out in one of the first destructive hostile takeover fights, many expressed moral indignation. When animators from Disney studios broke away to form a new studio in the summer of 1983, those of us who remember *Bambi* sensed a moral victory in the air.

Our moral intuitions about these cases cannot be completely explained by appeal to the effects of such corporate realignment on the lives of individual human beings. In some sense, it is the corporate person that is the focus of our concern.

We can explain our intuitions about these cases by appeal to Peter French's picture of the corporation as a moral person. He argues that corporations are persons in much the same sense as you and I and

are entitled to the same rights as human beings.[1] In this paper, I want to explore the consequences of his view for each of the cases mentioned above. I shall argue that, though French can explain why our moral intuitions seem to arise in response to some concern about the corporations themselves, his analysis commits us to the "wrong" intuitions. I shall then offer an account of these intuitions which focuses on the character of the corporations.

If corporations are moral persons entitled to the same rights as human persons, what should we say about the dismemberment of ATT? One might argue that this would be a clear case of cruel and unusual punishment. The right being violated here would be the right to bodily integrity. Dismembering a human person for the sole reason of controlling his behavior would be viewed as an obvious violation of this right. Even if we argue that ATT was dismembered as a punishment for its illegal acts, we

From *Journal of Business Ethics* **7** (1988) 639–643. © 1988 by Kluwer Academic Publishers. Reprinted by permission.

could not justify this response in the case of a human person. One could argue here that "dismemberment" is simply the wrong description. ATT was instead forced to sell many of its subsidiaries. A similar punishment for a human person would be seen as appropriate in similar cases. Hence, no rights are violated.

I'm not convinced that this is the right description of what happened to ATT. In some sense, ATT is no longer the same company after it sells off a sufficient number of subsidiaries. No one talks about "Ma Bell" anymore, and along with losing this nickname, ATT has lost its image as an all powerful monopoly. ATT is no longer exclusively identified with phone service, but is beginning to be identified with new products, e.g. computers. This marks a profound change for ATT, from monopolistic utility to competing producer. ATT could change sufficiently that we could say of it "the only thing this new company has in common with the old ATT is its name." This claim could not be made about a human person. A human person would also change if faced with the loss of all his property, but a central core would remain the same. The person would retain, among other things, his body, his relationship with certain other persons, and his memories. What would we have to do to a human person before we would say, "the only thing he has in common with the old Jack is the name"? Perhaps a serious injury would do. A burn which would change a healthy, active, outgoing pilot into a reclusive, introverted, essentially inactive person might count as forcing the victim to undergo a rebirth.[2] A lobotomy might also justify the claim that Jack is a new person. A deliberate burning would surely be morally repugnant in large part because of the pain, but even a relatively painless lobotomy as punishment for human indiscretion would be morally repugnant, so French would presumably be unwilling to settle for this description of what happened to ATT.

French could insist that I've overstated the case. ATT is still ATT; it just lacks its local subsidiaries. I agree that we are not justified in saying that the only thing the new ATT has in common with the old ATT is the name. The point I want to make is that there is a point at which the forced selling of subsidiaries

would justify the claim. This would not be true for the forced sale of the property of a human person. So the analogy with the forced sale of the property of a human won't work.

If we agree that "dismemberment" is the right description, and if we agree with French that ATT is a person with the same rights as a human person, then we should be appalled at the action of the SEC. In fact, the intuitions of many were just the opposite. They greeted the news of the dismemberment with satisfaction. I think that French is right to insist that this reaction cannot be explained by saying that these critics were thinking ahead to better days for all current and future customers and employees. Instead, they saw it as a just punishment for the misdeeds of ATT. This suggests that we do in fact commonly think of corporations as responsible agents. French's analysis provides a justification of such ordinary intuitions. He argues that corporations do have moral obligations because they can recognize the immorality of their actions, and because they can choose to do otherwise.[3] Though I do want to endorse this analysis, I want to stop short of saying that corporations also share the same rights as human persons.[4] It seems to me that French has three options here. The first is to say that "dismemberment" is not a strong enough description for what the SEC did to ATT. "Killing" might be a better description. The analogy with capital punishment could then be made. This would explain why the intuitions of many were that the SEC action was appropriate. On this analysis, ATT would be seen as a murderer of its potential competitors. Many share the same intuition about the appropriateness of capital punishment for a particularly vicious murderer. The problem with this response is that the descriptions of ATT as a murderer of potential competitors and of the SEC's action against ATT are too strong. ATT is not dead, and it's not clear how anyone can murder a potential person. Even if we view the competitors as actual persons, it's hard to see how ATT's protection of its monopoly status, no matter how zealousy and wickedly defended, would count as murder. Competitors had the option of choosing to go head to head with ATT or producing another service. If these actual persons were killed in combat with ATT, it was because they kept getting up after the knockout punch. They could have thrown in the towel. We could blame ATT for the deaths, but I'm not convinced that we would call the deaths murder. Anyway, I'm not convinced that many people cared about ATT's competitors. They were incensed by ATT's treatment of its customers, and no one would want to argue that ATT was killing customers. If this is right, we can't explain our intuitions about ATT as repugnance at its murder of competitors.

The second option for French is to urge that we reject our intuitions as a source of moral insight. I'm inclined to sympathize with this response. I do think that the appeal to intuition is suspect. After all, where do these intuitions come from? Unless we accept some account of intuition as an infallible source of moral knowledge, we must take an intuition with a grain of salt. If the intuition fits in with a theoretical account which we find persuasive, then we can save the intuition. If not, then so much the worse for our intuitions. If we accept this answer, then we need to answer the question of whether ATT is a person whose dismemberment ought to bother us by a dispassionate assessment of French's analysis of the corporation as a moral person. Since I've made this argument in another paper, I won't repeat it here.

The third option for French is to agree that dismemberment is the right description, but that dismemberment need not be morally repugnant. The reason why we consider dismemberment morally repugnant is because it would cause severe pain and it would interfere with proper functioning. If we were to find a human person who felt no pain and who could function in a reasonable way without the use of all four limbs, we would not find dismemberment so awful. ATT is just such a person. It does not suffer physical pain at being dismembered, and its functioning may even improve after the dismemberment. It seems to me that we would still be appalled by the dismemberment of a human, even if such dismemberment was not felt and caused no significant impairment of function. I suspect that this is so because we take it that our limbs are not property, but part of us, and that we wouldn't be the same

persons without them. I think that this is the right thing to say about corporations too, but we still don't find the dismemberment of a corporation necessarily morally repugnant. One explanation for the difference in intuition is that corporations are not moral persons in the same sense as human persons.

If we view Bendix and Martin Marieta as persons with the same rights as human persons, we should be appalled at the takeover fight because it is either an attempt to kidnap a person into slavery, or an attempted murder. If Martin Marieta planned to sell off all of Bendix's assets after the takeover, then this would look like an attempted murder. Bendix would cease to exist if all its assets were sold. If Martin Marieta planned to keep Bendix as a subsidiary, then it would look like slavery. Bendix would be working for the enrichment of Martin Marieta. Both of those descriptions are fanciful, and they are fanciful precisely because we don't view these, or any, corporations as persons with rights against bodily harm, or against involuntary servitude. I think that we can object to this takeover attempt because of its harmful effects on the shareholders, employees and customers. In addition, there is legitimate concern about the effect on the economy of such unproductive ways of creating assets. We can make the same point about any takeover attempt. If we find it objectionable, it is in virtue of the consequences of such takeovers, and, to a lesser extent, in virtue of the character of the respective firms.

French could take some comfort in the Martin Marieta — Bendix case. Our intuitions would correspond to the intuitions which his analysis would support. On this view, hostile takeovers are either murders or enslavements of persons. I am not convinced, though, that we ought to accept this result. Suppose that the Morally Upright Corporation takes over the Morally Bankrupt Corporation with a hostile bid. If the Morally Bankrupt Corporation is discriminating against employees, cheating customers and ignoring the safety of the workers, and the Morally Upright Corporation maintained a willingness to end these practices, we would probably applaud the takeover. We wouldn't view it as a murder even if Morally Upright swallowed up Morally

Bankrupt, nor would we see it as slavery if Morally Upright forced Morally Bankrupt into line. I think that the right thing to say about hostile takeovers is that where the characters of each firm are equivalent from a moral point of view, we have moral grounds for objecting only if the takeover would have a negative impact overall. By character, I mean the morally relevant properties that are exemplified by a firm. These properties can be either virtues or vices. A company can exemplify avarice, whether or not it makes sense to say that the company can actually be avaricious. I think that it does make sense to make the latter claim; I am convinced by French that a company can be said to exhibit behavior properly described in moral terms. Here, I need only defend the weaker claim, *viz.* that firms can exemplify moral properties. On my view we would have to settle the issue of whether a hostile takeover was morally permissible on a case by case basis, unless we had reason to think that such takeovers were generally likely to create negative utility. I am beginning to think that such evidence is forthcoming. The poison pill strategies, the golden parachutes, and the emphasis on the short term bottom line which are going on in virtually every firm which considers itself a possible takeover victim attest to the negative utility of allowing hostile takeovers. On French's view, we would have a *prima facie* reason to see any hostile takeover as morally repugnant.

The Disney case arouses our sympathies because the traditional Disney concern with high quality, innovative animation was being lost in the new Disney Studios. Animators who shared this concern broke away to create a new studio dedicated to this goal. How would we describe this case if we viewed Disney as a person in the same way as you and I? Divorce is the metaphor which comes to mind, but divorce requires at least two parties to begin with. A person cannot divorce herself. I suppose we could view this as a possession case. Disney is taken over by evil forces bent on destroying cartoons, but the real Disney triumphs and escapes. This implies that the animators are the real Disney, and the official Disney is the interloper. Though this captures my feeling about this case, it won't help us because it is not a description that most of us would be willing to apply to human persons. It commits us to an inter-

esting claim about human persons, *viz.* that they can be possessed and exorcise themselves. Another option is that Disney divided into two persons. This is not a dramatic feat for corporations, but it's currently practically, though not theoretically, impossible for human persons.

Even if we could make the claim that one person could be possessed or divided in two, it's not clear what our moral intuitions about these possibilities would be. I suspect that we would applaud the exorcism, but regret the fact that the real person had to leave too much of her body behind. We would probably object to dividing a person in two and creating two persons even if we could do this without harming the original person, but my intuitions about this possibility are not at all clear. If I have correctly described this case, then, on the French analysis, we should have the same unclear intuitions about Disney Studios.

There are three rejoinders to this analysis of the Disney case. First, one might argue that I have not described the case accurately. I'm not quite sure how to respond to this objection because I cannot imagine another possible description. This might be a failure of imagination on my part, and I am willing to be persuaded if someone comes up with a better description. The second possibility is that the appeal to intuition is illegitimate. We simply haven't gotten used to thinking of corporations as moral persons, and, if and when we do, we will begin to have different intuitions about this and similar cases. This would be a telling objection if there weren't theoretical objections to the view of the corporation as a moral person. I won't rehearse these arguments here. The last option is to suggest that not all corporate acts will have a description which could apply to human persons, and this may be one of those cases. If this is right, then we can't test our moral intuitions about corresponding acts involving human persons. There are things that a corporation can do that a human person cannot do, and perhaps dividing into two is one of them. If there is no human parallel, then there can be no appeal to intuition. I agree that corporations and human persons differ widely, and I do not suppose that the French analysis is committed to anything more than the claim that they are similar in respect to moral personhood. Still, it seems to me that there are actions which are at least theoretically possible for both corporations and human persons, and that the Disney case involves such an action.

It appears then that our intuitions about all of these cases do not correspond to the intuitions we ought to have if we shared French's belief that corporations have the same moral rights as human persons. If we shared his view, we would be aghast at what happened to ATT, unhappy at what happened at Disney Studios, and enraged at the Bendix — Martin Marieta slugfest. In fact, these are not the intuitions shared by all who watched these events. Still, we do sometimes care about the corporation itself, not just because what happens to the corporation affects the economy and the lives of its employees, customers, and shareholders. I think that we can explain this concern as a concern that certain values be protected or rejected. I am borrowing this analysis from Mark Sagoff's defense of wilderness preservation. Sagoff says of obligation to protect natural environments:

> We have an obligation to protect natural environments insofar as we respect the qualities they express. We have seen that these qualities do actually belong to some environments, which are their paradigms; and the discovery or identification of these qualities is effected in our language and by our arts. Preserving an environment may be compared to maintaining an institution, for symbols are to values as institutions are to our legal and political life. The obligation to preserve nature, then, is an obligation to our cultural tradition, to the values which we have cherished and in terms of which nature and this nation are still to be described.[5]

In the case of Disney Studios, we value the innocence and simplicity of Bambi, and the concern for animals and nature expressed by a whole tribe of talking animals. Many of us cried along with the boy who had to kill his rabid dog, Ole Yeller, and none of us emerged from a screening of *Bambi* without shedding a tear. We also value the artistry and the imagination which made *Fantasia* possible. This is not to say that all Disney creations exemplified such important values, but that Disney was unique as a corporation for expressing these values. Our desire to see this company continue in this tradition is a desire to see these values reflected and respected. We rejoiced at the end of Ma Bell because we rejected the capricious, arrogant posturing of this corporation. In this case, we rejected arrogance and capriciousness. In both cases, we can explain why our intuitions concerned the corporations themselves.

If French were right, and if there were a general recognition that corporations were persons entitled to the same rights as human persons, then our intuitions about ATT and Disney would be very different. One might argue that French is right, and that our ordinary intuitions about corporations are suspect. I have argued elsewhere[6] that there are theoretical reasons for rejecting the claim that corporations share the same moral right as human persons, but I want to suggest here that my analysis of our concern for corporations themselves is less ambitious and more consistent with our common evaluations of corporations.

ENDNOTES

1. Peter French, "The Corporation as a Moral Person," *The American Philosophical Quarterly*, Vol. 16, No. 3 (July 1979). (See this text p. 85 ff.)

2. Professor Amnon Goldworth describes the Coward case, a famous case in Medical Ethics, in this fashion.

3. French.

4. See my "Corporate Responsibility and Corporate Personhood," *Journal of Business Ethics* 3(1), 1984, pp. 77–84.

5. Mark Sagoff, "On Preserving the Natural Environment," in Richard A. Wasserstrom, ed. *Today's Moral Problems*, pp. 613–622.

6. I argue for this in "Corporate Responsibility. . . ." There I argue that corporations lack the features necessary for being moral rightholders. If I were writing this paper now, I would argue that rights are founded on certain properties, and that absence of the relevant property made the rights claim invalid.

9

Criminal Prosecution of Corporate Wrongdoing

HARRY J. GLASBEEK

. . . What has to be done is to urge the use of criminal law where there is little question that the conduct of the corporation and its agents was akin to that which we normally agree is immoral, that is, committed with an intent to harm personal integrity or property rights or, at least, with careless disregard and contempt for the physical integrity or property rights of others. Such situations are not hard to find. Consider these examples: harm in the workplace because of knowing non-adherence to established safety standards; deceptive advertising causing prejudicial investments; non-compliance with existing pollution control orders; conscious entry into resale price maintenance agreements or deliberate predatory pricing techniques. All of these are, in conventional moral terms, not to be differentiated from behaviour that consensus theories have no difficulty in calling criminal, such as physical assault, obtaining by false pretences, public nuisance or mischief, fraud and theft. The second step, then, is to make it difficult to mount an argument that, in these cases, criminal prosecution would serve no purpose. What follows is a series of proposals that may help to attain this goal.

1. One of the major arguments against punishing the corporation as such is that fines are usually inadequate to achieve standard criminal law objectives and, if sought to be made, they will break the corporation, negating the purpose of the exercise. I agree that it is not very productive to fine the corporation as such, but . . . not for these so-called pragmatic reasons. A better argument is that the corporation does not exist for its own sake and that it should not be punished unless this makes available the means to get at those who profit directly from its existence — the flesh and blood accumulators and controllers of capital. After all, if the corporation is punished, it does not necessarily follow that those who profited from its wrongful behaviour will be adequately punished or will not err in the future, perhaps even in a new corporate guise. In some situations, there will be this trickle-down effect, but it cannot be counted on. The logic of this argument requires the imposition of punish-

From H.J. Glasbeek, "Why Corporate Deviance is Not Treated as a Crime — The Need to Make 'Profits' a Dirty Word," *Osgoode Hall Law Journal* Vol. 22, No. 3 (Fall 1984) Copyright © 1984. H.J. Glasbeek. Reprinted by permission.

ment which overcomes this practical problem of applying ordinary sanctions. I offer the following.

A corporation should only be convicted and punished if some of its members are also convicted and punished as individuals. This would ensure both that the trickle-down effect could operate by affecting corporate capital (and thus the profits of voting members and officers of the corporation) and by subjugating obviously responsible people directly to the rigours of criminal law. Inasmuch as the latter occurs, Braithwaite and Geis have shown that the educational effect of such punishment is likely to be greater than it is in the case of street criminals. The executive suite criminals have conventional bonds of great importance, prestige to protect and are unlikely to learn bad habits from their peers when languishing in gaol.[1]

It will have been noted that the suggestion is that there should be no "either/or" premise. It is crucial that the corporation should not be prosecuted and convicted if individuals are not. One reason for this has already been given: the mythology of the corporation being an individual in its own right should be attacked.[2] More importantly, as has been pointed out above, it is precisely the combination of relatively low fines and the ineffectuality of the hoped-for trickle-down phenomenon which makes it impractical to use criminal sanctions against corporations. It is routine for corporations to plead guilty in return for clemency for individuals who may have participated in the culpable conduct as corporate members. The recent *Amway Corporation* case illustrates this point neatly. A fine of $25,000,000[3] was imposed when the corporation pleaded guilty to having practised a conscious fraud on Canadian customs laws. The two main directors of the corporation were, as a result, not prosecuted. The court, in accepting the plea, left no doubt that it attributed criminal blame to the directors:

> The two men involved, Mr. Humphrey has given, as I would expect, his usual very excellent presentation in mitigation, that these are men who are very responsible citizens in the United States. Well they weren't very responsible corporate directors in Canada. . . .

I have some difficulty in accepting that these sophisticated frauds are the responsibility of Mr. Discher or the lawyer who was advising them. The directing minds of these two corporations involved many others in their web of deception: the shell companies, the dummy invoices, the false price lists and the fraudulent oral and written representations and the cross-checking operations, were all part of a *modus operandi* by which the scheme functioned and could only have led to the corruption of employees who were necessarily implicated in furthering the operation of these frauds.[4]

To further emphasize how important it is not to let the corporate form obscure the fact that there are real people who act wrongfully and benefit from errant behaviour, note that the two directors concerned were principal owners of the corporation and had built vast fortunes. *Fortune* listed them amongst the four richest Americans, being worth between $300 and $500 million each. So much for the trickle-down effect. While this is a dramatic example, the point it permits to be made is of general application.

2. In some situations, however, corporate wrongdoing may not be attributable to what the law characterizes as a guiding mind. Setting aside, for the sake of argument, that that definition is elastic and can be made to fit many more circumstances than it presently does without offending legal principle, it may still be possible to identify some individuals who acted criminally. Every breach of a legal proscription requires the doing of an act by one or more persons. There is no reason that they should not be prosecuted as individuals. This may have the desired effect of deterring them and others. Inasmuch as these miscreants are in inferior positions in the corporate hierarchy, this may be unfortunate. If an argument is raised which suggests this is unfair because the accused may have been coerced into the commission of wrongs, with no hope of personal gain (other than security and advancement in the corporation!), the individual's position is not morally different from that of many people convicted as property offenders. Further, if this is a serious objection, it ought to inspire investigative forces to look thoroughly for decision-makers with discretion, and to lay their prosecutions accordingly. Moreover, if the tenets of deterrence attributed to criminal law make the sense which conventional wisdom assumes, when it becomes known that those who actually commit wrongful acts will be punished, the result will be a lower level of corporate agents having a real stake in setting up lines of communication within the corporation to identify the responsibility for decision-making.[5]

The counter-argument is that this will create corporate scapegoats and that middle management and subordinate personnel will be victimized, while senior officers will be blithely permitted to go on as before, enlarging the coffers of the corporation with ill-gotten gains. This is not a contention which should defeat the proposal. It signifies merely that, in some cases, an additional mechanism must be found to bring the right people to account. Certainly, there are many large corporations which have senior executive officers who can be identified as the actual wrongdoers, as in the *Amway* case.[6] In any event, the corporate world is made up not only of giants. There is an enormous number of middlesized and truly small corporations in which the senior officers and active personnel are very closely connected — indeed, they are often the same persons. The suggested approach should be fully effective in these situations.

3. Even in those circumstances where the senior officers of the corporation are truly removed from the departments and the many sub-departments which commit wrongful acts while pursuing relatively narrow and immediate goals, there is a plausible line of reasoning which would permit the prosecution and conviction of such senior officers for wrongful conduct. This arises from the recent revelations of the earnings of some chief executive officers in those very kinds of corporations. The general public has been agog at the numbers, ranging as they do from salaries of one half to thirteen million dollars per year.[7] The business community takes a more matter-of-fact approach: the dollar amounts by themselves mean little. Rather, the issue is whether or not the rate of increase or decrease bears any relation to the economic per-

formance, particularly the market-share performance, of the corporation.[8] Now, if chief executive officers are permitted to claim that they contribute to the overall performance of the corporation because they control its operations, there is no obvious reason why they should not be held responsible for its daily operations.

I concede that contributing through policy development is not the same as supervising ongoing function and, therefore, the step in the argument may be too big to take, but this is an empirical question. For instance, if a large portion of profits is derived from wrongful conduct, or if the corporation is a frequent violator of legal standards,[9] why should a chief executive officer who is credited (with money as well as prestige) for being prescient, be presumed unaware of this propensity of the organization for deviance? Thus, while the argument is not automatically applicable, there are no impenetrable legal or moral obstacles to its use. Where it is so used, it should most ably meet the needs of standard criminal law precepts, as well as attract attention to the fact that the corporation is a device which is used by individuals for their advantage, *not* the reverse.

4. More directly, where a corporation is truly large, differentiated in functions and segmented in its division of labour, there may be sense in the argument that it is inconceivable for senior officers to be deemed to have had the necessary criminal intent and that it would be pointless to punish mere replaceable cogs in the ever-spinning corporate wheel. However, there is another way to get at major, individual actors. Important shareholders could be, and should be, held personally responsible for corporate wrongdoing. This suggestion directly confronts the proposition that, because some shareholders may be innocent, none should be prosecuted. Shareholders benefit from unredressed corporate wrongdoing, whether or not they took an active part, whether or not they were conscious of the illicit behaviour. But this is not the basis of the proposition. A narrower group of shareholders may be isolated: those who have a controlling interest in the affairs of the corporation.

The idea that controlling shareholders should be identified does not present legal or conceptual problems. It is done every day when protection is sought for the investor class. Thus, the purpose of the *Securities Acts* is to ensure that shareholders with more clout than others will not use their holdings and any associated knowledge to their own advantage and to the detriment of the corporation and other shareholders. Insider trading is regulated by subjecting persons with a prescribed amount of equity to certain rules. Similarly, the buying and selling of shares by shareholders is of no particular interest until a major shareholder does it, and then the distribution of shares is subjected to controls, since a danger to be contained may arise when the person making the trade owns a certain amount of the corporation's equity. Shareholders' interests are to be protected when takeovers and mergers occur; the protective measures come into action when it becomes clear that a bidder will own a proportion of shares which will give that bidder control. Similarly, as for the purpose of securities' regulation it is necessary to discern corporate affiliations and relationships (such as parent/subsidiary, beneficial ownership) there is recourse to the notion of equity ownership. For example, when X owns Y% of another corporation, they shall be considered affiliates.[10]

The lesson is clear — in all these situations it is assumed that, where one shareholder has a certain amount of equity ownership (never all, and not necessarily half) that shareholder has sufficient power to control the affairs of the corporation and is subjected to certain restrictions on that control. If that assumption can be made in the sphere of regulation, why can it not be made in relation to corporate criminality? One argument might be that to have potential control is not the same as exercising that control, but this is not overly persuasive. Securities (and foreign investment) regulations assume that potential control is likely to be exercised. Controlling shareholders are given an opportunity to explain their conduct to the regulators. If it is considered benign, it will be permitted.[11] In the same way, the fact of control ought to permit the argument that shareholders who can have

managers and policies changed (hence the need to regulate their power) are to be held accountable for the corporation's wrongdoing unless they can show that they were uninformed about, and gave no approval to, the wrongful actors.

This raises a potential counter-argument. It is that shareholding is often a passive matter, something which gives the owner the right not to take an active interest.[12] This begs the question. The reason the controlling shareholders feel comfortable about leaving such issues to the managers is precisely because, fines being light, they can be confident that managerial wrongdoing is unlikely to impinge on them severely. As well, if any individuals are prosecuted, it will be employees rather than owners. Compare this argument about the assumed lassitude and apathy of major shareholders in respect of corporate affairs with the assumption of controlling shareholders' keenness to be informed when "their" corporation is being bid for, or its management seeks to buy into a totally different market. Would securities regulators, potential investors, newspaper reporters, politicians, *et al.* doubt that the major shareholders will be put on full alert? Indeed, as the argument is the essentially legal one which prides itself on understanding and propagating the distinction between ownership and management, will it not be a priority for those controlling shareholders' and the corporation's lawyers to investigate and advise their clients about such impending action? Thus, the assumption that controlling equity ownership is a passive thing, unless proved otherwise, turns the issue on its head. Ownership is always active in that it seeks to protect itself and to further its profitability. If the starting position is that it makes deliberate decisions about how capital is to be deployed, it is logical that it should be held responsible for any consequences. This is the argument which is used to protect the investor classes by means of the *Securities Act*, and it is an argument which thus can be used to protect the public at large, *if* this is a serious social objective.

Even if some shareholders have controlling power, it may be argued, they cannot be expected to exercise it to supervise the daily operations of the corporation. This contention is one which is often used to protect chief executive officers and (through them) the corporation from criminalization. In part, the answer must be as before: it is an empirical question. While often (perhaps, even, very often) the deviant conduct is the result of aberrant, peripheral actors, sometimes it is not. If, as is often true, the wrongdoing is alleged and publicized for a long time before it is finally legally proved, then the claim to ignorance, or the continued willingness to believe in the uprightness of management, is far from convincing. In part, the answer is that it would serve a valid purpose to prosecute and convict controlling shareholders, even for so-called peripheral behaviour. The reason that they do not involve themselves in routine operations of the corporations is because they are permitted to be exactly that: routine. Profit-making activity goes on and there is no concern with the actual processes. Attention is paid, and regulations imposed where necessary, when the business at hand is not routine, when it is likely to affect the controlling owners of the corporation or members of their class. The whole object of criminalizing corporate wrongdoing is to bring home the point that profit making cannot be insulated from restrictions imposed to protect the public from violations of morally important rights, in particular the right to physical integrity of self and property. The means of making profit must therefore be weighed directly against this goal. Making controlling shareholders responsible for what presently are seen as local, unauthorized peccadilloes would emphasize the fact that, if shareholders are willing to take the profit made on their investment, they are accountable for the method used in its generation. . . .

Finally, it is conceded that there may well be a great number of situations in these large, diffuse corporate organizations in which there are no controlling shareholders, at least to the extent that it would make sense to hold them responsible. Again, this is an empirical issue. What is certain is that the conventional wisdom that the equity in major corporations is widely-held and that, therefore, ownership and management are quite separate (which would make the argument in this section of theoretical interest only) is not borne out in Canada by the available data. Of the four hundred largest Canadian companies outside the financial sector, the equity of only twenty-two public corporations is widely-held. Another seventeen were held by other corporations and twenty-nine by the Government. The remaining 332 were controlled by one major shareholder.[14]

There are no serious legal or conceptual barriers to bring home corporate wrongdoing to appropriate actors. Most of the practical barriers are of the objectors' own making. In particular, isolation of the corporation as *the* actor, perception of the corporation as just another organization, the assumption that corporate structure is often too complex and denies discretion to individuals, are all unnecessary and misplaced assumptions. Further, there are no good reasons why individuals, who benefit from corporate wrongdoing (whether in terms of profit or sharing in the spoils by career advancement), should not be treated as responsible for the consequences of corporate wrongdoing. The adjustment required to do so does not necessitate radical departures from existing principles. They are just that: adjustments. A willingness to make them would indicate that the legal system treats all crime, no matter who commits it, equally.

ENDNOTES

1. Braithwaite and Geis, "On Theory and Action for Corporate Crime Control," (1982), 28 *Crime & Delinquency* 292.

2. In addition to the earlier argument, note that treating the corporation as an individual is one of the mechanisms by which the legal system removes class arguments from the adjudicative system. The wealth of the aggregation which is the corporation is ignored in its contests with individual human beings. More important is the fact that, by reifying the corporation, it is given human rights such as freedom of speech. It permits political participation by economic organizations which have access to much greater funds than do individual political actors; it also enhances anti-democratic practices because the individual corporation represents the views of the minority of its shareholders, as "democracy" in corporations is still of the one dollar — one vote variety.

3. *R.* v. *Amway Corporation and Amway of Canada Ltd.* (unreported, Nov. 10, 1983, Ont. S.C.). The accused had been charged with benefiting to the tune of $28 million from their fraud. The fine does not stand alone — the Canadian government will be able to levy the actual duty which should have been paid and could seek to have an administrative fine levied as well. Nonetheless, despite its absolute size, the fine was relatively light. *Macleans*, Nov. 21, 1983 at 44-45, reported Amway as being a $1.2 billion firm; *Time*, Nov. 29, 1982, at 54-55, reported that Amway's annual sales were $1.5 billion. Amway's counsel, on learning the amount of the fine, responded: "Thank you, my lord, I am in a position to pay that to-day." (Judgment transcript at 12.)

4. *Ibid.* at page 11 of judgement transcript.

5. This is the trickle-up theory — one way to tackle the need to restructure the corporation so that decision makers become visible.

6. See *R.* v. *McNamara et al.* (No. 1) (1981), 56 C.C.C. (2d) 516 (Ont. C.A.)

7. See *Business Week*, May 7, 1984; *Toronto Star*, June 3, 1984, at B1; *New York Times*, May 2, 1984 at P1.

8. *Business Week, ibid.*

9. In his work, Sutherland relied a great deal on corporate recidivism to prove his case; see Sutherland & Cressy, *Criminology* (9th ed., 1974) at 41. Corporations violated statutes of varying kinds, which means that senior executives did not necessarily know that the corporation as a whole was criminogenic. Yet there might be cases, especially if the penalties were significant, where this might come to their attention. Further, in some cases, the conviction for violations will demonstrate a long history of wrongful behaviour. This makes it less plausible that senior executives could claim that the matter was not, and should not have been, the focus of their attention. In addition, before charges are laid, there has frequently been longstanding public agitation about alleged corporate behaviour and its injury-causing nature, e.g. acid rain as a result of Inco's conduct; asbestosis as a result of Johns-Manville's mode of production. In such situations, officers who want to be praised for their managerial oversight and insight should not feel aggrieved if they are blamed for not taking an interest in these issues; see the moving appeal by Judge Miles W. Lord to corporate executives in just such a situation, reprinted *Harper's*, June, 1984, at 13.

10. E.g. *The Securities Act*, R.S.O. 1980, c. 466, ss. 1(1)(17)(iii), 1(1)(11)(iii), 88(1)(b), 1(2), 1(3), 1(4), 1(5), 1(6). For similar provisions defining controlling interests, other than by more than 50% equity ownership, see *Foreign Investment Review Act*, R.S.C. 1980, c. 46, *e.g.* s. 3(2).

11. *E.g.* s. 118, The Securities Act.

12. This accords with notions inherent in the absoluteness of private property ownership.

13. *Financial Post 1980: Annual Reports* as offered in evidence by Pierre Lortie, President of the Montreal Stock Exchange, before the Standing Senate Committee on Legal Constitutional Affairs, Nov. 30, 1982, Hearings on Bill S-31, *An Act to Limit Shareholding in Certain Corporations*. Similar figures are to be found in Toronto, Montreal and Vancouver Stock Exchanges and the Investment Dealers' Association, *The Regulation of Take-over Bids in Canada — Report of the Securities Industry Committee on Take-Over Bids,* (1983). To be sure, often the controlling shareholder is another corporation which, if it is American, may be diffusely held, but it is clear that, in Canada, to begin with the Berle & Means argument is to begin from a totally wrong perspective.

SUGGESTED FURTHER READINGS

CLEMEMT, WALLACE. *The Canadian Corporation Elite: An Analysis of Corporate Power.* Toronto: McClelland and Stewart, 1975.

DONALDSON, THOMAS. *Corporations and Morality.* Englewood Cliffs, N.J.: Prentice-Hall Inc., 1982.

FRENCH, PETER. "Institutional and Moral Obligations". *Journal of Philosophy* Vol. 74 (1977).

—————————. "The Principle of Responsive Adjustment in Corporate Moral Responsibility: The Crash on Mount Erebus". *Journal of Business Ethics* 3 (1984).

LAW REFORM COMMISSION OF CANADA. Working Paper 16, *Criminal Responsibility for Group Action* (1976).

PORTER, JOHN. *The Vertical Mosaic.* Toronto: The University of Toronto Press, 1965.

ROSS, MURRAY. *Canadian Corporate Directors on the Firing Line.* Toronto: McGraw-Hill Ryerson Ltd., 1980.

SMYTH, J.E. "The Social Implications of Incorporation" in J.S. Ziegel (ed.). *Canadian Law.* Toronto: Butterworths, 1967.

10

Rex v. *Fane Robinson Ltd.*

FORD J.A. (for the Court): This is an appeal by the Crown from the dismissal by Tweedie J. of two charges preferred against Fane Robinson Ltd., a corporation, of (1) conspiracy to defraud and (2) obtaining money by false pretences, which that learned Judge dismissed on the ground that, *mens rea* being an essential element of both offences, a corporation cannot be guilty of either. In the course of his reasons Mr. Justice Tweedie says that "even if the directors or the shareholders themselves had passed any resolution authorizing such act, in my opinion, that could be of no effect as there is no power in a corporation to commit criminal acts in which *mens rea* is a material element, even with the authorization of the shareholders or the directors."

The question is, in my opinion, one which in Canada may be treated as not being settled by any binding authority.

After reading and considering, with many others, the cases cited on the argument I have, not without considerable hesitation, formed the opinion that the gradual process of placing those artificial entities known as corporations in the same position as a natural person as regards amenability to the criminal law has, by reason of the provisions of the *Criminal Code*, reached that stage where it can be said that, if the act complained of can be treated as that of the company, the corporation is criminally responsible for all such acts as it is capable of committing and for which the prescribed punishment is one which it can be made to endure . . .

. . . As stated by Viscount Haldane, L.C., in *Lennard's Carrying Co.* v. *Asiatic Petroleum Co.*, [1915] A.C. 705 at p. 713: "A corporation is an abstraction. It has no mind of its own any more than it has a body of its own; its active and directing will must consequently be sought in the person of somebody who for some purposes may be called an agent, but who is really the directing mind and will of the corporation . . . his action must, unless a corporation is not to be liable at all, have been an action which was the action of the company. . . ."

. . . As stated by Lord Blackburn in *Pharmaceutical Soc.* v. *London & Provincial Supply Ass'n* (1880), 5 App. Cas. 857 at p. 869: "A corporation cannot in

Reported in (1941) 76 C.C.C. 196. Alberta Court of Appeal.

one sense commit a crime — a corporation cannot be imprisoned, if imprisonment be the sentence for the crime; a corporation cannot be hanged or put to death if that be the punishment for the crime; and so, in those senses a corporation cannot commit a crime. But a corporation may be fined, and a corporation may pay damages."

. . . I find it difficult to see why a corporation which can enter into binding agreements with individuals and other corporations cannot be said to entertain *mens rea* when it enters into an agreement which is the gist of conspiracy, and if by its corporate act it can make a false pretence involving it in liability to pay damages for deceit why it cannot be said to have the capacity to make a representation involving criminal responsibility.

It is perhaps unnecessary to add that a corporation like any other "person" is entitled to all the safeguards which the law provides before anyone can be found guilty including, of course, that cardinal rule that guilt must be proved beyond a reasonable doubt.

. . . The facts are that Fane Robinson Ltd. was incorporated in 1935 and has since carried on the business of garaging and repairing automobiles. It took over shortly after its incorporation two businesses one of which was that previously carried on by George Robinson who with Emile Fielhaber were its incorporators and provisional directors. At all material times George Robinson, Emile Fielhaber and Adolph Fielhaber were the directors of the company, George Robinson being its President and Emile Fielhaber its Secretary-Treasurer. Adolph Fielhaber took no active part in the operation of the company. There was only one other shareholder. Since its incorporation the company has held only three meetings of directors, the first that of the provisional directors, held July 13, 1935, the second being the First Meeting of Directors held on the same day and the third on April 2, 1940. Only one meeting of shareholders has been held, being that held on the same day as, and between, the meeting of the provisional directors and the first meeting of directors.

At the first meeting of directors George Robinson was appointed manager of the company's plant and was instructed to take possession as soon as possible and commence operations. He was at all material times the "service manager in charge of repairs" to automobiles and Emile Fielhaber the "bookkeeper in charge of accounts."

In 1937 on the instructions of an adjuster for the Saskatchewan Mutual Fire Ins. Co., a motor truck, which had been damaged in a collision and which that company had insured against collision damage, was taken to the garage of the respondent company and was there repaired on the account of the adjusters. On the books of the respondent company the actual account for labour and material and profit was charged as $339.80.

It was orally agreed by George Robinson, Emile Fielhaber and the representative of the firm of adjusters having charge of the adjustment of the loss that the account of the respondent company for repairs should be increased fictitiously to the sum of $404.80 and the adjuster should represent to the Insurance Company that the sum was the cost of the repairs of the truck and that Fane Robinson Ltd. should pay him the sum of $30.

In pursuance of the oral agreement as above, Fane Robinson Ltd., the respondent, rendered to the firm of adjusters an account for the repairs at the agreed amount of $404.80 and the individual in charge of the adjustment represented in writing to the Insurance Company that that sum was the cost of the repairs by Fane Robinson Ltd. and that the net cost of repairs for which the Insurance Company was liable to the assured was $379.80 after deducting $25 under the terms of the insurance policy.

The Insurance Company in reliance on the report of its firm of adjusters, which was signed by the individual in charge of the adjustment, and in reliance on the *bona fides* of the account of $404.80 furnished by Fane Robinson Ltd., paid by cheque to Fane Robinson Ltd., the sum of $379.80 and in pursuance of their oral agreement, out of the proceeds of the cheque for $379.80, George Robinson paid to the individual adjuster $10 and Emile Fielhaber paid him $20. It would appear that the respondent company benefited to the extent of $10 by the fictitious increase in its account for repairs. The first count in the charge is that between October 12th and December 31st Fane Robinson Ltd., did conspire with R. Noel Saunders, who is the individual adjuster above mentioned, and divers other persons unknown, by deceit and falsehood to defraud the Insurance Company by falsely and fraudulently representing that the costs of the repair of an automobile owned by one G.F.W. Otto was $404.80 instead of $339.80 the actual cost of repairs; contrary to the provisions of the *Criminal Code* of Canada and amendments thereto.

The second count is that between the same dates the respondent did by false pretences and with intent to defraud, procure the sum of approximately $40 from the Insurance Company, contrary to the provisions of the *Criminal Code* of Canada and amendments thereto.

The respondent appeared by attorney, pleaded not guilty to both charges and elected for trial by a Judge without the assistance of a jury.

. . . In my opinion George Robinson and Emile Fielhaber were the acting and directing will of Fane Robinson Ltd. generally and in particular in respect of the subject-matter of the offences with which it is charged, that their culpable intention (*mens rea*) and their illegal act (*actus reus*) were the intention and the act of the company and that conspiracy to defraud and obtaining money by false pretenses are offences which a corporation is capable of committing.

I would allow the appeal and direct a conviction to be entered against Fane Robinson Ltd. on both counts and sentence it to a fine of $150 on each.

LUNNEY J.A., dissenting, agreed with the trial judge that: "A corporation acts through its directors. There is no evidence whatever disclosed in the minutes of the meetings of the directors or the shareholders which are in evidence, that any authority by resolution was ever given to the directors acting in their official capacity to enter into the conspiracy alleged in the first count, or to procure by false pretences the money alleged in the second count. . . . *Mens rea* being an essential element of the charge as preferred and there being no expressed statutory provision making the corporation criminally responsible for the acts of its officers or servants in a case in which *mens rea* must be established, both charges against the accused will be dismissed."

Appeal allowed.

11

Regina v. Andrew Weatherfoil Ltd.

Eveleigh J. (for the Court): On March 23, 1971, at the Central Criminal Court, in a trial which lasted over six weeks, Andrews Weatherfoil Ltd., Sidney Frederick Charles Sporle and Peter George Day were charged with bribery and corruption under the Public Bodies Corrupt Practices Act 1889, s. 1, in relation to council building contracts of the Battersea Metropolitan Borough Council and the London Borough of Wandsworth Council when Sporle was member and chairman of the housing committee or member of the council. [Only the appeal by Andrews Weatherfoil Ltd. is set out below.]

Andrews Weatherfoil were given leave to appeal against conviction on two grounds of their notice of appeal.

The prosecution's case was that Sporle used his position on the council to obtain sums of money in return for support in obtaining building contracts from the council. The evidence showed, it was said, a systematic course of conduct to show favour where he had financial expectations and that when he acted in purported discharge of his duties to the council he failed to disclose his interest. In this way

it was sought to show that he acted intending to benefit his employers or their nominees without regard to the interest of the council. Once his support for candidates for contracts from the council was shown to be given with improper intentions or motives (it being too much of a coincidence that so often those he supported turned out to be his employers), there was material relevant to the question of the existence of an antecedent agreement to do so in return for benefits to himself which the evidence showed he received.

In this connection the fervour of his support for the cause of his employers was also relied upon. Thus it was said he was so determined to assist Ellis (Kensington) Ltd. that he even threatened Culpin — independent architect appointed to carry out some of the council's plans — with the possible loss of council work unless Ellis (Kensington) Ltd. were given sub-contracts. So too, in relation to Andrews Weatherfoil Ltd., he made a similar threat to Harding. Both of these gentlemen refused to be coerced.

The grounds upon which Andrews Weatherfoil were given leave to appeal were: (1) Failure properly

Reported in (1971), 56 Cr. App. R. 31. Court of Appeal (Criminal Division), England.

to direct on law as to the criminal responsibility of a limited liability company for the act of a servant. (2) Failure to deal with the correct factors that in law determine the question whether a criminal intention in an employee is also that of the company.

On examination these two grounds overlap, for in the present case the offence was not an absolute statutory offence, but involved criminal conduct and a guilty mind on the part, it was said, of the company's senior employees. The question therefore of the status and authority of the person or persons responsible was of great importance. The prosecution concedes and, in the view of this Court, rightly concedes that the learned judge's direction was not adequate.

There were three people who were alleged by the prosecution to have the status and authority to involve the company itself in criminal liability for corruption in connection with the offer of employment to Sporle as a reward for anticipated favours from him. Those three were Mr. Neuman, the managing director, Mr. Allen, a "technical director," and Mr. Williams, the manager of the or *a* housing division. That these three were concerned in the engagement of Sporle there is no doubt. The actual offer of employment was made by Mr. Neuman in a letter which Allen had some part in drafting. Whether or not it was one, two or all of these three who sought or were party to seeking favours for Andrews Weatherfoil from Sporle as a return for the offer of employment was, as is usually the case, a matter of inference from the evidence. The learned judge directed the jury as follows: "If an act is done by anyone who is in control of a company and who is in authority to perform an important act of that sort, then that act of that person can be the act of the company itself . . . if an act is done by a responsible agent of a company, if in the course of that act that agent commits an offence and he does it in the name of the company, then the company is liable . . . if an agent acts corruptly on behalf of the company, the corruption of the agent is the corruption of the company. That is not an absolute rule; it is a principle which depends on the circumstances of the offence." And again: ". . . if one of these people, Williams or Allen or Neuman or any combination

of them acting as a high executive of Andrews Weatherfoil, indulges in the employment of a person to act corruptly to further the interests of the company of which that man is one of the executive directors, the company is responsible and the company is guilty of a criminal offence."

On counsel drawing the judge's attention to the fact that Williams was not a director, he continued: "There is no magic in being a director. If you are the manager of the housing department or in any high executive position in such a way that you can recommend to your managing director that someone should be employed, as it is said Allen [*sic*] recommended Sporle, in those circumstances the person who recommends it, who is in a high position, if you are satisfied that he did that in the name of the company and it was corrupt, the company can be liable." And finally: "That is a matter for you as to whether or not you are satisfied that that employment by Sporle was done with the approval and knowledge of a high executive of Andrews Weatherfoil acting as an agent of the company for the purpose of his employment to the knowledge of the executive or executives and was corrupt."

It is not every "responsible agent" or "high executive" or "manager of the housing department" or "agent acting on behalf of a company" who can by his actions make the company criminally responsible. It is necessary to establish whether the natural person or persons in question have the status and authority which in law makes their acts in the matter under consideration the acts of the company so that the natural person is to be treated as the company itself. It is often a difficult question to decide whether or not the person concerned is in a sufficiently responsible position to involve the company in liability for the acts in question according to the law as laid down by the authorities. As Lord Reid said in *Tesco Supermarkets Ltd* v. *Nattrass*, [1971] 2 W.L.R. 1166 at p. 1176: "it must be a question of law whether, once the facts have been ascertained, a person in doing a particular thing is to be treated as the company or merely as the company's servant or agent. In that case any liability of the company can only be a statutory or vicarious liability." At p. 1179 Lord Reid added: "I think that the true view is that the judge must direct the jury that if they find certain facts proved, then as a matter of law they must find that the criminal act of the officer, servant or agent including his state of mind, intention, knowledge or belief is the act of the company." It follows that it is necessary for the judge to invite the jury to consider whether or not there are established those facts which the judge decides as a matter of law are necessary to identify the person concerned with the company. This was not done in the present case.

The Court was invited to apply the proviso to section 2 (1) of the Criminal Appeal Act 1968. It is not possible, however, to decide whether or not the jury regarded Mr. Neuman, Mr. Allen or Mr. Williams, or any or what combination of them, as responsible for the criminal act. Mr. Williams' position in the company is not at all clear and the description "housing manager" does not succeed in making it so. To a lesser extent this is true of Mr. Allen. Consequently it is impossible to say that the jury would have arrived at the same verdict if properly directed and it follows that this appeal must succeed.

Appeal allowed.

SUGGESTED FURTHER READINGS

CLEMENT, WALLACE. *The Canadian Corporate Elite: An Analysis of Corporate Power.* Toronto: McClelland and Stewart, 1975.

CORLETT, J. ANGELO. "Corporate Responsibility and Punishment." *Public Affairs Quarterly* **2** (1988).

DONALDSON, THOMAS. *Corporations and Morality.* Englewood Cliffs, NJ: Prentice-Hall, 1982.

FRENCH, PETER. *Corporate and Collective Responsibility.* New York: Columbia University Press, 1984.

_____. "Institutional and Moral Obligations." *Journal of Philosophy* **74** (1977).

LAW REFORM COMMISSION OF CANADA. "Working Paper 16." *Criminal Responsibility for Group Action.* (1976).

MAY, L. *The Morality of Groups: Collective Responsibility, Group-Based Harm, and Corporate Rights.* South Bend, Indiana: Notre Dame Press, 1987.

PORTER, JOHN. *The Vertical Mosaic.* Toronto: University of Toronto Press, 1965.

R. v. *MACNAMARA,* (No. 1) (1981), 56 C.C.C. (2d) 193 (Ont. C.A.).

R. v. N.M. PATERSON AND SONS LTD. (1980), 117 D.L.R. (3d) 517 (S.C.C.).

SMYTH, J.E. "The Social Implications of Incorporation." In J.S. Ziegel (ed.) *Canadian Law.* Toronto: Butterworths, 1967.

PART THREE

Morality
and
The Professions

INTRODUCTION

Let's begin with two observations. First, perhaps a distinction should be made between what it would be proper to do as a moral agent (that is, in one's role as a member of "the moral community") and what it would be proper to do as a professional (that is, in one's role as a professional lawyer, teacher, accountant, and so on). Secondly, the standard of behaviour for professionals is often higher than that for non-professionals. These two features of the professional's working life often pose problems for the professional not often faced, at least to the same degree, by "ordinary" people. The professional might be faced, for instance, with a difficult choice between, on the one hand, seriously jeopardizing her or his career prospects by reporting the questionable accounting practices of a corporate client, and on the other, violating principles of professional integrity by not reporting such practices. Professionals may be required to make sacrifices and shoulder burdens which would not otherwise be expected.

But why are professionals placed in situations where they have to shoulder special burdens? Why have a separate chapter on ethics and the professions? What's different about being a professional? The answers to these questions lie, no doubt, in the social role played by the professional. Professionals have specialized knowledge, knowledge of which the average person is, to a large extent, simply ignorant. In medicine, for example, surgeons daily make decisions which have life

117

or death consequences for other individuals. Specialized knowledge and the skills essential to the successful exercise of that knowledge come with a considerable amount of power. This power enables the professional, more easily than most people, to take advantage of others. These others are, of course, those of us who are dependent upon the professional for the essential service he or she provides and who are therefore vulnerable to potential abuses of power, whether the service provided is medical, legal, educational, technical, or of some other kind, and whether the professional is a doctor, nurse, lawyer, teacher, engineer, systems analyst, computer analyst, marketing specialist, accountant, business manager, priest, or minister. It may even be true for an automobile mechanic or TV repair-person. In each case, the professional's special knowledge and expertise give him or her power and advantage. But with special power and advantage must go special responsibilities and expectations, and higher standards of behaviour.

Professionals are specialists with particular expertise and particular responsibilities, yet they generally do not have expertise as ethicists or moral philosophers. As noted in the general introduction to this text, "Ethical Theory in Business," while most of us agonize over what is right and wrong, few of us are specialists in the critical theories of moral philosophy. Many codes of ethics for professionals operate as what was referred to in "Ethical Theory in Business" as the pre-reflective level of moral response; that is, they embody conventional norms or standards for moral behaviour (e.g. honesty, integrity, promise-keeping, etc.). Such standards or broad guidelines cannot, however, take the place of critical reflection when a complex moral question arises. An appeal to a code of ethics cannot take the place of reasoned justification for a moral position, nor can codes of ethics absolve one from providing relevant grounds for a particular action or practice.

In this chapter, a range of issues related to ethics and professions is presented. As you read these articles, keep in mind the introduction to moral philosophy at the beginning of this book. Are the authors appealing to different ethical theories in the various articles presented? Are some authors making intuitive or common-sense appeals with regard to morality and the professions?

In the first paper, Conrad Brunk describes the limitations of so-called "professional ethics." Brunk argues that we rightly expect professionals to be persons of "extraordinary integrity and altruism," and rightly hold them to a "professional ethic of special virtue."

Despite all this, Brunk detects in our society a concept of professionalism which encourages professionals to abdicate their moral responsibility — or at least to define its limits far too narrowly. He sees a conception of professionalism which encourages a kind of "ethical isolationism" insulating professionals from worries about the broad impact of their activities upon the welfare of persons other than those whom they directly serve. Recall here the argument of Friedman in Part One that the responsibility of business managers is to further and protect the interests of those they serve — the owners. This kind of isolationism, Brunk argues, encourages professionals to view themselves wholly as *instruments* serving the designs and purposes of others. And much as the pickaxe is not morally responsible for the death brought about through its use, the professional, on this view, is not morally responsible for any harm brought about through his being used by others. As Brunk notes, these "others" can range from the corporation with its goals and objectives, to the system of military technology with its potentially catastrophic "needs." The harm can range from the pollution of a river to the annihilation of our human species through chemical or nuclear warfare.

So, far from living up to higher standards of responsibility, professionals are, in Brunk's view, abdicating their responsibility almost entirely. They are becoming mere instruments and role-players oblivious to the morally repugnant ends to which their skills are being put. It is this conception of "professionalism" which must be eliminated. In Brunk's view, it is morally incumbent upon professionals that they expand their moral horizons and "take their social responsibilities seriously." The "narrow blinkers" of professional ethics must be abandoned and replaced with an "ethic of conscientious professionalism" which is always prepared to assess whatever tasks are assigned. If they, the only ones with the requisite skills and expertise, do not assume this responsibility, then we may all fall prey to forces that are anything but benign.

James Gaa and Charles Smith are also concerned, in "Auditors and Deceptive Financial Statements," with the possible abdication of moral responsibility by professionals. The focus of their concern is the public accountant or auditor. As they note, auditors do not prepare the financial statements of their clients (managers) and cannot, therefore, be held *directly* responsible for them. Nevertheless, if management's statements are deceptive, say to Revenue Canada, or to actual or potential shareholders, then the question of the auditor's *indirect* responsibility for the uses to which they might be put arises. Gaa and Smith document a wide variety of ways in which deception can occur in these contexts. The possibilities range from out-and-out lying to the selective application of competing, generally acceptable principles of accountancy. To what extent, they ask, can a professional accountant absolve herself of responsibility for any deception which might be caused? Is she as the "traditional professional ethic" suggests, nothing more than an instrument whose responsibility is merely to fulfill in a narrowly "professional manner" the assignment she has been given? Or must she herself assume partial responsibility for that assignment and in particular the means — deception — employed to assure its acceptance? Their conclusion, based upon an analysis of deception and a wide variety of arguments sometimes offered to excuse or justify deceptive actions, is that responsibility and blame cannot always be avoided. Professional auditors are indeed responsible for managerial deception to the extent that they knew, *or should have known*, about management's deceptive intentions and actions. As professionals, they must be prepared to accept this responsibility.

In "Regulation, Deregulation and Self-Regulation: The Case of Engineers in Ontario," Jack Stevenson, cognizant of the current climate favouring deregulation, argues against the deregulation and self-regulation of engineers. Stevenson analyzes the Staff Study of the Professional Organizations Committee set up by the Ontario government and criticizes it on three grounds: theoretically, empirically, and normatively. Stevenson goes on to address two broader issues: 1. "A failure to consider the proposal's effects on the internal political economy and sociology of the major employers of engineers leads POC Staff to neglect a very important source of third-party protection against externalities;" and 2. "The move to proletarianize a significant occupational group ignores the wider social implications of that move."

Beth Savan takes on a different aspect of professional ethics and provides a descriptive analysis of various "ginger groups," groups of professionals who take on voluntary lobby efforts as professionals concerned about larger ethical questions. Canada has a number of such groups, including scientists and medical doctors concerned about nuclear disarmament and environmental issues. While Savan clearly believes that such activities are praiseworthy, not everyone would agree. Controversy rages over the global activism of Dr. Helen Caldicott, a woman who has mobilized medical doctors internationally against nuclear proliferation. Dr. Henry Morgentaler has been repeatedly attacked for his advocacy of women's reproductive rights and his civil disobedience in performing illegal abortions. Should professionals use their professional authority in advocating and lobbying for beliefs which transcend the boundaries of professional ethics? What are the various approaches professionals use to justify their moral stances?

This section concludes with what is essentially a detailed case study. While the case is American, the issues raised are universal. The article details the ethical dimensions of the Challenger disaster and relates the experience of senior scientist Roger Boisjoly and other colleagues who repeatedly tried to convince authorities of the fatal flaw in the design of the Challenger's O-rings. Both before and after the disaster, Boisjoly found his knowledge questioned, ignored, and suppressed. As the authors note, "Boisjoly's experiences could well serve as a paradigmatic case study for . . . ethical problems, ranging from accountability to corporate loyalty and whistle-blowing."

12

Professionalism and Responsibility in the Technological Society

CONRAD G. BRUNK

In late 1984 Canada's first astronaut rocketed into space aboard the American space shuttle Challenger to help demonstrate to the world, or at least to his own countrymen, the technological wonders of the Canadian-built "Canadarm" — the robotic arm with which the astronauts launch and retrieve satellites of various kinds. As the shuttle circled the earth, performing with an uneven degree of success its televised tasks, rumours began to circulate in the media that this mission included darker and more ominous purposes than the official space administration statements cared to mention.

Of course, these rumours were not news to anyone who had taken the time to read behind the superficial headlines about the space shuttle project. It is well known that the shuttle is a central element of the American drive to place in space military weapons of various kinds, ranging from military intelligence and missile guiding satellites to anti-satellite weapons and eventually President

Reagan's "Star Wars" anti-ballistic-missile defense system.

Soon after Marc Garneau's triumphant return, he was asked by an unusually probing CBC interviewer how he felt about the military aspects of the space mission in which he had just participated. Garneau responded that he was opposed to the militarization of space, but that he did not see his participation in the shuttle mission as inconsistent with this view. He had not himself worked directly with any weapon, he explained, but only with "space technology, space science, and life science experiments."[1] These he considered purely "civilian" tasks. He expressed no ethical qualms at all about the fact that the space shuttle was by nearly all accounts the primary vehicle for the American militarization of space. He seemed able to view his own participation in the project in isolation from the larger system of which his role was an integral part. He was a professional merely doing his job

Adapted from "Professionalism And Responsibility in the Technological Society," Conrad G. Brunk, Benjamin Eby Lecture, February 3, 1985, Conrad Grebel College, Waterloo, Ontario. Originally published in *Conrad Grebel Review*. Copyright © 1985, Conrad Grebel College. Reprinted by permission.

and doing it well; and the job he defined, not as assisting in the militarization of space but as contributing to human scientific and technological understanding. All potential cognitive dissonance in this man appeared on the surface to be neatly resolved.

There is, unfortunately, nothing unusual in this regard about Marc Garneau. This story repeats itself countless times in the lives of professionals — scientists, engineers, lawyers, doctors, professors — and many others in our society, including many non-professionals. The story merely illustrates the complexity of society and the moral ambiguity of the situations in which we have to make many of our moral choices. Garneau, like most of his colleagues in the various professions, appears to be a man of high moral conscience, who seeks to live according to the system of values he espouses. We have no reason to charge him with "hypocrisy" in the sense that he is publicly espousing a commitment to moral values belied by his own behavior. His situation is not so simple as that. Garneau, if pushed on the matter, would probably be able to give a consistent justification for what might appear to some to be inconsistent behavior, and his justification would be found to be perfectly acceptable by most of his professional colleagues. His justification could appeal to principles of professional morality widely accepted in our society. It is these principles of the prevailing professional morality in our society that are my concern. For it seems to me that this morality fails in certain significant ways to provide a responsible approach to some of the most pressing problems of the modern, technological age.

Garneau's situation is a paradigm of one of the most intractable problems of moral responsibility in our age. On the one hand, he expresses strong moral opposition to a policy pursued by the society of which he is a member — in this case the use of space for the proliferation of military weapons. On the other hand, he lends his personal participation to a project which is an integral part of the implementation of the very policy he opposes. He is just like the research biologist who, having devoted herself to the development, through recombinant DNA, of an artificial organism for the

production of insulin for diabetics, finds that she can fund her research only by participation in a project that is also using her findings to produce a new, and of course illegal, biological weapon. Or, he is like the lawyer who, perhaps motivated by a genuine concern to protect his client from a severe injustice, finds himself drawn into a legal battlefield where the rules of the system require him to suppress information he knows to be true, make insinuations about the opposing party and hostile witnesses which he knows to be false or misleading, and which may irreparably injure their reputations.

These examples could be multiplied by the thousands. They are part of the everyday experience of people, not only professionals, whose work involves them in one way or another in economic, social, and technological institutions and systems not of their own making. These institutions and systems, of course, are never perfect from the point of view of any one individual's moral outlook. They are always a mixture of good and evil, of justice and injustice, and thus participation in them is always fraught with moral ambiguity. There is really nothing new about this. From the first time human beings created social institutions and thought about their actions in moral terms they faced this ambiguity. For whenever people decide to act in cooperation with others to achieve some otherwise unattainable purpose they face the necessity of accommodating their own moral goals to those of the others with whom they cooperate.

But it is not just this kind of ambiguity which is involved in the situation of Marc Garneau and the others in the examples I have cited. There is a more significant aspect of these examples than the simple model of choosing the lesser evil or the greater good captures. It has to do with the way the individuals in these situations find ways to escape moral choice and moral responsibility altogether. In these cases the actors may not even see a tragic choice of the lesser evil or greater good. Rather, they fail to see any choice whatever. If pushed to make a judgment about the militarization of space, for example, Garneau might well agree that the escalating arms race, particularly its expansion into space, poses dangers to humanity that far outweigh the limited goods achieved by space technology generally. Even if he would not go this far, still, he apparently believes that the development of space technology for peaceful purposes *could* and *ought* to go forward without the military component. Yet he does not see this as *his own* moral responsibility in any sense. Hence, he does not see his decision to participate in the space shuttle venture as posing for him any significant moral problem. He does not feel morally or professionally compromised.

It is this escape from any sense of responsibility that is one of the most significant aspects of the morality of our age, and it is important to uncover the route of this escape if we are to understand why our social institutions move in the directions they do, even in the face of widespread moral uneasiness.

The political scientist and philosopher Hannah Arendt addressed this question in her profound book, *Eichmann in Jerusalem*, in which she attempts to understand the mind and moral rationalization of Adolf Eichmann, the self-proclaimed "construction engineer" who engineered the massive program of arrest and transportation of millions of German Jews to the Nazi death camps during the Second World War. What intrigued Arendt as she sat through the long Jerusalem trial in which Eichmann was convicted by an Israeli court of crimes against humanity, was how a man who evidenced virtually no hatred or even prejudice against the Jewish people rationalized his full and energetic leadership of this "Final Solution to the Jewish Problem." This was a problem for the court, for it is an established principle of all law, that people ought not to be found guilty of a crime unless it can be shown that they knew their actions in some sense to be wrong and that they acted intentionally. Eichmann's testimony at his trial and his statements to psychiatrists indicated that, although he knew full well that the Final Solution was, as he himself put it, "One of the greatest crimes ever committed in the history of humanity," nevertheless he did not consider his own participation in it to be wrong. It was not wrong because, he claimed, he had himself never killed, nor even borne ill-will

toward, any Jew. He had only done what any good professional who was given an assignment would have done, and he had done it to the very best of his ability. As Arendt put it, "Except for an extraordinary diligence in looking out for his personal advancement, he had no motives at all. And this diligence in itself was in no way criminal; he certainly would never have murdered his superior in order to inherit his post. He *merely*, to put the matter colloquially, *never realized what he was doing*" (emphasis in original).[2]

Adolf Eichmann was not the only one in the situation who "never realized what he was doing," according to Arendt. The tragedy of the situation was that Eichmann's excuse could have been made by not only many other German citizens and Nazi functionaries who participated in or condoned the atrocities, but even by some of the victims themselves, whose complicity with their executioners made the latter's job easier. This is the moral reality which Arendt attempts to capture in the subtitle of the book, "A Report on the Banality of Evil." It is the "banality" of even the horrendous evil of the Nazi holocaust that troubles her, for it is this banality that allows even well-intentioned and conscientious people in a society to participate in seemingly limitless evil. The banality of evil consists in the fact that there are evil consequences without evil actors, and often even without evil actions. And, where there are no evil actors or actions to be found, no one takes responsibility for the evil that is done.

What is it about our society that makes this escape from responsibility so easy and so pervasive? Arendt, along with many others, suggests that it is in the nature of any kind of bureaucratic structure to define responsibilities within each role or office of the bureaucracy so narrowly that few, if any, in the bureaucracy have any real control over the policies adopted and pursued by it. In other words, it is a function of *role specialization*. When any social task is divided up into smaller, specialized tasks, and different people are trained for the performance of only one of these tasks, the sense of participation in the larger task is dissipated. Persons see themselves as responsible only for their immediate task and less responsible for the larger one. The greater the specialization of the overall task, the less the sense of responsibility felt by those performing the specialized tasks.

It is commonly noted by social observers that among the most significant aspects of the industrial-technological society are specialization and its closely related partner, professionalism. It is important to look at these two phenomena together if we are to gain a deeper understanding of the way in which we exercise, or fail to exercise, responsible moral control over the institutions we create. As society becomes scientifically and technologically more advanced, it also requires at the same time greater degrees of specialization. No one can be an expert on many things in a time when the body of scientific and technical knowledge is so large and expanding so fast that it far outruns the ability of any one person to keep up with any more than a small portion of it. At the same time that greater specialization is required, so, it seems, more professionalization emerges.

There is not complete agreement about how to define a "professional." The claim to professionalism is made by increasing numbers of people in increasing kinds of activities, so that everyone from the plumber to the chimney sweep calls themselves "professionals." The claim to be a professional certainly arises in part out of the fact that more types of jobs in our society demand the kind of highly specialized training in an esoteric body of knowledge that was previously required only in the traditional professions of medicine, law, nursing, teaching, engineering, and the like. But it is not just specialized training in esoteric knowledge and skill that defines a professional in the traditional sense. In addition, professionals have usually been thought of as people who, because they perform an essential service to others who must rely upon their knowledge completely, and hence are in a position to take advantage of their clients, must be persons of extraordinary integrity and altruism. Since professionals are accorded a special place in society — usually including not only social and economic status, but also the right to exercise monopolistic control over entrance into the profession and the exclusive right to regulate and discipline themselves

— it is expected that in return they exercise special virtue in looking after the public good. The Hippocratic oath, which for centuries has been taken by initiates into the medical profession, is a classic expression of this "professional ethic of special virtue."

It is a common observation that the infamous scandals of the Watergate affair, involving professionals of every sort, from Agnew the engineer to the lawyers, Nixon, Mitchell, and Dean, began a major "crisis of confidence" in the professions in Western society. A major fallout from this era has been strong renewal of interest in "professional ethics" among nearly all the traditional professionals. Institutes of Ethics in the Professions have sprung up all over the North American continent, along with university courses in Business Ethics, Medical Ethics, Engineering Ethics, Legal Ethics, and so on. The Codes of Ethics of the various traditional professions have undergone more amending in the past 10 years since Watergate than they had in the entire previous history of the professions, in what appears to be as much a frantic attempt to restore public confidence in the virtue and reliability of the professionals as a *bona fide* attempt to restore professional accountability. The professions came quickly to the realization that if they did not maintain at least the appearance of ethical integrity in the exercise of their skill for the public good, society, through government regulation, would maintain it for them.

Out of this has arisen an important debate about whether professionalism is or is not a good thing. Does professionalism in fact instill a greater sense of responsibility for the social good in the professional, or does it merely provide a cloak for self-serving, monopolistic practices? I want to look at this question from the point of view of how professionalism functions in a technological society such as our own, with all the dynamics for degeneration into the banality of evil which Arendt observes. The question I want to address is whether "professional ethics" and the notion of "professional responsibility" involved in such ethics act in our society as a significant check upon the descent into the banality of evil, or whether they in fact accelerate and rationalize such a descent.

This question is important, if for no other reason than that the greatest dangers faced by humanity today are dangers posed by the development and use of technology. Nuclear technology, in both its military and civilian uses, carries with it, we now know with certainty, the possibility of human extinction on this planet. So does the new biotechnology of recombinant DNA, which many experts believe poses as great a risk to the human species as nuclear technology, if not greater. Some of the other risks imposed upon the human future by technological development, such as the degradation of the social and biological environments, may not be as dramatic or immediate, but they are serious risks nonetheless. In a very obvious and incontrovertible sense we are all dependent upon the professional technologists who develop, and to a greater or lesser extent preside over, these technologies. We all trust that the recombinant DNA researchers will take the precautions necessary to insure that a newly synthesized deadly organism will not be released uncontrolled into our environment. To what extent is our trust well-founded and to what extent is it a blind faith? Can we really rely upon "professional ethics" to save us? If not, upon what can we rely?

I have become increasingly convinced that if moral responsibility is not exercised by the professional technologists themselves, it is not likely to be exercised effectively by anyone else. If technology is to be brought under human control so that it serves legitimate human ends, it will be because those professional technicians — the scientists, the researchers, the engineers, and the advisors to the politicians — exercise responsible moral judgment at the very source of technological development itself. If moral responsibility is abdicated here, technology will certainly chart its own course independent of human purposes, and it will become the responsibility only of the great, anonymous "No One." And the great "No One," we know well from recent history, seems prone to misdeeds of limitless horror.

Whether or not even the exercise of professional responsibility can save us depends upon how professional responsibility is conceived. There is always a "professional ethic" at work among professionals. It is clear from the statements of Adolf Eichmann at his trial that he considered himself to have adhered scrupulously to the ethic of his profession. This is in the very nature of the self-concept of a professional. So, clearly, it is not professional ethics *per se* that are needed, but professional ethics of a certain kind — of a kind that actually takes responsibility in some way for the policies and practices of the system in which one plays a professional role. If we want to understand what kind of professional ethic we need, we must first understand what kind we now have, and why it is that this professional ethic leads to a kind of abdication of moral responsibility for the evil that our social and technological systems do.

It is my view that the prevailing conception of professional ethics and professional responsibility in our society is one that in fact serves to rationalize the kind of escape from responsibility that we see evidenced by Eichmann, Garneau, and all those professionals who define their sphere of moral responsibility so narrowly as to exclude everything beyond their actions in their immediate role. In doing so it gives over to the Anonymous Other — the "No One" — all responsibility for the ultimate corporate outcome. How does the prevailing professional ethic move in this direction?

One way it does so is by focussing moral attention upon the actions of *individuals* rather than upon the corporate actions of a whole profession or institution in which the professional functions. This focus is clearly evident in the traditional Codes of Ethics for various professionals, whether physicians, nurses, or engineers. A primary principle in these Codes is the principle of "loyal agency," or the duty always to serve the interest of the client or employer in a loyal and faithful manner. A clear implication of this principle is that when one acts as the agent of others, their values are the ones that ought to control the situation. If those values conflict with your own, you must, in the interest of professionalism, place your own values in suspension. Since you are acting on behalf of others, the action is in a sense *theirs*, not your own, hence the responsibility is *theirs*, not your own.

So, for example, the lawyer hired by a chemical company to defend the latter in a suit brought against it by the government for illegal dumping of toxic chemicals, if she is truly "professional," will not concern herself with whether the company really is guilty of the offense. Indeed, it would be considered by many of her colleagues extremely "unprofessional" if she conducted her defense of the company according to her own view of how laws should be applied to companies whose activities threaten the environment, especially if that view is not completely consonant with the interests of the company. Her proper professional role, it is said, is to represent *only* the interests of the company for whom she acts as an agent, not to represent all the interests relevant to a just settlement of the case. In this way the lawyer abdicates completely her responsibility for a just outcome in the case. She sees the responsibility lying somewhere else. She might well see it as lying with her client, whom she knows is secretly dumping toxic chemicals into the river from which the drinking water is drawn, and she might deplore this "irresponsibility," but not see it as her own. Or, she might reason that the responsibility to remedy the situation lies with the judge or with the whole of the legal system itself.

Of course everyone else, following their professional ethic, will reason the same way. They will see their moral responsibility being fulfilled if only they are loyal to the demands of their specific role as interpreted by their superior. Even the managers of the chemical company will not see it as *their* responsibility to clean up the river unless legally required to do so. Their professional managerial responsibility is to be loyal stewards of the stockholders who hired them to produce a maximum return on their investment in the company by producing chemical products in the most profit-maximizing way. The stockholders did not invest in an environmental protection agency.

How is this ethical isolationism justified in terms of conventional morality? What are the ways in which professionals, and others, reach the conclusion that the evil done by the institutions in which they play a role is "not their business"? It is impor-tant to look at some of the typical rationalizations or excuses called upon by the traditional professional ethic, and to see how they stand up to critical scrutiny.

One common rationalization is the "Appeal to Expert Authority," or what might also be called the "Appeal to Technical Ignorance." This excuse seems to be endemic to technological society with its high degree of specialization and division of labour. It reasons thus: "It isn't professional for me to make a firm moral judgment about what my profession or the institution of which it is a part is doing, even though privately I do have serious doubts about what it is doing. But I am not an expert in that kind of problem, so it is best to keep my mouth shut and leave it to the experts. I have no option but to trust their judgment since they know more than I do."

One of the most important features of modern technological society is that as more aspects of life become technically and politically sophisticated, the more we depend upon the technical experts to deal with more and more of our problems. Five years ago I would have written this article with a pencil. If it had broken down I would have been able to deal with the situation myself. But today I have written it on a computer. If it suddenly begins to scramble my text and print out nonsense, chances are I will be at a loss to repair the problem. I am dependent upon the computer expert. I have to defer to his judgment.

But suppose he tells me that he knows a quick fix for my problem. He knows how to break the protection code on a software package that will repair my program in a jiffy. Normally it sells for 200 dollars, but if he cracks the code he can copy it for me free. Now, who is the "expert"? He may know far more than I do about computer software, but does that mean he is a better judge than I am about the ethics of computer theft? In some respects he might be. For example, he may know more about the legality of computer theft than I do. He may know more than I do about what has come to be "accepted practice" in the computer industry. But is this reason for me to withhold my own judgment about the course of action in which I am about to participate?

The path of least resistance here, of course, is not to ask any questions, but to fall back upon the "Appeal to Technical Ignorance" which absolves me from all responsibility for the way this technical expert solves my problem.

The "Appeal to Expert Authority" is widespread in our society. It permits the nuclear scientist, the electronics engineer, the laser physicist, and the astronaut to avoid neatly any moral questions about their participation in a nuclear weapons system. They can rely upon the military strategist or the arms control experts to decide these questions for them, since the latter know more about the strategic situation in the world and the risks and benefits of the system than do the former. They may well know more than the electronics engineer about the strategic situation, and that is good reason to accord their opinions on the matter great weight. But "experts" are not necessarily in any better position to make a responsible moral choice than non-experts — in fact, in many cases they may be in a worse position, for their role may make them even less objective, more biased, and under greater pressure to tailor their opinion to the requirements of their role. Being a technical expert is not the same as being a moral expert. Neither is it necessarily true that because the technical expert knows more about the facts he or she is in a better position to make a reasoned moral judgment. It is important to know something about the facts (e.g., in cases of impact of technology on the environment and society, risks of nuclear war under certain conditions, etc.). But it does not follow from this that the more facts you know or the more of the subject you have studied, the more *morally relevant facts* you know. Even in highly technical matters it is possible for the non-expert to obtain at least as good an understanding of the morally relevant facts as the expert. And, the non-expert may have a far superior understanding of the relevant moral considerations. Technical experts can be moral morons just as ethics experts can be technical morons — and, of course, the latter can make mistakes as disastrous as the former.

Further, technical experts themselves do not agree about the moral implications of the technolo-gies they design and control. Their assessment of the risks and probable consequences of certain technical decisions can be as influenced by their own normative biases as the assessments of non-experts. In nearly every highly technical question, from energy policy through medical policy to strategic-military policy, experts disagree radically about the "facts" (e.g., consequences, risks, etc.). It is a grave mistake to believe that the experts are in a preferred position to make the most reliable moral judgment, and a society that leaves moral judgments up to the experts in their field is a society that is asking most of its members to abdicate moral responsibility. The late American President Eisenhower once said that "War is too important to be left to the generals." He was absolutely right, if only because all significant issues of social morality are too important to be left to any group of experts.

One version of this "Appeal to Expert Authority" is especially characteristic of the modern bureaucratic society. It appeals to the fact that since society has created other professional roles specifically to look after the larger social interests, it is not proper to concern oneself with this interest in one's own profession. It escapes moral responsibility by claiming, "It's not my role to look after the problem of long-term public welfare because it will be looked after by those trained for exactly that job." In our bureaucratic society this argument takes advantage of the fact that government establishes all kinds of regulatory agencies with their arsenals of regulations as a way of protecting society from the threat of unrestrained technological adventurism. So, one very influential writer on professional engineering ethics, Samuel Florman, has argued very persuasively in the engineering community that it is wrong to expect engineers to assume responsibility for the social impacts of their activities.[3] No one, he argues, wants to live in a society where the only technologies available are those that conform to the moral and political interests of engineers. So why should engineers be called upon to decide what is good for the rest of us? This is a "political" question, he says, and therefore it should be settled in the proper political forum — in the legislatures where there is full political participation from the entire spectrum of moral interests in the society. On this view, it is inappropriate for the engineer or the physicist to ask whether the weapons system on which he works is good or morally defensible, or if he does have an opinion, to let it influence his "professional" judgment on the job. This is a question to be decided by others.

It is commonly charged that extensive government regulatory intervention in society stifles creativity and initiative, and to some extent this is true. It may also be true that it stifles the sense of moral responsibility as well, by creating the expectation that "Big Brother" will look after the implications of our professional and technological activities. Even though I happen to believe that the price we pay for government regulation is often worth it, yet, on this issue government control may not be the solution because government regulation can never fully substitute for a sensitive and morally responsible professional conscience. This is so not only because government experts, too, are not always necessarily trustworthy in their moral judgment, but also because it simply is not always possible to counter the full weight of the technological establishment whose interests simply overwhelm the political power of the government regulatory bodies. I will have more to say on this problem later.

There is a second important rationalization for the ethical isolationism which refuses to take moral responsibility beyond the immediate professional role. It relies upon a very narrow definition of professionalism as the performance of purely technical skills. Thus, it claims that it is simply "unprofessional" to use one's professional status to make judgments about any issue that goes beyond one's own area of technical competence. It identifies professional responsibility with technical competence. This view is bolstered by the positivistic assumption, still embraced by many in the scientific and technological community, that normative judgments of any kind are subjective matters of opinion, and that it is an abuse of one's role to put them forward as "professional" opinions. Only those problems which can be reduced to their technical dimensions are amenable to professional judgment.

This rationalization can take several different courses. One is to turn every question of social or moral value into a purely technical question, thereby disguising a moral choice as a technical one. For example, physicians who sit on the therapeutic abortion committees of Canadian hospitals have to decide whether to permit any abortion to be performed in their hospital according to what appears to be a purely technical, that is to say *medical*, standard. They are supposed to decide whether or not the pregnancy in each case before them constitutes a threat to the life or health of the mother. Even though the choice the physicians are forced to make is clearly a value choice — between the severity of the risk to the mother and the life of the unborn child — both the Therapeutic Abortion Act and the professional ethic of these physicians conspire as best they can to make this appear as a purely "medical" decision. Everyone involved, including the patient and the public, feels more comfortable if the doctors can emerge from their deliberations to announce that an abortion is or is not "medically indicated" in this case. The comfort stems from the illusion that they avoided making a moral choice about abortion for which they have to take moral responsibility. There can be no moral blame or guilt where there has been no moral choice. Most significantly, the doctors here have avoided the appearance of "unprofessional action," which they would risk if they were to emerge with the announcement that in their opinion it would be *wrong* to perform this abortion even though, medically speaking, there is some risk to the mother's health (or that it would be *right* even though there is no significant risk).

A second way the "It's Not Professional" rationale is used in the prevailing individualist professional ethic is to admit the importance of both moral and technical questions, but to make a strong distinction between personal, professional morality and politics or political morality. Professional morality is then limited, as we have seen, to matters of personal conduct such as honesty, loyalty, collegiality, and reliability. Any evaluation of the professional role itself or the institution of which it is a part is considered "political," not moral, and therefore is beyond the bounds of professional morality. When one is making these "political" judgments, one is speaking not as a professional, but as a private citizen, a member of a public interest group, or in some other non-professional role. Hence, to speak out or take a stand on these matters "as a professional" is to abuse one's role — to pose as an expert in an area where one is not.

This rationalization divides the moral agent up into different insular roles. It allows the nuclear physicist to be concerned about the escalating arms race and the policies of his government with respect to it *in his role as private citizen*, but when he goes to the university lab to pursue his enhanced radiation research funded by the defense department, research which he knows is part of a larger project to develop a neutron bomb, he must not bring his moral convictions into that area of his professional life. That would be an abuse of his professional position. He might well vote for the peace candidate in the next election, and even write a letter on the issue to the newspaper as long as he could make it clear that he was not speaking "as a nuclear physicist."

None of these rationalizations of the denial of professional moral responsibility for one's role and its place in the larger scheme of things has the pervasive influence and appeal to deep-seated moral assumptions in our culture as the third and final one I would like to consider. This is the appeal to one form or another of what the classical economist Adam Smith called the "Invisible Hand." The Invisible Hand, for Smith, was that benevolent principle he believed to be at work in the capitalist free market whereby the unrestrained self-interest and greed of capitalists interested in nothing but the maximization of their own profits would mysteriously result in the maximum welfare of everyone in society. The Invisible Hand, in other words, turns selfish motivations into altruistic results. It was due to the working of this great Invisible Hand that Smith believed an unrestrained laissez faire economy, in which each entrepreneur sought only his or her own profit and ignored completely the good of others or of society as a whole, would ironically make everyone better off. A deep faith in the Invisible Hand has been the fundamental premise of laissez faire economists from Adam Smith to the contemporary "neo-classical" economists.

The dogma of the Invisible Hand has been invoked as a justification for radical individualism far beyond the province of economic behavior. Nowhere has its influence been felt more profoundly than in the area of professional ethics where it is believed to turn narrow professional self-interest on the part of each professional into the general good. Just as Adam Smith's Invisible Hand theory prompted businesspeople not to worry about the social consequences of the products they market, the production procedures they used, or the conditions of work in their establishment, because the marketplace will make it all turn out right, so it tells modern professionals not to make it their business to worry about the social consequences of their professional roles or the institutions of which those roles are a part, because in the whole scheme of things these problems are sure to take care of themselves.

The modern Invisible Hand is invoked in a variety of forms. One form is just an updated version of Adam Smith's benevolent free market, which recently has been revived by the "neo-classical" economists such as Milton Friedman and by the new so-called "economic theory of law," all of which has been bolstered by the libertarian philosophies of the New Right. In this view the Invisible Hand of the free market will turn professional as well as economic egoism and greed into social well-being. If only we insure that the market is really free and that all externalities are actually paid for, it will in the long run naturally weed out all the socially detrimental practices. If the chemical engineer develops insect control chemicals that are also carcinogenic, the consuming public will discover this soon enough, and their market behaviour will spur the development by another engineer of a less carcinogenic chemical. In the meantime, neither of them needs to worry about the problem of increasing cancer rates — it will look after itself. Neither, presumably, do nuclear physicists need to worry whether the risks of reactor melt-downs or accidental nuclear war are too high, since after a few such disasters or near disasters the market will demand safer systems if not different ones altogether. This assumes, of course, that there will still be a market around to make the demand.

A second form of the Invisible Hand argument invoked in modern professional ethics is a favorite of professional lawyers and journalists. In this form the Invisible Hand operates, not through the laissez faire economic marketplace, but through the so-called "free marketplace of ideas." Here the assumption is that it does not matter so much if the viewpoint expressed by each lawyer in the courtroom or the story published by the journalist is "the whole truth and nothing but the truth" as far as he or she knows it, because as long as everyone's else's viewpoint is freely fed into the system, the greatest approximation to the truth will emerge. One astute observer of the ethics of the courtroom has put it this way:

> The ethics of law emphasizes the adversarial relationship between the two parties and the duty of the lawyer to press the advantage of his particular party with 'zeal' and without remorse. It is presumed that the truth will emerge like a phoenix from the devastation wrought in trial by combat — a . . . presumption reminiscent of . . . 18th Century economics.[4]

This statement captures succinctly the concept of the faith in the Invisible Hand which allows the professional lawyer to justify to herself the suppression of truth or the badgering of credible witnesses in hopes of impugning what is known to be perfectly reliable testimony against her client, all in the name of that Invisible Hand which in the long run will assure the emergence of the truth. Whether the Invisible Hand works this way in fact is another question.

There is a third version of the Invisible Hand idea which is probably the most widely accepted or assumed by professionals in our day, especially by professional technologists. While it may not generally be thought of as an Invisible Hand, I think it

functions in the logic of justification for ethical isolationism much in the same way as the previously considered Invisible Hand arguments. It, too, is an article of faith in a benevolent force presiding over human actions and institutions which protects them from their own worst mistakes. It is faith in what Amatai Etzioni has called the "Technological Fix" — the belief that for every human problem, including especially the harmful and dehumanizing consequences of certain technologies, there is a technological solution. It is an Invisible Hand argument because it assumes not only that there is for every technological problem a technological fix *theoretically* available, but also that this fix will *actually* be implemented in time to prevent irremediable harm to the human community.

Upon this article of faith the nuclear physicists employed by the nuclear power industry almost unanimously support the increased reliance upon the nuclear production of electricity, despite the fact that there is not at present any known way to store safely the highly toxic radioactive waste. So the nuclear generating plants of the world are piling up this waste in temporary holding tanks in anticipation of the "inevitable" technological solution. Here is an example of blind and unshakeable faith in the Invisible Technological Hand, for in this case if the Hand is stayed and the technological fix does not present itself, the already existing stockpiles of nuclear waste are sufficient to poison the entire earth for the foreseeable future.

This faith in the technological fix spurs technological development in all directions, seemingly without regard to the potential hazards. And the faith is so deeply and firmly entrenched that any professional scientist or engineer who suggests seriously that research or development of certain technologies (e.g., recombinant DNA, biochemical weapons, etc.) are so inherently risky that they ought not to be pursued at all, is viewed by his or her colleagues as an irresponsible alarmist if not a traitor to the profession. Belief in the Invisible Technological Hand not only leads to abdication from responsibility for the risks imposed by one's own professional involvement in technology, but it can also spur the professional technologists and their political allies on to the serious advancement of technological solutions which are themselves fraught with even more serious risks — all in the belief that it may be the final technological fix. The apparently serious intention of the American government to develop a "Star Wars" anti-ballistic-missile defense system designed, in President Reagan's words, "to rid the world forever of the threat of nuclear weapons," is one of the most extreme examples of technological adventurism spurred on by faith in the Invisible Hand.

Do we have good reasons to share with the true believers their abiding faith in the benevolence and trustworthiness of the Invisible Hand in any of its guises? It seems to me that there are good reasons for skepticism. I will not rehearse here the arguments and evidence amassed by others against the efficacy of the Invisible Hand in its economic "free market" version though they seem to me to be thoroughly persuasive. The history of massive poverty and exploitation, to say nothing of unrestrained environmental degradation, produced by the free marketplace wherever it has been most closely approximated is too clear to be denied by anyone who is not so fervently committed to the dogma as to be blind to the facts.

But what about the great Invisible Technological Hand? Is there evidence to support faith in its benevolent touch upon the sweaty brow of the technological society? Or is there evidence to the contrary? In the remainder of this paper I want to advance at least one important ground for reasonable doubt. That there is an Invisible Hand at work in the technological institutions of our society I do not doubt. Indeed, I suspect that there likely are more than just one such Hand, and if only one of them is anything less than benign there is good reason to doubt that the technological institutions can take care of themselves apart from conscientious moral responsibility exercised by the technological professionals themselves.

There is, in my view, an important Invisible Hand at work in our technological society, which is not necessarily benign. It is that force at work

within technology itself which various writers from Jacques Ellul to Anatol Rapoport have referred to as the "Technological Imperative." It is a dynamic inherent within technology, (and essential to its growth and survival), which means that it is not morally neutral and is often morally detrimental. In a recent paper, Anatol Rapoport has illustrated the inherent dynamic of the technological imperative especially as it works in the case of military technology.[5] To understand what Rapoport means by the "technological imperative" one must also understand his "systems theory" approach to the problem. Within this approach, technology is viewed as a social system analogous to a biological system, and like the latter it evolves in certain directions depending upon the demands made upon it by its environment. The "environment" of technological systems, and of technology itself, is the human community, especially as it is represented by the professional technologists. Viewed in this way, technological evolution is a response to the needs of its environment, which in this case are the needs of the human community. This is the aspect of technology that the technological optimists see best — technology as the servant of humanity. This is the way we like to think about technology, and it is the traditional assumption underlying our conventional thinking about professional ethics and responsibility.

However, from the perspective of systems theory, it is possible to view the matter the other way around. A biological species evolves in response to the "needs" of the other biological systems in its environment, but it also becomes part of the environment in which the other biological systems evolve in response to *its* needs. The same thing is true of institutional — what Rapoport calls "symbolic" — systems. They too become an environment for the human beings who created them, and the human community then also evolves in directions which serve their needs. This is clearly true of the institution of technology and its various technological sub-systems such as the system of military technology. Viewed in this way, it can be seen that human beings, especially the technological professionals, adapt their behavior to the "needs" of the technological system. In this sense human beings become the servants of the technology.

Rapoport sees the technological imperative as the internal needs of technological systems which determine the responses of the successful, innovative technologist. So, for example, one can speak of the "need" within missile technology for accurate guidance systems, radar evasion or "stealth" techniques, increased speed, range and so on. These "needs" are all internal to the missile technology itself. The persons who then are "selected for" in the professional community are those persons who are most closely attuned to these technological "needs." In evolutionary terminology, the technological environment "selects for" those ideas crossing the minds of the scientists and technologists which best serve the needs of the technological system.[6] And, importantly, the needs of technology are not necessarily the real needs of the human community it supposedly serves, for technology has its own system of "needs."

What are some of the typical "needs" or values intrinsic to technology itself which can be identified as part of the technological imperative? I would identify the following ones: 1. *Efficiency*. Technologically speaking, performing a task in less time and with less human energy is intrinsically better. 2. *Complexity*. Higher technology is intrinsically better than lower technology (because it reflects an intellectual advance or "breakthrough"). 3. *Technical "Elegance."* This is an aesthetic quality similar to that which obtains in science or mathematics, so that the more elegant the system, the better. 4. *Self-perpetuation*. This is a value intrinsic to all organic and social systems. It is the inherent drive to survive, to grow, to gain power, and to reproduce oneself. In the case of technology it manifests itself in the following maxims: More technology is better than less; technology dependent upon yet more technology is better; the technically possible is good and should therefore become actual, etc.

These values intrinsic to technology, which give it the "imperative" to develop along certain paths, help to constitute what Robert Oppenheimer once called "the lure of the technically sweet." This lure is what most attracted the brilliant team of profes-sional scientists, mathematicians and engineers headed by Oppenheimer in the Manhattan Project to devote their energies to the development of the first atomic bomb. Said Oppenheimer later, in reflection upon what he came to see as a regrettable part of his professional past:

> It is my judgment in these things that when you see something that is technically sweet you go ahead and do it and you argue about what to do about it only after you have had your technical success. That is the way it was with the atomic bomb.[7]

It was this realization that led Oppenheimer to speak out against the further development of the far more powerful hydrogen bomb. Its development, too, was driven on by the technological imperative and the lure to the professional defence community of its "technical sweetness." On this issue Oppenheimer threw aside the canons of the isolationist professional ethic and publicly opposed the devotion of scientific energy to the development of the hydrogen bomb. But his voice and the voices of other technological professionals who followed him were silenced. They were silenced because their appeal to moral and political ends (i.e., that the hydrogen bomb would stimulate an open-ended arms race to mass suicide) did not, as Rapoport notes, fit the mentality of the professional elite who had become the servants of the technology. In his evolutionary terms, the dissenters were "selected against."[8] Those who were "selected for" were those who responded to Oppenheimer the same way Enrico Fermi did when his participation in the bomb project was questioned: "Don't bother me with your conscientious scruples! After all, the thing is superb physics!"[9]

What is the import of this "technological imperative" for professional responsibility? Some implications should be immediately obvious. First, if such an imperative operates within technology it means that the technological professionals are the primary instruments through which the technological systems will have their needs met. Or, put bluntly, the professionals are the primary servants of technology, and their professional success is a measure of the degree to which they have learned to serve their "master." However, they will not see it that way. Their view will be the one of human purposes being served by the technological servant, and they will always be able to cite the human, social and political purposes which, if realized, would justify the course already charted by the imperatives of the technology itself. So, the defense professionals are always able to cite the strategic considerations that demand a further buildup of their nuclear arsenal — it is essential to counter the technological developments on the other side. Of course, it is not only the *actual* developments of the other side that require our response, it is more importantly, the developments we know they have the *potential* to actualize that require our response. *We* are able to see that *they* will follow the course dictated by the technological imperative by actualizing the technically possible. But *we* view our response as guided by independent considerations of rational defence strategy, whose purpose is to increase our security. What we both fail to see is that we are both being driven by the technological imperative into courses of action that *decrease* our security.

Secondly, if the professionals are the primary instruments through which the technological imperative actualizes itself, we ought not to be surprised to find that the professional ethic which has evolved in the professional community tends to serve the demands of the technological imperative rather than to place effective limits upon it. This is precisely how, in my view, the canons of professional morality I have cited function. The various rationalizations for the restriction of one's professional moral choice to the narrow confines of loyalty, honesty, and technical competence in one's role are all ways in which the professional retreats from the opportunity to challenge or redirect the course of the technological imperative. The professional ethic relies upon the Invisible Hand, but this Hand may well direct society in a course oblivious to morally acceptable human purposes. The Invisible Technological Hand is not necessarily benign. In the case of some of the new technologies there is good reason to fear that it is downright malevolent. If this is true, any professional ethic

which relies upon the good graces of the Invisible Hand constitutes a form of moral irresponsibility founded upon false hope.

Third, if it is true that the prevailing professional ethic is the rationalization of the technological imperative, it means that the influence of this internal dynamic of technology is greatly strengthened and entrenched in our society through the community of technological professionals. The professional establishment itself becomes a powerful political force on the side of the technological imperative. This is one reason why some of the rationalizations I reviewed earlier, which escape personal responsibility by assigning it to other roles such as government regulators, other more knowledgeable experts, or to other nonprofessional roles like the role of responsible citizen, are not very reliable solutions either. For if our society becomes increasingly professionalized, and if this professionalism is guided by the traditional professional ethic, then as the power of the technological imperative expands, there will be fewer non-professional "others" left who are free to make moral judgments, and it will become more difficult for them to counter its influence. This certainly is one reason, among others, why government regulatory agencies have been notoriously limited in their ability to curb many of the well-known and foreseen detrimental impacts of technology upon the social and biological environments. As technological professionalism grows in our society, it is not likely that the power of the technological imperative over other forces at work against it will diminish.

Is there any solution to this problem? Can the combined forces of the technological imperative and the professional establishment which serves its needs be countered effectively so that technology truly does serve the moral ends of humanity? The prospects, I think, are not good. But I have one suggestion which I think would constitute an important step in the direction of technological responsibility. That step is the adoption of a new professional ethic which rejects the rationalizations for ethical isolationism and escape from responsibility characteristic of the prevailing professional ethic, and infuses the technological establishment itself with a moral conscientiousness that places limits upon the Invisible Technological Hand *from the inside*. That is to say, professionals cannot place in abeyance their convictions about the moral implications for society of the roles and institutions in which they function. They must carry their convictions straight into their professional roles and allow them to influence the design and use of those projects in which they choose to participate. Moral convictions must be applied at the point where the technological imperative is actually realized in human affairs — namely at the point where professional design and manipulation of the technology actually takes place.

A responsible professional ethic, then, must be an Ethic of Conscientious Professionalism, which always takes a broader, structural view of the system or institution in which the professional role functions, and takes as *at least one* important consideration in decision-making, the moral significance of the larger system. It is willing to ask, "What contribution does my role make to the whole? Is this role one that itself is making an overall contribution to society? Are there ways to perform this role that would make it less destructive, or more conducive to the social good? What influence can I exercise which will make the role more socially beneficial?"

An Ethic of Conscientious Professionalism must always be prepared to address and answer the question, "How far am I prepared to go in participation with this system? Where do I draw the line in my participation with a system I can no longer justify?" The tragedy of a person like Adolph Eichmann is not just that he was not prepared to answer this question with conscientious refusal to participate, but that it did not even occur to him to *ask* the question. True conscientious professionalism is, in contrast, exhibited by the three nuclear engineers at General Electric's nuclear energy division in California, who several years ago announced their resignation from the company on the grounds of what they considered to be the "immorality" of reactor building and the immense risks to mankind that can result from technological mistakes."[10] Even if one does not agree with their assessment of

the immorality of nuclear power, one can applaud their courage to act on the strength of their convictions. In this respect, Greg Minor, Dale Bridenbaugh, and Richard Hubbard exhibited responsible professionalism. It is not surprising, however, that the general assessment of their action by their engineering colleagues is the same as that expressed by GE — unprofessional religious fanaticism.

An Ethic of Conscientious Professionalism must be prepared to take the difficult step of conscientious refusal to participate in the system or in aspects of the system. This is not an easy thing to do, because it almost always implies great personal sacrifice, including often the loss of professional standing in the eyes of one's colleagues, and even banishment from the profession. This is the price one pays as well for even the lesser "offense" of blowing the whistle on actions of one's professional colleagues or employers that pose grave threats to the public welfare. Conscientious Professionalism does not always require the professional to act in ways that require great sacrifice to herself or her family — no ethic that requires this level of commitment is likely to be widely embraced or followed — but it does require that the professional be confronted with that option and consider what level of response is required.

A responsible Ethic of Conscientious Professionalism embraces the principle that with increased knowledge and power comes increased responsibility. So, it is precisely because the professional has greater understanding of the implications for good or ill of the technology or skill she practices that she also has a greater responsibility to protect the social good. The Ethic of Conscientious Professionalism also accepts the Biblical principle that from those to whom much is given, much also is required. This means that insofar as the professional derives personal benefits from the advance of technology she also then carries a greater share of the responsibility to see that the technology is used in a socially beneficial way than does someone else who does not benefit in the same way. Thus, not only is it not *inappropriate* for the professional to take public moral stands on matters concerning the moral impact of her profession on society (as we have seen the traditional professional ethic says), but it is a positive professional *responsibility*. It is as appropriate for the nuclear physicist to warn of the dangers of nuclear power plants and nuclear weapons as anyone else, indeed, she usually has a greater obligation than anyone else to do so.

One of the positive developments in the direction of a more responsible professional ethic in our society has been the recent phenomenon of professionals organizing themselves *as professionals* to exercise an influence upon the political decisions being made affecting the use of their profession for the public good. We know well the phenomenon of professionals organizing themselves to speak out on matters affecting their own professional self-interest — the Canadian Medical Association, the Canadian Association of University Professors, and the like. But the new phenomenon is something very different. Here the concern is not professional self-interest, but public interest. The organization of academics into Science for Peace, medical doctors into Physicians for Social Responsibility, and even very recently, retired NATO military generals into Generals for Peace, are important examples of professionals taking their social responsibilities as professionals seriously. What is of interest here is especially the phenomenon of professionals such as scientists and military people organizing to assess critically the social consequences of *their own* profession and the actions of *their own* colleagues in the profession.

This sense that the narrow blinkers of traditional professional ethics must be removed and the horizon of moral responsibility expanded is finding its way even into the center of the traditional professional establishment. It is reflected in the fact that the Codes of Ethics of various professions have begun to shift their emphasis from the narrow concerns about loyalty to client or employer, honesty in dealing with one's colleagues, bringing honor upon the profession, and so on, to a recognition of the duty to use the profession in the service of the

public good. The Codes of Ethics of the various professional engineering associations have made dramatic changes in this regard in recent years. Nearly all of them expound the principle that the engineer shall "regard his duty to public welfare as paramount."[11] Whether, or to what extent, this sentiment will actually translate itself into practice remains to be seen. It is nevertheless significant that the profession has at least come to acknowledge the principle.

Another encouraging development, again within the engineering profession, is a movement among professionals to pressure their professional associations to support actively a member of the profession who takes conscientious action in defense of the public welfare at great personal sacrifice to him or herself.[12] Moral conscientiousness is far easier to practice if there is a community of support among one's colleagues than if one is required to act as a lone individual. In addition, a profession committed to supporting the ethical action of its members is much more likely to become sensitized to the social and moral implications of its role in the larger scheme of things.

I have argued that the traditional professional ethic and its typical rationalizations for not taking seriously a profession's broad impact upon the social welfare of the practice of that profession constitutes a serious avoidance of moral responsibility. It is an escape that permits other forces, whose influences are not always for the social good, to take over and determine the course of our social development, independent of the very values we espouse. The traditional ethic may even be the rationale by which professionals become the blind servants of such alien forces as the Technological Imperative. What is needed is a new Professional Ethic which sensitizes us to the way in which we are drawn into the service of these forces, and instills in us a vigilant responsibility for the future of humanity and its habitat.

ENDNOTES

1. *Engineering Dimensions* 6 (January/February, 1985) p. 22.

2. Hannah Arendt, *Eichmann in Jerusalem: A Report on the Banality of Evil* (New York: Viking Press, 1963) p. 287.

3. Samuel Florman, "Moral Blueprints," *Harpers* 257:30-33 (October, 1978) p. 30.

4. Michael J. Rosanova, "Divorce Related Mediation," *Perspectives on the Professions* 2 (September/December, 1982) p. 2.

5. Anatol Rapoport, "The Technological Imperative." Unpublished paper presented at the University of Waterloo Conference on Philosophy and Nuclear Arms, September 28-30, 1984.

6. *Ibid.*

7. Robert Jungk, *Brighter Than a Thousand Suns* (Harmondsworth: Penguin Books, 1964) p. 266.

8. Rapoport, *op. cit.*

9. Jungk, *op. cit.*, p. 184.

10. C. Barnett, "Three Leave GE," *New Engineer* (May, 1976) pp. 34-42. Reprinted in J. Schaub and K. Pavlovic (eds.), *Engineering Professionalism and Ethics* (New York: John Wiley & Sons, 1983) p. 246.

11. See, for example, the *Code of Ethics*, Association of Professional Engineers in Ontario, Sec. 2a.

12. Stephen H. Unger, *Controlling Technology: Ethics and the Responsible Engineer* (New York: Holt, Rinehart and Winston, 1982).

13

Auditors and Deceptive Financial Statements: Assigning Responsibility and Blame

JAMES C. GAA

CHARLES H. SMITH

Introduction

It is generally agreed that managers of firms can use financial statements to deceive readers of those statements, e.g., investors and creditors, about the health of the firm. Deception is a serious issue because of its effects on "dupes". Violence and deception are "the two forms of deliberate assault on human beings. Both can coerce people into acting against their will" (Bok 1978, p. 18). That is, deception reduces people's ability to act freely or voluntarily, and therefore, needs to be justified.

Managers produce financial statements, and are responsible to readers for deceptive information (i.e., misinformation). They may be also subject to blame for such deception. Auditors do not produce financial statements for their clients, although they are associated with them via their audit activity and report. To what extent are auditors also to be held responsible and/or subject to blame for managerial deception?

This paper is a detailed analysis of this issue.[1] The basic concepts used to judge auditors' behaviour are responsibility and blame, which are ethical concepts, and are concerned with the principles governing the actions of people that have an effect on others. Thus, blaming an auditor for deception is a form of ethical censure.[2]

Responsibility and blame are related to each other in the following way. Blaming someone for one's actions presupposes responsibility for them, since it does not make sense to blame someone for acts for which that person is not responsible. Thus, responsibility is a necessary condition for blameworthiness. However, it is not a sufficient condition, since the action (for which the individual is responsible) may be justifiable. In short, blaming an auditor for deception requires both that the auditor is at least partially responsible for deception, and that the actions are not justifiable. A broad range of possible defenses of auditors, seeking

From *Contemporary Accounting Research*, Vol. 1, No. 2. Reprinted by permission.

to defend them from responsibility and/or blame, will be examined. The basic conclusion of the analysis is that auditors may be relieved of responsibility and therefore blame for managerial deception, to the extent that they have been coerced (perhaps unknowingly) into acquiescing to management. However, the auditor is blameworthy to the degree that he *should have known* about the deceptive act.

Auditors who are members of a professional society are bound by its code of ethics.[3] The purpose of such codes is to provide a guide to auditors in making decisions having ethical (rather than merely technical) content. These codes play an important role in the production and communication of financial information. Therefore, this paper uses the analysis of auditor responsibility and blameworthiness to assess the content of two similar, but subtly different, code of ethics: the Institute of Chartered Accountants of Ontario (ICAO) code and the American Institute of Certified Public Accountants (AICPA) code. This assessment is important since codes of ethics are supposed to govern the behavior of auditors, particularly in difficult cases. If a code does not adequately codify the ethical principles underlying the auditor's role, then it may be expected that the risk of unethical behavior is increased.

The ICAO Rules of Conduct conform more closely than the AICPA's to the result of the analysis in this paper. Both the ICAO and AICPA maintain that their rules of conduct define practices at a minimum level of acceptability. The AICPA code is shown to set the minimum level too low. Since the U.S. Securities and Exchange Commission already holds auditors to a standard of behavior consistent with the results of the present analysis, tightening up the AICPA Rules of Conduct would extend the scope of the higher standard to all audit engagements. In any case, it would be difficult to justify on ethical grounds the existence of more than one set of standards. Thus, the analysis may lead to the recognition of needed changes.

The section immediately following is a description of some of the problematic situations in which auditors may find themselves, and which may

involve deception of financial statement readers. The next section analyzes the concept of deception itself. Following that is an examination of the problem of justifying or defending acts of deception. General criteria for evaluating such acts are provided. In the fourth section, portions of a framework developed by Bok (1978) are used to draw conclusions about auditors' responsibility and blameworthiness for deception practised by their clients. The comparison and evaluation of relevant portions of the ICAO Code of Professional Ethics[4] and the AICPA code is the topic of the fifth section. A summary and conclusion is provided in the last section.

PROBLEMATIC SITUATIONS

Before analyzing the concept of deception more closely, it will be worthwhile to describe some of the ways in which financial statements may be deceptive, even if Generally Accepted Accounting Principles (GAAP) have been followed in their preparation. This will provide an initial focus for the analysis of auditors' responsibility and blameworthiness. The issue to be addressed below is the following: Supposing that an auditor is not intentionally deceiving financial statement readers, and that the financial statements conform to GAAP, are *auditors* subject to blame if *management* tries to mislead readers of its financial statements?

Choices among alternative accounting methods are allowed within GAAP. For example, management can choose from among a number of inventory valuation procedures. Thus, the LIFO and average-cost cost flow assumptions can be used in conjunction with the timing of purchases, so as to modify the cost of goods sold figure, resulting in a smoother income stream.

Over time, and especially in the last few years, there has been less and less flexibility available to management and auditors in the selection of accounting methods.[5] However, even when uniformity is mandated, i.e., where judgments as to the methods used are not required or even allowed, management may be able to "gerrymander" their affairs in order to escape the application of unwanted standards, by meeting or failing to meet conditions specified by a financial reporting standard. The leasing issue demonstrates firms' ability to engineer contracts, so that the cost of acquiring rights to use property are not capitalized. The game of developing novel financing arrangements, to escape the already detailed rules of the Canadian Institute of Chartered Accountants (CICA) and Financial Accounting Standards Board (FASB), can be played *ad infinitum*.

Other examples of this sort of opportunity include manipulation of the "cutoffs" for use of the equity method, accounting for business combinations, and for computing earnings per share.[6] Since no financial accounting standard can be completely conclusive in determining appropriate financial reporting, professional judgment (and not just technical analysis) will always be required. Such cutoffs can be no more than guidelines for the application of GAAP. It will be shown below that auditors must look past these guidelines. They must look to the opportunities and intentions of management, to the circumstances, and to the anticipated effects of alternatives, in judging management's choice of reporting methods.

Financial reporting standards may provide little or no guidance in specific situations. For example, it was a common practice in the 1920s to write up the value of assets; half of the write-up would be credited to a capital surplus account, against which debt discount would be amortized.[7] The revenue recognition scandals of the 1960s and 1970s provide examples of *intentional* deception of investors through the medium of financial statements.[8] The recognition of revenue at the earliest possible time and in maximum amounts shows that questionable sale "transactions" could be made to fit the comparatively lax standards for revenue recognition then in effect. The conglomerate movement of the late 1960s, and the attendant purchase-pooling controversy, are other areas in which investors were deceived by financial statements into believing that conglomerates were more prosperous than they really were (See Briloff 1976; Chatov 1975).

Another sort of case concerns the level of aggregation of numbers in financial statements, e.g.,

whether a particular income statement item should be shown in a separate line. It is clear that judgment is required here. Aside from APB Opinion No. 30 and Section 3480 of the CICA *Handbook* on extraordinary items, auditors are given little guidance regarding the separate disclosure of particular items. If the issue were simply technical, the proper course of action would be clear; such an item would not have to be shown separately since GAAP does not provide specific and explicit guidelines for such disclosures.

The point is that adherence to a financial reporting principle or standard does not *ipso facto* make the resulting income statements any less deceptive. Indeed, at least in the case of Stirling Homex, a dubious land sales transaction was restructured *on the auditor's advice*, so that it *would* fit the standards (Briloff 1976, p. 419f). The auditor's difficulty cannot be eliminated by simply writing a better accounting or auditing standard. That is, auditors are often faced with situations where the mechanical application of a rule is insufficient. An auditor ought not to do anything for which he is subject to blame. Therefore, the criteria for establishing responsibility and blameworthiness given below serve at the same time as criteria for auditors in deciding on appropriate courses of action.

DECEPTION

It is necessary to clarify the concept of deception, in order to consider the conditions under which auditors may be excused from responsibility or blame for deceptive financial statements. Because the subject is highly complex, no attempt will be made to provide a general definition of the term. Instead, the simpler concept of lying will be analyzed first, as a framework for examining those aspects of deception which are important with regard to financial reporting.

Consider the following definition of 'lie': 'a statement made by one who does not believe it with the intention that someone else shall be led to believe it' (Isenberg 1973, p. 248). This definition is simple and workable, but it ignores important aspects of the problems auditors face. First, while lying is a central form of deception, it can take other forms, such as remaining silent when one has information which would be important to someone else. Both kinds of deception have been clearly recognized as issues in accounting. For example, Section 17 of the U.S. Securities Exchange Act of 1934 prohibits making "any untrue statement of a material fact or to omit to state a material fact necessary in order to make the statements made, in the light of the circumstances under which they are made, not misleading . . .".

Deception is a particular kind of use of the communication process. The general model of the communication process consists of a sender and a receiver, who are connected by a communication channel, over which signals are transmitted from the sender to the receiver (See Leonard 1967). In general, the intention of the sender in transmitting a message is to affect the receiver in some way, causing the latter either to *act* in a more or less specific way ("pragmatic communication") or to change his *dispositions* to act ("cognitive communication"). An act of communication is *successful*, insofar as the signal does affect the receiver in the way intended by the sender.

Success and intention   *Deceptive communication* is successful, from the sender's point of view, insofar as it actually causes people to be misled, or misinformed, i.e., to act or to be disposed to act in ways in which they would not, were they to possess or acquire more reliable information. Whether it is *actually* deceptive depends on its effects upon reception. Whether it is *intentionally* deceptive depends on the conditions of the production of the signal, and especially on whether the sender acts with the knowledge that the receiver is likely to be deceived. Therefore, a sender may intend to deceive someone else, but fail to do so successfully. Conversely, the sender may successfully deceive someone, without having intended to do so.[9] Since intentional deception is an "act of commission", it needs (from an ethical point of view) to be justified or excused. Unintentional deception also needs to be excused, insofar as one is obligated not to be deceptive. Suppose that management intends to deceive

readers of its financial statements. The auditor may himself have no such intention. If the act or practice of deception is successful, what are we to conclude about the auditor?

The importance of these two characteristics (success and intention) is reflected in the Continental Vending Case (*U.S.* v. *Simon*). The judge's instructions to the jury included two issues: "whether the financial statement as a whole 'fairly presented the financial position of Continental as of September 30, 1962 and whether it accurately reported the operations for fiscal 1962'. [i.e., were readers likely to be misled?] If they did not, the basic issue became whether defendants acted in good faith [i.e., what were their intentions?]" (Quoted in Liggio 1974, p. 103f).

Expectations of readers   It is the normal business of auditors to make reports of a certain sort to readers of financial statements; so that there is a more or less permanent communication channel between them and the auditor. The existence of such a channel may create a definite expectation on the part of receivers that, if the sender possesses relevant information, a certain sort of message will be sent along the channel. Thus, while it might be thought that because silence is a "nonaction", silent deception is less serious than deception through lying, the relationship between auditor and reader implies that *not* sending such a message on this established channel may be highly deceptive (whether intentional or not). In the Continental Vending case, readers presumably took the auditor's silence as evidence that the financial statements were not misleading. The fact that the auditor acted within the rules was not exculpatory, because strict adherence to the rules did not take into account the *expectations* of readers. According to Isenberg, (1973, p. 249) one of the essential parts of a lie is "a set of estimates by the speaker, apart from his main opinion of the statement he makes, of the existing evidence for that statement, the probability [of the truth] of the statement upon various portions of that evidence, the listener's mentality and cognitive situation". This applies as well to this kind of "passive" deception via silence. The reader's expectations and beliefs are thus a crucial factor in evaluating auditors' behavior.

The above analysis of deception supports Bok's (1978) view mentioned at the outset that the receiver of an intentionally deceptive message is not merely *unable* to act in ways he would act if given nondeceptive information, but is *prevented* from doing so. Since the receiver is not completely free in his actions, the victims of intentional deception are coerced into involuntary actions. This lack of freedom is central to deception.

The decrease in freedom changes the distribution of power between liar and dupe — the former having increased power and the latter less (Bok 1978, p. 19). The value of accounting information (including the auditor's report) is normally thought to accrue primarily to the receiver, by providing a reliable input into the decision making process of the receiver. But the value of intentionally deceptive information lies primarily in its benefit to the sender. Indeed, the purpose of intentional deception is just to affect the relative power of people.

THE JUSTIFICATION OF DECEPTION

Immanuel Kant (translation, 1949) argued that it is always wrong to lie; even if a person intending to murder a friend asks where the friend is, one is morally obligated to respond truthfully. There can be no conflict, according to Kant, between the duty to tell the truth and any other duty, such as to protect one's friends from wrongful death. However, this absolute prohibition of deception is too extreme. Since it is similar to violence, deception is at least *sometimes* justifiable. For if violence is sometimes acceptable as a means of self-defense and defense of others, then deception may also be used in such situations (Bok, 1978, p. 41).

Justifiable deception   Beyond such extreme and clearcut cases, the difficulties of justifying deception increase rapidly. For now one must begin to look carefully at diverse circumstances and at what kinds of considerations are relevant to particular cases.[10] Auditors are constrained to give

unqualified opinions only to financial statements which are prepared in accordance with GAAP. As described in the first section, managers can use financial statements to serve their own ends, by casting themselves in a favorable light. Abuses of GAAP (i.e., violations of "the spirit of the law") occur principally either because financial accounting standards allow management to choose from among a set of allowable alternatives, or because a pronouncement is written at a sufficiently high level of generality that a significant amount of judgment is required in applying GAAP to specific situations.

Judgment in applying GAAP   The possibility of intentional deception by management is always present. Therefore, an auditor's assent to the client's choice of an accounting principle is, to a significant degree, an ethical issue. While judgment is necessary in the application of GAAP, technical considerations — i.e., whether a specific accounting method is in accordance with GAAP in the sense that it follows "the letter of the law" — play an important role in judgments concerning the appropriate application of GAAP. However, because of their social role, auditors should view the technical matters as minimum requirements. In light of the analysis in the preceding sections, auditors need to make judgments, in addition, about (1) the *opportunities* for deception available to management, (2) the *intentions* of management with regard to deception, and (3) whether a particular reporting method provides the best information under the circumstances.

The perspective of the deceived   Three basic principles underly the defense of auditors against blame for deceptive financial statements, and therefore serve as guidelines in evaluating auditors' judgments. The most basic element concerning the justifiability of intentional deception is that there is an important difference between the perspective of the deceiver and the perspective of the deceived. From the deceiver's point of view, acts of deception are often well intentioned, and may be thought to be harmless (e.g., white lies), or even to produce more good than harm. A weakness in the deceiver's perspective is that it is easy to overestimate the good, and underestimate the bad results of deception. It is thus easy to justify them to oneself.

The perspective of the deceived is less positive toward lying, as may be seen in the observation that liars do not want to be deceived themselves (Bok 1978, p. 27). Dupes and others affected by lies are commonly resentful, disappointed, and suspicious — witness the lawsuits in the United States concerning the highly publicized "accounting failures" of the 1960s. (See Briloff 1976.) In such cases, auditors were sued on the grounds that they were supposed to act in the investors' interests by detecting and controlling corporate deception. Investors may thus feel doubly deceived, once by management and once by the auditor.

The importance of the perspective of the deceived is revealed in a statement of Harold M. Williams, (1980) a former Chairman of the SEC:

> The objective of each auditor should be to ensure that the profession's standards and conduct of its members comports — not merely with the letter of the law — but with the changing expectations and needs of users of financial information and the public.

Veracity   We all share the perspective of the deceived. A second principle, the Principle of Veracity, dating back to Aristotle, is important for justifying deception. The principle is "that lying is 'mean and culpable' and that truthful statements are preferable to lies in the absence of special considerations" (Bok 1978, p.30). This implies that deception is not neutral; there is a presumption against deception. The burden of "proof" or justification is on the would-be deceiver, whereas truthfulness does not ordinarily require any justification. "... It is the normal thing to demand a reason *for* lying, not a reason why one should not tell a lie" (Isenberg 1973, p. 259). Note that the Principle of Veracity does not rule out deception altogether, as Kant would have had it. Nevertheless, even if a lie is justifiable, one should at least seek truthful alternatives. (Bok 1978, p. 31.)

Publicity   A third principle, the Principle of Publicity, expands this idea beyond the burden of proof. It is that "a moral principle must be capable of public statement and defense" (Bok, 1978, p. 92). The principle, which applies to any ethical claim, is based on Rawls' (1971, p. 582) concept of publicity: anyone must be able to justify his actions, without the justification itself causing undesirable consequences, such as being self defeating. One implication of the publicity principle is that acts and practices of deception must "survive the appeal for justification to reasonable but independent persons" (Bok, 1978, p. 93).[11]

The primary purpose of the publicity principle is to reduce or remove personal bias. Therefore, personal soul-searching is insufficient. Likewise, appeal to friends, colleagues, and experts — which, as Bok notes, is common to professional groups — is generally inadequate because personal biases tend to be shared. A better approach is either to consult all classes of people who have an interest, or at least provide easy opportunities for them to make their views known. Doing so would help the people making decisions to continually seek to maintain the perspective of the deceived. This is especially so in such areas as auditing and financial reporting, where the focus of debate can easily settle on technical issues involving GAAP.

Consequences   In order to evaluate specific acts or practices of deception, a general criterion needs to be advanced, against which they are to be judged. A common view is that the *consequences* of a given act or practice of deception are fundamental. Since truth telling and lying differ in their consequences, consequentialism leaves open the possibility that some lies will be judged as justifiable, and some not. For example, it would not preclude an argument that the omission of lease information from the balance sheets of firms in the trucking industry is justifiable on the grounds that it would increase the ability of those firms to obtain financing (Hawkins 1975). Although such a practice would presumably yield less desirable consequences for readers of such statements (including the suppliers of capital) *through deception*, it might be defensible because of desirable "economic consequences" at a more general level.[12]

THE BLAMEWORTHINESS OF AUDITORS FOR DECEPTIVE FINANCIAL STATEMENTS

Bok distinguishes three types of arguments regarding lying, which might be used in defense of auditors to excuse them in one way or another from the responsibility or blame for deception by management. These arguments will be examined in this section.

First, it might be argued either that financial statements are not really deceptive, or at least that they cannot be proven to be deceptive. If this were the case, we might in some cases criticize management for *trying* to deceive financial statement readers. However, the fact that management does not, or cannot be shown to, succeed, is sufficient to defend the auditor against a charge of responsibility. On this argument, the issue of auditors' responsibility is moot, as long as they did not participate with management in its behavior. We may criticize management with respect to their intentions, but the fact that the consequences of their actions are not as intended means that there are no material consequences for which the auditor could be held responsible. *Ipso facto*, there is nothing to blame them for.

The second type of defense assumes, rather than disputes, that a set of financial statements is deceptive. Nevertheless, the argument would go, auditors are not *responsible* for what has occurred. Hence, they again would be relieved of blame. The traditional separation of the roles of preparer and auditor of financial statements has been used to claim that auditors are responsible only for their own attestation, and not responsible (and therefore not blameworthy) for managerial deception.

As with the second kind, the third type of argument excusing auditors assumes that deception has occurred. However, it would also be granted that the auditor is (at least partly) responsible. Yet, it would be claimed, the act or practice of deception was justified. In this way, the auditor takes responsibility for what has happened; but he should not be *blamed*, since there are good reasons for allowing the deception to occur.

These forms of arguments are schematized as follows:

A   Deception did not occur, or cannot be proven to occur.
     Therefore, responsibility for deception is a moot issue.
     Therefore, the auditor is not subject to blame.

B   Deception did occur.
     However, the auditor is not responsible for the deception.
     Therefore, the auditor is not subject to blame.

C   Deception did occur.
     The auditor and client share responsibility for the deception.
     However, the deception is justified or defensible.
     Therefore, the auditor is not subject to blame.

The remaining possibility assigns blame for deception to auditors:

D   Deception did occur.
     The auditor and client share responsibility for the deception.
     The deception is not justified or defensible.
     Therefore, the auditor is subject to blame.

The first three forms of argument in defense of auditors are in order of decreasing strength (from the auditor's point of view). By taking the "high ground", the first type shifts the burden of proof of blame furthest away from the auditor. Furthermore, the job of defending the auditor is easiest, in the sense that the other types require a more complex analysis. The second requires a theory about the conditions under which an auditor is or is not responsible for the actions of others. The third presupposes a theory about the justifiability of deception. The basic relationship between responsibility and blame is also revealed: blame presupposes responsibility, but responsibility does not imply blame. These defenses will be examined in turn.

A Deception cannot be proven

If a financial statement either is not or cannot be proven to be deceptive, a claim that the author is responsible for deception will not succeed. Several arguments of this type may be proposed.

One might claim that the specific financial statements in question are not really deceptive, although they may *exaggerate* (either overstate or understate) some important aspect of the company's financial position or changes in financial position. The burden of proof is important here, because exaggeration might be excused on the ground that a clear line between truthfulness and deception cannot be drawn. Exaggeration is somewhere in between; whether an act of exaggeration is deceptive may be anything but clear.

It is generally accepted that financial statement figures are at best finitely accurate. Therefore, exaggeration is possible when estimates of any sort are required, e.g., of uncollectible accounts, unsalable merchandise, or the useful life and salvage value of plant and equipment. Or one might attempt to defend a specific act of exaggeration on the ground that the estimate is subject to so much uncertainty that one number is "as good as" another, in the sense that using one number rather than the other would not be likely to cause a reader of the resulting financial statements to act differently.

In response to this, it may be agreed that there are "high" estimates and "low" estimates.[13] This does not imply, however, that a firm is free to adopt a practice of consistently using estimates or accounting principles which produce the highest of a range of possible income figures (e.g., the Westec case (Reiling and Taussig 1970)). The fact that the distinction between deception and nondeception is difficult to make in a specific instance does not relieve the auditor from having to decide whether a financial statement is deceptive. If it turns out that a statement is deceptive, then arguments of this type are not sufficient to exonerate the auditors.

The argument may be made in a stronger form, i.e., that financial statements as presently constructed are meaningless, or nearly so. For example, it may be claimed that the historical cost basis of accounting yields statements having no economic referent, and thus do not constitute measurements of anything. Therefore, it might be claimed, the responsibility of auditors for managerial deception is not an issue. For if a statement is sufficiently vague we may be unable to determine whether it is deceptive (Isenberg 1973, p. 25).

It needs to be said, of course, that the meaningfulness of some presently mandated income statement and balance sheet items is unclear. The "truth" of such items as goodwill, book value of operational assets, and retained earnings, is problematic, if for no other reason than because we may have little understanding of what the numbers are supposed to represent. At the same time, other items are pretty clearly true or false. Cash on hand, gross accounts receivable, current monetary liabilities, and many revenues and expenses are examples in which the amount of cash which has or will change hands (current cash equivalent) is determinable to a high degree of precision. The existence of a large amount of uncertainty for other financial statement items makes the auditor's job more difficult, insofar as attesting to all and only nondeceptive financial statements is concerned. However, that does not leave the field clear.

The perspective of the deceived is important in evaluating these claims, because of the importance of intention. In the case of a particular act or practice, one needs to know something about the receiver of the information, and what he may be presumed to know. The Continental Vending case revolved around the question of whether a financial statement *can be* deceptive if it is based on the use of GAAP, and whether the auditor obeyed Generally Accepted Auditing Standards. The Court's answer to the first question was yes. It may be that vagueness is an inescapable consequence of uncertainty regarding the use of financial information by a diverse group of readers. However, controversy concerning the exact meaning and *truth* of financial statements does not relieve auditors and firms from the responsibility to be *truthful*. As Bok (1978, p. 13) says, "As dupes we know what as liars we tend to blur — that information can be more or less adequate; and that truthfulness can be required even where full 'truth' is out of reach." Even vague statements, for which we have no clear meaning, can be deceptive.

Acting in accordance with Generally Accepted Auditing Standards (GAAS) includes the requirement that the financial statements be prepared in accordance with GAAP. GAAP is a *guide* to the auditor in making decisions; but one should not expect it to be a sufficient guide, since the principles do not refer to the relevant facts of individual cases.[14] Instead, in light of those facts — which may include information about management's intentions regarding deception — the auditor must make a judgment as to the appropriate application of GAAP in the specific situation. The general criterion is whether readers of financial statements are likely to be misled by a particular application of GAAP. Mere obedience to GAAP disregards the perspective of the deceived.

B Auditors are not responsible for deception

The second type of defense against blame is that while deception did occur, the auditor is not responsible for it, and therefore not blameworthy.

It might be claimed that, while it may appear *prima facie* true, auditors are not really a party to the publication of deceptive financial statements *via* their audit involvement. Once one distinguishes between the production of financial statements by the client, and the audit report, it is clear, according to this view, that management is completely responsible for any deception resulting from the publication of financial statements. Auditors are responsible only for the proper (i.e., in accordance with GAAS) conduct of the audit and the resulting audit report, and thus are not responsible for deceptive financial statements.[15]

Whatever the value in other contexts of the traditional distinction between these tasks and responsibilities, it is an artificial one in the present context. To see this, one need only appeal again to the perspective of the deceived. For the auditor's report is appended to the financial statements, and

reports something about them. They are thus, from the reader's point of view, intimately related. Since the perspective of the deceived should be the central concern of the auditors, the auditor's proper role is to reduce the risk that shareholders will indeed be deceived by management's application of GAAP. If readers are deceived, then the auditors are to some degree responsible — though they are not *ipso facto* to be blamed for it.

The major responsibility for deception does fall on management. The amount of responsibility of auditors depends on the degree to which they participate with, or acquiesce to, management in the production of financial statements. For example, if the public accounting firm were to perform a sizable amount of management advisory services for the client, then it could be actively involved in the design of the financial reporting system, including the choice of accounting methods, and so share responsibility for deceptive results. Indeed, if the auditors were to actually help in the process of producing deceptive information (as in the Stirling Homex case described above), then they may have a large degree of responsibility. Thus, the responsibility of the auditor for deceptive financial statements is a matter of degree. The crucial factor in determining the degree of responsibility in specific cases is the importance of the auditor in the "causal chain" whose outcome is deception of the readers of the financial statements.

Implicit here as a criterion of responsibility is the degree to which the auditor was aware, or should have been aware, that management intended to deceive the readers of its financial statements. This may range from active involvement of auditors in criminal conspiracy, such as apparently occurred in the Equity Funding case (Briloff 1976, pp. 339-341), down to cases in which an auditor's best efforts fail to prevent or detect deception — cases where the auditor is as much a dupe as the reader. In the middle ground is an area in which it would be said that the auditors were responsible to some degree, just because of their presence in the causal chain. They would be (partially) responsible even though they themselves had no intention of deceiving, because they allowed someone else to deceive, perhaps through negligence, weakness, or chance.

Another possible way of defending an auditor from responsibility for deceptive financial statements would be to claim that he was powerless to prevent the deceptive acts. In other words, the auditor himself would have been coerced, and in that sense, would have been an unwilling participant in the causal chain. Auditors are technically and legally independent contractors, providing a service to their clients (i.e., management). However, they are not in reality equally and totally independent (economically) of their clients.[16]

It might seem an attractive way out to excuse the auditor in such a situation, on the grounds that he is merely a passive instrument of his client. The auditor would be regarded as a neutral third party, and therefore free of responsibility. Such a view would allow shifting blame completely onto the client, in whose interest he acts, for both deception of financial statement readers and coercion of the auditor.

Sterling (1973) and Goldman and Barlev (1974) have argued that a major problem for auditors is their lack of power *vis-à-vis* management, with the attendant challenge to their independence. The importance of this economic relationship between auditors and clients, which forms the center of their arguments, is not to be minimized in considering the responsibilities of auditors. We should not rely on abstract notions of professional engagements, but include as a part of the analysis the realities of the economic pressures on auditors. That is, if we agree that clients are in at least a potentially coercive position with respect to their auditors, then we must also recognize that any exercise of coercive power may affect the degree of responsibility assigned to auditors for deceptive financial statements. It may be only an irrelevant abstraction of economic ideology to say that the auditor is free to withdraw from the engagement. Thus, the auditor's situation cannot be judged simply in terms of an analysis of the costs and benefits of retaining the client. Interestingly, the proposed solution of both Sterling, and Goldman and Barlev is to redress the balance by giving auditors more power over their clients.

In addition to the potentially coercive power of the economic relationship, there is the possibility of another means of coercion of auditors, i.e., coercion through deception. To the extent that an auditor is himself deceived by the client in the course of performing an audit, the client coerced him. The effect of this is to decrease the auditor's ability to act in accordance with his ethical responsibilities, which are to the readers. Because he will have been prevented from acting in the readers' interest, his responsibility for deception would be decreased.

A defense based on coercion would relieve an auditor of responsibility for deception. The Principle of Veracity implies that the auditor as well as the reader have a *prima facie* right to nondeceptive information. The auditor is obligated to act in the interest of external financial statement readers, and to avoid being deceived.[17] Suppose the auditor acts in their interests by attempting to avoid being deceived, but is nevertheless deceived. Then, to some extent, the auditor is relieved of blame for management's deception. Likewise, if the auditor was coerced *via* the economic relationship, he would be excused from blame for deception.

This excuse is a two-edged sword, however, because it simultaneously leaves the auditor subject to blame for subordinating his judgment to others. That is, he could be blamed for a failure to be independent, instead. The obligation to be independent is an important part of codes of ethics for auditors. The foregoing analysis supports that view. As currently codified in codes of ethics, independence (or the appearance of independence) is questionable if certain economic or family relationships exist between auditor and client. But the concept of independence is a good deal more complex than this, for it is possible that an auditor should have known about a deceptive act, but did not know about it because of an inability to make a disinterested judgment as a neutral third party. For example, through a sympathetic, personal relationship, an auditor could deceive himself into believing that management does not have questionable intentions. Thus, the concepts of self-deception and independence are closely interwoven, quite apart from the possible exercise of economic power.

C   Deception is justified

The last type of defense which might be offered consists of justifications *per se*, i.e., reasons why deception is the best, or at least an acceptable, course of action.[18]

One type of possible defense is, somewhat paradoxically, deception for the sake of the truth. Included here would be manipulations or misstatements of the facts in order to get a "truer picture." A possible example is the use of LIFO inventory valuation in periods of increasing prices in order to give a more realistic measurement of the current cost of goods sold, under the constraint of historical cost valuation of assets. As with other forms of deception, whether this is justifiable is a complicated question.

First, one must consider whether anyone is likely to be misled by this. If not, then no explanation or justification is needed. Assuming that such a practice is deceptive (perhaps because readers do not understand the effect of LIFO on the balance sheet), a second issue is whether there is a truthful and feasible alternative. In order to answer this, a clear concept of what cost of goods sold and inventory values are supposed to represent would have to be provided. The reason for this is that it is necessary to determine the exact nature of the deception, if any. Third, the level of understanding [among] financial statement readers would have to be taken into account.

Another type of defense is the claim that an act of deception could actually produce benefits. An example of this is the practice of mutually beneficial deception. However, examples of this are hard to devise. In the case of financial accounting and reporting, one might argue that intentional deception in the securities markets is justifiable because of the benefits produced. If this position could be sustained, then auditors might not be subject to blame, whether or not they were aware of management's intentions and actions.

It is true that securities transactions are voluntary, in the sense that an investor or potential investor freely enters the securities market in the first place. In light of this voluntariness, it might be claimed, investors have implicitly consented to

whatever formal and informal standards of financial reporting and auditing prevail at the time, both for specific firms and in general. The operative principle in the market would be "Let the Buyer Beware."

Those who would excuse deception as a general practice in external reporting are caught in a dilemma: either financial reports are not relied upon and therefore not (successfully) deceptive; or they are deceptive, but not justifiably so. The problem with this argument is that the mere fact that an investor purchases shares of a particular business does not thereby imply consent to be deceived. Two possible situations in the securities market need to be distinguished. Suppose first that relatively few corporations issue deceptive financial statements. Then investors can hardly be said to have consented to deception by an individual firm, since that firm has not adhered to the Principle of Publicity, by asking investors for their consent. Indeed, the strength of the incentive for an individual firm to engage in deceptive practices is inversely related to the number (or proportion) of firms which report truthfully. For, as more firms report truthfully, trust in the truthfulness (reliability) of financial statements in general is enhanced. A firm whose deception goes undetected is then a "free rider" in the securities market, once it is seen that the aggregate level of quality of information of all firms is a public good. The deceptive firm benefits from its actions, at the expense of both investors and truthful firms. While managers thus have an incentive to practice deception, the Principle of Publicity implies that it is not morally justified. Therefore, auditors cannot escape blame because of the voluntary nature of securities transactions.

It is also possible that firms are alike with regard to the truthfulness of their financial statements, i.e., that there are no free-riding firms.[19] Uniformity of information quality is consistent with any (aggregate) level of quality, and also with any perceived level of quality. Suppose first that a preponderance of investors do not have much faith in the truthfulness of financial statements in general, and therefore do not rely on them to any appreciable extent. Then, to that extent, investors would not be deceived by them. Even if management had intended to deceive the readers of their statements, they would not have succeeded. Therefore, the auditor's actions do not need to be justified; the justification of unsuccessful deception is not practically important. Indeed, the rationale for attempting to deceive investors who do not depend on financial statements in the first place, is not obvious. However, it may still matter whether investors consented to this state of affairs. Evidence that they do not rely much on financial reports as they currently exist does not imply that they would not rely on nondeceptive reports, i.e., reports of higher quality.

Suppose instead that investors generally do have faith in the truthfulness of, and rely on, financial statements. If they are in fact truthful, there is of course no problem of justification. However, if they are not truthful (or to the degree they are not), deception is successful, and must be justified. The Principle of Publicity again obviates the possibility of consent. Because of the nature of the case, seeking the consent of investors would give the game away, leaving firms without an incentive to deceive investors.

A third category of justifiable deception is deception in the interest of fairness, i.e., lies to promote justice or to prevent injustice. If justifiable, deception or acquiescence to it in order to protect confidentiality, e.g., between auditor and client, would fall under this rubric. This might appear to provide a defense for an auditor's participation or acquiescence in deception, since it would obligate him to remain silent, apparently without qualification. Auditors would be partly responsible for deception, through their silence. However, they would not be blamed for deception, because they would have been acting justifiably.

The existence of such an obligation to their clients only shows that auditors are faced with conflicting responsibilities: to the client, on the one hand, and to the readers of financial statements and auditors' reports, on the other. Silence would be justified only if either there were no conflicting responsibilities, or if the client's right to silence has priority over readers' rights. However the clear implication of the AICPA Code of Ethics is that the outsiders' interests are paramount. To remove blame from auditors using this argument requires showing either that this principle should be rejected, or that the deception itself, through silence, is justifiable. The former is unlikely, since, as noted above, the cornerstone principle of independence implies that the interest of some outside party takes priority over the interests of the client. The latter requires showing that silence (and therefore deception) is in the interests of financial statement readers.[20]

THE TREATMENT OF DECEPTION IN CODES OF ETHICS

Rules of conduct

In order to evaluate the rules of conduct governing auditors with regard to deceptive financial statements, it will be useful first to clarify the nature and role of such rules. If asked, most people will express an opinion on ethical issues: often, this will be a relatively simple and absolute position, and usually without any justification. The rules of conduct contained in codes of professional ethics are codifications of such opinions. For example, Rule 213 of the Rules of Professional Conduct of the ICAO states that:

> A member or student shall not knowingly lend himself, his name or his services to any unlawful activity.

This rule appears to be unexceptionable, since it only forbids Institute members (including auditors) from performing acts which they should not do anyway, i.e., be a party to unlawful acts. Anyone who violates this rule is subject to blame for his actions, in addition to any legal and professional sanctions which may be imposed.

Rules of conduct are intended to establish socially desirable practices on the part of Institute members. Generally, they do so by constraining members to a limited range of actions, and thereby forbidding behavior which some individual members may find to be in their own personal interest.

Rules of conduct are known as practice rules (Rawls 1971), because they *define* a practice (e.g., acting in accordance with the law) rather than describe it. Practice rules have two common characteristics (Diggs 1971). First, they provide guides to auditors to aid them in making decisions, by defining what is acceptable behavior. Second, they provide standards for evaluating the "correctness" of behavior. Merely stating a rule of conduct will not, of course, cause the complete elimination of unacceptable behavior. Nevertheless, both characteristics of practice rules encourage desirable behavior because a rule is used as "a *conventional* (symbolic) incentive to action (. . . a kind of linguistic prod)" (Black 1962, p. 122). If nothing else, a rule provides a basis for possible sanctions against transgressors.

Evaluation of rules governing deception

Rule 213 quoted above is an example of a simple rule regarding a straightforward relationship. In general, however, ethical issues are more complicated than that. For one thing, the scope of a rule (i.e., what it applies to) may be subject to uncertainty. Second, even within the scope of a rule, there may be difficult problems of interpretation and judgment. Consider rule 102 of the AICPA Code:

> A member shall not knowingly misrepresent facts, and when engaged in the practice of public accounting . . . shall not subordinate his judgment to others.

The first part of the rule suggests that members may be excused from blame for misrepresentation if it is "unknowing." But how is one to determine whether a statement is a misrepresentation or a "nonmisrepresentation"? Moreover, how is one to distinguish knowing from unknowing misrepresentation?

Indeed, the problem is even more complicated than this. The ICAO analog to the first part of this rule extends auditors' responsibilities in two ways. Rule 205 states that:

> A member or student shall not
>
> (1) sign or associate himself with any letter, report, statement, representation, or financial statement which he knows, or should know, is false or misleading, whether or not the association is subject to a disclaimer of responsibility, nor
>
> (2) make any oral report, statement or representation which he knows, or should know, is false or misleading.

According to this rule, a member is responsible for deceptive statements made by others (their clients). Furthermore, the fact that misrepresentation is unknowing (on the part of the auditor) is not sufficient to escape blame. If the auditor did not know, but *should have known*, he is still responsible. Deciding whether an auditor should have known something is problematic, and inevitably based on hindsight. Notwithstanding such difficulties, the AICPA rule is too narrow, since it would excuse auditors who unknowingly had a causal role in management actions, even if they should have been able to detect it. The ICAO rule corresponds more closely to the analysis in the third section. The SEC holds auditors to a similar standard, i.e., that unknowing association with misrepresentations is not sufficient to escape blame. While recognizing that deliberate deception of the auditor by the client is a factor in determining the responsibility of auditors, the SEC stated the following about the auditors in the Westec case:

> Respondents have stressed throughout this proceeding that they were the victims of management's fraud and deception. That they were deliberately deceived and that material information was kept from them is clear. But such deception did not relieve them of their responsibility to perform audits in conformity with generally accepted auditing standards. Their failure to fulfill that obligation resulted in their certification of financial statements which were materially false and misleading. [ASR No. 248].

With respect to the second part of AICPA Rule 102, we need to know how to determine whether an auditor has subordinated his judgment to others.

This is problematic because there may be honest differences of opinion in the application of GAAP. Many financial accounting and reporting standards are open to interpretation, because they have a "gray area" such that a unique course of action cannot be conclusively established. If auditor and client agree that there are two defensible positions on an accounting and reporting issue, has the auditor subordinated his judgment if he makes an unqualified report about financial statements employing GAAP with which he disagrees? In the case of knowing misrepresentation, there are at least actions (or the lack of action) taken by the auditor about which to form a judgment. But subordination of judgment is a much more amorphous thing to evaluate. Furthermore, given the complex relationship of public accountant and client, subordination (when it occurs) is undoubtedly a matter of degree. Indeed, its complete absence may be more than we can realistically expect of auditors. If so, where (and how) do we draw the line between acceptable and unacceptable behavior?

ICAO Rule 205 and AICPA Rule 102 concern acts of *commission* by auditors. Rule 205.1 of the ICAO Code explicitly bans acts of *omission* as well, such as failure to qualify or disclaim an opinion:

> In expressing an opinion on financial statements examined by him, a member shall not
> (1) fail to reveal any material fact known to him which is not disclosed in the financial statements, the omission of which renders the financial statements misleading, nor
> (2) fail to report any material mis-statement known to him to be contained in the financial statements.

The AICPA code is less clear. Rule 102, discussed above, is silent on acts of omission. Rule 301, however, commands silence:

> A member shall not disclose any confidential information obtained in the course of a professional engagement except with the consent of the client.

The auditor's obligation is not absolute.[21] However, an ethics ruling reveals that the obligation to silence is intended to have a wide scope:

Rule 301 is not intended to help an unscrupulous client cover up illegal acts or otherwise hide information by changing CPA's. If the member is contacted by the successor, he should, at a minimum, suggest that the successor ask the client to permit the member to discuss all matters freely with the successor. (Sec. 391.005)

The notion that an auditor should obtain permission from an unscrupulous client, before discussing (even on a confidential basis) deceptive (or any other) actions of the client, with a second involved auditor is difficult to defend in light of the analysis above. The inadequacy of this ruling is also revealed by noting that the successor auditor is bound to confidentiality with regard both to public disclosures and, should he resign in turn without permission for free discussion, to his successor. Adherence to the rules could cause an unbroken chain of fired auditors.[22]

In summary, the ICAO code is a better codification of the obligations to the readers of financial statements, because it requires more of Institute members in acting from the perspective of the deceived.[23]

SUMMARY AND CONCLUSION

Managers are responsible and subject to blame for deceptive financial statements which they provide to others. This paper provides an analysis of whether and to what degree auditors are also responsible and subject to blame. Auditors may share responsibility for deception in some circumstances, without necessarily being subject to blame for it. They are blameworthy in such cases only if the deception is not justifiable.

The concept of deception was analyzed, and the general principles for evaluating deception were presented. In addition to the perspective of the deceived, they are the nonneutrality of deception, and the Principle of Publicity. Together, they imply that deception is *prima facie* improper because of its effects on the readers of financial statements, and that it needs to be justified publicly from the readers' point of view.

A variety of possible arguments for defending an auditor from blame for managerial deception, categorized into three basic types, were examined. It is concluded that an auditor is not responsible, and therefore not subject to blame, only to the extent that he himself has been deceived (or coerced in some other way) by management. Even this defense is not air tight, however, since the auditor is still responsible to the degree that he *should have* known about management's deceptive intentions and actions. The inescapable vagueness attached to the notion of what they "should have known" reveals once again that auditors cannot complacently follow "the letter of the law" (as stated in a set of rules and interpretations), if they wish to act in an ethically appropriate manner. The concept of independence is also shown to be crucially important in evaluating the actions of auditors *vis-à-vis*

their clients. These observations are similar in spirit to those made by Kirk (1984), that detailed ethical and accounting standards have been written largely because of the failure, partly through client pressure, of auditors to act ethically.

The provisions of two codes of ethics were evaluated on the basis of the analysis. Rules of conduct contained in those codes are supposed to define a level of minimally acceptable behavior. The AICPA code is shown to set the minimum too low, while the ICAO code (and Securities and Exchange Commission standards) set an appropriate standard of behavior. This implies that the AICPA should consider tightening its rules, in line with the results provided here.*

*The comments of H. Falk and A.W. Richardson and two reviewers of this Journal are greatly appreciated.

ENDNOTES

1. The analysis is strictly limited to the audit activities of public accountants. Public accountants may also provide management consulting, tax and recordkeeping services. Their responsibilities with regard to nonauditing services and, particularly, any possible conflict between them and their role as auditor, are beyond the scope of this paper.

2. Legal censure, such as the sanctions found in legal proceedings and in the action (based on a code of ethics) of professional organizations, is also beyond the scope of this paper. Many of the issues addressed have legal aspects, but legal answers are not of primary concern here. While some legal cases are addressed below, it is to show that the law itself observes certain relevant ethical principles.

3. Such codes generally contain a set of fundamental principles defining the ethical responsibilities of auditors, a set of rules of conduct defining the standards of "minimally acceptable" professional behavior, and a set of interpretations which are intended to provide operational guidelines as to the meaning of the rules.

4. In Canada, each Province's Institute has its own Code of Ethics. Ontario's Code is chosen here because it is similar to the other codes, and because it governs the activities of more accountants than the other Provincial Codes.

5. The portion on research costs of section 3450 of the CICA Handbook (of the Canadian Institute of Chartered Accountants) and Financial Accounting Statement No. 2 on research and development costs (of the Financial Accounting Standards Board) are excellent examples.

6. An example of this form of cutoff is the guideline that ownership of more than 20-25% of another firm's shares outstanding provides reasonable assurance that the investor exerts significant influence on the firm's actions. Suppose Company A owns 19.9% of the shares of Company B, and that (on economic grounds) the equity method is the better way of accounting for the investment. Company A might use the cost method on the grounds that GAAP does not require that the equity method be used.

7. In the case of Northern States Power Company, the effect on income in 1935 was $5 million. Although Northern States disclosed its accounting practices, the question arises whether its financial statements may have been misleading (See Chatov 1975, pp. 107-109).

8. Land sales companies often "front ended" revenues on installment sales by recognizing the full purchase price at the date a sales contract was signed, even if substantial development work was yet to be performed. Sales revenue was also overstated by applying a nominal interest rate to the installments. The provision for uncollectible notes was understated, in view of the fact that down payments were frequently small, no credit investigation of the buyer was performed, and the company retained title to the land until payment was complete (Briloff 1970). See SEC, ASR No. 95 for more examples. Other frauds involved income derived from non-arms-length transactions (Republic National Life Insurance Company and the Penn Central Company), and accelerated recognition of income using percentage-of-completion accounting via overstating costs incurred (Stirling Homex) (SEC, ASR No. 173).

9. An important instance of this is that one may (unintentionally, but successfully) deceive oneself, e.g., into thinking one's lies (intentional deceptions) are harmless.

10. Even in such an intuitively clear case as the above, we may still lack a good reason for claiming that deception is acceptable. For one thing, the above justification does not explain why violence is sometimes acceptable; perhaps, even if acceptable in some general sense, some forms of violence may yet be unacceptable. The problem is to decide which forms are acceptable, and why they are.

11. Note the similarity between this ethical concept and the legal concept of the reasonable, prudent person.

12. An alternative approach would be to ignore the consequences of acts or practices, and claim instead that the act or practice in question is right or wrong, regardless of the consequences. Consequences simply do not count in moral evaluation, in this view. Instead, appeal to a framework of ethical principles concerning perhaps the rightness or wrongness of acts and practices, and concerning the justice of given social relations, underlies such evaluations. Kant's ethical theory, and position on lying in particular, is an excellent example of this, the deontological

approach. Deontologists make the important point that sometimes the welfare of one group or individual cannot be simply traded off for that of another. In the case of financial reporting, the Principle of Veracity is a way of saying that stockholders have a *prima facie* right to truthful financial information. Thus, a deontologist might hold that the rules of conduct examined in Section 5 below follow directly from a conception of individual rights, including a right not to be deceived. A difficulty with the deontological approach is how to argue that specific rights exist, without appealing in any way to the consequences of alternative assignments of rights. It may be that stockholders have a right to truthful financial information; but how could one argue that such rights exist, except by consequentialist considerations? (Scanlon 1978).

13. Indeed, the principle of conservatism which is at the heart of conventional accounting, demands systematic exaggeration.

14. This is particularly true of the *CICA Handbook*, which emphasizes more than the Financial Standards Board the importance of professional judgment by the auditor.

15. This position is similar to legal defenses, sometimes used by auditors, that the auditor's actions accorded with GAAS. An example is *Herzfeld* v. *Laventhol, Krekstein, Horwath & Horwath*. The auditor issued a qualified opinion, based on the uncertain collectibility of receivables. The qualification was sufficient evidence for the judge to conclude that there was an intention to mislead. A similar argument was used in the Continental Vending case. In *Hochfelder* v. *Ernst & Ernst*, the AICPA argued successfully in an *amicus curiae* brief that, even if the auditor's actions were not in accordance with GAAS, civil liability requires knowledge that the client's conduct was fraudulent. [See Olson (1982) pp. 16-22].

16. This defense may be important regarding the major clients of an accounting firm.

17. This is implied by the concept of independence. The concept only makes sense if there is some third party in whose interest the auditor is supposed to be acting.

18. The defense examined just above, powerlessness, consists of explanations why an act or practice of deception has in fact taken place, rather than a justification of deception. That is, an explanation is a characterization of what actually moved someone

to act in the way he did (Baier 1966, pp. 40-48). In providing reasons why deception is to be allowed, a justification presumes (as does an explanation) that deception did or will take place. Unlike them, though, a justification claims that even though an auditor is partially responsible, he is still not blameworthy.

19. This situation could occur through auditing, for example. At the same time, insofar as audits do increase investors' general faith in financial statements, the incentive to free ride is all the stronger.

20. The problem of determining what is in the interest of outsiders is complex. For one must also look beyond the immediate circumstances of specific cases. For example, one might try to show that disclosure of an illegal payment to officials of a foreign country is unnecessary because the size of the payment is immaterial, and because public disclosure of the payments would adversely affect the firms' stockholders. However, as events in the United States in the last few years have demonstrated, this is too narrow a view. For one thing, it fails to take into account the possible major long-run financial effects (e.g., lost sales, and lost markets) of such seemingly minor acts on the firm. Second, it fails to take into account the effects of deceptive reporting practices on the institution of financial reporting — i.e., the practice of financial reporting in general. Taken in isolation as individual acts, one might argue for nondisclosure and silence by the auditor. However its justifiability, as part of a general practice, is quite another matter.

21. For example, AICPA rules 202 and 203, regarding conformity to Generally Accepted Auditing Standards and Generally Accepted Accounting Principles respectively, take precedence. However, these rules do not explicitly consider this issue.

22. The SEC again holds auditors to a higher standard. "When one auditor succeeds another, . . . it is important that the successor obtain access to and carefully review the results of the predecessor's work. . . . If a client refuses to permit such discussions [with the predecessor], such a denial should constitute a reason for rejecting the engagement" (ASR No. 153). Clearly, the predecessor's cooperation is necessary in order for the successor to act as he ought.

23. This is reinforced by part 17 of Council Interpretation CI 201: ". . . the auditor of a company is appointed to represent the shareholders and has a duty to them, he should never lightly resign his appointment before reporting and should not resign at all before reporting if he has reason to suspect that his resignation is required by reason of any sharp practice, impropriety or concealment, which it is his duty to report upon." Furthermore, if there is a change of auditors, the successor is supposed to inquire of his predecessor whether there are any circumstances about which he should know; the successor is supposed to respond if such circumstances exist (although the nature of the response may be colored by a need for confidentiality) (Council Interpretation CI 302, part 2). Council Interpretations are issued to provide information and guidance for application of the Rules of Professional Conduct.

REFERENCES

American Institute of Certified Public Accountants (AICPA) "Code of Professional Ethics". In *AICPA Professional Standards, Vol. 2*. (Commerce Clearing House: Chicago).

Baier, K. *From a Moral Point of View*. (Harper & Row: New York 1966).

Black, M. "The Analysis of Rules." In M. Black, *Models and Metaphors* (Cornell University Press: Ithaca, NY 1962) pp. 95-139.

Bok, S. *Lying: Moral Choice in Public and Private Life* (Pantheon: New York 1978).

Briloff, A. "Castles of Sand?" *Barron's National Business and Financial Weekly*. (Feb. 2, 1970).

————. *More Debits than Credits*. (Harper & Row: New York 1976).

Canadian Institute of Chartered Accountants. *CICA Handbook*. (Canadian Institute of Chartered Accountants: Toronto).

Chatov, R. *Corporate Financial Reporting*. (The Free Press: New York 1975).

Diggs, B.J. "Rules and Utilitarianism." *American Philosophical Quarterly* (1964) pp. 32-44. Reprinted in S.

Gorovitz, ed. *Mill: Utilitarianism.* (Bobbs-Merrill: Indianapolis 1971) pp. 306-323.

Goldman, A. and B. Barlev "Auditor-Firm Conflicts of Interest." *The Accounting Review* (October 1974) pp. 707-718.

Hawkins, D. "Financial Accounting, The Standards Board and Economic Development." Emanuel Saxe Distinguished Lectures in Accounting. (Baruch College, City University of New York, 1975).

Institute of Chartered Accountants of Ontario *Members Handbook.* (Institute of Chartered Accountants of Ontario: Toronto).

Isenberg, A. "Deontology and the Ethics of Lying." *Philosophy and Phenomenological Research* (1964) pp. 463-480. Reprinted in W. Callaghan et al., eds. *Aesthetics and the Theory of Criticism: Selected Essays of Arnold Isenberg.* (University of Chicago Press: Chicago 1973) pp. 245-264.

Kant, I. "On A Supposed Right to Tell a Lie from Altruistic Motives." in L.W. Beck (ed. and trans.), *Critique of Practical Reason and Other Writings in Moral Philosophy* (University of Chicago Press: Chicago 1949) pp. 346-350. Reprinted in Bok (1978) pp. 285-290.

Kirk, D.J. "Enhancing Professionalism in Financial Reporting." *FASB Status Report* (June 28, 1984) pp. 4-8.

Leonard, H.S. *Principles of Reasoning,* 2nd ed. (Dover: New York 1967).

Liggio, C.D. "The Accountant's Legal Environment for the Next Decade." In R. Sterling, (ed.) *Institutional Issues in Public Accounting.* (Scholars Book Co.: Houston 1974) pp. 99-121.

Olson, W.E. *The Accounting Profession Years of Trial: 1969-1980.* (American Institute of Certified Public Accountants: New York 1982).

Rawls, J. *A Theory of Justice.* (Harvard University Press: Cambridge 1971).

Reiling, H.B., and R.A. Taussig "Recent Liability Cases — Implications for Accountants." *The Journal of Accountancy* (March 1970) pp. 39-53.

Scalon, T.S. "Rights, Goals and Fairness." In S. Hampshire (ed.) *Public & Private Morality.* (Cambridge University Press: Cambridge 1978) pp. 93-111.

Securities and Exchange Commission. *Accounting Series Releases and Staff Accounting Bulletins.* (Commerce Clearing House: Chicago).

Sterling, R. "Accounting Power." *The Journal of Accountancy* (January 1973) pp. 61-67.

Williams, H.M., Quoted in *The Week in Review*, April 25, 1980 (Deloitte Haskins & Sells).

SUGGESTED FURTHER READINGS

BAUM, ROBERT and FLORES ALBERT (eds.). *Ethical Problems in Engineering.* Troy, N.Y.: Center for the Study of the Human Dimensions of Science and Technology, Rensselaer Polytechnic Institute, 1978.

BOK, SISSELA. "Whistleblowing and Professional Responsibility," in T. Beauchamp and N. Bowie (eds.). *Ethical Theory and Business* (2nd ed.). Englewood Cliffs, N.J.: Prentice-Hall, Inc., 1983.

BAYLES, MICHAEL. "A Problem of Clean Hands: Refusal to Provide Professional Services." *Social Theory and Practice* 5 (1979).

——————— . *Professional Ethics.* Belmont, Ca.: Wadsworth Publishing Co., 1981.

FREEDMAN, BENJAMIN. "A Meta-Ethics for Professional Morality." *Ethics* 89 (1978).

GOLDMAN, ALAN. *The Moral Foundations of Professional Ethics.* Totowa, N.J.: Rowman and Littlefield, 1980.

14

Regulation, Deregulation, Self-Regulation: The Case of Engineers in Ontario[1]

J.T. STEVENSON

I. INTRODUCTION

For some thirty years or more the conventional wisdom in Western economics and politics has been in favour of a mixed regime — a regime in which there is a public and a private sector; in which there is regulation *of* the economy through fiscal and monetary policy and regulation *in* the economy through a host of laws and regulatory agencies; in which the theory of production is divorced from the theory of distribution, allowing for resource allocation according to neo-classical principles and income redistribution according to social democratic principles. It has been the received view that unregulated free enterprise does not work well in a complex modern society: it fails on the production side due to cyclical fluctuations causing loss of production, and on the distribution side due to unjust distributions of wealth and power. One *locus classicus* for this 'liberal' view is, of course, John Rawl's *A Theory of Justice* in which a contractarian political philosophy, a maximim theory of distributive justice and the conventional, roughly Keynesian, eco-

nomic wisdom are woven together into a mixed regime in which wealth, justice and freedom are to be realized.

The contemporary liberal view and its embodiments have been under attack from ideologies of both left and right. The body politic is suffering from a socialistic malaise, says the right, and must be doctored with various nostrums from their favourite alchemist's shop — the magic elixir of free enterprise, perhaps with a tincture of monetarism, a soupçon of supply-side economics, and massive deregulations within the economy. Yes, he is sick, say some on the left, but must submit to a stern regimen of diet and exercise according to some left-wing health plan for a regulated life. Both extremes, however, seem to be in accord on a few things: we must all bow before the juggernaut of the technological imperative exemplified in the current microelectronic revolution; we must achieve security by playing the decision theorist's game of 'chicken' with ever-increasing numbers of weapons of mass destruction; we may and must make, by stealth or

From *Journal of Business Ethics* **4** (1985) 253–267. © 1985 by D. Reidel Publishing Company. Reprinted by permission.

force, the people of the world accept the theory of some "mad academic scribbler," whether it be Friedman or Marx.[2]

In this paper I focus on the question of regulation *within* an economy, more particularly on the regulation of the professions, and more particularly still on the regulation of engineers in Ontario. I hope in this way to do two things: to consider some matters of general and theoretical interest, on the one hand, and to subject the discussion to the hard discipline of empirical reality, on the other. In Section II I suggest that engineering is a strategic profession in discussions of professional regulation. In Section III I present, briefly, some salient features of the current regulatory regime for engineers in Ontario and the reasons why it came under an intensive theoretical and practical scrutiny. There follows an analytical and critical discussion of the Staff Study of the Professional Organizations Committee (hereafter referred to as POC Staff), comprising sections IV through VI. The discussion is focused on the policy recommendations, and the rationale therefor, of an industrial exemption provision for professional engineers. The final section, VIII Coda, recounts the dénouement of the POC inquiry and current status of the recommendations as contained in the Report of the Professional Organizations Committee (hereafter POC Report). It is hoped that this 'case study' will have both general philosophical import and particular practical significance.

II. ENGINEERING: A STRATEGIC OCCUPATION

Western culture is outstandingly promethean: we have wrested fire from the gods; we think we have mastered nature and have claimed dominion over it. The engineer has been one of our chief agents in this conquest. Now that we have come to regard scientists as our society's high priests, we may forget that it was engineers — a group evolving out of the class of artisans, craftsmen, mechanics and military men — who laid the foundations of the industrial revolution. They were the ones who made practical the unleashing of new forms of energy; who created

mass production; who made the mountains plain; who, by building ships, flinging railroads across continents, inventing aircraft, the telegraph, and so on, enabled us to transform a globe of villages into a global village; and who are now taking us, if only vicariously, into interplanetary space. Moreover, it was largely engineers who developed the new forms of social organization and control on which complex industrial society depends: it was, in large part, engineers who were the original managers of giant enterprises. These facts are the basis for the engineer as an important symbolic figure earlier in this century in Canada and the United States and still today in the U.S.S.R.: the engineer as a kind of Prometheus bending nature to his (now: his/her) will and organizing human energy for the benefit of mankind.

Yet we have been ambivalent about treating the occupation of engineering as a profession. Drawing its recruits, as it still does, largely from the working class, it does not have the social cachet of law or medicine; nor, since its services are largely on a public scale, does it have the intimacy and confidentiality associated with the personal services rendered by the older professions. Moreover, the relationships between engineering and science, on the one hand, and engineering and management, on the other, have been changing. In the complex synergistic relation between science and engineering the person in the white coat tends to be regarded as the partner senior to the person in the hard hat and boots. The ranks of senior management now tend to be filled with specialized generalists — persons with specialized training in commerce, business administration and finance — rather than with persons from production and engineering as in the past.

Nevertheless, engineering is still a strategic occupation. A good case can be made that technological change has been the deep, underlying force for economic growth and change.[3] And technology, as opposed to pure or theoretical science, is still mainly in the domain of engineering. Furthermore, engineering decisions still require a consideration of a complex variety of factors, so that the engineer plays a special co-ordinating role. As the *Manual of*

Professional Practice of the Association of Professional Engineers of Ontario says,

> Engineering is a profession in which each decision is a compromise, being affected by such constraints as economics, available materials, reliability requirements, market dictates, environmental considerations, societal effects, and even political realities.[4]

Given the importance of engineering in modern society, it seems not unreasonable to use this occupation as one special test case for the more general question of regulatory regimes for occupations, itself a case of the still more general question of regulatory regimes *within* an economy.

III. THE CURRENT REGIME IN ONTARIO

Regulatory regimes for engineers vary considerably from one jurisdiction to another, ranging from virtual nonregulation to certification, to reserved titles, to highly legalized and regulated licensure schemes. In Canada — although there is some variation since the regulation of occupations is a provincial responsibility — the Ontario regime of self-regulation and licensure is representative; and, since 50 000 engineers are involved, important. The salient features of the system are:

1. Legal status

There is a legal statute, the Professional Engineer's Act, that created the Association of Professional Engineers of Ontario (APEO) and assigned the APEO its power and responsibilities. In addition, certain regulations proposed from time to time by the Council of the APEO and accepted by the Lieutenant Governor in Council become Regulations under the Act. The objects of the APEO are, by statute:

(a) to regulate the practice of professional engineering and to govern the profession in accordance with this Act, the regulations and the by-laws;

(b) to establish and maintain standards of knowledge and skill among its members; and

(c) to establish and maintain standards of professional ethics among its members,

in order that the public interest may be served and protected.[5]

2. Self-Regulation

Under the aegis of this legislation, engineering is in Ontario a self-regulating profession *in the public interest*. The APEO controls a restricted title, 'engineer', and, through the control of licences, a set of activities under that title. In sum, the public, through the provincial legislature, has granted the privilege of self-regulation to an occupational group, with the proviso that this privilege be used in the public interest.

3. Code of ethics

The APEO is required to set and enforce standards of competence and good behaviour. One instrument it uses, and by law is required to have, is a Code of Ethics that states the paramount duty to the public welfare. The Code sets out duties to the public, to employers, to clients, and to other engineers; this can and does give rise to difficult problems of casuistry. Yet the thrust of the Code is to protect, not the self-interest of engineers, but the interests of those they serve. Considerable efforts have been made by the APEO in recent years to improve the efficacy of the Code through education (including, for example, the production of a filmed case study), through examination (a compulsory examination in professional ethics, practice and legal responsibility is now required of all entrants) and through enforcement (the 'Gazette' Section of *Engineering Dimensions* publicizes disciplinary actions, with details and sometimes names, taken against members).

4. Regulatory constraints

In addition to, and interacting with, the professional rules of competence and good behaviour, engineers are bound by civil liabilities under the common law of contracts and torts and a host of regulations under statute and administrative law. They must not only abide by various safety and environment laws, but also product standards laid down legally or by industry standards associations.

5. Professional economic interests

At a time when the ideologues of deregulation emphasize the guild aspect of the professions, i.e., the actions of professions to advance the economic interests of their members,[6] it is important to note how little Ontario engineers act collectively to self-interested ends. In the main, entrance to the profession has not been restricted either by controlling enrolments in engineering faculties, or by forbidding licencing of those without engineering degrees or by restricting immigrants. The APEO has cooperated in the development of para-professionals in the form of engineering technologists and technicians. The APEO has issued guidelines for advertising engineering services, but these are nonmandatory and do not basically restrict this activity beyond suggesting accuracy and good taste. It is permissible for engineers to enter into tendering systems and competitive bidding, and for one engineer to replace another, provided only the courtesy of notification is met. Engineers fall under the provisions of the Combines Investigations Act and its strictures against anti-competitive behaviour.

All this is not to say that the regulatory regime for engineers is perfect. Law suits brought by the Ontario Association of Architects against engineers engaged in the design and construction of certain types of buildings were found to expose inadequacies in the regulatory laws. These questions were referred by the Attorney-General to the Ontario Law Reform Commission which advised him to refer the whole matter to a special committee. Thus came into existence in 1977 the Professional Organizations Committee (POC) with a mandate to investigate and recommend on the regulation of the professions of law, accountancy, architecture and engineering, after the manner of the earlier Committee on the Healing Arts which led to the Health Disciplines Act of 1974.

IV. POC'S THEORETICAL POSITION

Those conducting a deep investigation of a regulatory regime may well start from some general philosophical or ideological presuppositions. These in turn will probably mesh with an economic and/or a legal theory. Thus will philosophy, economics and the legal justice system come to have intercourse each with the other. So the immediate questions about theory are: What school of legal theory dominates the POC Staff Report? and With what economic and philosophical theories does it consort?

The answers are: the 'economics and law' approach exemplified in the work of Richard Posner, consorting with neo-classical economics and utilitarianism. It must be added, however, that there was also a general deregulatory climate of opinion abroad, with different theoretical bases, sponsored by both far left and far right: the anarchism of the 'critical theory of law' (a left wing theory of law with adherents in bastions of conservatism such as the law faculties of Harvard and Stanford) and the anarchism or libertarianism of economists (such as Friedman) or philosophers (such as Nozick). The ironies of this meeting of extremes are best appreciated, perhaps, by Hegelians.

The economics and law approach has " . . . used the theoretical and empirical methods of economics to illuminate a variety of issues and problems in the law."[7] I cannot go into a general critique of that movement here; but I will record my view that some of its adherents have been given to crude, sweeping arguments of dubious probative force, and that it is often unclear whether they are attempting a descriptive, explanatory account of legal decisions in western societies or whether they are offering a justificatory, normative account of them. In the case of the POC Staff Study, an economic theory seems pretty clearly to be taken as normative. It is the economic theory of competitive markets.

> In general, in a free enterprise economy, the government is willing to let market forces determine the allocation of factors of production and final products, and it does this because of a conviction that the free interaction of producers and consumers will best promote efficient production and economic well-being.[8]

In a familiar manner, five conditions are laid down that are sufficient for Pareto optimality, according to a fundamental, demonstrable theorem of theoretical economics:

(1) There are numerous buyers and sellers in the market, such that the activities of any one economic actor have only a negligible effect on the total market.

(2) There is free entry into and exit from the market.

(3) The commodity sold in the market is homogeneous; that is, essentially the *same* product is sold by each of the sellers in the market.

(4) All economic actors in the market have complete information about the nature and value of the commodities traded.

(5) All the costs of producing a commodity are borne by the producer and all the benefits of a commodity accrue to the consumer; that is, there are no externalities.[9]

If it exists, this "...perfectly competitive market achieves an optimal allocation of factors and products of its own accord — Adam Smith's 'invisible hand' works without the necessity for central direction towards the 'common good'."[10] Here then is a connection between philosophy, economics and the justice system: a utilitarian philosophy of a maximized 'common good', combines with neoclassical economics and a consequent ideal of minimal interference by the apparatus of the political-legal system. This utilitarian deregulatory approach should be contrasted with the libertarian approach, which may reach similar conclusions from different premises.

Although libertarians often belabour regulatory regimes with charges of allocative inefficiency, their basic premises are often drawn from, not an axiologically based theory such as utilitarianism, but rather a deontological theory of property rights and freedom. Thus Friedman, discussing whether free enterprise (the 'capitalistic ethic') is acceptable, says:

> I find it difficult to justify either accepting or rejecting it, or to justify any alternative principle. I am led to the view that it cannot in and of itself be regarded as an

ethical principle; that it must be regarded as instrumental or a corollary of some other principle such as freedom.[11]

From a theory of freedom is conjured a theory of distributive justice based on property rights and a factor of production contribution theory in true neo-classical style. "To each according to what he and the instruments he owns produces."[12] Our utilitarian 'economic analysis of the law' theorists in POC Staff do not share this view and it might be well to indicate why by reference to what I believe is a fundamental problem in economic theory.

Coincident roughly with the period of 'high capitalism' in the United States, the neo-classical theories of production and distribution formed a seamless web. The theoretical models seemed, more or less, to be empirically substantiated and to have predictive value.[13] Furthermore, the resulting system in the real world had, at least in the eyes of some, positive normative merit, both axiologically and dikaiologically: the system maximized overall welfare, so that it was good, and distributed this welfare according to a contribution canon of distributive justice, so that it was just.[14] A social-darwinian and Panglossian world.

Yet at least since the time of J.S. Mill, a deviant view — that the theory of production and the theory of distribution were distinct and that the latter depended upon the institutions of society, especially property schemes — had been abroad. So welfare could be maximized according to classical economic principles and justice could be achieved, independently and according to social democratic schemes, by redistribution measures. By this much, at least, was the classical faith diminished. It was further diminished by the recognition that neither the presuppositions about exogenous variables nor the explicit postulates of production theory were empirically satisfied in the world of the twentieth century.

So classical economic theory lingers on in some quarters only as a model, much divorced from reality, having normative force as a welfare maximization scheme. Pure economic theory, then, becomes an ideology, while practical economics becomes a matter of bullying and chivying the system towards its ideal productive norm with the one hand and dispensing largesse according to need and equity criteria of distributive justice with the other.

It is this perspective, I believe, that the position of POC Staff's legal-economic-philosophic theory must be seen. It should not be confused with the position of more radical libertarian deregulators, who, I think it not unfair to say, embrace with fervour a social-darwinian theory of justice and property rights as primary and who, secondarily, have a pious faith, currently expressed in 'supply-side' and 'trickle-down' theory, that their distributive scheme will, as a matter of fact, produce Pareto optimality. And then there are those who think contemporary economics empirically bankrupt and normatively vicious — but I leave them aside.

Given the centrality of their welfare norm, the question facing the POC Staff theorists was whether the postulates of their production theory were satisfied empirically. To what extent do concentration, barriers to entry, product heterogeneity, lack of information and externalities mean that there is an imperfect market in professional services? They conclude:

(1) Excessive concentration does not appear to be a serious problem in any of the four markets.

(2) Barriers to entry and exit exist by virtue of the large investment in 'human capital' of most professionals, but no artificial barriers seem to exist.

(3) Product heterogeneity is endemic to professional markets.

(4) Informational problems seem to be significant only in the market for legal services, though there are some problems in architecture and accounting as well.

(5) Third party effects constitute a serious problem in accounting, architecture and engineering and a secondary problem in law.[15]

These facts, although necessary, are not sufficient conditions for regulatory interference with imperfect markets, for the costs and effectiveness of regulations must also be taken into account.

The quantity, quality and price of professional services must be taken into account in view of various regulatory options — output regulations through civil liability and through performance standards, input regulation through certification or licensure, external regulation by the state or self-regulation by the profession — and in the light of the empirical circumstances of each profession.

> The selection of a regulatory option requires the application of priorities and weights across various interests and principles. . . . These are matters of judgement, to be defended and debated, and ultimately to be resolved by government authorities in framing legislation.[16]

Different patients will require different medicines. What did the doctors recommend for the engineers?

V. POC STAFF'S RECOMMENDATIONS

Some recommendations do concern matters of justice, for instance, procedural justice. But, because of its theoretical basis, the thrust of POC Staff is not towards questions of distributive justice *per se*; these questions are a secondary matter in a lexical ordering of problems. On the other hand, regulatory regimes may be said to be concerned with a form of corrective justice. In POC Staff the emphasis is on correcting deviations from full efficiency. Given that reality departs from the efficiency norm postulated, what corrective measures can be taken to rectify the situation?

The original conflict between engineers and architects is to be resolved by the restriction of engineers involved in designing buildings to a new group of 'Licensed Building Engineers', governed by a board of engineers, architects and laypersons. In general there should be non-professional members, appointed by the Lieutenant Governor in Council, on all governing councils of professional bodies. There are other recommendations, but I wish to focus on four that I think are particularly important for present purposes.

5.9 Except for engineering services specifically required by statute or regulation, all engineering work done by employees of industrial, commercial or government enterprises (not professional firms), should be exempt from the scope of the license to practice professional engineering.

6.4 No designation involving the use of the terms 'certified', 'registered', 'accredited', 'chartered' or 'professional' other than those established in the licensing statutes proposed [in certain other recommendations], should be established in the professions under review.

6.8 Engineering and architectural technologists and technicians ought not to be licensed to practice 'in parallel' and/or independently of engineers and architects. However, in engineering, the industrial exemption will have the effect of allowing partial parallel practice in industry and government.

13.2 The professional exclusions in *The Ontario Labour Relations Act* and *The Crown Employees Collective Bargaining Act* ought to be removed.[17]

(The last proposal, 13.2, would extend the right of engineers to unionize. In the POC Staff discussion it is suggested that such unions might negotiate employment clauses protecting the right to conform to professional ethics.)[18] These linked proposals focus on a form of deregulation, the industrial exemption, that allows firms and government agencies to decide who amongst their employees will perform 'engineering' tasks and under what conditions.

These proposals, deregulating the activities of most engineers and blocking the expansion of the professional self-regulation to engineering technologists and technicians, are important, I shall argue, because if they were to be adopted they would be a significant step towards the proletarianizing of professionals and would weaken the protection of third-party, public interests against negative externalities. Before addressing this practical issue, I shall make some critical remarks on POC Staff's theoretical and empirical position.

VI. CRITIQUE OF POC STAFF'S POSITION

The economic model can be taken as a purely theoretical deductive exercise: if the five conditions were to hold, the property of Pareto optimality would obtain. But the model has two practical uses. It can be used as an engine of description, explanation and prediction, or it can be used as an ideal, norm or goal. *In POC Staff these two uses interact.*

In the model, five conditions, given certain background assumptions, are logically sufficient for the achievement of a form of efficiency. When the model is used normatively for the formation of policy, efficiency is taken as a goal, as a good thing. The question is, 'Has the goal been achieved?' If the answer is 'Yes', one may go on to other goals. If the answer is 'No', one can formulate policies which if followed will be sufficient, insofar as the model has empirical predictive power, to achieve the goal. (It should be noted that although the postulates are *sufficient* for Pareto optimality, it would be another matter to show that they are *necessary* for it. Furthermore, if we are interested in 'efficiency' or maximization, there may be other ways to achieve these ends.)

In critizing the model's use in policy formation one might (1) question the desirability of the goal postulated, (2) question the compatibility of this goal with other goals, (3) question the empirical adequacy of the model, (4) question whether the evidence indicates that the goal has not been met so that reforms are required, (5) question whether the policy prescriptions will have undesirable side effects.

(1) I have doubts about the appropriateness of *Pareto* optimality as a goal and doubts about what priority should be given to maximization or efficiency *vis à vis* other goals. But I shall assume efficiency is, *ceteris paribus*, a desirable feature of a system of production and that we should carefully examine the efficiency consequences of regulatory regimes.

(2) I have already alluded to what I perceive as a difficulty in the received view that separates the theory of production from the theory of distribution and attempts simply lexically to order the prob-

lems, so I shall leave this issue aside. I shall take up the other sorts of criticisms *seriatim.*

(3) The model's postulates come into play only against other background assumptions or assumed exogenous variables: e.g., the distribution or purchasing power, the configuration of individual preferences and the technology of production are taken as givens. As the authors of the Staff Study admit,

> It is, however, heroic in the extreme to assume that technology, tastes and distributive shares are determined *outside* the economic system and they cannot then simply be taken as given in the assessment of perfect markets.[19]

To this I would add three other considerations: legal, psychological and sociological.

The legal system, especially the property regime, is — like technology, tastes and shares — a variable not empirically independent of the postulates. Likewise, the theory presupposes a certain conception of personality and agency — in the form of a 'rational' maximizer of a given personal preference structure. This again is not an empirically independent variable, for there is some reason to suppose that personality formation is influenced by expectations within an economic system. I believe, furthermore, certain sociological considerations are important in examining economic models and their application to the regulation question. I shall concentrate on what I have here called 'sociological considerations'.

I am aware, however, that this sort of attack on the 'assumptions' of classical economics has been replied to by some economic theorists, notably Milton Friedman in his essay *The Methodology of Positive Economics*.[20] Since I have limited space here, I will simply state that I believe this essay is unsuccessful because it contains a lot of bad epistemology and philosophy of science. For example, it waffles between realism and pragmatism concerning theoretical entities; it supposes that if a postulate of a theory can be tested indirectly, it should not be tested directly or through some other theory; and its general thrust is to protect a theory adopted on philosophical grounds from empirical refutation.

I have already raised a question about the nature of economic agents or the nature of the economic unit. Sometimes the economic unit is taken to be the 'individual human being' (perhaps exclusive of children and the handicapped); sometimes it is 'the family' (whether nuclear or extended); and sometimes 'the firm' (or some other similar social group). The individual, assumed to be a rational maximizer, is taken as primary, i.e., the other 'units' are treated *as though* they were individual rational maximizers.

This leads to the neglect of what I might call 'internal political economies', which are very important, I believe, for the regulation question in today's society. Sometimes it is admitted that the internal political economy of the family is based, not on the maximization of self-interest, but on social principles of trust, love, co-operation and the like that are different from and not derivable from self-interest together with, say, contractarian principles. The family, then, internally may constitute a sphere of the private, immune to standard economic analysis. There may be other spheres of private and 'non-economic' life such as friendship circles, clubs, churches and other voluntary social groups. Externally they must be treated as though they were individual rational maximizers — if they are to count as economic agents — but internally they are a 'black box' immune to internal understanding by the standard economist and his philosophical cousins. To a student of contemporary society, not blinded by occupational specialization or ideological zeal, it must be a source of amazement to observe the myriad of human associations apparently neglected by those who would explain, predict and prescribe for humans affairs in terms of classical economics and its theoretical relatives. Of course they are not really neglected, for a process of *engloutissement* by the theory of 'rational' choice is applied to the motives of these agents: other-regarding or altruistic motives simply become part of one's 'preference' structure. The psychology of motivation is turned from an empirical matter into an *a priori* normative one. That is, that one always acts so as to maximize one's interests is made trivially true by definition and then this is taken as a norm for rational behaviour. Of particular concern must be the firm or corporation or Crown (State) corporation — a human association that is, on any realistic view, a principal economic agent on the contemporary scene. What of its internal political economy?

There are those who would on *a priori* grounds, given their theoretical or philosophical views, treat the firm simply as a collection of individuals, bound by contractual ties entered into voluntarily by these individuals as economic agents. There are those who would, given their practical concerns and guided by ideology, try to organize large scale enterprises into 'profit centres' as subunits — the ideal limit being the individual as a profit centre. Yet, at the descriptive level, is it not true that the internal political economy of the modern corporation presents a very complex and mixed scene? To be sure, there are 'profit centres' and it is assumed, part of the time, that individuals are motivated as pure economic agents — provided that many non-monetary and intangible factors are included in his/her preference structure. But why is it that practical managers, while paying lip-service to pure economic theory as a matter of ideology and social acceptability, flit from one managerial panacea to another — in current jargon, from theory X to theory Y to theory Z? Why is it that the ideology of 'the bottom line' is transmuted into 'management by objectives' — where the objectives are quite multifarious?[21]

Is it not a sociological fact that the 'command economy', condemned and eschewed by standard economic theorists, has been internalized in the interior political economy of the firm, with its *el supremo*, the CEO (buttressed of course by phalanxes of vice-presidents), who is the brains and command centre directing and controlling an army of hands and legs? And does not the legal system, with its verbally anachronistic terminology of masters and servants, reflect the same state of affairs? And is it not a matter of sociological fact that 'countervailing centres of power', in the form of trade unions and other quasi-legal associations, have arisen, which interact with management/ownership in relations ranging from outright violence to subtly nuanced mutual accommodation? And is it not a matter of

sociological fact that the political economy of the family and other non-economic associations have also been internalized within firms, with their networks of mentors and students, priests and acolytes? These are, I think, matters of sociological fact that should not be ignored by an economic theory that pretends to empirical significance. And they are, I think, matters of sociological fact that would be ignored by prescriptivist philosophers and economists on pain of their offering useless nostrums or, worse yet, of causing iatrogenic disease. My particular point here is that in the modern industrial world many of the most important economic units do not conform to the ideal type presupposed in the background sociology of classical economics. The internal economy of these powerful economic agents is important, as I shall indicate, in considering the effects of deregulation questions.

More generally, there are a number of reasons, then, to believe the model to be flawed as an instrument of empirical prediction and hence flawed as an element in the policy formation process.

(4) I turn now to the question whether any policy prescriptions are necessary. What empirical evidence is there that the current regulatory regime in Ontario causes inefficiency in production? POC Staff does find three major deviations from the model: there are 'natural' barriers to entry and exit because of the large investment in human capital required by engineering; product heterogeneity is endemic; and third party (externality) effects constitute a serious problem. But these facts do not prove that the current regime is inefficient. The absence of certain conditions sufficient for a given effect does not prove that the given effect is absent. (There may be more than one way to skin a cat.) In any case, it is not at all clear that the industrial exemption recommendation would remedy these deviations. The reason for the industrial exemption is stated by the POC Staff thusly:

> . . . it appears that engineering work performed in industrial enterprises is characterized by a significant amount of substitution between professional engineers and other technical personnel. Knowledgeable employers adjust the mix of professional and non-professional inputs into their 'production process' in

such a way as to be most efficient. The rapid pace of technological change carries with it the requirement of flexibility in the use of technical resources, if maximum efficiency is to be achieved; such flexibility is often at odds with the rigidities imposed by a licensed regime.[22]

The industrial exemption would, it is claimed, increase flexibility in labour inputs; this would increase efficiency; and this in turn would be in the public interest.

The salient fact is that the overwhelming majority of engineers are employees of corporations, public or private. In a variety of estimates I have seen from various sources, formal and informal, the number of engineers as employees ranges from 90% to 98%. By whatever estimate, a small minority of engineers are self-employed, principals in professional engineering firms or employees in such firms. The removal of the requirement for licensure with its limitations on the reserved title of 'engineer', together with blockage of some variety of professionalization for paraprofessionals, as entailed in recommendations 5.9, 6.4 and 6.8 of POC Staff, would result in the proletarianization of a young profession. As part of this process, engineers would be given an extended right to unionize.

My reading of the voluminous staff studies and the summary of them is that, as say compared to the legal profession, engineering comes out with a comparatively clean bill of health as measured by various criteria such as: public interest versus economic self-interest, institutions and procedures for self-governance, submission to market forces, freedom of entry, encouragement of paraprofessionals, certification of specialists, education in professional responsibilities, policing or disciplining of members in a broad range of public responsibilities, and general openness to change. And yet, as compared again with the legal profession, engineering is singled out for what, I think, would be, in practice, a draconian change of status. One would expect strong empirical evidence adduced to justify the change.

It appears, however, that POC Staff's position is an expression of an ideologically based faith or a generalization applied without warrant to a particular case. For no empirical evidence is offered that the current regime in Ontario *in fact* prevents efficient adjustments in labour inputs. The fact is that provincial authorities, by creating a network of Colleges of Applied Arts and Technology, have greatly increased the supply of technologists and technicians — and they are being employed as such. The fact is that the APEO has been co-operative in this change in the number and use of these paraprofessionals, and has not attempted to enforce a narrow interpretation of the definition of 'engineering' in the Act. On this last point POC Staff goes so far as to admit:

> Anecdotal evidence suggests that in some employed contexts the restrictions imposed by the engineering license are honoured as much in the breach as in the observance.[23]

Perhaps there is some 'stickiness' in changes in labour inputs, perhaps caused by the aforementioned 'natural' barriers to entry and exit, but we are given no evidence that any significant 'stickiness' is caused by the regulatory regime or that an industrial exemption is needed to correct the situation. The proposal, then, has not been adequately justified.

(5) I turn finally to what I think are two important probable consequences of the industrial exemption proposal. The first concerns the problem of externalities, especially as these affect third parties, such as the general public. The second concerns the welfare of the engineers affected, but also, indirectly, other professionals and workers in general.

Externalities. Employed professionals face conflicts more complex than their self-employed counterparts. The traditional self-employed professional may have faced a potential conflict between his/her self-interest and the interest of the client, and, more rarely, third party interests. The employee-engineer, however, is often faced with conflicts amongst his/her self-interest, the interest of the employer, the interests of the direct client and the interests of fourth parties such as the general public. The latter, the public impact, is often of major importance and long range significance. Difficult decisions must be made using good judgement in the application to particular cases of general principles and guide- lines — *the very sort of judgement that is regarded as a hallmark of the professional.* The professional engineer in Ontario dealing with these problems and interacting with the employer has a position with *some* (not much but some) power and authority.[24] This engineer has professional duties to abide by and has a professional organization, created and backed by statute and regulations, for background support. This engineer has an important role in the internal political economy of large organizations.

But the industrial exemption proposal would in practice strip most engineers of their special legally based occupational duty to the public interest as well as the privilege of effective participation in a form of self-government. Engineers, technologists and technicians would become or remain proletari- ans — servants in a master/servant relationship. The effect of the change would be to tip the balance of power internally further in the direction of 'man- agement perogatives'. By changing the internal political economy of industrial enterprises further in favour of what I have called the 'command sys- tem', the proposal would tend to remove a small voice of conscience from the internal working of that system. By making 'whistle-blowing' even more hazardous for the engineer than it is at present, it would make the veil of corporate secrecy even more opaque than it now is, thus lowering still further the practical efficacy of the 'demand-side' regulation favoured by POC Staff. Let me illustrate with a well- known case from the USA, where the industrial exemption is commonly used.

In the BART affair three employee engineers 'blew the whistle' on safety defects in the design of the Bay Area Rapid Transit system. They were fired for, in effect, insubordination and subsequently brought suit for damages due to wrongful dismissal. The Institute of Electrical and Electronic Engineers, in an *amicus curiae* brief to the California Superior Court, argued that the right to adhere to its Code of Ethics should be considered an implied term of employment, so that an employer violating that right would be in breach of contract.[25] Unfortu-

nately, the suit was eventually settled out of court, so no precedent has been set. There is still little institu- tional or legal support, then, for professional ethi- cal conduct in a regime involving an industrial exemption. Indeed, I have some anecdotal evidence that some large firms in the U.S. strongly discourage their engineers from joining voluntary professional organizations, because they prefer no question of divided loyalties to arise. The current Ontario (and in general the Canadian) regime provides an insti- tutional and legal basis for actions favouring the public interest.

Proletarianization. I have suggested that engi- neers are a strategic group, because by occupation they are custodians of technology, a major force for social-economic-political change. But increasingly engineers are not alone in working in the context of large institutions, rather than in solo practice servic- ing individual clients with few third-party interests to be considered. The health professions, for instance, now operate in a context of large hospitals, clinics and group practice, where third-party inter- ests (at least financially through public or private insurance schemes) are involved. In partly similar ways, the same can be said of many lawyers, account- ants and architects. A combination of this sort of change in the conditions of professional practice, together with deregulation could lead to the prole- tarianization of virtually all professionals. And let libertarian academics who cherish personal free- dom of opinion and action ask themselves whether they would like to work in institutions that are run internally on command economy principles.

Many occupational groups have been engaged in a drive to obtain 'professional' status in some form or other.[26] The motive behind this may be, in part, a desire for monopolistic economic advantage and may be, in part, a desire for social prestige. Cynics — right-wing deregulators are a case in point — may suggest that that is all there is to the matter. I suggest there is something more. In a complex society of unprecedented wealth and high levels of education, many people, for the first time since the industrial revolution, have the potential to achieve *mundigkeit* (the age of majority, the age of both autonomy and responsibility) in that portion of their lives that comprises half their waking hours — their work life. Many want what professionals traditionally have had: a position of *responsible* freedom or autonomy, the status of an equal, the opportunity to exercise judgement — rather than the position of one who obeys, the status of a servant, the duty to perform routine tasks according to rule and command for most of the day in return for the wherewithal to engage in private pleasures in the remaining hours. I think it more than slightly paradoxical that some of those most concerned to cry "Freedom" and "Efficiency" advocate institutional arrangements that would condemn all but a few to conditions of servitude, and that would 'foster efficiency' through a wasteful system of command and confrontation (e.g., management *vs.* unions) rather than co-operation amongst co-workers.

So I hold no special brief for the welfare of established professionals. I would much prefer to see forms of 'professionalism' spread to other occupational groups.[27] The form that this 'professionalism' would have and the institutional bases for it could vary widely — corporatism, industrial democracy, participatory management, quality circles are some of the options. We need to experiment to discover workable arrangements to foster human dignity in the workplace. And let us see, empirically, whether these arrangements will also foster efficiency, as in at least some cases they do, rather than rule them out as inefficient on dogmatic, *a priori*, ideological grounds. At the very least let us not take retrograde steps, such as the introduction of the industrial exemption for engineers where it does not exist and is not needed.

VII. SUMMARY

I don't think, then, that a good case has been made out for the industrial exemption proposal on which I have focused. The economic model utilized is, as an engine of analysis and prediction, inadequate and misleading. There is a paucity of empirical evidence to support a corrective application of the economic theorem used by POC Staff as the main criterion for its normative position. A failure to consider the proposal's effects on the internal political economy and sociology of the major employers of engineers leads POC Staff to neglect a very important source of third-party protection against externalities. The move to proletarianize a significant occupational group ignores the wider social implications of that move. And finally, a matter I have not had space to discuss, the efficacy of 'demand side' or 'output' regulation in which POC Staff relies for third-party protection is something we are asked to accept on faith. ("To conduct a thoroughgoing review of the structures and processes of demand side requirements would involve nothing less than an analysis of the legislative and administrative processes of the Ontario government — needless to say, a task far beyond the scope of this Study."[28]) The POC Staff Study, impressive and useful in so many ways, is deeply flawed, in at least one case, by what the evidence I have adduced suggests is ideological bias.

Through an examination of some local proposals for deregulation measures for engineers in Ontario, I have tried to illustrate: how social philosophy, economic theory and a theory about the justice system can interact in a manner both theoretical and practical; how ideological abstractions can masquerade as realistic philosophy, sound jurisprudence and empirical economics; and how a study of the particular and local can illuminate some questions of wider human significance.

VIII. CODA

The discussion so far has centred exclusively on material from the POC Staff Study. This was so mainly for two reasons: the Staff proposed a major change in the regulatory regime for engineers in Ontario and, secondly, it provided an elaborate, general, theoretical rationale for its proposals that encouraged a philosophical analysis. It may be of interest to indicate what happened subsequent to the publication of the POC Staff Study.

Normally a committee, such as POC, commissions staff studies and consultants' reports which are prepared while public hearings are held. Then a final report is prepared with an eye to both sources of information and opinion. In the present case POC departed from the norm by holding private consultations with affected parties while staff research went on and then held public meetings and received public briefs after the Staff Report had been released. This enabled the public to react to Staff research and proposals, although it also engendered fear that Staff recommendations foreshadowed and embodied POC's final recommendations. The *Report of the Professional Organizations Committee*, however, departs significantly from the Staff Study and thus the fears proved groundless. I shall mention three changes relevant to the previous discussion.

(1) The basic rationale for determining regulatory regimes provided by the Posnerian 'economics and law' theory completely disappears in the final report. What replaces this rationale — or more accurately what remains in the way of theory from POC Staff — are

> . . . four principles to guide the formation of policy vis à vis the professions: The Protection of Vulnerable Interests; Fairness of Regulation; Feasibility of Implementation; and Public Accountability of Regulatory Bodies.[29]

Why this major change occurred, I cannot really say for lack of specific evidence available to me. I can only speculate that commonsense and political reality prevailed over ideology. (This would not be an uncommon occurrence in a province ruled for four decades by a marvellous contradiction in terms, the Progressive Conservative Party. Red Tories — another logical delight — comprise an important faction of the Progressive Conservative Party.) The cautious ruminative approach of POC, as contrasted with its more theoretically inclined staff, is indicated in the following paragraph:

> To adopt a set of principles entails more than an exercise in identification. It is a quest for content, balance, and relevance that requires many personal judgements. The extent to which this is so became clearly, sometimes painfully, apparent as our quest proceeded, forcing us to grapple with fundamental questions. With respect to content, we were asking what we believed our principles stood for. As for balance, we

were prodding the extent to which any given principle could or should be satisfied in deference to the others. And as to relevance, we were not dealing in bloodless abstractions, but in working principles applicable to very real professions existing in the complex society that is contemporary Ontario.[30]

(2) The original bone of contention concerning jurisdictional disputes between engineers and architects was worried to a division between the two parties through negotiations conducted during the writing of the final report. The compromise, too complex to relate here, satisfied not only the APEO and the Ontario Association of Architects, but, in the judgement of POC, (a) preserves an important element of choice for clients regarding prime consultants, (b) is adequate to the complex teamwork required in modern large scale buildings, and (c) protects the public against professional featherbedding.[31] So the Licensed Building Engineer proposal of POC Staff was dropped.

(3) The industrial exemption proposal against which I have inveighed was also dropped. The reasons given in the POC Report are these:

> In their briefs to the Committee and in appearances at the public meetings, individual professionals and their representative organizations were virtually unanimous in rejecting this proposal. We feel the force of some of the arguments presented against it; for instance, that an industrial exemption system would rely heavily on extensive and complex demand-side regulation to ensure adequate protection of public safety and welfare, and that it might run counter to efforts aimed at attaining nationally uniform licensing standards.
>
> We have also been made aware that similar exemption provisions found in a large number of U.S. state registration laws have been a source of considerable controversy and friction between the profession and the enterprises which employ engineers. Again, we are impressed by the fact that technical employees, who would gain appreciably more freedom to practise independently in the workplace under such an exemption, have been unenthusiastic about the proposal. Meantime, commercial, industrial, and government employers of engineers and technologists who might have expressed an interest in de-regulation, did not come forward to support it.

All these considerations lead us to reject the industrial exemption in favour of alternative approaches to the problems involved in the interface between engineers and technical personnel.[32]

In its place are recommended changes in the Professional Engineers Act which (a) recognize the reality of a teamwork approach involving a flexible division of labour in engineering work, (b) codify the current *de facto* position sanctioned by the APEO, and (c) protect the public interest by requiring that, whether or not the persons actually *doing* 'works of engineering' are professional engineers, there must be involved a licensed engineer "professionally responsible to the APEO for the maintenance of engineering standards in the performance of the work."[33] In my opinion these proposals are sensible, reasonable and fair: they are adequate to foster commonsense notions of efficient production, offer some protection of third-party interests and are consistent with the development of the sort of workplace relations I have advocated.

At the present time (July, 1983) the POC Report is in the hands of the Government and awaits legislative enactment. It does not seem unlikely that the final POC recommendations will be accepted.

Finally, given the current situation, one might well ask whether the foregoing analysis and critique of the POC Staff Study is of any interest or utility. A simple answer is this: the industrial exemption provision for engineers is a live issue. A serious proposal was made for its introduction in Ontario which, if adopted, would have had repercussions in the rest of Canada. Similar proposals are under debate in the United Kingdom.[34] And, of course, the industrial exemption, commonplace in the United States, has aroused concern amongst American engineers.[35] A careful discussion of one rationale for proposing such a regulatory regime, then, can be of some interest and utility, even if the particular proposal is a dead issue. For we live in a time in which ideological rationales have become, once again, important determinants of public policy. And as a philosopher once said, "Those who do not learn from history are condemned to repeat it."

ENDNOTES

1. An earlier version of this paper was presented to a conference, "Economics, Philosophy and Justice," at University of Waterloo, May 1983. I am indebted to Lawrence Haworth, University of Waterloo, for helpful criticisms. A shorter version was presented to a conference sponsored by the Society for Business Ethics at de Paul University, Chicago, July 1983. I thank Conrad Brunk, Conrad Grebel College, Waterloo for further helpful comments. The paper draws primarily on two documents: (a) Michael J. Treblicock, Carolyn J. Tuohy and Alan D. Wolfson, *Professional Regulation: A Staff Study of Accountancy, Architecture, Engineering and Law, prepared for The Professional Organizations Committee*, Ministry of the Attorney General of Ontario, 1979. (Hereafter referred to as POC Staff); (b) H. Allen Leal, J. Alex Corry, J. Stefan Dupré, *The Report of the Professional Organizations Committee*, Ministry of the Attorney General of Ontario, 1980. (Hereafter referred to as POC Report). The first work brings together material from sixteen staff working papers, to which I have had access through the courtesy of Professor John Swan, Faculty of Law, University of Toronto. I have also made use of *The Professions and Public Policy*, edited by Philip Slayton and Michael J. Treblicock (Toronto: University of Toronto Press, 1978) and, for American perspectives, *Regulating the Professions*, edited by Roger D. Blair and Stephen Rubin (Lexington: D.C. Heath and Company, 1980).

2. The reference to mad academic scribblers is from a well-known passage in Keynes' *General Theory*.

3. I have in mind, for instance, the theory of Joseph Schumpeter in the *Theory of Economic Development* that emphasizes entrepreneurial application of technological innovations.

4. *Manual of Professional Practice*, published by the Association of Professional Engineers of Ontario, p. 3.

5. RSO (1980), Ch. 394, S.3(3). See also RRO (1980) Reg. 804.

6. See, for example, Milton Friedman, *Capitalism and Freedom* (Chicago: The University of Chicago Press, 1971), Ch. IX, "Occupational Licensure."

7. Richard A. Posner, *Economic Analysis of Law* (Boston: Little, Brown and Company, 1972) p. ix.

8. POC Staff, p. 45.

9. *Ibid.*, p. 47.

10. *Ibid.*, p. 45.

11. Friedman, *op. cit.*, pp. 164–165.

12. *Ibid.*, pp. 161–162.

13. I have been influenced by Adolf Lowe, *On Economic Knowledge: Toward a Science of Political Economics* (New York: Harper and Row, 1965).

14. I have in mind, for instance, John Bates Clark's *The Distribution of Wealth*, 1899.

15. POC Staff, p. 59.

16. *Ibid.*, p. 85.

17. POC Staff, Chapter 14.

18. This matter is discussed at some length in Working Paper No. 13, *The Employed Professional*, by Katherine Swinton.

19. POC Staff, pp. 45–46.

20. Milton Friedman, *Essays in Positive Economics* (Chicago: The University of Chicago Press, 1953).

21. From a voluminous literature that has influenced my perceptions I shall cite only three classic works: Herbert H. Simon, *Administrative Behaviour* (Toronto: Collier-Macmillan of Canada Ltd., 1965), esp. Ch. VII, "The Role of Authority"; Peter F. Drucker, *Management: Tasks, Responsibilities, Practices* (New York: Harper & Row, 1975); and Alfred D. Chandler, Jr., *The Visible Hand: The Managerial Revolution in American Business* (Cambridge: Harvard University Press, 1977).

22. POC Staff, p. 118.

23. *Loc. cit.*

24. I have presented my views on this issue and suggested improvements to several chapters of the APEO. They are reported in an issue of the APEO journal, *Engineering Dimensions*, 1982.

25. The brief was filed in 1975. I have drawn my information from the IEEE journal *Spectrum*, which has had a series of articles on the case.

26. For some empirical information, see René Dussault, "The Office des Professions du Québec in the Context of the Development of the Professions," in Slayton and Treblicock, *op. cit.*

27. For a broader perspective of this question I am indebted to Lawrence Haworth, *Decadence and Objectivity* (Toronto: University of Toronto Press, 1977).

28. POC Staff, p. 237. In addition to common law remedies available under tort law, POC Staff favours, in general, 'demand side' or 'output' regulation. Others have favoured taxing schemes; see, for example, J.H. Dales, *Pollution, Property and Prices* (Toronto: University of Toronto Press, 1968).

29. POC Report, p. 7.

30. *Loc. cit.*

31. POC Report, Chapter 5.

32. *Ibid.*, p. 86.

33. *Loc. cit.*

34. England, Committee of Enquiry into the Engineering Profession, *Engineering Our Future* (London: Her Majesty's Stationery Office, Cmnd. 7794, 1980), Chapter V, "The Organization of Engineers."

35. U.S. National Society of Engineering Examiners, *Position Paper on Industrial Exemption in Registration Laws for Professional Engineers*, Washington, D.C., IM. 3/76 Corp. N.S.P.E. Pub. No. 2212, 1976.

15

Beyond Professional Ethics: Issues and Agendas

BETH SAVAN

INTRODUCTION

In George Bernard Shaw's play *The Doctor's Dilemma*, Sir Patrick Cullen, an elderly doctor, declares that: "All professions are conspiracies against the laity."[1] This is, of course, an outrageous statement, now just as much as in 1906 when Shaw wrote his play. Indeed most professions have as their mottoes some maxim that urges their members to serve, protect, or defend their clients; and no doubt most professions do try to serve their clients as well as they can, according to their own particular lights.

But what Shaw's doctor points out is that the interests of the clients, or laity, and the vested interests of the professionals who set out to serve them may not be entirely consistent: in fact, Sir Patrick is suggesting that they are quite contrary. It's clearly flippant and misleading to go as far as Shaw does, but it is certainly worthwhile to examine what the interests of the public or various publics are, and what exactly the interests of professionals and their organizations might be.

In this paper I briefly examine these interests, and then describe and discuss the efforts of various professional "ginger groups" to better serve the broad public interest. (For this purpose I define "the professions" as groups which apply special knowledge in the service of a client . . . which I take to include academic "experts" working on fields relevant to public policy as well as doctors, lawyers, engineers, nurses, dentists, *et al.* I will concentrate primarily on activist groups in science, since this is where my background and interest lie.)[2]

. . . most professional bodies now include committees or sub-groups devoted to encouraging the honest, decent, ethical delivery of professional services; they expect their clients' interests and more general concerns of social welfare to guide *how* their members work.[3] In some cases, though, these groups or others are also attempting to watch *what* they do with the broader public interest. This is a much more profound and difficult demand, and can affect almost every aspect of professional practice. I will discuss some of the groups and individuals that have embarked on this path, and explain how it changes their careers and their working lives. Finally, I will conclude with a plea for better integration of the personal, political, and technical aspects of professional work.

From *Journal of Business Ethics* **8**: (1989) 179–185.
Reprinted by permission of author.

BACKGROUND

The professions are among the most respected groups in society. People with professional careers generally enjoy the unusual status and credibility reserved for those with specialized knowledge and mastery of a particular area essential to our well-being. Public credibility can lead to lots of perks, some more desirable than others. (Many professionals may be less than delighted to have various friends, relations, and acquaintances line up to have their passport applications signed.)

Partly because they are seen (and like to be perceived) as indispensable, professional groups have often established special positions for themselves in society — they have more independence in terms of practice, self-regulation, fees charged and range of services provided.

Professional training is gruelling, underpaid, stressful, and often exploitive, engendering alienation from clients and outsiders and encouraging a sense of group identity and common experience. Trainees form a sort of underclass, essential for the smooth operation of the profession. They perform many routine, arduous, but necessary tasks, such as carrying out most of the repetitive lab work in many fields of experimental science. This is justified as an essential learning experience. It forms part of the strict hierarchy existing in most professions, in which the senior members profit by the efforts of their more junior partners who are, in turn (provided they dutifully toe the line) rewarded with good references and the support of their supervisor for their future career advancement.

I have described elsewhere the relationship between scientific research supervisors and their post-doctoral assistants as a kind of unwritten contract between the junior and senior scientist: the senior scientist secures the research funds, using his or her reputation to ensure generous grants to cover the cost of equipment, chemicals, and even the junior researcher's salary. In exchange, the junior investigator churns out data and drafts the papers, which he or she and the senior scientist co-author, to provide the senior scientist with proof that research funds are well spent. The senior researcher's reputation eases publication and also greatly enhances the

job prospects of the junior researchers working in the lab.[4] In a system where promotion and success depend on an established group of prestigious individuals in the profession, challenging the priorities and/or practices of the group is strongly discouraged. This kind of isolated, stressful training does not encourage, and may even discourage, a sense of responsibility to the wider community.

Powerful professional bodies are largely autonomous — lawyers, doctors, dentists, and engineering groups operate with little outside scrutiny and negotiate (like powerful unions) directly with government to guarantee continued perks. Professionals contribute enormously to society but only on their own terms, as free agents, answerable directly to their internal governing bodies and with little contact, as individuals or as associations, with their client communities. As a result of these favourable arrangements professional groups are usually bulwarks of the *status quo*. As the recent brouhaha preceding the Province of Ontario's ban on extra-billing by doctors demonstrated, professionals will strenuously resist attempts to wrest control from their own internal hierarchies, and will insist on their nominal "self-employed" status. Professional bodies appear to feel responsible primarily to their peers rather than to the wider lay community that they serve.

Doctors, lawyers, nurses, and engineers, and various expert policy advisors, can have a strong influence and sometimes indirect power over the lives of their clients and the political and social choices affecting us all. An example is the medical profession's vigorous protection of its own turf in lobbying against giving more responsibility to nurses and midwives, and the recently established task force to investigate spiralling health-care costs set up by the Ontario government, with a membership composed mainly of doctors![5] Of course, it is inevitable that professional bodies will use their knowledge and influence to promote certain perspectives; but, because their self-interest usually coincides with the social and political *status quo*, and because the professionals themselves usually deny any bias at all, these subtle lobbying efforts can go unnoticed.

Not all professionals subscribe to the values and attitudes fostered by the official professional organizations. Many individual professionals lead double lives: in mainstream jobs, serving their bureaucratic masters; and surreptitiously blowing the whistle by smuggling out heavy brown paper envelopes containing confidential information on matters of public import, or gently discouraging the worst excesses of their colleagues.

More relevant to [this discussion] are the various special-interest groups or splinter groups that have been formed with their own social, political, and moral perspectives. I will devote the rest of this paper to an exploration of these groups and their members, the mavericks in these professions: those who are willing to make their professional work in some way an extension of their personal convictions, and who may thereby sacrifice many of the benefits usually accruing to professionals. It is always more difficult to be in the minority, and groups which break ranks with the prevailing professional dogma — political, technical, or social — do so at considerable risk.

In the largely conservative professions, which pretend to maintain a certain reserve on social issues or a veneer of "objectivity", such activist groups stand out; their members can be isolated, labelled as "unprofessional" or "subjective", or seen as inappropriately using their status to promote personal interests. Movements to explore and act on the wider social responsibilities of professionals can be seen as attempts to act separately from the larger, established professional hierarchy, to set up different rules governing professional practices, and to establish new links with the communities of clients. Ultimately this can lead to an effort to take some of the power and knowledge of the profession and pass it on to a larger lay group — to demystify the profession and undermine its status as the exclusive guardian of certain knowledge, judgements, and authority.

ISSUES AND AGENDAS: WHAT IS THE GOAL OF THE ACTIVIST GROUP?

Obviously, activist groups have very different goals, and each kind of coalition or committee of professionals can be useful. I will try to outline below some

of the different ways I see such groups operating, and I will focus on those which encourage an integrated view of their values, their politics, and their professional endeavours. I have divided professional activist groups into two general categories: those dealing mainly with standards of professional practice, matters relevant primarily to persons *within* particular professions, and those which take professionals *beyond* their own practices to deal with political and social issues relevant to the larger milieu.

Professional standards groups

This kind of group, which deals with activities within the discipline, is by far the most common and accepted form of professional ginger group. It would include the sub-committees of the American Association for the Advancement of Science (AAAS), the medical, engineering, and dental associations that deal with ethical professional practice. For example, the AAAS has an Office of Scientific Freedom and Responsibility, and it has sponsored workshops on whistle-blowing and a special project on professional ethics in scientific and engineering societies.[6] Many scientific or academic associations have developed conflict-of-interest and publishing guidelines that deal with such issues as plagiarism, republication of work, criteria for co-authorship, and measures for fairer and more effective peer review of publications by the professional association's journals.[7]

Beyond professional standards groups

There are several sorts of activities relating a profession and its functions to the broader social or political context. These can be intended to benefit society as a whole, on matters of universal relevance, like nuclear war. Alternatively, an activist group may have goals which are geared to a segment of the population which is particularly needy or deprived of professional services. The range of projects undertaken by such a group can be divided into three categories: collective advocacy and action on single, focussed issues; support and assistance to individual professionals determined to make their careers socially constructive; and public education and empowerment, to enable lay clients to assume more power and responsibility in their dealings with professionals. These categories are somewhat artificial, and several professional groups engage in two or all of them; nonetheless it is useful to distinguish between these various endeavours in order to observe the evolution of particular groups and their members.

1. Many professional organizations take part in focussed, issue-oriented collective activities, like anti-nuclear lobbying (Science for Peace), lobbying against extra-billing (the Medical Reform Group), and medical and legal assistance to prisoners of conscience and torture victims (the Medical and Legal Networks of the Canadian branch of Amnesty International).

2. Several of these groups also provide important support for individuals devoting themselves to lines of professional work chosen on the basis of personal convictions. These include:

   (a) *Not* doing work that is harmful (e.g., not accepting or applying for defence research contracts, and blowing the whistle on socially irresponsible activities in the profession); and

   (b) *Doing* work which has as its goal some social or political goal grander than effective and ethical delivery of professional services (e.g., lawyers working with the poor and the disenfranchised, academics carrying out peace research as Anatol Rapoport advocates,[8] doctors working to return medical decisions to the patient in community health settings where the doctors are staff and not free agents).

In one of the rare commentaries on these ginger groups in science Dot Griffiths, John Irvine, and Ian Miles describe the evolution of the British groups advocating socially responsible science, from the view that scientists must merely avoid harmful work to a much stronger commitment to positive, socially constructive professional activity.[9] A rather broad range of concerned scientists established the British

Society for Social Responsibility in Science (BSSRS) in 1969. Initially many members of this group articulated a use/abuse model of professional activity, arguing that science had the potential to be enormously beneficial but that it was often abused; and this abuse was the focus of their early efforts. Science and technology themselves were perceived as being either value-free or inherently good, and it was only those using (or abusing) the science who were to blame for the nasty outcomes of scientific work. Proponents of this view argued that individual professionals should produce honest "objective" work and should merely inform themselves on the uses to which it could be put. They actively avoided doing work which could be harmful.

More radical scientists, however, questioned this model, arguing that their work inevitably served social and political purposes and that the scientific bureaucracy itself reflected undesirable social and political assumptions. They supported the active pursuit of work which would directly benefit socially or politically deprived communities. This radical group gained control of the BSSRS, and the other, "liberal", group left to form the Council for Science and Society. Yet another group of British scientists and historians forms the Radical Science Collective, which argues that the very act of scientific inquiry must be political. They dispute the view that science can ever be "objective" or that it is only the products and applications of science that are political, and they suggest instead that the process of science inevitably incorporates the scientist's values, assumptions, and ideology.

3. Taken to its logical conclusion, professional activity which is devoted to social and political goals rather than merely the delivery of good-quality, non-harmful professional services can lead to public education and empowerment. Professional groups may share their knowledge and skills, making their expertise accessible to the public which needs it. This then places decisions in the hands of the public rather than in those of the professionals, and it allows the client groups to direct their professional employees and to participate in interpreting the results of professional intervention. Professional

determination to share authority also leads to public education and to work with the media in order to correct the public view of the profession as a monolith with a uniform view of the world and itself. Professional groups with these goals operate, by necessity, outside the official professional bodies, trying to forge independent links with clients and client groups.

An excellent example of a professional body devoted to work which is explicitly useful to socially disadvantaged groups is the International Institute of Concern for Public Health (IICPH), based in Toronto. The IICPH is directed by Dr. Rosalie Bertell, a biometrician, assisted by various medical consultants who provide their services to the institute for a pittance as well as by several administrative and support staff. Collectively, they work with groups of radiation victims and residents of polluted communities on their agendas and concerns. The IICPH has a strong commitment to respecting the priorities of its clients, as was reflected in Dr. Bertell's speech accepting the Right Livelihood Award (termed the "Alternative Nobel Prize"), in December 1986. The quotations she used in that speech were not from respected experts, statesmen, or religious leaders, but from the words of a woman who was a non-fatal casualty of the 1979 reactor accident at Three Mile Island.

Current IICPH projects include an International Conference on Radiation Victims and assistance to people in Malaysia who are suing the Asian Rare Earth Company for careless dumping of radioactive and chemical toxic waste.[10] IICPH has also contributed to the Ontario Nuclear Safety Review and has assisted the Serpent River Indian Band in carrying out a local health survey. I discuss this last project at length below, as an example of the kind of interactive professional work which allows the client, rather than the professional, to retain authority over the expert work which is carried out.

An example of client-professional interaction

In 1981 the IICPH was approached by the Serpent River Band, which has had more than the usual

share of the hard times experienced by native people. Over the past decade members of this band have been particularly concerned about an abandoned acid plant on their reserve. Initially the IICPH developed a health questionnaire for them to administer to members of three bands on the north shore of Lake Huron: the Serpent River, Mississagi, and Spanish River bands. This survey established a very rough indication of the background level of health in these communities and provided a basis for more detailed medical examination of individual band members. Follow-up activities included screening clinics for high blood pressure and diabetes, and educational programs focussed on alcoholism and other public health problems. The project was very unusual in that only the band office had the lists which identified participating households: the band, and not the experts it had hired, retained control over the survey. The band then wanted to find out whether the abandoned acid plant site presented a health hazard or could safely be used for residential or commercial purposes. Dr. Bertell and her team carried out further investigations and concluded that the old acid plant indeed posed a health threat to band members, and that no homes or workplaces should be built on the site until the plant residue had been removed; they also recommended that further investigations were required to determine how best to protect public health now and during the cleanup.

This work helped the Band to press for cleanup of the plant site and compensation for past suffering and damage. Inevitably, however, given the sparse resources and records to which the IICPH team had access, its reports were not without weaknesses. Their summary of the report concluded that: "The limitation of this report is obviously its lack of clinical medical studies and its inability to quantify the extent of the medical problems identified as of concern to the Band. These aspects await further authorization and financial assistance from Health and Welfare Canada." Clearly surveys like this one, carried out by non-experts and without external validation, are subject to serious reporting errors; nevertheless such preliminary indications of the nature and prevalence of local health problems can be the basis for subsequent more rigorous and expensive work.

Other cases, which as the work of Beverly Paigen on the health effects of Love Canal chemicals on local residents,[11] and that of Michael Rachlis (another participant in the "Activist Groups" session of the Waterloo Conference) with the Environmental Health Committee of the South Riverdale Community Health Centre on local lead pollution,[12] offer further examples of sympathetic professionals putting their expertise at the service of community groups with the specific purpose of helping them improve their local situations. In these cases the professionals invest their time in the pursuit of agendas which have largely been set outside the profession; and goals for particular pieces of work are developed interactively, with full participation of the lay clients.

A common pattern is revealed here: citizens raise an issue that intimately concerns them and their families and neighbours, and sympathetic experts and professionals respond to this concern, helping the citizens to study the problem, suggest remedies, and lobby to remove the cause. Sometimes the experts involved are criticized for employing "unscientific" or "unprofessional" methods, because the work is often carried out by volunteer citizens rather than by well-paid experts.[13] The fact remains that in many cases the citizen-instigated preliminary studies have indicated problems or alarming trends which have later been substantiated by government agencies with more time and resources. Of course, the government or agency officials rarely acknowledge their debt to the earlier studies; rather, they claim the hypotheses of those studies as their own. Official recognition and measurement of the problem may nonetheless then pave the way for action to remedy the situation or to compensate those who have suffered from it.

But there is another, more important, consequence of expert involvement in citizen advocacy. Ultimately, this kind of work encourages a critical public view of the role of the profession. It sows the seeds of a change in the popular perception of how professionals should behave. Experts dedicated to serving the broad public interest may be ignored or

even ridiculed by their colleagues; but the public will take notice. Eventually other public groups will demand similar treatment from members of the profession and, whether they like it or not, the more traditional professionals will have to alter their practices and their relationships with their clients.

It is no coincidence that the scientists or professional experts involved with citizen groups are often women. Women are likely to feel a greater responsibility to the lay communities to which they belong because they are usually more integrated into them: children ensure contacts with other parents in libraries, pools, community centres, schools, and daycares. This integration of the professional and the personal is important; it may be valued most by women, who often have to struggle to balance the demands of their careers and those of their families. Projects which combine these interests hold a natural appeal for many women.

DISCUSSION AND CONCLUSION

Women may deliberately seek a consonance between their professional and personal priorities, but there is a sense in which the values an individual holds most dear will unavoidably direct his or her career, whether this is welcome or not. I believe that professional behaviour is inescapably political, not in any partisan sense but because the choices that professionals make — in the work they pursue, the clients they cultivate, and the relationships they develop with those clients — inevitably reflect their values and the larger social goals they consider desirable. Indeed, professionals should recognize the responsibility they bear for the outcomes of their personal work, not merely in terms of traditional professional ethics but in terms of the goals and impacts of their particular professional practice on society. As individuals, or by participating in activist groups, they can give the public an alternative view of their profession and set the stage for public demand for more responsive, socially controlled professional practices.

This is an ambitious and demanding view of the social responsibilities of professionals and the groups to which they belong, but it is one which should, ultimately, be satisfying for those professionals adopting it. If professional work becomes more of an extension of the individual lives of the professionals, the professionals themselves become, in a sense, members of the communities that they also serve. And then they will never, in Shaw's words, "conspire against the laity."

ENDNOTES

1. George Bernard Shaw, *The Doctor's Dilemma* (London: Constable and Co., 1911, rev. 1932), Act I, p. 106.

2. Jack Stevenson, "Professionals and social responsibility: Conflict or congruence," *Journal of Business Ethics* **8**, 1989.

3. Note, for example, other papers in the same issue of the *JBE* by Mark Frankel and Leonard J. Brooks.

4. Some of the above passage was taken from Chapter 5 of my book, *Science Under Siege*, (Toronto: CBC Enterprises, 1988).

5. "OMA — Ministry of Health Task Force to analyze use of medical services," 12 February 1988 press release from the Ontario Ministry of Health.

6. See, for example, *Agenda Book* of the Workshop on Whistle Blowing in Biomedical Research, 1981, sponsored by the President's Commission for the Study of Ethical Problems in Medicine and Research, the American Association for the Advancement of Science Committee on Scientific Freedom and Responsibility, and Medicine in the Public Interest, all in Washington, D.C.; and R. Chalk, M. Frankel and S. Chafer, *The AAS Professional Ethics Project* (Washington: AAAS, 1980).

7. See, for example, Mark Frankel's "Professional codes: Why, how and with what impact," also in these proceedings.

8. Anatol Rapoport, "The redemption of science," in the *JBE* proceedings.

9. D. Griffiths, J. Irvine, and I. Miles, "Social statistics: Toward a radical science," in *Demystifying Social Statistics*, (J. Irvine, I. Miles, and J. Evans (eds.) (London: Pluto Press, 1979).

10. For more information contact Institute of Concern for Public Health, 830 Bathurst Street, Toronto, Ontario M5R 3G1.

11. B. Paigen, "Controversy at Love Canal," *The Hastings Centre Report* 12:3 (June 1982), pp. 29–37.

12. South Riverdale Community Health Centre, *Submission from the Environmental Health Committee of the South Riverdale Community Health Centre to the Royal Society of Canada Commission on Lead in the Environment*, 13 June 1985 and then again on 18 March 1986.

13. The inadequacies in the resources and time available to lay groups attempting or assisting with professional work often lays them and their professional allies open to accusations of bias and lack of rigour; but these criticisms can also be seen as a difference in outlook, a difference in the values and priorities of the professionals involved. Advocates of "complete evidence" or "clear statistical significance" are sometimes more willing to risk being wrong in saying that a problem does *not* exist than the responsible professional may be to risk being wrong in saying that a problem *does* exist. In one case, the error involves misspent public funds; in the other, damaged human health. See, for example, B. Paigen, 1982, *op. cit.*, and N. Ashford, "Ethical problems in using science in the regulatory process," *Natural Reserves and the Environment* 2:2 (Fall 1986), a publication of the American Bar Association.

16

Roger Boisjoly and the Challenger Disaster: The Ethical Dimensions

RUSSELL P. BOISJOLY
ELLEN FOSTER CURTIS
EUGENE MELLICAN

Introduction

On January 28, 1986, the space shuttle Challenger exploded 73 seconds into its flight, killing the seven astronauts aboard. As the [American] nation mourned the tragic loss of the crew members, the Rogers Commission was formed to investigate the causes of the disaster. The Commission concluded that the explosion occurred due to seal failure in one of the solid rocket booster joints. Testimony given by Roger Boisjoly, Senior Scientist and acknowledged rocket seal expert, indicated that top management at NASA and Morton Thiokol had been aware of problems with the O-ring seals, but agreed to launch against the recommendation of Boisjoly and other engineers. Boisjoly had alerted management to problems with the O-rings as early

as January, 1985, yet several shuttle launches prior to the Challenger had been approved without correcting the hazards. This suggests that the management practice of NASA and Morton Thiokol had created an environment which altered the framework for decision making, leading to a breakdown in communication between technical experts and their supervisors, and top level management, and to the acceptance of risks that both organizations had historically viewed as unacceptable. With human lives and the national interest at stake, serious ethical concerns are embedded in this dramatic change in management practice.

In fact, one of the most important aspects of the Challenger disaster — both in terms of the causal sequence that led to it and the lessons to be learned

From *Journal of Business Ethics* **8**: (1989) 217–230. © 1989 Kluwer Academic Publishers. Printed in the Netherlands. Reprinted by permission.

from it — is its ethical dimension. Ethical issues are woven throughout the tangled web of decisions, events, practices, and organizational structures that resulted in the loss of the Challenger and its seven astronauts. Therefore, an ethical analysis of this tragedy is essential for a full understanding of the event itself and for the implications it has for any endeavor where public policy, corporate practice, and individual decisions intersect.

The significance of an ethical analysis of the Challenger disaster is indicated by the fact that it immediately presents one of the most urgent, but difficult, issues in the examination of corporate and individual behavior today, i.e., whether existing ethical theories adequately address the problems posed by new technologies, new forms of organization, and evolving social systems. At the heart of this issue is the concept of responsibility. No ethical concept has been more affected by the impact of these changing realities. Modern technology has so transformed the context and scale of human action that not only do the traditional parameters of responsibility seem inadequate to contain the full range of human acts and their consequences, but even more fundamentally, it is no longer the individual that is the primary locus of power and responsibility, but public and private institutions. Thus, it would seem, it is no longer the character and virtues of individuals that determine the standards of moral conduct, it is the policies and structures of the institutional settings within which they live and work.

Many moral conflicts facing individuals within institutional settings do arise from matters pertaining to organizational structures or questions of public policy. As such, they are resolvable only at a level above the responsibilities of the individual. Therefore, some writers argue that the ethical responsibilities of the engineer or manager in a large corporation have as much to do with the organization as with the individual. Instead of expecting individual engineers or managers to be moral heroes, emphasis should be on the creation of organizational structures conducive to ethical behavior among all agents under their aegis. It would be futile to attempt to establish a sense of ethical responsibility in engineers and manage-

ment personnel and ignore the fact that such persons work within a socio-technical environment which increasingly undermines the notion of individual, responsible moral agency (Boling and Dempsey, 1981; DeGeorge, 1981).

Yet, others argue that precisely because of these organizational realities individual accountability must be re-emphasized to counteract the diffusion of responsibility within large organizations and to prevent its evasion under the rubric of collective responsibility. Undoubtedly institutions do take on a kind of collective life of their own, but they do not exist, or act, independently of the individuals that constitute them, whatever the theoretical and practical complexities of delineating the precise relationships involved. Far from diminishing individuals' obligations, the reality of organizational life increases them because the consequences of decisions and acts are extended and amplified through the reach and power of that reality. Since there are pervasive and inexorable connections between ethical standards and behavior of individuals within an organization and its structure and operation, "the sensitizing of professionals to ethical considerations should be increased so that institutional structures will reflect enhanced ethical sensitivities as trained professionals move up the organizational ladder to positions of leadership" (Mankin, 1981, p. 17).

By reason of the courageous activities and testimony of individuals like Roger Boisjoly, the Challenger disaster provides a fascinating illustration of the dynamic tension between organizational and individual responsibility. By focusing on this central issue, this article seeks to accomplish two objectives: first, to demonstrate the extent to which the Challenger disaster not only gives concrete expression to the ethical ambiguity that permeates the relationship between organizational and individual responsibility, but also, in fact, is a result of it; second, to reclaim the meaning and importance of individual responsibility within the diluting context of large organizations.

In meeting these objectives, the article is divided into two parts: a case study of Roger Boisjoly's efforts to galvanize management support for effectively correcting the high risk O-ring problems, his attempt to prevent the launch, the scenario which resulted in the launch decision, and Boisjoly's quest to set the record straight despite enormous personal and professional consequences; and an ethical analysis of these events.

Preview for disaster

On January 24, 1985, Roger Boisjoly, Senior Scientist at Morton Thiokol, watched the launch of Flight 51-C of the space shuttle program. He was at Cape Canaveral to inspect the solid rocket boosters from Flight 51-C following their recovery in the Atlantic Ocean and to conduct a training session at Kennedy Space Center (KSC) on the proper methods of inspecting the booster joints. While watching the launch, he noted that the temperature that day was much cooler than recorded at other launches, but was still much warmer than the 18 degree temperature encountered three days earlier when he arrived in Orlando. The unseasonably cold weather of the past several days had produced the worst citrus crop failures in Florida history.

When he inspected the solid rocket boosters several days later, Boisjoly discovered evidence that the primary O-ring seals on two field joints had been compromised by hot combustion gases (i.e., hot gas blow-by had occurred) which had also eroded part of the primary O-ring. This was the first time that a primary seal on a field joint had been penetrated. When he discovered the large amount of blackened grease between the primary and secondary seals, his concern heightened. The blackened grease was discovered over 80 degree and 110 degree arcs, respectively, on two of the seals, with the larger arc indicating greater hot gas blow-by. Post-flight calculations indicated that the ambient temperature of the field joints at launch time was 53 degrees. This evidence, coupled with his recollection of the low temperature the day of the launch and the citrus crop damage caused by the cold spell, led to his conclusion that the severe hot gas blow-by may have been caused by, and related to, low temperature. After reporting these findings to his superiors, Boisjoly presented them to engineers and management

at NASA's Marshall Space Flight Center (MSFC). As a result of his presentation at MSFC, Roger Boisjoly was asked to participate in the Flight Readiness Review (FRR) on February 12, 1985 for Flight 51-E which was scheduled for launch in April, 1985. This FRR represents the first association of low temperature with blow-by on a field joint, a condition that was considered an "acceptable risk" by Larry Mulloy, NASA's Manager for the Booster Project, and other NASA officials.

Roger Boisjoly had twenty-five years of experience as an engineer in the aerospace industry. Among his many notable assignments were the performance of stress and deflection analysis on the flight control equipment of the Advanced Minuteman Missile at Autonetics, and serving as a lead engineer on the lunar module of Apollo at Hamilton Standard. He moved to Utah in 1980 to take a position in the Applied Mechanics Department as a Staff Engineer at the Wasatch Division of Morton Thiokol. He was considered the leading expert in the United States on O-rings and rocket joint seals and received plaudits for his work on the joint seal problems from Joe C. Kilminster, Vice President of Space Booster Programs, Morton Thiokol (Kilminster, July, 1985). His commitment to the company and the community was further demonstrated by his service as Mayor of Willard, Utah from 1982 to 1983.

The tough questioning he received at the February 12th FRR convinced Boisjoly of the need for further evidence linking low temperature and hot gas blow-by. He worked closely with Arnie Thompson, Supervisor of Rocket Motor Cases, who conducted subscale laboratory tests in March, 1985, to further test the effects of temperature on O-ring resiliency. The bench tests that were performed provided powerful evidence to support Boisjoly's and Thompson's theory: Low temperatures greatly and adversely affected the ability of O-rings to create a seal on solid rocket booster joints. If the temperature was too low (and they did not know what the threshold temperature would be), it was possible that neither the primary or secondary O-rings would seal!

One month later the post-flight inspection of

Flight 51-B revealed that the primary seal of a booster nozzle joint did not make contact during its two minute flight. If this damage had occurred in a field joint, the secondary O-ring may have failed to seal, causing the loss of the flight. As a result, Boisjoly and his colleagues became increasingly concerned about shuttle safety. This evidence from the inspection of Flight 51-B was presented at the FRR for Flight 51-F on July 1, 1985; the key engineers and managers at NASA and Morton Thiokol were now aware of the critical O-ring problems and the influence of low temperature on the performance of the joint seals.

During July, 1985, Boisjoly and his associates voiced their desire to devote more effort and resources to solving the problems of O-ring erosion. In his activity reports dated July 22 and 29, 1985, Boisjoly expressed considerable frustration with the lack of progress in this area, despite the fact that a Seal Erosion Task Force had been informally appointed on July 19th. Finally, Boisjoly wrote the following memo, labelled "Company Private", to R.K. (Bob) Lund, Vice President of Engineering for Morton Thiokol, to express the extreme urgency of his concerns. Here are some excerpts from that memo:

> This letter is written to insure that management is fully aware of the seriousness of the current O-ring erosion problem . . . The mistakenly accepted position on the joint problem was to fly without fear of failure . . . is now drastically changed as a result of the SRM 16A nozzle joint erosion which eroded a secondary O-ring with the primary O-ring never sealing. If the same scenario should occur in a field joint (and it could), then it is a jump ball as to the success or failure of the joint . . . The result would be a catastrophe of the highest order — loss of human life . . .
>
> It is my honest and real fear that if we do not take immediate action to dedicate a team to solve the problem, with the field joint having the number one priority, then we stand in jeopardy of losing a flight along with all the launch pad facilities (Boisjoly, July, 1985a).

On August 20, 1985, R.K. Lund formally announced the formation of the Seal Erosion Task Team. The team consisted of only five full-time engineers from the 2500 employed by Morton Thiokol on the Space Shuttle Program. The events of the next five months would demonstrate that management had not provided the resources necessary to carry out the enormous task of solving the seal erosion problem.

On October 3, 1985, the Seal Erosion Task Force met with Joe Kilminster to discuss the problems they were having in gaining organizational support necessary to solve the O-ring problems. Boisjoly later stated that Kilminster summarized the meeting as a "good bullshit session." Once again frustrated by bureaucratic inertia, Boisjoly wrote in his activity report dated October 4th:

> . . . NASA is sending an engineering representative to stay with us starting Oct. 14th. We feel that this is a direct result of their feeling that we (MTI) are not responding quickly enough to the seal problem . . . upper management apparently feels that the SRM program is ours for sure and the customer be damned (Boisjoly, October, 1985b).

Boisjoly was not alone in his expression of frustration. Bob Ebeling, Department Manager, Solid Rocket Motor Igniter and Final Assembly, and a member of the Seal Erosion Task Force, wrote in a memo to Allan McDonald, Manager of the Solid Rocket Motor Project, "HELP! The seal task force is constantly being delayed by every possible means . . . We wish we could get action by verbal request, but such is not the case. This is a red flag" (McConnell, 1987).

At the Society of Automotive Engineers (SAE) conference on October 7, 1985, Boisjoly presented a six-page overview of the joints and the seal configuration to approximately 130 technical experts in hope of soliciting suggestions for remedying the O-ring problems. Although MSFC had requested the presentation, NASA gave strict instructions not to express the critical urgency of fixing the joints, but merely to ask for suggestions for improvement. Although no help was forthcoming, the conference was a milestone in that it was the first time that NASA allowed information on the O-ring difficulties to be expressed in a public forum. That NASA also recognized that the O-ring problems were not receiving appropriate attention and manpower considerations from Morton Thiokol management is further evidenced by Boisjoly's October 24 log entry, ". . . Jerry Peoples (NASA) has informed his people that our group needs more authority and people to do the job. Jim Smith (NASA) will corner Al McDonald today to attempt to implement this direction."

The October 30 launch of Flight 61-A of the Challenger provided the most convincing, and yet to some the most contestable, evidence to date that low temperature was directly related to hot gas blow-by. The left booster experienced hot gas blow-by in the center and aft field joints without any seal erosion. The ambient temperature of the field joints was estimated to be 75 degrees at launch time based on post-flight calculations. Inspection of the booster joints revealed that the blow-by was less severe than that found on Flight 51-C because the seal grease was a grayish black color, rather than the jet black hue of Flight 51-C. The evidence was now consistent with the bench tests for joint resiliency conducted in March. That is, at 75 degrees the O-ring lost contact with its sealing surface for 2.4 seconds, whereas at 50 degrees the O-ring lost contact for 10 minutes. The actual flight data revealed greater hot gas blow-by for the O-rings on Flight 51-C which had an ambient temperature of 53 degrees than for Flight 61-A which had an ambient temperature of 75 degrees. Those who rejected this line of reasoning concluded that temperature must be irrelevant since hot gas blow-by had occurred even at room temperature (75 degrees). This difference in interpretation would receive further attention on January 27, 1986.

During the next two and one-half months, little progress was made in obtaining a solution to the O-ring problems. Roger Boisjoly made the following entry into his log on January 13, 1986, "O-ring resiliency tests that were requested on September 24, 1985 are now scheduled for January 15, 1986."

The day before the disaster

At 10 a.m. on January 27, 1986, Arnie Thompson received a phone call from Boyd Brinton, Thiokol's Manager of Project Engineering at MSFC, relaying the concerns of NASA's Larry Wear, also at MSFC,

about the 18 degree temperature forecast for the launch of Flight 51-L, the Challenger, scheduled for the next day. This phone call precipitated a series of meetings within Morton Thiokol, at the Marshall Space Flight Center; and at the Kennedy Space Center that culminated in a three-way telecon involving three teams of engineers and managers, that began at 8:15 p.m. E.S.T.

Joe Kilminster, Vice President, Space Booster Programs, of Morton Thiokol began the telecon by turning the presentation of the engineering charts over to Roger Boisjoly and Arnie Thompson. They presented thirteen charts which resulted in a recommendation against the launch of the Challenger. Boisjoly demonstrated their concerns with the performance of the O-rings in the field joints during the initial phases of Challenger's flight with charts showing the effects of primary O-ring erosion, and its timing, on the ability to maintain a reliable secondary seal. The tremendous pressure and release of power from the rocket boosters create rotation in the joint such that the metal moves away from the O-rings so that they cannot maintain contact with the metal surfaces. If, at the same time, erosion occurs in the primary O-ring for any reason, then there is a reduced probability of maintaining a secondary seal. It is highly probable that as the ambient temperature drops, the primary O-ring will not seat; that there will be hot gas blow-by and erosion of the primary O-ring; and that a catastrophe will occur when the secondary O-ring fails to seal.

Bob Lund presented the final chart that included the Morton Thiokol recommendations that the ambient temperature including wind must be such that the seal temperature would be greater than 53 degrees to proceed with the launch. Since the overnight low was predicted to be 18 degrees, Bob Lund recommended against launch on January 28, 1986 or until the seal temperature exceeded 53 degrees.

NASA's Larry Mulloy bypassed Bob Lund and directly asked Joe Kilminster for his reaction. Kilminster stated that he supported the position of his engineers and he would not recommend launch below 53 degrees.

George Hardy, Deputy Director of Science and Engineering at MSFC, said he was "appalled at that recommendation," according to Allan McDonald's testimony before the Rogers Commission. Nevertheless, Hardy would not recommend to launch if the contractor was against it. After Hardy's reaction, Stanley Reinartz, Manager of Shuttle Project Office at MSFC, objected by pointing out that the solid rocket motors were qualified to operate between 40 and 90 degrees Fahrenheit.

Larry Mulloy, citing the data from Flight 61-A which indicated to him that temperature was not a factor, strenuously objected to Morton Thiokol's recommendation. He suggested that Thiokol was attempting to establish new Launch Commit Criteria at 53 degrees and that they couldn't do that the night before a launch. In exasperation Mulloy asked, "My God, Thiokol, when do you want me to launch? Next April?" (McConnell, 1987). Although other NASA officials also objected to the association of temperature with O-ring erosion and hot gas blow-by, Roger Boisjoly was able to hold his ground and demonstrate with the use of his charts and pictures that there was indeed a relationship: The lower the temperature the higher the probability of erosion and blow-by and the greater the likelihood of an accident. Finally, Joe Kilminster asked for a five minute caucus off-net.

According to Boisjoly's testimony before the Rogers Commission, Jerry Mason, Senior Vice President of Wasatch Operations, began the caucus by saying that "a management decision was necessary." Sensing that an attempt would be made to overturn the no-launch decision, Boisjoly and Thompson attempted to re-review the material previously presented to NASA for the executives in the room. Thompson took a pad of paper and tried to sketch out the problem with the joint, while Boisjoly laid out the photos of the compromised joints from Flights 51-C and 61-A. When they became convinced that no one was listening, they ceased their efforts. As Boisjoly would later testify, "There was not one positive pro-launch statement ever made by anybody" (Report of the Presidential Commission, 1986, IV, p. 792, hereafter abbreviated as R.C.).

According to Boisjoly, after he and Thompson made their last attempts to stop the launch, Jerry Mason asked rhetorically, "Am I the only one who wants to fly?" Mason turned to Bob Lund and asked him to "take off his engineering hat and put on his management hat." The four managers held a brief discussion and voted unanimously to recommend Challenger's launch.

Exhibit I shows the revised recommendations that were presented that evening by Joe Kilminster after the caucus to support management's decision

---

EXHIBIT 1:   MTI assessment of temperature concern on SRM-25 (51L) launch

---

- CALCULATIONS SHOW THAT SRM-25 O-RINGS WILL BE 20° COLDER THAN SRM-15 O-RINGS
- TEMPERATURE DATA NOT CONCLUSIVE ON PREDICTING PRIMARY O-RING BLOW-BY
- ENGINEERING ASSESSMENT IS THAT:
    - COLDER O-RINGS WILL HAVE INCREASED EFFECTIVE DUROMETER ("HARDER")
- "HARDER" O-RINGS WILL TAKE LONGER TO "SEAT"
    - MORE GAS MAY PASS PRIMARY O-RING BEFORE THE PRIMARY SEAL SEATS (RELATIVE TO SRM-15)
    - DEMONSTRATED SEALING THRESHOLD IS 3 TIMES GREATER THAN 0.038″ EROSION EXPERIENCED ON SRM-15
  - IF THE PRIMARY SEAL DOES NOT SEAT, THE SECONDARY SEAL WILL SEAT
    - PRESSURE WILL GET TO SECONDARY SEAL BEFORE THE METAL PARTS ROTATE
      - O-RING PRESSURE LEAK CHECK PLACES SECONDARY SEAL IN OUTBOARD POSITION WHICH MINIMIZES SEALING TIME
- MTI RECOMMENDS STS-51L LAUNCH PROCEED ON 28 JANUARY 1986
    - SRM-25 WILL NOT BE SIGNIFICANTLY DIFFERENT FROM SRM-15

Joe C. Kilminster, Vice President Space Booster Programs

to launch. Only one of the rationales presented that evening supported the launch (demonstrated erosion sealing threshold is three times greater than 0.038″ erosion experienced on SRM-15). Even so, the issue at hand was sealability at low temperature, not erosion. While one other rationale could be considered a neutral statement of engineering fact (O-ring pressure leak check places secondary seal in outboard position which minimizes sealing time), the other seven rationales are negative, anti-launch, statements. After hearing Kilminster's presentation, which was accepted without a single probing question, George Hardy asked him to sign the chart and telefax it to Kennedy Space Center and Marshall Space Flight Center. At 11 p.m. E.S.T. the teleconference ended.

Aside from the four senior Morton Thiokol executives present at the teleconference, all others were excluded from the final decision. The process represented a radical shift from previous NASA policy. Until that moment, the burden of proof had always been on the engineers to prove beyond a doubt that it was safe to launch. NASA, with their objections to the original Thiokol recommendation against the launch, and Mason, with his request for a "management decision," shifted the burden of proof in the opposite direction. Morton Thiokol was expected to prove that launching Challenger would not be safe (R.C., IV, p. 793).

The change in the decision so deeply upset Boisjoly that he returned to his office and made the following journal entry:

> I sincerely hope this launch does not result in a catastrophe. I personally do not agree with some of the statements made in Joe Kilminster's written summary stating that SRM-25 is okay to fly (Boisjoly, 1987).

The disaster and its aftermath

On January 28, 1986, a reluctant Roger Boisjoly watched the launch of the Challenger. As the vehicle cleared the tower, Bob Ebeling whispered, "we've just dodged a bullet." (The engineers who opposed the launch assumed that O-ring failure would result in an explosion almost immediately after engine ignition.) To continue in Boisjoly's words, "At approximately T—60 seconds Bob told me he had just completed a prayer of thanks to the Lord for a successful launch. Just thirteen seconds later we both saw the horror of the destruction as the vehicle exploded" (Boisjoly, 1987).

Morton Thiokol formed a failure investigation team on January 31, 1986 to study the Challenger explosion. Roger Boisjoly and Arnie Thompson were part of the team that was sent to MSFC in Huntsville, Alabama. Boisjoly's first inkling of a division between himself and management came on February 13 when he was informed at the last minute that he was to testify before the Rogers Commission the next day. He had very little time to prepare for his testimony. Five days later, two Commission members held a closed session with Kilminster, Boisjoly, and Thompson. During the interview Boisjoly gave his memos and activity reports to the Commissioners. After that meeting, Kilminster chastised Thompson and Boisjoly for correcting his interpretation of the technical data. Their response was that they would continue to correct his version if it was technically incorrect.

Boisjoly's February 25th testimony before the Commission, rebutting the general manager's statement that the initial decision against the launch was not unanimous, drove a wedge further between him and Morton Thiokol management. Boisjoly was flown to MSFC before he could hear the NASA testimony about the pre-flight telecon. The next day, he was removed from the failure investigation team and returned to Utah.

Beginning in April, Boisjoly began to believe that for the previous month he had been used solely for public relations purposes. Although given the title of Seal Coordinator for the redesign effort, he was isolated from NASA and the seal redesign effort. His design information had been changed without his knowledge and presented without his feedback. On May 1, 1986, in a briefing preceding closed sessions before the Rogers Commission, Ed Garrison, President of Aerospace Operations for Morton Thiokol, chastised Boisjoly for "airing the company's dirty laundry" with the memos he had given the Commission. The next day, Boisjoly testified about the change in his job assignment. Commission Chairman Rogers critized Thiokol management, ". . . if it appears that you're punishing the two people or at least two of the people who are right about the decision and objected to the launch which ultimately resulted in criticism of Thiokol and then they're demoted or feel that they are being retaliated against, that is a very serious matter. It would seem to me, just speaking for myself, they should be promoted, not demoted or pushed aside" (R.C., V, p. 1586).

Boisjoly now sensed a major rift developing within the corporation. Some co-workers perceived that his testimony was damaging the company image. In an effort to clear the air, he and McDonald requested a private meeting with the company's three top executives, which was held on May 16, 1986. According to Boisjoly, management was unreceptive throughout the meeting. The CEO told McDonald and Boisjoly that the company "was doing just fine until Al and I testified about our job reassignments" (Boisjoly, 1987). McDonald and Boisjoly were nominally restored to their former assignments, but Boisjoly's position became untenable as time passed. On July 21, 1986, Roger Boisjoly requested an extended sick leave from Morton Thiokol.

Ethical analysis

It is clear from this case study that Roger Boisjoly's experiences before and after the Challenger disaster raise numerous ethical questions that are integral to any explanation of the disaster and applicable to other management situations, especially those involving highly complex technologies. The difficulties and uncertainties involved in the management of these technologies exacerbate the kind of bureaucratic syndromes that generate ethical conflicts in the first place. In fact, Boisjoly's experiences could well serve as a paradigmatic case study for such ethical problems, ranging from accountability to corporate loyalty and whistleblowing. Underlying all these issues, however, is the problematic relationship between individual and organizational responsibility. Boisjoly's experiences

graphically portray the tensions inherent in this relationship in a manner that discloses its importance in the causal sequence leading to the Challenger disaster. The following analysis explicates this and the implications it has for other organizational settings.

By focusing on the problematic relationship between individual and organizational responsibility, this analysis reveals that the organizational structure governing the space shuttle program became the locus of responsibility in such a way that not only did it undermine the responsibilities of individual decision makers within the process, but it also became a means of avoiding real, effective responsibility throughout the entire management system. The first clue to this was clearly articulated as early as 1973 by the board of inquiry that was formed to investigate the accident which occurred during the launch of Skylab 1:

> The management system developed by NASA for manned space flight places large emphasis on rigor, detail, and thoroughness. In hand with this emphasis comes formalism, extensive documentation, and visibility in detail to senior management. While nearly perfect, such a system can submerge the concerned individual and depress the role of the intuitive engineer or analyst. It may not allow full play for the intuitive judgment or past experience of the individual. An emphasis on management systems can, in itself, serve to separate the people engaged in the program from the real world of hardware (Quoted in Christiansen, 1987, p. 23).

To examine this prescient statement in ethical terms is to see at another level the serious consequences inherent in the situation it describes. For example, it points to a dual meaning of responsibility. One meaning emphasizes carrying out an authoritatively prescribed review process, while the second stresses the cognitive independence and input of every individual down the entire chain of authority. The first sense of responsibility shifts the ethical center of gravity precipitously away from individual moral agency onto the review process in such a way that what was originally set up to guarantee flight readiness with the professional and personal integrity of the responsible individuals, instead becomes a means of evading personal responsibility for decisions made in the review process.

A crucial, and telling, example of this involves the important question asked by the Rogers Commission as to why the concerns raised by the Morton Thiokol engineers about the effects of cold weather on the O-rings during the teleconference the night before the launch were not passed up from Level III to Levels II or I in the preflight review process. The NASA launch procedure clearly demands that decisions and objections methodically follow a prescribed path up all levels. Yet, Lawrence Mulloy, operating at Level III as the Solid Rocket Booster Project Manager at MSFC, did not transmit the Morton Thiokol concerns upward (through his immediate superior, Stanley Reinartz) to Level II. When asked by Chairman Rogers to explain why, Mr. Mulloy testified:

> At that time, and I still consider today, that was a Level III issue, Level III being a SRB element or an external tank element or Space Shuttle main engine element or an Orbiter. There was no violation of Launch Commit Criteria. There was no waiver required in my judgment at that time and still today (R.C., I, p. 98).

In examining this response in terms of shifting responsibility onto the review process itself, there are two things that are particularly striking in Mr. Mulloy's statement. The first is his emphasis that this was a "Level III issue." In a formal sense, Mr. Mulloy is correct. However, those on Level III also had the authority — and, one would think, especially in this instance given the heated discussion on the effects of cold on the O-rings, the motivation — to pass objections and concerns on to Levels II and I. But here the second important point in Mr. Mulloy's testimony comes into play when he states, "there was no violation of Launch Commit Criteria." In other words, since there was no Launch Commit Criteria for joint temperature, concerns about joint temperature did not officially fall under the purview of the review process. Therefore, the ultimate justification for Mr. Mulloy's position rests on the formal process itself. He was just following

the rules by staying within the already established scope of the review process.

This underscores the moral imperative executives must exercise by creating and maintaining organizational systems that do not separate the authority of decision makers from the responsibility they bear for decisions, or insulate them from the consequences of their actions or omissions.

Certainly, there can be no more vivid example than the shuttle program to verify that, in fact, "an emphasis on management systems can, in itself, serve to separate the people engaged in the program from the real world of hardware." Time and time again the lack of communication that lay at the heart of the Rogers Commission finding that "there was a serious flaw in the decision making process leading up to the launch of flight 51-L" (R.C., I, p. 104) was explained by the NASA officials or managers at Morton Thiokol with such statements as, "that is not my reporting channel," or "he is not in the launch decision chain," or "I didn't meet with Mr. Boisjoly, I met with Don Ketner, who is the task team leader" (R.C., IV, p. 821, testimony of Mr. Lund). Even those managers who had direct responsibility for line engineers and workmen depended on formalized memo writing procedures for communication to the point that some "never talked to them directly" (Feynman, 1988, p. 33).

Within the atmosphere of such an ambiguity of responsibility, when a life threatening conflict arose within the management system and individuals (such as Roger Boisjoly and his engineering associates at Morton Thiokol) tried to reassert the full weight of their individual judgments and attendant responsibilities, the very purpose of the flight readiness review process, i.e., to arrive at the "technical" truth of the situation, which includes the recognition of the uncertainties involved as much as the findings, became subverted into an adversary confrontation in which "adversary" truth, with its suppression of uncertainties, became operative (Wilmotte, 1970).

What is particularly significant in this radical transformation of the review process, in which the Morton Thiokol engineers were forced into "the position of having to prove that it was unsafe instead of the other way around" (R.C., IV, p. 822; see also p. 793), is that what made the suppression of technical uncertainties possible is precisely that mode of thinking which, in being challenged by independent professional judgments, gave rise to the adversarial setting in the first place: groupthink. No more accurate description for what transpired the night before the launch of the Challenger can be given than the definition of groupthink as:

> . . . a mode of thinking that people engage in when they are deeply involved in a cohesive in-group, when the members' strivings for unanimity override their motivation to realistically appraise alternative courses of action.

> . . . Groupthink refers to the deterioration of mental efficiency, reality testing, and moral judgment that results from in-group pressures (Janis, 1972, p. 9).

From this perspective, the full import of Mr. Mason's telling Mr. Lund to "take off his engineering hat and put on his management hat" is revealed. He did not want another technical, reality-based judgment of an independent professional engineer. As he had already implied when he opened the caucus by stating "a management decision was necessary," he wanted a group decision, specifically one that would, in the words of the Rogers Commission, "accommodate a major customer" (R.C., I, p. 104). With a group decision the objections of the engineers could be mitigated, the risks shared, fears allayed, and the attendant responsibility diffused.[1]

This analysis is not meant to imply that group-think was a pervasive or continuous mode of thinking at either NASA or Morton Thiokol. What is suggested is a causal relationship between this instance of groupthink and the ambiguity of responsibility found within the space shuttle program. Whenever a management system, such as NASA's generates "a mindset of 'collective responsibility'" by leading "individuals to defer to the anonymity of the process and not focus closely enough on their individual responsibilities in the decision chain," (N.R.C. Report, 1988, p. 68) and there is a confluence of the kind of pressures that came to bear on the decision making process the night

before the launch, the conditions are in place for groupthink to prevail.

A disturbing feature of so many of the analyses and commentaries on the Challenger disaster is the reinforcement, and implicit acceptance, of this shift away from individual moral agency with an almost exclusive focus on the flaws in the management system, organizational structures and/or decision making process. Beginning with the findings of the Rogers Commission investigation, one could practically conclude that no one had any responsibility whatsoever for the disaster. The Commission concluded that "there was a serious flaw in the decision making process leading up to the launch of flight 51-L. A well structured and managed system emphasizing safety would have flagged the rising doubts about the Solid Rocket Booster joint seal." Then the Commission report immediately states, "Had these matters been clearly stated and emphasized in the flight readiness process in terms reflecting the views of most of the Thiokol engineers and at least some of the Marshall engineers, it seems likely that the launch of 51-L might not have occurred when it did" (R.C., I, p. 104). But the gathering and passing on of such information was the responsibility of specifically designated individuals, known by name and position in the highly structured review process. Throughout this process there had been required "a series of formal, legally binding certifications, the equivalent of airworthiness inspections in the aviation industry. In effect the myriad contractor and NASA personnel involved were guaranteeing Challenger's flight readiness with their professional and personal integrity" (McConnell, 1987, p. 17).

When the Commission states in its next finding that "waiving of launch constraints appears to have been at the expense of flight safety," the immediate and obvious question would seem to be: Who approved the waivers and assumed this enormous risk? And why? This is a serious matter! A launch constraint is only issued because there is a safety problem serious enough to justify a decision not to launch. However, the Commission again deflects the problem onto the system by stating, "There was no system which made it imperative that launch constraints and waivers of launch constraints be considered by all levels of management" (R.C., 1986, I, p. 104).

There are two puzzling aspects to this Commission finding. First, the formal system already contained the requirement that project offices inform at least Level II of launch constraints. The Commission addressed the explicit violation of this requirement in the case of a July 1985 launch constraint that had been imposed on the Solid Rocket Booster because of O-ring erosion on the nozzle:

> NASA Levels I and II apparently did not realize Marshall had assigned a launch constraint within the Problem Assessment System. This communication failure was contrary to the requirement, contained in the NASA Problem Reporting and Corrective Action Requirements System, that launch constraints were to be taken to Level II (R.C., 1986, I, pp. 138–139; see also p. 159).

Second, the Commission clearly established that the individual at Marshall who both imposed and waived the launch constraint was Lawrence Mulloy, SRB Project Manager. Then why blame the management system, especially in such a crucial area as that of launch constraints, when procedures of that system were not followed? Is that approach going to increase the accountability of individuals within the system for future Flights?

Even such an independent minded and probing Commission member as Richard Feynman, in an interview a year after the disaster, agreed with the avoidance of determining individual accountability for specific actions and decisions. He is quoted as saying, "I don't think it's correct to try to find out which particular guy happened to do what particular thing. It's the question of how the atmosphere could get to such a circumstance that such things were possible without anybody catching on." Yet, at the same time Feynman admitted that he was not confident that any restructuring of the management system will ensure that the kinds of problems that resulted in the Challenger disaster — "danger signs not seen and warnings not heeded" — do not recur. He said, "I'm really not sure that any kind of simple mechanism can cure stupidity and dullness. You can make up all the rules about how things should be, and they'll go wrong if the spirit is differ-

ent, if the attitudes are different over time and as personnel change" (Chandler, 1987, p. 50).

The approach of the Rogers Commission and that of most of the analyses of the Challenger disaster is consistent with the growing tendency to deny any specific responsibility to individual persons within corporate or other institutional settings when things go wrong. Although there are obviously many social changes in modern life that justify the shift in focus from individuals to organizational structures as bearers of responsibility, this shift is reinforced and exaggerated by the way people think about and accept those changes. One of the most pernicious problems of modern times is the almost universally held belief that the individual is powerless, especially within the context of large organizations where one may perceive oneself, and be viewed, as a very small, and replaceable, cog. It is in the very nature of this situation that responsibility may seem to become so diffused that no one person IS responsible. As the National Research Council committee, in following up on the Rogers Commission, concluded about the space shuttle program:

> Given the pervasive reliance on teams and boards to consider the key questions affecting safety, 'group democracy' can easily prevail . . . in the end all decisions become collective ones . . . (N.R.C. Report, pp. 68 and 70).

The problem with this emphasis on management systems and collective responsibility is that it fosters a vicious circle that further and further erodes and obscures individual responsibility. This leads to a paradoxical — and untenable — situation (such as in the space shuttle program) in which decisions are made and actions are performed by individuals or groups of individuals but not attributed to them. It thus reinforces the tendency to avoid accountability for what anyone does by attributing the consequences to the organization or decision making process. Again, shared, rather than individual, risk-taking and responsibility become operative. The end result can be a cancerous attitude that so permeates an organization or management system that it metastasizes into decisions and acts of life-threatening irresponsibility.

In sharp contrast to this prevalent emphasis on organizational structures, one of the most fascinating aspects of the extensive and exhaustive investigations into the Challenger disaster is that they provide a rare opportunity to re-affirm the sense and importance of individual responsibility. With the inside look into the space shuttle program these investigations detail, one can identify many instances where personal responsibility, carefully interpreted, can properly be imputed to NASA officials and to its contractors. By so doing, one can preserve, if only in a fragmentary way, the essentials of the traditional concept of individual responsibility within the diluting context of organizational life. This effort is intended to make explicit the kind of causal links that are operative between the actions of individuals and the structures of organizations.

The criteria commonly employed for holding individuals responsible for an outcome are two: (1) their acts or omissions are in some way a cause of it; and (2) these acts or omissions are not done in ignorance or under coercion (Thompson, 1987, p. 47). Although there are difficult theoretical and practical questions associated with both criteria, especially within organizational settings, nevertheless, even a general application of them to the sequence of events leading up to the Challenger disaster reveals those places where the principle of individual responsibility must be factored in if our understanding of it is to be complete, its lessons learned, and its repetition avoided.

The Rogers Commission has been criticized — and rightly so — for looking at the disaster "from the bottom up but not from the top down," with the result that it gives a clearer picture of what transpired at the lower levels of the Challenger's flight review process than at its upper levels (Cook, 1986). Nevertheless, in doing so, the Commission report provides powerful testimony that however elaborately structured and far reaching an undertaking such as the space shuttle program may be, individuals at the bottom of the organizational structure can still play a crucial, if not deciding, role in the outcome. For in the final analysis, whatever the defects in the Challenger's launch decision chain were that kept the upper levels from being duly informed about the objections of the engineers at Morton

Thiokol, the fact remains that the strenuous objections of these engineers so forced the decision process at their level that the four middle managers at Morton Thiokol had the full responsibility for the launch in their hands. This is made clear in the startling testimony of Mr. Mason, when Chairman Rogers asked him: "Did you realize, and particularly in view of Mr. Hardy's (Deputy Director of Science and Engineering at MSFC) point that they wouldn't launch unless you agreed, did you fully realize that in effect, you were making a decision to launch, you and your colleagues?" Mr. Mason replied, "Yes sir" (R.C., 1986, IV, p. 770).

If these four men had just said no, the launch of the Challenger would not have taken place the next day. Could there have been any doubt about what was at stake in their decision, or about the degree of risk involved? Not in view of the follow up testimony of Brian Russell, another Thiokol engineer present at the teleconference. Mr. Russell was asked by Mr. Acheson to give his recollection of the thought process followed in his mind "in the change of position between the view presented in the telecon that Thiokol was opposed to the launch, and the subsequent conclusion of the caucus within the company" (R.C., 1986, IV, p. 821). In the course of his response, Mr. Russell stated:

> But I felt in my mind that once we had done our very best to explain why we were concerned, and we meaning those in the camp who really felt strongly about the recommendation of 53 degrees, the decision was to be made, and a poll was then taken. And I remember distinctly at the time wondering whether I would have the courage, if asked, and I thought I might be, what I would do and whether I would be alone. I didn't think I would be alone, but I was wondering if I would have the courage, I remember that distinctly, to stand up and say no . . . I was nervous . . . there was a nervousness there that we were increasing the risk, and I believe all of us knew that if it were increased to the level of O-ring burnthrough, what the consequences would be. And I don't think there's any question in anyone's mind about that (R.C., 1986, IV, pp. 822–823).

Some pertinent observations that have direct implications for managers in any organization must be made about where the principle of individual responsibility intersects with the structural flaws and organizational deterioration that have been attributed such a prominent role in the Challenger disaster. While it is on the basis of these flaws that the Rogers Commission absolved NASA officials of any direct responsibility for the disaster, it must nevertheless be pointed out that such officials "act in the context of a continuing institution, not an isolated incident, and they or other officials therefore may be culpable for creating the structural faults of the organization, or for neglecting to notice them, or for making inadequate efforts to correct them" (Thompson, 1987, p. 46). While it is true that attributing responsibility demands precision in determining the consequences of acts as much as in identifying the agents, this specificity of outcomes "does not preclude responsibility for patterns of decision and decision making" (Thompson, 1987, p. 48). Therefore, among the outcomes for which managers are held responsible, the continuing practices, standards, and structures of their organizations should be included.

Of all the descriptions of the flaws, break downs, and deterioration of NASA's managerial system, none point to any failures that fall outside the well-documented pathologies of bureaucratic behavior (e.g., lack of communication, distortion of information as it passes up the hierarchy, jealousy of existing lines of authority, bias in favor of the *status quo*, bureaucratic turf protection, power games, inclination to view the public interest through the distorted lens of vested interests, the "think positive" or "can-do" syndrome), and, as such, they can be anticipated. That bureaucratic routines "have a life of their own, often roaming beyond their original purpose, is a fact of organizational behavior that officials should be expected to appreciate. The more the consequences of a decision fit such bureaucratic patterns, the less an official can plausibly invoke the excuse from ignorance" (Thompson, 1987, p. 61).

So much has been made of NASA's top officials not being fully informed of the extent of the problems with the O-rings, and specifically of the Thiokol engineers' objections to the Challenger launch in cold weather, that an analysis of the disaster in *Fortune* magazine had as its title, "NASA's Challenge: Ending Isolation at the Top" (Brody, 1986). The actual extent of their isolation has been questioned, and even the Rogers Commission is not consistent on this issue. In its findings for Chapter V, the Commission states, "A well structured and managed system emphasizing safety would have flagged the rising doubts about the Solid Rocket Booster joint seal." Nevertheless, it concludes in the next chapter that "the O-ring erosion history presented to Level I at NASA Headquarters in August 1985 was sufficiently detailed to require corrective action prior to the next flight" (R.C., 1986, I, pp. 104 and 148).

Whatever the extent of their ignorance, an important principle comes into play in determining the degree of individual responsibility. It is implied in Richard Feynman's position where he drew the line in not ascribing accountability for the Challenger disaster to specific individuals. Referring to Jesse Moore, Associate Administrator for Space Flight, the Level I manager with whom final approval for launch rested, Feynman maintained, "the guy at the top never should have an excuse that nobody told him. It seemed to me he ought to go out and find out what's going on" (Chandler, 1987, p. 50). The moral principle underlying Feynman's position here and which must be considered in tracing the boundaries of individual responsibility *vis-à-vis* the question of ignorance is the principle of "indirect responsibility."

As applied to the issue of ignorance, this principle confronts anyone in an organization with the inherent expectations of his or her position of power and level of expertise. The contours of indirect responsibility follow in the wake of these expectations because the standards against which to measure a claim of ignorance are precisely the standards of a given position and requisite knowledge. Therefore, to reject an excuse from ignorance it is sufficient to say: You are indirectly responsible for what has transpired because, given your position and professional experience, if you didn't know, you should have (Rosenblatt, 1983).

Although this principle operates in a gray area where the difference between indirect responsibility and pardonable ignorance can be marginal, a tragic, complex event like the Challenger disaster demands its application. Like the law, ethical thought must not be willing to accept ignorance as a sufficient excuse when it can be reasonably established that those in the causal sequence or in positions of authority should have known, or found out before acting or rendering decisions. This is especially true for managers who become instruments of their own ignorance whenever they prevent the free and complete flow of information to themselves, either directly by their acts, or indirectly through the subtle messages they convey to their subordinates, in their management style, or by the organizational climate they help create (Thompson, 1987, pp. 60–61).

Although fragmentary and tentative in its formulation, this set of considerations points toward the conclusion that however complex and sophisticated an organization may be, and no matter how large and remote the institutional network needed to manage it may be, an active and creative tension of responsibility must be maintained at every level of the operation. Given the size and complexity of such endeavors, the only way to ensure that tension of attentive and effective responsibility is to give the primacy of responsibility to that ultimate principle of all moral conduct: the human individual — even if this does necessitate, in too many instances under present circumstances, that individuals such as Roger Boisjoly, when they attempt to exercise their responsibility, must step forward as moral heroes. In so doing, these individuals do not just bear witness to the desperate need for a system of full accountability in the face of the immense power and reach of modern technology and institutions. They also give expression to the very essence of what constitutes the moral life. As Roger Boisjoly has stated in reflecting on his own experience, "I have been asked by some if I would testify again if I knew in advance of the potential consequences to me and my career. My answer is always an immediate 'yes'. I couldn't live with any self-respect if I tailored my actions based upon the personal consequences . . ." (Boisjoly, 1987).

ENDNOTE

1. A contrasting interpretation of the meeting the night before the launch given by Howard Schwartz, is that NASA began to view itself as the ideal organization that did not make mistakes. According to Schwartz, "The organization ideal is an image of perfection. It is, so to speak, an idea of God. God does not make mistakes. Having adopted the idea of NASA as the organization ideal it follows that the individual will believe that, if NASA has made a decision, that decision will be correct" (Schwartz, 1987).

In his testimony before the Rogers Commission, Roger Boisjoly indicated the extent to which NASA procedure had changed: "This was a meeting (the night before the launch) where the determination was to launch, and it was up to us to prove beyond the shadow of a doubt that it was not safe to do so. This is the total reverse to what the position usually is in a preflight conversation or a flight readiness review" (Boisjoly, 1986).

As Schwartz indicates: "If it was a human decision, engineering standards of risk should prevail in determining whether it is safe to launch. On the other hand, if the decision was a NASA decision, it is simply safe to launch, since NASA does not make mistakes" (Schwartz, 1987).

REFERENCES

Boisjoly, Roger M.: 1985a, Applied Mechanics Memorandum to Robert K. Lund, Vice President, Engineering, Wasatch Division, Morton Thiokol, Inc., July 31.

Boisjoly, Roger M.: 1985b, Activity Report, SRM Seal Erosion Task Team Status, October 4.

Boisjoly, Roger M.: 1987, Ethical Decisions: Morton Thiokol and the Shuttle Disaster. Speech given at Massachusetts Institute of Technology, January 7.

Boling, T. Edwin and Dempsey, John: 1981, "Ethical dilemmas in government: Designing an organizational response," *Public Personnel Management Journal* 10, 11–18.

Brody, Michael: 1986, "NASA's challenge: Ending isolation at the top," *Fortune* 113 (May 12), pp. 26–32.

Chandler, David: 1987, "Astronauts gain clout in 'revitalized' NASA," *Boston Globe* 1 (January 26), 50.

Christiansen, Donald: 1987, "A system gone awry," *IEEE Spectrum* 24 (3), 23.

Cook, Richard C.: 1986, "The Rogers commission failed," *The Washington Monthly* 18 (9), 13–21.

DeGeorge, Richard T.: 1981, "Ethical responsibilities of engineers in large organizations: The Pinto Case," *Business and Professional Ethics Journal* 1, 1–14.

Feynman, Richard P.: 1988, "An outsider's view of the Challenger inquiry," *Physics Today* 41 (2), 26–37.

Janis, Irving L.: 1972, *Victims of Groupthink*, Boston: Houghton Mifflin Co.

Kilminster, J.C.: 1985, Memorandum (E000–FY86–003) to Robert Lund, Vice President, Engineering, Wasatch Division, Morton Thiokol, Inc., July 5.

McConnell, Malcolm: 1987, *Challenger, A Major Malfunction: A True Story of Politics, Greed, and the Wrong Stuff*, Garden City, NJ: Doubleday and Company, Inc.

Mankin, Hart T.: 1981, "Commentary on 'Ethical responsibilities of engineers in large organizations: The Pinto Case,'" *Business and Professional Ethics Journal* 1, 15–17.

National Research Council: 1988, *Post-Challenger Evaluation of Space Shuttle Risk Assessment and Management*, Washington, D.C.: National Academy Press.

Report of the Presidential Commission on the Space Shuttle Challenger Accident: 1986, Washington, D.C.: U.S. Government Printing Office.

Rosenblatt, Roger: 1983, "The commission report: The law of the mind," *Time* 126 (February 21), 39–40.

Schwartz, Howard S.: 1987, "On the psychodynamics of organizational disaster: The case of the Space Shuttle Challenger," *The Columbia Journal of World Business*, Spring.

Thompson, Dennis F.: 1987, *Political Ethics and Public Office*, Cambridge: Harvard University Press.

Wilmotte, Raymond M.: 1970, "Engineering truth in competitive environments," *IEEE Spectrum* 7 (5), 45–49.

SUGGESTED FURTHER READINGS

BAUM, ROBERT AND FLORES ALBERT (eds.) *Ethical Problems in Engineering*. Troy, NY: Center for the Study of Human Dimensions in Science and Technology, Rensselaer Polytechnic Institute, 1978.

BAYLES, MICHAEL. "A Problem of Clean Hands: Refusal to Provide Professional Services." *Social Theory and Practice*, 5, 1979.

_____. *Professional Ethics*. Belmont, Ca.: Wadsworth Publishing Co., 1981.

BOK, SISELA. "Whistleblowing and Professional Responsibility." In T. Beauchamp and N. Bowie (eds.) *Ethical Theory and Business*, 2nd ed. Englewood Cliffs, NJ: Prentice-Hall, 1983.

BENSON, GEORGE. "Codes of Ethics." *Journal of Business Ethics*, Vol. 8, No. 5, May 1989.

BROOKS, L.J. "Corporate Ethical Performance: Trends, Forecasts and Outlooks." *Journal of Business Ethics*, Vol. 8, No. 1, January 1989.

_____. "Corporate Codes of Ethics." *Journal of Business Ethics*, Vol. 8, Nos. 2 & 3, Feb. and March, 1989.

Journal of Business Ethics, Professionals and Social Responsibility, Special issue, Vol. 8, Nos. 2 & 3, Feb. and March, 1989.

FREEDMAN, BENJAMIN. "A Meta-Ethics for Professional Morality." *Ethics* 89, 1978.

GOLDMAN, ALAN. *The Moral Foundations of Professional Ethics*. Totowa, NJ: Rowman and Littlefield, 1980.

KULTGERN, JOHN. *Ethics and Professionalism*. Philadelphia: University of Pennsylvania Press, 1988.

LADD, J. "Philosophical Remarks on Professional Responsibility in Organizations." *Applied Philosophy*, 1, 1982.

PART FOUR

Health and Safety in the Workplace

INTRODUCTION

Every year workers all over the world die or are permanently disabled from work-related diseases or injuries. In many cases, both workers and employers have long been aware of the relationship between working in an industry and developing a particular disease. In the asbestos industry, for example, there is a well-established, very high correlation between working in the industry and developing asbestosis, lung cancer, gastro-intestinal cancer, and mesothelioma.

The question is: Who is responsible for such work-related diseases? If an employee chooses to work in an industry with serious and proven health hazards, can the company be held responsible for any related health problems which the employee subsequently develops? Some labour advocates argue that the most hazardous jobs are those which require the least education. Consequently, workers in these jobs tend not to have the resources to acquire safe work. If this is the case, employees may believe that they have little choice but to work in dangerous work environments if they are to be employed at all. Should employees be held responsible for their decisions to work in hazardous conditions or do corporations have a responsibility to minimize the hazards in the workplace? If employers do have that obligation, how can we establish what is minimally safe? But in many cases, workers are not even aware of the dangers in their work environment. Do employers have a moral responsibility to provide employees with information concerning all of the possible hazards of the workplace?

Apologists for the business-as-usual outlook would argue that the employer has a primary responsibility to maximize profit. To minimize the danger to employees in some industries would be extremely expensive. Consequently, it is argued, the employer has conflicting responsibilities if she or he is required both to maximize profit and to provide a safe work environment for employees. Besides, some occupations have inherent risks. The questions arise: How does a corporation, or its executives, balance these conflicting responsibilities? And again, what is an acceptable risk? Who is responsible for risk-taking?

In "The Worker as Victim," Harry Glasbeek argues that as long as risk is assessed in terms of an underlying "pure market" ideology, workers will suffer. Since market ideology panders to the consumer, "profitability over safety" is favoured. Glasbeek argues further that market ideology results in a number of "fictions," the dominant one being that "workers, like consumers, may bargain for more safety." The consequence of this fiction is that it is believed that "whatever conditions prevail must be the result of trade-offs workers make between wages and . . . job security, on the one hand, and safety on the other." This type of victim-blaming will continue as long as the root of the problem remains uncovered. One route to exposing the "inhumanity of profiteering at the expense of human life" is to hold employers personally responsible for harm done to employees. Glasbeek believes that once it is recognized that "the infliction of harm on workers may be classified as criminal," the preconditions for change will be present.

In this regard, it is worth mentioning a recent Illinois case in which three company officials were each found guilty of murder in the work-related death of their employee, Stefan Golab, a Polish immigrant who died in February, 1983, from exposure to hydrogen cyanide fumes. In June of 1985, the former president, plant supervisor and foreman of the now-defunct Film Recovery Systems Inc. were each sentenced to twenty-five years in prison and fined $10 000 (U.S.). They had argued that Stefan Golab died of a heart attack. The three defendants were also found guilty of fourteen counts of reckless conduct related to injuries suffered by other workers at the plant. The trial judge ruled that the conditions under which Golab and his co-workers performed their duties were "totally unsafe" and that the three officials were "totally knowledgeable" of the hazardous situation. During the trial, it was discovered that the plant's workers, most of whom were illegal aliens and spoke little English, were not warned that cyanide was dangerous. Nor did company officials respond to repeated instances of vomiting and nausea among workers. It was further established that a readily available and inexpensive antidote to cyanide poisoning was not kept at the plant. The three defendants are, as of July, 1986, free on bail while their case is under appeal.

Do employees have the right not to have certain diseases or harms inflicted upon them? Alan Gewirth begins his article by asserting that they do have such a right, at least with respect to cancer. Gewirth states that "every person has a basic right not to have cancer inflicted on him by the action of other persons." He further states that since it is fairly well established that 80–90% of all cancers are caused "by the controllable actions of human beings," those human beings who contribute to the causation of cancer and who do so knowingly can be held to be both causally and morally responsible for their actions. Gewirth argues that, according to what he calls *the informed control criterion*, individuals can be held morally responsible for knowingly inflicting a harm they could prevent.

But is such a right defensible, and if so, what does it entail? Some would argue that although we have a right to life, that right no more entails protection of the environment to guarantee our health, including the workplace, than it entails an obligation not to choose to self-induce disease (e.g., an obligation not to smoke). Gewirth discusses these and related difficulties, such as whether workers have the right to choose to work in dangerous environments, in "Human Rights and the Prevention of Cancer."

A deeply ironic aspect of these issues surfaces in Frances Early's article, where she discusses the problem of equal access to *unsafe* working conditions. Ontario Hydro's 1983 decision to utilize an employment equity policy in nuclear reactors raises the question of whether *anyone* should be exposed to these high-risk jobs with the inherent danger of ionizing radiation leaks. Traditionally, women have been kept out of these high-paying jobs due to possible harm to the fetuses of women of reproductive age. Early notes that concern for the genetic damage which might be carried in the sperm of a *male* exposed to radiation has not been of concern in the nuclear industry. Early's position is that standards of acceptable risk must be raised for all individuals working in the nuclear industry. Only then can equality of opportunity offer real choices for all prospective employees.

The above-mentioned articles discuss such issues as employer liability, personal responsibility, acceptable levels of risk in the workplace, freedom of choice, and conflicting interests. You would do well to keep in mind, while reading these articles, the issues raised in Parts One and Two; namely, are corporations, as such, moral agents, and if so, what degree and type of responsibility do they have?

In the case study at the end of this part, Lloyd Tataryn brings home poignantly the tragedy of work-related disease and death in the Canadian asbestos industry. For over a hundred years, Quebec's Thetford Mines has been the centre of asbestos production in Canada. Tataryn underlines the long-standing deceit and misinformation which falsely reassured workers that their health was not seriously threatened by their work. He notes that, as early as 1918, insurance companies were fully aware of the health hazards of the asbestos industry. Years later, physicians at Thetford Mines were still knowingly misinforming workers. Tataryn writes, "The evidence continues to mount showing that asbestos companies maintained a policy of not telling workers they were suffering from asbestos-related diseases until the men became physically disabled." Is this one of those cases where Glasbeek would argue that employers should be held criminally liable for harm to workers? Or are the workers themselves at least partially to blame for the results of their own ignorance?

17

The Worker as Victim

HARRY J. GLASBEEK

The newspapers carried the news. The television cameras whirred. A fusillade of fierce questions was directed at the government at Queen's Park. It had been revealed that asbestos, widely used in the construction industry in Ontario, was now leaking through its encasing materials, entering the atmosphere and endangering the public including, heaven preserve us, schoolchildren! This shocking discovery led to some monitoring, the temporary closing of some public schools and inevitably, to mendacious reassurance by government officials.

Without minimizing the potential danger of asbestos, it seems trivial compared to the risks workers have been exposed to in the workplace for years. Perhaps the most useful aspect of the publicity surrounding the asbestos-in-the schools issue is that a more hospitable climate for the airing of workers' grievances has been created. Certainly, the newspapers have carried more items recently on occupational health problems, particularly where asbestos has been involved.

There is much to agitate about. Hard figures about carnage in the workplace are difficult to come by, especially as the connection between work environment and debilitating disease is often disputed or unrecognized. But carnage it is. Dr. Paul Rohan has shown that from 1973 to 1976 one work injury happened every seven seconds, while an accident causing death occurred every 129 to 130 minutes in 1968, 1970, 1971 and 1976 — and these were the "best" years in his 10 year study![1] As many as 10,000 workers per annum suffer from job-related cancers, asbestosis, silicosis and others. These figures do not include many diseases not yet acknowledged as work-related, just as various cancers now recognized were once omitted.

Increased public awareness of industrial health could be beneficial depending on what the public is asked to do by reformers. Two demands are repeatedly made: one is for improvement in compensation schemes for disabled workers and their dependents; the second is for a better regulatory scheme to include appropriate safety standards and enforcement. The quest for more stringent administration has been and will be unrewarding if some basic premises are not challenged. Saskatchewan, Manitoba and Ontario, for instance, have well-designed statutory schemes obliging employers to provide an environment satisfying the required standards. The employer must give workers access

From *The Canadian Forum*, March 1981. Reprinted by permission of the author.

199

to information about processes and materials used in the workplace as well as levels of exposures to toxic substances. Workers must be represented on joint employer-employee committees which have investigatory, monitory and recommendatory powers. In addition, government inspectors have inquisitorial, reporting and sanctioning powers. The government agency can also set ideal standards, including the proscription of certain activities, processes, and substances. The schemes, however, will not significantly reduce workplace hazards unless officials publicly recognize that *the assumptions of the capitalist mode of production are challengeable.*

All enterprise, no matter who owns the means of production, creates risk. To declare that a work environment with an acceptable risk level must be created is to beg the question. An acceptable risk depends on the balance achieved when the legitimacy of an enterprise is weighed against physical integrity. As long as the legitimacy of the enterprise is judged by market criteria of the Adam Smith type, that is, accepting the notion that any enterprise which can compete and survive is legitimate, the balance will favour profitability over safety. This is so because profitability is seen as directly related to acceptability by informed consumers of the product or service. It does not take an economic genius to note the many deviations from this model. Yet this pristine approach is used as an unarticulated premise when industrial health and safety standards are regulated. But reliance on the market argument is even more inappropriate here than in other facets of the economy. The dominant fiction is that workers, like consumers, may bargain for more safety, thus, whatever conditions prevail must be the result of trade-offs workers make between wages and say, job security, on the one hand, and safety on the other. The absurdity is obvious. While the state, through its regulatory agencies, provides minimum safeguards — in much the same way as it provides for minimum wage rates — it never withdraws from the precept that the antediluvian, pure market doctrine should be the governing assumption. This rigid ideological perspective can only harm workers.

The assumption that certain enterprises should not be undertaken at all is seen as beyond the realm of options available to the state. Only enterprises acknowledged as immoral, in a very particular sense of that word, will be inhibited: for instance, brothel keeping or contract killing. This assumption also greatly inhibits the state's will to require entrepreneurs to obtain permits ensuring that a plant is designed with sufficient ventilation, proper sound systems and other safety measures *before* it operates. One industrial engineer in Quebec said that if design engineers had a legal duty to build in safety systems rather than to save employers money the industrial accident rate could be halved.[2]

There are usually some safety requirements which entrepreneurs must satisfy before they can set up business. But these are trivial, seldom ensuring a safe environment for workers. These entry barriers for manufacturers and miners are very low compared to those which have to be cleared by entrepreneurs whose activities may affect consumers rather than workers. For instance, note the quality and quantity of state control over entry into medicine, law and dentistry, or over the creation of banks. Look at the state's insistence on land developers' compliance with building and zoning regulations. These controls while often benefitting the controlled groups constrain human and other capital which the state is reluctant to fashion merely to protect workers.

The third adverse effect of the market ideology is that the efficiency of any regulatory mechanism will depend on *the nature* of the standards set and their enforcement. Standard-setting takes place in the context of two assumptions: the need to preserve profitability and a preference for letting individuals voluntarily *come to terms.* One of the wondrous by-products of the application of this naive free enterprise model is that there is no such notion as a "reasonable" profit. The market makes the decision about what is acceptable. Hence, regulators are regularly met with the argument that more stringent safety regulations may eliminate profit or reduce it to a level where investment would diminish, market activity would decline and unemployment would be caused. Administrators who accept this line of argument — as is the unsurprising norm, given that the nastier employers occasionally fortify the abstract theory by closing down plants, as Johns Manville has done in Scarborough, do so without regard for, or a realistic appraisal of, whether the assets and profitability of an industry can weather the storm of new regulations. Anyone who doubts this proposition should simply think of the way environmental agencies act when setting out to control polluters and killers like Inco and Dow Chemical. These economic giants are treated by the regulators as if the slightest imposition would drive them out of business.

In the occupational health and safety sphere the results are there for all to see. Given the context in which these decisions are made, we expect to find standards slow to evolve, inadequate, and that enforcement will leave a lot to be desired. All these expectations are realized. For instance, the predecessor of the present Ontario Occupational Health and Safety Act, Bill 139, was introduced in 1976 with great governmental flourish. The minister, Bette Stephenson, said that standards for 14 substances known to be toxic and extremely disabling unless controlled (such as asbestos, arsenic and lead), would be set immediately. To *date no such new standards have been promulgated*. Similarly, the debate about standards for particular substances seems to assume as a basic premise that the balance between profitability and safety will always lead to the conclusion that there is a safe level of exposure to all substances. Administrators, not having workers' safety as their own priority, are encouraged in this view by *hired gun* scientists. It is ludicrously easy for entrepreneurs to find apparently respectable experts who will say that it has not been proven beyond all doubt that there is a substantial causal link between a process or material and a particular disease. Faced with such an argument, regulators not ready to confront the issue that there may be unreasonable profit, are loath to impose serious restrictions on the existing *modus operandi* of employers. If safety, however, were the higher priority and profit were not treated as sacrosanct, the burden would shift. Rather than having to be overwhelmingly convinced that there is a causal connection

between a toxic substance and a disease, the regulators might set a tough standard, or even prohibit use of a toxic substance altogether, until it were proved truly safe at a particular level of exposure. That capitalists well understand the significance of supporting the idea that the burden to inhibit use should be on workers, is regularly demonstrated by the advertisements run by safety associations (read employers' representatives) in conjunction with the Workers' Compensation Board of Ontario. These ads stress that severe injuries could largely be avoided if only workers used more care. If they wore their helmets, the right boots, put ladders away, safety would be assured! *There has never been an advertisement emphasizing that plant design, speed-up or undermanning causes accidents.*

Finally, enforcement by the government agencies of their own standards leaves much to be desired. Unions tell of instances in which a sudden clean-up of the workplace occurs because the employer has apparently been forewarned of an inspection. But even where the inspectors seek to do their job diligently, enforcement will not be strict. The number of inspections depends in the first place on the number of inspectors available which is determined by the political will of the government. When Sterling Lyon's government took power in Manitoba, it left intact a legislative scheme which looked good, but diminished the inspection force so much that the scheme was left relatively toothless. In the USA inspectors considered 98 percent of all violations non-serious and imposed an average fine of $18.00.[3] This suggests another built-in problem with enforcement. Sociologists have repeatedly found that inspectors see fines as a final resort, one which stigmatizes and blames employers. Inspectors prefer voluntary co-operation.[4] The notion that the workplace relationship is a collaborative one plays a large role in fortifying this attitude. It also accords with the view that, wherever possible, individuals should be given the opportunity to settle their own problems.

This precept of the importance of self-determination is also reflected in the newer and more promising legislative schemes. Much of the monitoring and correcting is now left to joint committees of employers and employees, supported by inspectors and administrative standard-setters. Because this system fails to challenge the right of a capitalist to be enterprising until the governing authorities are satisfied that restraint is needed, substantive progress towards a safer work environment will be exceptionally slow. Joint committee members have to learn what to look for and, even then, it is unlikely that, in anything but the most egregious circumstances, will a *joint* committee make a recommendation costly to the employer. Secondly, standard-setters will be very cautious about imposing restrictions on entrepreneurs. The battle of expertise, with its skewed burden of proof, ensures such wariness. For instance, it takes the US National Institute of Occupational Health and Safety approximately six years to devise an optimal level of exposure to a toxic substance. The proclamation of this standard is then subjected to political lobbying, dilution and further delay.[5] (It is worth noting that there are thousands of known toxic substances already in use.) Further, the inherent barrier to regulation is heightened by the general reluctance to regulate entrepreneurs in the prevailing conservative climate which opposes governmental intervention. Thus, while new legislative schemes appear better than old, the outlook for workers remains grim. What is to be done?

The welcome publicity given to the dangers inherent in many substances now used in the workplace should be used to direct an attack on the root of the problem, the reverence for profit-making rather than seeking to make current regulations more sophisticated. The revolution of the proletariat is the ideal solution. While waiting for it (but without holding our collective breath), we need to adopt strategies aimed at revealing the class nature of the work relationships and the inevitable results of the dominance by the capitalist class and the destruction of workers.

Under the new pieces of legislation, workers have been given the right to refuse to work in dangerous conditions, but they have to be reasonable in their refusal. They will be represented by an employee safety representative when arguing that their refusal is reasonable. Even if their refusal is

deemed unreasonable at this juncture, they are not to be punished for it. How long they can insist on their right to refuse further is still problematic. There are still many legal difficulties, the foremost being the question of what is a reasonable refusal; others include whether an assignment to another task is a penalty and whether a refusing worker is to be paid. To evaluate the advantage bestowed by these kinds of provisions, it is pertinent that the right to refuse to work in unsafe conditions was recognized nearly 100 years ago and was not very helpful to workers then. What is new is the removal of fear of punishment if the worker turns out to have been wrong but reasonable in his assessment of this situation. Unchanged, however, is that the assessment of what is reasonable still depends on considerations which place productivity above safety. The trick is to change this. This might be done if all workers in a plant downed their tools when one or more of them felt that unsafe conditions existed. This would be, on the face of it, flaunting the processes setting up a right to refuse to work. Those processes, however, are ideally suited to cause as little interruption in productivity as possible.

In this light, a recent decision by the Ontario Labour Relations Board to uphold the right of 12 Inco workers to refuse to work because they could reasonably have believed that conditions were unsafe is welcome. But the decision stopped well short of granting permission to all workers in a plant to refuse, in concert, to work until conditions are made safe. The emphasis of the board's rather unexpectedly benign interpretation was still that the refusing workers must have reason to fear for their own safety. Workers are not to be encouraged to support others in their quest for greater safety. It could, after all, lead to a collective questioning of the practice of balancing employer profit against workers' welfare. It is unlikely, given the prevailing ideology of trade unions in Canada, that this interpretation of the law will be challenged. A strategy must be fashioned which will demonstrate that the root of the health and safety problem is the inhumanity of profiteering at the expense of human life. This can be done by teaching the public that if the cold balancing of monetary advantage against physical well-being occurred outside the work place, it would attract the strongest condemnation which society can bestow: *it would be treated as criminal behaviour.* Today, even when public and politicians accept the need and desirability of enforcing regulatory schemes vigorously, even if it means fining people, they do not think of this in the same way as they do about the enforcement of society's regulations against rape, dope peddling, arson or murder. This instinctive differentiation between "real" crimes and mere breaches of administrative rules is due to the pervasive effect of the ideology which inhibits more stringent controls over employers. It should be attacked.

Charles Reasons has shown that if we chose to categorize injuries at work as assaults upon workers, the chance of injury to a worker because of a work-related assault is twenty-five times higher than his or her chance of being the victim of an offense classified under the *Criminal Code.* Similarly, he found that workers are more than three times as likely to die as a result of working than as a result of acts committed by assailants away from work. He also calculated that death from occupational disease is more than ten times that resulting from homicide. The difference in our treatment of assailants outside the work force and of those in it must, in law, be justified by an argument that conduct, to be adjudged criminal, must be intentional. That is, it must be carried out with the intent to hurt, to maim, and therefore, employers are not to be compared to street offenders because they never actually want to hurt their workers: injury is inflicted incidentally. Ironically this justification is one of the strengths of the suggestion that criminal law proper should be used against employers. Successful prosecution will alert the public to the fact that failure to provide safeguards for workers' safety is so immoral as to be criminal in the same sense as rapes and murders are criminal.

The technical difficulties which have to be overcome to use the criminal law to this effect are significant, but not insurmountable. While lawyers deem it necessary to talk as if no person could ever be convicted of a crime if his or her conduct did not render him or her personally blameworthy according to society's accepted mores, the courts have given several shades of meaning to the word *intentional.* One result is that it is possible to convict drivers of criminal negligence who injure someone while drunk; that is, at a time when they may not have had a subjective intent to harm or may have been incapable of wilfully disregarding anyone's safety. In effect, they are held culpable in such cases because they should have known, while still sober, that if they drank before driving they might cause grievous injury. The real blameworthiness in such cases lies in deliberately putting oneself in a position where a reasonable standard of care could not be achieved. It is quite possible that certain workplace circumstances can, by analogy, lead to successful criminal convictions. For instance, as a matter of criminal law, there is no *a priori* reason why an employer who ignores recommendations about safety by a joint committee, or by an inspector, or who ignores emissions or noise statutes, should not be held criminally responsible. There are many provisions of the *Criminal Code* which can be interpreted as characterizing such behaviour as criminal; to cite but a few: criminal negligence (section 202), the unlawful endangering of a servant or apprentice by a master (section 201), wilfully breaching a contract (section 380) and criminal conspiracy (section 423).

There are difficulties in making such provisions applicable to work situations, but they are not overwhelming. They have been discussed at length elsewhere. For the moment, it suffices that these well-established heads of acknowledged criminal liability are technically available to be used against employers who harm workers.

The most important of the possible gains to be made by the use of this tactic is that once the public becomes aware that the infliction of harm on workers may be classed as criminal, it will be easier for politicians to accede to workers' demands that the burden of proof be changed. That is, the reasonableness of profitability, even if profit-making is still seen as a good idea, may be differently assessed because it will be understood that the side effects of the garnering of profit may be so immoral as to be criminal. Secondly, there is something very satisfying about using the criminal law, normally used to oppress the working class, against the establishment which created it. (The use of the criminal law against trade unions is well-known, and let it be noted that the majority of people in jail are former unemployed or poorly paid persons.) Furthermore, even if few prosecutions actually lead to convictions, the fear put into the occupants of executive boardrooms will bear useful fruit. Criminal convictions of crimes — other than *normal* business crimes such as bribery and corruption — carry a real stigma in that segment of our class-ridden society: note Ford Motors' violent reaction to the criminal charges laid against it in the Pinto case. There had been many civil actions against Ford over the exploding car before this prosecution, but none caused anything like the eruption of fear and anger which the Indiana criminal charges produced. There was much public rejoicing by Ford spokespersons and financial editorial writers when Ford was acquitted. This raises the spectre that failing criminal prosecutions may legitimate unacceptable employer practices. They may. But take comfort from the fact that since Ford's acquittal in Indiana, several other states' attorneys-general have spoken about initiating their own criminal prosecutions against Ford. They seem to feel that the Indiana

case was lost because of the limited resources of the county prosecutorial offices in that case and because of a significant procedural ruling by the trial judge which removed much damaging evidence from the jury's ken. But it may be true that only the spectacular nature of the Pinto case has led to this promising attitude in public officials who sense there may be political mileage in taking on an undoubted villain. Such enthusiasm is not likely to be found in provincial crown offices in Canada toward criminal charges in occupational health cases. But, again, this is not a negative aspect of the strategem. The very reluctance the powers-that-be are likely to evince when asked to prosecute employers in the same way as garden-variety criminals may well lead to greater public awareness of the class bias of the legal system and its functionaries.

The use of criminal prosecutions will not bring about the millenium. But it may lead to a heightening awareness and then to more beneficial standards being set more quickly and being enforced more effectively, without our having to wait for a change in ownership of the means of production, or the total discrediting of the god profit.

Most importantly, it is action, not reaction.

ENDNOTES

1. Paul Rohan, "The Trend of Work Injuries in Canada," and "Les accidents du travail: la situation au Quebec," *Canadian Family Physician*, Vol. 24 (June 1978).

2. Mr. Claude Lajeunesse as reported in *The Gazette*, Aug. 12, 1975.

3. Per Senator Harrison A. Williams, Jr. (Dem.-N.J.), Chairman of the Senate Committee on Labor and Public Welfare, *Trial Magazine*, Sept.–Oct. 1975.

4. E.G. Carson, "Some Sociological Aspects of Strict Liability and the Enforcement of Factory Legislation," 33 *Modern Law Review*, p. 396, and "White Collar Crime and the Enforcement of Factory Legislation" (1970), 10 *British Journal of Criminology*, p. 383.

5. United States, General Accounting Office, Report to the Senate Committee on Labor and Public Welfare: *Slow Progress Likely in Development of Standards and Harmful Physical Agents found in Workplaces* (1973), p. 7.

6. Data from Reasons, Patterson & Ross, *Assault on the Worker*, Occupational Safety and Health in Canada (Toronto: Butterworths, 1981).

7. Glasbeek and Rowland, "Are Injuring and Killing at Work Crimes?" (*Osgoode Hall Law Journal*, 17, 1979), pp. 506–594.

18

Human Rights and the Prevention of Cancer

ALAN GEWIRTH

Every person has a basic human right not to have cancer inflicted on him by the action of other persons. I shall call this right the RNIC (the Right to the Non-Infliction of Cancer). Since it is a species of the right not to be killed or severely injured, the RNIC is perhaps too obvious to need any justificatory argument. Nevertheless, it raises questions of interpretation that have an important bearing both on the ascription of responsibility and on the requirements of social policy.

Closely related to the RNIC is a further right, which I shall call the right of informed control. Each person has a right to have informed control over the conditions relevant to the possible infliction of cancer on him or herself. This is also a basic human right not only because of its connection with well-being but also because informed control is a component of freedom, which is a necessary condition of action and of successful action.

To understand the RNIC, we must consider what it is to inflict cancer on other persons, who is responsible for this infliction, and how it can be prevented.

Although the RNIC requires that all persons refrain from inflicting cancer on others, as a practical matter it is only some persons who are in a position to do such inflicting and to prevent it, so that they must especially be viewed as the respondents having the correlative duty to forbear and to prevent. The above questions about infliction hence come down to the issue of the causal and moral responsibility for other persons' getting cancer.

According to current estimates, 80% to 90% of all cancers are caused by the controllable actions of human beings. In the case of cigarette smoking the victims may be held to inflict the cancer on themselves. But in very many cases, it is other persons who cause the victims to get cancer, and it is to such cases that the RNIC directly applies. So far as our present knowledge goes, this causation occurs from an increasingly familiar variety of interrelated policies and situations, stemming in part from the vast explosion of physiochemical technology since World War II, that expose the recipients or victims to carcinogenic dangers: in industrial occupations,

From the *American Philosophical Quarterly*, Vol. 17, No. 2 (April 1980). © *American Philosophical Quarterly*, 1980. Reprinted by permission.

through air, water, and land pollution, by food additives and pesticides, and in many other ways. The victims include workers in factories producing asbestos and vinyl chloride, consumers of sodium nitrite and various chemical emissions, and very many other workers and consumers. Bioassays have shown the cancerous effect of various substances on test animals, and epidemiological studies have shown the relative distribution of cancerous effects or symptoms among persons who are exposed to the substances, as contrasted with persons not so exposed. In this way we have learned which substances are correlated with which symptoms — for example, vinyl chloride with cancer of the liver, asbestos with certain forms of lung cancer, and so forth — and we can thereby come considerably closer to establishing causal connections.

Serious efforts to prevent these cancers must be determined by the specific principles that underlie the RNIC and the right of informed control. First, if we know which substances are causally related to cancer, then exposure to these substances must be prohibited or carefully regulated. Second, every effort must be made to acquire the relevant knowledge and to publicize the results. Hence a major part of the causal and moral responsibility for inflicting various cancers can be attributed to manufacturers, employers, and sellers of various products who control the situations in which the cancers are caused if these persons are made aware of the causal connections and do nothing to stop the actions and policies, in the industrial processes and in marketing, which lead to the cancerous effects. A secondary responsibility can also be attributed to government officials, ranging from legislators to administrators charged with enforcing already existing laws, if, while having knowledge of these carcinogenic dangers, they do not take adequate steps to prevent them.

The basis of this responsibility is similar to that which applies to other forms of killing. The general prohibition against killing innocent humans extends not only to murder but also to manslaughter and other kinds of homicide, including those that stem from advertently negligent and other actions whose likely or foreseeable outcome is the death of their recipients. The general point is that if someone knows or has good reasons to believe that actions or policies under his control operate to cause cancer in other persons, then if he continues these actions or policies, he is in the position of inflicting cancer on these other persons, and he violates a basic human right: he is both causally and morally responsible for the resulting deaths and other serious harms. I shall refer to this as the *informed control criterion* for attributing responsibility.

This criterion is distinct from the criterion of intentionality. To be responsible for inflicting lethal harms, a person need not intend or desire to produce such harms, either as an end or as a means. It is sufficient if the harms come about as an unintended but foreseeable and controllable effect of what he does. For since he knows or has good reasons to believe that actions or policies under his control will lead to the harms in question, he can control whether the harms will occur, so that it is within his power to prevent or at least lessen the probability of their occurrence by ceasing to engage in these actions. Thus, just as all persons have a right to informed control, so far as possible, over the conditions relevant to their incurring cancer and other serious harms, so the causal and moral responsibility for inflicting cancer can be attributed to persons who have informed control over other persons' suffering the lethal harms of cancer.

There is a problem about the informed control criterion for attributing responsibility. Consider, for example, the case of automobile manufacturers. They know, on the basis of statistics accumulated over many years, that a certain percentage of the cars they make and sell will be involved in highway deaths and crippling injuries. Hence, since the actions and policies of making automobiles are under the manufacturers' control, why can't we say that they too are causally and morally responsible for inflicting these deaths and injuries on the victims and hence violate their basic human rights? Or consider the case of the civil disobedients during the 1950s and 1960s who knew or had good reasons to believe that their unauthorized marches, demonstrations, sit-ins, burning of draft cards, and similar activities frequently led or threatened to lead to riots, bloodshed, and other serious harms, including deaths. Since the actions and policies of engaging in such activities were under the control of the civil disobedients, why can't we correctly say that Martin Luther King and the other demonstrators also were causally and morally responsible for inflicting these injuries and deaths on the respective victims and hence violated their human rights?

To answer these questions, I shall refer to a certain principle, [relevant to] the attribution of legal and moral responsibility, which, paraphrasing Hart and Honoré, I shall call the "principle of the intervening action."[1] The point of this principle is that when there is a causal connection between some person A's doing some action X and some other person C's incurring a certain harm Z, this causal connection is "negatived" or removed if, between X and Z, there intervenes some other action Y of some person B who knows the relevant circumstances of his action and who intends to produce Z or who produces Z through recklessness. For example, suppose Ames negligently leaves open an elevator shaft — call this action X — and Carson falls through the shaft and is severely injured — call this harm Z. According to the principle, the causal connection between X and Z is negatived or removed, so far as moral and legal responsibility is concerned, if some other person Bates, who knows the elevator is not there, intentionally or recklessly entices Carson to step into the elevator shaft. Here it is Bates's intervening action Y that is the direct cause of Carson's falling through the elevator shaft and suffering the harm Z, and for purposes of assigning responsibility this action Y removes or "negatives" the causal connection between X and Z, and hence also removes Ames's responsibility for the injuries suffered by Carson. The reason for this removal is that Bate's intervening action Y of enticing Carson to step into the absent elevator is the more direct or proximate cause of his getting hurt, and unlike Ames's negligence, Bate's action is the sufficient condition of the injury as it actually occurred. Even if Bates does not intentionally bring about the injury, he is still culpable according to the informed control criterion, for he knows that the

elevator is not there and he controls the sequence of events whereby Carson is injured.

The principle of the intervening action enables us to see the difference between the case of the producers of carcinogens and the cases of automobile manufacturers and the civil disobedients. In the latter cases, an intervening action Y of other persons occurs between the initial action X and the harms suffered, Z. When the automobile manufacturers turn out cars, this does not itself usually cause or explain the suffering of injuries by the drivers and car occupants. There intervenes the reckless car operation of the drivers — their going too fast, not using seat belts, driving while drunk, and so forth, all of which are under the drivers' own direct and informed control. Similarly, when the civil disobedients staged demonstrations and there ensued riots and injuries, it was their vehement, determined opponents whose intervention directly operated as the sufficient conditions of the riots and injuries. These opponents voluntarily and with relevant knowledge engaged in the violent resistance and counteraction, which were hence under their control; and this counteraction negatived or removed the causal connection between the demonstrations and the injuries. Thus it was not the auto manufacturers and the civil disobedients who can correctly be held to have inflicted the respective injuries, but rather the drivers and the counter-demonstrators, so that, on the informed control criterion, the causal and moral responsibility lies with them.

In the case of the producers of most carcinogens, on the other hand (omitting for now the manufacturers of cigarettes), there is no similar intervening action between their production or marketing activities and the incurring of cancer. The workers, consumers, and other persons affected do not actively and knowingly contribute to their getting cancer in the ways in which the drivers and the rioting opponents actively and knowingly contribute to the ensuing injuries. To be sure, the workers work and the consumers eat and so forth, and these actions are under their respective control. But such actions are part of the normal course of everyday life; they do not involve new intervening actions that go outside the presumed normal cause-effect sequences on the part of persons who are informed about the carcinogenic properties of the substances they use; hence, their actions do not break or "negative" the causal connection between the exposure to carcinogens and the getting of cancer. It is for this reason that these cancers may correctly be said to be other-inflicted, i.e. inflicted on the victims by other persons, the manufacturers or distributors, who hence are guilty of violating the RNIC, as against the self-inflicted cancers that result from such actions as cigarette smoking, or the self-inflicted injuries that result from reckless car-driving.

It may still be contended that part of the causal and moral responsibility for inflicting cancer on workers and consumers rests with the victims themselves, in that they have at least a prudential obligation to use due caution just as motorists do. There is indeed some merit in this contention; but it is important to note its limits. The contention may be viewed as resting in part on the hoary maxim *caveat emptor*. Since workers and consumers are buyers or takers of offers made by employers, distributors, and so forth, the maxim says that it is these buyers who must exercise proper caution in accepting the offers.

While the maxim has much plausibility as a counsel of prudence, it has serious limitations when viewed morally. We can especially see this if we look at a general point about the moral principle which is at the basis of a civilized society. This is a principle of mutual trust, of mutual respect for certain basic rights: that persons will not, in the normal course of life, knowingly inflict physical harm on one another, that they will abstain from such harms insofar as it is in their power to do so, insofar as they can informedly control their relevant conduct. The normal course of life, in a society like ours, includes hiring persons for work and selling substances for use, including consumption of food and other materials. Hence, when workers agree to work for others and when consumers agree to buy various products, they have a right to assume, on the basis of this moral principle, that the work and the products will not be physically harmful to them in

ways beyond their normal ability to control, or at least, if there is knowledge or good reason to believe that the products are harmful, as in the case of cigarettes, that full knowledge and publicity will be given to this fact. Failing this knowledge and publicity, the primary responsibility for inflicting cancer on workers and buyers, and thereby violating a basic human right, rests with the employers and producers, since it is they who knowingly offer the conditions of work and the products for sale. What is especially serious about this infliction, by contrast with cases to which the principle of the intervening action applies, is that there is not the same opportunity on the part of the victims to control, with relevant knowledge, the causal factors that proximately impose the cancerous harms on them, so that their own right of informed control is violated.

The most direct requirement that the RNIC lays on the responsible agents is simply that they cease and desist from these lethal policies. This requirement must be enforced by the state because of the pervasiveness and seriousness of the harms in question, especially where the actual or potential victims lack the power and the knowledge to enforce the requirement themselves, and because the voluntary cooperation of the agents in stopping such infliction cannot be assumed. Whether this enforcement takes the form of an outright ban on the use of certain substances or the setting of standards that specify the levels at which various potential carcinogens may be used, in either case there must be appropriate sanctions or penalties for the violators. In addition, sufficient information must be made available so that all persons potentially affected may be able to help to control the conditions that affect them so severely. Thus both the state and the various employers, manufacturers, and distributors are the respondents of the RNIC, and their correlative duties have to an eminent degree the moral seriousness and coercibility that go with all basic human rights.

I have thus far presented the RNIC as an absolute right not to have cancer inflicted on one by the action of other persons. I now want to look more closely at the respects in which it is indeed absolute.

To say that someone has an absolute right to have or do something X means that his having or doing X cannot justifiably be overridden by any other considerations, so that there is a completely exceptionless prohibition on all other persons against interfering with the right-holder's having or doing X. Now there are familiar difficulties with trying to show that any right is absolute, including not only the First Amendment rights to speech, press, and assembly but even the right to life, including the right of innocent persons not to be killed. Without going into these, we must note the more specific difficulties that arise if we try to construe the RNIC as an absolute right.

The difficulties I have in mind are not those that may stem from certain utilitarian consequentialist ways of overriding the RNIC whereby it might be argued that cancer may justifiably be inflicted on some persons in order to maximize utility, if great goods may be attained or great evils avoided thereby. Such arguments may take either the science fiction form, whereby inflicting cancer on one person would somehow lead to eternal bliss for everyone else, or a somewhat more sober form whereby, for example, injecting cancerous cells into someone's bloodstream would somehow help to provide an experimental basis for finding a cure for certain cancers. While the right even of an innocent person to life may not be absolute, the kinds of crisis situations in which this right might be overridden are not applicable to violating any person's right not to have cancer inflicted on him, no matter how many other persons might be benefited thereby.

It must also be noted that the RNIC deals only with the infliction of cancer on some person without his consent or against his will. Thus it does not directly apply to a case where someone may give his informed, unforced consent to have cancer cells injected in him in the context of experimental research toward finding an effective cure or therapy. In such a case the cancer that may result is to be regarded as self-inflicted rather than other-inflicted. I shall deal below with some other aspects of such presumed consent.

There appear, however, to be ways of overriding the RNIC that appeal neither to the kind of utilitarian consequentialism just mentioned nor to presumed consent. These ways may seem to lead to the conclusion that the prohibition against inflicting cancer on other persons should be *prima facie* and probabilistic rather than absolute and apodictic.

We may distinguish two areas of such probabilism. The first bears on the cause-effect relation between exposure to various substances and the incurring of cancer. It will be recalled that in explicating the RNIC I said that if someone "knows or has good reasons to believe" that actions or policies under his control operate to produce cancer in other persons, then he is in the position of inflicting cancer on these other persons. The question now is: when can someone be said to know or to have good reasons to believe that his actions inflict cancer?

The difficulty here is that the causal relation in question seems to be one of degree. Some substances, such as β-naphthylamine and asbestos, have a very high ability to induce cancer. But with other substances the ability and the correlative risk, as determined on a statistical frequency basis, are much lower. There is a currently unresolved controversy on this question of degrees. One view holds that there is a threshold of dosage of carcinogens, below which they do not induce cancers; the other view holds that there is no such threshold, in that any amount of a carcinogen, no matter how small, may lead to cancerous tumors. This latter view is reflected in the Delaney clause that deals with food additives: "no additive shall be deemed safe if it is found to induce cancer when ingested by man or animal, or if it is found, after tests which are appropriate for the evaluation of the safety of food additives, to induce cancer in man or animal. . . ."[2] Here, then, use of the additives in question is strictly prohibited without regard to the degree of risk to humans at any level of use, and without regard to possible benefits.

The merits of such a blanket prohibition, in the case of other substances as well as food additives, are clear. So long as it is not known which particular workers in the various potentially lethal occupations will get cancer and which not, and similarly which consumers of the various suspect food additives and other substances, the only completely safe course would seem to be a blanket prohibition of the respective exposures. To the objection that such absolutism would entail prohibiting the use of automobiles and of many other modern conveniences, since these too carry the risk of death, the reply is, as before, that automobiles do not usually become harmful apart from the controllable, variable actions of the persons who use them, so that they do not pose the risk of death from external causes, i.e. causes external to their users, in the way that carcinogens do.

On the alternate view of the threshold controversy, it is maintained that just as automobiles may be made safer by a variety of devices that are within the power of their makers and users, so too the risks of getting cancer from various substances may be reduced by lowering the degree of exposure to them. For example, even in the case of vinyl chloride, an exposure standard of one part per million is thought to render it relatively even if not absolutely safe for the workers who are exposed to it, especially by contrast with the previous unregulated concentration of 200 to 5,000 parts per million.

I have two conclusions on this issue, one firm, the other tentative. The firm conclusion is that, in keeping with the right of informed control, it is necessary to try to reduce further the ignorance reflected in the varying probabilities of the cause-effect relations involved in carcinogenesis. For this purpose, intensive research must be pursued, within the limits of safety to humans, to ascertain the more specific causal variables, so that we understand more fully just which substances, at what levels of exposure, carry what risks of cancer to which persons. And the results of this research must be fully disseminated and used both in manufacturing and marketing operations and in appropriate legislation.

My more tentative conclusion is that, in contrast to construing the RNIC as an absolute right against even the slightest risk of cancer, a sliding scale may be introduced. Whether the use of or exposure to some substance should be prohibited should depend on the degree to which it poses the risk of cancer, as shown by bioassays and epidemiological studies. If the risks are very slight, so that, for example, use of the substance increases the chance of getting cancer from 1 in 10,000 to 2 in 10,000, or if the risk can be made very slight by drastically reducing the level of exposure, as in the case just cited of vinyl chloride, and if no substitutes are available, then use of it may be permitted, subject to stringent safeguards.

Does this conclusion entail that the RNIC is not an absolute right? The answer depends on how the word "inflict" is construed. If "inflict" is viewed solely as causal, with no reference to moral responsibility of the agent, then there is a sense in which the tentative conclusion I have reached would remove the absoluteness of the RNIC. For while the conclusion does not say that there may be exceptions to the prohibition against actually inflicting cancer, it does say that certain minimal risks of inducing cancer may be allowed, or that the risk of cancer may be increased so long as the level attained is still very low in the way just indicated.

The case is otherwise, however, if the RNIC's prohibition against inflicting cancer is viewed in the light of the ascription of moral responsibility. Since the RNIC is a strict right, it entails that persons strictly ought to refrain from inflicting cancer on other persons. Now this "ought," like other moral "oughts" addressed to agents, is limited by the possibility of informed control, and hence of knowing the likelihood of one's actions causing such infliction. For insofar as "ought" implies "can," to say that A ought not to do X implies that he can refrain from doing X and also that he can have the knowledge needed for such refraining. Thus, the extent of the RNIC's requirement and of the moral responsibility that stems from violating it is likewise limited by this possibility of knowledge.

In this context of moral responsibility, then, the RNIC is to be construed as entailing: Don't inflict cancer on other persons so far as you know or have good reason to believe that any of your actions will constitute or produce such infliction, and don't increase the risk of cancer for other persons beyond the minimal level just indicated. On this construal, the RNIC remains an absolute right even where it allows certain minimal risks of persons' getting cancer as a result of the actions of other persons. For the latter are morally responsible only if they can know or can have good reasons for believing that their action will lead to other persons' getting cancer. Where they do not and cannot have such knowledge, the informed control criterion for ascribing responsibility does not apply, nor, usually, does the intentionality criterion. This point is a quite general one. In the case of every moral precept addressed to actual or prospective agents, there is the limitation of their being able to know whether the actions they perform are or are not instances of what the precept prescribes or prohibits. The degree of such knowledge may vary with different circumstances. But especially in cases where the prohibition is as important as in the case of not inflicting cancer, there also remains the requirement that one must try as fully as possible to ascertain whether one's actions will in fact constitute an infliction of cancer, so that the right of informed control is again of central importance.

Let us now turn to a second area of probabilism that may be invoked to mitigate the absoluteness of the RNIC's prohibition against inflicting cancer, and that has been implicitly present in my preceding discussion. This area bears not on the varying probabilities of the cause-effect relations themselves in the production of cancer, but rather on a weighing of certain values in reaction to those probabilities. The weighing in question is concerned with the relation between the benefits obtained by prohibiting carcinogenic exposures and the costs of such prohibitions; or alternatively with the relation between the benefits obtained by accepting certain risks of cancer and the costs of accepting those risks. It is here a matter of the cost-benefit analysis dearly beloved of economists, which is simply the contemporary version of the pleasure-pain calculus long pursued by utilitarians.

In view of the extreme importance for human well-being of preventing cancer, and the human right to the non-infliction of cancer, how can the avoidance of such infliction be legitimately subjected to a cost-benefit analysis whereby its benefits are weighed against various costs? The better to understand this question, let us compare the problem of preventing cancer with such a situation as where coal miners are trapped in a mine by an explosion. So long as there is any hope of rescuing the miners, all possible means are used to effect a rescue. Except where other human lives are at stake, questions of cost are deemed irrelevant, and so too is the number of miners; less effort would not be made to rescue one miner than to rescue fifty, except insofar as less equipment might be needed to rescue the one. The basis of such unlimited effort to save human lives is that the right of an innocent person to continue to live is normally regarded as absolute, being limited only by the right to life of other persons, and human life is considered to be priceless, in the literal sense of being without price: it is incommensurable with, cannot be measured in terms of, money or any other material goods that might be needed to preserve the life or lives that are endangered.

There are obvious dissimilarities between such a situation and the prevention of cancer. In the former case the lethal danger is actual and immediate, not potential and remote; it is a danger to determinate individuals, not to some general percentage or statistical frequency out of a much larger, less determinate population; and the life-saving operations that are called for are similarly determinate and immediate. Partly because of these differences and partly for other reasons, economists and others have engaged in the cost-benefit analyses mentioned before. There is, after all, time for calculation, and the calculation bears especially on how much, from among the total values both of the individuals directly concerned and of society at large, it is worth spending in order to avoid the risks of cancer and other lethal harms.

To see how such cost-benefit analyses are even minimally plausible in this context, we may note that many kinds of human decisions involve at least implicit views as to the monetary value of human life. Examples are when someone takes out a life insurance policy, when society takes or fails to take measures to improve automobile safety, and when a court awards money damages to a family one of whose members has been killed through someone else's fault. Morally repugnant as it may be, then, putting a specific money evaluation on human life seems to be a feature of at least some segments of individual and social decision-making.

Accepting for the present at least the possibility of such a procedure, we may ask how the money value of a human life is to be estimated. Economists have answered this question in different ways, but the way that is most favoured is based on the familiar idea of a Pareto improvement.[3] According to this, one allocation of resources is an improvement over another if it involves at least one person's being made better off while no person is made worse off. The criterion of being made better off consists simply in the preferences of the person concerned, so that if some person prefers allocation X to allocation Y, then he is made better off by X than by Y. And if no person prefers Y to X, then the change from X to Y is a Pareto improvement. Thus if some person A is willing to accept some life-risking situation R on payment to him of a certain sum of money S by another person B who is willing to make this payment, then A's having R and S together is to that extent a Pareto improvement over the situation or allocation where he does not have R and S. On this view, the monetary value of A's life to himself is measured by the minimum sum of money he is willing to accept to compensate for the risk of losing his life in some activity or other.

There is a direct application of this Pareto criterion to the case of cancer, especially as this is incurred by industrial workers in various occupations. According to the criterion, the risk of cancer may be imposed on some worker in some job if he is willing to accept that risk on payment to him of a certain sum of money. Since he prefers a situation where he works at some carcinogenically risky job and hence earns money to a situation where he has no job at all, or since he prefers a carcinogenically riskier job at more pay to a less risky job at less pay, while in each case no one else is made worse off, it follows that the former situation is in each case a Pareto improvement over the latter. Hence, in con-

trast to the earlier position whereby human life is priceless and the RNIC is an absolute right, according to this new position human life turns out to have a price, and the right to the noninfliction of cancer is now limited not only by unavoidable deficiencies of knowledge but also by the willingness of potential victims to accept financial compensation.

There are, however, serious difficulties with this probabilistic alternative. I shall waive the question of whether the risk of getting cancer can be rationally compensated for by any amount of money or other satisfactions. It might be thought that the RNIC is not affected by such cases, since the risk of cancer is here assumed to be imposed on some person with his consent. But there still remain the questions of whether this consent is informed and unforced. Is each of the persons who chooses among alternatives able to know the degree of risk of the possibly carcinogenic alternative for which compensation is required? In the case of the industrial workers in factories making asbestos, kepone, vinyl chloride, and other lethal substances, they were surely not aware of the risks during the years that elapsed between their initial exposure and the time when some of them came down with cancer. For them, consequently, the Pareto criterion would not apply insofar as it assumes that the persons who express their preferences by their acceptance of compensation for risks are aware of the magnitude of the risks. And even when, as is increasingly the case in recent years, research is pursued into carcinogens and its results are made public, there remains the question of whether complicated statistical calculations can be understood and used by the workers who are most vulnerable to their possibly varying implications. In such circumstances it becomes very difficult to apply the right of informed control.

The Pareto criterion's applicability is also dubious over a wide range of cases because of a difficulty bearing on distributive justice. Since the poorer a person is, the greater is the marginal utility for him of a given sum of money, whereas the opposite is true the richer a person is, the poor are willing to accept much greater risks for considerably less money. Thus, in effect, they and their relative poverty are exploited as a way of getting them to do dangerous work far beyond what others will accept. While this is, of course, a very old story, it casts doubt on the economists' model of citizens' sovereignty where workers "voluntarily" accept compensation for risks and thereby show that they consider themselves to be better off than they would be without the risks and the compensation. For many workers are in effect confronted with a forced choice, since the alternative to their taking the risky job with its slightly added compensation is their not having any job at all. Where workers and others do not have the power to ward off such risks by themselves, it is an indispensable function of government to protect such persons from having to make such forced choices, and hence to protect their right both to the non-infliction of cancer and to the non-imposition of serious risks of cancer. This function can be generalized to the more extensive duty of the supportive state to try to provide opportunities and means of knowledge and well-being so as to reduce the vulnerability of poorer persons to such coercive alternatives. In this and other respects, the prevention of other-inflicted cancers merges into more general issues of the distribution of power and wealth in a society.

A quite central difficulty with this application of cost-benefit analysis is that human life or health is not a commodity to be bought, sold, or bid for on the market. Thus the Pareto criterion is mistaken in principle insofar as it assumes that any great risk of death can be compensated for by any amount of money. There are important differences in this regard between engaging in carcinogenic work risks, on the one hand, and buying life insurance, driving cars, or doing aerial acrobatic stunts, on the other. Even though in buying life insurance one implicitly places a certain monetary value on one's life, this is different from undertaking the risk of carcinogenic work for pay. In buying life insurance one recognizes that death is inevitable for everyone sooner or later, and one does not thereby voluntarily incur the serious risk of death. But to undertake the risk of cancer by one's work is not itself inevitable, so that the compensation involves putting a market price on one's life in the context of a con-

trollable, avoidable choice. In addition, the worker in a carcinogenic industry usually does not have the same kind of control over his degree of risk as does the driver of a car or an aerial acrobat. Hence the case for outright prohibition of more than minimal risk in the former case is much stronger than it is with regard to auto driving or aerial acrobatics despite the dangers of death common to these kinds of cases.

A further issue about the economic valuation of human life bears on who does the valuing. It is one thing for a person to put a money value on his own life where he has a relatively unforced choice between alternative ways of life and work. It is another thing for other persons to put this money valuation on his life, as is done when the benefits of making jobs less risky and hence prolonging workers' lives are weighed against alternative uses of public money, such as building new roads or ball parks. In such cases the worker and his life are made economic objects vulnerable to the preferences or choices of other persons rather than of himself. The very possibility of making such choices on such grounds represents a drastic lowering of public morality.

A related criticism must be made of the suggestion that the Pareto criterion should be applied to tax firms or manufacturers so as to encourage them to remove or lower the levels at which their workers are exposed to cancer. For a firm may choose or prefer to pay the tax rather than remove the risk, while passing the tax on to its customers and, under conditions of oligopoly, suffering little or no financial drain. Such payment would be small comfort to the workers who continue to be exposed to the lethal dangers. This taxational incentive approach also has the severe difficulty previously noted, that it makes persons' lives and health matters of bargaining or purchase rather than viewing them as basic goods and rights not subject to such cost-benefit calculation.

Thus far I have been dealing with a view of cancer as inflicted on persons against their will by the direct or indirect actions of other persons. It is to these interpersonal transactions that the RNIC directly applies. As against such other-inflicted cancers, let us briefly consider the lung cancer derived from cigarette smoking as a self-inflicted kind of harm. This distinction between other-inflicted and self-inflicted harms may be contested in the case of cigarettes on the ground that the blandishments of advertisers and, for young people, the models set by their peers constitute externally-caused incentives to smoke, so that the resulting lung cancers are here also other-inflicted. There is indeed some truth to this, especially in the case of the cigarette manufacturers. Since the lethal impact of smoking cannot be controlled by individual smokers in anything like the same degree that motorists can control the dangers of auto driving, cigarette manufacturers bear a much heavier responsibility for the resulting deaths than do auto manufacturers. The principle of the intervening action applies in much lesser degree to the former than to the latter because the actions of making cigarettes easily available and attractive have a much closer causal connection to the ensuing lethal harms, despite the intervention of the victims' choices to smoke.

I shall here assume, however, that the final choice to smoke rests with the individual himself, and that he is capable of withstanding the advertisers' blandishments. The fact remains that his smoking may be morally wrong because he may impose serious burdens on others. If he becomes hospitalized, his family suffers and he uses extremely valuable and costly facilities and services for which he may not be able to pay, or even if he can, he still makes extremely stringent demands on others which his knowing, controllable actions might have prevented. He also violates both an important prudential duty to himself and also a moral duty to himself as a rational person who is aware of the moral requirements of not burdening others.[4]

How, then, should the self-inflicted carcinogenesis of cigarette smoking be dealt with? While outright prohibition is a possibility, it would perhaps be too violative of individual freedom and, as with the 18th Amendment [to the U.S. Constitution]*, there would be too many possibilities of abuse and evasion. On the other hand, simply to leave the smoker alone would also be unacceptable because, even if we give up all paternalistic concern for his own well-being, there would still remain the problem of externalities, the costs he imposes on others.

The solution I suggest is that the smoker should be made to bear the full cost of his habit, including its external effects. These could be calculated in terms of the excess medical facilities, support of his dependents, and other costs he imposes on others. This would be an application of the Pareto criterion in that the smoker would have to compensate those who would otherwise bear the costs of his habit. If he chooses to pay this compensation, the outcome is a Pareto improvement, since he prefers his smoking together with paying the extra money for it to going without smoking, while, since other persons are compensated, they are not made worse off.

Why is such a compensation permissible in the smoker's case and not in the case of workers in carcinogenic industries? In each case it is the inflicter of cancer who has to pay. There is, however, a difference between a person paying others in order to inflict cancer on himself and his paying his workers in order to inflict cancer on them. The latter, as we have seen, violates the RNIC while the former does not. There is also a difference between the potential cancer victim's paying others, as in the smoking case, and others' paying him, as in the occupational health case. But there is also a more important difference. The industrial worker who is allowed to take money compensation for working in a high-risk industry is told, in effect, that he must choose between losing his job or livelihood and risking his life to cancer. This is an inadmissible choice. The smoker, on the other hand, is confronted with a choice between saving his life from cancer and saving his money, or, alternatively, between continuing his enjoyment of smoking, thereby risking his own life, and paying a larger

---

* Refers to the prohibition on the "manufacture, sale or transportation of intoxicating liquors . . .". — ED.

sum of money. This choice, whatever its psychological hardship for the smoker, is not of the same order of extreme objective adversity as in the case of the high-risk worker. The initial much greater relative economic vulnerability of the unskilled industrial workers makes a crucial difference.

I conclude, then, that the probabilistic issues of the carcinogenic cause–effect relations and cost–benefit analysis do not materially affect the conclusion drawn earlier. So far as the moral responsibility of agents is concerned, the Right to the Non-Infliction of Cancer is an absolute human right, and it requires the most determined efforts both to ascertain when such infliction is likely to occur and to take all possible steps to prevent it, and thereby to make its respondents fulfill their correlative duties.

ENDNOTES

1. See H.L.A. Hart and A.M. Honoré, *Causation in the Law* (Oxford: Oxford University Press, 1959), pp. 128 ff., 195 ff., 292 ff.

2. *U.S. Code* 21, 348 (c) (3). For this reference and for a valuable discussion of related issues I am indebted to Jerome Cornfield, "Carcinogenic Risk Assessment," *Science*, Vol. 198 (18 November 1977), pp. 693–699.

3. cf. E.J. Mishan, "Evaluation of Life and Limb: A Theoretical Approach," *Journal of Political Economy*, Vol. 79 (1971), pp. 687–705; M.W. Jones-Lee, *The Value of Life: An Economic Analysis* (Chicago: The University of Chicago Press, 1976), Chs. 1–3.

4. See Albert L. Nichols and Richard Zeckhauser, "Government Comes to the Workplace: An Assessment of OSHA," *The Public Interest* no. 49 (Fall 1977), p. 64 ff.

19

Reproductive Health Hazards at Work: The Canadian Atomic Industry*

FRANCES H. EARLY

In the early eighteenth century at the onset of the Industrial Revolution in the West, social tolerance of life-endangering work environments was high. Employer responsibilities were few, worker risks many. Over the past century and a half social critics of the high human costs of industrialization have been active both in documenting the prevalence of unhealthy worksites and in lobbying governments for appropriate regulation of industry. Labour unions have a long history of negotiating with employers for safe, healthy working conditions and at times have worked alongside concerned citizens' groups for protective legislation — laws designed to safeguard occupational health for special groups of workers.[1]

Historically — from the late nineteenth century onwards in North America — protective legislation has been applied primarily to women workers in certain industries, those industries like lead production, where a relationship has been seen to exist between exposure to chemical agents and malfunctioning of reproductive capability.[2] This "protection," however, has been incomplete. While women's health in some cases has been safeguarded by excluding them from jobs which have been traditionally male, in many traditional female occupations health hazards, particularly reproductive health hazards, have been ignored. Women beauticians, nurses, and dry cleaners, for instance, routinely come into contact with carcinogenic and mutagenic substances.[3] Men, ironically, have frequently suffered adverse health effects, including impaired reproductive functioning, from working at jobs that women have been kept from "for their own good."[4]

Exclusionary policies which seek to keep certain

This essay first appeared in the first edition of this book.

216

occupations "for men only" are at present under attack. In Canada the new Charter of Rights adds legitimacy to feminist demands that women by right must be accorded equality of opportunity in the labour market. However, as women begin to be employed in what formerly were all-male jobs, the issues of occupational safety and health become urgent concerns for employers and employees alike. Two related questions emerge in this context of a changing composition of the work force. Firstly, are these liberated positions safe for women, particularly in relation to their reproductive health? Secondly, if jobs are unhealthy for women, what does this mean for men who are similarly employed?

The recent decision of the Canadian nuclear industry to permit women to work in jobs from which they were previously excluded presents a case in point. Ontario Hydro in the fall of 1983 announced that it intends to employ women inside its twenty-two nuclear reactors at high skill, well-paid jobs. At the same time, its spokesperson pointed out that new regulations for the nuclear industry would soon be in place which would enable the company to safely hire women. Current regulations, promulgated by the federal government's Atomic Energy Control Board (AECB), are based on the theory that women could be pregnant unknowingly; they set limits on the amount of radiation any woman can receive to her abdomen in two-week and three-month intervals.[5] The new proposed regulations specify that both men and women will now have the same 5-rem annual whole-body exposure limit to ionizing radiation; women will no longer be restricted to the two-week and three-month limits.[6]

This move on the part of Ontario Hydro, in concert with the AECB, marks a dangerous new departure in public policy regarding occupational safety. A consensus is emerging in Canada among prominent scientists, labour unions, and well-informed members of the environmental and women's movements that "equality of opportunity for women" as articulated by the nuclear industry is, in effect, "equal opportunity for biological harm."[7] A careful perusal of the new regulations

reveals that the AECB is actually raising the permissible limit of exposure to ionizing radiation for many workers in the industry at a time when the health hazards associated with radiation exposure are well known. (Individual organ dose limits are in some cases much higher than under the older regulations.)[8] Men, as well as women, have cause to worry.

It has long been appreciated that exposure to ionizing radiation results in adverse health effects. Shortly after the discovery of radium in 1898 by Marie Curie and her husband, the health of a number of physicists, chemists, and radiologists working with X-rays deteriorated in various ways. By 1911 it was recognized that exposure to ionizing radiation could cause cancer. In the 1920s the case of the women radium dial painters who suffered radiation-related sicknesses from their work made front-page headlines in the United States.[9] After the bombing of Hiroshima and Nagasaki, massive amounts of documentation on the short-term and long-term effects of exposure to ionizing radiation became available for scientific scrutiny.[10]

Within the past decade, many more scientific studies and government reports have appeared which demonstrate that there are serious side-effects inherent in radiation exposure to humans (and animals), whether from diagnostic medical X-rays, work with radioactive substances, or from exposure to ionizing radiation at nuclear industry worksites.[11] In addition to the danger posed to present individuals, studies confirm that effects of ionizing radiation may be visited upon future generations. Indeed, the potential danger to "species survival" has become an important theme in recent literature. Several years ago the Norwegian government conducted an inquiry into health hazards associated with their nuclear industry. The published study, *Nuclear Power and Safety*, declared that there is no safe threshold of radiation exposure for individuals in terms of the effects of such exposure on future generations:

> There are no lower limits to effective doses for genetic effects. All doses, even the smallest, are significant, all the time from conception until the next generation is born.[12]

Certain kinds of hereditary defects appear in the first generation following irradiation, but owing to the nature of the mechanism of heredity, the genetic effects do not become fully manifest in a population until many generations have passed.[13]

A study by Ikuro Anzai and Rosalie Bertell reinforces the findings of the Norwegian government's report:

> The health effects of 10,000 man-rem exposure include 5.3 to 15.8 radiation induced cancers, 37.5 reproductive losses, and an eventual 3.8 to 79.7 genetic diseases per generation of offspring. There will be milder aging effects among those exposed and other probable effects in first generation offspring such as childhood cancers, asthma, allergies, and depressed immune systems. These latter effects will most likely be first generation effects only, and are difficult to quantify. However, each is a unique personal and family tragedy.[14]

Persuasive evidence exists that exposure to ionizing radiation may have untoward congenital and genetic effects in addition to the more readily detectable somatic effects.[15]

Because of increasingly sophisticated scientific understanding of the harmful effects of ionizing radiation on human beings, the international standard for permissible annual exposure for individuals has been steadily decreasing: 60 rems in 1934, 15 rems in 1950, and 5 rems since 1956. In 1982, Bo Lindell, Chairperson of the International Commission on Radiological Protection (ICRP), the body which has traditionally set annual standards, declared that 5 rems should be viewed as a "worst case" limit and that one rem "would . . . be about right, perhaps a little more."[16] The British National Radiological Protection Board has stated that 1 rem rather than 5 rems should be the effective limit, with .5 rem a target limit.[17] Why, then, critics are asking, is the AECB maintaining, and in some cases raising, exposure levels for atomic radiation workers?[18]

As mentioned, the AECB has proposed to eliminate the present limits of radiation exposure women can receive in any 2-week and 3-month period. In the proposed regulations a woman, upon discovering she is pregnant, should "forthwith inform her employer of her pregnancy."[19] She would then be transferred to a low-level radiation exposure environment.[20] The scientific literature demonstrates, as the AECB itself makes clear, that exposure to ionizing radiation during the period of "organogenesis," from two to eight weeks after a woman becomes pregnant, may have serious negative consequences for the fetus.[21] Since a woman may not realize that she is pregnant until she is well into the period of organogenesis, it appears imperative that no woman who is attempting to become pregnant should be employed in areas of the industry where she is in danger of being exposed to any amount of ionizing radiation.[22] Otherwise women may find themselves unwittingly inflicting damage on fetal life. The nuclear industry should not expect women to risk any chance however small, of genetic or health damage to their offspring.

Given the reproductive hazards involved in work in the nuclear industry it is not surprising that many critics of the AECB's new regulations are now insisting that any worker, woman or man, who is even planning to procreate, must be automatically able to transfer to on (or extremely low) exposure areas with no loss of pay or seniority.[23] This demand points to another ethical dimension to the question of worker rights: the right of men, as well as women, to reproductive health. For too long men have assumed that reproduction was basically women's sphere and that man's reproductive health was not at risk. However, scientific evidence — which has often been simply ignored — underscores the inherent dangers men face in this respect. It cannot be too strongly stated that radiation-damaged sperm as well as radiation-damaged ova in cases where conception occurs and pregnancies go to term will result in infant deaths or congenitally impaired offspring.

Another group of workers in the nuclear industry who are at risk are young people under the age of twenty, as radiation is more damaging to growing cells than to mature ones. At present, no one under the age of 18 can work in the nuclear industry. However, in the proposed regulations, the 18-

year-old requirement has been dropped.[24] This change is irresponsible since radiation exposure limits in the new regulations are the same for all workers (except those known to be pregnant), regardless of age.

Another problem with the new regulations is that, as in the present ones, there does not exist a comprehensive radiation-exposure record-keeping scheme at the national level. The federal government needs to assume responsibility on this issue. Accurate, longitudinal record-keeping is absolutely necessary to protect the health of atomic radiation workers, the offspring of workers, and future generations. Particularly relevant here are so-called "transient workers" in the nuclear industry, who, to date, experience less protection through record-keeping than regular workers employed in relatively long-term jobs.

The AECB must revise its regulations to bring them into line with current scientific knowledge on the effects on human health of exposure to ionizing radiation. At present, regulations do not adequately protect workers. The dosage limits are too high and must be scaled down substantially in order to safeguard workers' health. Even so, atomic radiation workers must be made aware of the occupational health risk associated with their work, especially the reproductive health risk, through regularly updated written information and routine briefings. The scientific community is on record as stating that there is no safe level of radiation exposure for human beings. And as articulated in the Norwegian government's report, this includes future generations: "All doses, even the smallest, are significant, all the time from conception until the next generation is born."[25]

It is crucial, too, for the AECB and the nuclear industry to recognize that they have been designing safety regulations for workers which are based on a standard "Reference Man" who is assumed to be male, a mature adult, healthy upon being first employed as an atomic radiation worker, and so forth. In reality, very few workers meet this standard. Instead, as enunciated by the Canadian Labour Congress: "All workers are not the same."[26]

The AECB and the nuclear industry must break out of a conceptual trap which dictates one standard of protection for all workers, and must instead accept the principle that there must be "protection for all workers according to their special needs," and begin to act upon it.[27] For the nuclear industry this requires devising exposure limits for some categories of workers who do not fit the Reference Man stereotypes, examples being pregnant women, all workers in their reproductive years, those not in "perfect" health to begin with, and minors. Furthermore, the industry must reject the notion that providing women with "equality of opportunity" means subjecting them inevitably to the risk of damaging potential offspring.[28] This kind of thinking is leading, in the present case of the nuclear industry, to a failure to develop a safe work environment for women. This same line of reasoning may also, in other contexts, deprive women absolutely of the right to work. Women make up roughly forty per cent of the total Canadian labour force. Two-thirds of gainfully employed women are between the ages of twenty and forty-four, the reproductive years. Studies show that industries concerned with reproductive hazards in their establishments (and possible future law suits) are increasingly barring women of this age group from employment.[29] More and more women of reproductive age are either facing serious discrimination in the job market or are being subjected to unhealthy working conditions. They lose either way.

To reiterate: Until the nuclear industry rejects the standard Reference Man concept and accepts the concept of protection for all workers in accordance with their special needs, atomic radiation workers, as a group, will not enjoy adequate health protection. The Canadian Labour Congress put it well: "Equality of opportunity must be based on *equal opportunity to a safe workplace*, not equal opportunity to biological damage."[30] In this instance of the nuclear industry, the principle of an equal opportunity to a safe workplace involves more than today's workforce: it involves the healthy survival of the human species.

ENDNOTES

1. See the entire issue of *Feminist Studies* 5 (Summer, 1979) which deals with the topic "Workers, Reproductive Hazards, and the Politics of Protection."

2. Vilma R. Hunt, "A Brief History of Women Workers and Hazards in the Workplace," *Feminist Studies* 5 (Summer, 1979): 274-80.

3. Michael J. Wright, "Reproductive Hazards and 'Protective' Discrimination," *Feminist Studies* 5 (Summer, 1979): 304-05.

4. Nancy Miller Chenier, *Reproductive Hazards at Work: Men, Women and the Fertility Gamble* (Ottawa: Canadian Government Publishing Centre, 1982), pp. 44-5. Prepared for the Canadian Advisory Council on the Status of Women.

5. Ibid., p. 44.

6. See AECB's Consultative Documents Numbers 47 and 78. Issued for public release November 14, 1983. A rem is a measure of the biological damage inflicted on the human body by radiation.

7. "Submission of the Canadian Labour Congress to the Atomic Energy Control Board on Proposed Revisions to Regulations Under the Atomic Energy Control Act," January, 1984, p. 24.

8. Ibid., pp. 15-24, and Frances Early, Susan Holtz, and Gwen Phillips, "Response to Atomic Energy Control Board Consultative Documents C-47 and C-78," Task Force on Radiation Exposure and the Atomic Radiation Worker representing: Canadian Research Institute for the Advancement of Women (Nova Scotia Chapter); Voice of Women, Nova Scotia; and Ecology Action Centre, April 13, 1984, pp. 6-7.

9. Hunt, *Feminist Studies*, pp. 280-81.

10. Committee for the Compilation of Materials on the Damage Caused by the Atomic Bombs on Hiroshima and Nagasaki, *Hiroshima and Nagasaki: The Physical, Medical, and Social Effects of the Atomic Bombings* (New York: Basic Books, 1981).

11. Rosalie Bertell, "Radiation Exposure and Human Species Survival," *Environmental Health Review* (June, 1981): 43-51; John Gofman, *Radiation and Human Health* (San Francisco: Sierra Club Books, 1981); and P. de Bellefeuille, "Genetic Hazards of Radiation to Man, Part II," *Acta Radiologica* 56 (1961): 145-59.

12. *Nuclear Power and Safety* (Oslo: Universitetsforlaget, 1978), p. 77.

13. Ibid., p. 76.

14. Ikuro Anzai and Rosalie Bertell, "Risks Expected from Radiation Exposure to Workers of Light Water Power Reactors," *Journal of Japanese Scientists* 18 (February, 1983): 4.

15. See Gofman, *Radiation and Human Health*.

16. Bo Lindell, Statement to Public Forum on Nuclear Power, Middletown, Pennsylvania, 1983. Cited in "Submission of the CLC to the AECB," p. 28. The AECB uses ICRP guidelines to establish permissible radiation exposure limits in its old and new regulations. Critics of the ICRP point out that it is a self-appointed, self-perpetuating body; Dr. Rosalie Bertell comments that "No outside medical or health related body, even the World Health Organization, can name a member for ICRP." See Rosalie Bertell, "Comments on Limitation of Exposure to Ionizing Radiation, Consultative Document C-78," January 10, 1983, p. 1. For a brief but excellent discussion of what critics have to say about the ICRP see "Submission of the CLC to the AECB," pp. 16-24. The AECB has also come under attack of late by the group "Energy Probe"; it feels that some of the board members of the AECB are too closely linked with the nuclear industry to serve as impartial protectors of workers and the public at large. See *The Citizen* (Ottawa), September 22, 1983, p. 10, and September 24, 1983, p. 24.

17. *The Nuclear Free Press*, Winter, 1984: 15.

18. For detailed discussions see "Submission of the CLC to the AECB"; Early, et al., "Response to AECB"; Canadian Union of Public Employees, Health and Safety, "Brief to the Atomic Energy Control Board on Proposed Regulations of Radiation"; and Bertell, "Comments on Limitation of Exposure to Ionizing Radiation."

19. AECB, C-78, Sec. 3, p. 6.

20. Ibid., Sec. 4.1, p. 8. The allowed radiation exposure would be .6 mSv (1 mSv = 1/10 of a rem) per 2-week period.

21. AECB, C-78, Sec. 4.5, p. 22. The Ontario Hydro Employees Union is appalled at the proposed standard: "The new standards allow women to be exposed to doses which during pregnancy will increase the risk of childhood cancer by 1,250 per cent. What's more, this proposal is being made under the guise of human rights!" Quoted in *The Nuclear*

Free Press, p. 15. See as well "Submission of the CLC to the AECB," p. 24.

22. See Bertell, "Comments on Limitation of Exposure to Ionizing Radiation," and Early, et al., "Brief to the AECB."

23. See particularly "Submission of the CLC to the AECB" and CUPE, "Brief to the AECB."

24. AECB, C-78, Sec. 3.1, p. 6.

25. *Nuclear Power and Safety*, p. 77.

26. "Submission of the CLC to the AECB," introductory section, unpaginated, and p. 24.

27. The term "conceptual trap" is borrowed from Elizabeth Dodson Gray's book, *Patriarchy as a Conceptual Trap* (Wellesley, Massachusetts: Roundtable Press, 1982), p. 17. Dodson defines a conceptual trap as "a way of thinking." It is like being in a room which — once inside — you cannot imagine a world outside. See also Chenier, *Reproductive Hazards at Work*, p. 65. Chenier points out that in Sweden the Working Environments Acts of the 1970s are based on the principle of "protection for all workers according to their special needs."

28. In an article in the *Globe and Mail* (Toronto), October 19, 1983, two Ontario Hydro employees of the health and safety division were reported as being concerned that the company was assuming some risk that an employee's pregnancy could be adversely affected by radiation exposure. Ontario Hydro has created a task force to study the probability of occupational risk in terms of women's reproductive health. The findings, according to Ontario Hydro, are in the company's favour. Rosemary Petrovich, a technical safety supervisor at Hydro, was quoted as saying: "It's sort of like a paternity suit — you can't prove it was you who did it, but you can prove it wasn't."

29. Chenier, *Reproductive Hazards at Work*, pp. 52-3 and p. 46.

30. "Submission of the CLC to the AECB," p. 24.

*I am indebted to Susan Holtz and Gwen Phillips for their invaluable help in preparing a brief to the Atomic Energy Control Board in response to proposed amendments to the atomic industry's regulations regarding employee radiation exposure limits. Many of the points raised in that brief are reflected in this article. I gratefully acknowledge the funding support from the Canadian Research Institute for the Advancement of Women (Nova Scotia Chapter) provided for the writing project.

20

From Dust to Dust

LLOYD TATARYN

Every time a life insurance company shoves another sky-scraper into the air, it acts as a reminder that every year millions of dollars are made from making book on people's lives. But general run-of-the-mill bookies are clearly not in the same league as those who gamble on life expectancy rates. Insurance companies refuse to take the same risks as even the most conservative bookmakers. Skilled actuaries are paid handsome salaries to calculate the odds on who will fully pay their insurance premiums before reaching life's finish line, and who, on the other hand, are bad life risks. Actuaries take the guesswork out of dying. Insurance companies simply refuse to play hunches or to finalize deals when the odds are not in their favour.

Consider workers who make a living in the asbestos industry. As early as 1918, North American insurance companies were declining to insure asbestos workers. The companies had stumbled onto certain facts of death — facts of death which governments and industries were not willing to acknowledge until decades later.

Asbestos workers die at high rates from asbestosis, a disease caused by severe scarring of the lung. They die at excessive rates from lung cancer, gastro-intestinal cancer (cancer of the colon, rectum and oesophagus), and mesothelioma, a cancer of the lining of the chest and abdominal cavities. It is little wonder that back in 1918 asbestos workers were considered bad insurance risks. Unfortunately, as we shall see, the odds against them are little better in the 1970s. In Canada, governments and corporations have casually gambled with the health of asbestos workers. Asbestos workers have had to pay with disease-wracked bodies when the health wager was lost.

The use of asbestos dates back to Greek and Roman times when it was known as the "magic mineral". Asbestos has amazing filtering powers, can withstand the fiercest heat, and is almost immune to the forces of corrosion and decay. Yet asbestos is so pliable that it is the only mineral that can be spun into thread and woven into cloth. In fact, the Emperor Charlemagne amused himself and convinced visiting knights of his magical powers by throwing an asbestos table cloth into a fire and removing it unscathed. But asbestos was a suspected health hazard even in those bygone days. As early as the first century A.D., Pliny the Elder, after a trip through the Roman Provinces, confirmed reports by Strabo, the Greek geographer, that slaves who wove asbestos into cloth were suffering from a sickness which left them short of breath. Years later, the disease was labelled asbestosis.

Asbestos remained a novelty mineral, primarily woven into prized robes for priests and kings or rare cremation garments for deceased monarchs, until 1879, when it was first mined for wide commercial use in Thetford Mines, Quebec. Canada has since become the world's largest producer of chrysotile (white) asbestos, accounting for over 40 per cent of world production. In 1973, close to two million tons of asbestos were shipped out of Canada, bringing in over $243 million. Approximately 80 per cent of Canada's total asbestos production is mined and milled in Quebec. As in 1879, the town of Thetford Mines is the heart of Quebec's asbestos production.

Given the long association between asbestos and ill health and given the fact that the commercial production of asbestos originated in Thetford Mines, it would be logical to assume that the Canadian and Quebec asbestos industries would have taken every conceivable step to clean up their environments and prevent the development of asbestos-related disease. Not so. According to a 1976 federal report on asbestosis, ". . . ample evidence exists that workers are being subjected to substantial levels of asbestos in their workplace, resulting in increased incidents of asbestos-related disease."[1]

In April, 1976, Judge René Beaudry released an interim report of his investigation into the Quebec asbestos industry. The report was sharply critical of the asbestos industry's attempts to duck its responsibility to improve working conditions. According to

Beaudry, asbestos companies "tended to *medicalize* the problem of air quality in the asbestos industry." The companies' approach to health was "based on medical compensation rather than the protection of workers' health . . .". Beaudry observed that the asbestos entrepreneurs channelled their industrial health efforts into fighting legal battles against compensation claims rather than into cleaning up hazardous work environments. Medical doctors were hired to contest asbestosis claims submitted to the Workmen's Compensation Commission, although "all the necessary data exists to initiate the technological control of asbestos dust." This led Beaudry to conclude:

> The industry seems to think that the number of compensated cases represents the air quality in the work environment. It seems that the [asbestos industry] wanted to prevent the payment of compensation more than the prevention of asbestosis.[2]

Judge Beaudry was appointed to investigate the Quebec asbestos industry shortly after an embarrassed provincial government was publicly accused of collaborating with the asbestos industry to cover up dangerous working conditions in Thetford's mines and mills. The Quebec asbestos unions based their allegations on asbestos air samples which had been collected illegally and in secret from the work environment. In 1976, the gathering of those samples led to the longest strike in the town's history. . . .

Since the 1949 recognition that "asbestos dust is harmful", the asbestos companies have indeed acted as if no "contractual obligation" exists to eliminate asbestos exposure. Quebec workers have continued to endure death and disease due to asbestos exposure. In the years 1970 to 1974, over two hundred and fifty asbestosis cases were compensated in Quebec.[3] In 1974 alone, eighty-five workers were so severely damaged by asbestos fibres that they were awarded lifetime indemnities by the Workmen's Compensation Commission. Many more have succumbed to asbestos-related cancer.

Knowing what we know about the effects of asbestos on the body, it would seem sensible to have at least provided workers with precise information about the asbestos dust levels they worked in. Yet before the 1975 strike, access to government and company dust surveys had been repeatedly denied to Thetford workers — which explains Paul Formby's furtive air-sampling activity in Thetford's asbestos operations and the union militancy which resulted from the secret testing. . . .

The findings convinced the CNTU [Confederation of National Trade Unions] that a clinical survey of Thetford's asbestos workers was essential, and the union grimly urged Mount Sinai's [New York] experts to visit their area. Formby, who agreed to handle the logistical details of the proposed expedition, lobbied on behalf of the CNTU and helped tip the hospital's decision in favour of a Quebec visit.

In the fall of 1974, a team of seven doctors and a group of technical experts openly travelled to Thetford Mines to examine the area's asbestos workers. Two Canadian doctors assisted the New York team. More than twelve hundred men who had drilled, blasted, and sweated a living in Thetford's mines and mills for twenty or more years were carefully examined.

Dr. Donald Haigh was one of the Canadian doctors who helped examine the workers. His initial evaluation was not comforting. "They were pretty sick people," he says, "and some of them were sick and didn't realize it. I met one fellow who had a symptom in his fingernail beds called clubbing[4], which is a peripheral sign of lung disease. I said to him 'You have clubbing; you're sick; you have lung disease.'

"He was shocked! He was surprised! Then the man told me, 'I thought my fingers were like this because it was hereditary. You see, my father and all my brothers have clubbing.'

"To this man, being sick was part of his life. Everybody around him was sick. To him sickness was a natural way of life." . . .

"These people," says Haigh, "are required to have a yearly examination and a chest X-ray at the industrial clinic, which is a clinic in Thetford supported by the companies. The industrial clinic classifies these men. People who are Class A have no disease and are allowed to work in the dust at their regular jobs. But I know that many of the people who were Class A, or at least Class A a few months before we saw them, were sick. And a lot of them knew they were sick. You would ask somebody if they had shortness of breath, and they'd say sure they had shortness of breath. You'd ask them if they had trouble climbing stairs, and they'd say sure they had trouble climbing stairs. These people weren't normal! How the industrial clinic arrived at their Class A classification I haven't any idea."

Jean-Baptiste Fortin, a former Thetford asbestos worker, insists that doctors at the medical clinic run jointly by the asbestos companies — Asbestos Corporation, Lake Asbestos of Quebec, Carey Canadian Mines, National Asbestos Mines, Bell Asbestos Mines — minimized the workers' health problems in order to protect the companies. Ever since his sixtieth birthday, Fortin has lived with a five-foot-high oxygen tank resting in the corner of his bedroom. Asbestosis has left him continually short of breath. He is forced to replenish his lungs with gulps of oxygen from the tank when his breathing problems intensify. The shortest walks leave him breathless. Even talking can be an effort and, as he relates his experience, beads of sweat glisten on his forehead.

"Every year we went for tests at the companies' clinic," he says, "and I was always Class A. I was always Class A until 1971 when I went to Montreal to get another opinion on asbestosis. There they decided to re-class me. The first time I went to Montreal they declared me 50 per cent incapacitated. In 1972, they declared me 100 per cent incapacitated. That's why I say the clinic was working for the companies, not for us."

On January 12, 1972, Emile St. Laurent received a Class A classification from the Thetford industrial clinic. On August 20, 1974, at the age of fifty-nine, Emile St. Laurent died of asbestosis. Asbestosis does not creep up on its victims. A person is not free from asbestosis one day and debilitated with the lung disease the next. Mount Sinai doctors say that lung scarring due to asbestos exposure would be readily apparent on one's chest X-rays long before the disease snuffed out one's life.

Emile's widow, Dolores St. Laurent, is extremely bitter. "We never heard about it at all," she says. "He was always fine, classed as 'number one'. But since his last visit to the clinic you could see his health wasn't getting better. He was going from worse to worse. His breathing was really difficult. Most of the time he had trouble. And I'll tell you that most of the time around the house he did nothing. . . .

"I knew that there was dust and that he worked there thirty-eight years, but I still blame the clinic because they gave these regular tests and we learned nothing from them. If only the industrial clinic had said something. They could have mentioned a spot on the lung or something like that. If only they'd said something. But they never did. Every year they never did."

Hervé Boutin is yet another asbestosis victim. His face is the colour of chalk and his conversation is liberally sprinkled with coughing and wheezing. "I went to the industrial clinic and they always told me I didn't have it," he says. "I even asked them once if I had it and they said, 'Oh, only a touch. Nothing worth mentioning.'

"Then I decided to go to Montreal. They told me I had it and classed me as having 25 per cent. The second year I went they classed me at 40 per cent. And the third time I returned, they put me at 60 per cent.

"I never believed them at the clinic and I told them so a few times. They said there's no dust on my lungs, but I knew there was anyway. Even better, I said to one of them, 'It's there but you don't want to tell us.' 'But sir,' he said, 'if we classified you anything other than A, you'd have to change jobs. That's why we classify you as A. But there's not enough dust to harm you.' That's what they told me," says Boutin, with a touch of irony. "Not enough to harm you."

Dr. Paul Cartier ran the companies' clinic from 1940 until 1974. When the results of the Mount Sinai study were finally made public, Dr. Cartier openly stated that he hadn't always informed workers suffering from asbestosis of the full extent of their illness on humanitarian grounds: "I figured it was in their best interests to stay at their jobs. Besides, they didn't want to be reported ill and transferred to a lower-paying job where they might have earned as much as fifty dollars less a week." Cartier also noted that "even if they had left their work completely and gone on to drive cabs, for instance, it might not have arrested the progressive effects of asbestosis." . . .

The evidence continues to mount showing that asbestos companies maintained a policy of not telling workers they were suffering from asbestos-related diseases until the men became physically disabled. In 1949, Dr. Kenneth Wallace Smith, then the medical officer for Johns-Manville Canada in Asbestos, Quebec, filed a health report with the asbestos company's head offices in the United States. The report indicates that Dr. Smith discussed the potential asbestos danger with Johns-Manville (JM) executives and records their reaction, which, according to Smith, was: "We know that we are producing disease in the employees who manufacture these products and there is no question in my [our] mind that disease is being produced in non-JM employees who may use certain of these products." Smith noted in his report that asbestosis was "irreversible and permanent" and added "but as long as a man is not disabled it is felt he should not be told of his condition so that he can live and work in peace and the company can benefit by his many years of experience."

Smith's report to Johns-Manville came to light through a series of recent lawsuits filed against U.S. asbestos companies by American asbestos disease victims. The victims allege that asbestos companies deliberately withheld information on the deadly effects of asbestos exposure from them.

ENDNOTES

1. Canada, Department of National Health and Welfare, *Report of the Asbestosis Working Group*, P. Bergeron, L. Guinton, G. Schreiber and J.H. Smith (Ottawa, 1976), p. 5.

2. T. Beaudry, G. Lagace and L. Jakau, *Rapport Préliminaire: Comité d'étude sur la salubrité dans l'industrie de l'amiante* (Avril, 1976), p. 39.

3. G. Schreiber *et al.*, *Report of the Asbestosis Working Group*, p. 23.

4. Finger clubbing is a thickening of the tissue at the fingertips which often occurs with asbestosis.

SUGGESTED FURTHER READINGS

BADARACCO, JR. *Loading the Dice: A Five-County Study of Vinyl Chloride Regulation*. Boston: Harvard Business School Press, 1985.

BEATTIE, MARGARET. "Women, Unions, and Social Policy." *Journal of Business Ethics*, Vol. 2, No. 3 (August 1983), pp. 227–231.

BERMAN, DANIEL. *Death on the Job*. New York: Monthly Review Press, 1978.

CURRAN, DANIEL. "Regulating Safety: A Case of Symbolic Action." In J. Desjardins and J. McCall (eds.) *Contemporary Issues in Business Ethics*. Belmont, California: Wadsworth Publishing Company, 1985.

DEUTSCH, STEVEN. "Introduction: Theme Issue on Occupational Safety and Health." *Labor Studies Journal*, 6, 1, pp. 3–6.

DEWEY, MARTIN. *Smoke in the Workplace*. Toronto: Non-Smokers' Rights Association Smoking and Health Action Foundation, 1985.

FADEN, RUTH R. "The Right to Risk Information and the Right to Refuse Health Hazards in the Workplace." In T. Beauchamp and N. Bowie (eds.) *Ethical Theory and Business* 2nd ed. Englewood Cliffs, NJ: Prentice-Hall, 1983.

HITT, MICHAEL, AMOS ORLEY, JR., and LARKIN WARNER. "Social Factors and Company Location Decisions: Technology, Quality of Life and Quality of Work Life Concerns." *Journal of Business Ethics*, Vol. 2, No. 2 (May 1983), pp. 89–99.

HITT, MICHAEL. "Technology, Organizational Climate and Effectiveness." *Journal of Business Research*, 1976, pp. 378–397.

JAIN, HARISH C. "Management of Human Resources and Productivity." *Journal of Business Ethics*, Vol. 2, No. 4 (November 1983), pp. 273–289.

MacCARTHY, MARK. "A Review of Some Normative and Conceptual Issues in Occupational Safety." In J. Desjardins and J. McCall (eds.) *Contemporary Issues in Business Ethics*. Belmont, California: Wadsworth Publishing Company, 1985.

NEYMAN, J. "Public Health Hazards from Electricity-Producing Plants." *Science*, 1977.

NIELSEN, RICHARD P. "Should Executives Be Jailed for Consumer and Employee Health and Safety Violations?" *The Journal of Consumer Affairs*, 13, 1979, pp. 128–134.

RASHKE, RICHARD. *The Killing of Karen Silkwood: The Story Behind the Kerr-McGee Plutonium Case*. Boston: Houghton-Mifflin Co. 1981.

TREMBLAY, HENRI. "Organizational Development at Steinberg's Limited: A Case Study." In H. Jain and R. Kanungo (eds.) *Behavioural Issues in Management: The Canadian Context*. Toronto: McGraw-Hill Ryerson, 1977.

Employee Loyalty
and
Moral Independence

INTRODUCTION

In Part Two of this text, various authors discussed the moral status of corporations. They asked such questions as, "Can corporations be considered to be moral agents in the same way in which persons are considered to be moral agents?" and "Who should be held accountable for corporate wrongdoing?"

In Part Five, we will discuss these and similar issues from the perspective of the worker. What, for example, are the limitations a corporation may justifiably impose upon individual decision-making? Does loyalty to a company which is, after all, performing a useful service to the public by its business activity, require the individual to support company policy even when the policy contravenes the individual's personal beliefs? Should there be legal protection for employees who "blow the whistle" on corporate wrongdoing?

You will recall from the introduction to this text, "Ethical Theory in Business," that contemporary moral philosophy as well as common parlance about morality stresses the notion of rights. Generally speaking, when individuals refer to rights in the context of expressing personal beliefs or values which are contrary to those of an employer, they are referring to Hohfeld's concepts of liberties or privileges as outlined in the introduction. A Toronto police officer who refused to enforce a trespassing law because he did not agree with the law concerning access to abortion argued that his paid occupation did not involve duties to act in ways contrary to his religious belief system. The officer believed that in such a case, he should have a "freedom from duty" or the liberty to follow his own conscience. Conversely, companies have in past argued that they should not be held responsible for individuals' decision-making on behalf of the company when that decision-making is illegal and/or immoral.

All of these questions take on even greater significance in the case of the government employee upon whom the demands of loyalty may pull in more than one direction. One might ask whether civil servants are, for example, employees of the people or of the political party in power? Government employees are, needless to say, often required to enforce laws and carry out policies that have considerable impact on the social and economic conditions of life in Canada. And, of course, political elections often result in new governments with new policies. In the light of these facts, important questions arise. For instance, should government employees be permitted publicly to question government policies with which they disagree? Do they have the right to campaign actively against those policies? If so, do those rights extend as far as the rights of people who do not work for their government?

Unions and professional groups often demand unconditional loyalty as well. The 1986 Ontario doctor's strike raised serious questions about demands which are sometimes made in the name of group solidarity or loyalty. In this case, physicians were asked to support a province-wide strike and to force the closure of emergency hospital wards, despite the acknowledged risks to patients. Are such demands morally defensible on grounds of loyalty? Should a doctor feel obliged by membership in a collegial association to pursue a course of action she or he might otherwise find morally objectionable? These are some of the many questions we will explore in this section.

In our first article, "Organizational Ethics: A Stacked Deck," Smith and Carroll discuss the basic question about the ability of employees to make independent, free moral choices within the corporate context. They are interested not only in the absence of individual moral decision-making within corporations but in the mechanisms which operate to keep moral autonomy within corporations at a minimum. Smith and Carroll claim that employees are chosen, socialized, groomed, and rewarded according to how well they fit with the company's goals and values. This "organizational socialization" results in a "form of 'group think'" which mitigates moral decision-making.

In "The Loyal Agent's Argument," Alex Michalos argues that even in a hypothetically simplified case where we assume that an individual blindly and unthinkingly attempts to serve her or his company's interests, the appeal to loyal agency as a defence will not make sense, logically.

Deborah Poff extends Michalos' argument in "The Loyal Agent's Argument Revisited," and states that even if we examine complex appeals to loyal agency on the part of more intelligent loyal agents, the appeal will still not work. Poff's contention is that loyal agency arguments are never adequate to absolve individuals from responsibility for knowingly doing what is wrong.

In our last article, Frederick Elliston discusses whether employees are justified in anonymously blowing the whistle on employers who are engaged in immoral and/or illegal activities. Blowing the whistle on an employer can result in the loss of a job or the possibility of being harassed in the workplace or discriminated against in future employment. This would seem to suggest that employees should be allowed to blow the whistle on company wrongdoing anonymously. However, this leaves the door open for a hostile employee to abuse the employer with false accusations of wrongdoing. If an employee wants to get even with a company (perhaps for overlooking him or her in job promotion), the employee could falsely accuse the company of wrongdoing. Elliston reviews many of the arguments for and against anonymous whistle-blowing and concludes with a defence of the practice as a means to redresss corporate wrongdoing.

This part ends with a case study highlighting the issue of whistle-blowing in all of its complexity. The case of Tim and Sam helps us to understand how difficult it sometimes is to weigh conflicting interests and to do what is right.

21

Organizational Ethics:
A Stacked Deck

H.R. SMITH

ARCHIE B. CARROLL

ORGANIZATIONAL ETHICS:
A STACKED DECK

Sometimes there is value in presenting the bottom line first. Much of our 'bottom line', in this look at organizational ethics as a 'stacked deck', is captured in some words of wisdom offered to the victim when the Ford Motor Company fired its chief economist:

> In the meeting in which I was informed that I was released, I was told, Bill, in general, people who do well in this company wait until they hear their superiors express their view and then contribute something in support of that view.[1]

The idea of a 'stacked deck' has three elements which are of significance here. There is (1) a magician, the 'deck stacker', (2) a 'straight man', the member of the audience asked by the magician to 'pick a card', and (3) a situation in which the straight man's choice turns out to be exactly the card the deck stacker had intended to be chosen.

Similarly, in organizational ethics there is (1) an organization which has so structured relationships within it that (2) members in the performance of their responsibilities typically choose (3) the organization's preferred way of doing rather than alternative behaviors which might be thought by some to be ethically superior. The result is a pattern of powerful pressures which needs to be thoroughly understood by whoever has responsibilities for the management of human resources.

Employees are supposed to be helpful not dangerous

The existence of a 'stacked deck', of course, presupposes a process by which it became that. In this study we will primarily look at this history. And the central focus of this investigation will be the individual decision maker. For it is necessarily individuals who, in [situations where the ethical standard is tipped in favour of the organization, must] exer-

From *Journal of Business Ethics*, Vol. 3, No. 2 (May 1984) pp. 95-100. © 1984 by D. Reidel Publishing Company, Dordrecht, Holland. Reprinted by permission.

cise the volition that has carefully been pro-grammed toward behaviors more rather than less acceptable to the organization.

The reason organizations often feel the need to 'stack' the ethical behavior 'deck' begins with the fact that the individuals who make organization decisions have already been basically shaped before they become employees. This happens through a process we call 'socialization'. That is, earlier gen-erations — particularly parents — teach newcomers what to believe and how to behave to be members in good standing of their society. Most concretely, from the standpoint of this presentation, children are taught by their elders what to believe and how to behave in that potentially very treach-erous realm we think of as ethics.

But that is only a beginning. The key difficulty [in] organizations and individuals coming to terms with one another in that realm arises because indi-viduals socialized by society must be more specifi-cally 'socialized' for their roles as employees. This necessity is, of course, quite matter of fact when the focus of attention is workers' and managers' compe-tence within the organizations employing them. We are less [likely to realize] that employees' ethical outlook and propensities can also be critically important to their contribution to the success of their organizations. A little close thinking about these things, however, quickly reminds us that organizations would ideally want members who are congenial with their operations in *every* way. And at that point ethical deck stacking becomes part and parcel of all kinds of ways in which organ-izations work to get the best help they can. As in the experience of the victim of a firing at Ford Motor Company, people are very likely to get along best in/with their organization when the latter feels that what they are doing is supportive.

The organizational 'right thinking' enterprise

One of the most significant ways in which this organizational socialization process occurs is in the

pressures, expectations, or 'messages' that are sent to the individual by his or her superiors, subordi-nates, and peers. We will deal with the question of superiors and subordinates later as we consider hierarchical influence, but let us face the issue of peer influence presently. We need to be mindful of the fact that peers, too, are subjected to many of these same influences, and the result is a kind of self-reinforcing organizational mind-set.

The organizational socialization process addresses a multitude of potential behaviors. The new employee must learn not to drive a Ford if he works for GM, not to be publicly critical of the organization, not to be seen in the wrong places or with the wrong kind of people, not to cash company checks in bars, and so on. Beyond this, the organ-izational member learns, frequently from his peers or colleagues, the basic values and behavior pat-terns of what is acceptable or unacceptable prac-tice. Is it acceptable to pad expense accounts? If so, to what degree? Is it acceptable to use company resources for personal use? Should hidden product dangers be kept to yourself? Should you report others' violations of company rules or policies?

Organizational socialization has as one of its principal functions the creation of loyalty and com-mitment to the organization. This is accomplished through a variety of techniques, some of which involve peers and colleagues. One technique used by peers (as well as superiors) is to get the new employee to make a series of small behavioral com-mitments that can only be justified by him [if he accepts and incorporates] organizational values. The individual then becomes his own agent of socialization.[2] An effect similar to this can be achieved by promoting a rebellious person into a more responsible position. Values once criticized from a lower position look more acceptable once he has subordinates of his own whose commitment must be obtained. One manager put this quite poignantly: "My ethical standards changed so gra-dually over the first five years of work that I hardly noticed it, but it was a great shock to suddenly realize what my feelings had been five years ago and how much they had changed."[3]

TO BE, OR NOT TO BE
(MORE ETHICAL)

When the individual in the organization is confronted with these pressures/expectations from others in their socialization efforts, at least three basic responses are possible. One, the individual can rebel — reject those values and norms being communicated. Two, he can engage in creative individualism — accept only pivotal values and reject all others. Three, he can conform — accept all the values and norms.[4]

The third response, conformity, is an especially enticing alternative given the pressures one receives from peers and superiors. It has been suggested that a 'club' psychology engenders a conformity ethic in organizations and that this preconditioning reinforces a bottom-line morality — results are what counts.[5]

Conformity shows its sometimes ugly head in the form of 'groupthink'. Groupthink is a quick and easy way to refer to a process that people engage in when concurrence seeking becomes so dominant that it overrides realistic appraisal of alternative courses of action. The term carries a negative connotation in that it typically refers to a deterioration in [decision-making] efficiency, reality testing, and moral judgment as a result of group pressures. Victims of groupthink frequently believe unquestioningly in the inherent morality of the group and this belief inclines the members to ignore the ethical consequences of their decisions.[6]

In addition to 'deck stacking' being further advanced by peers and colleagues through socialization, conformity, and groupthink processes, the task itself that the individual faces frequently encourages less ethical behavior or decisions. Pertinent here would be [such factors as] the type of industry and its ethical traditions, the type of job or position one has and its ethical traditions, the amount of power the individual has that may be abused, the problem the individual is faced with, and the frequently present pressure of time. Thus, the deck is stacked against careful, thoughtful deliberation by situational circumstances that do not always permit superior ethical views to surface.

Forces emanating from the organization's environment have the potential of moving behavior and decisions in a more or a less ethical direction. Of special concern here are those [forces] which further stack the deck against ethical behavior. We live in a society that reveres and rewards performance. Since ends are frequently valued more highly than means, this performance ethic is further institutionalized. The performance ethic is the heart of America. Growth, wealth-creation, achievement, and performance are some of the principle reasons we created organizations.

Beyond this emphasis on results, there seems to be a prevailing view that if something is not expressly prohibited by law, then it is permissible. Though society perhaps did not intend for this to be one of the consequences of an increasingly legalistic existence, it inevitably becomes one of the realities. Such rationalization creates a climate in which the organization's pursuit of profits is legitimized, and ends become more important than means.

'Men of conscience' as 'The Enemy'

Therewith we come to hierarchy as a particularly explicit and powerful dimension of deck stacking. And to focus on this context especially clearly, it will be useful to refer to Becker's concept of the "moral entrepreneur".[7]

Becker's point of departure is that standards of behavior, be they organization rules or the dictates of conscience, cannot be depended upon to enforce themselves. Thus, if rewards can be achieved by violations of behavior standards — and this would mean at a minimum that ignoring these guidelines is reasonably safe — there will be systematic violations. An important preventive may be the 'conscience-stricken' observer or associate who is unwilling to be an accomplice to this immorality by remaining silent. By, therefore, being instrumental in bringing those who flout standards of right and wrong to justice, these people quite literally do become 'moral entrepreneurs'.

Of course, if organizations are to remain free to pursue their interests, they must be able to protect themselves from internal 'conscience heroes'. Put differently, organizations' flexibility to take advantage of their opportunities may often depend in substantial part on their capacity to prevent moral entrepreneur members from 'blowing the whistle' on organization behavior these people see as ethically inferior. In a word, organizations must be able, over a wide range of relationships, to resolve internal conflicts between 'business as usual' and a higher level of morality in such a way that the organization's affairs, as these are understood by its leaders, do not seriously suffer.

In a multitude of ways the concentration of power toward the top of organizations is able to make this contribution to deck stacking — to help members be 'moral cowards' where the organization's affairs are involved. And let us be quite explicit about this. To bring about this 'they made me do it' situation is one of the reasons the hierarchical form of organizations was created and has been so successful. Just as organizations must see to it that employees are sufficiently competent and motivated, they must go to great pains also to make sure that these people are 'loyal' enough. And we all recall within the quite recent past several classic cases in which moral entrepreneur 'tattlers' were later dealt with quite harshly by their organizations.

The 'What is really right?' confusion

Interestingly enough, however, there is an almost opposite way in which the large, complex organization minimizes moral entrepreneurship. And this variety of [subtle corporate coercion] may be equally pervasive and significant.

The conscience enterprise, more easily than might be supposed, gets caught up in an intricate network of confusions, ambiguities, and uncertainties which severely cloud what ethical purists are inclined to think of as the real issues. A first key aspect of this difficulty asks, what is the ethical thing to do when what is easily advertised as an unambiguous principle stands side by side with some perhaps even more certain personal damage which will likely follow from a vigorous defense of that principle? What middle ground is ethically acceptable, when caring for others brings us into tension with our 'instinct' for self(-image) preservation? At what points in our relationships do our advantage and our conscience interests become all but inseparable?

Second, and similarly, what is the ethical thing to do when what is easily advertised as an unambiguous principle stands side by side with some perhaps even more certain damage to friends which will likely follow from a vigorous defense of that principle? What middle ground is ethically acceptable, when caring for more distant others brings us into tension with a more intimate need for a few of those others? What are we to do when the conscience which is supposed to guide us through our value conflicts commends to us competing definitions of the higher level of behavior it speaks for?

Third, how is one to be sure of what is ethical from the perspective of a professional living in one corner of an organization — and therefore understanding correspondingly little of the 'big picture?' Thus, whereas an organization's leaders are necessarily in a position to see the implications of what the organization is doing in a number of directions, the work of professionals/specialists is systematically designed so that incumbents have no need to see many implications either inside or outside the organization. Furthermore, those highest up in the organization must live as responsibly/constructively as they can with the consequences of what the organization is doing. In short, it might often seem quite presumptuous for those with much less organizational understanding to pass seriously consequential judgments on those who can see so much more clearly what is involved.

And let us mention one other complexity in the realm of organizational ethics, this one picking up on the theme that 'we are all sinners'. How can one be comfortably sure what is realistically ethical for someone else today — in the shadow of one's own vividly remembered transgressions of yesterday?

Who among us is so upright that we can remain unmoved by the question, "Are you so perfect that you can with clear conscience urge that particular sins of your fellows must be stringently dealt with?" As the 'Good Book' put it, "Judge not that ye be not judged". And of course forgiveness is itself a major ethical principle.

'Leave the driving to us'

How do professionals employed by large organizations respond to these confusions, ambiguities, and uncertainties in the ethics realm? It is our hypothesis that out of this situation fraught with so much (potential) discomfort will emerge — among other things — a quite basic reciprocity in which many organization members will be eager to 'delegate' ethical responsibilities to their leaders.

The principal dynamics here emerge from the need of so many of us to find a bed-rock of (even artifical) certainties on which to build our lives. Thus, in large, complex organizations, just as many employees are quite content to leave the difficult business decisions such as handling the perspective of the organization — consensus/political maneuvering, and guessing toward a highly uncertain future and so on — to their leaders, so are many of them quite content to let ethical decision making be their bosses' challenge. Just as many professionals are happy to 'nest in task' — find as much security as they can in the definiteness of their specialization — so are many organization members happy to enjoy another kind of security by letting leaders make the organization's conscience determinations. Not only are we sometimes quite willing to do little more than mind our own business; often we are willing in the bargain for 'our own business' to be defined fairly narrowly.

Let's particularly note three things about this variety of very human avoidance of ambiguity and confusion. First, while it is true that hierarchy can and often does create moral cowardice, just as often, the hierarchy is rather ministering to a sort of cowardice which is already there. Second, though there are, no doubt, frequent attempts to hide behind the 'they made me do it' excuse in the organization world, the abdication of responsibility for moral decisions more nearly comes down to the *abdicator*, in effect, forcing others to do the hard moral work. Third, as these dynamics work themselves out, the organization's 'business' problem is not to prevent moral entrepreneurship but to rescue members from the burden of discomfort. In short, given an inescapable confusion and uncertainty, is it not easily understandable that — just as in the world of bus transportation as we sometimes see advertised on our television screens — many people would be warmly responsive to an invitation in the ethical penumbra of their work to 'leave the driving to us'.

This really is a quite basic reciprocity, a very pragmatic *quid pro quo*. On the one hand, organization members lower in the hierarchy are protected from uncomfortable ambiguities and uncertainties — and thereby relieved of the burden of being moral guardians of their organizations. In exchange for this relief and protection, these subordinates give their superiors full 'loyalty', conformity, in this realm. Which is to say that organization leaders become, through this transaction, that much more free to decide among themselves how the organization will define the moral standards to which it will adhere. And again, from the perspective of those responsible for the management of human resources, there is a powerful and ever-present undercurrent almost imperceptibly shaping what is happening.

ENDNOTES

1. William A. Niskanen, Jr., quoted in *Wall Street Journal*, July 30, 1980, p. 18 (column by Robert L. Simison).

2. E.H. Schein, 'Organization Socialization and the Profession of Management,' *Industrial Management Review* (Winter, 1968), Reprinted in B.M. Staw (ed.), *Psychological Foundations of Organizational Behavior* (Goodyear Publ. Co., Santa Monica, California, 1977), p. 216.

3. *Ibid.*, p. 217.

4. *Ibid.*, p. 218.

5. Carl Madden, 'Forces Which Influence Ethical Behavior', in Clarence Walton (ed.), *The Ethics of Corporate Conduct* (Prentice-Hall, Englewood Cliffs, N.J., 1977), p. 59.

6. Irving L. Janis, 'Groupthink', *Psychology Today* (1971), in Staw, pp. 407-410.

7. Howard S. Becker, *Outsiders: Studies in the Sociology of Deviance* (Free Press, New York, 1963), esp. Chapter 8.

22

The Loyal Agent's Argument

ALEX C. MICHALOS

INTRODUCTION

According to the Report of the Special Review Committee of the Board of Directors of Gulf Oil Corporation:

> It is not too much to say that the activity of those Gulf officials involved in making domestic political contributions with corporate funds during the period of approximately fourteen years under review [1960–1974] was shot through with illegality. The activity was generally clandestine and in disregard of federal, as well as a number of state, statutes.[1]

Nevertheless, and more importantly for our purposes, the Committee apparently endorsed the following judgment, which was submitted by their lawyers tò the U.S. Securities and Exchange Commission.

> No evidence has been uncovered or disclosed which establishes that any officer, director or employee of Gulf personally profited or benefited by or through any use of corporate funds for contributions, gifts, entertainment or other expenses related to political activity. Further, Gulf has no reason to believe or suspect that *the motive of the employee or officer* involved in such use of corporate funds was anything other than *a desire to act solely in what he considered to be the best interests of Gulf and its shareholders.*[2] [Emphasis added.]

If we accept the views of the Committee and their lawyers, then we have before us an interesting case of individuals performing illegal actions with altruistic motives. What they did was admittedly illegal, but they meant well. They had good intentions, namely, to further "the best interests of Gulf and its shareholders." Furthermore, there is no suggestion in these passages or in the rest of the report that the officials were ordered to commit such acts. They were not ordered. On the contrary, the acts seem to have emerged as practically natural by-products of some employees' zeal in looking after their employer's interests. They are, we might say, the result of overzealous attempts of agents to fulfill their fiducial obligations.

This paper was written for the Conference on Ethics and Economics at the University of Delaware, Newark, Delaware, November 10-12, 1977. Copyright © 1978 by Alex C. Michalos. Reprinted by permission of the author.

In the following paragraphs I am going to pursue this apparently plausible account of overzealous behavior to its bitter end. That is, I'm going to assume for the sake of argument that there really are reasonable people who would and do perform immoral and illegal actions with altruistic motives, i.e., there are people who would and do perform such actions with reasons that they regard as good in some fairly general sense. It's not to be assumed that they are shrewd enough to see that their own interests lie in the advancement of their employer's or clients' interests. They are not, I'm assuming, cleverly egoistic. If anything, they are stupidly altruistic by hypothesis. But that's beside the point now. What I want to do is construct a generalized form of an argument that I imagine would be attractive to such agents, whether or not any of them has or will ever formulate it exactly so. Then I want to try to demolish it once and for all.

THE ARGUMENT

What I will call the Loyal Agent's Argument (LAA) runs as follows:

1. *As a loyal agent of some principal, I ought to serve his interests as he would serve them himself if he had my expertise.*
2. *He would serve his own interests in a thoroughly egoistic way.*

   Therefore, as a loyal agent of this principal, I ought to operate in a thoroughly egoistic way in his behalf.

Some clarification is in order. First, in order to make full use of the fairly substantial body of legal literature related to the *law of agency*, I have adopted some of the standard legal jargon. In particular, following Powell, I'm assuming that "*an agent is a person who is authorised to act for a principal and has agreed so to act, and who has power to affect the legal relations of his principal with a third party.*"[3] The standard model is an insurance agent who acts in behalf of an insurance company, his principal, to negotiate insurance contracts with third parties. More generally, lawyers, real estate agents, engineers, doctors, dentists, stockbrokers, and the Gulf Oil zealots may all be regarded as agents of some prin-

cipal. Although for some purposes one might want to distinguish agents from employees, such a distinction will not be necessary here. The definition given above is broad enough to allow us to think of coal miners, Avon Ladies, zoo attendants, and Ministers of Parliament as agents.

Second, as our definition suggests, there are typically three important relationships involved in agency transactions, namely, those between agent and principal, agent and third party, and principal and third party. The law of agency has plenty to say about each of these relationships, while LAA is primarily concerned with only the first, the fiducial relation between agent and principal. It would be a mistake to regard this as mere oversight. Few of us are immune to the buck-passing syndrome. Most of us are inclined to try to narrow the range of activities for which we are prepared to accept responsibility and, at the same time, widen the range of activities over which we are prepared to exercise authority. Notwithstanding the psychological theory of cognitive dissonance, most human beings seem to have sufficient mental magnanimity to accommodate this particular pair of incompatible inclinations. Like the insects, we are very adaptable creatures.

Third, I imagine that someone using an argument like LAA would, in the first place, be interested in trying to establish the fact that agents have a moral obligation to operate in a thoroughly egoistic way in their principals' behalf. If most LAA users in fact are primarily concerned with establishing their legal obligations, then perhaps what I have to say will be less interesting than I imagine to most people. Nevertheless, I'm assuming that the force of "ought" in the first premise and conclusion is moral rather than legal. For our purposes it doesn't matter what sort of an ontological analysis one gives to such obligations or what sort of a moral theory one might want to use to justify one's moral principles. It only has to be appreciated that LAA is designed to provide a moral justification for the behavior prescribed in its conclusion.

Fourth, an agent may be regarded as operating in a thoroughly egoistic way if all his actions are designed to optimize his own interests and he has no inclination at all to identify the interests of anyone else with his own. (Throughout the essay I usually let the masculine "he" abbreviate "he or she.") He may very well be a self-confident, self-starting, self-sustaining, and self-controlled individual. These are all commendable personal characteristics. But he must be selfish, self-centered, and/or self-serving. In conflict situations when there are not enough benefits to satisfy everyone, he will try to see that his own needs are satisfied, whatever happens to the needs of others. He is more interested in being first than in being nice, and he assumes that everyone else is too. He may harbor the suspicion that if everyone behaved as he does, the world's resources would be used in a maximally efficient way and everyone would be materially better off. But these are secondary considerations at best. His first consideration, which he regards as only prudent or smart, is to look out for *Numero Uno*, himself.

Fifth, to say that an agent is supposed to operate in a thoroughly egoistic way in behalf of his principal is just to say that the agent is supposed to act as he believes his principal would act if his principal were an egoist. The agent is supposed to conduct the affairs of his principal with the single-minded purpose of optimizing the latter's interests and not yielding them to anyone else's interests.

THE SECOND PREMISE

Now we should be talking the same language. The question is: Is the Loyal Agent's Argument sound? Can its conclusion be established or even well-supported by its premises? I think there are good reasons for giving a negative answer to these questions. Moreover, since the argument has been deliberately formulated in a logically valid form, we may proceed immediately to a closer investigation of the content of its premises.

Let's consider the second premise first. This premise can only be regarded as true of people *a priori* if one of the assumptions we have made for the sake of argument about human motivation is false. Following the quotations from the Special Review Committee, it was pointed out that the case involved agents who apparently performed illegal actions with altruistic motives. What they did wrong, they did in behalf of Gulf Oil Corporation. Fair enough. However, if it's possible to perform illegal but altruistically motivated acts, it must be possible to perform legal but altruistically motivated acts as well. The very assumption required to give the argument initial plausibility also ensures that its second premise cannot be assumed to be generally true *a priori*. Since some people can perform nonegoistically motivated actions, the second premise of LAA requires some defense. Moreover, broadly speaking there are two directions such a defense might take, and I will consider each in turn.

Granted that users of LAA cannot consistently regard every individual as a thoroughly egoistic operator and hence guarantee the truth of the second premise *a priori*, it is still possible to try to defend this premise as a well-confirmed empirical hypothesis. That is, admitting that there are exceptions, one might still claim that if one acted as if the second premise were true, much more often than not one would be right. This is the sort of line economists have traditionally taken toward their idealized rational economic man. They realize that people are capable of altruistic action, but they figure that the capability is seldom exercised and they design their hypotheses, laws, and theories accordingly.

So far as business is concerned, the egoistic line seems to be translated into profit maximization. According to Goodman, for example:

> The Wall Street rule for persons legally charged with the management of other people's money runs as follows: Invest funds in a company with the aim of gaining the best financial return with the least financial risk for the trust beneficiaries. If you later come to disagree with the company's management, sell the stock.[4]

Similarly, in a cautious version of LAA, Friedman has claimed that:

> In a free-enterprise, private-property system, a corporate executive is an employee of the owners of the

business. He has a direct responsibility to his employers. That responsibility is to conduct the business in accordance with their desires, which generally will be to make as much money as possible while conforming to the basic rules of the society, both those embodied in law and those embodied in ethical custom.[5]

Instead of challenging the accuracy of these assessments of the motives of people generally or of businessmen in the marketplace in particular now, I want to grant it straightaway for the sake of the argument. The question is: How does that affect LAA?

As you may have guessed, users of LAA are not much better off than they were. If it's a good bet that the second premise is true, then it's an equally good bet that anyone inclined to defend his actions with LAA is not an altruistic operator. No one can have it both ways. Evidence for the empirical hypothesis that people generally act as egoists is evidence for the truth of the second premise and the falsehood of the alleged altruistic motives of anyone using LAA. In short, the premise is still self-defeating.

Corporate Principals

Instead of regarding the second premise as an empirical claim about real people and attempting to support it inductively, one might treat it as a logical claim justifiable by an appeal to the definitions of some of its key terms. This looks like a very promising strategy when one considers the fact that many contemporary principals, like Gulf Oil Corporation, for example, are abstract entities. Corporate persons are, after all, nothing but fictional persons invented by people with fairly specific aims. In particular, corporations have been invented to assist in the accumulation of material assets. While they typically accomplish many different tasks, the accumulation of assets is generally regarded as their basic aim. Thus, if one's principal happens to be a corporation, one might reasonably argue that it is by definition thoroughly egoistic. The business of such entities is certainly business, because that is

their very reason for being, the very point of inventing them in the first place. So, the second premise of LAA could be substantiated by definitional fiat. . . .

Apparently, then, morally conscientious corporate agents may find themselves facing lawsuits if they assume their principals are not self-serving profit maximizers and act accordingly. Legal niceties aside, there is a thought-provoking moral argument in favor of agents acting as if their principals were just as the designers of corporate law imagine them. That is, if any particular stockholder wants to give his money away or to pursue any aims other than profit maximization, he is free to do so. Investors should be and almost certainly are aware that corporations are designed to make money. If they have other aims, they shouldn't be investing in corporations. If they don't have other aims and they go into corporations with their eyes wide open, then they should appreciate and respect the interests of others who have gone in with them.

In principle, the defense of the second premise of LAA on the grounds of the defining characteristic of corporations may be challenged as before. Insofar as corporations are defined as egoistic corporate persons (a rough abbreviated definition, to be sure), a serious question arises concerning the morality of becoming an agent for them — not to mention inventing them in the first place. The evils of unbridled egoism are well known and they aren't mitigated by the fact that the egoist in question is a corporate person. If anything, they are magnified because of the difficulties involved in assigning responsibility and holding corporations liable for their activities. It is demonstrably certain that if everyone only attends to what he perceives as his own interests, a socially self-destructive result may occur. That is the clear message of prisoner's dilemma studies. It's also the message of two kids in a playpen who finally tear the toys apart rather than share them.

As before, it will not help to argue that in developed countries most people work for corporations or they don't work at all. Again, self-preservation is not altruism. To serve an evil master in the interests of survival is not to serve in the interests of altruism, and users of LAA are supposed to be motivated by altruism. On the other hand, insofar as corporations are not defined as egoistic corporate persons and are granted more or less benevolent if not downright altruistic aims, the truth of the second premise of LAA is again open to question. In either case, then, an agent trying to salvage LAA with this sort of definitional defense is bound to find the task self-defeating.

THE FIRST PREMISE

Let's turn now to the first premise of LAA. In a way it's as innocuous as motherhood and apple pie. Every discussion I've read of the duties of agents according to agency law in North America and the United Kingdom has included some form of this premise. For example, Powell says, "An agent has a general duty to act solely for the benefit of his principal in all matters connected with the execution of his authority."[6] The *American Restatement of the Law of Agency* says that "an agent is subject to a duty to his principal to act solely for the benefit of the principal in all matters connected with his agency."[7] According to a standard Canadian textbook on business law, "Good faith requires that the agent place the interest of his principal above all else except the law."[8]

The only trouble with the premise is that its limitations are not clearly built into it. In this respect it is like most moral principles and rules of law. Short of turning every principle and rule into a self-contained treatise, it's impossible to indicate every possible exception. . . . However, the *American Restatement of the Law of Agency* makes it quite clear that "In no event would it be implied that an agent has a duty to perform acts which . . . are illegal or unethical."[9] Moreover, "In determining whether or not the orders of the principal to the agent are reasonable . . . business or professional ethics . . . are considered."[10] Powell also remarks that agents have no duty "to carry out an illegal act."[11] . . . Thus, there is no doubt at all that the first premise of LAA cannot be regarded as a licence to break the law. No respectable court would permit it. In fact, although the courts have no special jurisdiction

over moral law, they have shown no reluctance to condemn immoral acts allegedly performed in the interests of fulfilling fiduciary obligations.

Illegality and immorality aside, the first premise still gives up much more than any sane person should be willing to give up. It virtually gives a principal licence to use an agent in any way the principal pleases, so long as the agent's activity serves the principal's interest. For example, suppose a life insurance agent agrees to sell State Farm Insurance on commission. It would be ludicrous to assume that the agent has also committed himself to painting houses, washing dogs, or doing anything else that happened to give his principal pleasure. It would also be misleading to describe such an open-ended commitment as an agreement to sell insurance. It would more accurately be described as selling oneself into bondage. Clearly, then, one must assume that the first premise of LAA presupposes some important restrictions that may have nothing to do with any sort of law.

Since they are apparently drawn from and applicable to ordinary affairs and usage, perhaps it would be instructive to mention some of the principles developed in the law of agency to address this problem. You may recall that the definition of an agent that we borrowed from Powell explicitly referred to a person being "authorised to act for a principal." An agent's duties are typically limited to a set of activities over which he is granted authority by his principal. . . . [This] . . . would be sufficient to prevent the exploitation of the hypothetical insurance agent in the preceding paragraph.

Besides a carefully developed set of principles related to the granting of authority, the law of agency recognizes some other general duties of agents like the previously considered duty of good faith. For example, an agent is expected to "exercise due care and skill in executing his authority."[12] This obviously serves the interests of all concerned, and there are plenty of principles and precedents available to explain "due care and skill." . . . He is expected to "keep proper accounts," i.e., accounts that clearly distinguish his principal's assets from his own. . . .[13]

Keeping the preceding guidelines in mind, perhaps some form of LAA can be salvaged by tightening up the first premise. Let's suppose I'm in the advertising business and I want to use LAA by suitably restricting the scope of the first premise thus:

> 1a. *As a loyal advertising agent of some company, I ought to advertise its products as they would advertise them if they had my expertise.*

That would require a consistent modification of the second premise and conclusion, but we need not worry about that. The question is: Does this reformulated premise 1a escape the kinds of criticism leveled against premise 1?

Certainly not. If the company happens to be run by a bunch of thoroughly unscrupulous thugs, it could be immoral and illegal to advertise their products as they would if they had the agent's expertise. Even if the company is run by fools who really don't know what they make, it could be immoral and illegal to advertise their products as they would if they had the agent's expertise. For example, if the company's directors are smart enough to know that they can make more money selling drugs than they can make selling candy, but dumb enough to think that the candy they make is

an effective drug, an agent could hardly be under any obligation to advertise their product as a marvelous new drug, i.e., assuming that the agent was smart enough to know that his employers were only capable of producing candy.

If you think the agent could have such an obligation, what would be its source? Clearly it is not enough to say that the agent is employed by the company. That would be tantamount to appealing to LAA in order to establish a version of its own first premise, i.e., it would be a circular salvaging effort. Something else is required to support premise 1a. . . .

CONCLUSION

The announced aim of this essay was to destroy LAA once and for all. I think that has been done. It is perhaps worthwhile to emphasize that if people use LAA when, as we saw earlier, the real reason for their actions is fear (or job preservation) then they will be circulating a distorted view of the world and decreasing the chances of reform. Thus, in the interests of a clear perception and resolution of social problems related to responsible human agency, LAA deserves the sort of treatment it has received here.

ENDNOTES

1. J.J. McCloy, N.W. Pearson, and B. Matthews, *The Great Oil Spill* (New York: Chelsea House, 1976), p. 31.

2. *Ibid*, p. 13.

3. R. Powell, *The Law of Agency* (London: Sir Isaac Pitman and Sons, Ltd., 1965), p. 7.

4. W. Goodman, "Stocks Without Sin," *Minneapolis Star and Tribune Co., Inc.* Reprinted in R. Baum (ed.) *Ethical Arguments for Analysis*, (New York: Holt, Rinehart & Winston, 1975), p. 206.

5. M. Friedman, "The Social Responsibility of Business Is to Increase Its Profits," see p. 41 ff. of this book.

6. Powell, *The Law of Agency*, p. 312.

7. Section 387 as quoted in P.I. Blumberg, "Corporate

Responsibility and the Employee's Duty of Loyalty and Obedience: A Preliminary Inquiry," *The Corporate Dilemma*, ed. D. Votaw and S.P. Sethi (Englewood Cliffs, N.J.: Prentice-Hall, Inc., 1973), p. 87.

8. J.E. Smyth and D.A. Soberman, *The Law and Business Administration in Canada* (Toronto: Prentice-Hall of Canada, Ltd., 1968), p. 360.

9. Section 385 as quoted in Blumberg, "Corporate Responsibility," p. 86.

10. *Ibid.*

11. Powell, *The Law of Agency*, p. 302.

12. *Ibid*, p. 303.

13. *Ibid*, p. 321.

23

The Loyal Agent's Argument Revisited

DEBORAH POFF

Michalos has done an admirable job of illustrating the flaws in the reasoning of the "illogically altruistic" loyal agent. Though there may be some cases of such stupidly altruistic loyalty, I don't think that such altruism accounts for all or for the most interesting loyal agents. It is the more complex, intelligent loyal agent that I wish to discuss in this paper.

Michalos' naively altruistic loyal agent argues as follows:

1. As a loyal agent of some principal, I ought to serve his interests as he would serve them himself if he had my expertise.
2. He would serve his own interests in a thoroughly egoistic way.

    Therefore, as a loyal agent of this principal, I ought to operate in a thoroughly egoistic way in his behalf.[1]

It certainly does seem imprudent to accept this argument so unconditionally: it matters not what the interests of the principal are, the loyal agent will serve them. More interesting, I believe, are the cases of the intelligent misinformed (or willfully ignorant, or, even perhaps, evil) loyal agent. This loyal agent might argue as follows:

1. As a loyal agent of this specific principal (in whose aims and goals I believe) I ought to serve that principal's interests as she or he, given my expertise, would serve them.
2. The principal would serve them in a single-minded way to achieve her or his goals maximally.

    Therefore, as a loyal agent of this principal, I ought to operate in a single-minded way to achieve her or his goals maximally.

Now let's fill out our intelligently misinformed loyal agent's story. In this case, the ILA (Intelligent Loyal Agent) believes in the supremacy of the white race. The ILA believes that god and science have proven this to be true and is well-versed in both theological and bio-determinist accounts which support these beliefs. Consequently, the ILA has chosen to work for and help build a multinational corporation which exploits non-whites globally.

This article was written especially for the first edition of this book.

242

This not only serves to maximize profit for white stockholders, it also serves to preserve the proper order of things. Let's further assume that the global community has finally resolved to condemn apartheid and through a global resolution begins court trials to assess the legal responsibility of key players in corporations which supported apartheid in South Africa. The ILA finds her/himself on the stand. The ILA trots out the ILAA (Intelligent Loyal Agent's Argument). Premise 1 of the ILAA states that as a loyal agent of this specific principal (in whose aims and goals I believe) I ought to serve her or his interests as she or he would serve them if she or he had my expertise. However, just as in Michalos' case, the ILA finds that premise 1 of the ILAA will not absolve her/him from responsibility.

To the extent that this premise is appealed to solely on the grounds of loyal agency, it won't wash for the same reasons that Michalos cited. As Michalos argues, in addition to considerations of illegality and immorality, "the first premise gives up much more than any sane person should be willing to give up". If Premise 1 is accepted on the grounds of loyal agency, its perimeters are unlimited. Thus, Premise 1 implies that the loyal agent could give up all possibility of future rational decision-making (perhaps through the ingestion of loyal agents' loyalty potion). No premise with such unlimited scope can be appealed to on rational and moral grounds.

On the other hand, if the ILA appeals to Premise 1 because she or he personally believes in what the principal stands for, then the ILA is stating a personal belief for which she or he can and should be held responsible. To appeal to loyal agency in such a case, is subterfuge. In this case, the alleged loyal agent is loyal because of that agent's acceptance of apartheid. Put another way, the agent's loyalty is fundamentally to apartheid and secondarily to her or his principal. The agent's primary interest is precisely the same as that of her or his principal, namely, apartheid. The agent's appeal to loyal agency is a misleading and unsuccessful (logically) attempt to win support for the morally unacceptable institution of apartheid.

Hence, both stupid and intelligent loyal agents find themselves on the hook. Michalos notes that in many discussions of loyal agency it is explicitly stated that there are limits to loyality, whether these be stated as legal or ethical limitations. This is what we would and should expect. We have no evidence to believe that individuals as a rule become morally impaired when they work. However, we do have evidence to believe that some individuals find reason to join certain companies, to support certain practises and to benefit from certain immoral and/ or illegal acts.

If we have reason to believe, which I doubt, that corporations brainwash those who enter them, we may have further reasons for substantially revising and strengthening our structures to ensure corporate moral accountability. In any case, we should demand that individuals, whether employed or not, assume responsibility for their decision making.

ENDNOTE

1. Alex C. Michalos, "The Loyal Agent's Argument." See p. 236 ff., this text.

24

Anonymity and Whistleblowing

FREDERICK A. ELLISTON

A. IDENTIFYING THE PHENOMENON

Whistleblowing is a practice that can be defined in various ways. In the literature to date, the following four definitions are among the clearest:

(a) going public with information about the safety of a product;[1]

(b) sounding an alarm from within the very organization in which [an employee] works, aiming to spotlight neglect or abuses that threaten the public interest;[2]

(c) (when) the employee, "without support or authority from his superiors . . . independently makes known concerns to individuals outside the organization."[3]

(d) A whistle blower is an employee or officer of any institution, profit or non-profit, private or public, who believes either that he/she has been ordered to perform some act or he/she has obtained knowledge that the institution is engaged in activities which (a) are believed to cause unnecessary harm to third parties, (b) are in violation of human rights or (c) run counter to the defined purpose of the institution and who informs the public of this fact.[4]

My purpose in this first section is not to appraise the practice but identify it. Accordingly, in discussing these definitions and other elements of the concept, I shall 'build in' no prejudices or biases — either in favor of or opposition to the practice, for otherwise the argument over justification becomes merely a verbal quibble.

To begin with, we must recognize we are dealing with a metaphor. Though 'whistleblowing' serves to connote an *action*, the reality is quite different. Typically several actions are involved in a *process* of blowing the whistle — even if we exclude those events which lead up to the 'act' and follow it: someone calls a meeting of fellow employees, arranges interviews with the media, responds to questions, qualifies statements and counters objections.[5] Though we can treat whistleblowing as one act, to be more precise we should from the outset be aware that we are dealing much more with a *series*

From the *Journal of Business Ethics*, Vol. 1, No. 3, 1982, pp. 167-177. Reprinted by permission of the author.

of actions, a process. With this *caveat*, what are the features of this process that distinguish it from others?

All four definitions refer to the transfer of information. Accordingly, whistleblowing can be characterized as a mode of *communication*. But it is distinctive in several respects.

First, what is communicated? De George identifies the subject of the communication as the *safety* of a product. Clearly this is one possible content, and typical for his domain of inquiry — engineering. But it is not the only one. Bok speaks of *abuses* and *neglect*. In view of Frank Serpico, the cop who blew the whistle on New York City's finest, one can add *corruption*.[6] And if one thinks of Ernest Fitzgerald, who blew the whistle on illegal or unwarranted payoffs to Lockheed, one can speak of *bribery, mismanagement*, and *inefficiency*.[7] Is there a more precise way to characterize the common elements in the above cases and definitions that is more informative than Chalk/von Hippel's 'concerns'? Bowie's definition attempts this.

He stipulates the information must concern activities believed to cause unnecessary harm to third parties. Consider each element of his definition in turn. First, the information deals with activities — not natural disasters, but human actions or practices: one may blow the whistle only on events or conditions that involve people as agents who are affected by or perform these activities. Second, these activities must be harmful, or more precisely, believed to be harmful; in fact they may not harm others and the whistleblower's dilemma is that the harm may not be actual but only threatened. Accordingly, one must assess both the *amount* of harm, in terms both of the number of people harmed and the extent of the harm, and the *probability* of this harm's occurring.

What is meant by 'harm'? The second condition in Bowie's definition provides one answer: an action is harmful if it violates human rights. What these rights are is a difficult philosophical question to which we must return. De George's reference to safety suggests one kind of right-violation: putting others at risk — to their lives or health — without their consent, actual or proxy. Graft in the New

York City Police Department violates another right: the public's right to fair value in police services for their tax dollar, distributed in an equitable way. Moreover, because this violation is typically hidden, their right to know whether paid government employees are doing their job is further violated.

Bowie stipulates this harm must be of a certain sort: *'unnecessary'*, and to *third parties'*. Clearly, if the harm could be avoided at no cost, and hence is not necessary at all, it should not occur. But an organization may claim that its dumping toxic chemicals into public waters is necessary if it is to operate at a profit. Hence, more generally, whether one regards a harm as necessary depends on one's goals. It is the conflicting goals of institutions, their members and the public that generates the dilemma of the whistleblower. In claiming the harm is unnecessary one may have presupposed the priority of one group's interest — a third party or more generally the public.

From this it follows that I cannot accept Bowie's third condition, that the activities on which one blows the whistle "run counter to the defined purpose of the institution." If one of the purposes of private organizations is to make a profit (note I do not say this is the sole purpose, or that the profit must be maximized), then dumping toxic substances into the water may indeed be necessary for achieving this. Its consonance with institutional objectives is not relevant to either the definition or evaluation of whistleblowing — especially in private organizations. In public organizations the situation is different: their main objective (in principle) is to serve the public — at least some segment in some fashion. For this reason whistleblowers in public institutions have to take the interest of the public more seriously: private organizations may be allowed some small measure of harm to the public (e.g., dumping small amounts of toxic substances into the water, at a level below that judged to pose a threat to the health of citizens). To insist that they could not harm, or threaten to harm, the public in any way would curtail their activities too severely. Some measure of harm is allowed to be offset by the benefits from the activities of private organizations to the public generally. Inevitably, one is committed to a balancing act: how much harm to whom vs. how much benefit to whom. One must weigh both the net benefit in a utilitarian calculus and the distribution of benefits in a non-utilitarian deontological fashion to reach a decision on acceptable levels of harm to third parties.

So far I have analyzed whistleblowing as a *process*, which conveys *information* about activities producing a net harm to third parties. The information can be couched in different grammatical forms: (1) as a question, "Did you know that . . .?" (2) as an exclamation, "That . . . is terrible!" (3) as an injunction, "Do something about . . .!" (4) or as a mere statement of fact, "It is the case that . . . ." Typically, whistleblowing approximates the third, informing the public about an act or practice, and enjoining them to do something about it.

But if we think of whistleblowing only in these terms, we miss an important element. Consider the injunction: "Look out for the car!" It satisfies the four conditions listed so far — to inform third parties of an activity that threatens some harm. Clearly something is missing: what we have so far is not whistleblowing but warning.

The difference is that whistleblowing involves an *accusation*. It is directed to people — not just in the sense of warning those who are in danger, but in the sense of locating responsibility for the danger. The whistleblower need not identify one person who is responsible, though he may. Rather he may target a group who share responsibility, or who include someone likely to be responsible.

Responsibility has two dimensions. Consider an example. Someone in a chemical factory dumps toxic substances into the water which an engineer in the city's water department discovers is beyond acceptable risk. His boss tells him not to inform the residents, but when asked directly while testing the water in someone's house replies that he would not drink it — it's dangerous! He has blown the whistle — and gets fired.[8] His superior has the responsibility of informing the public when the water is unsafe, and the engineer blows the whistle on him for failing to perform his duties. But his superior is not responsible for the unsafe water in a causal sense: he did not put the toxic substances in it. Responsibility thus has two dimensions: a *descriptive* one referring to those who cause something to happen; and a *normative* one identifying those who should do something about it. The first sense looks to the past, as part of an explanation. The second looks to the future as a coping strategy. Whistleblowers must to some degree locate responsibility in at least one of these senses if their statements are to be more than mere warnings. Moreover, if one speaks purely of the past, one is not and cannot be a whistleblower. Of course, if one reveals a problem in the past which still persists, or the conditions which produced it still persist, then one warns of the recurrence of that problem in the future.

The whistleblower also differs from the spy: the latter belongs to the organization responsible for the harm, but owes his allegiance to another organization — one thinks of counter-espionage agencies and undercover police officers. In a sense he is a member of two organizations — spying on one to transmit information to the other. If one thinks of this other 'organization' as society, then the whistleblower is in a similar situation of divided loyalties: in the case of both public and private organizations, he owes allegiance to his co-workers and obedience to his superiors. But as a citizen in the society, he also owes allegiance to people outside the organization: he has a commitment to the public good. In public agencies, dependent on public funds and serving a public purpose, protecting the public interest is an even higher duty.

Organizational membership turns out to be a complicated issue. Consider the question many whistleblowers confront: Should I go public *before* or *after* I change jobs? The question raises issues like those raised by anonymity because the whistleblower who acts after he has left the organization (like the one who remains anonymous) does so to protect himself. Yet at the same time he risks loss of credibility: people may dismiss his accusations as the product of resentment and frustration in a disgruntled employee, an unfair counter-attack on those he has left behind. If the whistleblower has no choice in the matter because he has been fired, his charges may all too easily fall on deaf ears. In identifying whistleblowers, organizational membership must be taken broadly to include those who are no longer members of the organization on which they blow the whistle but who were in the not too distant past.

The central dilemma that defines whistleblowing has already been mentioned: the conflict in loyalty to one's employer (past or present) and to the public who has been or will (probably) be harmed.

Can one blow the whistle on one's employer without going public — restricting one's dissent to internal affairs? The issue of conflicting loyalties might then be recast: one owes obedience to one's immediate superior, but might blow the whistle on that person by 'going over his head'. One could do this in several ways: by going to his boss; by going right to the top — the president or chairman of the board; by going to the stockholders; by going to watchdog agencies which in a public agency might be regarded as still part of one's organization. The conflict is then between loyalty to one's *immediate superior* and loyalty to one's *organization*. One blows the whistle on one's immediate superior when one goes to someone else within the organization.

A final point about whistleblowing can be made, citing Alan Westin's recent book.[9] As he points out, the classic whistleblowers within organizations differ from referees, linesmen and traffic cops. The latter have the authority to have their decisions enforced whereas figurative whistleblowers do not. In a football game, when the referee blows the whistle, the play is supposed to stop: if it does not, players can be penalized; if someone scores a touchdown [after the referee has blown the whistle], their team receives no points. In the case of the traffic officer, the motorist who deliberately disobeys his directions can be fined, and for refusing the fine, imprisoned. Such literal whistleblowers have the power to have their decisions enforced, and are recognized by others as having this power.[10]

In the case of metaphorical or figurative whistleblowers, this authority is lacking. Indeed, blowing the whistle is a 'power-play', an effort to enlist the support of others to achieve social objectives. They act in the hope that if others co-operate,

worthwhile ends can be accomplished. Their plight is typically that of the powerless: as employees they have very few rights and can be dismissed at will by most employers. Consequently, they have much to fear: those whom they oppose are much more powerful, and [the employee has] few defenses.

The public is a defense of sorts. Often people hesitate to do in public what they would otherwise do behind a veil of secrecy. In going public in the act of whistleblowing, the individual not only seeks greater power, but seeks the protection that public scrutiny brings.

B. JUSTIFYING ANONYMITY

Should people who blow the whistle do so publicly? Are they obliged to make their identity known or may they remain anonymous? The prohibition on anonymity is pervasive and strong. My purpose is to sound out and assess alternative rationales for it.

Before turning to an appraisal of anonymous whistleblowing, we need to distinguish it from related phenomena. In general, someone acts anonymously when his (or her) identity is not publicly known. For example, a bomb threat is anonymous when no one knows who wrote the letter or made the telephone call. Yet clearly, to say literally that *no one at all* knows is mistaken: the writer himself knows he sent the letter, and therefore at least one person knows.

Is an action done anonymously when no one but the agent knows? This notion comes close to the extreme form of secrecy: the greatest secret concerns information I share with no one else. But secrecy in this sense is too extreme, for how did I come by this information? If someone told me, at least one other person knows. Paradigmatically, information is secret when shared among few people, with two as the limiting case. But it does not suffice that only these two people know and merely by chance no one else. Such 'accidental secrets' are not secrets in the strict sense. To qualify as a secret, there must be a conspiracy of silence. It is the exclusion of others, the denial of access by them to information, that marks a secret.

Yet something more is built into the notion of secrecy that becomes clearer if we consider a related concept — privacy. Information is private when I justifiably deny the right of others to share it. The facts about my sex life or income tax return are private in that others (ordinarily) cannot demand access to them. The domain of privacy is one in which I claim *a right* to exclude others, unless they can invoke a higher right to override mine.[11]

In the case of privacy, the burden of proof rests with those who would secure access to what is protected under this rubric. In the case of secrecy, the burden of proof is reversed: those who would withhold information must provide the justification. In the case of privacy, the presumption is that others should not intrude. In the case of secrecy, the presumption is that something be shared. This presumption is countered by 'Top Secret' documents with an appeal to national security. In the case of secret acts of espionage, the presumption is not met: information not shared should be, but is wrongfully and deliberately kept from others.

Is anonymity more like privacy or secrecy? First one needs to note that the information kept from others is of a particular sort — namely about a person's identity. Moreover the sharing of this information may be limited or extensive. For one to be anonymous, the public must be precluded from knowledge of the individual's identity, but their exclusion does not entail no one else knows. Anonymity is neutral, lying in the middle ground between secrecy and privacy: it entails that the public does not know or have access to the identity of an individual, but does not locate the burden of proof in withholding this information.

Accordingly, one can ask: Does the public have a right to know the whistleblower's identity, or does he (or she) have a right to withhold it? Withholding such information strikes many as wrong. But why is it wrong, and in what sense?

A refusal to let one's identity be known could be construed as bad manners. Blowing the whistle anonymously is like snitching on someone behind his back. As kids we were all taught that such tattle-tailing is wrong. It is a paradigm of bad manners to say nasty things about people not present to defend

themselves. Anonymity in whistleblowers is a breach of manners — faulty etiquette in people who should know better as they act in the more consequential professional world. But why are such breaches of etiquette condemned so harshly, and is this harshness justified?

Typically, the answer is couched in terms of loyalty.[12] To be a faithful member of a group is to protect the interests of that group as a whole and of its members individually. Saying nasty things about people behind their backs disrupts the cohesion of the group, undermining trust in each other and threatening the group solidarity. As a threat to the welfare of the group, individually or collectively, as well as to the very basis of its existence, tattle-tailing is severely condemned.

Yet clearly a blanket prohibition on tattle-tailing is unwarranted, as three analogies can serve to demonstrate.

(1) Suppose my older sister is about to swallow some pills I think may be dangerous. To tell mother may not be wrong, but right and indeed obligatory. Though I have 'blown the whistle' on my sister, if I am doing so for her own good in a situation that is serious and urgent, it is not objectionable — even if I ask mother not to tell on me. Clearly, it is preferable to saying or doing nothing at all. My sister's ignorance may help us to live together, to get along in situations where her anger might be disruptive and counter-productive for each of us. Since my sister does not know what I did, I have acted anonymously — at least as far as she is concerned. Even though mother knows, her knowledge, like that of the closed Congressional Committee to which a whistleblower testifies *in camera*, does not totally dispel anonymity.

Typically the boyhood scenario is less serious: my sister takes a cookie from the cookie jar without asking, and I squeal on her. My action may be condemned because the incident is trivial. But as the *seriousness* of the incident increases, the condemnation of anonymous whistleblowing weakens. The extent of the harm threatened is one factor to be weighed in making a moral judgment. The seriousness of the harm the whistleblower seeks to disclose and thereby curtail may be measured in several ways: the number of people affected; the extent to which they are hurt, physically or psychologically. Alternatively one might appraise this seriousness in less consequentialist terms by invoking deontological principles: perhaps someone's rights are denied — such as the right to privacy — even though no physical or psychological harm ensues. Whichever approach one takes, the more serious the offense, the less stringent the prohibition on anonymity.

One might respond that my analogy confuses two different concepts: whistleblowing and anonymity. Conceding that one is more obliged to blow the whistle the greater the harm threatened, one could nevertheless insist that one should always do so publicly and never anonymously. Consider three possibilities: P_1 blowing the whistle publicly; P_2 blowing the whistle anonymously; and P_3 not blowing the whistle at all. *Prima facie* P_1 is morally preferable to P_2, and P_2 is morally preferable to P_3. Though this ranking holds at the *individual* level, one can adopt a rule-utilitarian perspective on the effects of the *practice* of whistleblowing from acting anonymously: anonymity is justified if it increases the number who with good reason blow the whistle, that is, if anonymity promotes the practice of effective warranted whistleblowing.[13] Accordingly, the first analogy asserts that blowing the whistle anonymously is preferable to not blowing it at all — especially when the particular harm threatened is serious; and it hypothesizes that if a veil of ignorance increases the number of effective and legitimate whistleblowers, the principle of anonymity has a rule-utilitarian defense. But the analogy does not show that anonymously blowing the whistle is always preferable to blowing the whistle publicly. Consider now a second case to elicit a second factor in addition to seriousness.

(2) The school bully is about to beat up a new kid who looks very frail and helpless. Since I am unable to stop him, I run to the teacher to report the incident. After the teacher has intervened, I ask him not to say I reported the incident: to protect myself from retaliation, I want to remain anonymous. If the bully is very strong and I am very weak, my request is justified: there is no moral reason why I too should suffer unfairly at his hands. By the same

token, corporations bully employees who cannot easily defend themselves. Because of their vulnerability, anonymity is warranted. As a second thesis I propose that the greater the *probability of unfair retaliation*, the weaker the prohibition on anonymity should be.

The literature to date suggests that most whistleblowers — even those who act for good moral reasons — pay a very high price for dissenting.[14] In many cases they are fired or demoted, transferred to unattractive assignments or locales, ostracized by their peers and cast into psychological and professional isolation. Should they try to obtain another job in the same field, they often find they are 'blacklisted': many employers do not want to hire someone who 'caused trouble' on his (or her) last job. Moreover, under the prevailing legal doctrine of 'employment at will', fired whistleblowers have only limited legal recourse: in most jurisdictions the courts uphold an employer's right to fire someone for almost any reason.[15] In the absence of such legal protection, the burden of defending himself falls very heavily on the shoulders of the whistleblower alone.

In asserting that the probability of unfair retaliation decreases the strength of the prohibition on anonymity, I do want to distinguish two concepts: permissible and obligatory. My point, to put it briefly, is that moral heroism is not and should not be mandated. Though we praise the courage of a professional engineer who speaks out regarding dangerous practices when he (or she) risks his job, to require extraordinary self-sacrifices demands too much. His unwillingness to risk his career, his personal livelihood and the means whereby he supports his family are perfectly understandable reasons for remaining silent. Indeed, they may justify silence. When such individual self-sacrifice is the only way to protect the public, one must look instead to the development of other mechanisms — the law, the courts, unions, the press, professional associations or watchdog agencies.

To return to the earlier threefold distinction, blowing the whistle publicly may be ideal but one cannot demand it. One cannot condemn the persons who act anonymously to protect themselves, those who depend on them, love them and care for them. There is a limit to what we can ask a person to give up in order to do the right thing. Insofar as anonymity reduces what may be an unfair burden to begin with, it reduces an evil promoting a good.

So far I have identified two factors that enter into an appraisal of anonymous whistleblowing: the seriousness of the harm threatened, and the probability of unfair retaliation.

(3) A third moral factor can be elicited with the following modification in the second analogy: Suppose the bully is my friend. This social relationship places an obligation on me to go to my friend. Even if I am frail and helpless, given that he is my friend, I am duty bound by friendship to ask him to stop. Even if he is not my friend but only is a member of my gang, I should not blow the whistle straight away but go to our leader first — ask him to intervene. If that is not possible or fails, recourse to an outside group may be warranted. My third thesis is that the strength of the prohibition on anonymity is a function of the *social relationship*: the closer the whistleblower stands to the accused, the stronger the prohibition on anonymity.[16] Most whistleblowers feel an 'I vs. them' or 'us vs. them'. Within polarized groups, whistleblowers discuss problems with other members of their group, but hesitate — legitimately I contend — to go outside it without the protection anonymity brings.

This third factor is related to the second: social distance affects the probability of retaliation. If an intermediary can ensure that justice is done within the group, anonymity is less warranted — if not unwarranted. If the Federal Office of Professional Responsibility can guarantee that whistleblowers protesting unfair, illegal or corrupt practices will not suffer for their efforts to correct them, anonymity is less warranted. It is also less needed. But until employees' rights are secure, a veil of ignorance is one of their few safeguards.

Anonymity may be condemned because it impedes the pursuit of truth. The person who levels accusations against another while withholding his own identity makes it difficult to determine whether what he charges is true or false: we cannot question him, ask for his sources of information,

verify his accusations — or so it may be argued.

But to assert that we cannot verify anonymous charges at all, is too strong and unfounded. Verification, if it is to count as a proof, must be public and repeatable.[17] Consequently, the means whereby the whistleblower verified *to himself* that what he suspected was true must be available *to others* . . . if indeed he knows the truth. Those who would learn the truth can discover it by the same means the whistleblower used — even though they do not know his identity.

In the movie and book *All the President's Men*, the character called 'Deep Throat' played this role. Without revealing his own identity, he led the two reporters Bernstein and Woodward along a path that provided the evidence they needed to implicate the President in the Watergate break-ins. He did not need to reveal his own identity. It was enough that from the darkness he provided clues that would trace out a path, perhaps the one he followed but perhaps not, to the truth.

Admittedly, in some cases it may be difficult if not impossible for the whistleblower to provide any conclusive evidence that will not reveal his own identity. In such cases, the choice is not between blowing the whistle anonymously and blowing it publicly. Rather, the choice is between blowing it publicly and not blowing it at all. Accordingly, I do not assert that anonymity is always possible. But I do assert that where it is possible we cannot always fault it as a breach of professional etiquette or because it conceals the truth.

Therefore, I conclude that the blanket condemnation on anonymity is not warranted. Rather, its justification depends on three factors: the seriousness of the offense, the probability of unfair retaliation, and the social relationships. Let me now turn to some practical considerations.

C. ANONYMITY AND PERSONAL INTEGRITY

Perhaps anonymity is not a breach of professional etiquette or an obstacle to the truth but an act of foolishness. The individual who tries to shield himself may find anonymity makes his action *self-defeating*: to be effective one must act publicly — or so one argument may run. What can be said for or against it?

First, one must concede a paradox. The whistleblower attempts to draw public attention to an action he regards as wrong, yet is not willing to make his own identity public. His means and ends conflict: he uses ignorance to promote knowledge, identifies others while hiding himself. What he is trying to do is refuted by the way he does it. This paradoxical juxtaposition of means and ends raises our suspicions. It reminds us of those who make war to end war, who deceive to get at the truth, who use force to protect freedom.

Though our suspicions are justifiably aroused, they may turn out to be unjustified. Society may need an institution like the police, based on the legal use of physical force, to protect the freedom of its members. It may indeed be necessary to reveal less than the whole truth to determine if others are telling the truth. We are right to be suspicious when the means contradict the ends, but may find the contradiction only apparent: the whistleblower may succeed at uncovering abusive practices without blowing his cover.

Alternatively, our suspicions may be aroused not by the logical paradox but by the questions of motives: Why does the whistleblower conceal his identity — what does *he* have to hide? To show his intentions are pure, we demand that he stand up for his actions and not hide from public view. Hiding makes us uneasy that he seeks some private gain rather than the public good, that he himself may be implicated and protecting himself by pointing at others.

A sharp distinction can be drawn between reasons and causes,[18] the justification and the motivation, the evidence that proves a statement true or false and the personal considerations that lead a person to utter it. Anonymity calls the latter into question but need not affect the former. Whether the charges are true or false does not depend on the motivation of the individual who levies them. One can appraise the truth of accusations knowing nothing of motives. Whether the whistleblower draws attention to corruption out of spite or altruism makes no difference in one respect: if corruption exists, it should be ended.

Naturally our attitude towards the whistleblower depends very much on his motives. If he genuinely seeks the public good, he should be held in high esteem. If he does not benefit in any way, his altruism is commendable. In appraising his character, his motives are of the utmost importance. But in appraising his *charges*, his motives are logically irrelevant.[19] Anonymity helps guard against a fallacious counter-attack — an *argumentum ad hominem*.[20] Individuals called to account by the whistleblower may try to protect themselves by diverting attention to him, by shifting the issue from what he says to why he says it. They may seek to redirect attention from the truth of his claims to the truthfulness of the claimant. But logicians have long recognized this strategy as fallacious: whether or not what someone says is true does not depend on his personal motive for saying it.

Anonymity may be treated as self-defeating because it calls into question the motives of the whistleblower, but I contend it is wrong to insist it must. However, one genuine issue is raised by this attack on anonymity: How do we distinguish the accusations that should be investigated from those that need not be? A filtering process is needed to make this determination. Anonymity is not and should not be the main factor in the filter: one should not decide to investigate a charge only if the person who makes it identifies himself publicly. One is less inclined to investigate anonymous charges because of difficulties anonymity creates — the problems of gathering data, identifying the relevant participants, fixing the time, location, and extent of the act or practice. But then it should be for these reasons, and not because of anonymity *per se*, that no further action is taken.

From what I have said already, several factors emerge in the determination of the point at which the whistleblower's charges should be investigated. The main factor is the seriousness of the harm to others if the charges are true. Clearly, if the risk to their lives and health is very great, steps must be taken to protect them. The first step is to determine whether the risk is real or imaginary — and this requires investigating the whistleblower's accusations. If he claims that money has been misspent, stolen or siphoned off for illegal purposes, then the greater the amount involved, the more serious the charge and the greater the need to verify it.

In judging the harm to be done, one must also weigh the costs of determining this harm. If an investigation is likely to destroy the morale of an otherwise socially useful and productive organization, an investigation is probably not warranted. If it is likely to cost more money than might be saved, then it is likewise unwarranted. It is the *net harm*, after the costs of an investigation have been subtracted, that must be given moral weight in fixing the threshold.

Should the likelihood that the charges are true be considered? The objection to giving this probability estimate any weight is that the whistleblower's dilemma arises precisely because people do not know. An estimate based on ignorance is unreliable, and acting on it irrational. But at the other extreme, to investigate charges that are preposterous, about events logically impossible or astronomically remote, will be wasteful if not harmful. Accordingly, the probability that the charges will prove unfounded should serve as a factor only to eliminate extreme cases of the preposterous, impossible, or improbable.

So far I have offered three interpretations of the thesis that whistleblowers should not remain anonymous. On the first, anonymity is in bad taste — it offends our sense of etiquette in saying nasty things about someone behind their back. On the second, it is a barrier to the truth. And on the third it is self-defeating. I want now to consider several moral objections.

Fair Play.   It may be argued that everyone has a right to confront their accusers. If someone claims I have done something wrong, I should be allowed to question him face to face. It violates our sense of fairness to have accusations levelled against someone with no opportunity to defend themselves. Does this sense of fair play preclude anonymity among whistleblowers?

In fact we do not always regard concealing one's identity as morally bad. Quite the contrary, we sometimes regard it as good and proper. For example, within academia blind reviewing is a widespread practice: members of an editorial board passing judgment on an article submitted for publication may find the author's name removed. Conversely, the reviewers of manuscripts for publication may not reveal their name. In the first case the practice is justified on the grounds that it equalizes the competition: established authors can less readily exploit their reputation, and the decision to accept or reject an article is made on the basis of quality alone. The second practice supposedly allows more candor: reviewers can offer an honest evaluation without fear of reprisals or alienating a colleague with whom they may need to cooperate in the future. Note that in the first case anonymity serves as an equalizer to factor out extraneous and unwarranted influences like reputation. And in the second case it produces harmony. Insofar as it promotes fairness, equality or harmony, the practice of concealing one's identity has a moral justification.

The objection to anonymity can likewise be rebutted on the grounds that it promotes other values, or that the rights of the accused can be protected in other ways. It allows individuals to come forward who would otherwise remain silent for fear of reprisals. In so doing it promotes the *public welfare* which may be subverted by abuses of power by government officials, or the *public safety*, which may be threatened by dangerous practices of private industry. It may also promote *honesty* and *accountability* among managers who know they will find it difficult to conceal their indulgences. Admittedly, individuals have a right to protect themselves against false accusations that can ruin their careers and compromise their good name. But to guarantee this right, the identity of whistleblowers need not be known: it is only necessary that accusations be properly investigated, proven true or false, and the results widely disseminated.

If the whistleblower and the accused confronted each other as equals, anonymity would be unnecessary. But typically the power differentials are enormous, and most whistleblowers pay dearly for the action: they lose their jobs, get transferred to a less attractive if not unattractive locale and assignment, find their family life disrupted and their friends and colleagues less amiable.[21] The taunt of the accused that the whistleblower come forward and 'face him like a man' is a bully's challenge when issued by the powerful. In a court, where the judge, lawyers and legal process serve as an equalizer, anonymity is less warranted. The prohibition on anonymity denies employees one of their few safeguards from retaliation of powerful, aroused enemies. Until positive steps have been taken to protect employees' rights to dissent, the condemnation of anonymity discourages one of the few checks on the abuse of power by corporate or government officials.

The Slippery Slope.   Behind the prohibition on anonymity lurks the fear: What if everyone does that? The need to come forward and be identified acts as a check on a practice that threatens the day to day operation of bureaucracies, corporations and institutions. People have jobs to do, and precious time is wasted in unproductive activities if they go about secretly complaining of others — or so the argument may run. Furthermore, to continue this attack, damage is done to the moral fabric of an organization by anonymous whistleblowers who destroy the peace and harmony on which a smooth operation is based. To keep this practice within reasonable bounds and limit its corrosive impact, we must insist that whistleblowers publicly identify themselves. Without this restriction we slide down a slippery slope into corporate chaos and institutional anarchy.

What can be said against this slippery slope argument? First, it is important to maintain a realistic perspective: How many more employees are likely to blow the whistle if anonymity protected them? The simple answer is: We do not know. Clearly, to argue rationally against a practice, our argument should be based on information — not misinformation, suspicions and fears. Logically, the slippery slope contention is an

argumentum ad ignoratiam[22], a fallacious inference from our ignorance.

Second, it is important to locate clearly the burden of proof: Does it lie with the defenders of anonymity or its critics? As a form of dissent, whistleblowing is an exercise of a highly valued right — freedom of speech. Admittedly, the context is not political but bureaucratic, not dissent against one's government but against one's employer, (though for some whistleblowers the two are the same). Insofar as whistleblowers are speaking out, the burden of proof rests with those who would restrict them from exercising their freedom of speech. Until they can demonstrate clear and present danger to society — and not just themselves, their fears or hysteria will not serve as an adequate moral basis for restricting the rights of others to dissent.

Third, it is important to be clear that this burden will be difficult to sustain for the right to dissent is not easily overridden. For example, though an organization might be destroyed by the actions of an anonymous whistleblower, proving this would not necessarily establish the moral right of the institution's executives to silence the whistleblower. For suppose the institution is a chemical company, polluting the water the public drinks with toxic substances. Given that they have no moral right to endanger the health of others to begin with, they have no right to silence a whistleblower from disclosing this danger — even if his actions threaten their corporate existence.

To establish a right of corporations to silence whistleblowers, one would have to show that *society* would be better off if corporations had such a right. The very claim that they do or should have it sounds dangerously close to the rhetorical flourish: What's good for General Motors is good for the country. Today we recognize the dangers of air pollution from automobiles, and the harm of gas-guzzlers to the nation's economy. Such claims can now more readily be seen for what they are: self-deluded or hypocritical attempts to equate corporate profits with the social good. For a utilitarian the burden of proof can be sustained only by demonstrating that restricting the whistleblower's right of dissent will work to the long-term advantage of society, rather than the corporation. I for one do not think that the empirical evidence can be marshalled to establish this claim.

ENDNOTES

1. Richard De George, 'Ethical Responsibilities of Engineers in Large Organizations'. Paper presented at the National Conference on Engineering Ethics; Troy N.Y.: June 20-22, 1980, p. 8.

2. Sissela Bok, 'Whistleblowing and Professional Responsibility', *New York Univ. Educ. Quarterly* XI (1980), pp. 2-10.

3. Rosemary Chalk and Frank von Hippel, 'Due Process for the Bearers of Ill Tidings: Dealing with Technical Dissent in the Organization', *Tech. Rev.* 81 (1979), pp. 49-55.

4. Norman Bowie, *Business Ethics* (Prentice-Hall, Englewood Cliffs, N.J., Prentice-Hall, 1982).

5. Jackeline Varret's case follows this pattern. See Ralph Nader *et al.*, *Whistleblowing* (Grossman Publishers, New York, 1972), pp. 90-97.

6. See Peter Maas, *Serpico* (Bantam Books, New York, 1974).

7. See Nader *op. cit.*, pp. 39-54, and Fitzgerald's autobiography *The High Priest of Waste* (Putnam and Sons, New York, 1968).

8. This case is adapted from Nader. See *op. cit.* (Note 5).

9. Alan Westin, *Blowing the Whistle* (McGraw-Hill, New York, 1980).

10. I am here using Robert Paul Wolff's definition of authority. See his essay 'On Violence' reprinted in *Obligation and Dissent*, ed. by Donald W. Hansen and Robert Booth Fowler (Little Brown & Co., Boston, 1971), pp. 242-258.

11. St. Augustine confuses this distinction between privacy and secrecy in his analysis of sexual intercourse, with the result that he regards all sex as evil. See Augustine's 'Sexual Lust and Original Sin', in *The City of God* trans. by Philip Levine (Harvard Univ. Press, Cambridge, Ma., 1966), 4:345-401.

12. See *Divided Loyalties* by Robert M. Anderson *et al.* (West Lafayette, Ind., Purdue U. Press, 1980).

13. The experience of France, where civil servants are encouraged to report abuses on government by calling an investigation office, has proven an effective curb on abusive actions and practice. A similar hotline exists in the United States Federal bureaucracy.

14. One has only to look to those cases cited by Nader (*op. cit.*, Note 5 above) as well as those that typically make the newspaper headlines.

15. For an excellent discussion of this doctrine, see J.P. Christiansen's 'A remedy for the Discharge of Professional Employees Who Refuse to Perform Unethical or Illegal Acts: A Proposal in Aid of Professional Ethics', *Vanderbilt Law Review*, 28 (1975), 805-841.

16. Very little has been written on stratified moral obligations (and rights) that vary according to one's social relationship or role, though the issue is omnipresent in the fields of professional and applied ethics. For four notable exceptions, see R.S. Downie's *Roles and Values* (Methuen & Co., London, 1971) and Stuart Hampshire (ed.), *Public & Private Morality* (Cambridge, N.Y., 1978), Charles Fried's 'Rights & Roles', in *Right and Wrong* (Harvard Univ. Press, Cambridge, Ma.), pp. 167-195 and Alan Goldman's *The Moral Foundations of Professional Ethics* (Littlefield Adams, Totowa, N.J., 1980).

17. For a more detailed analysis of the philosophical issues involved in confirmation, see Carl G. Hempel's *Philosophy of Natural Science* (Prentice-Hall, Englewood Cliffs, N.J., 1966), Chap. 4.

18. For a discussion of these and related concepts see Richard Taylor's *Action & Purpose* (Prentice Hall, Englewood Cliffs, N.J., 1966), Chap. 10.

19. John Stuart Mill recognizes this distinction between judgments about actions and judgments about agents. See Chapter II of his *Utilitarianism*, ed. by Samuel Gorovitz (Bobbs-Merrill, New York, 1971), p. 25.

20. See Irving Copi's *Introduction to Logic*, 3rd edition (Collier Macmillan, New York, 1968), p. 61.

21. See Nader's examples (Note 5).

22. See Copi (*op. cit.*), p. 63.

25

Tim and Sam

WILFRID J. WALUCHOW

Tim Jones has been employed by Star Chemical for twenty years. Upon graduation from high school with a degree in general arts and sciences, Tim had joined Star Chemical as a laboratory assistant. His job was to clean test tubes, sweep up, run errands for the lab technicians, and in general to provide a set of young helping hands and legs. Tim worked contentedly as an assistant for two years, at which time he thought he might like a job with more interest and responsibility. Lacking qualifications for any job but lab assistant, however, Tim was in a fix. With two young children at home and another on the way, he was simply unable to quit his job to enroll in a one-year course of study being offered at the local community college. Successful completion of this course would have qualified Tim as a level-1 laboratory technician with Star Chemical.

One day, however, Tim discovered a notice on the lunch-room bulletin board announcing a new programme sponsored and funded jointly by the Federal Government and Star Chemical. According to the terms of this new programme, lab assistants employed by Star Chemical for more than one year were eligible for a full leave of absence with pay to enroll in the local lab technician's course. Tuition fees were to be paid by the joint sponsors. Tim, of course, seized the marvelous opportunity provided to him, graduated at the top of his class, and became a level-1 lab technician with Star Chemical. Having cleared his first major hurdle, Tim advanced rapidly through the rank and file. A week ago he made the leap from union to management ranks, assuming the role of Manager of Emissions Control. Tim's responsibility now is to oversee testing of industrial waste products emitted into the St. Clair River, to ensure that they are within recommended but non-mandatory federal guidelines.

Tim has spent the first week of his·new assignment learning the ropes. Having worked for the past twenty years on the production side, he is

This case, though it parallels many "real life" situations, is purely hypothetical. It was written for the first edition of this text.

unfamiliar with emissions control. Toward the end of his first week, Tim notices some anomalies in the testing procedures being carried out by the men he is now supervising. They are purposely "fudging" the tests to make it appear as if emissions are within the federal guidelines. Tim confronts the technicians and they explain that this fudging has been going on for months now, on the orders of Tim's retired predecessor. Tim is aghast. He marches off to report his discovery to the Director of Operations, Sam Brown, only to find that Sam is fully aware of and condones the fraudulent practices. He explains that, in the view of Star Chemical, federal emissions guidelines are far too stringent; that Star Chemical's levels of emissions are well within any reasonable levels of tolerance; and that to bring those emissions within the federal guidelines would require a costly six-month shut-down to modify production lines.

In response, Tim points out that Star Chemical has a social obligation, as a corporate citizen, to abide by federally recommended guidelines; that it is not up to Star Chemical to judge what is a "reasonable" level of tolerance; that the comparative costs of a shut-down are negligible when weighed against the harm to the community that could result from Star Chemical's hazardous emissions.

Sam counters by suggesting that the notion of "corporate citizenship" is mysterious — how can corporations, which are, after all, abstract entities and not real persons, be said to have social obligations? That, in any case, business is business — their responsibility is not to try to promote community welfare (that's better left to the politicians) but to promote, as best they can, the welfare, that is, profits, of Star Chemical.

At this stage of the discussion, Tim expresses amazement at Sam Brown's apparent lack of moral conscience. Sam doesn't seem to realize that there is a significant moral issue at stake here. Sam replies: "Business is business. Questions of ethics are better left to philosophers, theologians and people in pubs." Believing that any further attempts at moral suasion will prove fruitless, Tim decides to resort to more coercive measures. He threatens to

report Star Chemical both to the press and to the federal authorities unless something is done to bring emissions within the recommended guidelines. Sam becomes indignant, claiming that Tim is a fine one to speak of moral conscience. Doesn't Tim realize that his "whistleblowing" will cost Star Chemical millions of dollars in lost revenues? Doesn't he realize that, as a member of the management team of Star Chemical, he has a fiduciary responsibility to protect the interests of the company? It is one thing for a union member to engage in whistleblowing; it is quite another for a member of the team in whom considerable faith and trust have been placed, to do so. Sam also mentions that Tim has an even stronger obligation than most. Wasn't it Star Chemical who, twenty years ago, helped provide Tim with a year's paid leave of absence — plus tuition — so that he might advance his career? Where would Tim be today without the benevolent, helping hand of Star Chemical? Is this how Tim proposes to demonstrate his loyalty, let alone his gratitude?

Tim has by this point become a little uneasy. He sees now that his position is not quite as unshakeable as he had thought. But he remains convinced that he is in the right and says so to Sam. He adds that when it comes to a conflict between, on the one hand, his obligations to an impersonal entity such as a corporation (which Sam himself admitted earlier is a problematic notion) and, on the other, his responsibilities to people, he will always side with the latter.

Now Sam is infuriated. He is quick to point out that, when companies are hurt, people get hurt. Tim has said his whistleblowing will harm only the abstract corporate entity called Star Chemical. What this means, in effect, is that the shareholders in Star Chemical will suffer significant losses in profit; that Tim's fellow employees and their families will suffer considerably from the lengthy layoff which will take place while the required alterations are made; that those involved in the fudging of emissions control tests will be disciplined, perhaps even fired; and that, needing a scapegoat to shoulder responsibility before the media, the Board of Directors of Star Chemical will, in all probability, demand the resignation of Sam Brown. If Tim wants to consider his responsibility to people, shouldn't he consider these people too? Doesn't he have special obligations to his friends and colleagues, and to those who, for twenty years, have provided him with a means to support himself and his family?

The uncertainty Tim felt earlier has now permeated to the very foundations of his moral position. He no longer knows what he ought to do. He is in a state of moral quandary; the kind of quandary which provides the major impetus behind the study of business ethics.

SUGGESTED FURTHER READINGS

BOK, SISELA. *Secrets: On the Ethics of Concealment and Revelation.* New York: Pantheon Books, 1983.

_____. *Lying: Moral Choice in Public and Private Life.* New York: Pantheon Books, 1978.

_____. "Whistleblowing and Professional Responsibilities." *New York University Education Quarterly*, Vol. II, 4, 1980.

GLAZER, M. "Ten Whistleblowers and How They Fared." *The Hastings Center Report*, Vol. 13, December 1983.

GREENBERGER, DAVID, MARCIA MICELI AND DEBRA COHEN. "Oppositionists and Group Norms: The Reciprocal Influence of Whistle-blowers and Co-workers." *Journal of Business Ethics*, Vol. 6, No. 7, 1987.

ISENBERG, ARNOLD. "Deontology and the Ethics of Lying." In William Callahan (ed.) *Aesthetics and the Theory of Criticism: Selected Essays of Arnold Isenberg.* Chicago: The University of Chicago Press, 1973.

JENSEN, J. VERNON. "Ethical Tensions in Whistleblowing." *Journal of Business Ethics*, Vol. 6, No. 4, 1987.

LOEB, S. AND SUZANNE CORY. "Whistleblowing and Management Accounting: An Approach." *Journal of Business Ethics*, Vol. 8, No. 12, December 1989.

MICELI, M. AND JANET NEAR. "The Relationship Among Beliefs, Organizational Position, and Whistle-blowing Status: A Discriminant Analysis." *Academy of Management Journal*, 27, 1984.

NEAR, JANET AND MARCIA MICELI. "Organizational Dissidence: The Case of Whistle-blowing." *Journal of Business Ethics*, Vol. 4, No. 1, 1985.

WESTIN, A. *Blowing the Whistle.* New York: McGraw-Hill, 1980.

_____. *Whistleblowing: Loyalty and Dissent in the Corporation.* New York: McGraw-Hill, 1980.

PART SIX

Employee Equity

INTRODUCTION

On April 17, 1985, clause 15 of the Canadian Charter of Rights and Freedoms came into effect. Clause 15 states,

> (1) Every individual is equal before and under the law and has the right to the equal protection and benefit of the law without discrimination and, in particular, without discrimination based on race, national or ethnic origin, colour, religion, sex, age or mental or physical disability.
> (2) Subsection (1) does not preclude any law, program or activity that has as its object the amelioration of conditions of disadvantaged individuals or groups including those that are disadvantaged because of race, national or ethnic origin, colour, religion, sex, age or mental or physical disability.

This clause has prompted considerable debate about its implications for hiring, promotion, training and retirement practices in Canada. The debate is not peculiar to the Canadian situation, however, and many of the issues which have been and will continue to be raised are familiar to both philosophers and those concerned with equality issues in law.

Some of the classic questions which arise and which will be dealt with in this section involve an examination of the rights of individuals to fair treatment in employment situations. Such questions as "What counts as equality in employment?" and "Do individuals have the right not to be discriminated against in hiring and promotion practices?" will be discussed. Other issues to be raised include the justifiability of affirmative action policy and the imposition of quotas when such policy and quotas may inadvertently result in discrimination against otherwise qualified candidates. Is it justifiable to deny a qualified white male a position in senior management if a less qualified member of a group which has been discriminated against applies for the same position? More generally, the issue might be stated in terms of means and ends. Is policy which may be unjust to some individuals justifiable as a means to achieving an overall more just society?

Another related issue is whether it is reasonable to try to remedy past injustices done to particular groups by preferentially treating members of those groups now. The principle appealed to as justification for such policy is called the *principle of compensatory justice* (i.e., the rule that one must rectify past wrongs). This principle is generally considered to be problematic since those receiving the preferential treatment were not the ones initially discriminated against. A policy of preferential hiring for women, for example, if strictly applied, may result in the hiring of an upper-middle class privileged woman over an under-privileged male.

There is currently employment equity legislation in place in Manitoba, Nova Scotia, the Yukon, Ontario, and Prince Edward Island. As well, federal legislation imposes national employment equity policy on all Crown corporations and private companies with more than one hundred employees and contracts in excess of $200 000. Legislation covers the four disadvantaged target groups identified by the Abella report. None of the policies involve quotas for the target populations, and it is as yet unclear what these various policies will mean, if anything, with respect to changing Canadian views about employment equity and employee rights.

In "Defining Equality in Employment," Judge R. Abella provides an introduction to some of these issues. Abella begins with a discussion of the concept of equity as it relates to employment practices. This article is excerpted from the report of the Royal Commission on Employment Equity which the Canadian government set up to examine the implications of clause 15 of the Charter on employment in Canada. As Abella notes, consensus about the definition of equality is difficult to achieve, and, in fact, what individuals have thought and what nations have decided was equitable treatment for persons has changed radically over time and differs from nation to nation. Abella suggests that, minimally, equality is "freedom from adverse discrimination." However, what freedom from adverse discrimination means is not all that clear either.

To complicate things further, some people argue that no one has a right to non-discrimination. This position is represented in Jan Narveson's article, "Have We a Right to Non-Discrimination?" Narveson argues that there is no basic right to non-discrimination and that, in fact, "there is no such thing as obligatory basic non-discrimination." Narveson states further that "to require persons to perform all sorts of actions despite the fact that the actions they might instead prefer are not literally harmful to anyone is surely to violate their liberty."

Mary Hawkesworth presents a somewhat different perspective on these issues in her paper on affirmative action. Hawkesworth's article looks at the "conflicting conceptions of individuality" which underlie the affirmative action debate. Hawkesworth's contention is that "the intensity" of the affirmative action debate is "related to divergent assumptions about the fundamental nature of human rights." Specifically, Hawkesworth argues that the major dissension in the affirmative debate is between those who "incorporate a conception of atomistic individualism within their work and those who adopt a conception of socialized individualism." While proponents of both positions are committed to equity and the protection of the rights of individuals, their underlying ideological commitments lead to different perceptions and different solutions to problems of inequity in the workplace. It is because of the underlying ideological disparities between the proponents of these two positions that there is not only a lack of consensus about solutions to the problems but also a lack of accord in perceiving the problems. Thus, Hawkesworth contends, atomistic individualists do not perceive much of the discrimination against groups in hiring and promotion practices.

This section concludes with a case study, *Canadian National Railway Company* v. *Canadian Human Rights Commission et al*, which vividly illustrates the difficulty in rectifying acknowledged group discrimination through the legal process. Although CN was found to have discriminated against women on the basis of sex, the Order of the Human Rights Tribunal to cease discriminatory practice and to instate a 13 percent quota for women in blue collar positions was overruled by the Federal Court of Appeal on July 16, 1985. The grounds of the appeal were that imposing the principle of compensatory justice on CN was beyond the mandate of the Human Rights Commission. According to the Federal Court, the Commission is empowered only to recommend measures ensuring that future discrimination does not occur; its mandate does not extend to the rectification of past discrimination.

26

Defining Equality in Employment

ROSALIE ABELLA

The law, in its majestic equality, forbids the rich as well as the poor to
sleep under bridges, to beg in the streets, and to steal bread.[1]

Equality is, at the very least, freedom from adverse discrimination. But what constitutes adverse discrimination changes with time, with information, with experience, and with insight. What we tolerated as a society 100, 50, or even 10 years ago is no longer necessarily tolerable. Equality is thus a process — a process of constant and flexible examination, of vigilant introspection, and of aggressive open-mindedness.

One hundred years ago, the role for women was almost exclusively domestic; 50 years ago, some visible minorities were disenfranchised; 25 years ago, Native people lacked a policy voice; and 10 years ago, disabled persons were routinely kept dependent. Today, none of these exclusionary assumptions is acceptable.

But the goal of equality is more than an evolutionary intolerance to adverse discrimination. It is to ensure, too, that the vestiges of these arbitrarily restrictive assumptions do not continue to play a role in our society.

If in this ongoing process we are not always sure what "equality" means, most of us have a good understanding of what is "fair." And what is happening today in Canada to women, Native people, disabled persons, and visible minorities is not fair.

It is not fair that many people in these groups have restricted employment opportunities, limited access to decision-making processes that critically affect them, little public visibility as contributing Canadians, and a circumscribed range of options generally. It may be understandable, given history, culture, economics, and even human nature, but by no standard is it fair.

To attempt to unravel the complex tapestries that hang as a background to discriminatory attitudes can be an unproductive exercise. It is undoubtedly of interest to know why certain attitudes or practices were allowed to predominate; but in devising remedies to redress patently unfair realities, sorting through the malevolent, benevolent, or pragmatic causes of these realities is of little assistance. One

From *Equality in Employment, A Royal Commission Report*
by Judge R. Abella. © 1984 Government of Canada.
Reprinted by permission of the Minister of Supply and
Services.

can assume that the unfair results would not have occurred without the nourishing environment of limited sensitivities. But as we have these sensitivities educated, we must concentrate not on the motives of the past but on the best way to rectify their impact. And one of those ways is to appeal to our collective sense of fairness.

Equality in employment means that no one is denied opportunities for reasons that have nothing to do with inherent ability. It means equal access free from arbitrary obstructions. Discrimination means that an arbitrary barrier stands between a person's ability and his or her opportunity to demonstrate it. If the access is genuinely available in a way that permits everyone who so wishes the opportunity to fully develop his or her potential, we have achieved a kind of equality. It is equality defined as equal freedom from discrimination.

Discrimination in this context means practices or attitudes that have, whether by design or impact, the effect of limiting an individual's or a group's right to the opportunities generally available because of attributed rather than actual characteristics. What is impeding the full development of the potential is not the individual's capacity but an external barrier that artificially inhibits growth.

It is not a question of whether this discrimination is motivated by an intentional desire to obstruct someone's potential, or whether it is the accidental by-product of innocently motivated practices or systems. If the barrier is affecting certain groups in a disproportionately negative way, it is a signal that the practices that lead to this adverse impact may be discriminatory.

This is why it is important to look at the results of a system. In these results one may find evidence that barriers which are inequitable impede individual opportunity. These results are by no means conclusive evidence of inequity, but they are an effective signal that further examination is warranted to determine whether the disproportionately negative impact is in fact the result of inequitable practices, and therefore calls for remedial attention, or whether it is a reflection of a non-discriminatory reality.

Equality in employment is not a concept that produces the same results for everyone. It is a concept that seeks to identify and remove, barrier by barrier, discriminatory disadvantages. Equality in employment is access to the fullest opportunity to exercise individual potential.

Sometimes equality means treating people the same, despite their differences, and sometimes it means treating them as equals by accommodating their differences.

Formerly, we thought that equality only meant sameness and that treating persons as equals meant treating everyone the same. We now know that to treat everyone the same may be to offend the notion of equality. Ignoring differences may mean ignoring legitimate needs. It is not fair to use the differences between people as an excuse to exclude them arbitrarily from equitable participation. Equality means nothing if it does not mean that we are of equal worth regardless of differences in gender, race, ethnicity, or disability. The projected, mythical, and attributed meaning of these differences cannot be permitted to exclude full participation.

Ignoring differences and refusing to accommodate them is a denial of equal access and opportunity. It is discrimination. To reduce discrimination, we must create and maintain barrier-free environments so that individuals can have genuine access free from arbitrary obstructions to demonstrate and exercise fully their potential. This may mean treating some people differently by removing the obstacles to equality of opportunity they alone face for no demonstrably justifiable reason.

People are disadvantaged for many reasons and may be disadvantaged in a variety of ways — economically, socially, politically, or educationally. Not all disadvantages derive from discrimination. Those that do demand their own particular policy responses.

At present, society's disadvantages are disproportionately assumed by the four designated groups. Clearly, some distinctions have been made or overlooked in the past that have resulted in the disproportionate representation of Native people, visible minorities, disabled persons, and women on the lower rungs of the ladder to society's benefits. By reversing our approach and by using these same distinctions to identify, confront, and eliminate barriers these distinctions have caused in the past, we can reverse the trends, provide access, and open the door to equality.

To create equality of opportunity, we have to do different things for different people. We have to systematically eradicate the impediments to these options according to the actual needs of the different groups, not according to what we think their needs should be. And we have to give individuals an opportunity to use their abilities according to their potential and not according to what we think their potential should be. The process is an exercise in redistributive justice. Its object is to prevent the denial of access to society's benefits because of distinctions that are invalid.

Unless we reject arbitrary distinctions, these four groups will remain unjustifiably in perpetual slow motion. The objectives of breathing life into the notion of equality are to rectify as quickly as possible the results of parochial perspectives which unfairly restrict women, Native people, disabled persons, and visible minorities.

For women, equality in employment means, first, a revised approach to the role women play in the workforce. . . .

For Native people, equality in employment means effective and relevant education and training, accommodation to cultural and geographic realities, a primary voice in the design of the education, training, and funding programs established for their benefit, meaningful support systems, and the delivery of services through Native-run institutions.

For visible minorities, we must begin with an attack on racism, which though sometimes inadvertent is nevertheless pervasive. For immigrants, there is a need for adequate language training, for some mechanism to fairly assess the qualifications of those with non-Canadian experience or education, and for a program of information and counselling to teach and assist them to adjust to Canadian culture. . . .

For disabled persons, there must be as full accommodation as possible and the widest range of human and technical supports. . . .

For all groups, equality means an effective communications network whereby potential employee and employer can become aware of each other, a commitment on the part of educators, employers, and government to revise where necessary those practices that unfairly impede the employment opportunities of women, Native people, disabled persons, and visible minorities, and an end to patronizing and stultifying stereotyping. It means an end to job segregation and the beginning of an approach that makes available to everyone, on the basis of ability, the widest range of options. It means accommodating differences. . . .

If we do not act positively to remove barriers, we wait indefinitely for them to be removed. This would mean that we are prepared in the interim to tolerate prejudice and discrimination. By not acting, we unfairly ignore how inherently invalid these exclusionary distinctions are, and we signal our acceptance as a society that stereotypical attributes assigned to these four groups are appropriate justifications for their disproportionate disadvantages. . . .

It is probable that absolute equality is unattainable.[2] But even if it is, no civilized society worthy of the description can afford not to struggle for its achievement. We may not be able to achieve absolute equality, but we can certainly reduce inequality.[3]

EMPLOYMENT EQUITY/ AFFIRMATIVE ACTION

The achievement of equality in employment depends on a double-edged approach. The first concerns those pre-employment conditions that affect access to employment. The second concerns those conditions in the workplace that militate against equal participation in employment.

Efforts to overcome barriers in employment are what have generally been called in North America affirmative action measures. These include making recruitment, hiring, promotion, and earnings more equitable. They concentrate on making adjustments in the workplace to accommodate a more heterogeneous workforce.

The Commission was told again and again that the phrase "affirmative action" was ambiguous and confusing. . . .

The language that has collected around the issue

of equality often produces overwhelmingly emotional responses. Positions are frequently taken that have not been thought through either to their logical origins or conclusions, and this is true regardless of which side of the argument is being presented; yet they are so strongly held that they leave little room for the introduction of information or contrary judgements. . . .

People generally have a sense that "affirmative action" refers to interventionist government policies, and that is enough to prompt a negative reaction from many. For others, however, much depends on the degree and quality of the intervention. They may never agree to the concept, however reasonably argued, but at least a discussion of the issues will not have been foreclosed by the waving of the semantic red flag. In other words, there may be a willingness to discuss eliminating discriminatory employment barriers but not to debate "affirmative action" as it is currently misunderstood.

The Commission notes this in order to propose that a new term, "employment equity," be adopted to describe programs of positive remedy for discrimination in the Canadian workplace. No great principle is sacrificed in exchanging phrases of disputed definition for newer ones that may be more accurate and less destructive of reasoned debate. . . .

In default of some new verbal coinage, where this Report refers to affirmative action in the Canadian context, it is no more than a convenient way of identifying positive steps to correct discrimination in the workplace. Ultimately, it matters little whether in Canada we call this process employment equity or affirmative action, so long as we understand that what we mean by both terms are employment practices designed to eliminate discriminatory barriers and to provide in a meaningful way equitable opportunities in employment.

PURPOSE OF EMPLOYMENT EQUITY

Much legislative attention has been paid to eradicating and remedying discriminatory behaviour. Human rights acts, labour codes, and the Charter of Rights and Freedoms contain provisions to address the problem. By and large these provisions have been limited in two respects: they are restricted to individual allegations of discrimination; and they are potentially restricted, except under the Ontario Human Rights Code and the Canadian Human Rights Act, to cases of intentional discrimination.

This approach to the enforcement of human rights, based as it is on individual rather than group remedies, and perhaps confined to allegations of intentional discrimination, cannot deal with the pervasiveness and subtlety of discrimination.

Neither, by itself, can education. Education has been the classic crutch upon which we lean in the hopes of coaxing change in prejudicial attitudes. But education is an unreliable agent, glacially slow in movement and impact, and often completely ineffective in the face of intractable views. It promises no immediate relief despite the immediacy of the injustice.

The traditional human rights commission model, which valiantly signalled to the community that redress was available for individuals subjected to deliberate acts of discrimination, is increasingly under attack for its statutory inadequacy to respond to the magnitude of the problem. Resolving discrimination caused by malevolent intent on a case-by-case basis puts human rights commissions in the position of stamping out brush fires when the urgency is in the incendiary potential of the whole forest.

It is sometimes exceptionally difficult to determine whether or not someone intends to discriminate. This does not mean that there is no need for processes that provide remedies to individuals when intentional discrimination can be proven. On the contrary, the need is manifest, but these processes do not sufficiently address the complexity of the problem. There are those who are prejudiced in attitude but not in deed, and others who commit acts of flagrant discrimination out of obliviousness or misplaced benevolence. What we intend is sometimes far less relevant than the impact of our behaviour on others.

The impact of behaviour is the essence of "systemic discrimination." It suggests that the inexorable, cumulative effect on individuals or groups of behaviour that has an arbitrarily negative impact on them is more significant than whether the behaviour flows from insensitivity or intentional discrimination. This approach to discrimination was articulated in 1971 in the U.S. Supreme Court case of *Griggs* v. *Duke Power Co*.[4] The Court held that one should look at impact rather than motive in deciding whether or not discrimination has taken place. This approach has since been followed by the American courts and it is the one that should be followed here.

Systemic discrimination requires systemic remedies. Rather than approaching discrimination from the perspective of the single perpetrator and the single victim, the systemic approach acknowledges that by and large the systems and practices we customarily and often unwittingly adopt may have an unjustifiably negative effect on certain groups in society. The effect of the system on the individual or group, rather than its attitudinal sources, governs whether or not a remedy is justified.

Remedial measures of a systemic and systematic kind are the object of employment equity and affirmative action. They are meant to improve the situation for individuals who, by virtue of belonging to and being identified with a particular group, find themselves unfairly and adversely affected by certain systems or practices.

Systemic remedies are a response to patterns of discrimination that have two basic antecedents:

a) a disparately negative impact that flows from the structure of systems designed for a homogeneous constituency; and

b) a disparately negative impact that flows from practices based on stereotypical characteristics ascribed to an individual because of the characteristics ascribed to the group of which he or she is a member.

The former usually results in systems primarily designed for white able-bodied males; the latter usually results in practices based on white able-bodied males' perceptions of everyone else.

In both cases, the institutionalized systems and practices result in arbitrary and extensive exclusions for persons who, by reason of their group affiliation, are systematically denied a full opportunity to demonstrate their individual abilities.

Interventions to adjust the systems are thus both justified and essential. Whether they are called employment equity or affirmative action, their purpose is to open the competition to all who would have been eligible but for the existence of discrimination. The effect may be to end the hegemony of one group over the economic spoils, but the end of exclusivity is not reverse discrimination, it is the beginning of equality. The economic advancement of women and minorities is not the granting of a privilege or advantage to them; it is the removal of a bias in favour of white males that has operated at the expense of other groups.[5]

Nor should we be ingenuous in believing that once access is expanded, the equal opportunity will translate into treatment as an equal. It is not enough merely to tantalize the excluded groups with the idea that the qualifying education and training by themselves will guarantee employment opportunities. Individuals must be assured that the metamorphosis includes equality not only of access to the opportunities, but to the opportunities themselves for which their abilities qualify them. This is meaningful equality of opportunity.

Equality demands enforcement. It is not enough to be able to claim equal rights unless those rights are somehow enforceable. Unenforceable rights are no more satisfactory than unavailable ones.

This is where we rely on employment equity — to ensure access without discrimination both to the available opportunities and to the possibility of their realization.

EQUALITY IN THE CHARTER OF RIGHTS AND FREEDOMS

The genuine pursuit of equality is a litmus test that gauges our success as a liberal democracy. Canada has affirmed its commitment to this pursuit by the inclusion of section 15 of the Canadian Charter of Rights and Freedoms.[6]

Section 15 protects every individual's right to equality without discrimination. It states:

(1) Every individual is equal before and under the law and has the right to the equal protection and equal benefit of the law without discrimination and, in par-

ticular, without discrimination based on race, national or ethnic origin, colour, religion, sex, age or mental or physical disability.

(2) Subsection (1) does not preclude any law, program or activity that has as its object the amelioration of conditions of disadvantaged individuals or groups including those that are disadvantaged because of race, national or ethnic origin, colour, religion, sex, age or mental or physical disability.

Although the body of section 15(2) refers to actions that have as their object "the amelioration of conditions of disadvantaged individuals or groups," the marginal notes to section 15(2) use the phrase "affirmative action."

Under the Charter's legislative predecessor, the Canadian Bill of Rights, the Supreme Court of Canada restricted the definition of equality to "equality of process."[7] The wording of section 15(1) of the Charter attracts a more expansive interpretation, for it pronounces the right of equality to be one of process ("before and under the law") and also one of substance ("equal protection and equal benefit"). The law must not only be evenly available, it must be evenly applied.

Until any limits to equality are accepted as demonstrably justified by a court, the presumption is that equality as guaranteed by section 15(1) is unqualified. It is difficult in any case to see how equal freedom from discrimination in process or substance could be limited in a demonstrably justifiable way in a free and democratic society. Section 15 contains its own reasonable limits. It articulates the right to be equally free from discrimination.

As other parts of the Charter make clear, however, this does not mean that distinctions among individuals and groups are not to be recognized, or that everyone is necessarily to be treated indentically. Honouring and protecting diversity is also one of our deals as a liberal democracy.

Thus certain sections of the Charter reinforce the protection from enforced assimilation and provide rules of construction requiring that definitions of equality respect diversity. Section 23[8] protects language rights and freedoms, section 25[9] protects aboriginal rights and freedoms, and section 27[10] protects the diversity of cultural heritage. Section 28

reinforces gender equality. Section 36[11] reiterates Canada's commitment to the promotion of equal opportunity and the reduction of economic disparity. Equality under the Charter, then, is a right to integrate into the mainstream of Canadian society based on, and notwithstanding, differences. It is acknowledging and accommodating differences rather than ignoring and denying them.

This is a paradox at the core of any quest for employment equity: because differences exist and must be respected, equality in the workplace does not, and cannot be allowed to, mean the same treatment for all.

In recognition of the journey many have yet to complete before they achieve equality, and in recognition of how the duration of the journey has been and is being unfairly protracted by arbitrary barriers, section 15(2) permits laws, programs, or activities designed to eliminate these restraints. While section 15(1) guarantees to individuals the right to be treated as equals free from discrimination, section 15(2), though itself creating no enforceable remedy, assures that it is neither discriminatory nor a violation of the equality guaranteed by section 15(1) to attempt to improve the condition of disadvantaged individuals or groups, even if this means treating them differently.

Section 15(2) covers the canvas with a broad brush, permitting a group remedy for discrimination. The section encourages a comprehensive or systemic rather than a particularized approach to the elimination of discriminatory barriers.

Section 15(2) does not create the statutory obligation to establish laws, programs, or activities to hasten equality, ameliorate disadvantage, or eliminate discrimination. But it sanctions them, acting with statutory acquiescence. . . .

In contrast to the American system, a finding of discrimination is not a condition precedent under the Charter for approving an affirmative action plan. The judicial inquiry, if any, would be into whether or not the group was disadvantaged. Such an inquiry, in the employment context, would probably look for evidence that members of a particular group had higher unemployment rates and lower income levels, and tended to be clustered in jobs with lower occupational status. These have been referred to as the "social indicators" of job discrimination. They can also be characterized as systemic discrimination. . . .

ECONOMIC CONSIDERATIONS

. . . Full employment is desirable from every conceivable standpoint. In particular this Commission is aware of the advantages full employment would bring to the furtherance of its objectives. The fewer the jobs, obviously, the keener the competition, and the less probability of a generous and open-minded reception for proposals that the rules of the competition be changed. But the Commission must take the economy as it finds it. The fact that the economy is anaemic does not justify a listless response to discrimination.

The members of the four designated groups represent about 60 per cent of Canada's total population.[12] They have a right, whatever the economic conditions, to compete equally for their fair share of employment opportunities. As it is, the recession has only intensified their long penalization in the form of undertraining, underemployment, underpayment, and outright exclusion from the labour force.

The competition for jobs must be made an impartial one, open to all who are qualified or qualifiable regardless of gender, ethnicity, race, or disability. It is hard to imagine a valid excuse for postponement, given our avowed ideals and the commitments entrenched in the Canadian Charter of Rights and Freedoms. As for awaiting better times, the economic millennium may be further away than anyone comfortably projects.

The pursuit of policies that permit everyone who so wishes access to the realization of his or her full employment potential is not one that ought to be tied to an economic divining rod. The most positive way to prevent further irreversible human and financial costs to these four groups from accumulating is to impose employment equity. Under section 15 of the Charter it is permissible, and, while it is not the whole solution, it is a major step.

THE DESIGNATED GROUPS

The Terms of Reference of this Commission encouraged it to look into the most effective means of responding to "deficiencies in employment practices" since "the measures taken by Canadian employers to increase the employability and productivity of women, Native people, disabled persons and visible minorities have as yet not resulted in nearly enough change in the employment practices which have the unintended effect of screening a disproportionate number of those persons out of opportunities for hiring and promotion."

The Terms of Reference also referred to the government's "obligation to provide leadership in ensuring the equitable and rational management of human resources within its organizations." Eleven crown corporations were singled out for particular study.

In the cross-Canada meetings conducted by the Commission, much concern was expressed by the designated groups over the apparently restrictive focus of the mandate on crown corporations. Other studies had shown that the problems were far more generalized and not exclusive to government corporations, agencies, and departments. In the face of intractable barriers throughout the marketplace, groups made it clear that they were deeply disappointed at the government's apparent unwillingness to tackle in a meaningful way the problems in the private sector. They felt the credibility of a government's commitment to equality was undermined by approaching the issue in a limited way rather than one sufficiently comprehensive to meet the demonstrated need.

Two facts in particular fuel this disappointment and skepticism. The first is that the federal government has forcefully intervened on behalf of the employment needs of francophones. This served as a direct example to the groups with whom the Commission met of a strong and effective political will. The government concluded rightly that francophones had been unfairly, and often arbitrarily, excluded from access to many of the opportunities available in Canada, and it took strong corrective measures. Fifteen years later, the positive results of this political intervention are apparent, a message to Canadians that a government is prepared to take remedial legislative measures to ensure equitable access to the distribution of the opportunities this country generates.

To the four designated groups from whom this Commission heard, the absence of similar political will and leadership with respect to their own exclusion from opportunities was the subject of much discussion. The fact that one group had been able to attract effective political action while others had only managed to attract repetitive research was both frustrating and inspiring as an example of the art of the politically possible. . . .

The second pertinent fact to which these groups referred was that the country to which Canada has the closest physical and cultural proximity has had for two decades an intensive program of affirmative action. What was striking to them was that the American government had, for 20 years, made genuine efforts to rectify obvious employment inequities in the private sector, while Canadians were still wondering whether to take any steps at all. . . .

What follows is a consideration of the issues arising from the observations of the various groups. The issues concentrate on the observations members of these groups have about the way they are perceived by others. These collective perceptions were expressed as being determinatively inhibiting in defining the extent to which individuals felt they could maximize their employment opportunities.

A number of articulated employment barriers were common to all groups: insufficient or inappropriate education and training facilities; inadequate information systems about training and employment opportunities; limited financial and personal support systems; short-sighted or insensitive government employment counsellors; employers' restrictive recruitment, hiring, and promotion practices; and discriminatory assumptions.

Every study relevant to these groups in the past five years has urged the implementation of some form of interventionist measures to assist them in the competition for employment opportunities, yet in response, only peripheral adjustments to the sys-

tem have been made. The progress for these groups has ranged from negligible to slow, yet there is an unexplained apparent reluctance on the part of governments to address squarely the conclusions of their own research.

Women

According to 1982 data, about 52 per cent of Canadian women are in the paid labour force. They constitute 41 per cent of the workforce. Year after year, women make the case for better childcare facilities, equal pay for work of equal value, equitable benefits, equal employment opportunities, unbiased educational options, and an end to job segregation. Year after year, they are told by governments that measures are being looked into and solutions being devised. . . .

One of the major impediments to women having adequate employment opportunities, articulated by both women and employers, has to do with the education choices made by females. If these choices are based on an assumption by females that they need not seek paid employment, that their economic security will flow from a marriage, then clearly they will not address the issue of which educational options will provide them with better employment skills. Where they are interested, and most are, in seeking employment, they must participate in the full range of available educational opportunities. This will require dramatic changes in the school system.

For women interested in joining or rejoining the workforce later in life, training and educational opportunities must be made available so that they have a chance to work at the widest range of jobs. Nor should they be neglected in the wake of technological change. Every effort must be made to attempt to break the mold that results in job and economic segregation.

What precedes employment may be just as important as what occurs once employment is obtained. The cultural ambience from which men and women emerge affects what takes place in the workplace. How men and women perceive one another as spouses and how children perceive their parents both determine what happens to women in the workforce. If women are considered economic and social dependents in the home, they will continue to be treated as subservient in the workplace. If, on the other hand, they are perceived as social and economic equals in a partnership in the home, this will be translated into the practices of the workplace. Two issues must therefore be addressed simultaneously: the way women are perceived generally in society, and the employment practices that affect women in any given corporation.

The problem is one of assumptions, almost religiously held, about the role and ability of women in Canada. Many men and women seem unable to escape from the perceptual fallout of the tradition that expects women to behave dependently and supportively toward men.

The historic and legally sanctioned role of women in Canada has been as homemaker. For more than a century, in every province, the legal doctrines around marriage required that the legal personae of husband and wife merge into that of the husband. This obliterated the wife's identity as an independent legal entity. It also required, rather than permitted, the husband to be the breadwinner, resulting in the allocation of the homemaking function to the wife.

Only in the recent past have provinces begun to impose an equal obligation on husband and wife to be responsible for their own support. The right of one spouse to support from the other now flows mainly from economic need arising from the spousal relationship and its division of labour rather than from gender. Marriage is to be considered a partnership of social and economic equals, and the division of labour in marriage between breadwinner and homemaker is to be considered a division of two equally valuable contributions to this partnership.

Notwithstanding the existence of this legal requirement that no one gender should expect the other automatically to provide financial support, childcare, or household services, it will likely be generations before the impact of this newly sanctioned approach to marriage is reflected in society's other institutions. Nevertheless, it immediately requires courts to consider that although one

spouse, usually the wife, remains at home, the homemaking contribution is to be considered equally valuable to the spousal relationship whether or not its efforts generate income. There is no longer an automatic division of household responsibilities based on gender in spousal relationships. The responsibilities of economic self-sufficiency and parenting are bilateral.

At the same time, it would be wrong to undervalue the role of homemaking and to ignore its economic contribution simply because it is not "employment" as it has been traditionally defined. Homemakers, who have made choices authorized by law and justified by their own spousal relationships, should not be penalized economically because the majority of women are now making different choices.

The essence of equality for women, now and in the future, is that in their options, which may or may not include the selection of a "traditional" role, they face no greater economic liability than would a man, and that in whatever "employment" environment they choose, they receive the same benefit for their contribution as would a man. . . .

Although women have the same right to work and stay home as do men, until the legal directive in modern family law that each spouse is responsible for his or her own support takes root and inspires routinely in young girls and women the realization that they themselves, no less than any future spouse, must be financially self-reliant, women will likely be the gender performing the homemaking responsibilities.

In 1982, there were more than 70 000 divorces granted in Canada; about one in every three marriages now ends in divorce. Census figures show that the number of single-parent families increased from 477 525 in 1971 to 714 005 in 1981. Eighty-five per cent of single-parent families in 1981 were headed by a woman, and Statistics Canada data show that three out of five female-headed families were living below the poverty line. Women who have functioned primarily as homemakers may suffer enormously heavy economic penalties when their marriages unravel, and they should be assisted in the form of tax and pension measures as well as enforceable maintenance and support systems to help them resist poverty and achieve financial viability. When they apply for jobs, their homemaking and volunteer work should be considered legitimate work experience. If they work part-time, they should not bear the unfair financial brunt of a perception that part-time work is not serious work. They should be remunerated and receive benefits on a prorated basis with workers employed full-time.

But for all women, whether they work at home or in the paid labour force, it is crucial that they not be deemed for policy purposes as economic satellites of their partners. Tax laws, pension schemes, the public perception of parental responsibilities — all these need to be examined, and in some cases drastically revised, to confirm for women their status as independent individuals, to negate the perception of their dependency, and to discredit the assumption that they have a different range of options than men have.

Notwithstanding that there is an equal right to work, there is no avoiding certain biological imperatives. Women rather than men become pregnant. Children require care. An environment must therefore be created that permits the adequate care of children while also allowing the equal right of men and women to maximize their economic potential. This environment, however, is not possible if the public continues to assume that the primary responsibility for the care of children belongs to women. There is no mysterious chemistry that produces in one gender an enhanced ability either to raise children or to work at a paid job. . . .

Many women find that their current or prospective status as a mother is a powerful factor on a hidden agenda affecting hiring and promotion practices. Some companies fear hiring young women who, though otherwise qualified, are potential childbearers. The prospect of maternity leave appears to inspire alarm in a way that training leaves, extended vacations, or even lengthy illnesses do not. This alarm is communicated throughout the female candidate pool and results in a form of psychological contraceptive blackmail. . . .

Employers should presume no more about what mothers can, should, or should not do, than they do about fathers. Employers must operate on the assumption that their male and female employees have the same family responsibilities . . .

Most women work in the clerical, sales, and support services of any corporation. These are not only the lowest paying jobs, they also tend to be jobs limited in opportunities for promotion. Even where women perform managerial functions, as many secretaries do, they are not given credit for these responsibilities when candidates for promotion to management are sought. Nor do women get the same educational or training leaves in corporations as do men, and they are rarely selected by corporations for significant corporate policy task forces or committees. Women must train for, be hired in, and given opportunities for the full range of occupational categories in order to break out of the economically limiting job segregation they now experience. This means more than an occasional token appointment of a woman to a management position; it means the routine hiring of qualified women throughout the occupational layers of a workforce.

Their work, wherever they perform it, should be valued and remunerated no differently than work done by men. There is no excuse for excluding paid domestic workers from the protection of human rights or employment legislation. At the workplace, women should be free from sexual harassment. When sexual harassment has been proven, women should have available an effective and early remedy. They should be encouraged to qualify and apply for the widest range of jobs and careers, but where they choose to work in jobs traditionally held by women they should not, by virtue of working in a predominantly female occupation, be paid less than is paid for work that is no more valuable but is done predominantly by men.

Women should be encouraged to set up their own businesses and be assisted by banks and other lending institutions with no less serious consideration than that accorded men and no more onerous proof of their business potential than that required of men. . . .

Unless concentrated attention is given to all of these issues, little will change. Human rights commissions must have the resources they need to fulfil their mandate; women must be encouraged by all political parties to play an equal and effective role both as candidates and as policy advisers; the media must become more self-conscious about how they portray issues they consider "female"; businesses must be made to examine their practices to identify and eliminate barriers facing women; and the public must be taught to stop thinking in terms of how a particular gender ought to behave and to start thinking in terms of equal options. Until all these initiatives are undertaken, women and men will be less than they could otherwise be. . . .

Native people

Native people in Canada include Status and non-Status Indians, Métis, and Inuit.

It is not new that their economic conditions are poor. Study after study has documented the facts. The unemployment rate of Native people is more than twice that of other Canadians. Those in the labour force are concentrated in low-paid, low-skill jobs. The average employment income in 1980 for Native men was 60.2 per cent of the average income for non-Native men; for Native women it was 71.7 per cent of the average income for non-Native women.

Their economic plight has taken its inevitable toll on social conditions. Native people are angry over the disproportionate numbers of Native people who drop out of school, who are in prison, who suffer ill-health, who die young, who commit suicide. They are saddened by the personal, communal, and cultural dislocation of their people. . . .

There are insufficient numbers of Native people teaching, resulting in an absence of role models for young children. Curricula in the public and high schools do not reflect the cultural differences of Native persons, and therefore a sense of either alienation or unreality inhibits the development of the minds of children who are being taught about a world that often seems inhospitable or irrelevant to them. . . .

There is an inadequate supply of relevant training programs. Training programs designed with

insufficient input from Native people often result in skills developed for jobs that are either unavailable or low-paying. Waiting lists are often as long as two years. There is a strong unmet demand for trades and technical training, as well as for basic literacy training and for upgrading and preparatory courses, such as basic job readiness. The lack of training programs specially designed for Native people means that many existing programs are ineffective for them. Educational requirements for many of these training programs are felt to be unrealistically and inappropriately high and therefore arbitrarily exclude less educated Native people from participating. . . .

Native women feel that they are doubly disadvantaged — on one level because they are women and on another level because they are Native people. They feel that they are being constantly streamed into low-paying and irrelevant job opportunities. . . .

For Native women, particularly those living on reserves and in rural and remote areas, the lack of childcare acts as a barrier to training and employment opportunities. These women are also concerned that where childcare facilities do exist they tend not to be run by Native people who can enhance the cultural environment found in the child's home.

. . . The government agencies that provide services to adult Native people are generally staffed by non-Native persons who are often unable to understand the needs of Native persons. The most frequent use of Native persons is made in the Outreach program, whose workers perform many of the same functions as do regular government employees but are employed on a year-to-year contract position, with no benefits or security. They are perceived by Native people to be critical to the delivery of government-run services for Native people. There is resentment that Native Outreach workers are being paid at a lesser rate than government employees, most of whom are not Native people.

Native people living in urban areas encounter numerous difficulties. For Status Indians, some of these difficulties stem from the fact that they are not entitled to benefits that accrue to them if they live on reserves. This limits their options and is a disincentive to seeking job opportunities off the reserves, even if job opportunities are severely limited on the reserves. Status Indians requested amendments to the tax system to soften the impact of living off the reserves. . . .

Native people need better housing, services, and medical care. The Indian people want the paternalistic Indian Act abolished; it controls who can belong to Indian bands, the administration of reserves and reserve lands and resources, the ownership of reserve lands and education.

The central issues for Native people are their exclusion from relevant decision-making, the fragmented and uncoordinated programming, the problem of uncoordinated policy approaches, the absence of federal/provincial/municipal coordination of service delivery systems, and the constant sense that they are forever subject to the discretion of people who do not understand their culture. . . .

Disabled persons

The World Health Organization distinguishes among "impairment", "disability", and "handicap". An "impairment" embraces any disturbance of or interference with the normal structure and function of the body, including the systems of mental function.[13] Health and Welfare Canada statistics place the number of Canadians who have some form of mental or physical impairment at 5.5 million.[14]

"Disability", according to the World Health Organization, "is the loss or reduction of functional ability and activity" that results from an impairment. In other words, an impairment does not necessarily product a disability, a fact reflected in the Health and Welfare Canada statistics estimating that fewer than half (2.3 million) of impaired Canadians can be termed disabled.

A "handicap" is defined by the World Health Organization as the disadvantage that is consequent upon impairment and disability.

Persons with disabilities experience some limitation of their work functioning because of their physical or mental impairment. But the extent to which their disability affects their lives on a daily basis — that is, handicaps them — is very often determined by how society reacts to their disability. A disabled person need not be handicapped.

The significance of these distinctions lies in the fact that we have tended to consider disabled persons as a uniformly incapacitated group of people. Disability may or may not lead to a handicap affecting employment.

The issue must be examined from the point of view of the individual who has the disability rather than from the point of view of the assumptions of the employer. This is not to suggest that an employer's needs and concerns are not relevant; in fact, they may be critically so. But it is to suggest that the way one deals with this issue is first to determine whether or not the disabled person is qualified or qualifiable, and secondly to determine what measures are necessary to maximize the ability of a qualified disabled individual to perform the job for which he or she is being employed. . . .

There are many aspects of the systems and policy measures designed for disabled persons that have not been thought through. Generally, the problems include the fragmentation of policies, the short-term nature of many of the programs, the lack of continuity in these programs where they do exist, the uncoordinated approach among the various levels of government and within each level of government, and the lack of information about what programs in fact exist. . . .

Where training programs do exist, the waiting period is too lengthy and the programs inadequate or irrelevant. They rarely result in jobs. Many disabled persons feel they would benefit from more on-the-job training.

There is an overwhelming problem for disabled persons in the way welfare and disability pension systems operate in this country. Programs have been devised that operate as a disincentive rather than an inducement to entering the labour force. Most welfare and disability pension schemes under which disabled persons receive income require that they choose between the income from these schemes and from employment. The loss of a pension, for example, often results in the loss of medical and social support benefits. These may no longer be affordable once a disabled person is employed because the work opportunities available are often part-time and usually in low-paying jobs. There is rarely enough income from these jobs to pay for the benefits formerly provided by welfare or disability pensions. This means as well that there is rarely enough money to pay for work-related expenses such as transportation.

Moreover, welfare and disability pension schemes normally are set up so that an individual no longer getting the benefit of these schemes disqualifies herself or himself for a substantial period of time before becoming again eligible for these benefits. If a job does not work out for a disabled individual and he or she is again unemployed, there is the crucial problem of what the next source of income will be.

Unless these income systems are redesigned to take into account the financial reality disabled persons face, it is unreasonable to expect many disabled persons to risk economic security by seeking a job. When an individual has lived for years under the shadow of a public perception that he or she is incapable of functioning at the workplace in a meaningful way, that individual is likely to be insecure about having the ability to do so. The object of ameliorative programs, therefore, is to neutralize this insecurity, to encourage confidence, and to make the prospect of employment an economically and socially viable one. . . .

More employment training must exist, and on-the-job support in the form of technical aids, personnel assistance, and a sensitized able-bodied workforce must all be offered to make employment possible for disabled persons. Transportation systems have to be devised to ensure that physical access to employment is possible, and buildings must be constructed or retrofitted to be physically accessible in all respects to disabled persons. . . .

The problem of irrelevant job requirements affects all four designated groups. Job requirements that have a disparate impact on certain groups need to be analyzed to determine whether or not they are justified. Employment practices resulting in dispar-

ate impact are justifiable only if no reasonable alternative exists or if the practice is dictated by business necessity.

A related issue is the question of when an employer should be required to reasonably accommodate a disabled employee. Incentives must be given to employers to ensure that in those circumstances where accommodations should be made, it is economically feasible for the employer to make them. Amendments should be made to the Income Tax Act in order to permit employers to fully deduct these costs. . . .

There is an additional concern that not enough emphasis is placed on preparing these workers for and facilitating their entry into the general workforce. Sheltered workshops, where they exist, should provide job placement services so that a greater number of disabled persons who are trained in these facilities are able to enter the workforce. Workshops must be encouraged to seek opportunities for more relevant long-term work for disabled workers. There should be defined guidelines as to the duration, quality, and evaluation of training in sheltered workshop programs so that an individual's successful completion of the program may be determined. . . .

Although human rights statutes should continue to protect people with as wide a range of disabilities as possible from discriminatory acts or systems, employment equity programs should concentrate on attempting to increase employment opportunities for those persons whose permanent or long-term disabilities seriously handicap them in access to employment opportunities. Disabled persons should be defined for purposes of an employer's obligation to collect data under employment equity legislation as those persons whose general access to employment opportunities has been or has appeared to have been limited by the existence of a permanent or long-term disability. Because of the individualized approach employers must take in eliminating employment barriers for the different impairments a disabled employee may have, the emphasis in monitoring the success of employment equity systems for disabled persons should be less quantitative or data oriented. Disabled persons are so heterogeneous a group that each disability requires accommodation in a different way. This makes any emphasis on numerical change potentially unfair both to the disabled employee and to the employer. . . .

Therefore, [there is a need] for restricted and careful use of medical examinations as a pre-employment selection process to ensure that these examinations form only part of a *bona fide* occupational requirement and do not result in an arbitrary exclusion from employment. . . .

For disabled persons, as for other individuals, two stages in employment equality are called for. The first stage is the preparation for their eligibility to compete fairly and equally for jobs — qualifying the qualifiable candidate for employment. In the education of the disabled child, for instance, the child should be made to feel that he or she is an equal social participant, with access to whatever services and systems exist for the general public.

The second stage is in preparing the work environment itself, where the effectiveness of the disabled person's performance may be determined by the extent to which the disability is either ignored, accommodated, or over-emphasized.

This emphasis on integration should be carried into an examination of which institutions are properly providing the care disabled persons need and which are unfairly isolating them from general opportunities. In addition, the public should be educated against making stereotypical judgements about disabled persons which prevent them from gaining access to those things to which they are otherwise entitled. The best education is the employment of a qualified disabled person who can, by doing a job, teach able-bodied fellow employees and employers that what was thought impossible is not only possible but inevitable.

It is not just the opportunity of becoming employed that is at issue, it is the opportunity, once employed, of being able to move through a corporation with the same facility as would any other employee with a disabled individual's qualifications. . . .

Visible minorities

Visible minorities were defined by this Commission for purposes of the questionnaire requesting data from the designated crown corporations as "non-whites". . . .

Focusing on visible minority groups through employment equity programs does not relieve society of the responsibility to eradicate discrimination for all minority groups. It does not cancel the duty to provide for immigrants adequate language and skill training, bias-free mechanisms for determining the validity of foreign credentials and experience, and vigilant regard for whether employers are unreasonably making Canadian experience a job requirement. Nor does it absolve the school systems of their responsibility to ensure that minorities — visible or otherwise — are not being streamed routinely into certain types of courses. These are examples of the kind of measures that should be undertaken in any event to protect Canada's minorities from arbitrarily exclusionary systems. . . .

The problems for newly arrived immigrants are enormous. There is little information given to them prior to their emigrating to prepare them for living in Canada, and they often arrive completely unfamiliar with Canadian life and institutions. . . .

This has critical implications in employment contexts. In the interviewing process, for example, people are often hired on the basis of, among other things, an interviewer's perception of their ability to integrate easily into a given labour force. This may not be relevant either to the candidate's actual ability to integrate or to his or her qualifications.

Consistently across Canada the Commission heard that the language training an immigrant receives upon arrival is inadequate. The training tends to be too short; it tends to be English or French immersion which, for many immigrants, is an impossible pedagogical style; it is usually not taught by someone who speaks their own language; and it rarely provides instruction sufficient for them to be able to communicate with any degree of fluency. Moreover, an individual almost never receives language training in his or her own skill or profession. The absence of technical language training practically guarantees that the immigrant's job opportunities are severely restricted and that whatever qualifications he or she brought to this country will be underutilized.

Not only was the language instruction itself deemed to be a problem, the fact that full-time programs are offered mainly to persons expected immediately to enter the paid labour force means that some immigrant women learn little or no English. If they subsequently join the paid workforce, their lack of language skills means that they are reduced to applying for low-paying, ghettoized jobs with little prospect of economic advancement. They are ripe for exploitation.

Immigrant women are disadvantaged, too, by the lack of adequate childcare facilities. Without access to childcare, some immigrant women who want to work cannot and many are unable to take language or training courses even when these courses are available.

A further difficulty is created by the absence of language training as an alternative to, or in conjunction with, employment opportunities. It is difficult to learn a language while employed. Once an immigrant has entered the labour force there is no financial assistance available for him or her to stop work temporarily, either to complete language training or to learn the language of his or her own profession or skill. Very little on-the-job language training exists, a system that would be exceptionally helpful to people anxious to integrate and contribute economically as quickly as possible. The result for many immigrants is that they tend to be locked into whatever jobs they obtain when they first arrive. . . .

The problem of professional or career credentials from other countries is a serious one for many who try without success to find ways of satisfying an employer that their educational qualifications match those required to perform the job.

Many skilled and professional immigrants are frustrated by the absence of a mechanism to determine whether or not the professional qualifications they bring to this country qualify them to practise their profession in Canada or to determine what upgrading courses are necessary. The examinations and licencing requirements for many occupations and professions across Canada are prohibitively expensive. There is an additional problem of portability from province to province of professional qualifications. A system of qualification and credential assessment should be available so that recent as well as prospective immigrants can be advised accurately about exactly what is necessary in order to qualify them to practise their professions. . . .

The problem is essentially one of racism. Strong measures are therefore needed to remedy the impact of discriminatory attitudes and behaviour flowing from this problem.

What is clear is that many groups of people living in Canada despair about ever being able to avail themselves of the economic, political, or social opportunities that exist in this country. They increasingly experience a sense of futility. Nothing short of strong legislative measures is necessary to reverse, or at least inhibit, the degree to which members of visible minorities are unjustifiably excluded from the opportunity to compete as equals. . . .

ENDNOTES

1. Anatole France. *Le Lys Rouge (The Red Lily)*. Quoted in John Bartlett, *Familiar Quotations*. (Boston: Little Brown and Company, 1980), p. 655.

2. Jeremy Bentham, "Absolute Equality is Absolutely Impossible," in John Bowring (ed.), *The Works of Jeremy Bentham*. Vol. 1. (Edinburgh: William Tate, 1843), p. 361.

3. *Ibid.*, p. 311.

4. *Griggs* v. *Duke Power Co.* 401 U.S. 424 (1971).

5. Robert Belton, "Discrimination and Affirmative Action: An Analysis of Competing Theories of Equality and Weber", 59 *North Carolina Law Review* (1981), p. 537, footnote 28. Belton argues that "reverse discrimination" is a legal fiction.

6. *The Constitution Act 1982*, C. 11 (U.K.) Section 15 does not come into force until after April 17, 1985.

7. R.S.C. 1970 Appendix III. See *Attorney General for Canada* v. *Lavell*, [1974] S.C.R. 1349; *Bliss* v. *Attorney General for Canada*, [1979] 1 S.C.R. 183.

8. Section 12(1) states:

Citizens of Canada

(a) whose first language learned and still understood is that of the English or French linguistic minority population of the province in which they reside, or

(b) who have received their primary school instruction in Canada in English or French and reside in a province where the language in which they received that instruction is the language of the English or French linguistic minority population of the province,

have the right to have their children receive primary and secondary school instruction in that language in that province.

9. Section 25 states:

The guarantees in this Charter of certain rights and freedoms shall not be construed so as to abrogate or derogate from any aboriginal treaty or other rights or freedoms that pertain to the aboriginal people of Canada including

(a) any rights or freedoms that have been recognized by the Royal Proclamation of October 7, 1763; and

(b) any rights or freedoms that may be acquired by the aboriginal peoples of Canada by way of land claims settlement.

10. Section 27 states:

This Charter shall be interpreted in a manner consistent with the preservation and enhancement of the multicultural heritage of Canadians.

11. Section 36(1) states:

Without altering the legislative authority of Parliament or of the provincial legislatures, or the rights of any of them with respect to the exercise of their legislative authority, Parliament and the legislatures, together with the governments, are committed to

(a) promoting equal opportunities for the well-being of Canadians;

(b) furthering economic development to reduce disparity in opportunities; and

(c) providing essential public services of reasonable quality to all Canadians.

12. Women, Native males, and male members of visible minorities make up 57 per cent of the Canadian population. (Statistics Canada, *1981 Census of Canada*. Catalogue 92–911. Volume 1 — National Series (Population).) Although there is no precise data on the number of disabled males in Canada, it is conservatively estimated that 10 per cent of the Canadian population is disabled.

13. World Health Organization, Philip H.N. Wood, WHO/ICD9/REV. CONF/75.15.

14. Canada, Health and Welfare, *Disabled Persons in Canada* (Ottawa, 1981), p. 7.

27

Have We a Right to Non-Discrimination?

JAN NARVESON

1. Prefatory

Discrimination stands very high on the list of what is currently accounted injustice. Indeed, the pages of North American journals, at least, tend to be filled with articles addressing the issue of whether *reverse* discrimination is justified or not; but that discrimination itself is unjust is scarcely ever questioned. The point of the present essay is to question it anyway. I largely share the tendency to regard much of what is currently regarded as discriminatory as a bad thing, something to condemn and certainly to avoid. I am much less certain, though, that it is in addition something to prohibit by the machinery of the law. At a minimum — and this is the motivation for the essay — I am puzzled. So the reader may construe the following investigation as an invitation to come forth with a clear account of the matter, at any rate, for I am quite sure that none has as yet been given. And that seems to me to be a very bad thing. When we prohibit the activities of voluntary and rational human beings, we ought, one would think, to have a clear and compelling reason for it. The current tendency

seems to be to assume that the wrongness of discrimination is self-evident. That attitude, I am sure we'll all agree, will not do.

2. Initial Definitions

Discrimination requires three persons at a minimum: (1) the Discriminator, (2) The Discriminatee, the person discriminated against, and (3) the parties who have been favored in comparison with the discriminatees; perhaps we can call this class the Beneficiaries. Further, there has to be some characteristic possessed by the second class of persons on account of which they are treated less well than the third: being black, or a woman, or a foreigner, or non-Christian for instance. This property we might call the Discriminandum. Finally, note the expression 'discriminated *against*'. It is essential to the idea of discrimination, I take it, that the discriminatee is treated badly, adversely, or at any rate less well than the Beneficiaries.

All these are necessary conditions. I believe we have a sufficient condition if we add that to discriminate against someone is to treat that person in the undesirable way in question *because* the person has the property in question. But we should perhaps make room for a notion, presumably lower on the scale of moral culpability, of inadvertent discrimination. Here, the persons badly treated are not intentionally singled out for their possession of the Discriminandum in question; but it turns out that the class distinguished by possession of it is, nevertheless, coming out on the short end of the stick just as if they were intentionally thus singled out.

As with so many of the expressions we employ in day-to-day moral activity, it would be possible to expend time and energy deliberating about whether the word 'discriminate' is *logically* condemnatory or not. I don't think this time would be well spent. Smith may be complimented for being a discriminating judge of wine, or of music; Jones may be condemned for his discriminatory practices in business. I believe we can readily enough identify a sense of 'discrimination' which is logically neutral on the moral issue, and indeed, the proposed definition assembled above really is so. Confining ourselves to the more dominant intentional sense of the term, let us begin as follows:

> D_1: A discriminates against B in relation to C by doing x = (def.) There is a property, K, such that B has K, C does not have K, and A treats B worse than C by doing x, and does so *because* B is a K.

That A treats B worse than C is not, itself, a morally significant fact — a point I shall expand on below. And — as I shall also be at pains to point out — there are obvious cases of treatment fitting the above which no one would take to be unjust. There are two suggestions to consider for expanding the above in such a way as to bring it more nearly into line with that use of the term in which the current controversies are couched. Each deserves some further treatment of its own. Meanwhile, the partial definition given so far may serve as the basis for raising the important questions. What we want to know is: what values of K and x are such that to do x to a K *rather* than a non-K and *because* the person in question is a K rather than a non-K make the doing of x unjust?

Incidentally, I will tend to favor the term 'unjust' for these purposes because my main interest is in the moral status which would ground restrictive *legislation*. Whether some lesser charge than injustice might be brought against one who discriminates is not a matter I shall be much concerned to explore.

3. Non-Basic Discrimination

One way in which D_1 can be expanded would be by restricting the value of our act-variable, x, in such a way as to guarantee that discrimination is unjust. There are two ways to do this (at least). One would go like this:

> D_2: A discriminates against B in relation to C by doing x = (def.) B is a K, C a non-K, and because B is a K, A does x to B *and x is unjust*.

This makes discrimination unjust by definition, but also trivializes the matter. What we want to know is whether there are acts, x, such that x is unjust because x is discriminatory. We do not wish to know whether there are acts, x, such that x is unjust because x is unjust.

A more interesting way might go like this:

> D_3: A discriminates against B in relation to C by doing x = (def.) A does x to B and not to C because B is a K and C isn't a K, and x consists in harming B, e.g. by killing, torturing, maiming, depriving of rightful property, etc.

I leave an 'etc.' in this definition because my intention is to incorporate into the definition of discrimination a restriction on x to acts which are generally recognized to be morally wrong (and, indeed, are morally wrong, in my view). But I don't wish to incorporate a use of the term 'unjust' in the definition. The idea is to identify discrimination with the doing of evil acts, even though the evilness of those acts is not logically part of the description of those acts. (I have failed even so, in view of the reference to "depriving of rightful property"; finding a non-tendentious description of violations of property rights is not easy, and I request that this failing be overlooked for present purposes.)

D₃ makes discrimination wrong, all right, and it is not trivial either. But it has a different and crucial defect. For the restriction on the range of acts to be considered discriminatory according to it is now such that discriminatory acts are wrong, all right, but not *because* they are discriminatory. For they would be wrong even if they *weren't* discriminatory. We may call such acts acts of "non-basic" discrimination. Now, there are plenty of examples of non-basic discrimination, and indeed, I think that most examples of discrimination which one might be inclined to go to as paradigm cases of it would be non-basic discriminations. Think of black people being lynched, or Jews sent to the gas chambers at Auschwitz, for instance. It is quite true that the reason why these people were thus treated is that they were black or Jews, and quite true that they were discriminatory. But surely what makes it wrong to lynch an innocent person is not that that's no way to treat a *black* person, but rather that it's no way to treat *any* innocent person.

A good deal of the progress which, I think we'd all agree, has been made in the treatment of other races in North America (at least) in the last few decades has taken the form of getting people to appreciate that the basic principles of morality are color-blind. We think there are basic human rights, held by everybody of whatever race, color, etc., and we are at the point where even sheriffs in small towns in Alabama could probably be got to subscribe to that thesis, at least in point of lip service and maybe to some degree in action as well. All this is very real progress, and insofar as the hubbub about discrimination is about this sort of thing, the hubbub is justified. The trouble is, it seems clear that what I have called non-basic discrimination is not the sort of thing which we need [in order] to show that discrimination as such is wrong — that there is anything that is wrong just *because* it is discriminatory. 'Discrimination', given our new definition, D₃, has yet to signify a basic wrong, something which we have a right that others not do to us which we wouldn't have had anyway.

There is, no doubt, an interesting question on the matter of whether non-basic acts of discrimina-

tion are *worse* because they are discriminatory. It has been suggested to me[1], for instance, that if the Nazis had gassed people at random, or by lot, rather than picking on the Jews in particular, then that would strike us as being hideous and awful, but not *unjust*, or at least not *as* unjust as what actually happened. It is unclear to me whether this is so or not. Perhaps one reason why one might think so is that we tend to connect injustice with *unfairness*, and it may be agreed that it is unfair to gas people for being Jews, leaving non-Jews intact. And that defect could be rectified by establishing a lottery. But on the other hand, a just community will surely be just as concerned to prevent random gassing of innocent people as it will to prevent selective gassing of them, will it not?

Suppose that instead of gassing you because you are a Jew, I gas you because I dislike your taste in ties. Is this in the same boat, or not? Or suppose I gas you because I have embezzled your money and don't want you to tell the authorities I have done so. Gassing people at random is in one sense more terrible than any of these, in the same way that terrorism in general is terrible: it might befall anyone at any time. But all of these things are terrible, and I doubt that there's any point in trying to say in the abstract which is worst. In general, I suspect that the reason we are so impressed with the case of the Jews is twofold. First, antisemitism is popular, for some reason, whereas anti-tiewearing (to the point of gassing) is virtually unheard of, and random gassing is exceedingly rare, though random violence is not. And second, antisemitism is *divisive*. It sets people against each other. Policies of antisemitism will tend to produce in many people the attitude that there is actually something wrong with being Jewish, that Jewishness is a property which literally deserves extermination, or whatever. There is therefore a public interest reason for worrying about antisemitism that isn't there in regard to the other two practises.

4. Moral Irrelevance

The most popular candidate for a principle of non-discrimination, no doubt, would be one which makes use of the notion of "moral irrelevance." On this view, discrimination would be defined in some such way as the following:

> D_4: A discriminates against B in relation to C by doing x = (def.) A does x to B and not to C because B is a K and C is not, and K-ness is *morally irrelevant* to treating people in way x.

What is meant by 'moral irrelevance' here? I suppose that a property of a person is morally relevant to a manner of treatment if it is the case that by virtue of having that property, one is morally entitled to a certain sort of treatment. And indeed, we do frame some exceedingly high-level, abstract-sounding moral principles in some such manner as that. To use the words of Sidgwick, for instance: "If a kind of conduct that is right . . . for me . . . is not right . . . for someone else, it must be on the ground of some difference between the two cases, other than the fact that I and he are different persons."[2] This suitably self-evident-seeming idea readily lends itself to evolution into a principle about the treatment of others: if I am to treat B differently from C, then there has to be some difference, other than the fact that B is B and C is C, which justifies this difference of treatment.

Principles as abstract as this have some well-known demerits. Those, for instance, who practice racial discrimination are certainly not treating B differently from C just because C is a different person from B. They are treating B differently from C because (for instance) B is black and C isn't. Obviously a thicker theory about which properties are relevant to which sorts of treatment is required. But I think the plot can be thickened before we get into detail on that matter. We need at a minimum to distinguish two different levels of moral relevance. (1) A property might be morally relevant in the sense that we are morally *required* to treat people who have it differently from people who don't. Or (2) a property might be morally relevant only in the sense that it is morally *permissible* to treat people who have it differently from people who don't. And we may agree straight off that there must be morally relevant properties grounding any dif-

ferences of treatment in the *second* sense. For after all, if it is not morally permissible to treat B differently from C, then no doubt it is wrong to treat them differently; and if we confine ourselves to the sorts of wrongness which ground restrictive laws, unjust-making wrongnesses, then it is obvious that moral relevance in sense (2) is a necessary condition for treating people justly. But it is also trivial to say that, after all. What, however, about sense (1)?

It does, I must say, seem perfectly obvious that in order to justify difference of treatment of two persons, B and C, there does *not* need to be a *morally relevant* difference between them in sense (1). I do not mean merely that we might find different ways of treating B and C which treat them equally well, so that neither has any complaint coming on the score of having been less well treated. I mean, more interestingly, that we may very well treat one person less well than another without a hint of injustice, and without appealing to any differences between them which are morally relevant in the stronger sense. Moreover, I think we can find examples of this type which are also frankly discriminatory in the sense not only of D_4, but also relative to current thinking, in that they discriminate along the very lines which figure in many of our laws as well as private judgments.

Such, for instance, seems to me to be the case with marrying and offering to marry. It seems to me that there are virtually no morally relevant characteristics in this whole area. Suppose I decide to marry Jane on the ground that she has lovely blue eyes, whereas Nell has to make do with plain ol' brown ones. Well, where is the duty to marry blue-eyeds rather than brown-eyeds? Obviously nowhere: so do I perform an injustice to Nell in thus behaving? I think not. Nor is the situation any different if we think of the standard Discriminanda currently in the public eye. If I marry Amanda because she is black, I do not behave unjustly to Sue who is white; or if I marry Cathy because she is of the same religious persuasion as I — or because she is of a different persuasion, for that matter — I do not *thereby* wrong the unfortunate (or fortunate?) candidates who are thus rejected.

Similarly with friendship. If I like A because he is intelligent and charming, while refraining from befriending B because he is uninteresting, I do not thereby wrong B, despite the total lack of any moral duty to befriend all and sundry, or to befriend the intelligent, or the charming. In short, I think it clear that the general claim that we can justify treating one person less well than another only by invoking "morally relevant" characteristics in the interesting sense distinguished above simply will not wash.

It is manifestly clear that we can act well or badly, and in particular, intelligently or unintelligently, in these contexts. You may certainly criticize my taste if I marry someone because of the color of her eyes, or her skin, or even her choice of religion, perhaps. These decisions may be personally justified or not. But morally? It would take a special background to bring morality into it. Perhaps you have been dating Jane all this time, leading her to expect that you like people such as her, indeed leading her to expect a proposal from you; and instead, you turn around and propose to some total stranger. You may owe her an explanation. Or perhaps you promised your dear ol' Mum that you'd marry a fellow Seventh Day Adventist, and now you've gone and proposed to a Buddhist, yet. There's no end of what might bring moral considerations into these matters. But my point is that so far as it goes, morality has no bearing on it: marry whom you like, and Justice will not blink an eye, though Prudence might turn around and quietly vomit.

5. Is There Basic Discrimination?

Further reflection on the foregoing discussion of moral relevance raises the interesting question whether there really is any such thing as what I have implicitly identified as Basic discrimination. Non-basic discrimination, we recall, is where there is something wrong with what you are doing to B *anyway*; the fact that you do it to him because he is the possessor of some property (not common to all moral persons) which does not qualify him for that

treatment is not needed in order to condemn the action in question. Basic discrimination, then, would be where your act of treating B worse than C is wrong, not because it is to do something to B which you have no right to do anyway, but because it unjustly discriminates between B and C. What we would need here, evidently, is a principle calling upon us to do certain things to certain people if we also do them to certain others, but where there is in itself nothing wrong with doing it to anyone.

Yet there seems something odd about this. Here is something I can do to someone, something which there is no inherent moral objection to doing. Call this act x. Often x will be some negative action, a *non*action such as not offering the person in question a job. There is also, we are assuming, *no* moral duty to do not-x, to refrain from x, to *anyone*. How, then, can it suddenly be unjust if I choose to do x to B, and not-x to C? Doing it, to anyone, is not wrong; nor is doing it, to anyone, a moral duty, required. Nobody has the right that I do it to him or refrain from doing it to him. How can it be that it is, under the circumstances, wrong to do it to B rather than C?

The most interesting current context, I take it, is employment. We have in general no obligation to hire anybody for anything; nor have we in general any obligation to refrain from hiring anybody for anything. Yet it is widely supposed that if A hires C rather than B because C is, say, a male, or white, despite B's equal competence, then A has done B an injustice, and the law may properly descend upon A and make him toe the line of equality. Why? So interesting are these contexts that I propose to discuss them on their own for a few pages.

6. Public/Private

To begin with, we had better immediately take account of a distinction plainly relevant in this connection, namely the distinction between hiring in the public sector and private hiring. I mean this to be a conceptual distinction. Some might argue that the public sector is a fraud, or at any rate that there ought to be no such thing: you name it and "the public" has no business doing it. Others might say the same thing about the private sector. I do not intend either to affirm or deny either view here. I only wish to point out that if we acknowledge a public sector, it is easy enough to see why discrimination there would be something to make a fuss about.

The reason is simple enough. Suppose there are services which any member of the public has a right to, *vis-à-vis* the public generally. He has that right, then, *qua* member of the public. Moreover, those offering it to him are also acting as agents of the public. Now, the public consists of *everybody*. If, then, there is some service to which one is entitled *qua* member of the public, clearly it will be wrong for any agent of the public to give it to C but withhold it from B, so long as both are members of the relevant public. If there is a limited resource which the public is to expend — medical services, say — it is held that this is a public matter, so that all and only the medically needy have a claim on it, and demand exceeds supply, then it is also plausible to hold that the resources ought to be proportioned equally to the need, or perhaps that we ought to maximize the public health, but in any case not on a basis which favors some irrelevantly distinguished group in society. In fact, the criteria of relevance will be quite clear: if there is some need N to which some service S of the public is to cater, then factors other than N are irrelevant when it comes to administering S.

Prima facie, we also have a case for insisting that the agents administering S hire only on the basis of competence. If the idea is to maximize the satisfaction of N, then if applicant B promises to promote that goal better than C at the same cost, then the public would seem to have a right that B be hired rather than C. (The situation gets messy when we ask whether the public has the right that its servants reflect, say, the racial composition of the public they are to serve, particularly when perhaps the typical applicants from one readily-distinguished group are less competent than those of some other, since now there will be a clash between considerations of efficiency, which the public has a right to, and the interest in an equal share of the action,

which it may also have a right to. But we will not press these issues further here.)

What is important about the invocation of the public here is that it gives us a basis for nondiscrimination which again does not clearly show discrimination to be a *basic* injustice. For it seems, again, that if B can successfully claim to have been discriminated against in the public sector, there is also a claim on B's part to that which he was denied by virtue of the discriminatory act in question. It is not the case that there is no obligation to hire at all, nor that there is no obligation to provide the service for which hiring is being done. On the contrary, the thesis is that the public has the duty to provide the service, and is also entitled to it, on a basis that is equal as between persons of one color and another, one sex and another, etc.

But this is not true of the private sector in general. In that sector, the assumption is that those who hire do so in pursuit of private gain, or perhaps some other sort of private satisfaction. There is no obligation to set up any business whatever, no obligation to offer any particular service, or any service at all. That somebody didn't get hired by you, a private employer, is *prima facie* not something he can complain about, since you have no obligation to hire anybody at all — neither that person nor any other. More interestingly, it is by no means clear that he can complain even if he was of superior competence as compared with his competitors. Since you have no obligation to hire at all, it is hard to see why you should have an obligation to hire the most competent. What if you don't care about competence? Perhaps you'd rather that your employees were attractive, or devout Catholics, or tee-totalers, or males. So what? Again, it seems to me: if there is no right to a job at all, how can there be a right that people like you be hired rather than people like anybody else, if anyone is hired at all?

Again, there are certainly considerations of prudence; and it is possible that some will see considerations of morality entering here too. Let us see, beginning in particular with prudence. We turn, briefly, to the question the of economics of discrimination. Too briefly, no doubt, but the matter can afford some instruction anyway.

7. Dollars and Discrimination

Let us first consider the matter on what are usually thought of as classical assumptions, *viz.*, that everyone in the market is an economically rational agent interested in maximizing his dollar returns. (This assumption, as will be noted below, is unclear even if true; but one thing at a time. One good reason for starting with this assumption is that some people seem to think that discrimination is actually *caused* by the motive of gain.) Such agents will buy at the lowest price available for a given level of quality in the product, and will sell whatever they have to sell, e.g. their labour power, at the highest available price. If A wants an x and B, a black person, offers it to him at a lower price than C, who is white, then A will buy from the black person. (It should be noted that although, as I say, I will be questioning the above assumptions in some respects, there is plenty of empirical evidence that consumers, whether of labour or other things, will indeed buy from people they ostensibly despise if the price is right.)

Consider, then, the case of the Little Goliath Motor Company, a firm which makes no bones about its basic purpose: profit. And consider any position in this firm, call it P, forwarding some function, F, within this noble enterprise. The primary purpose of making money will determine both which subordinate functions will be values of F and, together with an understanding of how F fits in with the rest of the operation, the criteria of better and worse performance at P. The more efficiently per unit of pay F is fulfilled, the lower will be the firm's cost per unit, or the higher the quality, or some mix of the two; in either case it will do better on the market, being able to sell cheaper or higher quality goods than the competition, if the latter don't do as well on these scores. Applicants for P, therefore, will rationally be judged by those criteria.

Enter another classical assumption, *viz.*, that such factors as race and sex make no difference to efficiency on the part of employees. (Again, it is an assumption which is often certainly false to fact, but, again, one thing at a time.) On this assump-

tion, the people down at Little Goliath will not do well to have any interest in the race or sex of their applicants. For imagine what happens if they do. They begin, let us suppose, preferring males or whites. Preferring here means that they will hire them instead of females or blacks (or whatever). Now this presumably means that it will hire a less efficient white male at the same wage as it could get a more efficient black or female for the job at hand; which is equivalent, economically speaking, to paying more for an equally efficient one. On classical assumptions, what happens next? Well, the more persistently enterprising Universal Motor Co. up the road will begin to hire females and blacks, doing equally good work, for lower wages; it is in a position to do this, since the Goliath people insist on turning away perfectly good females with an interest in taking the best-paying job they can get. If this keeps up, and if, as our assumptions dictate, motor car purchasers are interested in quality for price rather than the color or sex of those who put the product together, then we shall expect the Universal people to do well, and the Goliath people to do badly.

Perhaps a case at a somewhat classier level will be still more perspicuous. Most firms, we are told, much prefer males to females for executive positions; and we are also told that this is in fact sheer prejudice, females being equally capable. Under the circumstances, we should expect cagey firms to be soon staffed, in their higher reaches, with high-powered women at half the pay which their competitors have to offer to their all-male staffs. If all firms were rational and our assumption about the relative abilities of the sexes correct, we should eventually see executives of both sexes at the same salaries more or less everywhere.

The moral is generalizable: if the criterion of discrimination in hiring is that criteria other than those relevant to job-performance are used for the sorting of candidates, then in free-market conditions, with economically rational consumers, the non-discriminating firm will be better. Discrimination does not pay.

Might things go severely otherwise? Might the assumptions be badly wrong? The situation is unclear. We can certainly imagine cases in which consumers are not out to maximize their returns. If consumers insist on buying grapes picked by unionized labour, we are into another ball game: not that storeowners really *mind* having customers who prefer paying more to paying less for the same goods, but it is all slightly puzzling. Likewise, it is possible that people would want to know whether the soap they buy was wrapped by lily-white rather than ebony hands. Possible, though unlikely. More likely, of course, is discrimination in service industries where the customer comes into direct contact with the supplier. People might like black waiters and butlers better than white ones, or pretty stewardesses better than plain though efficient ones, or whatever. In all such cases, economics will not erode discrimination. It will instead lead to the members of favoured classes being better off than members of unfavoured ones; and whether, for instance, wages in given industries will tend to equalize in a longish run is imponderable. But it should certainly be noted that there is no clear tendency toward reinforcing preexisting patterns of social discrimination, as anyone who has recently attempted to procure the services of Leontyne Price or Oscar Peterson will be acutely aware.

It is also essential to point out that the most scandalous cases in the past have been anything but cases of free market operation. Black slavery in the American South was *not* a free market institution. Neither is the situation in South Africa, where wage differentials between black and white workers are reinforced not only by law, but by unions.

I should like to explore this aspect of the matter much further, but space does not permit. Instead, I wish to turn to another crucial matter, closely related to that just discussed and, I think, offering perhaps the most puzzling challenge of all to those who think that there is a clear and straightforward underlying principle behind current attitudes about discrimination.

8. The Purposes of Firms

Competence is assessed by the criteria relevant to performance of the function which the position in

question is to serve. Which functions are to be served, depends in turn on the ultimate purpose of the firm in which the position is situated. Some firms are out to make money; but not all. Let us address ourselves to a couple of relevant cases. One of my favorites, for starters, is a small nonprofit organization known as the Equadorian Friendship Society. The E.F.S. has as its purpose the forwarding of friendship among Equadorians, and this purpose is not notably served by hiring, say, Bolivian janitors and secretaries, or even French chefs. We may well imagine that the management down at the E.F.S. will substantially prefer less competent Equadorians to more competent Bolivians when screening applications for those and other positions, right up to Vice President depending, no doubt, on the condition of its finances. But who is to say that the firm is acting irrationally in such practices? After all, it might be argued, given the purpose of this particular firm, that it is *not* efficient, looked at from the higher point of view, to hire Bolivian secretaries, however efficient they may be *qua* secretary. Under the circumstances, the hiring of Bolivians, however competent, is less than utterly Friendly.

Another of my favorites among these specialized nonprofit establishments is the Black Muslim Church of America, which may be presumed to look considerably askance at applicants of the Occidental persuasion for positions in their clergy, however eloquent and dedicated. The point, again, may be made that given the purposes of the firm, what would otherwise be discriminatory is legitimate, indeed efficient and thus mandatory. Thus it may be argued that these firms do not really violate the canon of hiring only on the basis of relevant competence: competence, as I say, is dictated by the purposes of the organization.

At this point, two questions loom before us. Both should tax us mightily, I think. The first point may be furthered by bringing up another example dear to my heart: the Irish-Canadian Distilleries Corporation. This amiable organization lets it be known to all and sundry that although it is happy to turn an honest dollar, it also has a pronounced interest in maximizing the percentage of persons of

Irish descent amongst its employees, even if this should cut into profits a bit. For its purpose is not simply to make money — this, they imply, is a motive reserved for the low of mind, such as the denizens of the Highlands. It is, rather, to be a sort of marginally profitable Irish-Canadian Friendly Society, a high purpose for which, indeed, its commercial product is peculiarly suitable. Its otherwise inefficient hiring practices, when viewed from this higher perspective, turn out to be perfectly efficient after all, and therefore, on the standard view which seems to prevail about what is "morally relevant", quite free of any taint of discrimination.

The second question follows naturally enough, *viz.*: what's so great about efficiency, anyway? Why not accuse those firms which hire exclusively on the basis of competence of discriminating unjustly against the incompetent? Why should competence be thought a "morally relevant characteristic"? It is not, incidentally, thought to be so when it comes to such elementary matters as the right to vote, or indeed, to stand for Parliament. From the point of view of the employer, of course, competence is highly desirable. So indeed is it from the point of view of the consumer. But why should only that point of view count? Aren't we supposed to be adumbrating an impartial standard of justice?

9. Advertising of Positions

One possible account of the injustice thought to be inherent in discriminatory hiring, and to some extent applicable in other contexts as well, is that those who are excluded for apparently irrelevant reasons have been dealt badly with because their expectations, engendered by the advertisement for the position or such other description of the opportunity regarding which the discrimination has taken place, have been disappointed. An applicant may well say, "Look, I've come all this way, taken all this time and trouble to get this job interview, and now you tell me that no X-ians will be considered. Why didn't you say so in the first place?"

Complaints of this kind, where applicable, may certainly be well-taken, and sometimes could be a basis for a claim of compensation. But so far as the

general issue of a basic right to nondiscrimination is concerned, it is surely too weak to do the job many people feel there is to be done. For one thing, it would be hard to specify the number of factors on the basis of which a candidate might be rejected in any satisfactorily general way. After all, if there is just one job and many candidates, several are going to be disappointed, however excellent the reasons for their rejection. And more generally, it is surely not true that the case against discrimination, in the minds of the many who think it a major context for social concern, would always be settled just by wording advertisements appropriately. The claim is that it's wrong to impose the condition that No Irish Need Apply, however well advertised that condition may be. We shall have to look elsewhere to find any deep principles against discrimination. (Nor should it be assumed *a priori* that we will succeed.)

10. Current Practice

It is perhaps not entirely out of order to ask whether our current practices in this area make all that much sense, taken in large. For one thing, it does seem as though discrimination is in fact quite all right when practiced by the allegedly downtrodden against the allegedly mighty majority (though the term 'majority' has come to have a somewhat non-literal usage, in view of the fact that, e.g., white Anglo-Saxon males must by now make up rather a small percentage of the Canadian or American populace, and women an outright majority). And do we not tolerate, indeed expect and encourage, discrimination as between members of our own family and others when it comes to the distribution of various economic and social benefits, including jobs, education beyond what is provided by the public, and so forth?

Another area in a more public quarter has to do with the matter of nationalism. At one time, discrimination on grounds of nationality was one of the standard bad examples, along with discrimination on grounds of sex, race and religion. But recently, one hears less about nationality, perhaps for the reason that every government so flagrantly violates any principle along this line. Not only public employers, but also employers in the private sector, are routinely required to discriminate very strongly against citizens of other countries (in Canada, this is true even of immigrants, whom employers are often required to rank second to citizens for employment). Goods made by foreign firms are, of course, routinely discriminated against by means of tariffs and other restrictions. Even the freedom to marry foreigners has been abridged by some nations, and immigration restrictions having this effect are not uncommon.

I have already mentioned churches in connection with employment. But the existence of organizations with special purposes seems quite generally to raise a question about the intent of nondiscrimination principles; for do not organizations routinely distinguish between members and non-members, persons who share their goals and persons who do not? And why on earth shouldn't they — indeed, how could they not do so? But that is just the point. A clear principle distinguishing between all these myriad cases of intentionally prejudicial bestowing of important benefits and the ones popularly frowned upon as discriminatory is what we need and, it seems to me, do not have.

11. A Note on Utilitarianism

Those who have felt that nondiscrimination is a basic right have often, I think, supposed that it is a right which exceeds the reach of utilitarianism. Partly for this reason, it is of some interest to observe that, while it is, if the foregoing arguments are as strong as I am so far persuaded they are, extremely difficult to find a plausible deep principle going beneath the level of utilitarian considerations, it is not difficult to give a pretty plausible account of our practices and currently professed principles in utilitarian terms. For one thing, the distinction between private and public in the hiring arena, which figures strongly in the foregoing, does not have all that much status for the utilitarian. From his point of view, one might say *all* activities are "public" in the sense that the public has a legitimate interest in how they are carried on. If there is to be a private

sector at all, from that point of view, it is because the public interest is served better by making some things private. That the wealth of a society is promoted by private enterprise, if true, is certainly important and creates a presumption in favor of private enterprise; but then, in cases where it is not so promoted, the utilitarian has no scruples about putting it back in the hands of the public. And if some other important public interest besides wealth comes into the picture, then the utilitarian will simply consider whether this other interest is sufficient to outweigh the lost prosperity resulting from catering to it, if indeed that is what would happen.

What other utilities might be at stake? Prominent among them, surely, are two, or perhaps two sides of a single one. First, there is the sheer fact that those discriminated against *feel* badly done by. If the public is upset by a certain practice — or indeed, if a smallish minority is upset by it, given that it is upset enough — then that creates at least some presumption in favor of altering the practice. And secondly, it is fair to argue that discriminatory practices, particularly in areas of such substantial concern to people as hiring, are socially divisive, as was noted in section 3 above. If sizable groups of people are clamoring for advancement, while others characteristically are preferred in those respects, even at some cost in efficiency, then the tendency will be for bad feeling to exist between the groups in question, and we may expect trouble. The fact that we can't identify, in principle and in general, any characteristics and range of practices such that the doing of those things to people with those characteristics and the nondoing of them to people without them is fundamentally wrong doesn't matter all that much; if we can deal with the situation pretty effectively with rather vague and unsatisfactorily messy principles, that is better than ignoring the problem.

It is to be expected, if utilitarianism is our guide, that there will be no stable list of Discriminanda such that nondiscrimination principles would always be stated in terms of them, nor any particular social context, such as hiring, where the wrongness of discrimination is permanently to be abhorred. It will depend on social conditions. Fifty years from now, perhaps some quite new contexts, new Discriminanda, will be where the focus of concern falls. And if we are interested in capturing current "intuitions" and predicting the way things will go, this aspect of utilitarianism seems likely to stand us in pretty good stead.

But there are some shortcomings. Naturally, the basic status of utilitarianism itself is one of them. Nor is it evident that the whole job to be done is to account for current practices; and if currently held beliefs are what are to be accounted for, then there is the widespread feeling that the right to non-discrimination does not wait upon social interest for its confirmation to consider: is that part of what is to be accounted for, or isn't it? More importantly, however, is that it seems to me questionable what the real outcome of utilitarianism is on such issues. To see this, we need to distinguish between two views about the operation of utilitarianism, or perhaps about its application. We might call these the "crude" versus the "sophisticated" form. The crude variety, which I have tacitly appealed to above, has it that we weigh any old interest, however derived. If interests in strawberry jam count, and interests in Mahler symphonies, so do interests in wife-beating, in keeping up with the Joneses, and in one's neighbors all being attired in identical seersucker suits. The sophisticated type, however, does not easily allow such interests to count, or discounts them as compared with others. If interests in others' having such-and-such interests count, and if interests in others having such-and-such relations to oneself count equally, that seems to make way for the kind of objections to utilitarianism trotted out in the standard textbooks and Introductions to Philosophy. And the difficulty is that it seems that the kind of interests catered to in non-discrimination principles are of that kind. In order to get very much weight behind the thesis that social utility will be further enhanced by A's electing to have B work for him rather than C, despite the fact that he'd prefer to have C, we have to attach a good deal of weight to the intensity of B's feelings of indignation at not being equally considered by A, and more weight to the fuss which will be caused by the objections of B's cohorts, etc. If, on

the other hand, we simply attend to what appears to be the fact, that whichever A hires, A will be doing that person a favor, but if he hires the one he likes he will in addition create more utility for himself, then it is unclear that we should allow the further fact that B doesn't like the situation to count.

It is characteristic of utilitarianism that once one sees that there are competing sources of utility to take into account, and these are not easily estimated, the argument could be taken either way. And often, the very utility being counted is due to the pre-existing moral beliefs of the persons involved. If B had the attitude that A has a perfect right to hire whomever he pleases, there wouldn't *be* the various political utilities to which the argument of crude utilitarianism appeals. And this means that utilitarianism may not be of much use in this matter after all.

12. And a Note on Contractarianism

Another of the most important theoretical bases for social philosophy to have been taken seriously in recent times, as well as times past, is the suggestion that the principles of justice are the principles for the structuring of society which would be accepted by rational individuals on a long-term basis, or perhaps an impartial one. Indeed, I would be inclined to argue this way myself. But some who have been of this persuasion have evidently supposed that principles of nondiscrimination are among those which would most fundamentally be opted for in this way; and unfortunately, I fail to see that this is obvious.

Presumably a main source of the view that non-discrimination would have such a status is the fact, which is not in dispute here, that the fundamental principles chosen would be, so to speak, color-blind (and sex-blind, etc.). Unfortunately, as has been in effect argued above, this is very far from supporting the very strong principles which are here being questioned. For it is one thing to say that the fundamental principles of morality will not favour any groups as compared with any other (except, of course, that it will disfavour those who don't comply with them), and quite another to say that those principles will require individuals not to favour other individuals on the basis of sex, color, race, religion, taste in wines, or whatever, when it comes to doing good things for them. When we are contracting for general rights, after all, we are contracting to give up certain liberties. The strategy of contractualism is to pick out those liberties which we are better off giving up, and thus to argue that the rational person will be prepared to do so, in exchange for certain benefits which cannot be had without giving up those liberties. In the case of the liberty to kill, or in general to inflict harms on people, it is plausible to argue that the advantage of being free from such depredations at the hands of others will outweigh, in any even modestly longish run, the disadvantage of giving up the liberty to commit them oneself. But it is a different story when what is at issue is how one is to dispose of one's various positive assets, one's capacity to benefit others. Here it is *not* plausible to argue that every rational person *must* find it to his or her advantage to forego the liberty to decide who will be the beneficiary of such activities, in return for the benefit of being assured of having an equal chance, along with others who differ in various respects, of winding up as the beneficiary of some other people's similar activities.

It has been the habit of Rawls and of theorists persuaded by his general views to speak rather vaguely about opportunities for realizing the benefits which one's 'society' has to offer. The trouble with this, as Nozick was at pains to argue, is that it seems to assume that society is a kind of organized club with certain rather specific purposes which all members in good standing must be interested in promoting, and having a variety of assets at its disposal for the promotion of these purposes. But since this is fairly obviously not so, and fairly obviously therefore not something which we can simply assume, it is clear that one would have to argue for the claim that everyone *ought* to look at it that way. And I don't see how such an argument is to go through in general. But 'in general' is what we are talking about here. It is not to the point to

observe that many people would see advantage in so viewing the matter; for manifestly some would not, and given that that is so, there is surely no prospect of a general agreement, reaching to all rational persons, on the point.

Even if we suppose that some progress along that line is possible, there is a further problem about the relevance of our results to the present issue. Suppose, for instance, that we can make some kind of case for, say, an assured minimal income for all — already an extremely implausible assumption. But still, although that would, by the reasoning of section 6 above, provide the basis for nondiscrimination in the administration of the program for securing that minimum to all, it does not seem possible that it would provide a basis for nondiscrimination as between candidates for very high-paying positions, or even most positions. Presumably the minimum must be set somewhere below the average income from employment, and then we have the question of why everyone's entitlement to this minimum should carry with it an entitlement to nondiscrimination at any of the levels above it.

Most contractualist arguments about social minima *et al* in any case run up against another problem. If people were so interested in security, including the particular kinds of security which nondiscrimination laws provide, why wouldn't they buy into insurance which provided that kind of security? Or form clubs whose members would agree to boycott those who practiced the types of discrimination they wished to avoid? Why, in short, are the kinds of benefits which nondiscrimination presumably provides of a type which justifies coercive methods for seeing to it that *all* persons avoid practicing the types of discrimination in question — not only those who do see it as a benefit, but also those who see it as just the reverse? Given contractarian premises, one would have thought that if one has one's choice between enabling some good to be brought about by voluntary efforts among those who want it and a system of imposing it by force, if need be, on all alike, the former would be preferable. When we disagree, the rational thing for us both to do is agree to disagree — *not* agree that something called 'society' will declare one of us out of bounds and impose the other's view on him willy-nilly.

13. A Note on Logic

The principal argument in the foregoing effort to establish that the foundations of our attitudes toward discrimination are insecure and obscure has been of the following general form: We do not (it is admitted) have any obligation to do anything of the kind in question — appointing to a position, say — to anybody at all; so why do we have an obligation not to do it to one person rather than another? If I don't owe *anybody* a certain benefit, x, how is it that I can owe it to everyone that if I do give it to some person other than he, it will not be because he has certain properties but rather because he has certain others? If I owe it to no one at all, then why can't I give it to whomever I please, since the option is to give it to nobody whatever?

The question arises how we are to formulate the principle thus implicitly appealed to. Very generally, no doubt, the idea is that found in Hobbes, to the effect that "Obligation and Liberty . . . in one and the same matter are inconsistent." However, there is the question of specifying the 'matter' in question. Perhaps it is the case that even though I have no obligation to do x to A or to B, I have an obligation to do it to A in preference to B if at all, because in doing x to B I would not simply be doing x, but also something else, y, which is forbidden. The trouble is, though, that in the foregoing I have argued that the cases in which there clearly is this other description of my act, this other fact about it, in virtue of which it is obligatory on me not to do it, we have what I called "non-basic" discrimination, and this, I observed, doesn't seem to be sufficient to account for standard attitudes and practices on this subject. Were it the case that, in declining to give the job to A, one also hit him over the head or heaped insults upon him, that would be wrong; but that is not the behavior at issue. It is felt that it is wrong to decline to give it to A at all, if A is in fact "better qualified" than B and one simply prefers to have B for extraneous reasons such as that one simply likes B, or people like B in certain respects, better than A or people like A in certain respects.

A slightly formalized representation of the principle behind the argument would go, perhaps, something like this:

(1) A's preferring B to C in context H consists in A's doing x to B rather than to C, if at all.

(2) A's being obliged to prefer B to C in context H = A's being obliged to do x to B rather than C, if at all.

(3) A's not being obliged to do x at all = A's not being obliged to do x to any person whatever, for any reason; i.e., there is no class of persons such that A is obliged to do x to any member of that class.

(4) Context H involves some purpose, P, such that pursuit of P would give a reason to prefer B to C.

(5) But A has no obligation to pursue P *at all*. (If P were obligatory, then A would have some obligation to do x to someone, if available. But by hypothesis, A has no such obligation.)

(6) Therefore (by 5), A has no obligation to prefer anyone to anyone with respect to x; and hence not to prefer B to C.

If this is right, then it also appears that there is no such thing as obligatory *basic* nondiscrimination. If we were obliged to prefer one person to another *vis-à-vis* doing of some act x, that would imply that we had some obligation to do x, or pursue some purpose such that x promoted it, though other acts y could be done instead, or in general to perform kinds of acts of which x was an example.

Do we think this to be so? I am hard put to decide, but let us consider a few examples. Many of us would accept a general obligation to treat our children equally, for instance: if we have some limited resource — money, for instance — which we can devote to promoting their welfare, we feel some obligation to divide that resource equally, or in such a way as to promote their respective welfares equally. True: but it is also true that we have an obligation to promote their welfare *at all*. How much is, of course, not entirely easy to say, but suppose that we say we are to promote each child's welfare maximally within some limit. If we have this for *each* of them, and the resources are only sufficient for some level short of what we would ideally like, then it is readily concluded that we should split the resource more or less equally, or aim at equal welfares. But if we had no such obligation at all, it is hard to see how any of them could reasonably complain if he or she were always passed over in favor of others.

In general, it seems to me that the claim to *equal treatment* rests on an assumption that there are equal *claims to that kind of treatment*; and hence, that there *are* claims to that kind of treatment. The right to *equal opportunity*, in particular, rests on an assumed *right to opportunity*. In the absence of the latter, it is hard to see how we can make much sense of the former.

14. A Note on Prejudice

One final matter should be mentioned. Very often, certainly, treatment of different large groups that is markedly unequal in the various respects we have in mind when we talk of 'discrimination' is based on beliefs about the relative merits of those different groups. When those beliefs are without foundation, we bring in the notion of 'prejudice', of judging people's merits before we actually know the relevant facts — if any. The subject of prejudice invites special comment; and doubtless some, though I think not all, of the prevailing beliefs about discrimination are accounted for on the basis of their relation to it. The following observations seem especially pertinent here.

(1) We must bear in mind that not all discrimination will be due to prejudice. Perhaps Brown doesn't believe that all X-ians are shiftless, immoral, or whatever: he may simply not much care for X-ians, or he may care for members of his own race (etc.) more. There is a difference between an attitude based on an unreasoned or baseless belief, on the one hand, and on no belief at all, on the other.

(2) When the attitudes in question are based on beliefs, those beliefs are, of course, capable of being

rationally appraised. Now sometimes — we ought to recognize — they might be based on pretty decent evidence. It may not be obvious that the different races, sexes, etc. do have the same degree of allegedly relevant properties. Possibly it is a matter on which reasonable people may differ. Where this is so, it is at least clear that one cannot convict, say, an employer who turns out to employ a quite different percentage of X-ians from that which X-ians bear to the whole population, of discrimination straight off. Perhaps the X-ians *are* a lot better, or a lot worse, at that sort of job than the average other person. (Obviously there might still be discrimination, for perhaps the employer follows a policy of not even considering non-Xians, when in fact a modest percentage of them are better at the job than a lot of X-ians. This raises further questions, prominent among them being how much trouble an employer could reasonably be required to go to to test persons directly rather than going by obvious qualities, such as sex, which are quite well correlated with them.) At any rate, the point is that we cannot assume *a priori* that various abilities and whatnot are distributed in a population independently of the popular discriminanda; it simply isn't an *a priori* matter.

(3) Even where it is quite clear that prejudice is at work, there are two questions to raise about it. In the first place, there is the question whether it is right to persecute people for their beliefs. We do not do so, or at least we profess to believe that we have no right to do so, in the case of religious beliefs, even though those beliefs are always, strictly speaking, baseless, and even though they often lead to very substantial kinds of discriminatory treatment. In the second place, and more important at least in practice, there is the fact that once the foundations, or lack of them, of a belief are out in the open where critics can assail them, it is not easy to maintain that belief with a perfectly straight face for very long. Why should we assume so readily that the proper way to deal with actions based on beliefs we think are baseless, illogical, or confused is by making laws against those actions? We can hardly think that generally appropriate. Do we not, after all, have a pretty well-grounded suspicion that most people's

practical beliefs are baseless, illogical, and/or confused? (Including, it will doubtless turn out, most of our own?) And are we not agreed that one does not properly outlaw the entertaining of that belief: that in fact the proper way to deal with it is to *refute* it, much to the psychic stress of the person who holds it?

At the risk of being embarrassingly obvious, I would just note that if we were to take seriously the suggestion that it is unjust to hold baseless beliefs, then any principle of freedom of religion would evidently have to go by the boards. Most religions, after all, are almost self-consciously mysterious, and do not even pretend to offer sound reasons, persuasive to any rational being, for holding their main tenets. For all that, these beliefs are obviously dangerous. It takes little investigation of history to see that any number of wars, including perhaps most of the messier ones, have been fought partly or wholly on religious grounds. If the sort of prejudices often leading to discrimination are a public menace, surely religion is even more so. Yet which tenets of liberalism have pride of place over religious freedom?

It may be urged that there is a difference between allowing someone to hold a belief and allowing him to act on it. Anyone seriously urging a strong principle of freedom of thought or of speech needs to make such a distinction, since otherwise he will find himself in the embarrassing position of having to allow any degree of iniquity whenever the agent in question does it on conscientious grounds. In those cases, of course, we need to establish the iniquitousness of the acts in question on independent grounds; and by and large, my argument in this paper has been that it is unclear that we have such grounds. Meanwhile, it in any case remains that employers frequently cannot be said to have clearly unreasonable grounds for their discriminatory beliefs; and when this is so, it is difficult to see how we could proceed against them on the ground that their beliefs were, as we in our wisdom have decreed, false. And on the other hand, we do allow people to act on their religious beliefs, within broad limits, and those beliefs don't have nearly so much to be said for them as some of the beliefs on which prejudices are based.

There is one particular kind of prejudice-supporting belief of which we may, I would agree, make a special case. This is the kind which consists in holding that certain groups of people are, without further explanation, "morally inferior". A belief so expressed might, of course, be an empirically based one, to the effect that the incidence of certain standardly recognized types of immoral behavior is greater in that group than in others — which in any case, of course, would not in fact justify across-the-board discrimination against members of that group. But the case I have in mind does not involve an explicable belief of that kind. It consists instead of simply holding that the group in question is not morally deserving of normally good treatment or of ordinary rights. Such a belief, we may certainly agree, is not only unintelligible but also immoral. It is unintelligible because it requires that there be a special, empirically undetectable property or set of properties that render their possessors eligible for inclusion in the moral community, and it is in principle erroneous to suppose that there is any such feature or features. And it is immoral because it would make it impossible for an accused person to defend himself against the "charge" of "inferiority" of that kind, even though its purpose is to justify the kind of treatment that is only properly administered to persons guilty of genuinely immoral behavior. But as with the kind of beliefs discussed previously, it must again be pointed out that persons engaging in that kind of treatment of others without a supportable charge of that kind are themselves guilty of violating the rights of others. What is wrong with the behavior in question is not that that is its motive, and it is unclear that the motive in question *adds* to the iniquity of the behavior. But certainly the spreading of such "beliefs", since it *can* only be used to promote evil behavior, may be condemned strongly enough.

15. Summary

The thesis of this essay is that the case for regarding discrimination, properly so called, as an injustice has not been clearly supported in western thought, despite its enormous impact on western practice. "Discrimination properly so called" marks an essential distinction here, for much discriminatory behavior, termed 'non-basic' in the foregoing, is undoubtedly wrong but not wrong by virtue of being discriminatory: killing or injuring people who are innocent of any morally sustainable crime is wrong, whatever the motive. But that leaves a great deal that *is* "properly so called", where the discrimination consists only in treating some people less well than others, and doing so for a reason that is not morally relevant, in the strong sense of that term in which a morally relevant distinction morally requires a corresponding distinction in treatment. Not giving one person rather than another a job in a company of which you are the owner, and where your reason for preferring the other has nothing to do with competence at that job, is an example. What is anomalous about classifying such behaviour as unjust, I have argued, is that there seems to be no *duty* to give anyone the job, in general; how, then, can it be unjust not to give it to one person rather than another? That is the central puzzle, and it seems to me to remain unanswered.

Cases can be made for the wrongness of what is ordinarily called discrimination on indirect grounds having to do with social harmony and the like. But such cases, unlike what can be said in the case of non-basic discrimination, run up against a serious barrier, *viz.*, the principle of liberty. To require persons to perform all sorts of actions despite the fact that the actions they might instead prefer are not literally harmful to anyone is surely to violate their liberty. It has been assumed throughout that that is a serious point against any requirement or prohibition, and perhaps some would be inclined to deny that it is. Arguing against those people would get us into another essay, and thus I let the case rest at this point.

ENDNOTES

1. In private conversation with G.A. Cohen.
2. Henry Sidgwick, *The Methods of Ethics*, 7th ed. (Indianapolis/Cambridge: Hackett, 1981), p. 379.

28

The Affirmative Action Debate and Conflicting Conceptions of Individuality

MARY E. HAWKESWORTH

. . . In this paper I shall attempt to demonstrate that the intensity of this debate among scholars and jurists committed to constitutionalism, justice and the protection of individual rights is related to divergent assumptions about the fundamental nature of individuality. I shall argue that two different conceptions of individuality replete with presuppositions about the nature of individual identity and individual freedom, the relationship of the individual to other people, to social groups and to impersonal forces, underlie the arguments of proponents and opponents of Affirmative Action. I shall attempt to show that the proponents of Affirmative Action tacitly adopt a conception of 'socialized individualism' which emphasizes the impact of cultural norms and group practices upon the development of individual identity and the pervasive influence of internal as well as external obstacles to individual freedom; while opponents of Affirmative Action adopt a model of 'atomistic individualism' which assumes that identity is a matter of individual choice and will — unconstrained by racial, sexual, or cultural experiences — and which posits a conception of freedom as simply the absence of external coercion. I shall further argue that the tacit acceptance of these divergent conceptions of individuality influences the very capacity to perceive the existence of discrimination . . . and hence, affects the assessment of the need for a remedy and of the propriety of Affirmative Action as such a remedy. Finally, having demonstrated the importance of these conceptions of individuality as a foundation for the moral and constitutional arguments concerning Affirmative Action and indeed, for the very perception of the existence of a problem of discrimination, I shall examine the theoretical adequacy of these two models of individuality in an effort to assess the merits of several arguments central to the Affirmative Action debate.

From "The Affirmative Action Debate and Conflicting Conceptions of Individuality," by Mary Hawkesworth. *Women's Studies International Forum*, Vol. 7, No. 5. © 1984. Reprinted by permission of Pergamon Press, Ltd., Oxford.

CONFLICTING CONCEPTIONS OF INDIVIDUALITY

'Individualism' as a social doctrine asserts the moral primacy of the individual in society and recognizes the right of the individual to freedom and self-realization. Yet, what it means to be an individual, the processes by which individual identity is constituted, the nature of the individual's relation to other people and to social institutions, the scope and depth of self-realization, may be topics of debate among those equally committed to the protection of individualism. Those who incorporate a conception of atomistic individualism within their work and those who adopt a conception of socialized individualism are equally committed to the protection and enhancement of individual freedom. They differ, however, in their understandings of the constitution of individual identity and the elements of individual liberty.

The atomistic conception posits the individual as radically independent, in the sense that the individual exists as a self-contained entity, impervious to history, culture or society, motivated solely by appetites or aversions which are subjectively determined and unalterable. Individuals differ from one another both in the objects they desire and in the amount of effort which they expend to satisfy their desires. Although a scarce supply of most goods dictates that competition will characterize the relations among individuals and that the outcome of such competition will be zero-sum, all individuals are endowed with fairly equal capacities and as such, all have an equal opportunity to emerge victorious from the throes of competition. Given the assumption of fairly equal natural assets, differences in outcomes can be attributed solely to variations in individual effort. But because intensity of effort is a matter of individual choice and because an individual who chooses to work hard can hardly be faulted for achieving a great deal, the unequal outcome of the competitive process is morally justifiable. Success is a function of individual initiative and effort and is, consequently, deserved.

The atomistic conception of the individual envisions self-realization as the satisfaction of sub-jectively determined desires. To achieve this goal individuals must devote their energies toward the achievement of success through competition. Precisely because scarcity and competition are accepted as given, obstacles to self-realization are defined solely in terms of external constraints intentionally imposed by other human beings. Thus the individual is free in the absence of the willful coercion of other persons. According to the perspective of atomistic individualism, human freedom is not incompatible with subjection to objective forces external to the individual as long as these objective forces are 'impersonal', such as the products of the market's 'Invisible Hand'. Although the market is acknowledged to be a stern task master, its functioning is deemed essential to the distribution of economic rewards on the basis of individual effort. Individuals are free to reap the rewards of their hard work if, and only if, the market distribution is safeguarded. Moreover, the only alternative to the market according to this view, is the arbitrary command of some self-serving decision-maker which would undermine the very possibility of freedom.

> Man in a complex society can have no choice between adjusting himself to what seems to be the blind forces of the social process and obeying the orders of a superior. So long as he knows only the hard discipline of the market, he may well think the direction by some other human brain preferable; but when he tries it, he soon discovers that the former still leaves him at least some choice, while the latter leaves him none and that it is better to have a choice between several unpleasant alternatives than being [sic] coerced into one. (Hayek, 1948: 24).

When the options available to individuals are construed this narrowly, either subordination to the command of a fallible decision-maker or open competition with the prospect of unlimited success, it is clear that only the latter sustains a conception of meaningful freedom. Thus it is not surprising that the market is depicted as a precondition of freedom, 'so essential that it must not be sacrificed to the gratification of our sense of justice or of envy'

(Hayek, 1948: 24). Within the parameters of the atomistic conception then, the individual is 'self-made': identity is a function of individual desire, will and effort; freedom is simply the power to do or forbear according to one's subjectively determined appetites or aversions unconstrained by other human beings; and self-realization is nothing more than success in the competition for necessarily scarce goods. The individual alone is responsible for choices made, for effort invested and for the outcomes achieved, be they successes or failures. Impersonal forces mediate the competition among individuals but because they cannot be controlled by humans and because they affect all individuals in the same neutral way, they cannot be considered to be constraints upon individual freedom. Impersonal forces may establish the rules of the game but it is individual effort which determines the outcome.

The conception of socialized individuality is premised upon an image of society and culture as a 'complex web of values, norms, roles, relationships and customs which do not merely confront the individual as external barriers or constraints but which are internalized by individuals' (Weaver, 1980: 197), shaping their self-understanding, their interests and their desires. The individual's identity, expectations and aspirations are formed within the context of a host of intersubjective understandings incorporated in a language, a culture, and a particular history. Whether described as a process of socialization or enculturation, individuals are taught determinate ways of being human. Although individuals are not merely passive recipients of cultural norms, their options for response to existing patterns of interaction are circumscribed by the range of possibility incorporated in the existing cultural universe. Any individual may choose to perpetuate or repudiate dominant cultural values, but no individual can escape altogether the legacy of membership in a particular community within a particular nation at a particular point in history.

The conception of socialized individualism suggests that freedom involves a great deal more than absence of coercion. The individual's capacity to act freely, to choose certain options, to undertake particular risks may be undermined by the internalization of images, insults and stigmas associated with group membership. The inculcation of cultural, ethnic, racial, or sexual norms may constitute formidable internal obstacles to individual freedom. The very meaning of self-realization may be unduly constricted by the tacit incorporation of derogatory stereotypes within the individual's self-understanding.

In addition to recognizing that certain cultural values may limit the range of individual freedom, the conception of socialized individuality suggests that 'impersonal' or 'objective' forces may also constitute an enormous impediment to personal liberty. Rather than accepting that 'impersonal' forces such as market mechanisms are a necessary evil which people must accept if they desire any freedom whatsoever, the conception of socialized individualism admits the possibility that human agency may underlie 'objective' forces. The 'Invisible Hand' can be conceived as a cultural creation which serves the interests of some to the detriment of others. Once conceived as cultural constructs, market mechanisms too can be considered targets for political action. If particular human actions responsible for the 'blind forces of the social process' could be identified, then it is possible that the intended and unintended consequences of such behavior could be isolated and altered. The modification of individual action in order to eliminate deleterious social consequences could thereby enhance the prospects for individual freedom. The perspective of socialized individualism then acknowledges individual identity, as well as the conceptions of personal liberty and 'objective' forces, to be social products, shaped by the beliefs and values of the prevailing culture. While such cultural constructs circumscribe the possibilities for individual choice and action, they are not invariable; they can themselves become the target for systematic criticism and reform. Existing beliefs and values may narrow the range of choice available to individuals, but they cannot foreclose choice or change altogether.

In the following sections of this paper, I shall

attempt to demonstrate that various arguments against Affirmative Action incorporate the conception of atomistic individuality, while arguments in favor of this policy are informed by a conception of socialized individuality. I shall argue that these conflicting conceptions of individuality color not only the moral and constitutional arguments which opponents or proponents of Affirmative Action advance, but they also shape the most fundamental perception of the 'facts' of the case, that is, the perception of the existence of discrimination as a social problem in the late twentieth century. . . .

ATOMISTIC INDIVIDUALISM AND THE REJECTION OF AFFIRMATIVE ACTION

A recurrent theme among opponents of Affirmative Action is the denial that discrimination in hiring, wage scales, promotion and admissions currently exists. . . . While they acknowledge that 'Blacks as a group earned less than Whites as a group, and women as a group earned less than men as a group and both minorities and women were a smaller percentage of the academic and other professions than of the general population' (Sowell, 1977: 119), they deny that the explanation of these facts lies in employer/admissions officers' deliberate discrimination. They suggest that a combination of two factors, personal choices made by individuals of their own free will and objective forces over which discrete individuals have no control, provide a more adequate explanation of these phenomena. Arguing that the inference that gross racial/sex differentials in admissions, employment, pay, and promotion reflect a deliberate policy of exclusion cannot be validly drawn from 'superficial, raw and uninterpreted statistical data concerning the relative distribution of members of minorities and women' (Hook, 1977: 89), opponents of Affirmative Action suggest that the problem of underrepresentation does not reflect discrimination against qualified applicants, but rather reflects the fact that women and minorities lack the requisite qualifications and therefore fail to apply. The problem is primarily one of inadequate supply of qualified

women and minority applicants, not one of demand hampered by willful discrimination (Lester, 1974). In its most extreme form this view claims that not only are there too few qualified women and minority applicants in general, but also that women and minority applicants who are hired in academia for example, are less qualified than their white male colleagues.

> Blacks or female academics have a Ph.D. less than half as often as the rest of the profession, publish less than half as many articles per person and specialize in the lowest paying fields — notably education, the social sciences and the humanities, with very few being trained in the natural sciences, medicine, law or other highly paid specialities. Thus even if no employer had a speck of prejudice, black and female academics would still have lower pay and promotion prospects (Sowell, 1977: 119–120).

It is lack of qualifications which impair the employment potential of women and minorities, not discrimination.

Two themes are reiterated in explanations of the lack of qualifications among women and minorities: individual choice and objective forces. Empirical evidence is said to indicate that women and minority individuals freely choose career patterns which differ from those of white males and 'this crucial element of individual choice is routinely ignored in syllogistic arguments that go directly from statistical "underrepresentation" to "exclusion" or "discrimination"' (Sowell, 1977: 129). A second approach to the explanation of lack of qualifications suggests that these deficiences may stem from either the 'lack of equitable social, economic and educational stimuli or opportunities, for which the entire community must accept the blame' (Hook, 1977: 90) or from the 'pervasive effect of social attitudes' concerning the proper role of women and minorities, both of which can be subsumed under the category of objective forces. But whether social attitudes or the absence of social, economic and educational opportunities is responsible for the dearth of qualified female and minority applicants, Affirmative Action is clearly a misguided and inappropriate remedy.

Affirmative Action is designed as a social policy to end intentional discrimination in admission, employment, pay, promotion, etc. Since any underrepresentation which currently exists can at best be described as the unintended consequence of social attitudes and is not related to any deliberate policies of discrimination, the disease and the cure are mismatched. The basic lack of correspondence between problem and solution stems from the failure to draw an important distinction between problems caused by deliberate individual actions, which are susceptible to solutions aimed at specific individuals, and problems caused by impersonal/objective social forces for which no individual can justly be held accountable. Imbued with the perspective of atomistic individualism, critics of Affirmative Action argue that since the lack of requisite qualifications is the unfortunate consequence of pervasive social attitudes, it falls under the category of 'objective forces' which lie beyond the scope of political remedies. Solutions to problems rooted in impersonal social processes are extraordinarily complex and elusive and unfortunately, political efforts to implement them frequently degenerate into hapless social engineering which strips individuals of their freedom and autonomy. If individual freedom is not to be sacrificed, the most acceptable remedies for problems caused by objective forces must be recognized to be time and education: with time and increasing education, social attitudes can be expected to change. As attitudes change even unintentional discrimination will be relegated to the museum of antique relics. Education is a comprehensive remedy which can influence the values and choices of the entire community. Furthermore, as the level of education of all community members is raised, the educational level and hence, the qualifications, of women and minority group members will simultaneously be raised, thereby eliminating the inadequate supply of qualified female and minority applicants. Affirmative Action, on the other hand, is a thoroughly inappropriate remedy for a problem caused by impersonal social forces for it arbitrarily imposes responsibility for a collective problem upon specific individuals; it requires preferential treatment for 'unqualified' women and minority group applicants and consequently, it discriminates in reverse against the 'best qualified' candidates who just happen to be non-minority men. Such reverse discrimination is all the more intolerable because it is not the result of the market's 'Invisible Hand' but the clear manifestation of government bureaucrats' attempts to impose their vision of the good upon the society at large. The bureaucracy's usurpation of the 'power of judge, jury, accuser and patron combined' (Todorovich [Todorovich and Glickstein] 1977: 34) places universities and employers in the position of having to placate federal officials under penalty of loss of federal contracts vital to their very survival. Thus bureaucratic whim becomes a tyrannical task master which strips would-be federal contractors of their autonomy and their fidelity to standards of pure meritocratic excellence.

Having diagnosed the cause of underrepresentation as an insufficient supply of qualified women and minority applicants, opponents of Affirmative Action insist that Affirmative Action is synonymous with reverse discrimination: government policies necessitate the use of 'quotas', the hiring of less qualified candidates, the obliteration of merit as a criterion of desert and consequently, the sacrifice of creative, hardworking individuals. Since qualified women and minority applicants are not available according to this analysis of the facts, it follows that school administrators and employers must engage in all these abuses in order to increase the number of women and blacks in their institutions as a demonstration to the government of their 'good faith'. Giving less qualified women and minority group members preference in admissions, hiring and promotion can only result in new forms of discrimination which will entail 'the erosion of the principles of merit, scholarly quality and integrity . . . which is not only unconstitutional, but immoral, for it makes a mockery of the principle of desert which was the basis of denunciation of past discriminatory practices.' (Hook, 1977: 90).

Opponents of Affirmative Action also argue that it is naive to believe that reverse discrimination can remedy the current effects of past discrimination;

on the contrary, they assert that it can only create further injustices:

> The belief that discrimination can be administered to the body politic in judicious doses in order to create non-discrimination is akin to the medical wisdom of curing an alcoholic with whiskey. Discrimination is addictive. Its use cannot be precisely controlled ... (It is wrong) to imagine that one discrimination can compensate for another. Discrimination causes individuals to suffer. If they can be individually compensated, well and good. But compensating their grandchildren at the cost of discriminating against someone else does not compensate them in the slightest. It does replace private discrimination (or at least supplement it) with public discrimination, sanctioned by the laws. It also sets up another imaginary debt for the social engineer, whose successors will one day have to compensate the grandchild of the one victimized today, at the expense of the one benefited today (Todorovich [Todorovich and Glickstein] 1977: 37 -38).

These objections to reverse discrimination express the belief of many opponents of Affirmative Action that in the absence of deliberate discriminatory policies in the contemporary United States, the only possible moral justification for the government's policies is compensatory justice for groups. They suggest that 'the entire early federal Affirmative Action drive was motivated and stimulated by the history of three hundred years of injustice against blacks. Only after the argument for reparation to blacks had prevailed as the single determining factor of overriding importance in justifying a temporary preferential treatment for aggrieved groups were the programs for minorities implemented. Women were added later.' (Hook, 1977: 20). Yet this concept of compensatory justice to groups for past injustices suffered by them as groups is completely foreign to the notions of morality associated with atomistic individualism; not surprisingly then, opponents of reverse discrimination have little difficulty identifying sufficient deficiencies in the arguments for compensatory justice to sustain its rejection.

The assault on compensatory justice for groups frequently begins with a brief reference to Aristotle who originally formulated the concept of compensatory justice as a rectifying or reparatory transaction between one person and another. The goal of corrective justice was to impose a penalty upon the party who inflicted the injury and confer a corresponding benefit upon the injured individual in order to restore the kind of equality which existed prior to the injury. Aristotle envisioned a close correspondence or proportionality between the harm suffered and the compensation received. Contemporary proponents of compensatory justice stray markedly from Aristotle's ideals; they insist upon blanket preferential treatment for certain persons on the basis of race, sex or minority group membership even if those persons did not personally suffer past injustices. Thus, preferential treatment for groups as a social policy is notoriously overinclusive. But it is simultaneously underinclusive, for, in providing compensation only for specific groups, it ignores the claims of other individuals who have personally suffered injustice, yet who are not members of the groups targeted for compensation. Furthermore, reverse discrimination imposes the cost of compensation upon individuals who did not perpetrate the injustice and who cannot fairly be dubbed beneficiaries of the injustice since they neither sought the benefit nor had the opportunity to reject it; in other words, reverse discrimination imposes the cost of compensation upon innocent parties. Thus reverse discrimination can be faulted as arbitrary both in the distribution of benefits to the disadvantaged and in the assignment of the costs of compensation (Blackstone, 1977). And such rampant arbitrariness seriously impairs its status as a persuasive moral argument or justification in that it substitutes concern with 'abstract groups and their purported rights' for concern with the atomistic individual; as such, it violates that 'essence of liberalism which has always been concerned with the welfare, rights and responsibilities of individuals *qua* individuals, not the masses or classes or other such linguistic abstractions (Nisbet, 1977: 52).

Those who accept the atomistic conception of

the individual cannot make sense out of the claims that certain groups have inflicted, and continue to inflict, sufferings upon other groups and that individuals experience injury as members of a distinctive group and therefore deserve to receive compensation as members of the group. Focusing solely upon individuals who 'make themselves', they reject any notion of a legacy of group injury, just as they reject any notion of collective guilt on the part of the group which historically imposed the suffering. They argue instead that preferential treatment for specific groups violates the 'spirit of the laws ... which assert that governments are created to assure individuals (not groups) the retention of their inalienable natural rights. . . .' (Todorovich [Todorovich and Glickstein] 1977: 38). To endorse a policy of preferential treatment for groups would be to subordinate individuals' rights to equal treatment to the broader social aim of making amends for a past injustice which they did not perpetrate, a policy which is clearly unconstitutional. According to the opponents of Affirmative Action, justice can require nothing more than the use of neutral principles, such as non-discrimination, in admissions and employment. Since deliberate discrimination is not a contemporary problem, the use of neutral principles will promote meritocratic decisions while simultaneously according justice to individuals regardless of the group to which they happen to belong. For it will allow each individual to 'make it' on his/her own. . . .

SOCIALIZED INDIVIDUALISM AND THE JUSTIFICATION OF AFFIRMATIVE ACTION

Proponents of Affirmative Action often introduce their arguments with the assertion that 'racial, sexual and no doubt other forms of discrimination are not antique relics but are living patterns which continue to warp selection and ranking procedures.' (Beauchamp, 1977: 90). Rather than assuming that the United States represents a just and primarily nondiscriminatory society, they suggest that empirical evidence supports the belief that

discrimination is currently widespread and that present discrimination differs from past discrimination only in the degree of subtlety and visibility. While this very subtlety makes present discrimination far more difficult 'to prove statistically', it renders the effects of discrimination no less pernicious. Acknowledging that statistics cannot provide decisive indicators of discrimination, proponents of Affirmative Action yet insist that the pervasiveness of statistical underrepresentation of women and minority groups in higher education, in higher paying employment and in positions of prestige and power is sufficient to establish a *prima facie* case of discrimination. But proponents of Affirmative Action do not rest their arguments concerning the persistence of discrimination upon a demonstration of underrepresentation alone, for as their opponents have argued, any number of variables can be introduced to explain such underrepresentation. Instead, they emphasize 'underutilization' in an effort to explode the myth that the principal cause of underrepresentation is the inadequate supply of qualified women and minority applicants. 'Underutilization is defined as having fewer members of the group in the category actually employed than would reasonably be expected from their availability, e.g. in universities, from the percentage of available Ph.D's in a given field' (Goldman, 1977: 194). The phenomenon to be explained, then, is not the dearth of minority or female professionals *per se*, but the dearth of such professionals given the availability of a certain percentage of qualified minority and female candidates. The pervasive underutilization of qualified women and minorities in the United States renders suspicious any explanation of the phenomenon which emphasizes personal choice. For it seems unlikely that individuals who have invested great effort to become qualified to apply for certain careers should suddenly choose not to pursue those professions.

Having challenged the adequacy of 'personal choice' and 'lack-of-qualified applicant' explanations of underrepresentation, proponents of Affirmative Action also challenge the assumption that all individuals have an equal opportunity to compete for economic and educational benefits in the contemporary United States, and that the differential rewards simply reflect differences in effort. Proponents of Affirmative Action argue that 'background conditions, such as unequal treatment relating to occupational preparation and expectations in the course of childhood, upbringing and education, ego development, psychological counseling, technical and higher education, etc., which would make it more difficult for women and nonwhites as a group than for white men as a group to succeed occupationally, are factors contributing to the denial of equal opportunity for occupational attainment' (Held, 1975: 33). In short, they argue that racist and sexist biases which pervade American culture establish a system of differential rewards which benefit certain individuals but not on the basis of neutral criteria of talent and effort. On this view, one great benefit of Affirmative Action's insistence that group results be considered stems from its demand 'that whites recognize that their own advantages are, in significant measure, group benefits, rather than individual achievements and that their own success has been, in part, a matter of their own superior group opportunities, purchased at the expense of opportunities for non-whites' (Livingston, 1979; 182). Opportunities accrue not to atomistic individuals but to individuals as members of particular families, particular communities, particular ethnic, racial and sexual groups.

Articulating the premises of socialized individualism, proponents of Affirmative Action emphasize that individual identity as well as preparation for educational and economic opportunities ordinarily develop within the confines of family life. 'The self-concept, life-style and careers of parents have a tremendous impact upon their children. Such factors greatly influence the home environment and in turn play a significant role in shaping a child's interests and motivations. The financial, intellectual and social resources accumulated by parents play a large role in determining the opportunities their children get' (Katzner, 1982: 75). To the extent that diet, housing, medical care, intellectual stimulation, cultural enrichment, and family connections can enhance the individual's chances for

success, mobility within the meritocracy is and will continue to be a function of luck in the birth lottery. Success will come more readily to the sons and daughters of the successful and disadvantage will remain a legacy to those born of the disadvantaged (Livingston, 1979: 120-128; Held, 1975; 33-34).

Proponents of Affirmative Action argue that racism and sexism may handicap minority and female applicants in a number of ways. Racist and sexist stereotypes may curb the expectations and aspirations of women and minorities. Disadvantaged backgrounds and inadequate education may make it more difficult for women and minorities to achieve particular goals than it is for a middle-class white male to achieve those same goals. But more importantly, when women, minorities and white males do achieve the same goals, racism and sexism may preclude recognition of the accomplishments as identical. The tendency to view women and minorities as less capable, less creative, less willing to work and less deserving of serious consideration and respect culminates in a refusal to acknowledge the merit of members of oppressed groups. Given identical qualifications or performance, psychologists have documented that 'there is a general tendency to give men more favorable evaluations than women' (Nieva and Gutek, 1980: 267-276) and to give whites more favorable evaluations than minorities. Moreover, 'there is psychological evidence to indicate that women and minority group members are systematically downgraded by school teachers (and graded higher when race or sex is unknown to the grader) . . . and that a woman's name on an assigned paper leads students to rate it lower than the same paper with a man's name on it' (Beauchamp, 1977: 110). Thus women and minorities experience a form of discrimination which is analytically distinct from the problems of under-representation and pay differentials (Hughes, 1975: 26). They are treated as beings less worthy of respect than the average white male, not because of any individual foible but simply because they are members of a particular group. The disrespect shown to women and minorities on the irrational basis of their sex, race or ethnicity highlights the fact that the competition for educational and economic opportunities is neither neutral nor fair, for women and minorities are judged by standards irrelevant to the competition (Livingston, 1979: 38). A tacit pro-white, pro-male bias in admissions and hiring procedures constitutes a form of discrimination which continues to harm women and minorities not because of their individual characteristics but because of their membership in particular groups. Thus, proponents of Affirmative Action, insist that:

> It is absurd to suppose that young blacks and women now of an age to apply for jobs have not been wronged. . . . It is only within the last 25 years (perhaps the last 10 years in the case of women) that it has become at all widely agreed in this country that blacks and women must be recognized as having, not merely this or that particular right normally recognized as belonging to white males, but all of the rights and respect which go with full membership in the community. Even young blacks and women have lived through down-grading for being black or female; they have not merely not been given that very equal chance at the benefits generated by what the community owns which is so firmly insisted on for white males, they have not until lately even been felt to have a right to it (Thompson, 1977: 36).

Discussions of continuing racist and sexist bias illuminate one other factor central to admissions and hiring procedures: neither the criteria employed nor the individuals employing them are neutral or 'impersonal'. It is not 'objective forces' which determine individual applicants' merit and prospects for success, but the decisions of fallible administrators. 'In the modern meritocracy, the process of selection is not made by nature or by Adam Smith's "Invisible Hand", but by admissions and personnel officers who apply cultural standards to applicants for admissions, appointment and promotion' (Livingston, 1979: 132). Thus, it is not 'blind social processes' which Affirmative Action must remedy, but rather the particular decisions of concrete individuals who serve as gatekeepers to the positions of power and privilege in contemporary society.

Given their diagnosis of the problem as on-going discrimination in the form of anti-minority, anti-female bias, those who accept the socialized conception of individuality suggest that Affirmative Action is a fair and appropriate remedy. As a mechanism for the cultivation of a 'mature recognition of the talent of all persons in society' (Pottinger, 1977: 49), Affirmative Action does not jeopardize principles of merit or standards of excellence; it simply prohibits situations in which 'the only ones allowed to demonstrate their "merit" are white males' (Glickstein [Todorovich and Glickstein] 1977:30). Through the establishment of fair hiring practices and competition open to public inspection, Affirmative Action ensures that 'men . . . compete fairly on the basis of merit, not fraternity; on demonstrated capability, not assumed superiority' (Pottinger, 1971). By focusing attention on admitting, hiring and promoting members of particular target groups, Affirmative Action draws attention to both the consequences of historic racism and sexism and to the extent, the gravity and the immediacy of the injuries still sustained by minorities and women. . . . (Livingston, 1979: 32).

Recognition of the tenacity of the presumption of racial and sexual superiority and of . . . pervasive discrimination . . . causes believers in socialized individualism to reject the claim that compensatory justice constitutes the only moral ground for the justification of social policies designed to ameliorate the conditions of women and minorities. They reject compensatory justice, in part, because it facilely perpetuates the myth that discrimination is a social atavism. Instead, they insist that the appropriate moral justification for contemporary programs to eliminate current discrimination lies in arguments for distributive justice. Both Affirmative Action and the more stringent policy of preferential treatment can promote the redistribution of income, power and prestige, reduce the distributive inequities which plague the present racist and sexist society and thereby enhance the freedom and the possibility for self-realization of women and minority group members. Concern with distributive justice focuses attention upon the crucial role which higher education performs in certifying individuals for positions of power and prestige. . . .

Affirmative Action and preferential treatment in admissions to higher education then is cast as one means by which to improve the employment prospects, income, status, security and chance for self-determination of women and minorities. Awareness of underutilization, of the truncated life prospects of women and minority group members who are qualified for but not employed in positions of power and prestige, however, cautions against too great a reliance upon Affirmative Action in educational opportunities as a remedy to racial and sexual discrimination. This awareness has culminated in the rejection of excessive reliance upon 'neutral' or 'color-blind' principles such as 'non-discrimination' as inadequate to accomplish the goals of distributive justice. For non-discrimination alone can make no assault upon the 'standards of excellence' devised by white middle-class males as admission criteria which have not been proven to have any direct relation to an individual's performance in a professional capacity but which have worked admirably to screen out minority candidates. . . .

Arguments on the grounds of distributive justice, therefore, justify not only Affirmative Action but also preferential treatment, emphasizing that without such stringent measures little progress will be made toward the elimination of racial and sexual inequality. The conception of socialized individuality allows a construction of the case for the legitimacy of preferential treatment which simultaneously recognizes that such a policy will cause white males to lose certain advantages, yet denies that the loss constitutes violation of individual rights. Socialized individualism suggests that the white men currently occupying favored positions in existing organizations have themselves been the beneficiaries of some preferential treatment: 'they are members of a group of persons who have been privileged in hiring and promotion in accordance with normal practices of long-standing, persons who have been offered better educational preparation than others of the same basic talents, persons

whose egos have been strengthened more than members of other groups' (Held, 1975: 34). Because these white males did not deserve such preferential treatment, because they had no right to the advantages afforded by a racist and sexist society, no rights are being violated by the removal of those advantages. Policies to promote justice for the victims of injustice may require that white men lose their unwarranted privilege in society but they do not strip these individuals of legitimate rights. . . .

THE DISPUTE LAID BARE

To this point, I have attempted to demonstrate that the dispute over the legitimacy of Affirmative Action involves more than a simple disagreement over the utility of a particular social policy; it reflects fundamental differences in the understanding of the nature of individual identity and freedom. Indeed, I have suggested that these basic conceptions of individuality so structure the interpretation of contemporary social life that the very capacity to perceive the existence of discrimination turns on the tacit acceptance of the socialized conception of individuality. It is important to stress that these conceptions operate at the tacit level, that most people are unaware of the influence of these presuppositions upon their perceptions and analyses of contemporary events and that this lack of awareness places these fundamental assumptions beyond examination and critical scrutiny. Now, there is more at stake in the explication of these divergent conceptions of individuality than a mere plotting of the conceptual terrain. For when these tacit assumptions about the nature of individuality are made explicit and subjected to critical assessment, it becomes clear that both conceptions are not equally capable of providing an adequate account of the formation and development of individual identity.

The atomistic conception of individuality misconstrues the individual's relation to self, others, society and tradition. In assuming that individual desires are subjectively determined, the atomistic conception overlooks the extent to which the individual's impressions, desires, sensations and aspirations are socially constructed, founded upon a host of intersubjective understandings incorporated in language, culture and tradition. The atomistic conception of the individual must deny the pervasive impact of history and culture upon the formation of individual identity if it is to retain its assumption concerning the radical independence of the individual and the primacy of choice and effort as determinants of individual success. Yet precisely this denial renders the atomistic ideal incapable of accounting for the ethno-cultural and historical diversity of individual personalities and self-understandings documented in anthropological and historical studies. The atomistic conception is at a loss to explain the shared values and valuations characteristic of distinct peoples, whether they be tribes, clans, nations, ethnicities, races, religions or genders. Moreover, in treating individual passions, appetites and desires as permanently fixed, the atomistic conception denies the individual's capacity to reflect upon, criticize and alter both desires and the behavior which is informed by those desires. In short, it denies what many philosophers have considered the essence of moral freedom. While this denial sustains platitudes such as, 'You can't change human nature,' which serve to challenge the efficacy of any political action designed to achieve social justice, its determinist roots drastically constrict both the meaning of and the possibility for individual freedom. The determinist underpinnings of the atomistic account of individual desire might well undermine the claim that choice and effort are the principle determinants of success. For a consistent determinism negates the possibility of choice and nullifies the effect of effort.

The atomistic conception of individuality is marred by its inability to provide an account of individual identity consistent with the empirical findings of anthropologists and historians and its theoretical foundations are endangered by the possibility of a logical contradiction. The prospects for future social policy founded upon atomistic assumptions are also problematic. For those who

build their political prescriptions upon the atomistic conception of individuality advocate the use of neutral principles as the sole constitutional remedy for racial and sexual inequality. If underrepresentations, underutilization and the irrational disrespect for women and minority individuals persist, on this view, they must be discounted as the private preferences of particular individuals or as the consequence of the inexorable workings of impersonal forces; in both instances they are beyond the scope of a political remedy. The atomistic prescription urges resignation to injustice as an inevitable aspect of the human condition. In denying the existence of culturally shared values, it denies the possibility that systematic racism or sexism can cripple the life prospects of entire groups of individuals. It renders humanity helpless in the face of grave social evils. It is ironic that the atomistic conception which flaunts a boundless confidence in the capacities of individuals to make anything of themselves as individuals simultaneously denies their capacity to achieve anything as a community.

It is time that the atomistic conception of the individual, replete with its empirical and theoretical defects and its overbearing pessimism concerning the possibility of collective choice and action be subjected to explicit criticism and public scrutiny. The implications which flow from the pervasive acceptance of the atomistic conception of individuality are manifest in the context of the Affirmative Action debate: the perpetuation of a systematic blindness to the pernicious consequences of racism and sexism, the toleration of racial and sexual inequality with an untroubled conscience, the denial of a wide range of opportunities to members of oppressed groups and the restriction of the sphere of freedom of the disadvantaged. Such policies challenge the authenticity of our commitment to the principles of liberty, equality and justice. Such policies should not be accepted as the only feasible political possibilities. Rigorous examination of the theoretical presuppositions of various policy prescriptions may contribute to the reconstitution of the very conception of political possibility.

ENDNOTES

Barasch, F.K. 1977. HEW., The University and women. In Gross, Barry R., ed. *Reverse Discrimination.* Prometheus Books, New York. Also published in *Dissent* (Summer, 1973).

Beauchamp, Tom L., ed. 1975. *Ethics and Public Policy.* Prentice-Hall, Englewood Cliffs, New Jersey.

Beauchamp, Tom L. 1977. The justification of reverse discrimination. In Blackstone, William T. and Robert D. Heslop, eds. *Social Justice and Preferential Treatment.* University of Georgia Press, Athens, Georgia.

Bernstein, Richard, 1976. *The Restructuring of Social and Political Theory.* Harcourt, Brace and Jovanovich, New York.

Blackstone, William T. 1977. Reverse discrimination and compensatory justice. In Blackstone, William T. and Robert D. Heslop, eds. *op. cit.*

Cohen, Marshall, Thomas Nagel and Thomas Scanlon. eds. 1976. *Equality and Preferential Treatment.* Princeton University Press, Princeton, New Jersey.

Dumont, L. 1965. The modern conception of the individual: notes on its genesis and that of concomitant institutions. *Contr. Indian Sociology* 8: 13-61.

Dumont, L. 1970. *Homo Hierarchicus: The Caste System and Its Implications* (trans. by Mark Sainsbury). Weidenfeld and Nicolson, London.

Dunn vs Blumstein. 1972. (405 U.S. 330).

Eisenstein, Zillah. 1981. *The Radical Future of Liberal Feminism.* Longman, New York.

Goldman, Alan H. 1976. Affirmative Action. In Cohen, Marshall, Thomas Nagel and Thomas Scanlon, eds. *op. cit.*

Gross, Barry, ed. 1977. *Reverse Discrimination.* Prometheus, Buffalo, New York.

Hayek, F.A. 1948. *Individualism and Economic Order.* University of Chicago Press, Chicago, Illinois.

Held, Virginia. 1975. Reasonable progress and self-respect. In Beauchamp, Tom L., ed. *Ethics and Public Policy.* Prentice-Hall, Englewood Cliffs, New Jersey.

Hobbes, Thomas. 1958. *Leviathan.* Bobbs-Merrill, New York.

Hook, Sidney. 1977. The bias of anti-bias regulations. In Gross, Barry R., ed. *op cit.* Also published in *Measure* 14 (October 1971).

Hughes, Graham. 1975. Reparations for Blacks. In Beauchamp, Tom L. ed. *op cit.*

Katzner, Louis. 1982. Reverse discrimination. In Regan, Tom and Donald Van de Veer, eds. *And Justice For All.* Rowman and Littlefield, Totowa, New Jersey.

Korematsu vs United States. 1944. (323 U.S. 214).

Lester, Richard. 1974. *Anti-Bias Regulations of Universities: Faculty Problems and Their Solutions.* McGraw-Hill, New York.

Lewis, Michael. 1978. *The Culture of Inequality.* New American Library, New York.

Lipset, Seymour M. and William Schneider, 1977. An emerging national consensus. *New Republic,* 177(16): 8-12 (October 15).

Livingston, John. 1979. *Fair Game: Inequality and Affirmative Action.* W.H. Freeman, San Francisco.

Lukes, Stephen. 1973. *Individualism.* Harper and Row, New York.

Macpherson, C.B. 1962. *The Political Theory of Possessive Individualism.* Clarendon Press, Oxford.

Nieva, Veronica and Barbara Gutek. 1980. Sex effects on evaluation. *Acad. Management Rev.* 5(2): 267-276.

Nisbet, Lee. 1977. Affirmative action—A liberal program? In Gross, Barry R. ed., *op. cit.*

Pottinger, J. Stanley. 1971. Come now, Professor Hook. *New York Times* CXXI: 29. (Saturday, December 18).

Pottinger, J. Stanley. 1972. The drive toward equality. In Gross, Barry R. ed., *op. cit.*

Price, Philip B., James N. Richards, Calvin W. Taylor and Tony L. Jacobsen. 1964. Measurement of physician performance. *J. Med. Educ.* 39: 203.

Regan, Tom and Donald Van de Veer, eds. 1982. *And Justice For All.* Rowman and Littlefield, Totowa, New Jersey.

Regents of the University of California vs Bakke. 1978. (438 U.S. 265; in *The United States Law Week* 46 LW 4896, June 27).

Sennett, Richard and Jonathan Cobb. 1972. *The Hidden Injuries of Class.* Alfred A. Knopf, New York.

Sleeth, Boyd C. and Robert Mishell, 1977. Black underrepresentation in United States Medical Schools. *New Engl. J. Med.* 297(21): 1146-1148 (November 24).

Sowell, Thomas. 1977. 'Affirmative Action' reconsidered. In Gross, Barry R., ed., *op cit.* Also published in *The Public Interest* (Winter 1976).

Thompson, Judith Jarvis. 1977. Preferential hiring. In

Cohen, Marshall, Thomas Nagel and Thomas Scanlon, eds. *op. cit.*

Todorovich, Miro M. and Howard Glickstein. 1977. Discrimination in Higher Education: a debate on faculty employment. In Gross, Barry R., ed., *op. cit.* Also published in *Civil Rights Digest* (Spring, 1975).

Unger, Roberto. 1975. *Knowledge and Politics.* Free Press, New York.

United States vs Iron Workers Local 86 443 F.2d 544 (9th Circuit, 1971). cert. denied. (404 U.S. 984).

Weaver, Mark. 1980. The concept of mind in political theory, Ph.D. Dissertation. University of Massachusetts, Amherst.

Wood, Ellen. 1972. *Mind and Politics.* University of Berkeley Press, Berkeley, California.

29

The Canadian National Railway Company v. Canadian Human Rights Commission et al.

Federal Court of Appeal, July 16, 1985.

Affirmative action — Canadian National found to have a practice of discriminating against women on the basis of sex in that few women were employed in "blue collar" positions — Human Rights Tribunal ordered Canadian National to cease discriminatory practice and to hire women until "blue collar" workforce 13 per cent female — Employer appeal allowed — Tribunal authorized to make order to prevent future occurrence of discriminatory practice not restitution for past wrongs — The required hirings not prevention but catch-up measures designed to remedy past discrimination — Hiring order set aside — *Canadian Human Rights Act*, S.C. 1976-77, c. 33, ss. 10, 15, 41(2)(a) (¶ 5110; 5115; 5141).

At Canadian National Railway less than one per cent of the blue collar jobs in the St. Lawrence region were held by women compared to 13 per cent for Canada as a whole. A complaint alleging discrimination on the basis of sex was filed citing Canadian National's hiring practices as depriving women of employment opportunities. A Canadian Human Rights Tribunal of Inquiry upheld the complaint, ordered the employer to cease the discriminatory practice, and ordered that one woman for every four blue collar jobs be hired until its blue collar work force was 13 per cent female. Canadian National appealed.

Held (one dissenting): The appeal was allowed. The Tribunal is authorized to make orders aimed at preventing the future occurrence of a discriminatory practice. The sole purpose of the order is prevention not cure. Even though the Tribunal may order the adoption of affirmative action programs it can only order the kind of program designed to prevent future occurrences, not restitution for past wrongs. The required hirings were not prevention but rather catch-up measures designed to remedy past discrimination. The part of the order requiring hiring was set aside.

A. Giard, Q.C. and R. Boudreau for the applicant; A. Trottier and R. Duval for the Canadian Human Rights Commission; L. Pillette and H. LeBel for Action Travail des Femmes; before: Hugessen, Pratte and MacGuigan JJ.

[Appeal]

HUGESSEN, J.: This section 28 application attacks a decision made by a Tribunal constituted under the *Canadian Human Rights Act*. By its decision, the Tribunal found that the applicant, "CN", had been guilty of discriminatory hiring practices, contrary to section 10 of the Act, by denying employment opportunities to women in certain unskilled blue-collar positions. The Tribunal issued an Order in three parts: the first, entitled "Mesures permanentes de neutralisation de politiques et pratiques courantes" (page 170), requires CN to cease certain discriminatory hiring and employment practices and to alter others; the second part sets a goal of 13% women in the targeted job positions and sets a quota of one female hiring in four until that goal is reached; the third part of the Order requires the filing of periodic reports with the Commission.

Insofar as the Tribunal's findings of discrimination are concerned, I am satisfied that no ground has been shown which would justify intervention by this Court under the provisions of section 28 of the *Federal Court Act*. Likewise, I have not been persuaded that the Tribunal committed any excess of jurisdiction in Parts 1 and 3 of the Order under review.

[Power to make orders]

The only part of the Order which gives me concern are the "Special Temporary Measures" contained in Part 2 and, in particular, paragraph 2 thereof, which imposes a hiring quota of 25% on

CN until such time as the goal of 13% has been achieved.

The Tribunal's power to make the order in question must be found in paragraph 41(2)(a) of the Act:

> 41. (2) If, at the conclusion of its inquiry, a Tribunal finds that the complaint to which the inquiry relates is substantiated, subject to subsection (4) and section 42, it may make an order against the person found to be engaging or to have engaged in the discriminatory practice and include in such order any of the following terms that it considers appropriate:
>
> (a) that such person cease such discriminatory practice and, in consultation with the Commission on the general purposes thereof, take measures, including adoption of a special program, plan or arrangement referred to in subsection 15(1), to prevent the same or a similar practice occurring in the future.

Reduced to its essentials, this text permits the Tribunal to order the taking of measures aimed at preventing the future occurrence of a discriminatory practice on the part of a person found to have engaged in such a practice in the past. The power to make such an order is defined by its purpose. This is clear enough in the English text ("take measures ... to prevent"), but clearer still in the French ("prendre des mesures destinées à prévenir").

The sole permissible purpose for the order is prevention; it is not cure. The text requires that the order look to the avoidance of future evil. It does not allow restitution for past wrongs.

This is not to say that such restitution is in every case impossible. On the contrary, paragraphs (b), (c) and (d) provide specifically for compensation, in kind or in money. Such compensation is limited to "the victim" of the discriminatory practice, which makes it impossible, or in any event inappropriate, to apply it in cases of group or systemic discrimination where, by the nature of things, individual victims are not always readily identifiable.

Paragraph 41(2)(a) goes further, however. It specifies that the measures ordered to be undertaken may include the adoption of a special prográm under subsection 15(1). That subsection deals with what are commonly referred to as "affirmative action programs":

15. (1) It is not a discriminatory practice for a person to adopt or carry out a special program, plan or arrangement designed to prevent disadvantages that are likely to be suffered by, or to eliminate or reduce disadvantages that are suffered by, any group of individuals when those disadvantages would be or are based on or related to the race, national or ethnic origin, colour, religion, age, sex, marital status or physical handicap of members of that group, by improving opportunities respecting goods, services, facilities, accommodation or employment in relation to that group.

Again reducing this text to what is essential, it declares certain programs to be non discriminatory provided they have one of the designated purposes (in English, "designed to . . ."; in French, "destinés à . . . "). Those purposes are the prevention of future disadvantages or the elimination or reduction of present disadvantages suffered by a protected group. The object of the subsection is obviously to prevent affirmative action programs from being struck down as constituting "reverse discrimination" against the majority.

Subsection 15(1) is not by its terms limited to the prevention of future evil although that is clearly included. The elimination or reduction of present disadvantages by the granting of improved opportunities to the disadvantaged group is specifically permitted. Manifestly such opportunities are aimed at reversing the consequences of past wrongs as well as at avoiding their recurrence.

The programs which subsection 15(1) protects as non discriminatory are voluntary in nature. By contrast, the measures which paragraph 41(2)(a) permits are imposed by order of the Tribunal. Likewise paragraph 41(2)(a) is limited to prevention in the future: subsection 15(1) allows the sins of the fathers to be visited upon the sons.

Ordinary grammatical construction requires that, when the Tribunal exercises its power under section 41 to order the adoption of a program envisaged by section 15, it can only order that kind of program which will meet the purposive requirements of section 41.

In the case at bar, the Tribunal leaves us in no doubt as to its purpose in issuing the order contained in paragraph 2 of the "Special Temporary Measures." First, it sets the goal:

Pour plus de clarté, précisons donc que dans le cas présent, l'objectif visé est d'augmenter à 13% la main-d'oeuvre féminine dans les postes non-traditionnels au CN dans la région du St-Laurent (page 169).

I am prepared to concede that the fixing of a goal such as this is a legitimate means of setting a measurable standard against which the achievement of the ultimate purpose of the order can be tested. That purpose remains however, as required by law, the prevention of future acts of discrimination.

The Tribunal goes on to require that, until such time as the required goal is achieved, CN must hire one woman for each four new entries into its unskilled blue-collar labour force. Thus a hiring rate of 25% is imposed in the target area. The justification for this is stated as follows:

Considérant qu'il nous apparaît que le processus de changement dans la région du St-Laurent au CN doit être accéléré et que des mesures préférentielles visant les femmes s'imposent (page 172).

In an earlier passage, the Tribunal states:

Il sera difficile dans le cas du CN de remédier à la disproportion marquée qui résulte de pratiques suivies depuis des années. Il faut espérer qu'avec le temps, le déséquilibre sera réduit, mais il nous apparaît que la chose ne sera pas possible sans l'imposition d'un programme d'action positive dans le cas qui nous occupe (page 166).

[Order not preventative]

There is nothing of prevention in this. The measure imposed is, and is stated to be, a catch-up provision whose purpose can only be to remedy the effects of past discriminatory practices. That purpose is not one which is permitted by section 41.

I confess to a certain sense of frustration in coming, as I do, to the conclusion that the Tribunal has exceeded its powers in making this order. On a purely impressionistic basis, neither the goal of 13% nor the imposed hiring quota of 25% strike me as being *per se* unreasonable. I would certainly not be prepared to hold, as a matter of law, that in order to meet the test of being preventive a hiring quota must always bear a one-to-one relationship with the ultimate goal; I would think, however, that any variance from that ratio would require some very specific findings by the Tribunal in order to justify it.

Likewise, I recognize that by its very nature systemic discrimination may require creative and imaginative preventive measures. Such discrimination has its roots, not in any deliberate desire to exclude from favour, but in attitudes, prejudices, mind sets and habits which may have been acquired over generations. It may well be that hiring quotas are a proper way to achieve the desired result. Again, however, one would expect a Tribunal to make clear findings supporting as preventive measures which are in appearance remedial.

I have searched in vain for any such findings in the impugned decision. No attempt is made to justify the order as being designed to prevent future discriminatory practices only. The Tribunal was perfectly aware that this case was the first in which quotas had been imposed in Canada and that the United States legislation, which it quotes at length, was very different in language from ours. Despite this, the order is expressed in terms that are purely remedial, almost as if the Tribunal had deliberately chosen to disregard the words of the statute.

Perhaps the legislation is defective in this regard and the scope of section 41 should be enlarged to encompass the whole range of affirmative action programs envisaged by section 15. It is not difficult to think of good policy reasons in favour of such action. But they are questions of policy and there

are arguments the other way as well. It is not for the Tribunal or for this Court to disregard the text of the statute and to prescribe that which, reasonable or otherwise, the law does not permit.

What I have said so far is limited to the hiring quotas imposed by paragraph 2 of the "Special Temporary Measures". Paragraph 1 of these measures requires CN to undertake a temporary publicity campaign with a view to encouraging women to apply for blue-collar jobs. While it is certainly arguable that this too is remedial rather than preventive, I have decided, on balance, that it should be allowed to stand. In the first place, the nature and cause of systemic discrimination are such that to prevent it may well require a change of attitudes and perceptions; seen in that light the publicity campaign can be readily justified as preventive. Secondly, while paragraph 1 is clearly closely associated with paragraph 2, it does not contain any of the latter's objectionable references to remedial action and the need for catch-up. Since the two paragraphs are severable, I would limit our intervention to paragraph 2. . . .

[Appeal allowed]

I would allow the application and set aside that part of the impugned order contained in paragraph 2 of the "Special Temporary Measures".

PRATTE, J.: I agree with most of what my brother Hugessen says in his reasons for judgment. Our only important difference of opinion relates to the extent to which the decision under attack should be set aside. He would merely set aside paragraph 2 of the second part of the Order entitled "Special Temporary Measures"; I would, in addition, set aside the first paragraph of that part of the Order as well as the whole of the third part requiring the filing of periodic reports with the Commission.

I agree with my brother Hugessen that, as paragraph 41(2)(b) of the *Canadian Human Rights Act* did not confer on the Tribunal the power to prescribe the temporary measures contained in the second part of the Order, the only question to be resolved is whether the Tribunal was given that power by paragraph 41(2)(*a*). I also agree that, under that paragraph, the Tribunal's power was limited to prescribing measures for the purpose of preventing the recurrence of the discriminatory practices which the Tribunal had found to exist (or, of course, the occurrence of similar practices). However, in my view, the whole of the second part of the Order, not only its second paragraph, was obviously prescribed for the purpose of remedying the consequences of past discrimination rather than preventing future discrimination. I would, therefore, set aside the second part of the Order in its entirety. As the sole purpose of the measures prescribed by the third part of the Order is to enable the Human Rights Commission to monitor the implementation of the prescription contained in the second part of the Order, the third part of the Order should also, in my view, be set aside.

I would allow the application and set aside the second and third parts of the Order of the Tribunal.

[*Dissent*]

MacGUIGAN, J: The Human Rights Tribunal order of which review is sought on this section 28 application is the first such order in Canada imposing a specific program of affirmative action on an employer. In one other case, *Hendry* v *LCBO* (1980), 1 CHRR D 33, a Tribunal under the Ontario Human Rights Code made a compulsory order, but it required the employer itself to design a specific program. Here, the program is imposed on the employer, and the essential question is whether a Human Rights Tribunal has the power under section 41 of the *Canadian Human Rights Act* to make such an order.

The complaint on which the Tribunal's order was founded was brought against Canadian National Railways ("CN") by Action Travail des Femmes ("ATF") on November 6, 1979, under section 10 of the *Canadian Human Rights Act*, an act which had come into effect on March 1, 1978. It alleged that:

ATF has reasonable grounds to believe that CN in the St-Lawrence Region has established or pur-

sued a policy or practice that deprives or tends to deprive a class of individuals of employment opportunities because they are female.

This complaint replaced an earlier one of June 1979. Both complaints were limited to blue-collar positions in the CN's St. Lawrence region, which comprises roughly the province of Quebec minus the Gaspé Peninsula. Not having resolved the matter by conciliation, the Canadian Human Rights Commission ("the Commission") appointed a three-person Tribunal in July, 1981, which after 5 months of hearings, rendered its decision on August 22, 1984.

The relevant portions of the *Canadian Human Rights Act* as of the relevant time were as follows:

2. The purpose of this Act is to extend the present laws in Canada to give effect, within the purview of matters coming within the legislative authority of the Parliament of Canada, to the following principles:

(*a*) every individual should have an equal opportunity with other individuals to make for himself or herself the life that he or she is able and wishes to have, consistent with his or her duties and obligations as a member of society, without being hindered in or prevented from doing so by discriminatory practices based on race, national or ethnic origin, colour, religion, age, sex or marital status, or conviction for an offence for which a pardon has been granted or by discriminatory employment practices based on physical handicap. . . .

10. It is a discriminatory practice for an employer or an employee organization

(*a*) to establish or pursue a policy or practice, or

(*b*) to enter into an agreement affecting recruitment, referral, hiring, promotion, training, apprenticeship, transfer or any other matter relating to employment or prospective employment, that deprives or tends to deprive an individual or class of individuals of any employment opportunities on a prohibited ground of discrimination.

14. It is not a discriminatory practice if

(*a*) any refusal, exclusion, expulsion, suspension, limitation, specification or preference in relation to any employment is established by an employer to be based on a *bona fide* occupational requirement;

15. (1) It is not a discriminatory practice for a person to adopt or carry out a special program, plan or arrangement designed to prevent disadvantages that are likely to be suffered by, or to eliminate or reduce disadvantages that are suffered by, any group or individuals when those disadvantages would be or are based on or related to the race, national or ethnic origin, colour, religion, age, sex, marital status or physical handicap of members of that group, by improving opportunities respecting goods, services, facilities, accommodation or employment in relation to that group.

(2) The Canadian Human Rights Commission established by section 21 may at any time

(*a*) make general recommendations concerning desirable objectives for special programs, plans or arrangements referred to in subsection (1); and

(*b*) on application, give such advice and assistance with respect to the adoption or carrying out of a special program, plan or arrangement referred to in subsection (1) as will serve to aid in the achievement of the objectives the program, plan or arrangement was designed to achieve.

41. (1) If, at the conclusion of its inquiry, a Tribunal finds that the complaint to which the inquiry relates is not substantiated, it shall dismiss the complaint.

(2) If, at the conclusion of its inquiry, a Tribunal finds that the complaint to which the inquiry relates is substantiated, subject to subsection (4) and section 42, it may make an order against the person found to be engaging or to have engaged in the discriminatory practice and include in such order any of the following terms that it considers appropriate:

(*a*) that such person cease such discriminatory practice and, in consultation with the Com-

mission on the general purposes thereof, take measures, including adoption of a special program, plan or arrangement referred to in subsection 15(1), to prevent the same or a similar practice occurring in the future;

(*b*) that such person make available to the victim of the discriminatory practice on the first reasonable occasion such rights, opportunities or privileges as, in the opinion of the Tribunal, are being or were denied the victim as a result of the practice;

(*c*) that such person compensate the victim, as the Tribunal may consider proper, for any or all of the wages that the victim was deprived of and any expenses incurred by the victim as a result of the discriminatory practice, and

(*d*) that such person compensate the victim, as the Tribunal may consider proper, for any or all additional cost of obtaining alternative goods, services, facilities or accommodation and any expenses incurred by the victim as a result of the discriminatory practice.

(3) In addition to any order that the Tribunal may make pursuant to subsection (2) if the Tribunal finds that

(*a*) a person is engaging or has engaged in a discriminatory practice willfully or recklessly, or

(*b*) the victim of the discriminatory practice has suffered in respect of feelings or self-respect as a result of the practice,

the Tribunal may order the person to pay such compensation to the victim, not exceeding five thousand dollars, as the Tribunal may determine.

(4) If, at the conclusion of its inquiry into a complaint regarding discrimination in employment that is based on a physical handicap of the victim, the Tribunal finds that the complaint is substantiated but that the premises or facilities of the person found to be engaging or to have engaged in the discriminatory practice impede physical access thereto by, or lack proper amenities for, persons suffering from the physical handicap of the victim, the Tribunal shall, by order, so indicate and

shall include in such order any recommendations that it considers appropriate but the Tribunal may not make an order under subsection (2) or (3).

The Tribunal distinguished three levels of blue-collar entry-level positions: skilled occupations requiring trade qualifications; apprenticeship occupations, for which trade training is also necessary; and positions which require no special qualifications. It is only entry-level occupations of the latter kind which it considered to be the subject of the complaint and to which its order applied. Examples of such occupations are brakeman, yardman, checker, bridge and building labourer, track maintainer, signal maintainer, signal helper, car cleaner, engine cleaner.

The Tribunal found as a fact that, despite the dedication of its executive management to equal opportunity for women, the CN nevertheless perpetuated traditional hiring practices which were unfair to women with knowledge of the consequences for women of these practices, that no marked change occurred after the entry into force of the *Canadian Human Rights Act* in the spring of 1978, and that the CN must be taken to have intended what it did. Therefore, even if section 10 of the Act is interpreted, following *Canadian National Railway Co.* v. *Canadian Human Rights Commission and K.S. Bhinder*, [1983] 2 F.C. 531, in this Court, as requiring intention for the commission of a discriminatory practice, the CN possesses the intention required for liability.

In addition, the Tribunal found that its analysis of intention was supported by statistical evidence: women in Canada occupy 13% of blue collar jobs, whereas in the St. Lawrence region, as well as in CN generally, the comparative figure is .7%. (All measurements are based on 1981.)

To ascertain whether the minute number of women in blue-collar positions could result from *bona fide* occupational requirements under subsection 14(*a*) of the Act, the Tribunal engaged in a painstaking examination of the totality of the CN's hiring process: recruitment, reception and hiring criteria, including the practice of compulsory promotion, the use of the Bennett Test, and the con-

duct of foremen and fellow workers. This analysis led it to the conclusion not only that the CN's policies and practices regarding the employment of women in blue-collar positions could not be justified on a *bona fide* occupational requirement basis, but that the discriminatory practices were so pervasive and so permanent and so deeply rooted that the discrimination could be said to be systemic, not in the sense that it lacked deliberation, but in that it was imbedded in the totality of the system and co-extensive with it. The Commission therefore concluded that the problem could be resolved only by a full-scale affirmative action program, though it decided to impose a hiring goal or temporary quota, which would lapse when a specified ration was achieved, rather than a more inflexible relatively permanent hiring ratio.

The terms of the Tribunal's order are as follows:

Order

FOR THE ABOVE REASONS this Tribunal, concluding that there are in the St Lawrence Region of CN certain hiring policies or practices that are discriminatory for the purpose of section 10 of the *Canadian Human Rights Act*, and that these practices are not based on *bona fide* occupational requirements for the purpose of section 14 of said Act, makes the following order, according to the powers conferred upon it by section 41:

Permanent Measures for Neutralization of Current Policies and Practices

1. CN shall immediately discontinue the use of the Bennett Test for entry level positions other than apprentice positions, and, within one year of the time of this decision and for the same positions, shall discontinue all mechanical aptitude tests that have a negative impact on women and are not warranted by the aptitude requirements of the positions being applied for.

2. CN shall immediately discontinue all practices pursued by foremen or others in which female candidates undergo physical tests not required for male candidates, mainly the test which consists of lifting a brakeshoe with one arm.

3. CN shall immediately discontinue the requirement for welding experience for all entry level positions, with the exception of apprentice positions.

4. CN must modify its system for the dissemination of information on positions available. More specifically, within the period of one year it shall take the most suitable measures to inform the general public of all positions available.

5. CN shall immediately change the reception practices in its employment office to give female candidates complete, specific and objective information on the real requirements of non-traditional positions.

6. CN shall immediately modify its system of interviewing candidates, in particular, it shall ensure that those responsible for conducting such interviews are given strict instructions to treat all candidates in the same way, regardless of their sex.

7. Should CN wish to continue to grant foremen the power to refuse to hire persons already accepted by the employment office, it shall immediately issue a specific directive to the effect that no one shall be rejected on the basis of sex.

8. CN shall continue to implement the measures already adopted in its directive on sexual harassment with a view to eliminating from the workplace all forms of sexual harassment and discrimination.

Special Temporary Measures

1. Within the period of one year and until the percentage of women in non-traditional jobs at CN has reached 13, CN shall undertake an information and publicity campaign inviting women in particular to apply for non-traditional positions.

2. Whereas we feel that the process of change in CN's St Lawrence Region must be accelerated and preferential measures for women are required;

— Whereas the employer must be given a certain measure of flexibility in view of the uncertainty surrounding the question of how many qualified female workers are available;

— Whereas ideally, in order to create as soon as possible a critical mass that would allow the system

to continue to correct itself, we would be inclined to require over the coming years, until the objective of 13% is achieved, the hiring of women to fill at least one non-traditional position out of every three;

— Whereas for the sake of giving more latitude and flexibility to CN in the methods employed to achieve the desired objective, we feel that it would be more prudent to require a ratio lower than one in three for the hiring of women for non-traditional positions at CN;

ACCORDINGLY, Canadian National is ordered to hire at least one woman for every four non-traditional positions filled in the future. This measure shall take effect only when CN employees who have been laid off but who are subject to recall have been recalled by CN, but not before one year has elapsed from the time of this decision, in order to give CN a reasonable length of time to adopt measures to comply with this order. When it is in effect, daily adherence to the one-in-four ratio will not be required, in order to give the employer more choice in the selection of candidates. However, it must be complied with over each quarterly period until the desired objectives of having 13% of non-traditional positions filled by women is achieved.

3. Within a period of two months of this decision, CN shall appoint a person responsible with full powers to ensure the application of the special temporary measures and to carry out any other duties assigned to him by CN to implement this decision.

SUBMISSION OF DATA
CN SHALL SUBMIT TO THE COMMISSION:

1. Within 20 days of the introduction of the above-mentioned special temporary measures, an initial inventory of the number of blue-collar workers in the CN's St Lawrence Region, by sex and by position.

2. Within 20 days of the end of each quarterly period after the above-mentioned special temporary measures have begun to be applied, and for the entire duration of the said measures, after forwarding a copy to ATF, a report containing:

(a) a list indicating the name, sex, title and duties, date hired and employment sector of every person hired in the St Lawrence Region during the previous quarter;

(b) a detailed statement of the efforts made by CN to recruit female candidates for non-traditional positions during the previous quarter;

(c) a breakdown, by sex, of: the total number of persons who applied for non-traditional positions at CN during the previous quarter; and the total number of persons who completed, underwent or failed every test or written examination to fill a non-traditional position. This list shall include the score and rank of every person who passed the test or examination;

(d) the name, sex and changes of titles and duties, or changes in status of every employee hired for non-traditional positions after the special temporary measures come into force.

3. A statement giving the name, official title and date of appointment of the person in charge of applying the above-mentioned special temporary measures, within twenty days of his or her appointment.

In its factum the applicant sets out five reasons for setting aside the Tribunal's order under section 28 of the *Federal Court Act:*

(1) The Tribunal erred in law in blindly applying the American jurisprudence.

(2) The Tribunal erred in law as to the legal meaning of section 10 of the *Canadian Human Rights Act.* According to the correct interpretation of the law, the complainant must establish the existence of systemic discrimination by a preponderance of proof.

(3) The Tribunal erred in law in its appreciation of the statistical evidence, it failed to consider important material before it, and it drew erroneous conclusions in a perverse way.

(4) The Tribunal failed to consider important material before it relating to the process of hiring and it drew erroneous conclusions in a perverse and capricious manner.

(5) The Tribunal erred in law in its interpretation of paragraph 41(2)(a) of the Act in arrogating

to itself the right to establish and to impose a detailed plan of action on the applicant, in ignoring the role of the Commission, and in confiding to the A.T.F. powers of supervision which are not conferred on it in conformity with the wording of the Act itself.

The first allegation, that concerning the blind use of American precedents, cannot be taken seriously in this context. The Tribunal introduces its reference to American experience in this fashion:

Since there are hardly any examples in Canadian law of the imposition of an affirmative action program such as that suggested by ATF and the Canadian Human Rights Commission, we think it is important, before considering the appropriateness of ordering CN to adopt such a program, to indicate the legal basis of affirmative action programs and to look at some examples of them. Accordingly, we will draw a comparison between the Canadian Human Rights Act and American legislation and then look at the American experience in imposing such programs. Lastly, we will give a few examples of voluntary affirmative action programs in Canada.

Not only was it not improper for the Tribunal to review the wider U.S. experience with affirmative action programs, but it might have been thought to have been delinquent not to do so. Similar considerations apply to other references by the Tribunal to U.S. material.

The second allegation raises the Tribunal's understanding of section 10 of the Act. Here, the CN takes exception to two passages in the decision. The first is as follows:

Section 10 [of the Act] requires that the complainant provide *prima facie* evidence that the disputed hiring practices are such as to deny a protected group the same employment opportunities as other applicants.

We have seen in the preceding part that the statistics would tend to provide such *prima facie* evidence, since the proportion of women hired by CN for the positions covered by the complaint was substantially lower than the average among employers in similar sectors.

In addition to such *prima facie* evidence, the complainant must also prove that the disputed hiring practices were adopted for the purpose of lessening the employment opportunities of a protected group.

The allegation is that the reference to a *prima facie* proof contradicts the required overall standard of proof on a balance of probabilities. But the compatibility of the two aspects of proof, the former referring to the onus of proof, the latter to the standard, is clearly shown by the words of McIntyre J. in the leading case of the *The Ontario Human Rights Commission et al.* and *The Borough of Etobicoke*, [1972] 2 S.C.R. 202, 208:

Once a complainant has established before a board of enquiry a *prima facie* case of discrimination, in this case proof of a mandatory retirement at age sixty as a condition of employment, he is entitled to relief in the absence of justification by the employer. The only justification which can avail the employer in the case at bar, is the proof, the burden of which lies upon him, that such compulsory retirement is a *bona fide* occupational qualification and requirement for the employment concerned. The proof, in my view, must be made according to the ordinary civil standard of proof, that is upon a balance of probabilities.

The second passage objected to by the applicant under the second allegation is as follows:

With respect, we believe that this decision [*Bhinder*], in which leave to appeal has been granted by the Supreme Court of Canada, is in error, and that the distinction that the Court attempted to make between section 10 and section 7.03 of Title VII rests on no solid foundation.

Nevertheless, it will not be necessary for us to distinguish that case since we believe that, here, Canadian National was aware of the consequences of its hiring practices. We have already shown, at the beginning of this judgment, that Canadian National knew several years before the complaint was filed that its hiring practices had a negative

effect on the employment of women and that women were under-represented at Canadian National compared with their general employment situation. Yet Canadian National continued these hiring practices, knowing their consequences. The proclamation of the Canadian Human Rights Act, which did not take Canadian National by surprise, as can be seen from the testimony in the proceeding, has not resulted in any marked changes in its hiring practices.

The CN argued before us that the Tribunal had no option but to follow the *Bhinder* decision. The problem with this argument is that, however unwillingly, that is exactly what the Tribunal did.

The CN argued, alternatively, that there was insufficient evidence on the basis of which the Tribunal could have found an intention to discriminate on the Railway's part. This variation of their second ground for review has, in my view, to be treated along with their third and fourth grounds, since all are founded on review under section 28(*c*) of the *Federal Court Act*.

This Court has frequently had the occasion to describe the limits on its intervention under section 28(*c*): *Armstrong* v. *The State of Wisconsin*, [1973] F.C. 437; *Re Rohm and Haas Canada Limited* v. *Anti Dumping Tribunal* (1978), 91 D.L.R. (3d) 212, will serve as examples. Perhaps the most succinct statement of the Court's jurisdiction is that of Urie J. in *In Re YKK Zipper Co. of Canada Limited*, [1975] F.C. 68, 75:

It would be quite improper, therefore, for the Court to disturb such finding unless it be satisfied that there was no evidence upon which it could have been made or that a wrong principle was applied in making it.

Here, the CN has been unable to show either that there was no evidence to support the Tribunal's findings or that it applied a wrong principle in the course of arriving at them. The CN took exception, for instance, to the Tribunal's categorization of statistics in arriving at its comparison between the .7% of women employees in its blue-collar occupations and the 13% in the labour force as a whole in the same occupations, but the Tribunal made use of the most accurate statistics available and its decisions on categorization were well within its non-reviewable discretion under section 28.

The principal ground of review urged by CN was its fifth, *viz*, that the Tribunal lacked jurisdiction under paragraph 41(2)(*a*) of the *Canadian Human Rights Act* to make the order it did. It alleges a lack of jurisdiction in three respects: the Tribunal's imposition of the detailed plan of action on the CN, its ignoring the role of the Commission, and its conferring supervisory powers on the ATF. Let me say at once that the third allegation is not a substantial one. The Tribunal requires the CN merely to transmit a copy of each quarterly report to the ATF, presumably so that it can make representations (to the CN itself, to the Commission, to the public) if it is not satisfied. This is far from a power of supervision, and, certainly if the Tribunal has the power to impose a detailed program of affirmative action on the Railway under its power under paragraph 41(2)(*a*) to "take measures . . . to prevent a similar practice occurring in the future," it does not lack the lesser power to keep the original complainant informed as to the progress of the program.

The heart of the CN's interpretation of paragraph 41(2)(*a*) is that the Tribunal is not itself authorized to prescribe the content of a special program but only to order the adoption by the employer, after discussion with the Commission, of such a special program. In other words, the content of such programs does not fall under the jurisdiction of the Tribunal. It must content itself with ordering the adoption of such a program and with determining the general object, which is specified by the Act as the prevention of similar discriminatory practices in the future.

Parliament's intention, the CN argues, was to accord some flexibility to the employer in the light of the characteristics of its enterprise, the state of the labour market, the impact on the employer's organization, the requirements of collective agreements, etc. In this way, with the aid of the expertise of the Commission, the employer itself taking account of all the circumstances would have

to establish an adequate plan of action to attain the objectives established by the Tribunal.

Such an interpretation is not without textual plausibility. But the respondents contend that the phrase "including adoption of a special program, plan or arrangement referred to in subsection 15(1)" must necessarily establish the Tribunal's power also to impose such a special program compulsorily, by way of contrast to the voluntary adoption of special programs under subsection 15(1). They also argue that the clear implication of the exemption of orders under 41(2) from the mere recommendations possible under subsection 41(4), where discrimination is based on a physical handicap, is that the 41(2) orders are compulsory.

However, this argument of the respondents does not quite meet the applicant's point, which is not to deny the validity of compulsory orders entirely under paragraph 41(2)(*a*), but only to limit them to the imposition of objectives rather than of content.

Nevertheless, it remains that the powers of a tribunal under 41(2)(*a*) are expressed in general and unrestricted language ("take measures . . . to prevent . . . a similar practice occurring in the future"). How should these words be interpreted?

Section 11 of the *Interpretation Act* provides that "every enactment . . . shall be given such fair, large and liberal construction as best ensures the attainment of its objects." The *Canadian Human Rights Act* includes an internal guide to its objects in section 2. This section gives an unmistakeable signal to Courts, in cases of doubt, to give the statutory words the interpretation that provides the greatest protection to protected groups against discriminatory acts. This Court should therefore not hesitate to interpret the phrase "take measures" as generously as is consistent with the context, and therefore to include the content as well as the objectives of an affirmative action program in the discretion of the Tribunal ("include in such orders any of the following terms that it considers appropriate").

This interpretation, which in my view is imposed by the language of paragraph 41(2)(*a*) read in the light of subsection 2(*a*), does not immediately resolve the question of what is intended by the consultative role of the Commission, but this is a secondary issue, and, however resolved, it cannot be allowed to frustrate the broad discretionary powers of a Tribunal. The respondents urge that what Parliament intended was that a tribunal should consult with the Commission before making its order. Such an interpretation of the text is not grammatically possible in either language:

a Tribunal . . . may make an order against the person found to be engaging or to have engaged in the discriminatory practice . . . *that such person cease* such discriminatory practice, *and, in consultation* with the Commission on the general purposes thereof, take *measures* . . . [emphasis added]

le tribunal . . . peut . . . ordonner . . . à la *personne trouver coupable* d'un acte discriminatoire . . . *de prendre* des mesures destinées à prévenir les actes semblables, et *ce, en consultation* avec la Commission relativement à l'objet général de ces mesures. [c'est moi qui souligne].

In English the subject of the clause in question, and therefore the party required to consult the Commission, is the person against whom the order is made. In French, the effect is similar, though the structure is different. The result is that the CN and the Commission are expected to consult on the general purposes of whatever program is adopted, but since this is already required by the statute, it does not necessarily have to be repeated in the Tribunal's order.

However, the most difficult aspect of the issue remains. Even if it is held to be bound as to the content of an affirmative action program, the CN maintains that such an order can include only measures aimed at prevention of similar acts and cannot be designed to more generally redress the disadvantages suffered by women in their labour market participation. In other words, it must be a preventive and not a catch-up or curative program.

Clearly, the Tribunal has not been given a general social mandate by the very precise words of paragraph 41(2)(a): "to take measures . . . to prevent the same or a similar practice occurring in the

future" ("de prendre des mesures destinées à prévenir les actes semblables"). The respondent Commission's argument that the powers conferred on a Tribunal under 41(2)(a) are co-extensive with the powers conferred by subsection 15(1) must therefore be rejected.

But one must beware of thinking too univocally about the concept of prevention. How does one 'prevent' systemic discrimination? The Tribunal found discriminatory practices in the CN to be pervasive, persistent and deeply rooted in the psychology of both people and workplace. So to assess the true dimensions of the problem it had to look back, even to the period when, in the absence of federal human rights legislation, discrimination was not illegal.

The Tribunal was well aware of the tightrope it was walking in this regard:

The complaint by Action Travail des Femmes is aimed primarily at CN's general hiring process for positions described as unskilled, as this was being carried out in the St Lawrence Region at the time the complaint was filed.

. . . .

As for the period of the complaint, the Tribunal is of the opinion that, for the purpose of determining whether CN's hiring process was legal or not under the *Canadian Human Rights Act*, we must adhere essentially to the period specified in the complaint. However, we shall consider the period prior to that of the complaint in order to show what developments occurred and to get a better idea of the hiring process in effect at that time. Finally, any changes that may have occurred since the filing of the complaint are also relevant, not for determining whether the hiring process was legal at that time, but for determining whether there are grounds for concluding that an affirmative action program should be adopted, and if one should, for determining its essential features.

This passage reveals that the Tribunal clearly understood that it was for legal purposes confined to the short period from the coming into effect of the Act to the time of the complaint, and that its recourse to any other period, either before or after, was for strictly limited ends. Nevertheless, a tribunal's power is retrospective with respect to the psychological dimension as well as prospective in relation to the remedy.

The ideal form of prevention would consist of radical improvement in attitudes within the CN, leading to an amelioration in behaviour, but no one has yet devised an assured technique of directly modifying the value systems of large numbers of people. However, since the solution must reach the problem, the prevention of systemic discrimination will reasonably be thought to require systemic remedies.

It must be admitted that the Tribunal did not attempt to provide a justification of the heart of its affirmative action program, *viz*, its special temporary measures (to hire one woman in four in non-traditional occupations until the desired objective of 13% is reached) in a form explicitly parallel to its powers under paragraph 41(2)(*a*), but that should not prevent the upholding of these measures by this Court if they can be interpreted to be within that paragraph. In my view, they can be so justified.

The essence of the affirmative action program is a limitation on the CN's discretion in hiring. The necessity of such a program for the CN was in fact stated in the Railway's own Boyle-Kirkman Report in 1974:

> Setting specific (name and number) targets is essential, as without these goals day-to-day priorities will take precedence over the more intangible employee development efforts.

The CN rejected this recommendation.

It must not be forgotten that the complaint here was brought by the ATF on behalf of women as a class. Indeed, the respondent ATF argued (without the support of the Canadian Human Rights Commission) that the Tribunal's order could be supported under paragraph 41(2)(*b*), with women as a class being recognized as the "victims" of the discriminatory practice. In view of my holding under paragraph 41(2)(*a*), I do not find it necessary to decide whether the meaning of "victim" in

41(2)(*b*) extends this far, but the argument serves to underline that the Tribunal's findings relate to women as a class. The prevention of discrimination has to be effective for women as a group.

As I read paragraph 41(2)(*a*), the limitation on a Tribunal in ordering an affirmative action program for systemic discrimination is that the measures ordered must be objectively intended to prevent such systemic discrimination in the future ("to prevent the same or a similar practice occurring in the future"), that is, they must bear an appropriate relationship or proportion to the problem. What sort of affirmative action goal would bear such a relationship in this case?

The Tribunal might arguably have set the goal for the hiring of women at 50% (or in fact a bit more) for an indefinite period, on the ground that women constitute that percentage of the Canadian population, or they might have set it at 40.7%, the percentage of women in the Canadian work force (1981). But it seems to me that such a goal would not observe a due proportionality to the observed discrimination because it would have to rely on too many unprovable assumptions, especially on the demand side — to say nothing of the onerousness of such a requirement on the employer. They might have established a goal of 6.11%, based on the percentage of women in the CN work force, but such a figure, drawn from the same company, might not unreasonably be suspected of also having been diminished by systemic discrimination.

The Tribunal, wisely in my view, chose to derive its goal from the most proximate independent generalization, *viz*., hiring in the same blue-collar occupations across Canada. I believe this figure contains the irreducible minimum of unprovable assumptions and hence is the least arbitrary and most proportionate goal. As I see it, whether the Tribunal then chose to move to this goal by a one-in-three or by a one-in-four ratio is within their reasonable discretion.

It seems to me this leaves only one difficulty — and that I believe merely an apparent one. The Tribunal expressed its goal, in terms, not of hiring, but of employment. This is undoubtedly what conjures up an image of a general social goal of employment of women out of proportion to the discrimination actually established here.

But in fact hiring and employment are opposite sides of the same coin. Employment is the consequence of, and the more permanent state resulting from, hiring. In the absence of discrimination, employment ratios probably roughly correspond to hiring ratios over a sufficient period of years. But what is key to the decision, and is a matter of which I believe this Court must take judicial notice, is that the only available official statistics on a scientific data base relate to employment. Statistics Canada does not publish general statistics either as to hiring (the "in" stream) or separation (the "out" stream) from employment, but only as to employment "stock". Since there was no other statistical basis available, there was therefore no other objective basis on which the Tribunal could have established its objective.

It may well be that the Tribunal's own motivation was mixed, and that it was as much aware of the fact that its order served the general interests of an egalitarian society as that it was based on the more limited mandate of paragraph 41(2)(*a*). But in my view it is not for this Court on a section 28 application to interfere with such a judgment call by the Tribunal unless it is shown to be clearly outside its statutory jurisdiction. Chouinard J. has spoken recently in *National Bank of Canada* v *Retail Clerks International Union* and *Canada Labour Relations Board* (1984), 53 N.R. 203, 227, of "the caution which the courts must exercise whenever the juris-diction of an administrative tribunal is questioned." In my view the CN has not been able to show that the terms of the order here cannot be said "to prevent the same or a similar practice occurring in the future." Given the more than five and a half years it has taken to bring the complaint to this point, the 31 volumes in the record before us, the Tribunal's decision of 175 pages, the public funds and the private effort expended, it is excessive to return the matter again to the administrative forum unless there is a compelling reason to do so. In my opinion there is no such reason.

I must leave unresolved any question as to the supervision and variation of the Tribunal's order. Since the Tribunal is *functus officio*, subject to the possibility of a temporary resurrection for the reconsideration of its order, and the law does not confer supervisory powers on the Commission, there is no apparent mechanism of supervision or variation. The provision in subsection 43(1) of the Act that "Any order of a Tribunal under subsection 41(2) . . . may, for the purpose of enforcement, be made an order of the Federal Court of Canada and is enforceable in the same manner as an order of that Court" clearly creates a power of enforcement in this Court, but does not confer any power of initiative or any flexibility in the approach to the order. But that is a policy matter beyond the competence of this Court.

Since in my opinion the order of the Tribunal is within its jurisdiction under paragraph 41(2)(*a*), I would dismiss the application.

SUGGESTED FURTHER READINGS

ABELLA, ROSALIE SILBERMAN. *Equality in Employment: A Royal Commission Report*. Government of Canada, 1984.

—————————. *Equality in Employment: A Royal Commision Report, Research Studies*. Government of Canada, 1985.

BLAKELY, JOHN AND EDWARD HARVEY. "Socioeconomic Change and Lack of Change: Employment Equity Policies in the Canadian Context." *Journal of Business Ethics*, Vol. 7, No. 3, 1988.

CHEGWIDDEN, P. AND WENDY KATZ. "American and Canadian Perspectives on Affirmative Action: A Response to the Fraser Institute." *Journal of Business Ethics*, Vol. 2, No. 3, 1983.

CLAIRMONT, DON AND RICHARD APOSTLE. "Work: A Segmentation Perspective." In K. Lundy and B. Warme (eds.) *Work in the Canadian Context*, 2nd ed. Toronto: Butterworths, 1986.

DWORKIN, RONALD. "What Is Equality? Part 1: Equality of Welfare." *Philosophy and Public Affairs*, Vol. 10, No. 3, Summer 1981.

ECONOMIC COUNCIL OF CANADA. *Towards Equity*. Ottawa, 1985.

GROARKE, LEO. "Beyond Affirmative Action." *Atlantis*, Vol. 9, No. 1, 1983.

POFF, DEBORAH. "Women and Economic Equity." *Canadian Issues*, Vol. 10, No. 1, 1988.

THOMPSON, JUDITH JARVIS. "Preferential Hiring." *Philosophy and Public Affairs*, 1973.

WALUCHOW, W. "Pay Equity: Equal Value for Whom?" *Journal of Business Ethics*, Vol. 7, No. 3, 1988.

WINN, CONRAD. "Affirmative Action for Women: More than a Case of Simple Justice." *Canadian Public Administration*, Vol. 28, No. 1, Spring 1985.

Environmental Effects of Business Activities

INTRODUCTION

You will recall the discussion of claim-rights from our introductory essay. Claim-rights are always paired with corresponding duties or obligations. A violation of a claim-right is always a violation of someone else's duty towards me. Part Seven of this text focuses on such claim-rights. It focuses on the rights of individuals not to have their economic livelihood and physical health threatened by environmental contaminants. You may want to review the introductory essay, "Ethical Theory in Business," prior to reading the articles in this section. These articles also focus on the often competing interests of business, government, environmental groups, and private citizens.

In November of 1985, two Native Indian bands secured a final out-of-court settlement worth $16.6 million in compensation for an environmental despoilment, the full extent of which has yet to be determined. Under the terms of this hard-fought settlement, two companies, Reed Paper Company (Dryden Division) and its successor, Great Lakes Forest Products, agreed to pay $6.2 million to the Grassy Narrows band and $5.5 million to the Whitedog band. In addition, the Government of Ontario made a commitment to provide each band with $1.08 million, the Federal Government, $1.37 million.

The story behind this historic settlement is steeped in tragedy. Between 1962 and 1970, Dryden Chemicals Limited, a mercury cathode chlor-alkali plant producing chlorine and other chemicals for use in the adjacent pulp and paper mill of Reed Paper, dumped an estimated 20 tons* of highly toxic inorganic mercury into the English-Wabigoon system of lakes and rivers (and discharged another 20 tons into the air). By March 1970, when the Ontario Ministry of Energy and Resource Management ordered a halt to the mercury discharges, extensive damage had already been done. In addition to the devastating effects of the methyl mercury poisoning on the health of their members, the Indian bands were forced to cope with the loss of their primary source of livelihood. Their rivers and lakes were closed to commercial fishing and their fishing lodges were shut down. As Anastasia Shkilnyk points out in "Mercury in the Environment," "Over three hundred miles of the English-Wabigoon river system, with all its life, would probably remain poisoned for half a century." Yet, as Shkilnyk also notes, the devastation extended far beyond physical health and loss of economic livelihood. To a much greater extent than the majority of their fellow citizens, the Native peoples of Canada share an intimate relationship or "partnership" with their natural environment — a relationship which Reed Paper all but destroyed. The bands could, she writes, "no longer draw strength either from their relationship to the land or from the well of their faith, which had once given meaning and coherence to their lives."

The shameful case of the Grassy Narrows and Whitedog Indians serves as an all too vivid illustration of the potentially destructive effects of individual activities on our natural and social environments — on what some environmentalists have termed our "ecosystems." The threat of acid rain provides yet another. As Environment Canada points out in its 1985 *Status Report*, Atlantic salmon runs have disappeared from seven rivers in Nova Scotia. Toxic metals which the acid leaches from the soils find their way into our lakes and rivers, deforming fish and other animals, clogging respiratory systems, and disrupting reproductive cycles. Metals, such as lead, mercury, and cadmium, find their way into the flesh of fish and ultimately onto our dinner plates. The list goes on and on.

Despite the clear and substantial threat it poses, however, industrial pollution is not at all easily curbed. In "Risks Versus Rights," Ted Schrecker outlines a number of forces that conspire to render environmental pollution an almost intractable problem. As Schrecker points out, a purely profit-oriented company has little if any economic motive to pursue costly pollution control measures. "Indeed, unless it occupies a monopoly position, it has excellent economic reasons to avoid doing so: the higher prices or lower returns on capital which result mean that it would soon be driven out of business by less altruistic competitors." In short, from the point of view of sheer profit, it simply pays to pollute.

As a result of this fact, governments have felt the need to intervene to protect us from the undesirable and inevitable impact of unconstrained industrial activities. But as Schrecker demonstrates, the cards are stacked in favour of companies

---

*1 ton = 907.2 kilograms

who often control, among other things, access to technical information which is essential to governments in the making of environmental policy. They are also able to exert considerable pressure on governments whose concern must extend not only to the elimination of damaging environmental effects, but also to sustaining economic growth capable of providing income and employment for citizens as well as essential funding for desirable state services of various kinds. Given these other serious interests, business can sometimes use implied threats of production cutbacks or plant closures (what some would like to call "job blackmail" or "extortion") to mobilize opposition to regulatory proposals on the part of governments — and affected workers and communities. As an example, Schrecker cites what for us is a highly relevant case. At hearings of an Ontario legislative committee held in 1979, the president of Reed Paper Company reportedly threatened that the firm would shut down its plant — Dryden's major employer — if the Ministry of the Environment held firm on a proposed deadline for pollution control measures. This clearly provides an example of what is aptly termed "the power position of business."

If economic forces conspire against morally responsible industrial activity, and we must rely instead on strong government intervention, then thorny moral and political questions arise. Precisely how do we, through our government agencies, determine the threshold of environmental despoilment beyond which companies will be prohibited from going? By what principles ought we to be guided and upon whom should we place the burden of proof: businesses, government agencies, environmental groups, or private citizens? And how are we to balance the "costs" of pollution in terms of health, safety, and perhaps even a whole way of life (as in the case of the Grassy Narrows and Whitedog Indians) against the substantial costs of measures to reduce or eliminate pollution? These latter costs must be absorbed not only by businesses but ultimately by consumers and employees who will inevitably be faced with higher prices, lower wages, and perhaps even the loss of a job. Some sort of balancing seems necessary here because, as the Law Reform Commission of Canada points out in "Crimes Against the Environment," it is generally acknowledged within our society that there are some valid social purposes which can justify, at least for periods of time and in varying degrees, industrial activities which pose threats to our ecological systems. For instance, it is sometimes accepted that the only way to establish a new industry in an economically depressed area and to develop and market local resources is to permit it to do some widespread ecological damage — damage which would normally be beyond the limits of tolerance. According to the Commission, whose concern is to establish a new category of criminal activity involving environmental despoilment, it would be naive and unrealistic to think that all such judgements are equally defensible. (The case of Grassy Narrows should make this plain.) However, they go on to note, "it would be equally naive and Utopian to expect that environmental decision-making can ever be completely insulated from economic and political considerations." So the economic costs of pollution control measures must not be underestimated in our thinking about how best to police the environmental effects of business activities.

Together with these questions of balance go very difficult questions of measurement. Precisely how do we go about measuring the environmental and social costs of pollution so that these can be balanced against the economic costs of regulatory measures? Can these be measured at all? Or are we perhaps here in an area where "incommensurable values (e.g., dollars versus lives) are being compared." Recall the position defended by Alan Gewirth in "Human Rights and the Prevention of Cancer" (see Reading 18) regarding the immeasurable value of human life. According to Gewirth, many of our social practices, e.g., our practice of sparing no effort to rescue trapped miners, reveal a commitment to the view that human life is "priceless, in the literal sense of being without price: it is incommensurable with, cannot be measured in terms of, money or any other material goods that might be needed to preserve the life or lives that are endangered." If this really is the case, and if we recognize the fact that environmental despoilment poses grave threats to our health and our lives, (as well as to the quality of the lives we lead), then it is questionable whether we can rationally measure the costs of industrial pollution in a way which will enable us to carry out the delicate balancing that seems to be required.

These questions of measurement and balance are explored in some detail by Schrecker in his insightful and informative article. He both outlines and submits to critical scrutiny popular attempts to invoke cost-benefit analysis to solve the problems we have posed. This is a form of analysis developed by economists to help determine the most cost-efficient means of securing desired ends. Schrecker's conclusion regarding the use of cost-benefit analysis in this context is clearly stated. "Quite apart from such issues as the value implications of methods for valuing health benefits and criteria for resolving scientific uncertainty," he writes, "the 'bottom line' is how much do we, as a society, really care whether regulations guarding against this sort of effect are economically efficient?" There is nothing irrational, he argues, in deciding to forego some wealth and some economic efficiency in favour of preventing adverse effects upon our fellow human beings, effects which may be incalculable or which we should not wish to inflict upon others at any cost. And this is especially clear when one considers that those affected adversely are sometimes people who (a) derive little, if any, of the offsetting benefits of industrial activities; (b) neither have nor would have chosen to assume the risks they entail; and (c) can in no real measure ever be compensated for the harms they have endured. One might ask whether the Grassy Narrows and Whitedog tribes stood to benefit from the economic activities of Reed Paper, whether they would have chosen to assume the risks to which they were subjected, or whether they can ever really be compensated. As Chief Roy McDonald of the Whitedog band said, "No amount of money will ever right the wrongs that have happened here" (*Toronto Star*, Dec. 1, 1985, p. H1). Cases such as this confront us again with the issues of responsibility — indeed, criminality — of employees of polluting companies. In the light of continuing human-made disasters (Union Carbide's Bhopal plant, the Soviet Chernobyl radiation discharges), these questions demand answers.

Harriet Rosenberg ends this section with a different perspective on the environment, the household as "intimately linked to . . . [the] . . . global process of commodification and danger." Rosenberg's article deals with the household in two different ways. First, she details the fight of a number of women in Whitchurch-Stouffville, Ontario, who became worried about the unusually high rates of miscarriage in their community and the possible link between those miscarriages and the "thousands of tons of toxic liquid industrial wastes . . . [which] . . . were poured into a farmer's field never designed as a landfill" between 1962 and 1969. She then goes on to discuss "exposure to less visible and less understood hazards stemming from the penetration of the home by the household products industry." Although causal relations between environmental contaminants and disease are often difficult to establish, there is continual and growing evidence of severe allergic reactions to the strong chemicals in household products. Rosenberg believes that women are the victims of advertising campaigns which equate "cleaning with caring" and which equate clean with industrially-produced solvents and cleansers. Women increasingly put themselves and their families at risk by exposing them to noxious cleansers, and they do so because they are convinced that this makes them better homemakers, argues Rosenberg.

Since the first edition of this text was published, interest in and anxiety over the environment have spread. While environmentalists have been concerned about global indicators which point to drastic erosion of the biosphere for over two decades, dire warnings and predictions did not always result in action on the part of governments and businesses. The 1990s have been declared by many world leaders to require interventionist and radical attention to environmental issues. All of Canada's main political parties have focused their attention on the development of stricter environmental policy. Multinationals, such as the Body Shop, are donating monies to protect areas such as the Amazon that are environmentally at risk. Large grocery store chains, such as Loblaws, have introduced lines of products labelled "environmentally friendly."

When reading the articles in this section, you may wish to consider the reasons behind the increasing concern for the environment. Is it that the costs have risen so significantly that, according to any utilitarian calculation, the costs to the environment and human well-being far outweigh the benefits? Or, is it that even the most narrowly focused, self-interested individuals and businesses recognize that there will be no profitable marketplace if the planet ceases to sustain life? Perhaps, as the "New Age" thinkers would like us to believe, there is a global shift in the orientation and value-system of people with relation to their environment.

30

Crimes Against the Environment

LAW REFORM COMMISSION
OF CANADA

Latency, Accumulation and the Ecosystem Approach

In many cases, the pollution activities which are potentially the most harmful are those involving damage, destruction or injury which is not immediate and not harmful to identifiable aspects of the environment or identifiable human victims. Yet the damage can nevertheless be very grave. Two of the reasons why this can be so have to do with *latency* and *accumulation*. Latency is the delay between the release of, or exposure to, a hazard and the appearance of its injurious effects. Some of the most catastrophic effects can take the longest time to appear. An example is some carcinogens which can be latent for up to thirty years. The mutagenic effect of some hazardous chemicals may only show up several generations after the initial exposure. The process of accumulation means, in effect, that while an individual release of a pollutant may not in some cases be seriously or obviously harmful, many such acts, from one or many sources, may in the aggregate produce an accumulated threat to the environment, health and property, one going well beyond the threshold of what a particular species, resource, ecosystem or human body can tolerate without serious harm. A lake can finally lose the ability to cope with accumulated acid rain, and will die. Or a child exposed to lead over a long period of time can finally become seriously ill and even die because too much lead has accumulated in the body.

One explanation of the mechanics and implications of environmental damage and destruction is that provided by the ecosystem approach. That approach is not without its limitations when pushed to extremes, and it is not our intention to promote it or to justify legal prohibitions and reforms purely on the basis of one or another environmental school of thought. Nevertheless, some findings of ecologists are not disputed, and the general lines of the approach help to underline the potential seriousness of some environmental pollution.

This relatively new approach is a synthesis of the insights and skills of a number of disciplines, especially biology, chemistry, geography, and climatology. Whereas those and other fields study the threads of nature, the ecosystem approach studies its "whole cloth". Its proponents insist especially upon two points. They argue first of all that it is erroneous to speak of man *and* environment, or of man as *external* to the natural environment. Rather, humans are internal to, and partners with, the rest of nature. They argue, secondly, that serious harm done to one element in an ecosystem will invariably lead to the damage or even destruction of other elements in that and other ecosystems.

What ecologists mean by an "ecosystem" is any relatively homogeneous and delineated unit of nature in which nonliving substances and living organisms interact with an exchange of materials taking place between the nonliving and living parts. The term "ecosystem" is somewhat flexible and the boundaries between them somewhat arbitrary. Those boundaries are generally based upon what is most convenient for measuring the movement of energy and chemicals into and out of the system. Typical and important interrelated and overlapping ecosystems are: units of land along with the surrounding air and water, or lakes, or river basins, or forests, or climatic zones, or the earth itself or the biosphere (the outer sphere of the earth inhabited by living organisms and including lakes, oceans, soil and living organisms, including man). Within each ecosystem there is, they maintain, a delicate balance and interdependence between all the elements. Systems can cope with and adapt to some interferences, but not others. The overall long-range effect of some intrusions is not yet known with certainty or in detail. Ecologists argue that ecosystems are now known to be subject to very definable and immutable processes, which impose corresponding ecological constraints. They stress two organizational rules, namely, the first two of the three laws of thermodynamics. The first rule (that of conservation of matter and energy) is that matter and energy cannot be destroyed, only *transformed*. The second (the law of entropy) is that all energy transformations are *degradations*, whereby

energy is transformed from more to less organized forms. In simpler terms, they explain those rules by the following principles and examples.

The first is that *everything in the environment or individual ecosystems is related*. If one breaks a link in the food-chain, for example, or introduces a substance not biodegradable, there are consequences for the entire ecosystem. Examples of the resulting serious and often irreversible harm are DDT and mercury. Since its massive use in the 1940s, the footsteps of DDT can be followed from wheat, to insects, to rodents, to larger animals and birds, and to man. In its wake it left whole species of animals more or less extinct or with serious reproductive problems. To illustrate the degree of interaction involved and the insignificance of time and distance, traces of DDT can now be found in the flesh of polar bears. The industrial discharge of *mercury* is another illustration. It has been followed from its discharge by pulp and paper industries into the air and water, to its transformation in the water into methyl-mercury by the water's micro-organisms, to its accumulation in the sediment of lakes or its absorption by the fish. Among its victims in the next stage, it is argued, have been the Indians of northern Ontario and Québec who eat those fish and are frequently inflicted with the horrors of what has come to be known as Minamata disease.

The second principle underlined by ecologists is that *unless neutralized, every contaminating substance remains harmful somewhere to something or someone* in the natural environment. Sooner or later we will pay, in some cases dearly, for discarding, for example, nonrecycled industrial toxins into rivers and dumps. Matter cannot be destroyed — only transformed. The atoms and molecules of matter are always preserved by ecosystems in some form. Moreover, if they are not or cannot be transformed, degraded, recycled or neutralized, it is an illusion to hope that that form will become a benign and harmless one.

Limitations of an Unqualified Ecosystem Approach

From the perspective of harm, however, there may

be some difficulties and limitations of the ecosystem approach pushed to its extreme. It has been observed that some (by no means all) of its proponents are unjustifiably pessimistic and too rigorous. Some imply that each now stable and healthy ecosystem has inherent worth, and must be preserved exactly as it is, that any harm or modification to it would be immoral, and that all human impacts upon, or changes to, an aspect of the environment are necessarily unnatural. However, that view has at least three limitations.

(1) Viruses and diseases: Good or bad?

First of all, if every ecosystem, every species, is to be preserved and protected "as is" in its natural state, if human values, human judgment and human benefit are to be considered irrelevant, we would be forced to *tolerate many threats and diseases* generally perceived to be themselves harmful if not attacked and even wiped out if possible. An unqualified ecosystem approach pushed to its logical extreme might, for example, force a conclusion that the extinction of the smallpox virus was not a good thing, or that grasshoppers, mosquitoes, noxious weeds, various pests and disease organisms should not be combatted but protected, or that the building of human settlements was wrong because some ecosystems were necessarily harmed in the process. Few if any ecologists seem actually to intend those conclusions, but they do perhaps illustrate the sort of dilemmas implicit in attempts to determine and evaluate environmental harm, and the need to qualify the "deep ecology" stance in the light of some other considerations.

(2) The adaptive capacity of the environment

A second limitation of an extreme and rigorous ecosystem approach used to measure environmental harm, is that ecosystems are not only in many respects vulnerable, but also *adaptive and evolutionary.* Up to a point and in some respects, ecosystems can respond to and accommodate change. Some man-made alterations of an element of the environment can, in particular cases, trigger adaptive responses. Ecosystems are not in all respects fixed; there is a

degree of rhythm and fluctuation. It becomes important in this regard to weigh impacts of polluting contaminants and activities as to whether they are degradable and noncumulative (for example, many pulp and paper wastes), nondegradable and cumulative (for example, mercury, lead, PCBs), reversible or irreversible, natural yet likely to cause damage to some environments in large concentrations (for example, sulphates, chlorides). There are undoubtedly good reasons for policy makers to give more attention to the "inherent worth" view of the natural environment, but this adaptive mechanism itself of ecosystems has an inherent worth and should be added to the calculations of harm. In some cases, the conclusion will be that a substance or activity goes well beyond the adaptive capacity of an ecosystem; in other cases it may not.

(3) Tolerating pollution for legitimate social purposes: Balancing the human health standard

There is yet a third and most important factor to be weighed in calculations of serious pollution harm, a factor more or less incompatible with an ecosystem approach which is strict and absolute. It is generally acknowledged in our political and economic system, and in our environmental policies and laws, that there are a number of legitimate social purposes which can justify, at least for a period of time, varying degrees of pollution, deterioration and risk — which permit downgrading the pollution harm and risk from serious and intolerable to less-than-serious and tolerable. It is not, of course, uncommon for the law to conclude that what would be reckless and unacceptable behaviour in some circumstances, can be justified if socially desirable for one reason or another. For example, a very risky medical operation can, in some circumstances, be acceptable and even desirable if it offers the only chance to save a life.

Primary among the goals and purposes implicitly or explicitly underlying environmental policies, regulations and statutes are economic ones. An environmental agency may judge, for example, that a particular existing industry should be allowed to exceed, at least for a specified time, the statutory emission standard for a particular contaminant, because there may be good reason to believe the expense of strict compliance will bankrupt the company and cause widespread unemployment. Similarly, it may be judged that the only way to secure the establishment of a new industry in an economically depressed area and to develop and market local resources is to permit it to do some widespread ecological damage, and/or, at least for a time, exceed by a considerable margin the statutory emission standards. It would, of course, be naive and unrealistic to assume that all such judgments are equally defensible, or that the economic viability and employment arguments of industry should be accepted uncritically by agencies. However, it would be equally naive and Utopian to expect that environmental decision making can ever be completely insulated from economic and political considerations.

It should be noted that the mere emission of a particular contaminating substance beyond the standard established in the relevant statute or regulations need not in itself always imply serious (or even minor) environmental and health harm. In the first place, the standard itself may be open to legitimate debate as to its accuracy and appropriateness. In some cases the standard may, by some criteria, be too strict, or based upon uncertain evidence. On the other hand, it may be felt by some to be not strict enough. Secondly, it is at least the intention of regulation and standard makers to build into the emission standards a certain margin of safety.

The "social utility" and other factors just indicated demonstrate that judgments before or after the event about the types and degrees of pollution which will be characterized and treated as serious and intolerable, as opposed to minor and tolerable within regulated limits, are not and cannot be strictly and exclusively "scientific" in nature. Determinations of harm and degree of harm are to a large degree value-judgments, rather than scientific calculations. More precisely, such judgments are based upon criteria which themselves imply or import value-judgments. Therefore, these judgments about the acceptability of harm and risk should not be made only by the scientist as scientist. . . .

In any event, the life and health of others cannot be traded off for other apparent benefits, whether economic or other. We do not permit such a trade-off for other criminal offences involving serious harms or dangers to human life and bodily integrity. That being so, we may formulate the following by way of a general criterion: (1) the more certain is the evidence or likelihood of present or future harm and danger to human life and health, and the more serious the nature of that harm and danger, the less legitimate and persuasive should be other socially useful goals as justifications for the pollution or for reducing its classification from serious to minor, and the more compelling would be arguments for the criminal nature of that activity; (2) the less likely are the serious present and future human health harms and dangers, and the more likely the interests affected are exclusively those of the use and enjoyment of the environment, the more relevant and legitimate is the weighing of other societal goals by way of mitigating its classification as potentially serious harm.

31

Risks versus Rights: Economic Power and Economic Analysis in Environmental Politics

TED SCHRECKER

INTRODUCTION

Environmental pollution is one of the most striking and omnipresent impacts of industrial activity on society. Since the revelations concerning careless disposal of hazardous industrial wastes at Love Canal, it has become apparent that such corporate disregard for public health and safety is distressingly widespread, not only in the United States but in Canada as well.[1] Emissions of literally millions of tonnes per year of sulphur dioxide from non-ferrous smelters and electrical generating plants, and of nitrogen oxides from automobile exhausts and various industrial sources,[2] are transported over long distances and return to earth as the acid precipitation which threatens the life of lakes and rivers and, quite possibly, the health of forests in much of eastern North America.[3] And as this paper is being written, news stories about the "toxic blob" in the St. Clair river are drawing long-overdue attention to industry's use of the Great Lakes, which provide drinking water for millions of Canadians, as a convenient dumping ground for vast volumes of chemical waste.[4]

Economists refer to environmental impacts such as those described in the preceding paragraph as negative externalities. They are "costs of production," much like labour and raw materials. However, rather than being "internalized" in the sense that they are reflected in product prices and are therefore borne by either producers or consumers, they are borne by third parties (sometimes including future generations) who are not *directly* involved in the market transactions.[5] In an unregulated market, expenditures on pollution control would rarely be made. A purely profit-oriented firm has no economic motive to increase its production costs by internalizing the costs associated with its

From Protection of Life Series, *Political Economy of Environmental Hazards* by T.F. Schrecker. © 1984 Government of Canada. Reproduced by permission of the Minister of Supply and Services Canada.

impacts on the environment. Indeed, unless it occupies a monopoly position, it has excellent economic reasons to avoid doing so: the higher prices or lower returns on capital which would result mean that it would soon be driven out of business by less altruistic competitors. Considerations other than profitability (such as the negative public image associated with being viewed as a major polluter) *may* temper this purely economic calculation somewhat. However, the concept of negative externalities emphasizes the fact that environmental protection requirements, like other forms of governmental intervention to protect health and safety, are inherently redistributive.[6] They represent attempts to shift some costs of production from those who are affected by environmental degradation to producers and consumers of the products and services whose production generates these externalities.

"Business" is, of course, not a homogeneous group which always speaks with one voice, although recent research has demonstrated a pattern of "classwide rationality" in which large corporations appear to defend at least a core set of common interests and priorities.[7] On strictly economic grounds, one of these common priorities clearly is opposing environmental control requirements, or (alternatively) minimizing their economic impact. The reason for this opposition is analogous to the reasons for resisting any other increase in costs of doing business which is unproductive from the point of view of the individual firm.

Part I of this paper is an extremely brief inventory of the political resources[8] which business brings to environmental policy and politics, in particular the leverage large corporations enjoy by virtue of their control over investment flows. In many cases, the deployment of these resources has enabled business successfully to resist potentially costly environmental regulation, to delay its implementation, and (when this is no longer possible) to shift the costs of compliance to the public purse rather than imposing them on shareholders or consumers.

A further, and philosophically more intriguing, aspect of environmental ethics and politics has to do with the way we (as citizens, as consumers, as decision-makers in business or government) think about the issue of environmental pollution. Cost-benefit analysis of environmental regulation is, superficially at least, a common-sense approach to setting or assessing objectives for environmental policy, and is attractive on that basis. However, Part II of the paper suggests that CBA contains a number of built-in biases which favor business' priorities — a fact which explains the frequent support for CBA of environmental regulations expressed by business, and by business' advocates within government.

Cost-benefit analysis, more generally, embodies an implicit (but by no means self-evident) conception of what environmental policy — indeed, public policy in general — ought to be about. Part III of the paper briefly critiques this conception, arguing that there is much more to environmental policy than just correcting for market failures, in economists' terminology. Cost-benefit analysis involves adopting the "conceptual lenses"[9] of economics in a way which essentially prejudges a number of important ethical and political questions, and which does so in a way which reinforces what might loosely be termed a business-oriented view of the political process as a whole. When we substitute other conceptual lenses, the relative importance of various aspects of environmental problems changes, as do problem definitions themselves. Exploring the biases of economics, *via* the implications of CBA, suggests the seriousness of some of the optical flaws in that particular set of lenses.

I. BUSINESS IN ENVIRONMENTAL POLITICS: HOW THE CARDS ARE STACKED

Given the economic analysis provided in the introduction to this paper, one would expect the relationship between business and environmental regulators to be an adversarial one. Yet despite occasionally bitter conflicts, it is generally characterized by a high degree of consultation and mutual accommodation between business and agencies charged with environmental protection.[10]

One reason for this coziness is information: regulated firms may control access to technical information which is essential to governments in the making of environmental policy. As an example of how this resource helps industry to defend its preferred status in the regulatory process, the head of Environment Canada's Environmental Protection Service (EPS) informed a Parliamentary committee in 1980 of EPS's fear that broadening public participation would "break down that relationship with industry that has served us very well in providing us with technical information."[11]

Another reason is the substantial financial and organizational resources of business, in particular of large corporations. The interests of these firms are articulated not just through individual representations to governments, but also by way of trade associations with substantial resources of their own. An extensive study of the 10 major chemical industry trade associations several years ago found that their average annual budget was roughly $350,000 — not counting the value of the time of corporate staff spent on association business.[12] Few if any organizations representing the constituency for environmental protection have resources even approaching this magnitude. In addition, as illustrated in the chemical industry study,[13] trade associations have more or less on-going contacts with government concerning a variety of issues, of which the environment is only one — providing business with a valuable resource in terms of its contacts with government departments such as those responsible for industrial expansion or resource development. The success of policies and programs administered by these latter departments is more or less inseparable from the activities of industry,[14] a fact which may make them indifferent if not actively hostile to environmental concerns which threaten those activities.

One effect of business' wealth and organization is to enable it to monitor and respond to governmental initiatives on an on-going basis. The result is, arguably, environmental policy whose major impact is largely symbolic: "'tough' legislation to satisfy environmental groups and the general public, and weak enforcements with many complex exceptions to provide an accommodation with the pollution sources themselves."[15] At the level of implementation and enforcement, the financial resources of business firms allow them to delay implementation of costly environmental requirements by forcing regulators either to accept promises of compliance at some future date or to become involved in protracted and costly litigation. Relative to the costs (to polluters) of litigation, "[t]he benefits of delay are typically so great in comparison with the costs of complying that . . . a regulatory agency faces the possibility not of a handful of violators that it could reasonably handle, but of tacit noncompliance by large segments of an industry."[16] This observation helps to explain why (for example) throughout the 1970s firms in the Ontario pulp and paper industry persistently failed to meet the deadlines for meeting effluent limits which they had negotiated with the province's Ministry of the Environment.[17]

Another essential factor in explaining such situations is the way in which the legal framework for environmental policy reflects and reinforces business power and influence.[18] There are several dimensions to this problem, only two of which are discussed here. First, most environmental legislation in Canada is structured along the same lines as the criminal law — meaning that penalties can only be imposed following conviction. Preparing a successful prosecution is time-consuming and expensive, and the actual resolution of the case may take several years.[19] Yet until a conviction is registered, the cost of violating the law is limited to the costs of litigation, which (as noted earlier) may be trivial relative to the economic benefits of noncompliance. In addition, the economic penalties (fines) provided for by legislation need not bear any relationship to the economic benefits from violating environmental law.[20]

A number of alternative mechanisms for imposing sanctions on polluting firms have been proposed to overcome these difficulties.[21] For example, frustrated by the pulp and paper industry's continuing indifference to its effect on the environment, economists with Ontario's Ministry of the Environment in the mid-1970s proposed a regime of pollution control delay penalties, which would *automatically* be levied against any company which failed to meet a deadline (negotiated with the Ministry) for meeting pollution control objectives.[22] The penalties would be based on a formula taking into account both the amount by which effluent discharges exceeded allowable limits, and the duration of the violation. Perhaps not surprisingly,[23] this proposal was never implemented, despite the subsequent success of a similar approach to sanctioning polluters in the state of Connecticut.[24]

Second, the effectiveness of the potential constituencies for environmental protection (environmentalist organizations and the general public in affected areas) is seriously compromised by the general absence of legally guaranteed opportunities for participation in policy and enforcement decisions.[25] Whereas industry enjoys an on-going consultative relationship with government, the situation in Ontario — in which public participation opportunities consist of meetings where audiences are treated to defences of positions previously negotiated between the Ministry of the Environment and the polluting firm — is more or less typical. As an extreme example of the effect of the absence of public participation on policy outcomes, in 1979 Amax Ltd. was given permission by Order-in-Council to dump more than 10,000 tonnes of heavy metal-laden tailings a day into the ocean from a mine in northern British Columbia, despite the fact that this dumping was clearly prohibited by one of the few sets of regulations under the federal Fisheries Act, and despite strong internal opposition within Environment Canada. The company was able to press its case in forums including a private meeting between its lawyers, Environment officials, and two Cabinet ministers; and the regulations permitting the dumping were developed on the basis of secret correspondence and exchanges of drafts between Environment Canada and Amax's lawyers.[26] Not only was there no "public participation" in this process, the very fact that there was a process going on was concealed from those outside the charmed government-industry circle until the regulations were published.

The law can provide for the public *some* portion of the status within the policy process which industry enjoys by virtue of wealth and organization. When the law fails to do this, as it does almost without exception in Canada, access to decision-making remains contingent on wealth, organization, and perceived legitimacy. Access therefore remains largely restricted to the industries whose activities create the need for government intervention in the first place. The extent of the perceived legitimacy of the priorities of business, and of business–government contacts, is indicated by the comments of Canada's Royal Commission on Corporate Concentration (the Bryce Commission) that:

> It is not surprising that there should be close contact between many businesses and the governments of Canada and the provinces in which they operate, for there is a common concern with a wide variety of economic and social problems and legislative and regulatory measures. The success of government measures requires knowledge of how they may be expected to affect particular industries or companies, while the success of business projects will require a knowledge of the laws and public policies that will apply to them. It is *in the public interest* that there should be consultation in these matters."[27] (Emphasis added)

But what are the roots of this equation of business priorities with the public interest, of the "common concerns" of business and government? And how do these affect environmental policy?

To address this question, it is necessary to consider the role of control over investment flows as a political resource for business (and for large corporations, in particular). In specific conflicts over environmental hazards, the ownership of capital (and its mobility) enable corporate polluters to use the implied or expressed threat of production cutbacks or plant closures to mobilize opposition to regulatory proposals on the part of affected workers and communities and to impose a particular set of tradeoffs between jobs and the environment on political decision-makers. Kazis and Grossman, who have analyzed this phenomenon extensively in the American context, refer to it as "job blackmail;"[28] and two Canadian examples suggest how the process works.

In the 1960s, the paper mill complex operated by Reed Ltd. at Dryden, Ontario was responsible for the contamination of the English-Wabigoon river system in northwestern Ontario with mercury, and the resulting destruction of the food supply of the local Native population.[29] The mercury problem was eventually remedied, but throughout the 1970s, Reed Ltd. made almost no changes to reduce its emissions of dissolved organic materials and suspended solids, with devastating effects on downstream waters, and the Ontario Ministry of the Environment made few serious efforts to induce such changes.[30] At hearings of an Ontario legislative committee held in 1979, partly to address Reed's pollution record, the president of Reed Ltd. threatened that the firm would shut down the plant (the community's major employer) if the Ministry of the Environment held firm on a proposed deadline for pollution control measures.[31] This threat, based on Reed's alleged financial weakness and the unwillingness of its British parent company to invest any additional money in its money-losing subsidiary, was effective in getting the legislators to recommend a compromise between the Ministry's proposed deadline and the three additional years Reed demanded for reducing discharges whose destructive efforts had been identified at least as early as 1968.[32]

Noranda, Inc., a firm indirectly controlled by one of the richest families in Canada[33], operates a copper smelter in Rouyn, Quebec which accounted in 1980 for roughly 11 percent of total Canadian emissions of sulphur dioxide, and roughly 30 percent of sulphur dioxide emissions from non-ferrous smelters.[34] Like other smelter operators (for example Inco Ltd. in Sudbury, Ontario[35]), Noranda has until recently been very successful in resisting public and governmental pressure for major emissions reductions, despite the contribution of smelter emissions to acid precipitation and despite evidence of elevated lung-cancer risk to residents of the Rouyn area.[36] The company's president warned in May, 1984 that the firm "could find itself caught between the 'politically unacceptable' choice of closing a smelter that employs 1,200 people" or investing in modernization which would have the added effect of reducing SO_2 emissions.[37] The impact of such statements in terms of allocation of the costs of emission reduction is discussed below.

The threat of disinvestment may be invoked in discussions of general policy directions as well as in firm-specific conflicts. One of the executives interviewed by Silk and Vogel in their 1976 study of American business argued that it should be used more extensively: "We need political sophistication. We have to tell a state considering additional restrictions on business: 'The next plant doesn't go up here if that bill passes'."[38] Such a capital strike does not appear to have occurred in Canada in response specifically to environmental policy initiatives. However, the use of such a tactic by the mining industry in resisting the tax reform recommendations of the Carter Royal Commission on Taxation[39] suggests that it might be employed under some conditions in the environmental policy context.

In terms of the overall development of environmental policy, it is less important to enumerate specific cases of job blackmail than to understand that conflicts in which the overt threat of disinvestment is invoked in response to environmental requirements are the exception, rather than the rule. Here we come back to the Bryce Commission's definition of the "public interest." Governments in capitalist or mixed economies rely heavily on the continued flow of private investment to sustain the economic growth which both provides income and employment for their citizens and finances the provision of state services of various kinds. Public policy in various areas must therefore reflect an underlying latent tension between the state's various other functions, such as eliminating the damaging effects of industrial activity on the environment, and the need to sustain the conditions for capital accumulation — or, in the more familiar terms often used by business organizations, to create and maintain a favorable business climate. Marxist analysts, of whom Offe is the most sophisticated,[40] have led the way in drawing attention to the importance of this constraint. At the same time, Lindblom's extremely perceptive account of the "privileged position of business" in public life[41] shows that it is possible to analyze the impact of corporate power on public policy starting from a thoroughly non-Marxist set of assumptions.

The powerful position of business is further enhanced when firms can allocate investment (and use their control over technology and expertise) in a way which maximizes returns on a transjurisdictional scale, whether the jurisdictions being played off one against another are provinces, states or nations. In the words of a leading text on international business: "Whenever a business has something of value that can be offered to several nations, the power to control can be eroded by competition between countries. And the limits on the exercise of this power are set by the weakest of the nations concerned."[42] This process becomes particularly significant in times of slow economic growth. Gladwin and Walter conclude, on the basis of extensive research on environmental conflicts involving large corporations, that "conditions of high unemployment [have] led to shifting environmental priorities and less opposition to new plant construction in some regions."[43]

An evocative illustration of the power of corporate managements and the shareholders they represent occurred in the United States, in 1983. Asarco, Inc. had threatened to shut down a copper smelter in Tacoma, Washington if further reduction in the smelter's arsenic emissions were required by the Environmental Protection Agency (EPA). EPA solicited the views of area residents on whether or not they were willing to accept the (estimated) additional cancer risks associated with the arsenic emissions in return for the 500 jobs and associated economic benefits provided by the smelter.[44] This is job blackmail, but in a particularly subtle and revealing form. Government, *via* the EPA, was not in a position to challenge Asarco's right to shut down the smelter if the firm considered the returns from its operation to be inadequate. Thus, the terms of the jobs-versus-environment tradeoff imposed by the corporation's management and shareholders could not be altered except by

compromising environmental and human health protection.

In the Canadian context, the control of emissions from copper and nickel smelters provides a fine illustration of another important aspect of business' power: the ability to recover from the public purse the cost of compliance with pollution restrictions. Copper and nickel smelters account for more than 40 percent of Canadian sulphur dioxide emissions[45] — the emissions which, along with nitrogen oxides emissions, are the chemical precursors of acid precipitation. The 1984 report of a Parliamentary Sub-committee on Acid Rain[46] pointed out that expenditures on modernizing Canadian non-ferrous smelters would result both in emissions reductions and in major economic payoffs for the industry. According to the report, "process changes in a number of smelters can significantly reduce SO_2 emissions and still be justified on purely economic grounds. In other words, the portion of cost which is attributable to SO_2 control can, in some instances, approach zero."[47]

Yet despite such economic benefits to polluting firms, *not one* of the report's recommendations for controlling smelter emissions suggested a stricter or more effective regime of regulation to require emissions reductions at the expense of the smelter operators. Rather, citing the poor profit position of the smelter operators, the legislators recommended far more generous tax writeoffs for pollution control investments and research, as well as a system of direct capital grants to the non-ferrous smelting industry for capital expenditures associated with pollution abatement.[48] Early in 1985, the Canadian government committed itself to providing up to $150 million in direct subsidies to smelter operators for pollution abatement, as part of an intergovernmental agreement under which provincial governments will be called on to provide further subsidies.[49]

As suggested earlier, direct job blackmail may have played a part in determining this outcome. Probably more important, however, was and is the fact that the redistributive nature of environmental policy means that it cannot be made in isolation —

at least not for long, or not by a government which intends to remain in power. In Lindblom's words, "even the unspoken possibility of adversity for business operates as an all-pervasive constraint on governmental authority."[50] In the environmental field, the most significant manifestation of business power is its effect in constraining the regulation of existing operations, or determining that some policy options (for example, requiring the shareholders of firms like Inco and Noranda or the consumers of their products, rather than the taxpaying public as a whole, to foot the bill for plant improvements which will reduce pollution levels) are *a priori* infeasible and therefore will not form part of the agenda of government. Feasibility in this context is defined not in a technical sense, or even on the basis of academic economic analysis, but rather by the wealth and power of the affected firms and industries.[51]

II. COST-BENEFIT ANALYSIS AND THE EFFICIENCY CRITERION

For most economists, the prevalence of environmental pollution is traceable to the absence of definable property rights to the use of common property resources like air and water, and to the consequent absence of a market in their use as a way of balancing competing uses.

> For example, people exposed to the effects of air pollution . . . have no recourse through the market to obtain financial compensation. This would not be the case if people owned a marketable right to clean air since, under those circumstances, industrialists wishing to pollute the air in their quest for profit would have to buy the right to do so in the same way as they must buy the right to use the other resources that are necessary for production."[52]

It is therefore plausible to take the view adopted by the Economic Council of Canada, in the final report of its Regulation Reference study, that "regulation has . . . to perform the function normally accomplished by market forces; that is, regulation

must establish the relative values of alternative uses of the environment if appropriate trade-offs are to be made."[53]

Cost-benefit analysis (CBA) was originally developed as a technique for evaluating major public works projects involving water development, for many of whose benefits (e.g. flood control, improved recreational opportunities) no markets existed.[54] CBA "is a procedure through which the analyst simulates the workings of a perfectly competitive market system;" it "addresses the question of how the market would decide an issue, such as whether and in what way to use a new pesticide, if the market was perfectly competitive and all effects were accounted for."[55] There is a commonsensical appeal to CBA: would "we," as a society, want to incur costs for environmental protection which are not justified by the corresponding benefit? However, the implications are too seldom examined of the implied endorsement of markets as the preferred way of deciding the worth of benefits like the improvements in human health and longevity which may result from environmental protection initiatives.

Utilitarian philosophers have long been bedevilled by the abstract nature of the concept of utility, the absence of natural units for interpersonal comparisons of utility, and the consequent elusiveness of the ideal of the greatest good for the greatest number. The corresponding concept for economists is that of Pareto-optimal allocations of resources,[56] and markets provide a solution to the problem of interpersonal comparisons of utility by allowing all participants to define welfare or utility on the basis of their own preferences, and to maximize their welfare (within the context of their limited individual resources) on the basis of willingness to pay to satisfy those preferences.

> An exchange takes place only when both parties feel they benefit by it. When no additional exchanges can be made, the economy has reached a situation where each individual in it cannot improve his own situation without damaging that of another. . . . When no one can be made better

off without someone else being worse off, Pareto optimality has been reached.[57]

In other words, perfectly functioning markets will generate optimal allocations of resources.

Situations in which no one is made any worse off (like perfectly functioning markets) are rare indeed in the real world of public policy. The response of welfare economists and policy analysts has been to evaluate policy alternatives on the basis of *potential* Pareto improvements. This criterion, known as the Kaldor-Hicks principle after its originators, requires only that aggregate welfare/utility gains outweigh aggregate losses, based on the ability of "gainers" to compensate "losers," once values have been attached to gains and losses. In theory, society *could* require that gainers compensate losers, thus achieving a Pareto-superior distribution of utility. However, the principle does not require that compensation actually be paid[58], and is thus normatively indifferent to questions of distribution or entitlement. "This is the efficiency criterion of the new welfare economics."[59]

As applied to environmental pollution, this efficiency criterion defines an appropriate level of pollution abatement in terms of the level of pollution control or hazard control expenditures at which the sum of the costs of pollution abatement and of the damage done by the remaining externality is minimized. The next increment of environmental improvement "purchased" through installing additional pollution control devices will cost more than it is worth in terms of the value of damage reduction, and at this point:

> Despite passionate prose to the contrary, society will lose less, or gain more, if it puts [the remaining] waste in the river and takes the money (land, labor and capital) it would have spent treating these units of waste and devotes it to building hospitals, homes, and hula-hoop factories, or whatever people indicate they prefer by their spending habits.[60]

Pollution is thus only one among many competing uses of the natural environment, and pollution control just one among many competing uses of society's resources, the balance among which is best decided on the basis of market mechanisms.

For several years during the 1970s, executive agencies like the Council on Wage and Price Stability (COWPS) and the Office of Management and Budget (OMB) in the United States attempted to force regulatory agencies like the Environmental Protection Agency (EPA) and the Occupational Safety and Health Administration (OSHA) to attach greater importance to the costs of compliance with their proposed standards.[61] The rationale for these attempts was concern for the inflationary impacts of such regulations. The Reagan administration in February, 1981 issued an Executive Order requiring formal CBA of major new regulations, specifically requiring that new regulations demonstrate a favourable benefit-cost ratio.[62] Tolchin argues that this progression was a direct result of industry resistance to regulation-imposed costs:

> The rush to deregulate was industry's answer to double-digit inflation, and its leaders convinced the leaders of both political parties . . . that they had a simple way of reducing product costs: reduce the onerous regulations, sometimes confusing and duplicative, and trust the free market to regulate itself.[63]

In Canada, CBA is a preferred, although not mandatory, technique for assessing the economic impacts of major new regulations under the Socio-Economic Impact Analysis (SEIA) requirements imposed by Treasury Board at the federal level.[64] Recent initiatives by a group of Canadian government departments including Environment, Agriculture, and Health and Welfare have strongly supported more extensive application of CBA to the choice of objectives in toxic substances policy.[65] Some of the reasons for the relatively less extensive reliance on CBA in Canadian regulatory decision-making, and for its attractiveness to industry, are discussed in Part III of this paper.

An extensive literature exists on the daunting practical limitations of trying to quantify the hazards of environmental pollution and the corresponding benefits of regulation — for instance, in terms of the improvements in water quality which will result from a specified level of effluent discharge reductions, or in terms of the reduced number of cases of lung cancer or premature mortality from respiratory disease which will be associated with controlling air pollution from a given source.[66] In the case of cancer, for example, uncertainties about actual human exposures are compounded by conflicting models of the relationship between disease incidence and exposure, meaning that numerical risk estimates may vary by several orders of magnitude.[67] In some instances, industries faced with absorbing the costs of regulation may argue that insufficient evidence exists for the *existence* of a health hazard. Industry spokesmen have claimed, for example, that insufficient evidence exists for a relationship among gasoline lead levels, blood lead levels in children, and behavior alterations and impairments in cognitive development in those exposed children[68] despite a large and growing body of scientific data.[69] In such situations of at least partial uncertainty about impacts (which are probably the rule rather than the exception in environmental policy) any CBA is only as good as the underlying quantitative risk estimates. The decisions which determine the outcome of the analysis do not involve readily and unequivocally quantified benefits. Rather, they involve policy decisions about how scientific uncertainty is to be treated for purposes of public decision-making.[70] The values brought to the resolution of such "science policy" questions[71], crucial through they are, are not discussed further here. However, it must be emphasized that crucial value judgments about how to resolve scientific uncertainty — in situations where waiting for more evidence itself implies a particular normative balancing of risks and benefits[72] — are part of almost every assessment of human health risk or environmental impact.

When we make decisions about, for example, the appropriate level of pollution prevention on the basis of CBA or of the efficiency criterion which underlies it, we are saying that we would be satisfied with the outcomes of markets for such amenities as environmental quality, if such markets could be established. But this point is hardly self-evident. We are uncomfortable with the implications of using "pure" markets to allocate such benefits (or hardships) as military service or scarce and expensive medical treatment,[73] largely because market-based resource allocations inevitably reflect the existing distribution of income and wealth. Willingness to pay implies ability to pay. Thus in environmental planning, as Kapp has noted:

> The logical and practical result of using willingness to pay as a criterion would be that public parks or clean air in the ghetto sections of a large city would yield a lower benefit-cost ratio than the marina for top management personnel. A mode of reasoning which leads to or indirectly supports such an outcome reveals its hidden, basically unequalitarian [*sic*] value judgments inherent in the compensation principle as a criterion of evaluating the 'worth' of environmental goals.[74]

This inseparability of benefit valuations from distributions of wealth and income is one general source of bias in CBA. Another has to do with the issue of what is to count as a cost of regulation (or a benefit of the regulated activity). Such costs include not only the direct expenditures made on complying with the regulation or policy (compliance costs), but also the foregone returns that the funds thus expended could have been earning in some other use (e.g. producing more hula hoops rather than reducing emissions of the pollutants produced by their manufacture). Thus, Weidenbaum argues that the costs of regulation include "[t]he new investments in plant and equipment that are not made" and "the factories that are not built, the jobs that do not get created, the goods and services that do not get produced, and the incomes that are not generated"[75] because of the diversion of investment capital for purposes which are unproductive (in market terms).

The discounting of future benefits and costs is a corollary of this preference for market outcomes. Benefits which result in the future from the expenditure of funds today (for example, on proper disposal of industrial wastes) must be discounted in order to assess the efficiency of resource allocations, because otherwise the funds could be earning a return in some other use.[76] This is the rationale for the choice of a discount rate for purposes of CBA based on average private-sector rates of return on capital. It is possible, of course, to specify a lower discount rate for certain kinds of benefits, such as protection of human health. However, the choice of a discount rate remains inescapably value-laden. Since many environmental impacts and human health effects (e.g., from the improper disposal of hazardous industrial waste) may take many years to materialize, a point of particular importance is that extremely painful and undesirable future consequences may appear insignificant once their dollar cost is discounted to arrive at the present value of avoiding future disaster. In the occupational health context:

> . . . consider the economic decision faced by a businessman who would need $200,000 to 'design-in' carcinogenic exposure controls for workers at a particular worksite. Given a current [1981] discount rate in the private economy of at least 12 percent, if the businessman put only $11,800 into an investment opportunity affording 12 percent interest, at the end of 25 years there would be a check for $200,000 waiting for him. So, for the businessman, clearly the preference would not be to spend $200,000 now in prevention, but to bank $11,800 now for compensation and after-the-fact expenditures.[77]

Such discounting is, in the context of CBA, rational for society as well as for the individual firm.

Some further philosophical implications of this preference for marketed goods and services are explored in Part III of the paper. A more immediate issue is: how are dollar values attached to the benefits of environmental control for purposes of cost-benefit comparisons? Here, in particular, only an outline of a very extensive literature can be provided. The value of recreational amenities preserved or improved has often been inferred on the basis of the amount of time and money individuals are willing to spend to take advantage of such opportunities.[78] And the difference in property values between areas of (for example) high and low air pollution areas can be used to provide a proxy measure for the amount people are willing to pay for cleaner air.[79] Such measures are at least vaguely plausible, but they also illustrate (as Kapp points

out) the biases which are related to income and wealth distribution. The fact that high-income areas generally enjoy cleaner air than poor areas of the same city[80] can be interpreted in terms of willingness to pay for air quality; it can also mean simply that the poor are victimized by their inability to pay the higher price of living in a cleaner, healthier area.

Benefit valuations become most questionable, and most contentious, when dollar values are determined for prevention of adverse effects on human life and health. One approach to valuing policy-related health improvements is to estimate direct cost savings on, e.g., doctors' fees, drugs, and hospital services.[81] Thus, the CBA produced by the U.S. EPA of its 1984 proposals for drastic reductions in allowable gasoline lead levels valued the benefits of regulation in terms of avoiding cognitive impairment among children with elevated blood lead levels in terms of the avoidance of costs for compensatory education and medical treatment which would otherwise be incurred.[82] Benefit valuations may also include the increased dollar earnings which are made possible by a healthier population — an approach which, admittedly, "discriminates against programs that improve the health of the non-working: children, the elderly, unemployed."[83] This is a specific variation of a general method for valuing the benefits of life-saving or health-protecting programs known as the "human capital approach," which values the saving of a life in terms of discounted future earnings. On this basis, the lives of men are worth more than those of women (who earn less money), children's lives are worth less than those of young adults and middle-aged people (because of the effects of discounting on nominally larger, but more remote, future earnings), and the life of an 85-year-old nonwhite American woman, in 1972, was worth US $128.[84] Yet despite such conclusions, and despite its repudiation by at least some economists,[85] the human capital approach was endorsed by a Canadian government interdepartmental working group on toxic chemicals policy in 1984.[86]

The human capital approach is not, in fact, an estimate of willingness-to-pay; rather, "it is derived from an alternative value judgment, namely, that . . . output is a measure of worth."[87] (It could, presumably, be argued that the maximum amount individuals will be *able* to pay for protection of life and health is a function of their discounted future earnings.[88]) Alternative approaches which attempt to generate estimates based on willingness to pay do not attach a value directly to life; rather, they assess expenditures directed toward improving health or incrementally reducing the risk of death — a subtle but important distinction.[89] As an extreme and barbaric example of such inferences, it has been seriously suggested that cosmetic losses resulting from illness or injury could be valued based on "an implicit price of personal attractiveness" based on "expenditures wholly designed to increase one's own attractiveness."[90] (A moment's reflection on the application of this criterion in a CBA of, say, a product safety standard designed to prevent disfiguring injury is sufficient to illustrate its absurdity). More humanely, analysts have attempted to infer valuations from the amounts people spend to protect their life and health (for example, by investing in home smoke detectors[91]) or, alternatively, from the amount they appear to demand as compensation for increased risk as measured by the wage differentials between more and less hazardous occupations.[92] (The "payment" in this case is not a direct one, but rather the foregone earnings in higher-paid, but more hazardous occupations).

Full information on the effectiveness of, e.g., smoke detectors may not be available. And full information on work-related hazards is probably never available.[93] (Indeed, employers have an obvious economic motive to restrict the supply of such information[94]). The "choice" facing workers may be seriously limited by such factors as skills, geographical location, the cyclical nature and dominant labour market position of local industries (alternative employment for uranium miners in Elliot Lake, Ontario; asbestos miners in Thetford Mines or Asbestos, Quebec; or loggers and pulp mill workers in northwestern Ontario and much of British Columbia may be hard to come by[95]) and regional and national unemployment levels. Since the distribution of wealth in economies like Can-

ada's means that most individuals must work for a living, many of those who enter risky occupations may have little *effective* choice in the matter.[96] A related weakness of wage differential studies, almost universally ignored, is that they have focussed on hourly-rated or working-class occupations[97] and have therefore restricted their scope to individuals whose alternative employment options are far less extensive than those of, say, senior managers (or university economists). People in these latter occupations might demand far higher compensation in return for additional increases in work-related risk. Indeed, it may well be that such occupations are not only much better paid but also safer than those included in wage differential studies. This observation illustrates the class bias of such studies, and suggests that "risk premiums" for hazardous work, if and when they exist at all, probably reflect only the relative power of buyers and sellers in a particular labour market. Here, again, valuations of life and health are "molded by the current distribution of wealth because behaviour and perceived opportunities depend on ability to pay. Thus, these methods have a status quo bias and cannot be expected to produce socially equitable resource allocations."[98]

III. COST-BENEFIT ANALYSIS, ETHICS, AND POLITICAL THEORY

An economist might respond to these criticisms, and others, by pointing out that society's material resources are finite. In one respect, society implicitly attaches a dollar value to human life and health (the most frequent criticism of CBA) every day, for example in deciding on the level of expenditure which will be made (or required) on various life- or health-protecting initiatives, ranging from occupational health standards to purchases of medical equipment for hospitals or improvements in highway guardrails.[99] Cost-benefit analysis, then, is merely a source of information which can be used to improve the "return" (in terms of protecting life, health and the environment) from the use of limited resources.

Few would deny the problem posed by finite resources, although (as suggested in Part I) limits to available resources in specific contexts are often a function of the wealth and power of those who might be adversely affected by the redistributive impact of a particular policy. However, there are several reasons to reject invocations of resource limitations in defence of CBA. First, Calabresi and Bobbitt have coined the phrase "tragic choices" to describe such decisions as the allocation of life-saving expenditures or scarce medical treatment.[100] CBA attempts to simulate a market allocation, but markets are only one of several ways of making tragic choices. (The choice of a market mechanism rather than some other kind is itself a value-laden and political one). At best, then, CBA is instructive as a way of determining how resources might be allocated *if* markets were used to make a particular tragic choice. And in the course of doing so, it arguably serves to camouflage the importance of the fact that incommensurable values (e.g., dollars versus lives) are being compared.

This weakness is important even in cases where CBA is only used (as some economists say it should be) to "organize available information"[101] for purposes of policy decisions. A second weakness emerges in cases where CBA is used as the basis for an actual decision rule — i.e. where market valuations are implicitly favoured as the basis for allocating resources. Requirements that policy measures show a favourable benefit-cost ratio foreclose serious consideration of the merits of decisions which would reduce the aggregate wealth of society but improve the situation of a particular set of victims. For example, a CBA might conclude that the costs of regulations which reduce or eliminate the use of lead additives in gasoline are not exceeded by the dollar benefits of associated improvements in the cognitive abilities of children who now are exposed, via a number of pathways, to considerable amounts of lead which originates from gasoline combustion.[102] Quite apart from such issues as the value implications of methods for valuing health benefits and criteria for resolving scientific uncertainty, the "bottom line" is: how much do we, as a society, really care whether regulations guarding against

this sort of effect are economically efficient? There is nothing irrational about a society which decides to forego some wealth in favour of preventing adverse health effects of this sort, unless "rationality" is *a priori* equated with wealth-maximization.[103]

To state this problem in another way, the efficiency criterion as embodied in CBA of environmental policy implies that the creation of any "cost," including pain, illness and death, can be justified (at least in principle) by the demonstrable creation of an offsetting benefit *somewhere* within the society or the economy, once both benefits and costs have been properly monetized. On the basis of the Kaldor-Hicks principle, this state of affairs is justifiable since losers *could* be compensated for their losses. But what if no mechanism exists for them to assert a claim for such compensation? (The inadequacy of existing legal entitlements to compensation for pollution damages in Canada has been extensively documented.[104]) Or, more seriously, what if the losers consider their losses non-compensable and would as individuals choose not to incur them, whatever the greater good in whose pursuit the costs are imposed? In such cases, a cost-benefit approach to choosing environmental policy objectives constitutes a form of technological conscription. As Bogen notes, the process " . . . goes farther than merely placing life on the market, it perforce places *all* lives on the market — in effect, transforming life into currency or legal tender which society is of right free to collect, like taxes, in order to pay off its technological debts."[105]

CBA, then, "solves" the problem posed for resource allocation (according to economists' analysis) by the absence of property rights in resources like air and water. But it does so by way of a powerful, implicit assignment of rights to the creators of environmental hazards, as a category, rather than to the potential recipients or victims of hazards, as long as economic benefits can be claimed to offset these risks. This is the same bias which is evident within the implementation of environmental policy, as typified by the case of Canadian non-ferrous smelter emissions, where the choice of accepting continued environmental destruction or bearing at least part of the cost of reducing those impacts is imposed by industry on other "users" of the natural environment.

At least some environmentalists have argued that the problem should be solved in quite a different way: some form of substantive and enforceable right to environmental quality, analogous in at least some respects to property rights, should be entrenched in law.[106] Examining the implications of this alternative approach serves to highlight the biases of the efficiency criterion. When a regulation prohibiting the release of a hazardous pollutant is not adopted because it cannot be shown to have a favourable benefit-cost ratio, government in effect allows the expropriation of the health of those individuals whose health may deteriorate as a result of exposure to the pollutant, based on an analyst's inference of the fair market value of their lives and health. The process is analogous to that of expropriation of real property. However, until and unless specific procedures for expropriation have been followed, our society defends your right to refuse to sell your house, whatever an economist's opinion of its fair market value. In Sax's words, society does not "leave the enforcement of an individual's property rights to some bureaucrat to vindicate when, and if, he determines them to be consistent with the public interest."[107] Procedural safeguards against unfair or arbitrary expropriation of property may be inadequate, but their perceived inadequacy highlights our general unwillingness to abandon a conception of property as an issue of *rights* for an alternative conception in which the entitlements to exclusion which consitute property rights are less firmly entrenched.

Why might industry support the application of CBA to environmental policy? The preceding analysis of the assignment of rights to the use of the environment suggests one important reason. Related, but probably more significant, is the way in which CBA's implied skepticism about the worth of benefits such as health protection which are inherently difficult to quantify and value serves to focus attention on the more "solid" and readily quantifiable costs (to industry) of regulation. In a perceptive comparison of American and British

regimes of environmental regulation, Vogel notes that the informal, consultative nature of the British regulatory process allows industry ample scope for articulating its priorities. On the other hand:

> American corporate executives, and academics sympathetic to them, urge the use of cost-benefit analysis precisely because so much of American environmental regulation is written and enforced without reference to the costs of complying with it. In a sense, the use of cost-benefit analysis represents a surrogate for the inability of American industry to have its interests taken more seriously.[108]

Tolchin similarly notes that CBA provides "a respectable methodological rationale" for opposition to the redistributive impacts of social regulation.[109] Vogel's analysis also suggests a reason for the relative scarcity of formal CBA requirements in Canadian regulatory mechanisms. The role played by CBA in the American context is made superfluous in Canada (as in Britain) by the routinely high degree of industry involvement in the policy process, and by the associated deference accorded to its priorities.

Related to the ethical assumptions embedded in CBA are implied propositions concerning political theory and the proper form of public decision-making. Environmental regulation is routinely justified as a necessary corrective for market failures. However, it is not self-evident that public policies which control environmental pollution should be evaluated on this basis. An alternative view, which emphasizes the redistributive aspects of environmental protection initiatives, is that "[t]he real purpose of government regulation in this field is not and never has been to correct deficiencies of markets but to transcend markets altogether." From this point of view, environmental policy "can be said to advance a conception of the public interest apart from, and often opposed to, the outcomes of the market place."[110] Beauchamp has made a similar point in analyzing public health policy: he contrasts the allocations of resources which result from the highly unequal distribution of market power ("market-justice") with what he sees as the basic direction of public health policy. That direction is "ultimately rooted in an egalitarian tradition that conflicts directly with the norms of market-justice."[111]

To oversimplify a highly complex set of comparisons, markets differ in several ways from non-market mechanisms (such as electoral politics) for making decisions and allocating resources. Although within an electoral system the impact of all franchised individuals is theoretically equal,[112] in a market setting power is directly proportional to wealth. One person, one vote as a basis for decision-making can yield outcomes strikingly different from those generated based on the (market) principle of one dollar, one vote.

More subtly, markets allocate resources based on the aggregation of (wealth- or income-weighted) individual preferences. Unlike at least some political decision-making mechanisms, they do not offer the opportunity for decisions based on collective choices about the proper direction and values of the community. This point has often been made with respect to decisions about the preservation of wilderness (whose direct economic worth may be relatively low) as opposed to its destruction for purposes of building dams or vacation resorts.[113] A dramatic contrast may well exist between individuals' willingness to pay for environmental protection (or to finance environmentally destructive activity!) as individual consumers, and their willingness *as citizens* to make decisions incurring a collective obligation (for example, preserving wilderness).[114] In Tribe's words, a decision-making process based on the "instrumental rationalty" of which CBA is typical

> ... could help the community draw various inferences from an assessment of how much its inhabitants *do in fact* value birds and other wildlife as compared, say, with boating and other activities; that is, the analysis could spin out the logical and empirical entailments of the value systems with which the community begins. But the analysis could *not* enable the community's inhabitants to think about *what those value systems ought to be* — about the extent to which theirs *should* be a wildlife-valuing community, with all that this might entail

for how its members view and value both nature and one another.[115]

Similarly, members of a community might decide on the need to guard against the health and environmental dangers of improper industrial waste disposal (for example) for reasons unrelated to the inferred willingness of any individual or set of individuals to pay for the benefits of those objectives as consumers, and unrelated to the number of dollars which can be saved for society (e.g. via reductions in health care expenditures).

It is not suggested here that political choice mechanisms in Canada routinely operate in the way idealized by Tribe. But they *can* do so, whereas markets cannot. The presuppositions underlying CBA and its application to public policy are therefore important as what Mueller has called a para-ideology.[116] For Mueller, ideologies in the traditional sense "justify the use of force to maintain the status quo, to initiate social change, and to suppress revolutionary activities."[117] Para-ideologies substitute, in functional terms, for such "integrated system[s] of meaning providing sociopolitical interpretations"[118]; they consist of "collective imagery rooted in material and social compensations"[119] which has the effect of structuring individuals' perceptions about the social order.

As an example of the contemporary significance of the concept of para-ideology, Mueller uses the acceptance of "rational" solutions derived by analogy with scientific and technological conclusions as a substitute for the outcome of conscious political choice. He is particularly concerned with the way such "rationality" can be used to obscure class conflicts — in Mueller's own words, to depoliticize politics.[120] The "rationality" embodied in CBA arguably has a similar effect, at the level of issue definitions, by (a) legitimizing existing distributions of wealth and rights, and (b) obscuring the potential for making tragic choices on some basis other than the aggregation of individual preferences.

There is nothing vicious or conspiratorial in business' defence of CBA and the associated norms of the marketplace. These are the norms according to which business must function, and according to which its success or failure is judged. One executive interviewed by Silk and Vogel succinctly argued that: "In the marketplace, every person gets a vote every day. The market is more democratic than the government."[121] There are a number of objections to this claim, only some of which have been discussed in this paper. More detailed examination would lead into a critical scrutiny of the concept of "democracy" itself.[122] The quotation is cited here to underscore the depth of potential conflict between markets and politics as alternative — if not competing — ways of making decisions about the direction of society, and the allocation of its admittedly finite resources. The greatest weakness of CBA as applied to environmental policy is simply that it presupposes the proper resolution of this competition. It does so in a way which reinforces, at the conceptual level, existing inequalities of wealth and power and which fails to acknowledge the legitimacy of views of public life as discerned through conceptual lenses other than those of economics.

ENDNOTES

1. J. Jackson and P. Weller, *Chemical Nightmare: The Unnecessary Legacy of Toxic Wastes* (Waterloo, Ont.: Between the Lines Press, 1982); S. Wolf, "Hazardous Waste Trials and Tribulations," *Environmental Law* 13 (1983), pp. 367-491. The province of Ontario alone generates more than 1.5 million tonnes of industrial wastes per year: D. Chant, "Ontario Generates 1.5 million Tonnes of Industrial Waste Annually," *Water and Pollution Control* (Directory and Buyers' Guide issue, 1983), pp. 17-21, 87-88.

2. *Still Waters: The Chilling Reality of Acid Rain*, Report of the Sub-Committee on Acid Rain, House of Commons Standing Committee on Fisheries and Forestry (Ottawa: Supply and Service Canada, 1981), pp. 19-47.

3. *Ibid.*, pp 51-59. See also M. Havas *et al.*, "Red Herrings in Acid Rain Research," *Environmental Science and Technology* 18:6 (June 1984), pp. 176A-186A; G. Likens *et al.*, "Acid Rain," *Scientific American* 241:4 (October 1979), pp. 43-51; G. Tomlinson II, "Air Pollutants and Forest Decline," *Environmental Science and Technology* 17:6 (June 1983), pp. 246A-256A.

4. Great Lakes Water Quality Board, International Joint Commission, *Inventory of Major Municipal and Industrial Point Source Dischargers in the Great Lakes Basin* (Windsor, Ontario: IJC, July 1979); M. Comba and K. Kaiser, "Volatile Hydrocarbons in the Detroit River and their Relationship with Contaminant Sources," *Journal of Great Lakes Research* 11:3 (1985), pp. 404-418; Y. Hamdy and L. Post, "Distribution of Mercury, Trace Organics and Other Heavy Metals in Detroit River Sediments," *Journal of Great Lakes Research* 11:3 (1985), pp. 353-365.

5. P. Victor, "Economics and the Challenge of Environmental Issues," in *Ecology versus Politics in Canada*, ed. W. Leiss (Toronto: University of Toronto Press, 1979), pp. 36-37.

6. R. A. Kagan, "On Regulatory Inspectorates and Police," in *Enforcing Regulation*, ed. K. Hawkins and J. Thomas (Boston: Kluwer-Nijhoff, 1984), p. 43.

7. M. Useem, "Classwide Rationality in the Politics of Managers and Directors of Large Corporations in the United States and Great Britain," *Administrative Science Quarterly* 27 (1982), pp. 199-226; M. Useem, *The Inner Circle* (New York: Oxford University Press, 1984).

8. R. Dahl defines political resources as "means by which one person can influence the behavior of another. Political resources therefore include money, information, food, the threat of force, jobs, friendship, social standing, the right to make laws, votes, and a great variety of other things." *Modern Political Analysis*, 4th ed. (Englewood Cliffs, NJ: Prentice-Hall, 1984), p. 31.

9. A concept drawn from G. Allison, *Essence of Decision* (Boston: Little, Brown, 1971), p. v.

10. J. Castrilli and C. Lax, "Environmental Regulation-Making in Canada: Towards a More Open Process," in *Environmental Rights in Canada*, ed. J. Swaigen (Toronto: Butterworths, 1981); R. Gibson, *Control Orders and Industrial Pollution Abatement in Ontario* (Toronto: Canadian Environmental Law Research Foundation, 1983), esp. chapter 4; J. W. Parlour, "The Politics of Water Pollution Control: A Case Study of the Canadian Fisheries Act Amendments and the Pulp and Paper Effluent Regulations, 1970," *Journal of Environmental Management* 13 (1980), pp. 127-149; W. Sullivan, "An Overview of the Background and Development of the Canadian Mercury Chlor-Alkali Air Emission Regulation," paper presented at the 73rd Annual Meeting, Air Pollution Control Association (Montreal, 1980), reproduced in *Proceedings* of the meeting.

11. Comments of R. Robinson, Assistant Deputy Minister, Environmental Protection Service, Environment Canada, in *Minutes of Proceedings* no. 6, House of Commons Special Committee on Regulatory Reform (September 24, 1980), p. 7.

12. W. Coleman and H. Jacek, "The Political Organization of the Chemical Industry in Canada," paper presented to the Canadian Political Science Association (Hamilton, Ont.: McMaster University, mimeo, 1981), pp. 36-37

13. *Ibid.*, pp. 24-29.

14. On such "functional relationships" between government departments and specific private-sector interests, see R. Presthus, *Elite Accommodation in Canadian Politics* (Toronto: Macmillan, 1973), pp. 212-216.

15. D. Dewees, "Evaluation of Economic Policies for Regulating Environmental Quality," Regulation Reference Working Paper No. 4 (Ottawa: Economic Council of Canada, 1980), p. 24.

16. F. Anderson, *Environmental Improvement Through Economic Incentives* (Baltimore: Johns Hopkins University Press, 1977), p. 16.

17. P. Victor and T. Burrell, *Environmental Protection Regulation, Water Pollution and the Pulp and Paper Industry*, Regulation Reference Technical Report no. 14 (Ottawa: Economic Council of Canada, 1981).

18. See generally T. Schrecker, "Mobilization of Bias in Closed Systems: Environmental Regulation in Canada," *Journal of Business Administration* 15:1, 1985, pp. 43-63.

19. See, e.g., "Long-Drawn Trial of Lead Company Adjourned Again," *Winnipeg Free Press*, October 18, 1984, p. 10; "Lead-Emission Case Goes to Judge," *Winnipeg Free Press*, December 7, 1984, p. 1 (on a prosecution under the federal *Clean Air Act* over regulations covering secondary lead smelters; which had dragged on for more than four years).

20. Gibson, note 10 above, p. 83; J. Swaigen, "Sentencing in Environmental Cases: A View from the Bar," in *Environmental Enforcement: Proceedings of the National Conference on the Enforcement of Environmental Law*, ed. L. Duncan (Edmonton: Environmental Law Centre, 1984).

21. For an overview see S. Baumol and W. Oates, *Economics, Environmental Policy and the Quality of Life* (Englewood Cliffs, NJ: Prentice-Hall, 1979), pp. 241-281 (on effluent charges); Dewees, note 15 above; Economic Council of Canada, *Reforming Regulation* (Ottawa: Supply and Services Canada, 1981), pp. 92-93; Peat, Marwick and Partners, *Economic Incentive Policy Instruments to Implement Pollution Control Objectives in Ontario* (Toronto: Ontario Ministry of the Environment, 1984), chapter III.

22. J. Donnan and P. Victor, *Alternative Policies for Pollution Abatement: The Ontario Pulp and Paper Industry* (Toronto: Ontario Ministry of the Environment, October 1976).

23. The cynical explanation is quite simply that such penalties would work — i.e., they would create much more reliable and consistent economic disincentives to the externalization of cost via pollution of the environment than do current legal regimes. See G. Majone, "Choice Among Policy Instruments for Pollution Control," *Policy Analysis* 2 (1976), pp. 590-613.

24. W. Drayton, "Economic Law Enforcement," *Harvard Environmental Law Review* 4 (1980), pp. 1-40.

25. Castrilli and Lax, note 10 above; Gibson, note 10 above; A. Lucas, "Legal Foundations for Public Participation in Environmental Decision Making," *Natural Resources Journal* 16 (January 1976), pp. 73-102; M. Rankin, "Information and the Environment: The Struggle for Access," in *Environmental Rights in Canada*, ed. J. Swaigen (Toronto: Butterworths, 1981).

26. This case is discussed in greater detail in K. Boggild, "The Amax Controversy," *Alternatives: Perspectives on Society and Environment* 10:2/3 (1982), pp. 40-46, 54; Schrecker, note 18 above, pp. 45-46, 54.

27. *Report of the Royal Commission on Corporate Concentration* (Ottawa: Supply and Services Canada, 1978), pp. 338–339.

28. R. Kazis and R. Grossman, *Fear at Work: Job Blackmail, Labor, and the Environment* (New York: Pilgrim Press, 1982).

29. W. Troyer, *No Safe Place* (Toronto: Clarke, Irwin, 1977).

30. *Final Report on Acidic Precipitation, Abatement of Emissions from the International Nickel Company Operations at Sudbury, Pollution Control in the Pulp and Paper Industry, and Pollution Abatement at the Reed Paper Mill in Dryden*, Standing Committee on Resources Development, Legislature of Ontario (Toronto, October 1979), pp. 85–90.

31. *Ibid.*, pp. 94–95.

32. *Ibid.*, pp. 115, 119–120.

33. B. Jorgensen, "Noranda Will Stick it Out Despite Debt," *The Globe and Mail*, June 29, 1985, p. 81.

34. *Still Waters*, note 2 above, pp. 19, 24.

35. B. Felske and R. Gibson, *Sulphur Dioxide Regulation and the Canadian Non-Ferrous Metals Industry*, Regulation Reference Technical Report No. 3 (Ottawa: Economic Council of Canada, 1980).

36. S. Cordier *et al.*, "Mortality Patterns in a Population Living near a Copper Smelter," *Environmental Research* 31 (1983), pp. 311–322.

37. K. Noble, "Noranda Links Pollution Control Costs to Fate of its Smelters," *The Globe and Mail*, May 31, 1984, p. 84.

38. L. Silk and M. Vogel, *Ethics and Profits: The Crisis of Confidence in American Business* (New York: Simon & Schuster, 1976), p. 66.

39. M. Bucovetsky, "The Mining Industry and the Great Tax Reform Debate," in *Pressure Group Behavior in Canadian Politics*, ed. P. Pross (Toronto: McGraw Hill-Ryerson, 1975).

40. C. Offe, *Contradictions of the Welfare State*, ed. J. Keane (Cambridge, MA: MIT Press, 1984).

41. C. Lindblom, *Politics and Markets* (New York: Basic Books 1977), pp. 170–221.

42. S. Robock *et al.*, *International Business and Multinational Enterprises*, rev. ed. (Homewood, IL: Irwin, 1977), p. 260. See also A. Martinelli, "The Political and Social Impact of Transnational Corporations," in *The New International Economy*, ed. H. Makler *et al.* (London/Beverly Hills: Sage, 1982).

43. T. Gladwin and I. Walter, *Multinationals Under Fire: Lessons in the Management of Conflict* (New York: Wiley/Interscience, 1980), p. 433.

44. P. Davis, "Arsenic and Jobs Trade-Off," *Nature* 304 (July 21, 1983), p. 200; B. Kalikow, "Environmental Risk: Power to the People," *Technology Review* 87:7 (October, 1984).

45. *Still Waters*, note 2 above, p. 19.

46. *Time Lost: A Demand for Action on Acid Rain*, Report of the Sub-Committee on Acid Rain, House of Commons Standing Committee on Fisheries and Forestry (Ottawa: Supply and Services Canada, 1984).

47. *Ibid.*, p. 32.

48. *Ibid.*, pp 34–36.

49. J. Sallot, "$150 Million Slated for Smelter Cleanup," *The Globe and Mail*, March 7, 1985.

50. Lindblom, note 41 above, p. 178.

51. "[T]he power position of private investors includes the power to *define* reality. That is to say, whatever they *consider* an intolerable burden in fact *is* an intolerable burden which will *in fact* lead to a declining propensity to invest. . . . " (Emphasis in original). C. Offe, "Some Contradictions of the Modern Welfare State," in *Contradictions*, note 40 above, p. 152.

52. Victor, note 5 above, pp. 36–37.

53. *Reforming Regulation*, note 21 above, p. 83.

54. A. Kneese and R. D'Arge, "Benefit Analysis and Today's Regulatory Problems," *The Benefits of Health and Safety Regulation*, ed. A. Ferguson and P. LeVeen (Cambridge, MA: Ballinger, 1981).

55. P. Victor, "Techniques for Assessment and Analysis in the Management of Toxic Chemicals," paper prepared for Agriculture Canada National Workshop on Risk-Benefit Analysis (Toronto: Victor & Burrell Research and Consulting, mimeo, March 1985), p. 7.

56. For a succinct explanation of the concept and its philosophical foundations, see N. Rescher, "Economics versus Moral Philosophy: The Pareto Principle as a Case Study," in Rescher, *Unpopular Essays in Technological Progress* (Pittsburgh: University of Pittsburgh Press, 1980).

57. A. Kneese, *Economics and the Environment* (New York: Penguin, 1977), p. 20.

58. A.M. Freeman, *The Benefits of Environmental Improvement: Theory and Practice* (Baltimore: Johns Hopkins University Press, 1979), pp. 54–57.

59. *Ibid.*, p. 55.

60. H. Macaulay and B. Yandle, *Environmental Use and the Market* (Lexington, MA: D.C. Heath, 1977), p. 49.

61. D. McCaffrey, *OSHA and the Politics of Health Regulation* (New York: Plenum, 1982), pp. 89-94, 113-122, 128-131; S. Tolchin, "Cost-Benefit Analysis and the Rush to Deregulate," *Policy Studies Review* 4:2 (November 1984), pp. 212-218; D. Whittington and W.N. Grubb, "Economic Analysis in Regulatory Decisions: The Implications of Executive Order 12291," *Science, Technology and Human Values* 9:1 (1984), pp. 63-71.

62. 46:33 *Federal Register* (February 19, 1981), pp. 13191-13198.

63. Tolchin, note 61 above, p. 212.

64. Treasury Board of Canada, *Administrative Policy Manual*, Chapter 490, "Socio-Economic Impact Analysis" (Ottawa: Supply and Services Canada, December 1979).

65. *Risk-Benefit Analysis in the Management of Toxic Chemicals* (Ottawa: Agriculture Canada, 1984).

66. Summarized in N. Ashford and C. Hill, *Benefits of Environmental, Health and Safety Regulation*, prepared for Committee on Government Affairs, U.S. Senate, 96th Cong., 2nd Sess. (Washington, D.C.: U.S. Government Printing Office, 1980). See also J. Haigh *et al.*, "Benefit-Cost Analysis of Environmental Regulation: Case Studies of Hazardous Air Pollutants," *Harvard Environmental Law Review* 8 (1984), pp. 395-434.

67. L. Fishbein, "Overview of Some Aspects of Quantitative Risk Assessment," *Journal of Toxicology and Environmental Health* 6 (1980), pp. 1275-1296.

68. Canadian Energy and Emissions Committee, International Lead Zinc Research Organization, "Response of the Canadian Lead Industry to Environment Canada's Proposal to Further Restrict Gasoline Lead Usage" (Toronto: ILZRO, mimeo, March 1984); H. Kelly, "The Misdirected War Against Leaded Gasoline," *ACSH News and Views* 6:1 (January/February 1985), pp. 1, 12-13 (New York: American Council on Science and Health).

69. See, e.g., *Low Level Lead Exposure: The Clinical Implications of Current Research*, ed. H. Needleman (New York: Raven Press, 1980); *Lead versus Health*, ed. M. Rutter and R. Russell Jones (London: John Wiley, 1983). A detailed discussion of the treatment of scientific uncertainty with respect to controlling lead pollution is provided in T. Schrecker, "Environmental Lead Pollution: A Public Health Issue in Social Context," submission to the Royal Society of Canada Commission on Lead in the Environment (Ottawa: Friends of the Earth, Canada, December 1985).

70. T. Page, "A Generic View of Toxic Chemicals and Similar Risks," *Ecology Law Quarterly* 7:2 (1978), pp. 207-244; T. McGarity "Substantive and Procedural Discretion in Administrative Resolution of Science Policy Questions," *Georgetown Law Journal* 67 (1979), pp. 729-810 (see particularly pp. 731-749).

71. McGarity, note 70 above.

72. Page, note 70 above; S. Jellinek, "On the Inevitability of Being Wrong," in *Management of Assessed Risk for Carcinogens*, ed. W. Nicholson, *Annals of the New York Academy of Sciences* 363 (1981); H. Latin, "The 'Significance' of Toxic Health Risks: An Essay on Legal Decisionmaking Under Uncertainty," *Ecology Law Quarterly* 10:3 (1982), pp. 339-395.

73. G. Calabresi and P. Bobbitt, *Tragic Choices* (New York: W.W. Norton, 1977), pp. 32-41.

74. K.W. Kapp, "Social Costs, Non-Classical Economics, and Environmental Planning: A Reply" [to W. Beckerman], *Political Economy of Environment: Problems of Method, Environment and Social Sciences* 2 (Paris/The Hague: Mouton, 1971), p. 120. (See also Kapp's essay "Environmental Disruption and Social Costs," in the same volume).

75. M. Weidenbaum, "The Continuing Need for Regulatory Reform," in *Use of Cost-Benefit Analysis by Regulatory Agencies*, Joint Hearings before the Subcommittee on Oversight and Investigations and the Subcommittee on Consumer Protection and Finance, Committee on Interstate and Foreign Commerce, U.S. House of Representatives, Serial 96-157 (Washington, D.C.: U.S. Government Printing Office, 1980), pp. 330-331.

76. T. Page, *Conservation and Economic Efficiency* (Baltimore: Johns Hopkins University Press, 1977), pp. 152-155.

77. R. Ruttenberg and E. Bingham, "A Comprehensive Occupational Carcinogen Policy as a Framework for Regulatory Activity," in *Management of Assessed Risk for Carcinogens*, ed. W. Nicholson, *Annals of the New York Academy of Sciences* 363 (1981), p. 18.

78. Freeman, note 58 above, pp. 195-233; E. Hyman, "The Valuation of Extramarket Benefits and Costs

in Environmental Impact Assessment," *Environmental Impact Assessment Review* 2:3 (1981), pp. 227–264 (see pp. 228–232); D. Tihansky, "A Survey of Empirical Benefit Studies," in *Cost-Benefit Analysis and Water Pollution Policy*, ed. H. Peskin and E. Seskin (Washington, D.C.: The Urban Institute, 1975).

79 Freeman, note 58 above, pp. 108–164; Hyman, note 78 above, pp. 233–235.

80. See, e.g., F. Handy, "Income and Air Quality in Hamilton, Ontario," *Alternatives: Perspectives on Society and Environment* 6:3 (1977), pp. 18–26; F. Muller, "Distribution of Air Pollution in the Montreal Region," *Canadian Public Policy* 3 (1977), pp. 199–204.

81. Freeman, note 58 above, p. 191; G. Torrance and D. Krewski, "Risk Assessment and the Evaluation of Toxic Chemical Control Programs," paper prepared for Agriculture Canada National Workshop on Risk-Benefit Analysis (Ottawa: Health and Welfare Canada, mimeo, March 1985), p. 9.

82. *Costs and Benefits of Reducing Lead in Gasoline: Final Regulatory Impact Analysis* (Washington, D.C.: Economic Analysis Division, Office of Policy, Planning and Evaluation, U.S. Environmental Protection Agency, February 1985). For another example of such an approach, see R. Dardis *et al.*, "Cost-Benefit Analysis of Flammability Standards" [for children's sleepwear], *American Journal of Agricultural Economics* 60 (November 1978), pp. 695–700.

83. Torrance and Krewski, note 81 above, p. 9. The authors note that such calculations do, however, "provide a measure of *productive* resources returned to society as a result of allocating other resources . . . to the program" (emphasis added).

84. Freeman, note 58 above, pp. 169–172.

85. E.g. Kneese and d'Arge, note 54 above, p. 85.

86. *Risk-Benefit Analysis*, note 65 above, p. 6.

87. Freeman, note 58 above, p. 171.

88. *Ibid.*, p. 170.

89. R. Howard, "On Making Life and Death Decisions," in *Societal Risk Assessment: How Safe is Safe Enough?* ed. R. Schwing and A. Albers (New York: Plenum, 1980); Kneese and d'Arge, note 54 above, pp. 84–85.

90. J. Bishop and C. Cicchetti, "Some Institutional and Conceptual Thoughts on the Measurement of Indirect and Intangible Benefits and Costs," in *Cost-Benefit Analysis and Water Pollution Policy*, ed. H. Pes-

kin and E. Seskin (Washington, D.C.: The Urban Institute, 1975), p. 121.

91. R. Dardis, "The Value of a Life: New Evidence from the Marketplace," *American Economic Review* 70 (December 1980), pp. 1077–1082.

92. Freeman, note 58 above, pp. 185–189; R. Thaler and S. Rosen, "The Value of Saving a Life," *Household Production and Consumption*, ed. N. Terleckyj, *Studies in Income and Wealth* 40 (New York: National Bureau of Economic Research/Columbia University Press, 1975); W.K. Viscusi, "Labor Market Valuations of Life and Limb: Empirical Evidence and Policy Implications," *Public Policy* 26 (Summer 1978), pp. 359–386. Viscusi has defended the validity of this approach as a basis for standard-setting in "Setting Efficient Standards for Occupational Hazards," *Journal of Occupational Medicine* 24:12 (December 1982), pp. 969–976.

93. Economic Council of Canada, note 21 above, p. 101; Viscusi, note 92 above, p. 365.

94. G. Reschenthaler, *Occupational Health and Safety in Canada: The Economics and Three Case Studies* (Montreal: Institute for Research on Public Policy, 1979), p. 11.

95. For a discussion and inventory of Canadian one-industry communities such as those named, see Department of Regional Economic Expansion, *Single-Sector Communities*, rev. ed. (Ottawa: Supply and Services Canada, 1979).

96. M. MacCarthy, "A Review of Some Normative and Conceptual Issues in Occupational Safety and Health," *Boston College Environmental Affairs Law Review* 9 (1981–82), pp. 773–814 (see esp. pp. 778–781).

97. Thaler and Rosen, note 92 above, pp. 287–289; Viscusi, "Valuations," note 92 above, p. 364.

98. Hyman, note 78 above, p. 252.

99. Freeman, note 58 above, p. 166; J. Graham and J. Vaupel, "Value of a Life: What Difference Does It Make?" *Risk Analysis* 1:1 (1981), pp. 89–95.

100. Calabresi and Bobbitt, note 73 above.

101. Freeman, note 58 above, p. 6.

102. The U.S. EPA's analysis of the costs and benefits of further limits on lead additives in gasoline (note 82 above) in fact found a strongly favourable benefit-cost ratio for further reductions in allowable lead levels.

103. N. Ashford, "Alternatives to Cost-Benefit Analysis

in Regulatory Decisions," in *Management of Assessed Risk for Carcinogens*, ed. W. Nicholson, *Annals of the New York Academy of Sciences* 363 (1981), p. 137.

104. S. Chester, "Class Actions to Protect the Environment," in *Environmental Rights in Canada*, ed. J. Swaigen (Toronto: Butterworths, 1981); P. Elder, "Environmental Protection Through the Common Law," *University of Western Ontario Law Review* 12 (1973), pp. 107-171; J. Swaigen, *Compensation of Pollution Victims in Canada* (Ottawa: Economic Council of Canada, 1981).

105. K. Bogen, "Public Policy and Technological Risk," *IDEA: Journal of Law and Technology* 21:1 (1980), pp. 37-74 (at p.56).

106. J. Swaigen and R. Woods, "A Substantive Right to Environmental Quality," in *Environmental Rights in Canada*, ed. J. Swaigen (Toronto: Butterworths, 1981).

107. J. Sax, *Defending the Environment: A Strategy for Citizen Action* (New York: Knopf, 1971), p. 60. Sax was the principal drafter of a statute (the Michigan *Environmental Protection Act*) which is widely cited as an adventurous attempt to extend to citizens the legal right to use the courts in defence of environmental quality: see Swaigen and Woods, note 106 above, pp. 212-223.

108. D. Vogel, "Cooperative Regulation: Environmental Protection in Great Britain," *The Public Interest* no. 72 (June 1983), pp. 88-106 (at p. 97).

109. Tolchin, note 61 above, p. 212.

110. D. Caplice, Regional Director, Central Region, Ontario Ministry of the Environment, "Role of the Senior Regulator: Practicalities and Pressures," presented to Canadian Environmental Law Research Foundation conference on Environmental Regulation: The Burdens and the Benefits, February 1981 (Toronto: Ontario Ministry of the Environment, mimeo), p. 5.

111. D. Beauchamp, "Public Health as Social Justice," in *Public Health and the Law: Issues and Trends*, ed. L. Hogue (Rockville, MD: Aspen Systems Corp., 1980), p. 6.

112. This equality seldom obtains in practice, because (for example) of the way in which electoral results in systems where legislators are elected individually by geographically defined constituencies tend to reward regional concentrations of support, but not to respond to diffuse national increases in party support. See R. Landes, *The Canadian Polity: A Comparative Perspective* (Scarborough, Ont.: Prentice-Hall, 1984).

113. M. Sagoff, "We Have Met the Enemy and He is Us, or, Conflict and Contradiction in Environmental Law," *Environmental Law* 12 (Winter 1982), pp. 283-315; L. Tribe, "Technology Assessment and the Fourth Discontinuity: The Limits of Instrumental Rationality," *Southern California Law Review* 46 (1973), pp. 617-660.

114. Sagoff, note 113 above; M. Sagoff, "Economic Theory and Environmental Law," *Michigan Law Review* 79 (June 1981), pp. 1393-1419.

115. Tribe, note 113 above, p. 656.

116. C. Mueller, *The Politics of Communication* (New York: Oxford University Press, 1973), p. 108.

117. *Ibid.*

118. *Ibid.*

119. *Ibid.*

120. *Ibid.*, pp. 109-111.

121. Silk and Vogel, note 38 above, p. 49.

122. J. Schaar, "Legitimacy in the Modern State," in *Power and Community: Dissenting Essays in Political Science*, ed. P. Gren and S. Levinson (New York: Vintage, 1970).

32

Acidic Precipitation

ENVIRONMENT CANADA

Acidic precipitation, generally defined as precipitation having a pH below 5.6, occurs in North America primarily within and downwind of the major industrial and population concentrations. More than two million square kilometres of North America now receive precipitation with a pH of 4.6 or lower. Composed mainly of man-made emissions of sulphur dioxide (SO_2) and nitrogen oxides (NO_X), acid emissions are able to travel long distances in the atmosphere before returning to the surface in rain or snow. Studies have shown that acid deposition adversely affects aquatic and terrestrial ecosystems, building materials and human health.

Emissions of sulphur dioxide and nitrogen oxides from industrial processes and motor vehicles increased greatly during the 1950s and 1960s. During the 1970s nitrogen oxide emissions continued to increase but sulphur dioxide emissions declined.

The major Canadian sources of sulphur dioxide include copper and nickel smelters, which contribute approximately forty-five percent, and utilities, such as thermal power plants, which produce fif-

teen percent. The transportation sector is the major source of nitrogen oxides; utilities and commercial and residential boilers are also significant contributors.

As improved technology and regulations to reduce emissions have come into effect, the rate of increase in emissions has declined. Recent reductions may also result from lower production levels following the downturn in the economy. One must be cautious in comparing data from various years, due to the use of different methods in determining emissions from specific sectors.

The impact of acidic precipitation upon aquatic and terrestrial ecosystems is greatest in the Canadian Shield and Atlantic Canada. There, granitic bedrock and soils derived from acidic parent material possess little buffering capacity to reduce the effect of acid rain. An estimated 2.5 million square kilometres in eastern Canada are believed to be particularly vulnerable to damage from acidic precipitation.

Adverse environmental impacts resulting from acidic precipitation have been observed in aquatic

From *Environmental Issues in Canada: A Status Report*, 1985, Environment Canada. Reproduced by permission of the Minister of Supply and Services Canada.

ecosystems. Water with a pH of 5.0 places severe stress upon most fish and amphibians; below pH 4.5 fish populations can no longer be supported. Of 5341 lakes tested in Ontario, 4.1 percent or 220 lakes were found to be acidified (pH less than 5.1 year-round) and supporting no fish or only acid-tolerant species. A further 14.8 percent were subject to deleterious pH levels during part of the year, often during the spring thaw. A similar situation exists in Quebec. It should be noted that it has long been recognized that some lakes on the Shield are naturally acidic. Lakes in the southern portion of Ontario, where limestone bedrock occurs, are comparatively insensitive to acidic precipitation.

In the geologically vulnerable area of southwest Nova Scotia, river pH readings have fallen significantly since the mid-1950s. Atlantic salmon runs have disappeared from seven rivers in which the mean annual pH is currently less than 4.7 and have substantially declined in rivers in which the pH ranges from 4.7 to 5.0.

Toxic metals which the acid leaches from the soils, find their way into lakes and rivers deforming fish and other species, clogging respiratory systems and disrupting reproductive cycles. Metals such as mercury, cadmium and lead concentrated in the tissues of fish can produce harmful effects if eaten by humans.

Acidic precipitation has the potential to harm vegetation by directly damaging plant tissue, interfering with normal plant metabolism and reproduction, increasing susceptibility to insect and disease damage and acidifying soil. Its potential effect on forest productivity is of particular concern as forest soils, acidic in nature, can lack the capability to buffer acidic pollutants. Approximately one-half of the forest resource in Canada is exposed to acidic precipitation and there is concern that serious soil and forest degradation will occur in some areas in future decades if emissions are not reduced.

Canada has made considerable progress in learning about acid rain and in developing a control strategy. In March 1984 federal and provincial environment ministers agreed to achieve a wet sulphate deposition level of 20 kilograms per hectare

Figure 1   Surface Wind Flow in July and Mean pH of Precipitation in 1979

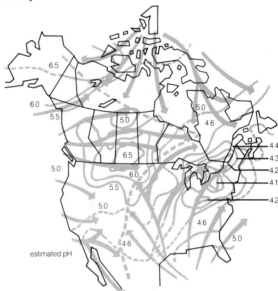

SOURCE: Canada Sub-committee on Acid Rain, Standing Committee on Fisheries and Forestry (1981), *Still Waters: The Chilling Reality of Acid Rain.*

Figure 2   Regions of North America Containing Lakes Sensitive to Acidification

SOURCE: Canada Sub-committee on Acid Rain, Standing Committee on Fisheries and Forestry (1981), *Still Waters: The Chilling Reality of Acid Rain.*

Figure 3 Sulfur Dioxide Emission Trends in Canada and the Eastern United States 1965-1980

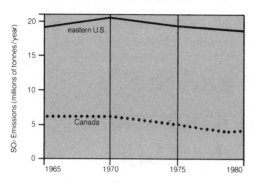

SOURCE: Environmental Protection Service, Environment Canada (1985) and adapted from Hidy, G.M., et al. (April 1984) "Trends in historical acid precursor emissions and their airborne and precipitation products", *Journal of Air Pollution Control Association*, 31(4).

per year. Attaining this level will require that sulphur dioxide emissions east of the Saskatchewan-Manitoba boundary be reduced to 2.3 million tonnes annually by 1994 or to approximately one-half their 1980 allowable level. A schedule for reductions was agreed to by the federal and seven provincial environment ministers in February 1985. Substantial federal financial support will be made available to industry for emission controls and technology development needed to meet this target.

In June 1984 the federal Ministers of Transport and Environment agreed to make automobile emission standards more stringent. Effective September 1, 1987, the new standards are projected to reduce automotive pollutants by 45 percent by the end of the century.

Acid rain is an international problem. Because over 50 percent of the pollutants contributing to Canada's acid rain originate in the United States, Canada will continue to press for constructive action by the United States. The appointment by our Prime Minister and the United States President in March 1985 of a special Envoy for each country (the Honourable William Davis for Canada) re-opens, at a high level, previously stalled bilateral discussions on acid rain. On the international scene, Canada will also continue to seek co-operative agreements on acid rain controls with North American and European nations.

The federal government is committed to maintaining the program of monitoring acid deposition and the effects of acid rain. Related scientific research will also continue.

Reducing the amount of acid emissions to an environmentally acceptable level will be an expensive undertaking. The costs of not acting and allowing our environment to suffer possible irreversible damage greatly exceed the cost of prudent controls. Attaining a sustainable balance will require the continued support of provincial and state governments and the North American public as a whole.

READING LIST

Environment Canada (1984) *The Acid Rain Story*, Ottawa.

Environmental Protection Service, Environment Canada (December 1983) *A Nationwide Inventory of Emissions of Air Contaminants (1978)*, Report EPS#-EP-83-10, Ottawa.

Government of Canada (1981) *Still Waters, The Chilling Reality of Acid Rain*, A Report by the Sub-committee on Acid Rain of the Standing Committee on Fisheries and Forestry, Ottawa.

Government of Canada (1984) *Time Lost, A Demand for Action on Acid Rain*, A Report by the Sub-committee on Acid Rain of the Standing Committee on Fisheries and Forestry, Ottawa.

33

The Kitchen and the Multinational Corporation: An Analysis of the Links between the Household and Global Corporations*

HARRIET ROSENBERG

INTRODUCTION

This paper will explore certain relatively unstudied aspects of the relationships between multinational corporations and the unwaged work that women do in their households. The activities of multinational corporations since the 1930s but especially in the last two decades have pushed them into far-flung areas of the world. This process of global penetration has seen pesticides, pharmaceuticals, chemical and nuclear wastes dumped in Africa, Asia and the Pacific (Melrose, 1982; Bull, 1982; Dinham and Hines, 1983). The Bhopal disaster is one horrifying example of the implications of this process but smaller-scale events occur on a daily basis. The Third World is not alone in being a dumpsite for global corporations. The household in North America is also intimately linked to this global proc-ess of commodification and danger. In large part it has been the unwaged workers within the house-hold who have come face to face with the contradic-tory tasks of trying to do their jobs as housewives and mothers, while encountering life-threatening hazards.

The social relationships that women manage in the home, especially as caregivers, are not commodi-fied, for the most part, even under the advanced capitalist conditions of North American society.[1] This separation from the commodity sphere has facilitated the mystification that the home is a haven from outside hazards and is protected from danger by the power of love, reciprocal human feelings, and kinship obligations. But the home is not really a private fortress: it is a sieve, open to all the excesses of industrial development. The household and its

From *Journal of Business Ethics* **6** (1987) 179–194. © 1987 by D. Reidel Publishing Company. Reprinted by permission.

environment are a dumpsite for thousands of untested, or undertested chemical products[2] which endanger the health and safety of its members. And since the sexist gender division of labour in North America has designated women as primary care-givers it is women — wives and mothers — who are responsible for the health and safety of household members. Women confront the contradictions of trying to do their unwaged work of nurturing while being undermined by the dangerous products and practices of capitalist industrial production. The confrontations that these contradictions produce usually come as great surprises to women who may have heard of health and safety dangers in factories or offices but have felt secure and protected in their own homes. Nevertheless, it is in their homes that women begin to piece together the statistics on local miscarriage rates, on high incidences of birth defects and chronic illnesses in the neighbourhood. It is over cups of coffee in their kitchens that women have mobilized and found themselves taking on some of the most powerful forces in our society.

Part I of this article deals with the households' exposure to external dangers such as chemical waste dumps. Part II concerns exposure to less visible and less understood hazards stemming from the pene-tration of the home by the household products industry. In both cases the household will be ana-lyzed in terms of its relationship to global corpora-tions.

PART I

The household as a dumpsite: Prelude to consciousness and action

Across the United States and Canada, thousands of housewives and mothers have become political activists. They have left their homes to become col-lectors and analysts of health statistics, writers of briefs, organizers of press conferences, public speakers, agitators and demonstrators. In Harde-man County, Tennessee; Rutherford, New Jersey; Pine Ridge Reservation, South Dakota; Alsea, Ore-gon; Harlem, New York; rural Nova Scotia; Niagara Falls, New York; Scarborough, Ontario; and Whitchurch-Stouffville, Ontario,[3] women have found their households exposed to toxins and pol-lutants. Their houses have been found to be built on or near nuclear waste dumps (Scarborough, Ont; Pine Ridge Reservation) they have found deadly pesticides blowing into their windows (Alsea, Ore-gon; rural Nova Scotia) and chemical residues seep-ing into homes and schools (Love Canal, Niagara Falls, New York). They have found their air and their water contaminated by lead, PCBs and dioxin[4] (Rosenberg, 1984, Table 2). Women have miscarried at alarmingly high rates, have seen their children born with defects or die of leukemia at early ages.

The women who pieced together the evidence of these disasters and organized grass-roots move-ments have been for the most part unwaged, full-time housewives. (See for example Freudenberg and Zaltzberg's 1984 survey of 110 grass roots groups in the U.S. and Jackson and Weller, 1984, for a discus-sion of some Canadian housewife/activists.) Those housewives from white middle class backgrounds rarely had any previous political experience and began their inquiries assuming that government agencies were on their side — and would support them. (Black and native women began with no such trust for politicians and bureaucrats.) These women soon became disillusioned with local and national politicians who treated housewives dismissively and sided with the large corporations. Encountering male dominated 'realpolitik' was a bitter but also energizing experience for many of the women involved in neighbourhood coalitions. They fre-quently became tougher and more self-confident in their own organizational and political abilities. The political implications of this transformation from isolated housewife to activist has had an important personal impact on the lives of many of the partici-pants and is also an important area for socialist/feminist analysis.

Let us consider in more detail the experiences of one such grass-roots alliance and trace out the course of events which brought housewives out of their kitchens and into major confrontations with big business and big government. My example is drawn from the Concerned Citizens of Whitchurch-Stouffville Inc.

Whitchurch-Stouffville is a small Ontario com-munity just north of Toronto. Between 1962 and

1969 thousands of tons of toxic liquid industrial wastes were poured into a farmer's field never designed as a landfill (i.e. no liners were used) near the community.[5]

> One particular site was called a "garbageman's delight" because "you could pour stuff in one day and when you came back the next it was empty." (Cited in Jackson and Weller, 1982, 62).

For years, local women who constantly used the water in their domestic routines, asked the Ministry of the Environment about the impact of the dump on their water supply. Groundwater was only 100 feet below the dump and supplied residents' wells and the town of Whitchurch-Stouffville. In the spring of 1981, a group of Stouffville mothers conducted a health survey and found an unexpectedly high number of miscarriages. Like their concerned counterparts in Oregon, Nova Scotia, New Jersey and Niagara Falls, New York, they went to what they thought would be the appropriate government agency with their health survey of the area. Except for one member of the group who had been vice-president of the Scarborough Progressive-Conservative association, they had had no previous political experience. "We were just your average Joe Citizen." Many have since come to the conclusion that "...government is nothing but bullshit and baffling brainlessness" (Interview, April 1984).

The group began as a Moms and Tots meeting in a United Church basement. Before they changed their name to the Concerned Citizens of Whitchurch-Stouffville they called themselves Concerned Mothers and conducted a health survey of a quarter of the homes in Stouffville. They found that the town's miscarriage rate was 26% compared to the provincial rate of 15%. Another survey within a two mile radius of the dump found 37 cases of cancer, 11 miscarriages, seven cases of birth defects and four cases of thyroid problems (*Globe and Mail*, May 12, 1982). Despite repeated statements by the Ministry of the Environment that the water was safe the group was far from reassured and decided to hire independent scientists to test the water. They raised money in the ways in which women raise money, through bake sales and entertainment

shows, and spent between $10 000 and $15 000 on tests whose findings were at complete odds with the Ministry's.[6] Furthermore the Citizen's group protested that the government was trying to intimidate them with wiretaps and threats (*Toronto Star*, March 10, 1982) and a barrage of demeaning remarks about housewives. One member of the group dealt with the pressure by wearing a T-shirt to meetings which read: THIS IS NO ORDINARY HOUSEWIFE YOU ARE DEALING WITH. Other grassroots groups in the U.S. and Canada experienced similar anti-housewife attacks. In Alsea, Oregon for example, women were organized in opposition to aerial spraying of forests with the herbicide 2, 4, 5–T manufactured by the Dow Chemical Company. Dow countered with accusations that the high miscarriage rates in the region were caused by alleged marijuana use among the mothers of Alsea (Freudenberg and Zaltzberg, 1984, 250).

In Whitchurch-Stouffville housewives have regarded themselves as fighting for life. "Our kids could get cancer . . . and that's a crime" (Interview, April 1984). Like their counterparts in other areas of Canada and the U.S. they soon realized that they had to form alliances with other groups (there are about 100 Environmental Non-Government Organizations in Ontario); they had to find out more about government,[6a] about power and about Waste Management Inc. (WMI), the multinational that they charged was polluting their neighbourhood.

Many people in Whitchurch-Stouffville no longer trust the Government of Ontario. They believe in ways that they never understood or believed before that the government is serving the interests of big corporations and finds the housewives to be a nuisance.[7] Said one member of the group protesting the dumpsite:

> Certain people had the rough luck to be situated near a landfill. Are they expendable because of that? (Fran Sainsbury cited in Jackson and Weller, 1981, 66)

The household and the multinational corporation

The question raised in Whitchurch-Stouffville is the crux of a global problem, in terms of health, responsibility and regulation. Capitalism has developed a new service — the disposal of dangerous industrial waste products. The corporations that deal in this service are enormously powerful in terms of size and profit margins. They view the world in terms of cheap and easily accessible dumpsites. They are "not in business for their health" as the saying goes; they are in business to make a profit. Here is a direct contradiction between the needs of capitalist accumulation and the needs of social reproduction: this contradiction pits the housewife and mother doing her unwaged job against global corporations.

It takes a great deal of digging to find out about such corporations. They purposefully keep very low profiles, and count on the fact that the average citizen is not an investigative reporter and will not be able to identify the dangerous cargo moving through their community in virtually unmarked trucks.

The company that the people of Whitchurch-Stouffville have been concerned about is called York-Sanitation and is a subsidiary of Waste Management Inc. (WMI). WMI of Oak Brook Illinois is currently the largest waste disposal company in the world. The company had a profit margin of 20.4% in 1980 representing $54.9 million (US) of revenue in excess of expenditures (Moody's handbook of Common Stocks). WMI has contracts for waste disposal all over the world including Venezuela, Argentina and Saudi Arabia where they recently signed a $380 million (US) contract. In 1983 WMI purchased Chemical Nuclear Systems and is now involved in the disposal of nuclear wastes.

The corporation has been investigated and sued many times. For example, the state of Illinois has charged them with concealment of illegal toxic waste shipments and they are currently being prosecuted in Vickery, Ohio in a $400 000 suit which alleges that they violated environmental laws in relation to the disposal of PCBs and dioxin (*Wall Street Journal*, 29 March, 1983). In November (4th) 1984 both *Business Week* and *Fortune* reported that the U.S. Environmental Protection Agency had launched a $1.1 million suit against WMI for price fixing and illegal dumping. A year before (27 Dec. 1983) an Australian Court refused to allow a WMI contract

with Queensland to stand and they were not permitted to operate in that state (*Wall Street Journal*, 27 Dec. 1983). WMI's incinerator ships have been investigated by the United States Environmental Protection Association and even WMI shareholders have brought a suit against their company which "alleges failure to disclose environmental liabilities" (*Wall Street Journal*, 29 March 1983).

Because WMI operates around the world it can offset the problems caused by lawsuits in one place by new deals in another and can count on the fact that there is very little communication between the people of the different areas where it operates. Furthermore WMI has the money and power to launch appeals when and where it wants to. And as in the case of Whitchurch-Stouffville it has continued to operate while appeals are pending. In fact in this Ontario community residents have been greeted with the following picture since 1977. As the Hughes Commission Report put it:

> There is no doubt in my mind (Hon. S.H.S. Hughes) that a great deal of justifiable public resentment was occasioned by the spectacle of the dump trucks rattling past the building where a hearing was convened to entertain an application for authority to do what their owners were doing without any authority whatsoever, and by open violation of orders made by a ministry of the government on the grounds that either an appeal was pending or the officers of the ministry were trying to coax a recalcitrant operator into a mood of compliance with what had been ordered.
>
> (. . . *Royal Commission . . . into WMI*, 1978, 60–61)

The dumptrucks are continuing to operate in Whitchurch-Stouffville but the housewives have not given up. They are still concerned and still want the dumping to stop and they are willing to continue pushing public authorities to serve what they see as being the interests of the citizens rather than the multinational corporations. They still want regular health surveys of the region to test for changes in the levels of diseases and birth defects and they still want their water tested for mutagenicity and carcinogenicity. And they say, because they see the issue in terms of the health and lives of their children, that they have no intention of quitting their fight.

Politics

One of the most ingenious mystifications of capitalism has been to separate ideologically the economic from the political, making it appear as though power, the essence of politics, were somehow outside the realm of the process of capital accumulation (Wood, 1981). Companies as large as WMI, control enormous financial, legal and political resources. Compared to the millions that companies like this take in profits a year, the Concerned Mothers of a small Ontario community have very little in the way of resources. WMI, in an uncharacteristic breech of silence concerning their activities once accused the Whitchurch-Stouffville group of being "political elements" — clearly the most negative epithet they could come up with (*Globe and Mail*, 14 May 1982). And in essence the company was quite right, even though what they meant to imply was that the women of Whitchurch-Stouffville were using emotional pressure tactics to press their position with the Ministry. The 'politics' of this grassroots organization go well beyond such petty accusations. Lois Gibbs, the mother/housewife, who was president of the Love Canal Homeowners Association, a group that argued that 56% of the children born near the site were mentally or physically disabled has said, "'Birth defects have become a political issue'" (Cited in Norwood, 1985, 16).

Gibbs, who has now become a full-time activist, is involved with The Citizen's Clearing House for Hazardous Wastes (Arlington, Virginia) in the United States. This group has pressed for fuller studies of links between residential proximity to chemical dumpsites and birth defects. Thus far, U.S. Centers for Disease Control have been unwilling to undertake such surveys and have attributed higher rates of teratagenicity to improved reporting techniques by doctors. Gibbs' interpretation is different. She has argued that public health officials are deliberately refusing to continue monitoring hot spots, because epidemiological surveys may in fact confirm that industrial wastes are heavily implicated in causing birth defects (Norwood, 1985, 16).

If such correlations were confirmed the findings would be explosive. They would raise questions about the sanctity of the home — a discourse thus far staked out by political conservatives. The conservative symbolic geography of private home and safe family life separated from public and workplace activities is based on the image of home as reward for hard work and law-abiding (i.e. non-militant) habits. (See Wynn, 1985 for a brief history of separate spheres ideology.) Whitchurch-Stouffville, Love Canal and other activist groups have challenged that ideology and have shown that the home is not necessarily a sanctuary or a reward. They have argued that industry and government have lined up to attack the home, not defend it.

PART II

This section discusses factors that contributed to the social isolation of the housewife in the home and facilitated the household's colonization by home products manufacturers. I will analyze how the home came to be a dumpsite in which women/consumers have been actively and successfully encouraged to purchase large quantities of potentially hazardous substances in the belief that they are fulfilling supposedly innate feminine caregiving functions. The marketing of these products has involved the development of costly advertising campaigns but has also produced extremely high profits for multinational corporations who are among the largest and most powerful companies in the world.

The mortgage holding husband consumerist wife ideal: "Because cleaning is caring."

The home products industry began actively expanding in the 1920s and 1930s. Its development was interwined with political and ideological trends which devalued collectivist movements in relation to domestic labour. In post World War I North America, anything other than the isolated housewife managing her domestic world alone, came to be identified as politically subversive. The imagery and symbols of these decades continue to have profound effects on how domestic labour is organized and carried out today, and influence what has and what has not been problematized in relation to domestic labour in both personal and theoretical terms.

Extremely significant for Canadian and American domestic life had been the defeat of the collectivist branch of the home economics movement, which since the late 19th century had developed models of co-operative solutions to the problems of housework, food distribution (consumer's co-operatives) and preparation (co-operative dining clubs and cooked food delivery services) and childcare (daycare). By the 1920s individualist trends among home economists were in the ascendancy presenting models of the home as a private, feminized and isolated domestic sphere. The model of the private home paid for by the male breadwinner in long term installments and the female unwaged caregiver who maintained the home and raised children by herself became the dominant model, in North America, in conscious opposition to collectivist models which were being developed in Russia after the 1917 Revolution.

The concept of the mortgage-holding male appealed to industrialists who saw it is a way of taming an increasingly radicalized and militant labour force. In 1919 when over 4 000 000 workers were involved in demonstrations in the U.S. (and major strikes in Canada as well as mass rallies of unemployed veterans), industrialists became intrigued by the idea that labour peace could be bought by making small surburban homes available to white male workers. Representatives of the housing industry phrased it this way:

> Happy workers invariably mean bigger profits, while unhappy workers are never a good investment . . . A wide diffusion of home ownership has long been recognized as fostering a stable and conservative habit . . . The man owns his own home but in a sense his home owns him, checking his impulses. (Industrial Housing Associates, 1919, *Good Homes Make Contented Workers* cited in Hayden 1982, 283–4).

By 1931, this approach had been institutionalized in U.S. public policy. That year President Hoover convened the "Conference on Home Building and Home Owning" which put government support behind a national strategy of home ownership for men " 'of sound character and industrious habits' " (Cited in Hayden, 1982, 286). The coalition of those who favoured this policy included former campaigners against slums and even some feminists. But for the most part backing came from real estate speculators, housing developers and the manufacturers of consumer goods.

The involvement of this latter group is significant because the move to cheap urban housing which aimed at tying men to long-term mortgages also aimed at tying women to consumerism or 'consumptionism' as one of its leading advocates (Christine Frederick) in the 1920s and 30s called it (Hayden, 1982. See also Ewen, 1976). The gendered social division of labour was to work as follows. Men were to be breadwinners and homeowners able to liberate their wives and children from the evils and hazards of the workplace. The *dependent-wife family* (Cameron, 1983) meant not only the demobilization of women from the workforce and the closure of wartime daycare centres but the possibility that working class women could devote themselves fulltime to domestic tasks. Higher steady wages for husbands were still too small to pay for servants to help with the childcare and housework but North American industry in combination with the teaching of home economics in schools and community centres (see for example, Parkers, 1899, "Training for Housework in Canada") would create a class of "scientific household engineers" who did not need servants or collective social supports (Hayden, 1982, 386). Each woman was to become the epitome of Taylorist efficiency, alone, in her own home. (See for example Frederick's *Household Engineering: Scientific Management in the Home*, 1920.)

It has been pointed out that Taylorist techniques of efficiency were logically impossible in the home since scientific management required scale, specialization and the division of labour while the essence of privatized housework is precisely its isolated unspecialized character (Hayden, 1982; Wynn, 1985). Efficiency was a smokescreen, according to Hayden, for the real aim of the home economics movement as developed by Frederick and her colleagues which was to turn the household into a unit of consumption. Frederick and others worked as consultants to large corporations and advertising agencies becoming specialists on how to sell things to women, and developing advertising techniques aimed at women's supposed suggestibility, passivity and inferiority complexes. (See *Selling Mrs. Consumer*, 1928, dedicated to Herbert Hoover and for a later era see Janet Wolff, 1958, *What Makes Women Buy*.)

The world, in which men earned and women bought, did not become a widespread reality until the post-Second World War boom of cheap suburban housing supported by government policy in both the U.S. and Canada in the 1950s. The image of women's domesticated role which preceded that boom had decades to spread and fix itself in popular consciousness. Since the 1920s advertising and the household products industry had worked hard to stereotype housework as an extension of the feminine role, an expression of love of family and not socially useful work that could potentially be organized in a variety of different ways. Housework became conceptualized as a personal task made easier by the purchase of an ever-increasing array of products which women bought because they wished to care for their families in the best, most modern way possible.

An ironic boon to advertisers was the fact that despite it all women did not seem always to love isolated housework and often yearned to find ways to involve others, even though this upset the social conventions of a male-female division of labour. Colgate-Palmolive, for example, hit upon the sales advantages of this discontent years ago with its ads for a home cleaner that was symbolized by a white knight.[8] A Colgate vice-president explained the significance of the ad this way:

> We believe that every woman has a white knight in her heart of hearts. To her he symbolizes a good powerful force that can enter her life and clean up that other man in her life, her husband, who symbolizes exactly the opposite of what the white knight stands for (*Printer's Ink*, 1966, 85).

In the isolation of their housework, while serving their families women have been encouraged by advertisers to fantasize about other men but in ways that are not a threat to marital stability. The somewhat ambiguous figure of Mr. Clean has been consciously portrayed by advertisers as being a eunuch, and, therefore not a problem in terms of female alliances or male egos (*Ibid.*).

While variations on this theme of fantasy domesticity have continued to appear, one theme is never raised: women are discouraged from asking any questions about the safety of the products they buy. They are to concentrate on "ring around the collar," extra moist cake mixes and shiny floors that never yellow. They are never to ask questions about the chemicals used to attain these dazzling effects. They are never to ask questions about the unsafe and toxic qualities of what they bring into their homes because otherwise the whole myth of the home as separate sanctuary and reward might crumble.

Let the buyer beware

The development of the mortgage-holding consumerist household ideal has permitted manufacturers to dump an enormous variety of virtually untested chemicals into the home and to shift the responsibility for product safety onto the consumer rather than the producer. There are literally thousands of products that one could discuss. In the area of food, for example, housewives and health activists have been concerned with the issue of food additives — everything from salt, sugar, preservatives, artificial colours and flavours to lead leeching out of the solder of evaporated milk cans to hormones and antibiotics in meat.[9] These are not simple issues of the kind with which public health officials deal. These are issues which lead to the heart of major world corporations such as plantations, agribusinesses and food processing companies, and also have to do with the most fundamental organizational structures of production, advertising, distribution, and health. The presence of sugar, salt, caffeine, BHA, BHT, and pesticide residuals in food has raised key questions about social, economic and political organization as well as health concerns.

Other areas of concern are the dumping of pesticides, asbestos, lead, PCBs, formaldehyde, aerosols, vinyl chloride and appliances which pose carbon monoxide and radiation hazards in the home. (See Rosenberg, 1984 for a discussion of these hazards.) Also of concern are the products we use to clean our homes — the soaps, detergents, softeners, and polishes. This latter category will be discussed in some detail because these products are usually viewed as benign and the hazards they pose are generally unknown as are the connections between these products and multinational corporations.

I have argued that, for the last 50 years, the notion of the isolated housewife fulfilling her feminized caregiving destiny has been developed, used and refined to facilitate the dumping of mountains of unsafe products in the home. What is known about these products is that they are supposed to make women feel satisfied in the thought that they are creating comfortable happy homes.[10] (Of course we also know that a large percentage of women hate doing housework. See, for example Oakley, 1975; Luxton, 1980; Proulx, 1978.)

I have written about the health and safety problems that detergents, polishes and cleaners pose in the home elsewhere (Rosenberg, 1984). Table I (pp. 364-365) summarizes my findings. What is not known and as far as I can tell not being studied is what the impact of long term exposure to these products might mean. If two ounces of dishwashing detergent can be lethal to a small child, what is the health outcome of 30 years of exposure to detergent residue? If one or two drops of furniture polish can be fatal if ingested, if aspiration can cause a form of chemical pneumonia, if some products are routinely contaminated by cancer-causing nitrosamines; then what are the long term effects of spraying and inhaling while cleaning the dining room table? If a fifth of an ounce of disinfectant can kill a small child, which is more dangerous in the long run: the microbe or the disinfectant? And finally what are the combined effects of these cleaners, sprays, and pesticides?

The success of advertising in directing women away from health and safety questions is in large part attributable to the enormous size of the advertising budgets available to these corporations.

Soap business: Harvesting profits in households

Proctor and Gamble (as of 1978) is the biggest advertiser in the United States, spending $554 million (US) a year. This is more money than such major corporations as General Motors, AT&T or Gulf and Western spend in a year on advertising (Moskowitz *et al.* 1980, 359). Proctor and Gamble harvests enormous profits in the kitchens of the world. As of 1980, its sales were estimated at $9.3 billion (US), with profits at $557 million (US) (*Ibid.*, 499). In the United States Proctor and Gamble is the largest manufacturer of bar soap, cake mixes, laundry detergent, toilet tissue, toothpaste, diapers and deodorants and the third largest producer of mouthwash, salad and cooking oils, and coffee (*Ibid.*, 355). Its products are sold under a variety of different names suggesting to consumers that they are actually choosing from a variety are different products. However, only the names are different — the products are essentially the same.[11]

Most of the home cleaning and bar soap market is controlled by only three corporations: Proctor and Gamble, Colgate-Palmolive and Unilever. These three corporations accommodate each other and do not compete; the fiction of competition is maintained within the differently named soaps and detergents produced by each conglomerate. The real aim of advertising is not to promote Tide over Cheer but to constantly assert the need for these products.

Enormous profits have been made, but only by those companies that were big enough to market and promote them. Thus when chemists at Monsanto (the fifth largest chemical company in the U.S.) invented a lowsudsing detergent in 1957, they found that even they were too small to capitalize the marketing programme necessary to sell the detergent. "Monsanto people blanched" at the price and sold the product to Lever Bros (Moskowitz *et al.*, 1980, 611). Monsanto bowed out of sales and promotion and focussed its attention on making most of the chemicals which are used by the major manufacturers of soaps and detergents.[12]

In the past the advertising industry has expressed concern about the fact that there was very

TABLE I   Dangers of Home-cleaning Products

Product	Dangers	Alternatives
Drain cleaner (lye)	The most dangerous product in home use. Can eat through mouth, skin, stomach, or damage eyes. There is no effective antidote.	Rubber plunger or plumber's snake. Prevent clogging with drain strainer. Use hot water + ¼ cup washing soda.
Toilet bowl cleaner (ammonia)	Can burn skin on contact, or respiratory tract if inhaled. Liquid from intank cleaner harmful if swallowed. Fumes fatal if mixed with chlorine bleach.	Scrub with stiff brush.
Scouring powder	Rapidly absorbed through mucous membranes and scraped skin. Can cause red rash in any area that comes in contact with product.	Salt or baking soda clean and disinfect effectively.
Oven cleaner (lye)	Extremely dangerous. Can burn skin and eyes. Inhaling fumes is hazardous. Some brands don't have childproof closures.	Damp cloth and baking soda. Scrape hardened material with a knife. One commercial product contains no lye.
Chlorine bleach	Can cause corrosive burns if swallowed. Fumes fatal if mixed with ammonia.	Safer when diluted.
Window or glass cleaner	Swallowing can cause nausea or vomiting. Can irritate eyes. Lethal dose for a child is over one pint.	Warm tap water alone or ½ cup white vinegar mixed with 1 quart cool water. For chrome, use flour and a dry cloth.
Disinfectants	May irritate skin and eyes. Spray can irritate throat. May cause nausea and diarrhea if swallowed. Lethal dose for small child is ⅕ oz.	Soap and water.
All-purpose cleaner	Hazardous to eyes. Can burn throat and stomach lining if swallowed. Products containing petroleum distillates can cause a fatal lung condition.	Diluted bleach or detergent. A slice of potato removes fingerprints on painted wood.

Dishwashing detergent	A lethal dose for a small child is 2 oz. Enzymes can be highly irritating.	Use less. Rinse dishes immediately after use. Scour with a stiff brush and/or salt and baking soda. Soak burned pots overnight, boil, cool, and scour.
Automatic dishwashing detergent	Major cause of poisoning in children. Irritating to skin, eyes, respiratory tract. Residue on dishes may have long-term effects.	Use less. Vinegar in rinse cuts spotting, leaves less residue to be ingested.
Laundry detergent	A lethal dose for a small child is ½ oz. Swallowing can cause nausea, vomiting, diarrhea. A few grains can damage eye cornea if left untended.	Soap powders are safer. Liquid laundry detergents do not contain sodium carbonate, a corrosive present in detergent powders.
Furniture polish	A drop or two of solvent fatal if swallowed. Flammable. Aspiration can cause a form of chemical pneumonia. Nitrosamines (present in some brands) can be absorbed through skin and cause cancer in laboratory animals.	Tsp. of vinegar in a cup water; buff with a dry cloth for wood furniture. Use material oil for shine.

Sources:

On drain cleaners, see Calpirg Reports (June 1981). "Factsheet." Center for Science in the Public Interest, *The Household Pollutants Guide* (Garden City, N.Y.: Anchor Books, 1978), pp. 180–90, Joanne Robertson, "Housework is Hazardous to Your Health," Pollution Probe (Toronto), 1982, Women's Occupational Health Resource Center. "Factsheet for Women Who Work in the Home," January 1979. "Alkali Products Dangerous to Eyes," Occupational Health Bulletin 26, nos. 1–2 (1971): 4.

On toilet bowl cleaners, see Robertson *op. cit, Housework is Hazardous to Your Health, op. cit,* Center for Science in the Public Interest. *Household Pollutants Guide, op. cit.,* "Toilet Bowl Cleaners," *Consumer Reports* (4, 3), March 1975: 157.

On scouring powder, see Robertson, *op. cit.*

On oven cleaners, see Robertson, *op. cit.,* "Oven Cleaners," *Consumer Reports* (45, 10), October 1980: 598–99.

On chlorine bleach, see Calpirg Reports, *op. cit,* Robertson, *op. cit.*

On window and glass cleaners, see Calpirg Reports, *op. cit,* Robertson, *op. cit.*

On disinfectants, see Robertson, *op. cit,* "Household Cleaners," *Consumer Reports* (39, 9), September 1974: 677.

On all-purpose cleaners, see Calpirg Reports, *op. cit,* Robertson, *op. cit.,* "All-purpose Cleaners," *Consumer Reports* (44, 2), February 1979: 81.

On dishwashing detergent, see Calpirg Reports, *op. cit,* Robertson, *op. cit.*

On automatic dishwashing detergent, see Robertson, *op. cit.*

On laundry detergent, see Calpirg Reports, *op. cit.:* Center for Science in the Public Interest, *op. cit.,* pp. 149–50: Emmanuel Sommers, "Risk Assessment for Environmental Health," *Canadian Journal of Public Health* (7), November–December 1979: 389.

On furniture polish, see Calpirg Reports, *op. cit,* Robertson, *op. cit.,* "Furniture Polishes," *Consumer Reports* (44, 7), July 1979: 496.

little difference between the products on the market. *Printer's Ink*, a leading journal of the United States advertising industry noted in 1966:

> Is such advertising an economic waste — a drain on society? The differences in scents and the amount of chemical brighteners among brands are not regarded by many economists as justification for spending millions on advertising [just] to establish brand preferences.
>
> (*Printer's Ink*, 1966, 85)

The article went on to predict that the advertising structure as it then existed would inevitably collapse. Instead it has expanded. This is not only due to the expansion of selling techniques and the development of new "needs" and new products in North America but to the expansion of activities in the Third World.

In sales to the Third World it is the Unilever corporation which dominates,[13] through its subsidiaries Hindustan Lever and United Africa Company (Pedlar, 1974). On a world scale the Unilever Corporation is the ninth largest corporation on the globe, just after the major oil corporations. Women were from the beginning (1885) targeted by this international empire. Unilever (formerly Lever Brothers) was among the pioneers of market research. Between 1885 and 1905 Lever Brothers spent the sum of £2 million in advertising — an unheard of amount in those days, in campaigns directed against working class housewives.[14] Lever exhorted his managers to try to achieve "hypnotic effect" with their advertising, and to "build a halo around the product" (cited in Counter Information Services, n.d., 92). By 1899 soap advertising was directed at children ". . . so they will bother their mothers to buy some" (*Ibid.*, 23).

Unilever, with over 800 subsidiaries, has rarely identified itself as the parent company. Unlike the Nestlé Corporation for example, it has striven for a policy of anonymity so that workers and consumers in different areas rarely know with whom they are dealing. The company's activities range from owning plantations that supply palm oil, cocoa, tea and coffee to companies trading in agricultural commodities, shipping lines, warehouses; they own factories processing primary products into margarine, cooking oils and of course detergent, soaps and other cleaning products. They own supermarket chains and marketing organizations which distribute their products. Their subsidiaries handle every imaginable level of production, distribution and marketing from growing timber to designing wallpaper. They have a network of laboratories producing pesticides and conducting genetic engineering projects (*Ibid.*, 8). Unilever is the largest food company in the world. It has over 1000 products on the market; none of which bears the name Unilever.[15]

This company which touches the daily lives of millions amassed sales to third parties (i.e. excluding intracompany trading) in 1979 of £9 842 million — "an amount roughly equivalent to the GNP of Angola, Benin, Botswana, Burundi, the Central African Empire, Chad, Congo, Gabon, Gambia, Guinea, Guinea-Bissau, Lesotho, Malawi, Mali, Mauritania, Mauritius, Mozambique, Niger, Rwanda, Senegal, Sierra Leone, Somalia, Swaziland, Togo, and Upper Volta" (Dinham and Hines, 1983, 167).

Politics

What have been the responses to such power? In North America we often see the small scale skirmishes between mother/housewives and these major corporations acted out in women's pages of our local newspapers. Women write in to complain about faulty pouring spouts on bleach containers, or lung irritations caused by cleaning the oven, or baby bottle nipples contaminated by cancer-causing nitrosamines[16] (Fishbein, 126–127). The "consumer experts" hired by local papers treat each issue as an isolated problem. Consumer objections of this sort are easily absorbed into the mythology that corporations will always try to make their products better and safer if concerns are pointed out to them.

More subversive to the ideology of consumerism are public education activities carried out by ecology groups who are not dependent on advertising dollars for their existence. In this context just naming names and pointing out some of the dangers of these products can be very effective. It has been because of alliances between consumer groups, legal groups and ecology groups that such dangerous products as Captan, a fungicide, have come under government scrutiny and may eventually be banned.[17]

Other effective alliances have come from the international sphere where organizations like the International Organization of Consumers' Unions operate. In 1981 for example the IOCU with head offices in Brussels and Penang, launched Consumer Interpol.[18] There are about 52 groups working in 32 countries which are actively participating in this network. They are also in close contact with other highly successful coalitions like the International Babyfood Network, and Health Action International, which coordinated an informal grapevine of about 200 groups working on pharmaceutical issues and which is in contact with Pesticides Action Network, itself representing about 50 working groups. It is clear to Third World health activists that the multinationals are using their countries as dumpsites for hazardous wastes, for untested or banned pharmaceuticals, for toxic pesticides and for dangerous consumer products. In the summer of 1985, North American non-government organization (NGO's) delegates met with their Third World counterparts in the context of the Nairobi Conference to share information and discuss strategies in dealing with global corporations.[19] These coalitions are concrete examples of how groups have developed ways to expand and attack the practice of the multinationals of turning the home into a dumpsite.

Conclusion

Health issues and consumer issues have come to be defined as women's issues, because women act as our principle caregivers and are seen as being responsible for the reproduction of non-commodi-

fied reciprocal relationships in the home. Mothers, and wives are under social obligations to keep the family safe and nuture human feelings of intimacy, sharing and security. But this caregiving work is not done in a vacuum: world economic systems are dominated by capital accumulation and the spread of commodified relationships.

This process has been resisted in a variety of ways, as people have confronted not only exploitation in the workplace but also threats to themselves and their families at home. Love, attachment and security are still highly valued and these values in relation to the home have been politicized. The New Conservatives have characterized the discourse in terms of a defence of home and family as a private feminized sanctuary apart from the public masculinized domain. Separation of spheres and of gender roles are crucial to this conception. The New Right has attributed problems within the family to feminists defined by them as women who want abortions, sex-education, day care and non-gendered division of labour in the home and in the workplace (Freudenberg and Zaltzberg, 1984; Harding, 1978).

But the activities of the people and groups discussed in this paper have the potential for shifting the locus of the discourse to an examination of capitalism and the responsibilities of democratic governments. Environmentalist, consumer and health groups, dealing with essentially the same issues as the New Right in terms of concern with life, health, and caregiving have identified different enemies and are forging a different political discourse. They have found the home to be a contrived and inauthentic refuge and attribute this finding not to feminism but to corporate greed, and inadequate government regulation.

Such groups are amorphous; they do not form a coherent social movement. Often group structure is decentralized. Such groups, by their very existence provide lived alternatives to the alienating and oppressive conditions around them. Because they are usually composed of society's less powerful people, they are rarely taken seriously by those with power. Such grass-roots groups are like social guerrillas who deal in localized hit and run operations, not full-fledged battles. But herein may lie their advantage. They are harder for power structures to define, locate, co-opt or eradicate. They may be suppressed in one place but reform and reappear in another. They have the weapons of ridicule and embarrassment using the sacredness of motherhood ideology to confound their enemies. In the past (see for example, Kaplan, 1982) as well as in the present women transcending their domestic roles, formed coalitions and formulated radical social visions which have brought women into large scale collective action against economic and political power holders. Whether these actions are mobilized by the right or the left is historically contingent but the capacity of housewives to draw on social networks and personal resources holds out the promise of new patterns of empowerment and new alliances for social change.

ENDNOTES

* Paper presented at *Women and the Invisible Economy*, Conference, Institute Simone de Beauvoir, Concordia University, Montreal, Quebec, Feb. 22, 1985.

1. There are certain highly significant exceptions. Much that now relates to birth control, the management of dying and death is commodified, for example, in the marketing of contraceptives by multinational pharmaceutical companies or the franchizing of profit-making nursing homes. Also significant is the relatively new phenomenon of surrogate motherhood, although certain kinds of adoption, especially from Native reserves and overseas, has been and continues to be a means by which relatively wealthy white middle class people purchase children from the poor. While the sale of sex in the form of prostitution is ancient, the recent expansion of pornography has made it a major growth industry.

2. In the wake of the Bhopal disaster the *New York Times* published an article on potential chemical hazards. Citing a survey by the U.S. National Academy of Science, March 1984, the Times listed the following estimates about the quality of information available on the potential health hazards of selected chemicals, expressed as a percentage of the chemicals in each of the groups.

Group	Quality of Information			No. of Chemicals Studied
	A	**B**	**C**	
Pesticide Ingredients	10%	52%	38%	3,350
Pharmaceuticals	18%	42%	56%	3,410
Food Additives	5%	49%	46%	8,627
Other Commercial Chemicals (with sales of at least one million pounds a year)	11%	11%	78%	12,880

A = Adequate Information
B = Incomplete Information
C = No Information

Source: *New York Times*, Dec. 16, 1984; National Academy of Sciences 1984. Toxicity Testing: Strategy to Determine Needs and Priorities, Washington: National Academy Press.

3. Hardeman County, Tennesse was the site of chemical dumping by Velsicol Chemical Company. Local wells

were contaminated with twelve chemicals including 5 known carcinogens — benzene, chlordane, heptachlor, endrin, dioxin. Eighty residents have launched a $2.5 billion class action suit against the company (Freudenberg and Zaltzberg, 1984, 246–7).

Rutherford, New Jersey is a cancer hot spot. In this comfortable middle class suburb, the leukemia rate for children ages five to nineteen was six times higher than the U.S. national average. Causes for high cancer rates in this community include: 42 industrial concerns using organic chemicals including known carcinogens within three miles of the local school; intensive mosquito spraying yearly, including the use of DDT until 1967; exposure to high levels of automobile exhaust; exposure to microwave radiation from two airports and an industrial research facility. Parent activists in this community have forced a plant using benzene to shut down and with the support of labour and environmentalist groups have forced the state of New Jersey to establish a cancer registry to aid in epidemiological research (Freudenberg and Zaltzberg, 1984, 247–249).

Pine Ridge Reservation, South Dakota has been the site of high rates of miscarriage (38% in 1979 compared to generally acceptable rates of 10% to 20%). A local hospital has also reported extremely high rates of birth defects. Other studies have shown that the Reservation had higher than average rates of bone and gynecological cancers. Widespread spraying of pesticides and herbicides and exposure to uranium tailings and nuclear waste have been implicated in these health disorders. WARN (Women of All Red Nations) has been active in trying to improve health conditions on this reservation (Freudenberg and Zaltzberg, 1984, 249–250).

Alsea, Oregon is a rural logging community where high levels of herbicidal spraying have been linked to an elevated miscarriage and birth defects rate. Women in that community have taken on the Dow Chemical Corporation, manufacturers of the defoliant 2, 4, 5–T, the United States Forest Service and the United States Environmental Protection Agency to have spraying banned (Freudenberg and Zaltzberg, 1984, 251–252). A comparable event has occurred in rural Cape Breton, Nova Scotia where local residents have recently fought and lost a court case to prevent the spraying of a 2, 4, 5–T and 2, 4–D mixture. This mixture was known as Agent Orange when it was used by the United States army as a defoliant during the Viet

Nam war. It has been sprayed in Nova Scotia by Nova Scotia Forest Industries, a Swedish multinational to destroy competing hardwoods in areas reforested with the softwood cash crop. Herbicide efficacy has never been demonstrated. Critics contend that its use and putative value are aimed primarily at justifying unecological forest harvesting practices. Dioxin, a biproduct of this herbicide, is a carcinogen (Labonté, 1984, 4–9).

Recently Dow Chemical, involved in a major class action suit brought by veterans of the Viet Nam war who were exposed to Agent Orange, settled out of court. Dow agreed to pay the veterans and/or their survivors $180 million. The plight of women nurses exposed to Agent Orange during the Viet Nam war is discussed in *Family Circle* magazine (Distelheim, 1985).

In addition, the U.S. government has purchased the entire town of Times Beach, Missouri for $30 million. The town had been exposed to dioxin-laden oil which was sprayed on its streets to keep dust levels down (Labonté, 1984, 4). Niagara Falls, New York, site of Love Canal, Bloody Run Creek and other chemical dumps has been identified as releasing toxins into Lake Ontario. Dioxin may be among them. Citizens Rebelling Against Wastes in Ontario, Inc. and Operation Clean Niagara have been active on the Canadian side of the Niagara River (Jackson and Weller, 1984, 30).

The Love Canal Home Owners Association was influential in forcing the United States government to evacuate 239 families closest to a chemical dumpsite in 1980. Research at the Rosewell Park Memorial Institute in Buffalo, New York, indicated higher than accepted rates of miscarriage and birth defects including mental retardation (Orwen, 1985, *Toronto Star*, 26 January). Some Love Canal area residents who relocated three kilometres away now find themselves exposed to toxins from the Cecos dumpsite (Orwen, 1985, *Toronto Star*, 2 February).

In Harlem, New York City, mothers concerned over high levels of asbestos fibres in their children's school forced the city to spend $100 000 on repairs. A survey by the New York City Board of Education in 1977 showed that 400 New York Schools had asbestos problems (Freudenberg and Zaltzberg, 1984, 252–253). Asbestos is a potent carcinogen found in insulation products, dry-wall patching compounds, ceiling tiles as well as some baby powders, some hair driers, oven mitts and ironing board covers (Rosenberg,

1984, Table 2). The hazards of asbestos are well-documented. As early as 1913 both United States and Canadian insurance companies refused to sell life policies to asbestos workers (Epstein, 1978, 83–4). Johns-Manville is a leading manufacturer of asbestos products. Workers in its Scarborough plant have sustained high rates of disabling chronic respiratory diseases including lung cancer (*Ibid.*, 85). This multinational has recently been accused of dumping 300 000 tons of crushed asbestos in Scarborough near Highland Creek, a small stream flowing into Lake Ontario (*Toronto Clarion*, 1984, Vol. VIII, No. 4).

4. Concern over PCB exposure has mobilized citizens in the west-end of Toronto (who live near a CGE plant). Recently, high levels of PCBs have been identified in Pottersburg Creek in London, Ontario. Joseph Cummins, a geneticist at the University of Western Ontario, has called Potterburg Creek one of Canada's largest environment disasters. "It's unprecedented to have PCBs loaded with dioxins running through residential neighbourhoods," according to Cummins (Kenna, 1985, *Toronto Star*, 2 February).

5. In Dec. 1979 the *Globe and Mail* reported that the government had found 800 previously unrecorded dumpsites in southern Ontario (*Globe and Mail*, Dec. 11, 1979). The research team making that survey also estimated that there may be between 2000 and 3000 unrecorded dumps in Ontario as a whole. In 1979 the U.S. Environmental Protection Agency estimated that there were 50 000 chemical dumps in the U.S. Between 1200 and 2000 are thought to pose significant dangers (Hart 1979, 25). In the U.S., it has been argued that 125 billion pounds of hazardous wastes were produced in 1980 — enough to fill 2 000 Love Canals (Brownstein, 1981). In Canada, the federal government has estimated that as of 1982, there are 3.2 million tonnes of toxic wastes generated in this country (Environment Canada, 1982, Vol. 3, 8). About half of these wastes come from Ontario which produces 1 650 107 tonnes annually (Waste Management Corporation, 1982, 58).

6. The Minister of the Environment (Ontario) Keith Norton stated in 1981 that on the basis of "the most comprehensive testing of any water supply in the history of this province using some of the most sophisticated methods available to us" that there was "outstanding water quality in the community" of Whitchurch-Stouffville (Legislature of Ontario, Legislative Debates, 11 June 1981, p. 1486 and 16 June 1981 p. 1650).

6a. One thing they discovered was that York Sanitation, a subsidiary of Waste Management Inc. of Oakbrook, Ill., had made a $35 000 contribution to the Progressive-Conservative party of Ontario in 1977 which was laundered through Chicago, Luxembourg and Italy. The Royal Commission which investigated this unseemly donation in 1978 admitted that it contravened the Election Finance Act of 1975 but laid no criminal charges (Ontario, Report of the Royal Commission Appointed to Inquire Into Waste Management, Inc. etc. The Hon. S.H. Hughes, March 30, 1978).

7. Not all members of the community supported the efforts of the Concerned Citizens groups. According to Fran Sutton, some Stouffville residents thought of the women as "'mouthy dames,' and wished '. . . they would go . . . look after their pots and pans and children and keep out of this. They are just hysterical women'" (Jackson and Weller, 1984, 30).

8. Advertisement (television) for Pinesol cleaner, March 1985.

9. See for example, Hall, 1974, on the issues of additives overprocessing and the destruction of nutrition, carcinogens (DES) and antibiotics in meat; *Consumer Reports* on lead in evaporated milk, lowering sugar and salt content of baby foods etc. The Nestle boycott has generated important literature on multinational corporations, food and health. See also Weir and Schapiro, *Circle of Poison*, on the return of banned pesticides in food imported into North America from the Third World.

10. What is also mystified about these products is the conditions under which they are made and distributed both in terms of the working conditions inside the factories which produce them and in terms of the health and safety concerns within those factories. We don't normally pick up a box of detergent and ask what the hourly wage of the worker who made it was. In fact we have little knowledge of the production process involved in making laundry detergent. The whole process is socially and culturally camouflaged. Our schools do not tour detergent plants, or the chemical companies that make the dyes, emulsifiers and solvents that go into the detergent. There are no TV documentaries about the men or women in these plants. Are they unionized, do they have adequate health and safety equipment? These are questions totally absent from public discourse and in fact very hard for the specialist to investigate. The barriers preventing problematization and investigation are

socially constructed. Once questions are asked about the working conditions of lettuce pickers, for example, alarming truths about exploitation, child labour or the unsafe use of pesticides may emerge. Thus manufacturers must make a concerted effort to prevent consumers from asking: "Who made this? How did it get to my kitchen?"

One strategy of deflection has been to present the labour process as a fairy tale. Advertisements tell the public that products are made by elves. "Crans," giants or benign patriarchs like "Mr. Kraft," "Mr. Christie," and "Aunt Beatrice." Fantasy labour complements fantasy housework symbolized by blonde middle class mothers dancing or singing in glowingly well appointed homes as camera angles pan to describe the intense satisfaction they feel in cleaning, ". . . because cleaning is caring. . . ".

11. Among dish detergents P&G produces Ivory Liquid, Joy and Dawn. In laundry detergents P&G makes Bold, Cheer, Dash, Duz, Era, Gain Oxydol, Tide, Dreft and Ivory Snow. In bar soap Ivory, Camay, Coast, Lava and Safeguard are all made by P&G. And in general cleaners and softeners, P&G makes Mr. Clean, Spic and Span, Top Job. P&G toothpastes are Crest and Gleem; deodorants are Secret and Sure; diapers are Pampers and Luvs.

12. Monsanto is also a major producer of pesticides for agribusinesses and in this regard has become involved in advertising. As the pesticide industry came under increasing attack by environmentalists and health activists, Monsanto has launched a $45 million (US) campaign to assure consumers that chemicals are 'natural' and that its herbicides, like Vegadex discussed in TV commercials, are beneficial. In independent studies, Vegadex has been shown to be carcinogenic to rats and mice, including breast cancers in the females of both species, tumors of the stomach in male rats and of the lung in male mice. It is considered to be unsafe for agricultural workers (Epstein, 1978, 394).

13. In the United States, Proctor and Gamble, Colgate-Palmolive and Unilever control 90% of the market, Unilever has only 18% of detergent sales, Proctor and Gamble has 50% and Colgate-Palmolive has 22% (*Counter Information Services*, n.d. 12–13).

14. Global market penetration seems boundless. In the summer of 1983, while I was doing research in a remote corner of the Kalahari desert in Botswana, I found Bingo detergent available on the virtually barren shelves of a small store.

15. In some African countries a large percentage of the waged workforce is in some way dependent on Unilever (*Ibid.*, 7. See also R. Howard, 1978).

16. Former Consumer Affairs Minister Judy Erola set a limit for nitrosamines of 30 parts per billion in baby bottle nipples to be lowered to 10 p.p.b. in Jan. 1985 (*Toronto Star*, 16 February 1984).

17. Captan, a fungicide, is hazardous to pregnant women and young children. It has been found to cause cancer and birth defects in pregnant animals. It is used by home gardeners as well as commercial florists and gardeners and unbeknownst to most people, it is also found in cosmetics, wallpaper paste, vinyl textiles, and polyethylene garbage bags (Rosenberg, 1984).

Captan has been tested and approved by Industrial Bio-Test Laboratories in the United States and their findings on this and over 100 other chemicals were used by Canadian regulators to grant registration for the use of these chemicals in this country. Unfortunately IBT officials have been tried and found guilty of having falsified tests on more than 100 chemicals allowed for use in Canada by the Departments of Agriculture and Health and Welfare (Hall, 1981; Vigod and Woodsworth, 1982; Schneider, 1983). The Canadian government knew of this problem in 1977 but did not release details to the public until 1980 (Toronto Health Advocacy Unit, City Hall, 1981). Pressure by ecology groups after the IBT affair finally forced the Ontario Ministry of the Environment to act on Captan.

18. When a Consumer Interpol member learns of a potential hazard in his or her country, the member will investigate and if convinced that something is amiss, will notify the Consumer Interpol coordinator in Penang, sending along whatever evidence has been gathered. The coordinator drawing on the advice of experts on such issues as food, drugs, pesticides, consumer law will sift the evidence. If the suspected hazard is confirmed, the coordinator sends out Alert notices to all groups in the network. The message that goes out directs activists to contact manufacturers or distributers immediately, to contact the relevant government agencies and agitate loudly in the press (*New Internationalist*, 1983; 28–29).

19. Personal communication from a delegate from the Manitoba Council for International Co-operation on joint efforts between MCIC, IOCU, and HAI.

20. For a fuller discussion of recent patterns of organization in the United States see Freudenberg, 1984.

REFERENCES

Brownstein, Richard: 1981, "The Toxic Tragedy," in R. Nader *et al.* (eds.), *Who's Poisoning America?* Sierra Club Books: San Francisco.

Bull, David: 1982, *A Growing Problem: Pesticides and the Third World Poor*, Oxfam: Oxford, U.K.

Cameron, Barbara: 1983, "The Sexual Division of Labour and Class Struggle," *Social Studies/Études Socialistes: A Canadian Annual*, pp. 40–50.

Cyng-Jones, T.W.: n.d., *Unilever*, Geneva: International Union of Food and Allied Workers' Association.

Counter Information Services: n.d., "Unilever's World," *Report* No. 1.

Dinham, Barbara and Colin Hines: 1983, *Agribusiness in Africa*, Earth Resources Research: Birmingham: U.K.

Distelheim, Rochelle: 1985, "There's a Time Bomb Ticking Inside My Body," *Family Circle*, Oct. 89 (14): 46 and ff.

Dowie, Mark: Circle of Poison.

Epstein, Samuel S.: 1978, *The Politics of Cancer*, Sierra Club Books: San Francisco.

Ewen, Stuart: 1976, *Captains of Consciousness*, McGraw-Hill: New York.

Fishbein, Laurence: "An Overview of Potential Mutagenic Problems Posed by Some Pesticides and Their Trace Impurities," *Environmental Health Perspectives* **27**, 126–127.

Freudenberg, Nicholas and Ellen Zaltzberg: 1984, "From Grassroots Activism to Political Power: Women Organizing Against Environmental Hazards," in E. Chavkin (ed.), *Double Exposure: Women's Health Hazards on the Job and at Home*, Monthly Review Press: New York.

Freudenberg, Nicholas: 1984, *Not in Our Backyards*, Monthly Review Press: New York.

Gore and Storrie Limited: 1982, *Canadian National Inventory of Hazards and Toxic Wastes*, Ottawa: Environment Canada.

Hall, Ross Hume: 1974, *Food for Nought: The Decline in Nutrition*, Harper and Row: New York.

Hall, Ross Hume: 1981, "A New Approach to Pest Control in Canada," *Canadian Environmental Advisory Council*, Report No. 10, July: 48.

Hart, Fred C. Associates Inc.: 1979, *Preliminary Assessment of Cleanup Costs for National Hazardous Waste Problems*.

Hayden, Dolores: 1981, *The Grand Domestic Revolution: A History of Feminist Designs for American Homes, Neighborhoods, and Cities*, MIT Press: Cambridge, Mass.

Howard, Rhoda: 1978, *Colonialism and Underdevelopment in Africa*, Croom Helm: London.

Jackson, John, Phil Weller and the Ontario Public Interest Group: 1982, *Chemical Nightmare: The Unnecessary Legacy of Toxic Wastes*, Between the Lines: Toronto.

Jackson, John and Phil Weller: 1984, "Focus: Chemical Nightmare," *Homemaker's*, Oct. 19(8).

Labonté, Ron: 1984, "Chemical Justice: Dioxin's Day in Court," *This Magazine* **17**(16), 4–9.

Luxton, Meg: 1980, *More Than a Labour of Love*, Women's Press: Toronto.

Kaplan, Temma: 1982, "Female Consciousness and Collective Action: The Case of Barcelona. 1910-1918," *Signs* **7**(3), 545.

Melrose, Dianna: 1982, *Bitter Pills: Medicines and the Third World Poor*, Oxfam: Oxford, U.K.

Moskowitz, Milton, Michael Katz and Robert Levering (eds.): 1980, *Everybody's Business: An Almanac*, Harper and Row: San Francisco.

Norwood, Christopher: 1985, "Terata," *Mother Jones*, Jan. X(1), 15–21.

Oakley, Anne: 1975, *The Sociology of Housework*, Pantheon: New York.

Ontario Waste Management Corporation: 1982, *Waste Quantities Study*.

Ontario: Report of the Royal Commission Appointed to Inquire Into Waste Management Inc., *et cetera*: 1978, The Hon. S.H.S. Hughes, March 30.

Pedler, Frederick: 1974, *The Lion and the Unicorn in Africa: The United Africa Company, 1787–1931*, Heinemann: London.

Proulx, Monique: 1978, *Five Million Women: A Study of The Canadian Housewife*, Advisory Council on the Status of Women: Ottawa.

Rosenberg, Harriet: 1984, "The Home is the Workplace: Hazards, Stress and Pollutants in the Household," in W. Chaukin (ed.). *Double Exposure*, Monthly Review Press: New York.

Schneider, Keith: 1983, "Faking It," *Amicus Journal* **4**(4), 14–26.

Vigod, Toby and Anne Woodsworth: 1982, "Captan: The Legacy of the IBT Affair," Submission on Pesticide Law and Policy to the Consultative Committee on IBT Pesticides on Behalf of the Canadian Environmental Law Association and Pollution Probe.

Weir, David and Mark Schapiro: 1981, *Circle of Poison*, Institute for Food and Development Policy: San Francisco.

Wolff, Janet: 1958, *What Makes Women Buy: A Guide to Understanding and Influencing the New Woman to Today*, McGraw-Hill: New York.

Wood, Ellen: 1981, "The Separation of the Economic and the Political in Capitalism," *New Left Review* **127**, 66–95.

Wynn, Mona: 1985, "Selling Mrs. Consumer: Corporate Capitalism and the Domestic Labour Process," Paper presented at the Women and the Invisible Economy Conference. Simone de Beauvoir Institute, Montreal, February 20–22.

34

Mercury in the Environment

ANASTASIA M. SHKILNYK

Pijibowin is the word for poison. It is used by the people of Grassy Narrows to describe the mercury that now contaminates their sacred English–Wabigoon River. Between 1962 and 1970, Dryden Chemicals Limited, a pulp and paper mill located about eighty miles upstream from Grassy Narrows, dumped over 20,000 pounds of mercury into the river system as effluent from its chlor-alkali plant. By March 1970, when the Ontario Minister of Energy and Resource Management ordered the company to stop discharging mercury into the environment, the damage was complete and irreversible. Over three hundred miles* of the English –Wabigoon river system, with all its biological life, would probably remain poisoned for half a century or more.

------

* 1 pound = .45 kilograms; 1 mile = 1.6 kilometers.

An environmental disaster can be assessed in many ways. One can measure the sheer force of the impact, the extent of the damage, the effects on human health, the economic losses sustained, or the length of recovery time. Any major disruptive event, however, should also be judged by looking at the vulnerability of the people who are exposed to it. It seems logical that a community that has just suffered a traumatic upheaval in its way of life will experience the effects of yet another crisis much more acutely. In such a situation, environmental contamination can no longer be measured in isolation, for its impact interacts with previous events in a complex manner to form a pattern of cumulative injury.

Coming only a few years after the relocation, the discovery of mercury dealt a devastating blow to the community of Grassy Narrows. Having just been wrenched from their moorings on the old reserve, the people were ill prepared to cope with yet another misfortune. They had but a precarious hold on the conditions of their existence on the new reserve. They could no longer draw strength either from their relationship to the land or from the well of their faith, which had once given meaning and coherence to their lives. In the context of their traditional religious beliefs, the contamination of the river could only be interpreted as punishment by the Great Spirit for some serious violation of the laws governing man's relationship to nature. People had great difficulty comprehending this "unseen poison" of mercury, whose presence in the water and in the fish they could not see or taste or smell. They could not understand how something that happened so far away from them could hurt them. Many could not believe that the natural environment, which had nurtured them both spiritually and materially could suddenly betray them. To accept the fact that their "River of Life" had turned into a river of poison meant to lose forever their faith in nature and in the source of life itself.

In the community, the suspicion of *pijibowin* and the feeling of loss of control over the environment ran like a strong undercurrent beneath the tangible and measurable effects of the contamination. The tangible effects — the disruption in guiding, the loss of commercial fishing, the warnings against taking fish for food — struck a further blow to the people's already weakened ability to produce their own food and make an independent living from the resources of the land. Just as important were the intangible effects — the massive intrusion of outsiders, the confusion and misunderstanding about the effects on human health, the political manipulation of the mercury issue and the acceleration of government intervention in community life. Far from being just a medical and an economic problem, the pollution of the river became a serious psychological problem. The way in which the governments of Canada and Ontario handled the mercury issue and the exploitation of the Grassy Narrows people by self-seeking groups and individuals were in the end as severely demoralizing as the fact of the poison itself. Any analysis of the impact of this environmental disaster, therefore, has to take into account the relationship of Indian people to the Canadian society as a whole. Indeed, the way in which the mercury issue was defined, managed, and politicized mirrors much of what is so wrong with our own mainstream society.

While there is no way to measure with any precision how much of the current crisis at Grassy Narrows is attributable to mercury and how much to the collapse of a way of life, the people's own perception of the importance of mercury is significant. They speak of mercury poisoning as the event that pushed them over the edge of their ability to feel secure in nature, to relate to each other and to the world around them, and to be self-reliant in providing for their material needs. They call mercury "the last nail in the coffin."

Mercury is one of the oldest metals known to us. Aristotle described it as "liquid silver" in the fourth century B.C. Its ore cinnabar was used to make the red dye found in prehistoric cave paintings in Europe. During Roman times, it was used to purify gold and silver. In the first century A.D., Greek physicians used it to heal open sores and burns. Centuries later, mercury ointment became a treatment for syphilis. But the hazards of mercury, as well as its uses, were also well known from early times. The miners of this metal, for example, developed violent tremors, muscular spasms, and character disorders. The Romans therefore chose convicts and slaves to mine the metal, and this precedent of using forced labor was followed by the Spaniards in the mercury mines they developed in the New World.

Miners, however, were not the only ones susceptible to the toxic effects of exposure to mercury. In the eighteenth century, a physician called Ramazzini wrote that goldsmiths using mercury in their craft "very soon become subject to vertigo, asthma, and paralysis. Very few of them reach old age, and even when they do not die young, their health is so terribly undermined that they pray for death."[1] Of artisans who used mercury to coat the backs of mirrors, he wrote: "You can see these workmen scowling and gazing reluctantly into their mirrors at the reflection of their own suffering and cursing the trade they have adopted."[2]

The popular expression "mad as a hatter" grew out of the observation of tremors, manic-depressive behavior, and temperamental instability among hatmakers who used mercuric nitrate to improve the felting quality of wool and fur. The toxic and potentially fatal effects of working with metallic or inorganic mercury, therefore, have been well established in recorded history.

Today, mercury and its compounds are used in about three thousand industrial processes by over eighty industries. Mercury is a valuable element because it is the only metal that is liquid at room temperature, and it also has special electrical properties that make it almost irreplaceable. It is used in making dental fillings, paints, electronic controls, thermometers, disinfectants, preservatives, and lotions. It is a catalyst in many metallurgical processes, and it is used in the production of vinyl chloride, a component in the manufacture of plastics. The single most important use of mercury (prior to 1970) was in chlor-alkali plants that served the huge pulp and paper industry. Here, mercury was used in the electrolytic production of caustic soda and chlorine, and it was this industry that "lost" mercury in great volume both in wastewater and through exhaust gases.[3] While individual cases of industrial mercury poisoning have been fairly well documented,[4] it took the massive epidemic of poisoning in Minamata, Japan, in the late 1950s and 1960s to shake the world out of its complacency about the dangers of discharging mercury as industrial waste.

AN INSIDIOUS POISON

Minamata is a village of about forty thousand persons, located on the southernmost island of Japan, Kyushu, on the bay of the Shiranui Sea. Its inhabitants make their living by commercial fishing, tourism, and working in the giant petrochemical complex owned by the Chisso Corporation. The town is associated with Minamata disease, which is known to have taken 107 lives and by 1970 had left over a thousand people with irreversible neurological damage, crippled limbs, blindness, paralysis, internal disorders, and loss of bodily functions. The disease fell most heavily on the poorest people of the area, who were most dependent on a steady diet of fish and shellfish.

Signs of the poison appeared in 1950, when fish in the bay began to float to the surface, swim erratically, and thrash about wildly before dying. Two years later, cats began to leap up in the air and turn in feverish circles, like whirling dervishes, before dying. People call it "the cat-dancing disease." In April 1956, two victims of what was at first diagnosed as cerebral palsy were admitted to the Chisso Factory Hospital. By mid-summer, so many similar cases had been reported that the director of the hospital, Dr. Hosokawa, declared that "an unclarified disease of the central nervous system had broken out." By the autumn of that year, a research team of the Kumamoto University Medical School suspected that the mass poisoning was traceable to a heavy metal concentrated in the flesh of fish and shellfish taken from Minamata Bay. It took years of research to identify organic mercury as the cause of the disaster and to provide conclusive evidence that the source of the poison was the effluent from the chemical plant of the Chisso Corporation. Indeed, a full decade passed before enough evidence could be accumulated to establish Chisso's legal liability for the damages caused by industrial pollution. Meanwhile, the company's executives refused to cooperate with the scientists, continued to dump mercury as effluent until 1968, and used their considerable economic and political influence to stifle criticism and frustrate the research effort.[5] In the end, the Chisso Corporation was forced to pay compensation to the victims of mercury poisoning, but the cost in human life was staggering. It is estimated that, aside from the actual and potential cases of congenital mercury poisoning, the number of Minamata disease victims may ultimately exceed ten thousand because of the long-term effects of past exposure.

Although outbreaks of mercury poisoning have occurred elsewhere,[6] the disease is always associated with the Minamata experience. This tragedy was followed by an extensive investigation of the causal links between inorganic mercury dumped as industrial waste, the contamination of the marine food chain by methyl mercury, and the onset of clinical symptoms of poisoning in humans. Scientists discovered a rather extraordinary natural phenomenon whereby inorganic (or metallic) mercury, which settles into the sediment of a body of water, is transformed into the much more toxic form of organic (or methyl) mercury in a process known as biomethylation.[7] What happens is that microorganisms living in the sediment, in order to protect themselves, convert the inorganic mercury into methyl mercury, which is much less toxic to them. The transformed mercury is then absorbed by microscopic underwater life such as plankton or algae, which serve as food for insect larvae. The insects are consumed by little fish; the little fish are consumed by bigger fish; and in this manner, the burden of methyl mercury in fish increases in concentration and toxicity as it passes up the food chain. Once inorganic mercury has been added to a water system, it takes a very long time for the mercury to clear the marine biosystem. Scientists estimate that only about 1 percent of the sediment's burden of inorganic mercury is converted into methyl mercury each year. Further, the biological half-life of methyl mercury in fish is very long. As a result, the process of contamination of marine life is continuous, persistent, and irreparable.

Of the two kinds of mercury, methyl mercury is more dangerous to human beings. Structurally, it differs from inorganic mercury simply through the addition of one or more carbon atoms to the mercury atom. Although both types are toxic, inorganic mercury does not do as much damage when taken by mouth. It is not as readily absorbed by the body; it is much more easily expelled from the body; and it does not accumulate in the body's vital organs and brain. Methyl mercury, on the other hand, is quickly carried by the blood through body tissues, concentrating in the heart, intestine, liver, and kidneys. But its greatest damage is reserved for the brain, and most of the clinical symptoms of mercury poisoning are related to brain and nerve lesions.[8] Methyl mercury destroys cells in the cere-

bellum, which regulates balance, and the cortex, which influences vision. It finds its way to other regions of the brain like the frontal lobe, where it may cause disturbances in personality. The toxin is singularly difficult to trace as a cause of illness because the symptoms of poisoning are not very specific and may be simulated by alcoholism, diabetes, severe nutritional deficiencies, old age, and many other disorders of the central nervous system, Therefore, a complete assessment of mercury poisoning can be made only at autopsy. Postmortem studies of the brains of Japanese victims, for example, revealed a marked atrophy or shrinkage of the brain caused by the destruction of nerve cells; the remaining nerve cell tissue was characterized by a spongelike quality.

Neurologists have identified the clinical symptoms of Minamata disease as follows: numbness of the mouth, lips, tongue, hands, and feet; tunnel vision, sometimes accompanied by abnormal blind spots and disturbances in eye movement; impairment of hearing; speech disorders; difficulty in swallowing; loss of balance; a stumbling, awkward gait; clumsiness in handling familiar objects; disturbances in coordination; loss of memory, inability to recall basic things like the alphabet; loss of the ability to concentrate; apathy; feelings of extreme fatigue; mental depression; emotional instability; and a tendency to fits of anxiety and rage. These initial symptoms of mercury poisoning may eventually lead to severe disability, uncontrollable tremors and convulsions, deformity, paralysis, coma, and death. There are no remedies or therapy for the victims of mercury poisoning; the disease is considered to be irreversible.

Aside from these dreadful symptoms, methyl mercury has other characteristics that make it a particularly insidious poison. In the first place it has a special affinity for unborn children. In the body of a pregnant woman, not only is the mercury immediately passed from the placenta to the fetus, but the fetus actually concentrates the lethal toxin. In Japan, blood concentrations of methyl mercury in infants at birth averaged about 30 percent higher than in the mother. There were many cases of infants born with what seemed like cerebral palsy;

some had deformed limbs, showed uncontrollable muscle spasms, and were seriously mentally retarded. These were the congenital victims of Minamata disease who had acquired the poison prenatally. Postmortem studies of such children showed massive atrophy in brain size and underdeveloped and malformed tissues in the central nervous system. To illustrate: the normal brain weight for a two-year-old child is about 960 g; for a three-year-old child, about 1,125. Minamata disease victims aged two and three registered brain weights of only 650 and 630 g, respectively.

Second, mercury continues to affect brain cells even after a person has stopped eating contaminated food. It has a half-life of at least seventy days in human blood and perhaps longer in the brain. This means that after seventy days, half of the burden of methyl mercury still exists in the body; it takes another seventy days to eliminate half of the remaining burden, and the balance is halved again every seventy days. Yet brain damage can be caused by minute amounts of mercury.

Third, individuals have different tolerances for the toxin; some are so sensitive to methyl mercury that even very brief exposure to contaminated food can cause significant damage to the brain. Some people also retain the poison in the body for a much longer time than others. So there are no guarantees that an individual who is exposed to small amounts of mercury over a long period of time will escape the pitiless and progressive degeneration of the nervous system.

Fourth, methyl mercury is a poison that follows no specific timetable between the time of exposure and the onset of symptoms of neurological injury. The damage done to the brain may not be manifest for several years.[9] In Japan, some patients diagnosed initially as chronic cases of low-level mercury intoxication developed symptoms of acute poisoning three or four years later. Thus there are no assurances that cases of low-grade or subacute poisoning will not worsen later on.

Finally, since many of the first symptoms of mercury poisoning (a "pins and needles" sensation in the arms and legs, tunnel vision, tremors) are also characteristic of other illnesses and nervous afflic-

tions, it is very difficult to make a positive and early diagnosis of Minamata disease. No wonder, then, that the correlation between levels of exposure to methyl mercury and neurological symptoms of mercury poisoning has presented scientists with a formidable analytical challenge. It does not help matters when different laboratories use different units to measure the burden of mercury in the body or when significant differences appear in the interpretation of symptomatic evidence. But all scientists agree on one point: the amount of mercury in the blood is positively correlated with the potential health risk a person bears. Blood levels of mercury are indicated by the ratio of mercury to whole blood calibrated in parts per billion (ppb). In Canada, the norm for the level of mercury in the blood of persons who are not fish-eaters is considered to be about 5 ppb; this rises to about 20 ppb for people who eat a lot of fish. Some countries recognize 200 ppb of mercury in blood as a "safe" level. Others (for example, Canada, the United States, Sweden, Finland, and Japan) accept 100 ppb as a "safe" level; anyone with more than 100 ppb is considered to be at risk.

The body burden of mercury can also be measured by the analysis of mercury values in human hair. It so happens that as hair is being formed on the head, mercury is being incorporated from the bloodstream. Thus there is a constant concentration ratio between the amount of mercury in the hair and in the blood. Once in the hair, methyl mercury remains there unchanged. Since hair grows at the rate of about one centimeter per month, scientists have an inbuilt and permanent record of previous levels of exposure to the toxin.[10]

Because of individual variations in tolerance and in the length of the retention period, it has been very difficult to establish the precise relationship between blood concentrations of mercury and the incidence of symptoms of Minamata disease. The available data, gathered from an outbreak of mercury poisoning in Iraq, are shown in the table.[11]

Symptoms of poisoning, then, begin to appear when levels of mercury in blood fall in the range of 500–1,000 ppb. Studies published by the World Health Organization confirm that lower levels of

Table: Relation of Clinical Symptoms of Methyl Mercury Poisoning in Iraq to Blood Levels of Mercury

Whole Blood Methyl Mercury Concentration Levels (ppb)	Percentage of Patients Showing Symptoms					
	Paresthesia	Ataxia	Visual Changes	Dysarthria	Hearing Defects	Death
0– 100[a]	9.5	5	0	5	0	0
101– 500	5	0	0	5	0	0
501–1 000	42	11	21	5	5	0
1 001–2 000	60	47	53	24	0	0
2 001–3 000	79	60	56	25	12.5	0
3 001–4 000	82	100	58	75	36	17
4 001–5 000	100	100	83	85	66	28

Source: From F. Bakir, S.F. Damluji, L. Amin-Zaki *et al.* "Methylmercury poisoning in Iraq: An Inter-University Report," *Science* 181 (1973), as reproduced in David Shephard, "Methyl Mercury Poisoning in Canada," *Canadian Medical Association Journal* 114 (March 1976): 463–72.

[a]The data from Iraq suggest that the range of 0–100 ppb of mercury in whole blood is associated with a 9.5 percent incidence of paresthesia (numbness in the extremities) and a 5 percent incidence of ataxia (stumbling gait) and dysarthria (slurred speech). Medical authorities concluded, however, that at this concentration, the symptoms were probably caused by factors other than methyl mercury.

exposure are associated with a significantly decreased degree of risk; at mercury blood levels in the 200–500-ppb range, there is presumed to be a 5 percent chance that adults will show the initial symptoms of Minamata disease.[12] It is worth repeating that very little is known about the long-term effects of even very modest concentrations of mercury in the human brain. In Japan, a few particularly sensitive individuals developed initial symptoms of mercury intoxication at blood levels close to 200 ppb; in Sweden, some chromosome breakage was observed at the 400-ppb level. Autopsies have also shown brain damage in individuals whose exposure to methyl mercury was considered insufficient to provoke actual symptoms. In general, however, fully developed methyl mercury poisoning will occur only when the concentration of mercury in the blood is in the range of 1,230–1,840 ppb.[13] With prenatal exposure to the toxin, the risks of poisoning are considerably higher, perhaps three or four times.

AN ENVIRONMENTAL DISASTER

Following the dreadful experiences of Minamata and Iraq, a series of international conferences on heavy metals took place in the late 1960s to publicize the link between the industrial uses of mercury and the potential dangers of mercury contamination. At about the same time, Swedish scientists described the process of biomethylation and established that abnormally high levels of mercury found in fish and wildlife were related to upstream chlor-alkali and pulp and paper plants. In Canada, early warnings to government health officials about the hazards of mercury spills seem to have gone unheeded.[14] Then, in 1967–68, Norvald Fimreite, a Norwegian graduate student at the University of Western Ontario, studied the effects of industrial mercury losses on birds and fish. He found very high levels of mercury in the fish of the southern part of the Saskatchewan River, downstream from a pulp and paper mill and chlor-alkali plant. In

1969, he alerted the officials of the Ontario Water Resources Commission that the fish of Lake St. Clair had unacceptably high concentrations of methyl mercury. It did not take long to confirm that fish taken downstream from all the chlor-alkali plants in Ontario carried body burdens of mercury that were sometimes more than forty times the standard of 0.5 ppm set for export and human consumption by the federal government. The Lake St. Clair fishery was closed. In March 1970, the Ontario Minister of Energy and Resource Management ordered all the companies in the province with substantial industrial mercury losses to stop discharging mercury into the environment. One of these companies was Dryden Chemicals Limited, a subsidiary of Reed Paper Limited. In May 1970, the Ontario government banned commercial fishing on all lakes and tributaries of the English-Wabigoon river system.

There was cause for concern. Fish in the 300-mile river system, from Dryden to the Manitoba border, were found to contain mercury burdens comparable to those found in the fish of Minamata Bay. Levels of methyl mercury in the aquatic food chain of the system, including plankton, bottom-dwelling organisms, fish, wildfowl, and fish-eating mammals, were found to be ten to fifty times higher than those in surrounding waterways off the system. The greatest concentration of mercury was found among the organisms dwelling on the sediment bottom, particularly crayfish. In 1970, the average value of mercury in crayfish was 10 ppm, a value about twenty times greater than that in crayfish from unpolluted adjacent lakes and rivers.[15] Comprehensive studies of the mercury burden in fish in the early 1970s revealed levels of contamination so high that no species of fish from any lake on the river system was fit for human consumption. The range of mean mercury concentration (measured in parts per million, ppm) in the three most commercially viable species of fish found in the English–Wabigoon river system was as follows (1975 data): pike, 2.31-5.18 ppm; walleye, 1.58-5.98 ppm; whitefish, 0.47-2.01 ppm. The mean level of mercury in the same species and size of fish taken from off-system lakes was, by contrast,

several times lower: pike, 0.47-1.39 ppm; walleye, 0.38-1.08 ppm; whitefish, 0.04-0.24 ppm.[16]

Since these peak values were recorded, in the early 1970s, there has been a decline in the amount of mercury in fish, but it has not been of sufficient magnitude to inspire confidence that the river system will heal itself quickly.[17] Not only is the process of biomethylation singularly unenergetic, but there is also a great deal of inorganic mercury sitting on the bottom of the riverbed. It may therefore take anywhere from fifty to seventy years for the poison to clear the system. The pressing question is: Who is responsible for an environmental disaster of such proportions?

Between March 1962 and October 1975, Dryden Chemicals operated a mercury cathode chlor-alkali plant that produced chlorine and other chemicals for use as bleach in the adjacent pulp and paper mill of Reed Paper Limited (Dryden Division). During that period, scientists estimated that about 40,000 pounds of inorganic mercury were "lost" to the environment via aquatic and aerial discharges, of which about 20,000 pounds entered the English–Wabigoon river system.[18] Prior to the promulgation of the 1970 government control order to stop all mercury discharges into water systems, all the waste from the mercury cells was going into the air and the Wabigoon River. In 1970 -71, treatment systems were installed to isolate the heavy metal in the effluent. Although this resulted in a significant decline in the amount of mercury going into the river, aerial emissions continued. The loss of mercury to the environment was finally halted in 1975, when the company changed the technology in its chlor-alkali plant.

Executives of Dryden Chemicals and Reed Paper Limited have repeatedly insisted that mercury occurs naturally in the environment of the Canadian Shield and that therefore the effluent from the mill was not the only source of mercury in the river. But the sheer volume of mercury discharged as waste and the fact that fish taken from the polluted waters show much higher mercury levels than fish caught in adjacent lakes and rivers undermine this argument. After studying the problem, scientists of the Ontario government came to the conclusion that "factors such as mineralization, mining activities, and aerial fallout cannot account for the elevated mercury levels found in fish from the Wabigoon–English system of lakes. The major source of mercury pollution in the area is the chlor-alkali plant/pulp and paper complex in Dryden, Ontario."[19]

Throughout the 1970s, corporate executives continued to deny any culpability for the contamination. They pleaded ignorance of the process of biomethylation. They argued that the mercury in the Wabigoon system was less harmful than the mercury discharged in Minamata Bay. And they insisted that they had no records of how much mercury was purchased, used, or discharged into the environment. The litany of rationalizations in their public pronouncements sometimes bordered on the absurd.[20] But the strongest line of defense was marshalled around the idea that the company had "a license to pollute" from the Ontario government. It had, after all, respected existing environmental regulations and standards; therefore, it could not be held exclusively liable for the disaster.

Robert Billingsley, president of Reed Paper Limited, succinctly asserted the company's position in an interview filmed in September 1975. "I think there are many instances in our society where people are harmed in one way or another through no fault of their own, and it's particularly difficult where blame is not exclusive, where there is [sic] complicating factors; and since we operate on a principle of law in this country, then you almost have to define [blame] in the courts, split up where is the responsibility, do it on a legal basis and assign . . . the consequences. . . . I don't know exactly what we've done. Nobody has told us what the consequences of our actions were." The company's defense, then as now, rested on the premise that mercury pollution was a societal responsibility and that any claims for damages would have to be fought out in the courts. But as we come to understand the kind of injury and loss sustained by the Indian people, we will recognize the immense hurdles of definition, proof, and lack of precedent that would have to be overcome to obtain justice through the Canadian courts.

ENDNOTES

1. Bernardino Ramazzini, 1731 A.D., as quoted in Warner Troyer, *No Safe Place* (Toronto: Clarke, Irwin and Company Limited, 1977), p. ix.

2. Quoted in "Mercury and Its Compounds," *Occupational Health Bulletin* 25, no. 7-8 (1970).

3. Data on the volume of mercury emissions in Canada show that in 1970 the chlor-alkali industry accounted for about 32.1 percent of the total volume of mercury losses from all industrial plants. Inadvertent emissions of mercury from petroleum combustion constituted about 24.3 percent of the total. Paints, dental amalgams, instrumentation and electrical equipment, print manufacture, battery cathodes, pharmaceuticals, fungicides, and the recovery of gold, zinc, copper, and lead accounted for the remainder. Total emissions of mercury into the atmosphere in 1970 have been documented as 74.6 metric tons. Environment Canada, "National Inventory of Sources and Emissions of Mercury: 1970," Internal report APCD 73-6, 1973. See also L. M. Azzaria and F. Habashi, "Mercury Pollution — An Examination of Some Basic Issues." *CIM Bulletin* (August 1976), pp. 101-07.

4. Between 1955 and 1975, in the province of Ontario, for example, the Workmen's Compensation Board paid compensation to twenty-two workers who developed mercury poisoning. These workers held jobs in the following industries: hat manufacturing, gold refining, fungicides, battery manufacturing, and the electrical industry. Other cases of poisoning stemmed from working with mercury in a dental laboratory and from inhaling mercury vapor while firefighting. Two other cases of poisoning involved workers exposed to mercury in a chlor-alkali plant.

It is inorganic mercury that is most often responsible for mercury poisoning among industrial workers. Troyer, p. 10.

5. In 1969, attorneys representing disease victims came to see Hosokawa, who had retired as the director of the Chisso Factory Hospital. He was very ill and dying, but he made a sworn statement that in 1959 he had informed Chisso executives that his research had demonstrated a direct link between Chisso effluent discharges and Minamata disease. In response to this information, management had stopped him from doing any further research and had clamped down on scientists trying to take samples of the effluent water. In public and during the court case, the company continued to deny that it had any previous knowledge of the link between its chemical operations and Minamata disease.

6. In 1956, 1960 and 1971–72, there were outbreaks of mercury poisoning in Iraq, where seed grain treated with mercury to prevent spoilage was diverted and milled for flour. Smaller outbreaks caused by eating mercury-treated seed grain occurred in Guatemala (1963–65), Ghana (1967), and Pakistan (1969). In 1964, in Niigata, Japan, 120 persons died from eating poisoned fish and shellfish in an outbreak similar to that at Minamata.

7. The process of biomethylation was first described in 1965 by two Swedish scientists, Alf Johnels and M. Olsson, who suggested that inorganic mercury of the kind used in chlor-alkali plants could be converted to methyl mercury in muddy lake bottoms. Within a few years, two more researchers documented more precisely how biomethylation works. See Soren Jensen and Arne Jernelov, "Biological Methylation of Mercury in Aquatic Organisms," Institute of Analytical chemistry, University of Stockholm, 1969. In Canada, there is a continuing controversy as to when Canadian scientists were made aware of biomethylation and the dangers of polluting waterways with inorganic mercury.

8. A complete description of the type and distribution of lesions in the human brain caused by methyl mercury can be found in D. Hunter and D. Russell, "Focal Cerebral and Cerebellar Atrophy in a Human Subject due to Organic Mercury Compound," *Journal of Neurology, Neurosurgery, and Psychiatry* 17 (1954):235–41; and T. Takeuchi, "Biological Reactions and Pathological Changes in Human Beings and Animals Caused by Organic Mercury

Contamination," in *Environmental Mercury Contamination*, ed. R. Hartung and B. D. Dinman (Ann Arbor: Ann Arbor Science Publishers, 1972), pp. 247–89.

9. In 1953, in Niigata, Japan, a boy who had eaten large amounts of contaminated fish and shellfish over a period of only ten days was, seven years later, so severely affected by the poison that he could not attend school. Department of National Health and Welfare Canada, "Task Force on Organic Mercury in the Environment: Final Report (1973)," p. 6.

10. The level of mercury in hair is given in units of parts per million (ppm). The criteria for "safe" levels of mercury vary for hair as they do for blood, but generally, for persons having minimal environmental exposure to mercury, levels in hair are about 6 ppm. In Japan, people who had hair values of 200 ppm or more in 1965 are now seriously ill with Minamata disease; some of those who had hair levels between 100 and 200 ppm are now certified patients; and a few with hair levels between 50 and 100 ppm have the initial symptoms of mercury poisoning. Memorandum from the Mercury Team, National Indian Brotherhood, to the Standing Committee on Mercury in the Environment, October 9, 1975.

11. Iraq has had three outbreaks of organic mercury poisoning, two of which were major. In 1960, approximately 1000 persons were affected; in 1971 and 1972, 6430 cases were recorded, of which 459 were fatal. The 1971–72 outbreak followed the ingestion of bread made from grain treated with a methyl mercurial fungicide. The symptoms of poisoning were similar, but not identical, to those found at Minamata. Whereas blood concentrations of Japanese victims were not fully documented at the time of exposure, in Iraq, blood samples were taken an average of sixty-five days after people stopped eating contaminated food.

An important question is whether the Iraqi data are relevant as a baseline for other populations. What the data show is that there is a risk of neurological damage for persons whose blood levels of methyl mercury are in the range of 100–500 ppb. The difference between the Iraqi situation and that in northwestern Ontario lies in the temporal nature of the exposure to mercury. In Iraq, the exposure was a brief one, with relatively large doses of mercury ingested over a period of one to three months. In Canada, the exposure of the Indian people is seasonal, with the highest blood levels of mercury falling at the end of the summer guiding period.

12. World Health Organization, *Environmental Health Criteria: Mercury* (Geneva: World Health Organization, 1976) pp. 23–24.

13. B. D. Dinman and L. H. Hecker, "The Dose-Response Relationship Resulting from Exposure to Alkyl Mercury Compounds," in *Environmental Mercury Contamination*, p. 290.

14. In 1966 and 1967, the Department of Health and Welfare was apparently warned by several sources that mercury contamination could be a serious health hazard. Scientists from the National Research Council approached federal health authorities but were told that there was no problem. That same year, direct communication from the World Health Organization in Geneva failed to move the federal bureaucrats in Ottawa to action. Yet a full account of Minamata disease had been published in English as early as September 1961. Troyer, pp. 22–23.

15. A comprehensive survey of mercury accumulation by all organisms in the system was carried out by the staff of the Freshwater Institute of the Fisheries Marine Service in Winnipeg. See A. L. Hamilton, "A Survey of Mercury Levels in the Biota of a Mercury-Contaminated River System in Northwestern Ontario," The Freshwater Institute, report No. 1167, 1972.

   In 1971, Norvald Fimreite studied fish-eating birds and waterfowl on the English–Wabigoon river system. He found very high levels of mercury in the tissues of the birds. Similar mercury values were found in another study of birds around Clay Lake (K. Vermeer, F. A. J. Armstrong, and D. Hatch, "Mercury in Aquatic Birds at Clay Lake, Western Ontario," *Journal of Wildlife Management* 37 [1973]:58–61).

16. J. N. Bishop and B. P. Neary, *Mercury Levels in Fish from Northwestern Ontario 1970–1975*, Inorganic Trace Contaminants Section, Laboratory Services Branch, Ontario Ministry of the Environment, April 1976, p. 78.

17. After mercury discharges into a river system cease, natural restorative processes help to reduce the concentration of mercury in the sediment. These include the trapping and isolation of mercury by further sedimentation, the "flushing" of the system by the natural seasonal flow of water, and the transport of mercury further downstream. Between 1970 and 1975, for example, the level of mercury in the sediment twenty miles from the source of pollution in Dryden had decreased by half; further downstream, however, the level had increased. Recent indications are that the mercury burden continues to travel westward, downstream, away from the original source of the pollution.

18. J. A. Spence, "Inorganic Mercury Discharges and Emissions by the Dryden Chemical Co. Ltd., March 1962 to October 1975" (Unpublished paper, April 1977), p. 9. Estimates of mercury losses to the English–Wabigoon river system were based on known empirical relationships between chlorine production, mercury consumption, and mercury losses per ton of chlorine produced. Mercury was lost to the environment in wastewater from the plant, in sludge resulting from the precipitation of impurities in brine, and in atmospheric emissions from the mercury cell room. No direct estimate of aerial emissions of mercury has been made, although studies at similar plants have shown that such discharges form a substantial proportion of total losses; furthermore, they occur in the immediate vicinity and are then washed into the adjacent river system. The total inorganic mercury available to the English–Wabigoon river system (from both aerial and direct aquatic emissions) was estimated to be between 30,000 and 46,000 lbs (1962–75); the remainder (from estimated total losses of 50,000 lbs) was trapped in special disposal pits and buried.

19. Bishop and Neary, p. 78.

20. In describing the attempts to whitewash "the crimson history of mercury," Troyer includes the following excerpt from a press release prepared by Dryden Chemicals Limited "To dispell [sic] the notion that we have wantonly dumped mercury into the river, we should point out that the effluent from our plant even before the installation of the treatment system had a mercury concentration in the order of 1/30 the concentration of mercury in normal human urine." Troyer quips back: "The logic is not much better than the spelling — few of us manage to excrete 33 million gallons* of urine daily" (Troyer, p. 98).

---

* 1 gallon = 3.8 litres.

SUGGESTED FURTHER READINGS

BLACKSTONE, WILLIAM (ed.) *Philosophy and the Environmental Crisis*. Athens, Georgia: University of Georgia Press, 1974.

DOBELL, R. "The Global Bargain." *Options*, Vol. 10, No. 10, 1989.

DOERN, G.B. *Regulatory Processes and Jurisdictional Issues in the Regulation of Hazardous Products in Canada*. Background Study No. 41, Ottawa: Science Council of Canada, 1977.

GOODPASTER, K. AND K. SAYRE (eds.) *Ethics and Problems of the 21st Century*. Notre Dame, Ind.: University of Notre Dame Press, 1979.

HOLM, WENDY (ed.) *Water and Free Trade*. Toronto: James Lorimer and Co., 1988.

LEISS, W. (ed.) *Ecology Versus Politics in Canada*. Toronto: University of Toronto Press, 1979.

PASSMORE, J.E. *Man's Responsibility for Nature*. New York: Charles Scribner's Sons, 1974.

ROEMER, JOHN. "A Public Ownership Resolution of the Tragedy of the Commons." *Social Philosophy & Policy*, Vol. 6, No. 2, Spring 1989.

SCHERER, D. AND T. ATTIG (eds.) *Ethics and the Environment*. Englewood Cliffs, NJ: Prentice-Hall, 1983.

SCHRECHER, T. *Political Economy of Environmental Hazards*. Law Reform Commission of Canada Study Paper: Protection of Life Series, 1984.

SENTES, RAY. "The Asbestos Albatross." *Options*, Vol. 10, No. 10, December 1989.

SINGH, JANG. "Business Activity and the Environment: The Case of Guyana Sugar Corporation and Thallium Sulphate." *Journal of Business Ethics*, Vol. 7, No. 5, 1988.

SWAIGEN, JOHN (ed.) *Environmental Rights in Canada*. Toronto: Butterworths, 1981.

PART EIGHT

International Business

INTRODUCTION

Some people argue that a corporation is fulfilling its moral responsibility if it maximizes profit for its stockholders and obeys the law. As we saw in Part One, this is essentially the view defended by Milton Friedman. Others, however, while they agree that corporations should obey the law, point out that the law is often an inadequate guide to morally responsible behaviour.

In this section, we examine this debate in the context of international business. Companies often choose to operate in countries where the law is far less protective of workers than in Canada. A considerable amount of microtechnology, for instance, is manufactured for North American multinational corporations in Malaysia where wages are very low and laws governing working conditions are less than stringent. Many fashion houses have garments sewn in the Third World where women work for far less than the minimum wage in Canada and where the law does not protect them from having to work long hours without overtime pay. Are Canadian companies which faithfully obey the laws of these host countries, and which dutifully maximize the profits of their stockholders, fulfilling their moral responsibilities? Should there perhaps be universal guidelines or laws by which all companies must abide, regardless of the particular laws of their host country? Many answer yes to the first question and no to the second. In defence of this view, some simply reiterate the arguments of capitalists such as Friedman. Others argue that universalized laws would not in fact benefit workers in underdeveloped countries. Still others believe that offering wages similar to those received by the rest of the citizens in the country not only allows for the possibility of more jobs, which benefits the country as a whole, but also serves to prevent unrest among employees not working for the company. Others counter that this is merely a smoke-screen argument made by those who wish to exploit cheap labour in underdeveloped countries. What is clear is that the world has become in many respects a "global assembly line." The second edition of this text is going to press at a time when it is particularly difficult to predict what changes will occur in the global assembly line and whether the creation of (ever-changing) trade alliances and trading zones will ultimately harm or benefit workers in various parts of the world. Eastern bloc countries such as Poland are now going to be recipients of loans from the World Bank. Will such loans and the policy of the International Monetary Fund deflate domestic economies in Eastern bloc countries as they have in the Third World? Will structural adjustment policies continue to cause economic and social hardship in debtor nations, or will the international economy stabilize over the next decade?

And what about foreign-owned companies that exploit Canadian unemployment? There has been much public debate about the desirability of accepting foreign defence contracts to lessen the high unemployment rates in the Maritimes. The Federal Government has stated that, although it will not engage in Star Wars Research, it is permissible for Canadian companies and universities to do so. The Maritime provinces have disproportionately high rates of unemployment. In some ways, this puts unemployed Maritimers in much the same position as Third World workers.

A different set of issues in international business involves the standardization of behaviour in commercial negotiations. Is it acceptable to offer bribes to obtain contracts in another country if the practice is not only commonplace there but seems essential to any successful business negotiation? In our first selection, Henry Lane and Donald Simpson address this question and relate some of their own personal experiences. They also clearly outline the basic sides taken in the debate. On the one hand, some argue, "it is an accepted business practice in [some] countries, and when you are in Rome you have to do as the Romans do. 'Moralists', on the other hand, believe that cultural relativity is no excuse for unethical behavior." Lane and Simpson provide a theoretical discussion of the multi-faceted nature of bribery in global terms and argue that bribery is not only unnecessary for successful negotiation, it may not even be in one's own self-interest or the interests of one's company.

In a related article, Carson analyses both bribery and extortion in international business. He begins by offering definitions of these two activities. Bribery, he suggests, "is a payment of money (or something of value) to another person in exchange for his giving one special consideration that is incompatible with the duties of his office, position, or role." Carson contrasts this with extortion, which "is the act of threatening someone with harm (that one is not entitled to inflict on him), in order to obtain benefits to which one has no prior right." Although Carson believes that his definition is inadequate to cover all types of extortion, his claim is that anyone who does act in accordance with it would indeed be guilty of extortion. After providing his useful definitions, Carson proceeds to offer a conceptual analysis of the similarities and differences between bribery and extortion. He then makes an interesting case for the claim that, although we have strong *prima facie* reasons to believe that bribery is wrong, it is not so clear that succumbing to extortion is always morally wrong.

Michael Philips disagrees. While Carson argues that bribe-taking is *prima facie* wrong in all contexts, Philips wishes to argue that there are cases in which accepting a bribe violates no promises, and, further, that there are cases where there is no *prima facie* duty not to accept a bribe. Philips argues that "P accepts a bribe from R if and only if P agrees for payment to act in a manner dictated by R rather than doing what is required of him as a participant in his practice." The force of Philips' argument here hangs on whether or not all participants in some kinds of practices either explicitly or implicitly break promises or violate tacit expectations. Philips provides examples he believes support his case.

The next three articles involve the difficult issue of what theoretically and strategically is the best approach to the moral dilemma of divestment in South African assets. With the sole exception of Great Britain, there has been a general consensus among Commonwealth countries that economic sanctions must be sustained, if not increased, as a method of moral suasion against apartheid. However, while there is increasing international condemnation of apartheid, approaches to the issue vary. This variation will continue to be the case as the political situation in South Africa continues to change. As this book goes to press, governments around the world are still in the process of assessing what impact, if any, the release of Ne̶   ̶ould and will have on investments in South Africa.

The first of these   mic Sanctions and Political Change in South Af   historical context as part of colonized Africa. It   f, analysis of what apartheid means and stands fo   ts both for sanctions against and for investment   at "the highest ethical stance for international b   operation with the apartheid state and the instit   ng that they are the modern equivalent of the sl   d labour."

In "To Stay or   Divestment of South African Assets," Kenneth   apartheid is unquestionably immoral, firms wh   should stay while firms which benefit the goverı   sen challenges Bond. Madsen questions Bond's position on the grounds that strategically the consequences he projects and the assumptions he makes are not certain. Furthermore, he concludes that "divestment is not only a good, but . . . it is a *bona fide* moral duty which should be practiced regardless of its consequences." In so doing, Madsen reasons that there are more than consequentialist arguments for divesting in South Africa. There are also deontological arguments.

The last article in this section raises the general issue of universal standards of employment while asking the specific question, "Should there be equal pay for equal work in the developing world?" Lehman takes the somewhat controversial position that, while workers should receive equal pay for equal work according to the pay scale of their own country, there is no requirement that the pay scale of a developed industrial nation should apply to a developing country. This raises the issue of whether the multinational corporations of industrialized nations improve the quality of life when they locate in the developing world, or merely exploit a vulnerable population of workers who cannot afford to reject poor working conditions and salaries.

35

Bribery in International Business: Whose Problem Is It?

HENRY W. LANE
DONALD G. SIMPSON

Introduction

No discussion of problems in international business seems complete without reference to familiar complaints about the questionable business practices North American executives encounter in foreign countries, particularly developing nations. Beliefs about the pervasiveness of dishonesty and the necessity of engaging in such practices as bribery vary widely, however, and these differences often lead to vigorous discussions that generate more heat than light. Pragmatists or 'realists' may take the attitude that "international business is a rough game and no place for the naive idealist or the faint-hearted. Your competitors use bribes and unless you are willing to meet this standard, competitive practice you will lose business and, ultimately, jobs for workers at home. Besides, it is an accepted business practice in those countries, and when you are in Rome you have to do as the Romans do." 'Moralists', on the other hand, believe that cultural relativity is no excuse for unethical behavior. "As

Canadians or Americans we should uphold our legal and ethical standards anywhere in the world; and any good American or Canadian knows that bribery, by any euphemism, is unethical and wrong. Bribery increases a product's cost and often is used to secure import licenses for products that no longer can be sold in the developed world. Such corrupting practices also contribute to the moral disintegration of individuals and eventually societies."

The foregoing comments represent extreme polar positions but we are not using these stereotypes to create a 'straw-man' or a false dichotomy about attitudes toward practices like bribery. These extreme viewpoints, or minor variations of them, will be encountered frequently as one meets executives who have experience in developing countries. Some 'realists' and 'moralists' undoubtedly are firm believers in their positions, but many other executives probably gravitate toward one of the poles because they have not found a realistic

From the *Journal of Business Ethics*, Vol. 3, No. 1 (Feb. 1984), pp. 35-42. © 1984
D. Reidel Publishing Co., Dordrecht, Holland. Published by permission.

alternative approach to thinking about the issue of bribery, never mind finding an answer to the problem.

The impetus for this article came from discussions with executives and government officials in Canada and in some developing nations about whether a North American company could conduct business successfully in developing countries without engaging in what would be considered unethical or illegal practices. It was apparent from these talks that the question was an important one and of concern to business executives, but not much practical, relevant information existed on the issue. There was consensus on two points: first, there are a lot of myths surrounding the issue of pay-offs, and second, if anyone had some insights into the problem, executives would appreciate hearing them.

In this article we would like to share what we have learned about the issue during the two years we have been promoting business (licensing agreements, management contracts, joint ventures) between Canadian and African companies. Our intention is not to present a comprehensive treatment of the subject of bribery nor a treatise on ethical behavior. Our intention is to present a practical discussion of some dimensions of the problem based on our experience, discussions and in some cases investigation of specific incidents.

The problem is multi-faceted

It can be misleading to talk about bribery in global terms without considering some situational specifics such as country, type of business and company. Our discussions with businessmen indicate that the pay-off problem is more prevalent in some countries than in others. Executives with extensive experience probably could rank countries on a scale reflecting the seriousness of the problem. Also, some industries are probably more susceptible to pay-off requests than others. Large construction projects, turn-key capital projects, and large commodity or equipment contracts are likely to be most vulnerable because the scale of the venture may permit the easy disguise of pay-offs, and because an individual, or small group of people, may be in a strategic

position to approve or disapprove the project. These projects or contracts are undoubtedly obvious targets also because the stakes are high, the competition vigorous and the possibility that some competitors may engage in pay-offs increased. Finally, some companies may be more vulnerable due to a relative lack of bargaining power or because they have no policies to guide them in these situations. If the product or technology is unique, or clearly superior, and it is needed, the company is in a relatively strong position to resist the pressure. Similarly, those firms with effective operational policies against pay-offs are in a position of strength. Many senior executives have stated, with pride, that their companies have reputations for not making pay-offs and, therefore, are not asked for them. These were executives of large, successful firms that also had chosen not to work in some countries where they could not operate comfortably. These executives often backed up their claims with specific examples in which they walked away from apparently lucrative deals where a pay-off was a requirement.

Two other elements of the situational context of a pay-off situation that vary are the subtlety of the demand and the amount of money involved. All pay-off situations are not straightforward and unambiguous, which may make a clear response more difficult. Consider, for example, the case of a company that was encouraged to change its evaluation of bids for a large construction project. Some host-country agencies were embarrassed by the evaluation results since Company X, from the country providing significant financing for the project, was ranked a distant third. The agencies sought a re-evaluation on questionable technicalities. The changes were considered but the ranking remained the same. At this point pressure began to build. Phone calls were made berating the firm for delaying the project and hinting that the large follow-on contract, for which it had the inside track, was in jeopardy. [But] no one ever said [explicitly,] make Company X the winner or you lose the follow-on.

Although no money was to change hands, this situation was similar to a pay-off request in that the company was being asked to alter its standard of acceptable business practices for an implied future benefit. The interpretation of the "request", the response, and the consequences, were left entirely to the company's management. Refusal to change may mean losing a big contract, but giving in does not guarantee the follow-on and you leave the company vulnerable to further demands. In ambiguous situations, factors such as corporate policies and the company's financial strength and its need for the contract enter into the decision. In this case the company had firm beliefs about what constituted professional standards and did not desperately need the follow-on contract. Although it refused to change, another company might find itself in a dilemma, give in to the pressure, and rationalize its behavior.

Finally, pay-offs range in size from the small payments that may help getting through customs without a hassle up to the multi-million dollar bribes that make headlines and embarass governments. The pay-off situations we discuss in this article are more significant than the former, but much smaller and far less dramatic than the latter. These middle-range pay-offs (tens of thousands of dollars) may pose a problem for corporations. They are too big to be ignored but possibly not big enough to be referred to corporate headquarters unless the firm has clear guidelines on the subject. Regional executives or lower level managers may be deciding whether or not these 'facilitating payments' are just another cost of doing business in the developing world.

On the outside looking in (the North American perspective)

"It's a corrupt, pay-off society. The problem has spread to all levels. On the face it looks good, but underneath it's rotten." Comments such as these are often made by expatriate businessmen and government officials alike. The North American executive may arrive in a Third World country with a stereotype of corrupt officials and is presented with the foregoing analysis by people on the spot who, he

feels, should know the situation best. His fears are confirmed.

This scenario may be familiar to some readers. It is very real to us because we have gone through that process. Two cases provide examples of the stories a businessman may likely be told in support of the dismal analysis.

The New Venture: Company Y, a wholly-owned subsidiary of a European multinational, wished to manufacture a new product for export. Government permission was required and Company Y submitted the necessary applications. Sometime later one of Company Y's executives (a local national) informed the Managing Director that the application was approved and the consultant's fee must be paid. The Managing Director knew nothing about a consultant or such a fee. The executive took his boss to a meeting with the consultant — a government official who sat on the application review committee. Both the consultant and the executive claimed to remember the initial meeting at which agreement was reached on the $10,000 fee. A few days later the Managing Director attended a cocktail party at the home of a high ranking official in the same agency. This official recommended that the fee be paid. The Managing Director decided against paying the fee and the project ran into unexpected delays. At this point the Managing Director asked the parent company's legal department for help. Besides the delay, the situation was creating a problem between the Managing Director and his executives as well as affecting the rest of the company. He initially advised against payment but after watching the company suffer, acquiesced with the approval of the parent company. The fee was re-negotiated downward and the consultant paid. What was the result? Nothing! The project was not approved.

The Big Sale: Company Z, which sold expensive equipment, established a relationship with a well placed government official on the first trip to the country. This official, and some other nationals, assured Company Z representatives that they would have no trouble getting the contract. On leaving the country, Company Z representatives had a letter of intent to purchase the equipment. On the second trip Company Z representatives brought the detailed technical specifications for a certain department head to approve. The department head refused to approve the specifications and further efforts to have the government honour its promise failed. The deal fell through. Company Z's analysis of the situation, which became common knowledge in business and government circles, was that a competitor paid the department head to approve its equipment and that the government reneged on its obligation to purchase Company Z equipment.

While in the country, the visiting executive may even have met Company Z's agent in the *Big Sale* who confirms the story. Corruption is rampant, and in the particular case of the "Big Sale" he claims to know that the department head received the money and from whom. The case is closed! An honest North American company cannot function in this environment — or so it seems.

On the inside looking out (the Developing Country's perspective)

During his visit the executive may have met only a few nationals selected by his company or government representatives. He probably has not discussed bribery with them because of its sensitive nature. If the businessmen and the officials he met were dishonest, they would not admit it; if they were honest he probably felt they would resent the discussion. Also, he may not have had enough time to establish the type of relationship in which the subject could be discussed frankly. It is almost certain that he did not speak with the people in the government agencies who allegedly took the payoffs. What would he say if he did meet them? And more than likely he would not be able to get an appointment with them if he did want to pursue the matter further. So the executive is convinced that corruption is widespread, having heard only one side of the horror stories.

Had the visitor been able to investigate the viewpoints of the nationals what might he have heard? "I would like to find a person from the developed world that I can trust. You people brought corruption here. We learned the concept from you. You want to win all the time, and you are impatient so you bribe. You offer bribes to the local people and complain that business is impossible without bribing."

Comments like these are made by local businessmen and government officals alike. If the visiting executive heard these comments he would be confused and would wonder whether or not these people were talking about the same country. Although skeptical, his confidence in the accuracy of his initial assessment would have been called into question. Had he been able to stay longer in the country, he might have met an old friend who knew the department head who allegedly was paid-off in the Big Sale. His friend would have made arrangements for the visitor to hear the other side of the story.

The Big Sale Re-visited: After the representatives of Company Z received what they described as a letter of intent to purchase the equipment they returned home. On the second visit they had to deal with the department head to receive his approval for the technical specifications.

At the meeting they told the department head that he need not worry about the details and just sign-off on the necessary documents. If he had any questions regarding the equipment he could inspect it in two weeks time in their home country. The department head's initial responses were: (1) he would not rubber stamp anything, and (2) how could this complex equipment which was supposedly being custom made for his country's needs be inspected in two weeks when he had not yet approved the specifications.

As he reviewed the specifications he noticed a significant technical error and brought it to the attention of Company Z's representatives. They became upset with this 'interference' and implied that they would use their connections in high places to ensure his compliance. When asked again to sign the documents he refused, and the company reps left saying that they would have him removed from his job.

After this meeting the Premier of the country became involved and asked the company officials to appear before him. They arrived with the Premier's nephew for a meeting with the Premier and his top advisors. The Premier told his nephew that he had no business being there and directed him to leave. The company officials then had to face the Premier and his advisors alone.

The Premier asked if the company had a contract and that if it had, it would be honoured. The company had to admit that it had no contract. As far as the Premier was concerned the issue was settled.

However, the case was not closed for the Company Z representatives. They felt they had been promised the deal and that the department had reneged. They felt that someone had paid-off the department head and they were quite bitter. In discussions with their local embassy officials and with government officials at home they presented their analysis of the situation. The result was strained relations and the department head got a reputation for being dishonest.

Well, the other side of the story certainly has different implications about whose behaviour may be considered questionable. The situation is now very confusing. Is the department head honest or not? The executive's friend has known the department head for a long time and strongly believes he is honest; and some other expatriate government officials have basically corroborated the department head's perception of the matter. But the businessmen and government officials who first told the story seemed reputable and honest. Who should be believed? As the visiting executive has learned, you have to decide on the truth for yourself.

Patterns of behaviour

The preceding vignettes illustrate our position that bribery and corruption is a problem for North American and Third World businessmen alike. We also have observed two recurring behavioural pat-

terns in these real, but disguised, situations. The first is the predisposition of the North American businessman to accept the premise that bribery is the way of life in the developing world and a necessity in business transactions. The second behavioural pattern occurs in situations where payments are requested and made.

We believe that many executives visit Third World countries with an expectation to learn that bribery is a problem. This attitude likely stems from a number of sources. First, in many cases it may be true. In some countries it may be impossible to complete a transaction without a bribe and the horror stories about the widespread disappearance of honesty are valid. However, in some instances the expectations are conditioned by the 'conventional wisdom' available in international business circles. This conventional wisdom develops from situations like the ones we have described. As these situations are passed from individual to individual accuracy may diminish and facts be forgotten. This is not done intentionally but happens since it is rare that the story-tellers have the complete story or all the facts. Unverified stories of bribery and corruption circulate through the business and government communities and often become accepted as true and factual. The obvious solution, and difficulty, is learning how to distinguish fact from fiction.

Another factor influencing initial expectations are the unfavourable impressions of developing countries and their citizens that are picked up from the media. Often only the sensational, and negative, news items from these countries are reported in North America. We learn of bombings, attacks on journalists and tourists, alleged (and real) coup d'états, and major scandals. These current events and the conventional wisdom combined with an executive's probable lack of knowledge of the history, culture, legal systems or economic conditions of a country all contribute to the development of unfavourable stereotypes that predispose the executive toward readily accepting reports that confirm his already drawn conclusions: all Latin American or African countries, for example, are the same and corruption is to be expected.

The stories that constitute evidence of corruption may be tales of bribery like the *New Venture* or the *Big Sale*, or they may take other forms. The story we have heard most often has the "protect yourself from your local partner" theme. It goes like this: "If you are going to invest in this country, particularly in a joint venture, you have to find a way to protect yourself from your partner. He is likely to strip all the company's assets and leave you nothing but a skeleton. Just look what happened to Company *A.*"

On hearing the evidence, particularly from expatriates in the foreign country, a visiting businessman most likely accepts it without further investigation. He has forgotten the old adage about there being two sides to every story. His conclusion and conviction are most likely based on incomplete and biased data.

Is there another viewpoint? Certainly! Many nationals have expressed it to us: "The Europeans and North Americans have been taking advantage of us for decades, even centuries. The multi-nationals establish a joint venture and then strip the local company bare through transfer pricing, management fees and royalties based on a percentage of sales rather than profits. They have no interest in the profitability of the company or its long-term development."

The situation is ironic. Some local investors are desperately looking for an honest North American executive whom they can trust at the same time the North American is searching for them. Our experience indicates that this search process is neither straightforward, nor easy. And while the search continues, if it does, it is difficult for the North American to maintain a perspective on the situation and remember that there are locals who may share his values and who are equally concerned about unethical and illegal practices.

In summary, we would characterize the first observed pattern of behaviour as a preparedness to accept 'evidence' of corruption and the simultaneous failure to examine critically the evidence or its source.

The second behavioural pattern appears in the actual pay-off process. The request very likely comes from a low- or middle-level bureaucrat who says that his boss must be paid for the project to be approved or for the sale to be finalized. Alternatively, it may be your agent who is providing similar counsel. In either case you are really not certain who is making the demand.

Next, the pay-off is made. You give your contact the money, but you never really know where it goes.

Your expectations are obvious. You have approached this transaction from a perspective of economic rationality. You have provided a benefit and expect one in return. The project will be approved or the sale consummated.

The result, however, may be very different than expected. As in the case of the *New Venture*, nothing may happen. The only outcome is indignation, anger, and perhaps the loss of a significant amount of money. Now is the time for action, but what recourse do you have? Can you complain? You may be guilty of bribing a government official. And, you certainly are reluctant to admit that you have been duped. Since your direct options are limited, your primary action may be to spread the word: "This is a corrupt, pay-off society."

Why does it happen?

There are numerous explanations for corruption in developing nations. First, and most obvious is that some people are simply dishonest. A less pejorative explanation is that the cost of living in these countries may be high and salaries low. Very often a wage earner must provide for a large extended family. The businessman is viewed opportunistically as a potential source of extra income to improve the standard of living. Finally, some nationals may believe strongly that they have a right to share some of the wealth controlled by multi-national corporations.

Besides being familiar to many readers, these explanations all share another common characteristic. They all focus on the other person — the local national. Accepting that there may be some truth in the previous explanations, let us, however, turn our focus to the visiting North American to see what we find. We could find a greedy, dishonest expatriate hoping to make a killing. But, let us give him the same benefit of the doubt we have accorded to the local nationals so far.

On closer examination we may find a situation in which the North American executive is vulnerable. He has entered an action vacuum and is at a serious disadvantage. His lack of knowledge of systems and procedures, laws, institutions, and the people can put him in a dependent position. Unfamiliarity with the system and/or people makes effective, alternative action such as he could take at home difficult. A strong relationship with a reputable national could help significantly in this situation. Quite often the national knows how to fight the system and who to call in order to put pressure on the corrupt individual. This potential resource should not be dismissed lightly. Although the most powerful and experienced MNC's may also be able to apply this pressure, most of us must be realistic and recognize that no matter how important we think we are, we may not be among those handful of foreigners that can shake the local institutions.

Time also can be a factor. Often the lack of time spent in the country either to establish relationships, or to give the executive the opportunity to fight the system contributes to the problem. Because the North American businessman believes that time is money and that his time, in particular, is very valuable, he operates on a tight schedule with little leeway for unanticipated delays. The pay-off appears to be a cost-effective solution. In summary, the executive might not have the time, knowledge, or contacts to fight back and sees no alternative other than pay or lose the deal.

Some real barriers

If, as we think, there are many honest businessmen in North America and in the developing world looking for mutually profitable arrangements and for reliable, honest partners, why is it difficult for them to find each other? We believe a significant reason is the inability of both sides to overcome two interrelated barriers — time and trust.

Trust is a critical commodity for business success in developing countries. The North American going to invest in a country far from home needs to believe he will not be cheated out of his assets. The national has to believe that a joint venture, for example, will be more than a mechanism for the North American to get rich at his expense. But, even before the venture is established, trust may be essential if the prospective partners are ever to meet. This may require the recommendation of a third party respected by both sides.

Establishing good relationships with the right people requires an investment of time, money and energy. An unwillingness of either party to make this investment is often interpreted as a lack of sincerity or interest. The executive trying to do business in four countries in a week (the '5 day wonder') is still all too common a sight. Similarly, the successful local businessman may have an equally hectic international travel schedule. Both complain that if the other was really serious he would find time to meet. Who should give in? In our opinion, the onus is on whichever party is visiting to build into his schedule the necessary time to work on building a relationship or to find a trusted intermediary. Also, both parties must be realistic about the elapsed time required to establish a good relationship and negotiate a mutually satisfactory deal. This will involve multiple trips by each party to the other's country and could easily take 12 to 18 months.

The cost of bribery

The most quantifiable costs are the financial ones. The cost of the 'service' is known. The costs of not bribing are also quantifiable: the time and money that must be invested in long-term business development in the country, or the value of the lost business. However, there are other costs that must be considered.

(1) You may set a precedent and establish that you and/or your company are susceptible to pay-off demands.

(2) You may create an element in your organiza-

tion that believes pay-offs are standard operating procedure and over which you may eventually lose control.

(3) You or your agents may begin using bribery and corruption as a personally non-threatening, convenient excuse to dismiss failure. You may not address some organizational problems of adapting to doing business in the developing world.

(4) There are also personal costs. Ultimately you will have to accept responsibility for your decisions and actions, and those of your subordinates. At a minimum it may involve embarassment, psychological suffering and a loss of reputation. More extreme consequences include the loss of your job and jail sentences.

Conclusion

It is clear that bribery can be a problem for the international executive. Assuming you do not want to participate in the practice, how can you cope with the problem?

(1) Do not ignore the issue. Do as many North American companies have done. Spend time thinking about the tradeoffs and your position prior to the situation arising.

(2) After thinking through the issue, establish a corporate policy. We would caution, however, that for any policy to be effective, it must reflect values that are important to the company's senior executives. The policy must also be used. Window dressing will not work.

(3) Do not be too quick to accept the 'conventional wisdom'. Examine critically the stories of bribery and the source of the stories. Ask for details. Try to find out the other side of the story and make enquiries of a variety of sources.

(4) Protect yourself by learning about the local culture and by establishing trusting relationships with well-respected local businessmen and government officials.

(5) Do not contribute to the enlargement of myths by circulating unsubstantiated stories.

Finally, we would offer the advice that when in Rome do as the *better* Romans do. But, we would add, do not underestimate the time, effort, and expense it may take to find the better Romans and establish a relationship with them.*

---
*The authors wish to acknowledge the support of the Plan for Excellence and the Centre for International Business Studies at The University of Western Ontario's School of Business Administration and the Industrial Cooperation Division of the Canadian International Development Agency.

36

Bribery and Extortion in International Business

THOMAS L. CARSON

Bribery

Webster's New World Dictionary (1962) defines a bribe as a payment or inducement for someone to do something illegal or unethical. This definition is too broad; not all instances of paying someone to do something illegal or immoral count as cases of bribery. Hiring someone to murder one's spouse is not a case of bribery. Talk of bribery only makes sense in the context of positions or roles having special obligations. Central cases of bribery involve paying or inducing others to violate the fiduciary obligations of their offices or positions. Consider the following examples: (1) Paying a judge or juror to decide in one's favour; (2) Paying a policeman not to give one a traffic ticket; and (3) Paying a government official not to report violations of health and safety standards.

One can imagine cases of bribery in which the person being paid is not an agent or employee of a specific party. For example, it would be possible to bribe a self-employed professional tennis player or boxer to lose a match.[1] Bribery is also possible in the case of amateur athletics. However, in these cases the recipient of the bribe still has specific obligations attaching to his role that he is being paid to ignore. An athlete performing in public competition has an obligation (assignable to the sponsors of the competition, his fellow competitors, and to those who follow the sport) to do his best to win in that competition. Athletes participate in such competition on the understanding that they will do their best to win. On my view, it would not be a bribe for one to pay an athlete to lose a private match that was not represented as being a real competition. For example, it would not be a bribe if I paid Bjorn Borg to lose to me in a secret tennis match. Nor would it be a bribe if I paid him to lose to me in public, provided that our agreement was a matter of public record and the match was not represented to anyone as a true competition. I don't think that conventional usage of the word "bribe" gives us decisive reasons for either accepting or rejecting the consequences of my view for this kind of case. However, the fact that there is clearly nothing morally objectionable about paying someone to lose in a private athletic match that is not represented as true competition is a strong reason for thinking that a correct definition of the word "bribe" should not count such cases as bribes. I propose the following definition of bribery:

> A bribe is a payment of money (or something of value) to another person *in exchange for* his giving one special consideration that is incompatible with the duties of his office, position, or role.[2]

There are uses of the terms "bribe" and "bribery" that do not fit this definition. We speak of parents "bribing" their children to be quiet or to behave themselves. Children do not have any special position that obligates them to be noisy or misbehave. If we allow this as a genuine case of bribery then the foregoing definition is untenable. However, it seems more plausible to say that this is not a genuine case of bribery but rather an extended use of the term analogous to the use of the word "murder" in "your father is going to murder you when he sees this mess." Consider another possible objection to my definition. Suppose that I call a *self-employed* plumber and ask him to come and fix my pipes. He refuses to come on account of its being the weekend. Then I offer him extra money to come out anyway. Many would describe this case by saying that I bribed the plumber. However, I believe that this is just an extended use of the term "bribery." In any case, the kinds of examples considered here are not morally worrisome cases of bribery. Surely there is nothing morally objectionable about either my offering the plumber payment or his accepting it. My definition may not be adequate to all of the everyday uses of the word "bribery," but it covers all of the cases of bribery that raise ethical questions.

Bribery and Extortion

Here I will attempt to define "extortion" and contrast it with bribery. Before doing this, however, we should first have before us some clear cases of extortion: a gangster threatening to blow up my store unless I pay him for "protection" each month, and a policeman threatening to frame someone for a crime unless he pays him money. Extortion is sometimes construed in a very narrow sense as an official's demanding payment for services that he is obligated to perform without payment.[3] In cases of bribery someone offers an officer payment for doing something contrary to the duties of his position. According to the present definition, extortion occurs when an official demands payment for doing something that he ought to do without being paid. The proposed definition of extortion, however, seems excessively narrow. For as we ordinarily use the term "extortion" it is possible for someone who does not hold any official position to extort money from others. For example, the criminal who demands money from a merchant in exchange for not burning down his store is committing extortion even though he is not acting in any official capacity. Consider the following definition of extortion:

> Extortion is the act of threatening someone with harm in order to obtain payment or other benefits to which one has no prior entitlement.[4]

The expression "benefits to which one has no prior entitlement" in the above definition should be read as "benefits to which one has no prior *legal* right" as opposed to "benefits to which one has no prior moral right" or "benefits to which one has no prior moral or legal right." It is not a case of extortion if a slaveowner threatens his slaves with a beating unless they work hard, even though he is not morally entitled to the fruits of their labour. Similarly, a banker who threatens a poor family with foreclosure is not committing an act of extortion, even if he has no moral right to repossess their home. This definition is not intended to suggest that extortion is a purely legal concern; it may be morally wrong to threaten to inflict harm on someone unless he gives one something to which one is not legally entitled. It is also worth noting that this definition does not imply that it is necessarily illegal to extort things from others. Unless the harms threatened are either illegal for independent reasons or forbidden by specific statutes concerning extortion, extortion (as defined here) is not illegal.

There seem to be clear counterexamples to the

proposed definition. Suppose that I threaten to leave your employ unless you give me a 100 percent pay raise. I am threatening you with economic harm and I am not entitled to the extra money that I am demanding (I have no cause for complaint if you don't pay me), so this counts as a case of extortion according to the preceding definition. However, this is clearly not an instance of extortion, just fair bargaining. There is nothing morally or legally objectionable about my threatening to leave unless you pay me more since you have no right to my continued services. We might say that this is also what accounts for the fact that the case in question is not an instance of extortion. This suggests the following definition of extortion:

> Extortion is the act of threatening someone with harm (that one is not entitled to inflict on him), in order to obtain benefits to which one has no prior right.

However, this definition is also inadequate. Although the harms threatened in extortion are often ones that an individual is neither morally nor legally entitled to inflict, for example, murder or arson, this needn't be the case. My threatening to expose the official misconduct of a high government official unless he pays me $100,000 constitutes a case of extortion, even though exposing him would be both morally and legally permissible.

I am unable to formulate a fully adequate definition of extortion. However, nothing that I say in this article is dependent on my being able to do so. . . . All that I need to do is make the unproblematic claim that threatening someone with harm (that one is neither morally nor legally entitled to inflict on him) unless he gives one benefits to which one is neither morally nor legally entitled is *sufficient* for extortion. Given this, it follows that, contrary to most press reports, some of the most notorious foreign payments were not bribes, but rather extortion payments.[5]

Many of the most troubling cases . . . seem to lie near the border between bribery and extortion. Therefore, it would be helpful to inquire as to the nature of the difference or differences. Typically, in cases of bribery the payment in question is sug-

gested or offered by the party who makes the payment; in cases of extortion the payment is usually suggested or demanded by the party who receives it. However, these differences cannot serve as a basis for distinguishing between bribery and extortion. For an official might suggest payment of a bribe to him without threatening any harm for nonpayment, that is, without it being the case that this suggestion constitutes extortion.

Let us consider one of the sorts of cases that has been a matter of particular controversy. . . . Suppose that a salesman is told by the purchasing agent of another company that he (the purchasing agent) won't consider the salesman's product unless he receives a payment. To offer payment here would not constitute bribery since the salesman is not paying the officer to disregard his fiduciary obligations — to the contrary, the salesman is paying him to fulfill them by giving his product fair consideration. In this case the payment is merely for fair consideration and is not understood to guarantee one any special privileges. (To offer a larger payment than is requested and stipulate that one expects this payment to guarantee that one's own products will be purchased would constitute bribery.) Since the payment is a) for something to which one is legally entitled (one is entitled not to have it be the case that one's competitors gain an advantage over one through bribery), and b) made for the purpose of avoiding threatened harm, it constitutes an extortion payment. I am assuming that the purchasing agent will demand payment from all potential suppliers and then make an impartial decision from among those suppliers who pay. Perhaps a more likely scenario is that the purchaser will make an impartial rank ordering of suppliers, then demand payment from the leading candidate and buy from the first supplier on the list who is willing to pay. In neither case, however, can making the payment be considered bribery.

My contention that this is not bribery is somewhat vitiated by the following considerations. While the payment is not a case of paying someone to fail to fulfill his fiduciary obligations, it is presumably contrary to his fiduciary obligations for him to accept payments of any sort from potential suppliers. His firm may have explicit regulations forbidding such payments. Does this compel me to grant that payment here would constitute bribery? I think not. Not every inducement or temptation for one to violate one's fiduciary obligations is a case of bribery. It is not a bribe if I induce you to abandon your post and come and get drunk with me. A bribe must be a payment *for* actions that violate the recipient's fiduciary obligations.

Consider a slightly different case. Suppose that some of one's competitors, for whatever reasons, are not making the payments. Wouldn't offering payments in this sort of case constitute bribery? Payment would secure one special consideration over those competitors who don't pay and therefore it would be payment for acts that are contrary to the fiduciary obligations of the recipient. However, this argument is not entirely convincing. For it is not clear that a payment that can be *foreseen* to give one an unfair advantage over certain competitors always counts as payment for the purchaser to give one this advantage. Perhaps it is also necessary that the payment be *intended* to give one these advantages. Whatever one says about all of this (and I prudently propose to say nothing more), it is clear that one *could* offer the payment in such a way that it didn't constitute a bribe by stipulating that one doesn't want the payment to give one any advantages over those competitors who don't pay.

An Economic Analysis of Bribery and Extortion

Here I will propose an economic analysis of several common types of bribery and extortion.

Case 1. Suppose that a *firm* or *government* demands a substantial payment from a supplier as a condition of sale. This demand is not a solicitation for a bribe or an extortion demand; it is, in effect, a demand for a lower price. Therefore, for a supplier to offer payment in this case would not constitute either a bribe or an extortion payment; it would simply be tantamount to giving the firm or government a "rebate" or a lower price. (Similarly, for a supplier to offer payments to another company or government would not be an offer of bribery, but only an offer of a lower price. Only payments to individuals who have specific duties attaching to their positions or roles can constitute bribes.) There is no particular moral or economic objection to payments of the sort described in this case.

Case 2. Suppose that I am a sales representative for an aircraft corporation that is trying to market its products abroad. My company's planes are costlier and less fuel efficient than those of our major competitor. There are no significant respects in which our aircraft is preferable to theirs. If things function the way that they are supposed to according to economic theory, then our company's planes will not be sold. If I offer a substantial bribe to the government or corporate officer who is responsible for purchasing aircraft then he may decide to purchase our planes instead. In this kind of case a company that is willing to engage in bribery can gain considerable advantages over its competitors. It is precisely this kind of advantage that makes bribery such a tempting option. From a purely economic point of view such bribery is undesirable — optimal results will occur if agents act in the best interests of those whom they represent and make purchases that best further the economic interests of their principals.

Case 3. This is a variation of the preceding example. Suppose that our planes are the best buy, all things considered, and that the purchasing agent will probably choose them without receiving any payment from us. But just to be on the safe side we make him a payment. In that case the "right" decision from an economic point of view will still be made — they will buy the best planes. However, our costs will be higher than they should have been and the purchasing agent will get the extra money — this is also undesirable: if anyone gets the money it should be his firm or government.

Case 4. Suppose that I know that all of our competitors are offering bribery or extortion payments and that the person in charge of purchasing the aircraft is corrupt so that we cannot expect to sell our aircraft unless we do the same. In this case our offering payments will not disrupt the usual competitive constraints of the marketplace. In fact, it might serve to restore the competition. For, in this case, the purchasing agent might attempt to buy the best product from those suppliers who are willing to make him payments. (This is arguably a case of extortion. Although the purchasing agent doesn't actually threaten harm for non-payment, one can expect to suffer harm unless one pays.) Assuming that the purchaser will attempt to make the best choice from those companies that are willing to offer payments, an individual company can make it more likely that the "correct choice" will be made, that is, that the best product, all things considered, will be chosen, by being willing to make such payments itself. For it is conceivable that its product is the best or at least the best of those companies that are willing to pay and the company can sell its product only if it is willing to pay. If all potential suppliers offer payments (of roughly equal size), then there is no reason to suppose that the final decision reached will be any different from the one obtained under perfect competition. The scenario described here differs from a perfect market only in that the supplier will receive a lower net price (the difference between the selling price and the amount of the bribery or extortion payment) than he would have in a perfect market and the purchasing agent pockets the difference. Perhaps the fact that suppliers were willing to offer substantial payments shows that the selling price was pegged too high. In that case, the difference between our present scenario and a perfect market is that in a perfect market the company or government purchasing the product would reap the benefits of the lower net selling price.

Case 5. Suppose that only *some* of one's competitors are willing to make payments and that the individuals in charge of purchasing are corrupt and will only buy from a supplier who is willing to pay them. In this case it would also seem to be preferable (economically speaking) to offer payments oneself. Regardless of what one does oneself, the product purchased will be chosen from one of the companies that is willing to make payments. By offering payments oneself one increases the number of firms whose products will be given consideration,

and thereby increases the probability that the "best" product will be purchased. (There is some chance that one's own product is the best, or if not, one's product might still be better than those of the companies whose willingness to pay has kept them in the running.)

Case 6. Suppose that the purchasing agent informs us that he will purchase our product, but only on the condition that we make him a substantial payment.[6] Assume also that it is in the economic interest of our company to make the deal in spite of the payment. Then, if at least one of our competitors is willing to pay, it seems probable that the economic consequences of our making the payment will be preferable to those of our not making it. The product purchased will presumably be the one judged best of those companies that are willing to make extortion payments. If we don't pay, then the product chosen will be one judged to be inferior to ours.

From the foregoing it can be concluded that there are situations in which there would be good economic consequences if a company made bribery or extortion payments in order to help sell its products. Bribery and/or extortion payments to help make sales cannot be faulted on economic grounds if the following conditions are satisfied:

1. The person who is making the purchasing decision is corrupt and, if possible, will purchase only from firms that offer him payments.
2. At least some of one's competitors are willing to make payments so that the purchasing agent is in a position to refuse to buy from any company that doesn't offer him payment.
3. The supplier finds it advantageous to make the payment rather than not do business at all.
4. The payments that one makes are not greatly in excess of those made by one's competitors, so that making the payments does not put one in a position to get preference over other suppliers making smaller payments who may have better products.

It is worth noting here that it may often be difficult

for a company to *know* whether or not these conditions are satisfied. This suggests that the economic status of foreign payments (and their status as either bribes or extortion payments) is often unclear (see n. 5). I am assuming that no individual company has the power to end the practice of extortion and that any such attempt on the part of an individual company would be futile. (For further consideration of this assumption, see Section V.)

So far I have only considered examples of paying someone to purchase a product. There are many other types of payments that space does not permit an adequate discussion of here. However, I would like to consider briefly the economic consequences of three other important kinds of payments to government officials. . . .

1. "Grease payments" offered in order to facilitate or speed up routine bureaucratic decisions of a nondiscretionary nature, e.g., hastening the passage of goods through customs. . . .
2. Payments to insure nonenforcement of laws or regulations. . . .
3. Payments intended to influence officials possessing substantial discretionary powers in their interpretation of laws and regulations affecting one's business. . . .

1. In much of the world it is simply impossible for companies to do business without making grease payments to cut red tape and obtain routine governmental services within a reasonable amount of time. Clearly, the decision to make such payments cannot be considered undesirable from an economic point of view. Grease payments do not necessarily constitute bribes. If government officials routinely violate their duties by providing slow and inefficient services, then payments to insure more efficient service cannot be considered bribes; they would only be payments in exchange for the officials' fulfillment of their fiduciary obligations. There are some countries in which nominal payments to government officials are tantamount to tips. The payments are expected in exchange for the performance of routine tasks. They are not taken to entitle one to any special or unfair advantage over others, and (most importantly) the payments are tacitly condoned by those governments in question. The practice of tipping as we are familiar with it in the context of restaurants and taxicabs differs from grease payments in that it is at least semi-voluntary; since the tip is paid after the services are rendered it is possible to receive the services in question without making the payment. The involuntary nature of grease payments argues in favour of viewing them as extortion payments and, no doubt, they often are. However, when modest grease payments are tacitly condoned by foreign governments as a means for civil servants to supplement their incomes, such payments would be more plausibly viewed as fees paid for services to be rendered. (The withholding of services in the absence of such payments is a kind of harm that the officials have both a moral and a [*de facto*] legal right to inflict on one.) Not only is there no economic or moral objection to making grease payments when they are tantamount (or nearly tantamount) to tips, there is nothing inherently inefficient or immoral about a system in which government officials are paid in part through "tips." On the other hand it must be conceded that such a system is easily abused. There is a slippery slope leading from mere tips to payments intended to secure one special consideration over others.

2. If a company pays a government official not to enforce a particular law or regulation against it, then it is spared the costs of complying with the law or regulation. Often the social costs of noncompliance with regulations, for example, increased pollution, are greater than the costs of compliance. In such cases the payments will result in a net economic harm. However, there are presumably some costly regulations that are undesirable from an economic point of view, that is, regulations that are such that the cost of compliance with them greatly exceeds the benefits of compliance. Payments intended to secure the nonenforcement of such regulations may have desirable economic consequences.

3. There are situations in which government officials have very wide discretionary powers in interpreting laws and regulations affecting

businesses. For example, in Italy tax collectors have great discretionary power in determining the tax liabilities of individuals and corporations. Corrupt officials have the power to impose extremely heavy tax burdens on those who are unwilling to placate them with special favours.[7] It's hard to see how payments intended to avoid unfair treatment can be considered undesirable from an economic point of view. Of course, payments intended to give one favoured treatment in the interpretation of the law are most likely undesirable from an economic point of view.

What's Wrong with Bribery?

To accept a bribe is *prima facie* wrong because it involves violating the fiduciary obligations (or other obligations) attaching to one's office or role. The following are examples of fiduciary obligations. Attorneys are expected to act in the best interests of their clients; government regulatory officers are expected to enforce regulations impartially. Fiduciary obligations are central to cases of conflict of interest. It is thought to be wrong merely to allow oneself to be in a position in which one would be tempted to violate one's fiduciary obligations or fail to act in the best interests of one's principal. I take it that fiduciary obligations have their basis in implicit or explicit agreements. An employee works on the implicit or explicit understanding that he will do certain things. Other types of "positional obligations" also have their basis in agreements or understandings. A tennis player who participates in public competition does so on the understanding that he will do his best to win. So, accepting a bribe is wrong, in part, because it is a case of breaking an understanding or agreement. It is also wrong on account of the bad consequences that may result from it. There are two types of bad consequences that often result when people accept bribes: (a) Accepting bribes causes one to corrupt one's moral character; (b) The actions that the recipient is being paid to perform are likely to have bad economic consequences. For example, if a businessman accepts a bribe to purchase a product or service that is either inferior to or costlier than

something else that he could have purchased, then he is hampering the efficiency of his company and the efficiency of the marketplace itself. The acceptance of bribes by government officials may also lead to undesirable consequences such as the pollution of the environment, the endangerment of the health and safety of workers, or the noncollection of taxes.

There are several reasons for thinking that it is wrong or *prima facie* wrong to *offer* bribes in business contexts: (a) The bribery payments may be an attempt to gain an unfair advantage over one's competitors; (b) Bribery offers often serve to corrupt the character of those to whom they are made; (c) Bribery offers often cause the recipient to do things that have bad economic consequences. The bad consequences of the action that the recipient is being paid to perform also count as bad consequences of the bribery offer itself. In assessing the responsibility of the briber for the bad consequences of what the bribed party does, we need to ask what would have happened if the briber had not made his offer. Suppose that the bribed party has received other bribery offers to do things having the same sorts of bad economic consequences that he actually brought about by accepting the briber's offer. Suppose also that he would have accepted one of these other bribery offers, if he hadn't received the offer from the actual briber. In this case, the briber is not responsible for bringing about bad economic consequences that would not have occurred, were it not for him. Further, he is not responsible for any harm to the moral character of the bribed party that would not have occurred otherwise. However, if the briber makes the only bribery offer that the bribed party is willing to accept, then the briber is the cause of both harm to the bribed party's character and of economic harm that would not have occurred otherwise. (d) Offering bribes is wrong, because it compels one to falsify financial records in order to keep the bribery secret.[8] (e) It is often morally wrong for someone to fail to fulfill the obligations of his position. Therefore, offering bribes often involves enticing others to do what is morally wrong. As a general principle, if it is wrong for S to do x, then it is wrong to entice or induce him to do x. (This principle will be discussed and qualified at some length below.) So, it is probable that it is at least *prima facie* wrong to offer someone a bribe if what he is being paid to do is itself morally wrong. (Offering a bribe to a guard to let one out of a concentration camp would presumably not be *prima facie* wrong in this way.)

The Moral Status of Extortion Payments

Let us consider our example of offering extortion payments to corrupt officials in cases in which one knows that some of one's competitors are willing to offer similar payments, so that one has little chance of doing business unless one pays. What, if anything, is wrong with making such payments oneself? Are any of our four reasons for thinking that it is wrong to offer bribes also reasons for thinking that it is wrong to offer extortion payments?

(a) Making the payments in this case would not constitute an attempt to gain an unfair advantage over one's competitors for, by hypothesis, they are making, or are willing to make, the payments themselves. (b) Making an extortion payment cannot corrupt the extortionist's character, for the extortionist has demonstrated that he already has a bad character by demanding the payment. Paying him cannot cause him to be corrupted. (c) Such payments are not harmful from an economic point of view; to the contrary, they may help to restore a "fair" competitive balance. The corrupt officials may make a perfectly objective and impartial decision after receiving payment (or offers of payment) from all potential suppliers. (A more probable scenario is that the officials will compile a rank ordering of potential suppliers in an impartial manner and then purchase from the first of those on their list who is willing to make extortion payments.) From an economic point of view it would be best if there were no extortion at all. But no one company can eliminate the practice of extortion on its own and, given that others are willing to make extortion payments, it may be preferable that one do so as well.

(d) The practice of making extortion payments to corrupt officials may require companies to conceal or withhold certain information, but it does not require that they falsify their financial records. Companies involved in making extortion payments can make a full accounting of the existence and cost of such payments to stockholders. The experiences of those companies whose payments to foreign officials were revealed during the Watergate scandals suggest that such revelations have little effect on investor confidence and the value of stock.[9] Of course, a company may not be able to reveal the details of extortion payments. In particular, it may be unable to reveal the identities of the recipients of its payments; for most extortionists will presumably demand that their identities be kept secret. (There is nothing morally objectionable about withholding such information, except perhaps when the information in question can be used to remove extortionists from positions of authority — see below.) Given that there are laws against payments to foreign officials for "economic extortion," any company that makes such payments must falsify its books in order to avoid prosecution. . . .

(e) Do extortion payments of this sort constitute inducements for others to act immorally? It seems that they would not, provided that they are only intended to insure that one's own product will be given fair consideration. (If the payment is intended to give one special consideration over one's competitors, then that is another matter.) One is only paying the officials to do what they are morally obligated to do anyway. They aren't being *paid* to do anything that is either immoral or contrary to the duties of their positions. However, it might be objected that accepting the payment is itself both immoral and contrary to the duties of their positions. So, even if the money isn't offered as payment *for* doing anything wrong, the very act of offering the money is an inducement to do wrong. Offering someone money constitutes enticing him to violate his promise not to accept such payments. Generally speaking, if it's wrong for S to do x, then it's wrong to induce him to do x. However, we need to examine the status of this principle in some detail. Does it constitute an "ultimate" ground of obligation or is it merely a derivative principle? Consider the following:

(1) The act of inducing someone to do something that is morally wrong, all things considered, is itself *prima facie* wrong, that is, the fact that an act is one of inducing another person to do wrong is *always* a *prima facie* reason for thinking that the act is wrong.

Unless (1) is true, there is no reason to think that the payment to the corrupt foreign official is *prima facie* wrong on account of its being a case of inducing someone to do wrong. There is no way to make a fully adequate assessment of (1) in the absence of a thorough inquiry into general questions of normative ethics, which extends far beyond the scope of this article. Still, I think that it is possible to give cases that show that (1) is inconsistent with our considered moral intuitions. According to our considered moral intuitions, it is not *prima facie* wrong to induce someone to do wrong unless doing so has bad consequences (such as the corruption of the recipient's character), or constitutes a violation of some *other* ultimate moral principle.

Case 1.   Y is the flagrantly adulterous husband of X. Z meets Y at a singles bar and invites him to have sex with her. Y would have had sex with someone on that occasion, even if he hadn't received an invitation from Z. Z has not done anything to corrupt Y. She hasn't harmed his character or caused him to perform any wrong actions that he wouldn't have performed otherwise. (There is a pickwickian sense in which this just isn't so. Z has caused Y to perform the act of "committing adultery with Z" and this is an act that Y would not have performed if it hadn't been for Z. However, the wrongness of this act is derived *entirely* from its being a case of "committing adultery with someone" and this is an act that Y would have performed that night, regardless of what Z did.) There may be other reasons for thinking that what Z does is morally wrong, but we can't say that it's wrong on account of what she does to Y.

Case 2.   In city q police protection is almost nonexistent in certain neighborhoods on account of the corruption and inefficiency of the higher offici-

als of the department. Merchants in these areas receive little, if any, police protection. A merchant offers the police chief a large sum of money in exchange for a promise of protection. Even though the merchant is entitled to the protection, the offer is an inducement to do something that is wrong — the chief has a fiduciary obligation not to accept such payments. However, there is no moral presumption whatever against making the payment and it follows that (1) is false.

Should these arguments against (1) fail — and I do not concede this for a moment — I still have one further argument to show that the sorts of economic extortion payments considered in our example are permissible. Let us grant for the sake of argument that making extortion payments to corrupt foreign officials is *prima facie* wrong on account of being a case of inducing others to do wrong. The presumption against paying is still rather weak and can be easily overridden by the economic considerations that weigh in favor of paying. The economic extortion payments in question are analogous to the case of paying a corrupt police officer for protection that he ought to provide without receiving the payment. Although in each case offering the payments constitutes enticing someone to do something that he ought not to do, i.e., accept the payment, the recipients are still being *paid to do* things that they ought to do anyway — give one's product fair consideration or provide one with police protection. Since it is clearly permissible to pay the police, we are entitled to conclude that it is permissible to pay economic extortion in cases of the sort in question. It might be objected that there are relevant differences between the two cases; the harms averted by the payment to the police are much greater than those involved in the case of extortion payments. But this isn't necessarily the case. The merchant is justified in making payments to the police officers, even if the harms that he is seeking to avoid are of a relatively minor nature. For example, it is permissible to pay in order to help avoid vandalism or attract new customers who might otherwise be kept away out of fear of crime in the area.

None of the reasons proposed earlier for thinking that it is wrong to make bribery payments is a strong reason to think that it is wrong to make extortion payments. . . . However, one might argue that making bribery or extortion payments is morally wrong in this case because it abets and contributes to the harmful practice of extortion.[10] This argument raises the question of how much one is obligated to sacrifice to help eliminate harmful practices. For the sake of argument, let us suppose that a corporation is obligated to sacrifice whatever profits it obtains from making bribery or extortion payments in order to combat these practices. This may be conceding too much. However, I believe that I can defend my view without denying this. As stated, the foregoing principle is in need of qualification. It is plausible only if we make the further stipulation that no firm is obligated to keep its hands clean if doing so is completely futile (see principle P below). Suppose that a supplier is being subjected to extortion demands by an employee of another company. There is a very strong presumption against making the payments. Instead of paying him off, one should expose him to his employer. In ordinary contexts this is very likely to be effective — it is safe to assume that the other company doesn't want its employees to either demand or accept such payments. By revealing the extortion demands one can probably succeed in removing the corrupt employee and thereby the extortion itself.

The same remarks apply to many cases of extortion payments demanded by government officials. If the official in question is likely to be dismissed or reprimanded if exposed, then, allowing for exceptions in unusual cases, one should refuse to make the payment and expose the demand to the government in question. If a company makes extortion payments in these circumstances, we have good reason to suspect that it is seeking to obtain special advantages from the payments. For, by hypothesis, it can nullify the extortion demand simply by exposing it. However, there are many situations in which corrupt officials have little to fear from having their wrongdoing brought to light. In such cases the aforementioned remedies and recourses may be of no avail. In a limiting case, the corrupt official in question may be the head of a non-democratic regime and thus invulnerable to unfavorable publicity. Perhaps one should try to get all of one's competitors to refuse to do business with him. Failing this, one could pressure other . . . companies by threatening to report their violations. . . . However, in cases in which one is dealing with large numbers of foreign competitors this does not seem to be a viable option. (It is worth remarking here that if there were effective [and enforceable] international laws against bribery and extortion, then it might be nearly impossible to justify extortion payments for the purpose of making sales. Alas, however, there are no such laws.)

There seem to be cases in which any attempt on the part of an individual company to curb the practice of extortion will be completely futile. In such cases I believe that a company has no obligation to refrain from engaging in the practice itself. But, no doubt, there are many who would disagree. At issue is the following principle:

> P. A company or individual has no *special obligation* to sacrifice its own interests in order to refrain from participating in harmful practices if doing so will not help to curb those practices.

Let me consider some examples that might be thought to constitute objections to P:

1. A man in the deep South in the 1930s refuses to allow blacks to use the restrooms in his service station.
2. A soldier in the Waffen-SS takes active part in the massacre of civilians in a small village in Poland.
3. Following the example of his colleagues, a business executive "pads" his expense account for a business trip.

P might seem to commit me to saying that the actions described in 1, 2, and 3 are morally permissible. However, as I shall now argue, this is not the case. In all three cases the agent has the option to refuse to participate in a harmful practice. But his own nonparticipation is likely to be futile; he can do nothing to effectively curb these practices. P commits me to saying that the conduct described in 1, 2, and 3 cannot be criticized simply on the grounds that the agents are participating in practices that are generally harmful. However, it is perfectly open to me to say that there other reasons for thinking that the conduct in question is morally wrong. The actions described in these three examples are wrong for reasons that are independent of their being instances of harmful practices. The agents in 1 and 2 are unjustly harming others and denying them their rights. Case 3 involves lying, breach of promise, and the act in question results in direct economic harm to the agent's company. The cases of extortion payments in dispute are very different. As our earlier arguments have shown, it is only the fact that the acts in question are part of the harmful practice of extortion that makes it at all plausible to hold that they are morally wrong. Apart from their place in the practice of extortion, we have failed to find any reason for thinking that it is morally wrong to make the payments.

Example 2 deserves one further comment. It is quite possible that massacre of the people in the village will occur no matter what one does. Therefore in this case a utilitarian might reason as follows: "No matter what I do the people in the village will be killed, so I don't have a duty to refrain from participating in the massacre and thus risk my own life just to keep my hands clean." While this line of reasoning is consistent with P, P does not commit me to this. P does not commit me to be a utilitarian; it is consistent with principles that imply that one has a special duty not to be the immediate cause of harm or injustice oneself, as opposed to simply having the duty to minimize the incidence of harm or injustice.[11] P only says that one has no special duty to refrain from participating in practices that are *generally* harmful.

It remains for us to consider briefly a slightly different and, perhaps, more common sort of case. Suppose that most, but not all, of one's competitors are willing to make extortion payments to a corrupt foreign official who demands the payments as a necessary (but not sufficient) condition of doing business and that any attempt on one's own part to limit this practice will prove to be unavailing. The only morally relevant difference between this case and the one considered earlier is that in this case making the payment will give one an unfair advantage over some of one's competitors. Is this sufficient reason for saying that it would be wrong to offer the payments? I think not. Making the payment oneself will not harm those companies that don't pay; they will be unable to do business regardless of what one does. However, this is not enough to settle the issue, as the example of the soldier who is deliberating about whether to take part in the massacre should make clear. Still, in this case all companies are justified in making payments to avoid being placed at an unfair disadvantage relative to other companies, and no company is obligated to refrain from making payment. Those companies that don't pay might be motivated by moral considerations, but refusing to pay is not morally required. They cannot blame those companies that do pay for their unfair disadvantage relative to them. It is possible for them to remedy that situation, themselves, without doing anything that is morally wrong. By making payments in a case in which some of one's competitors do not pay, one is not placing them in the unacceptable situation of being forced to choose between being at an unfair disadvantage relative to others and acting immorally.

ENDNOTES

1. This example is taken from Michael Philip's article, "Bribery" (*Ethics*, 94, July 1984, pp. 621–636).

2. This is similar to one of the definitions given in *Black's Law Dictionary* (St. Paul, MN: West Publishing Company, 1968): "The offering, giving, receiving, or soliciting of anything of value to influence actions as official or in discharge of legal or public duty." See also the second definition of "bribe" in *The Oxford English Dictionary*, "a reward given to prevent the judgment or corrupt the conduct."

3. This sort of definition is also given in *Black*. On this broader definition of extortion, blackmail counts as a special case of extortion. Blackmail is extortion in which the harm threatened involves damage to one's reputation. (See the definition of "blackmail" in *Black*.)

4. See *Black's Law Dictionary*.

5. Between 1966 and 1970 the Gulf Oil Corporation paid $4 million to the ruling Democratic-Republican Party of South Korea. The late party chairman S.K. Kim once demanded $10 million from Gulf, warning that Gulf's continued prosperity and survival in Korea depended on its making this payment. (See Jacoby et al., pp. 107–108, and Yerachmiel Kugel and Gladys W. Gruenberg, *International Payoffs* [Lexington, MA: D.C. Heath & Co., 1977], p. 68.) Northrop Corporation's board member, Richard Miller, claimed that his company's highly publicized foreign payments were necessary for its sales and thus a form of blackmail or extortion. (See Kugel and Gruenberg, p. 13.) At the very least it seems plausible to suppose that its payments in the Middle East were extortion payments. (See Jacoby et al., pp. 8–9.)

The most notorious case of foreign political payments is that of Lockheed's payments in Japan to help sell its L1011 aircraft. The rough outlines of the case are as follows. In 1972 the two major Japanese airlines JAL and ANA were planning to make large purchases of the then new wide-bodied aircraft. Lockheed was in very bad financial shape, having only just recently avoided bankruptcy by receiving a government guaranteed loan. It was competing with Boeing and McDonnell Douglas for the lucrative Japanese market. Lockheed hired several highly-connected Japanese agents to handle the sale. The agents suggested several times that Lockheed make them large payments which would be channeled to high government officials, including Prime Minister Tanaka. Lockheed made all of these payments totaling about $7 million. The sale to ANA was completed in the following way. Lockheed's vice-president and head in charge of the Japanese sale, Carl Kotchian, was informed by the company's principal agent that the sale would be made provided that Lockheed did the following: 1. guarantee that its maintenance and fuel consumption estimates would not be exceeded; 2. assign 100 technical and maintenance personnel to ANA for a short period of time; and 3. make a final payment of about $400,000 to officials in ANA and the Japanese government. (Carl Kotchian, "Lockheed's 70-day Mission to Tokyo," *Saturday Review*, July 9, 1977, and Robert Shaplen, "The Annals of Crime: The Lockheed Incident," *The New Yorker*, Jan. 23 and 30, 1978.) From the facts of the case as we know them it cannot be determined whether it was a case of bribery or extortion. Did Lockheed's payments give it special advantages over Boeing and McDonnell Douglas or did the payments just insure it equal consideration? (In other words, would the Japanese officials have requested and received payments from either of the other companies if none had been forthcoming from Lockheed?) Lockheed made no attempt to answer these questions and can therefore be faulted for its *willingness* to make bribery payments — for all it knew its payments were bribes. However, Lockheed is not guilty of making payments that it *knew* to be bribes. It had reason to suppose that if it declined to pay it would lose the contract to another company from whom payment would be demanded and received. Boeing's history of foreign payments makes this supposition probable. (See Jacoby et al., pp. 117 and 256, and "How Boeing Passed $52 Million Under the Table," *Business and Society Review*, [Winter 1978–79].)

6. This is apparently what happened in the case of Lockheed's sale of its L1011 aircraft to Japan.

7. Jacoby et al., pp. 37 and 112; Arthur Kelly, "Italian Tax Mores," in *Ethical Theory in Business*, 1st ed., Donaldson and Werhane, eds. (Englewood Cliffs, NJ: Prentice-Hall, 1979).

8. Jacob Zamansky, "Preferential Treatment, Payoffs and the Antitrust Laws: Distortion of the Competitive Process Through Commercial Bribery," *Commercial Law Journal* 83, no. 10 (December 1978): 559, and

Judson Wambold, "Prohibiting Foreign Bribes: Criminal Sanctions for Corporate Payments Abroad," *Cornell International Law Journal* 10, no. 2 (May 1977): 234.

9. Jacoby et al., p. 57.

10. Cf. Kenneth Alpern, "Moral Dimensions of the Foreign Corrupt Practices Act: Comments on Hooker and Pastin," in *Ethical Issues in Business*, Donaldson and Werhane, eds. (Englewood Cliffs, NJ: Prentice-Hall, 1982).

11. Bernard Williams attacks utilitarianism on the grounds that it denies that one has special duties to avoid harming others or acting unjustly *oneself*. According to Williams, a utilitarian only recognizes the duty to minimize instances of harm and injustice. Among other things a utilitarian seems to be committed to the view that it would be permissible for an SS soldier to murder innocent civilians, provided that they will be killed by someone else regardless of what he does himself. Cf. *Utilitarianism For and Against* (with J.J.C. Smart) (Cambridge: Cambridge University Press, 1972), pp. 93–100 and "Utilitarianism and Moral Self-Indulgence," in *Moral Luck* (Cambridge: Cambridge University Press. 1982).

37

Bribery

MICHAEL PHILIPS

Although disclosures of bribery have elicited considerable public indignation over the last decade,
popular discussions of the morality of bribery have
tended largely to be unilluminating. One reason for
this is that little care has been taken to distinguish
bribes from an assortment of related practices with
which they are easily confused. Before we can be in
a position to determine what to do about the problem of bribery, we need to be clearer about what
count and ought to count as bribes. Unfortunately,
there is as yet very little philosophical literature on
this topic.[1] In this essay I shall remedy this defect by
presenting an account of the concept of bribery
and by employing that account to clarify matters in
three areas in which there is public controversy and
confusion.

At least some confusion in discussions of bribery
arises from a failure adequately to appreciate the
distinction between bribery and extortion. This is
true, for example, of accounts of the notorious case
of Lockheed in Japan. I shall attempt to show that
the morality of this and similar transactions is better

assessed if we are clear on that distinction.

A second problem area arises out of the fact of
cultural variability. As is generally recognized, the
conduct of business, government, and the professions differs from culture to culture. In some places
transactions that many Americans would consider
bribes are not only expected behavior but accepted
practice as well. That is, they are condoned by the
system of rule governing the conduct of the relevant
parties. Are they bribes? Are only some of them
bribes? If so, which?

A third problem arises out of the general difficulty of distinguishing between bribes, on the one
hand, and gifts and rewards, on the other. Suppose
that a manufacturer of dresses keeps a buyer for a
catalog company happy by supplying him with any
tickets to expensive shows and athletic events that
he requests. Are these bribes? Or suppose that a
special interest group rewards public administrators who rule in its favor with vacations, automobiles, and jewelry. May we correctly speak of bribery
here?

From *Ethics* 94 (July 1984) 621–636. © 1984 by The
University of Chicago. All rights reserved. Reprinted by
permission.

I

To answer such questions we need to say more precisely what bribes are. A bribe is a payment (or promise of payment) for a service. Typically, this payment is made to an official in exchange for her violating some official duty or responsibility. And typically she does this by failing deliberately to make a decision on its merits. This does not necessarily mean that a bribed official will make an improper decision; a judge who is paid to show favoritism may do so and yet, coincidentally, make the correct legal decision (i.e., the bribe offerer may in fact have the law on her side). The violation of duty consists in deciding a case for the wrong sorts of reasons.

Although the most typical and important cases of bribery concern political officials and civil servants, one need not be a political official or a civil servant to be bribed. Indeed, one need not be an official of any sort. Thus, a mortician may be bribed to bury a bodyless casket, and a baseball player may be bribed to strike out each time he bats. Still, baseball players and morticians are members of organizations and have duties and responsibilities by virtue of the positions they occupy in these organizations. It is tempting, then, to define a bribe as a payment made to a member of an organization in exchange for the violation of some positional duty or responsibility. This temptation is strengthened by our recognition that we cannot be bribed to violate a duty we have simply by virtue of being a moral agent. (Hired killers, e.g., are not bribed to violate their duty not to kill.) And it is further strengthened when we recognize that we may be paid to violate duties we have by virtue of a nonorganizationally based status without being bribed. (I am not bribed if — as a nonhandicapped person — I accept payment to park in a space reserved for the handicapped; nor am I bribed if — as a pet owner — I accept payment illegally to allow my dog to run free on the city streets.)

Still, it is too strong to say that occupying a position in an organization is a necessary condition of being bribed. We may also speak of bribing a boxer to throw a fight or of bribing a runner to lose a race.

These cases, however, are importantly like the cases already described. Roughly, both the boxer and the runner are paid to do something they ought not to do given what they are. What they are, in these cases, are participants in certain practices. What they are paid to do is to act in a manner dictated by some person or organization rather than to act according to the understandings constitutive of their practices. Civil servants, business executives, morticians, and baseball players, of course, are also participants in practices. And their responsibilities, as such, are defined by the rules and understandings governing the organizations to which they belong. At this point, then, we are in a position to state a provisional definition of bribery. Thus, P accepts a bribe from R if and only if P agrees for payment to act in a manner dictated by R rather than doing what is required of him as a participant in his practice.[2]

One advantage of this account is that it enables us to deal with certain difficult cases. Suppose that a high-ranking officer at the Pentagon is paid by a Soviet agent to pass on defense secrets. The first few times he does this we would not hesitate to say that he is bribed. But suppose that he is paid a salary to do this and that the arrangement lasts for a number of years. At this point talk of bribery appears less appropriate. But why should something that has the character of a bribe if done once or twice (or, perhaps, on a piecework basis) cease to have that character if done more often (or, perhaps, on a salaried basis)? In my account the explanation is that the frequency or basis of payment may incline us differently to identify the practice in question. Thus, if an American officer works for the Soviet Union long enough, we begin to think of him as a Soviet spy. In any case, to the extent to which we regard his practice as spying we are inclined to think of the payments in question as payments of a salary as opposed to so many bribes. A similar analysis holds in the case of industrial spies, undercover agents recruited from within organizations, and so forth.[3] We do not think of them as bribed because we do not think of them as full-fledged practitioners of the practices in which they appear to engage.

This practice conception is further supported by the fact that a person may satisfy my account of bribery on a long-term and regularized basis and still be said to be a recipient of bribes. This is so where his continued and regularized acceptance of payments does not warrant any change in our understanding of the practices in which he participates. Thus, we do not think of a judge who routinely accepts payments for favors from organized crime as participating in some practice other than judging, even if he sits almost exclusively on such cases. This may be arbitrary: perhaps we ought rather think of him as an agent of a criminal organization (a paid saboteur of the legal system) and treat him accordingly. My point, however, is that because we do not think of him in this way — because we continue to think of him as a judge — we regard each fresh occurrence as an instance of bribery.

The present account, however, is not entirely adequate as it stands. Consider the following counterexamples: *(a)* an artist is offered $5000 by an eccentric to ruin a half-completed canvas by employing an unsuitable color and *(b)* a parent is paid $500 for the use of his eight-year-old son in a pornographic film.

It might be argued in relation to *a* that it is consistent with the practice of being an artist that one accept payment to produce whatever a client is willing to pay for. However, the conception of a practice that underlies this response seems to me questionable. What seems to me counterintuitive about speaking of bribery in *a* is that the act in question is private. By this I mean, roughly, that it affects no one who is not a party to the transaction. If I pay an artist to ruin a painting that has been commissioned by a museum, the oddity of speaking of bribery disappears. In general, where there is no violation of an organizational duty, we might say that a payment is a bribe only if it affects the interests of persons or organizations who are not parties to the transaction. To forestall counterexamples based on remote or indirect consequences, we must add that the parties affected must be parties whose interests are normally affected by the conduct of the practice in question and that they must be affected in the manner in which they are normally affected.

It is tempting to go further than this and claim that a bribe occurs only when the act agreed to by the bribed party violates the moral rights of some third party or organization. But this seems to me mistaken. We may speak of bribing officers of terribly corrupt institutions (e.g., concentration camps), but it is not at all clear that these officeholders necessarily violate the rights of any person or organization by violating their institutional duties (e.g., by allowing prisoners to escape). Or consider a society in which slaves are used as boxers and masters wager on the bouts. It seems clear that one can bribe a slave to lose a fight here, but it is not at all clear that a slave violates anyone's rights by accepting payment for so doing. (To say this would be to imply that a slave boxer has a *prima facie* duty to try to win his fight, and this seems to me untenable.)

What, then, of the second counterexample? Why are we reluctant to speak of bribery in the case of parents? One way to deal with this case is to attribute this reluctance to an anachronistic linguistic habit developed and sustained by centuries of thinking according to which children are the property of parents. According to this outmoded way of thinking, either there is no such thing as the practice of parenting or that practice far more resembles an account that Thrasymachus might offer of it than an account most of us would now accept. It sounds odd to speak of bribing parents, then, because our linguistic habits have not caught up with our new vision of parenting. But this is something we should change: we ought to allow that parents may be bribed.

But I am uncomfortable with this reply. Most of us now agree that children have rights which ought to be protected by law and/or community pressure and that parents have duties not to violate these rights. To this extent, we are coming to understand families as organizations. Thus, if we allow that parents are bribed, we will almost certainly hold that they are bribed in the way that members of organizations are typically bribed, namely, they are paid to violate their positional duties. But there is something disturbing about this. For despite our conviction that children have rights, many of us are uncomfortable thinking of the family as just another organization and thinking of a parent as just another functionary. Our reluctance to maintain that parents may be bribed, then, may express a healthy resistance to thinking of a parent on the model of an official. Just how we ought to think of the family, I cannot say; the challenge is to arrive at a conception that acknowledges that children have legally enforceable rights without reducing the family to just another institution.

If we exempt the family from consideration and we build in the condition required by the second counterexample, we are now in a position to present a tentative definition of bribery. Thus, P is bribed by R if and only if (1) P accepts payment from R to act on R's behalf,[4] (2) P's act on R's behalf consists in violating some rule or understanding constitutive of a practice in which P is engaged, and (3) either P's violation is a violation of some official duty P has by virtue of his participation in that practice or P's violation significantly affects the interests of persons or organizations whose interests are typically connected to that practice.

At least two additional important features of bribery deserve mention. The first is a consequence of the fact that bribes are payments. For, like other kinds of payments (e.g., rent), bribes presuppose agreements of a certain kind.[5] That is, it must be understood by both parties that the payment in question is exchanged, or is to be exchanged, for the relevant conduct. In the most typical and important cases, the bribed party is an official and the conduct in question is the violation of some official duty. In these cases we may say simply that an official P is bribed by R when she accepts payment or the promise of payment for agreeing to violate a positional duty to act on R's behalf. This agreement requirement is of great importance. As I shall argue in Section IV, without it we cannot properly distinguish between bribes and gifts or rewards.

Such agreements need not be explicit. If I am stopped by a policeman for speeding and hand him a fifty-dollar bill along with my driver's license, and he accepts the fifty-dollar bill, it is arguable that we have entered into such an agreement despite what we might say about contributions to the Police Benevolence Association. As I shall argue, some of the difficulties we have in determining what transactions to count as bribes may stem from unclarity

concerning the conditions under which we are entitled to say an agreement has been made.

It is a consequence of this account that someone may be bribed despite the fact that she subsequently decides not to perform the service she has agreed to perform. Indeed, we must say this even if she has never been paid but has been only promised payment, or even if she has been paid but returns this payment after she decides not to abide by her part of the agreement. I see nothing strange about this. After all, if one accepts a bribe it seems natural to say that one has been bribed. Still, I have no strong objection to distinguishing between accepting a bribe and being bribed, where a necessary condition of the latter is that one carries out one's part of the bribery agreement. As far as I can see, no important moral question turns on this choice of language.

A final interesting feature of bribery emerges when we reflect on the claim that offering and accepting bribes is *prima facie* wrong. I will begin with the case of officials. The claim that it is *prima facie* wrong for someone in an official position to accept a bribe is plausible only if persons in official capacities have *prima facie* obligations to discharge their official duties. The most plausible argument for this claim is grounded in a social contract model of organizations. By accepting a position in an organization, it might be argued, one tacitly agrees to abide by the rules of that organization. To be bribed is to violate that agreement — it is to break a promise — and is, therefore, *prima facie* wrong.[6] While I concede that this argument has merit in a context of just and voluntary institutions, it seems questionable in a context of morally corrupt institutions (e.g., Nazi Germany or contemporary El Salvador). And even were it technically valid for those contexts, its conclusion would nonetheless be a msleading half-truth.

It is beyond the scope of this paper to discuss, in detail, the problems with the tacit consent argument in a context of corrupt institutions. In brief, my position is that actions which create *prima facie* moral obligations in just or ideal contexts do not necessarily create comparable obligations in unjust or corrupt contexts. Thus, for example, it does not seem to me that, if I join the Mafia with the intention of subverting its operations and bringing its members to justice, I have thereby undertaken a *prima facie* obligation to abide by the code of that organization. Of course, one could say this and add that the obligation in question is typically overridden by other moral considerations. But this seems to me an *ad hoc* move to defend a position. We use the expression "*prima facie* duty" to point to a moral presumption for or against a certain type of action. And surely it is strange to insist that there is a moral presumption, in the present case, in favor of carrying out the commands of one's Don.

But even if we grant that there is a *prima facie* duty here, we must be careful to qualify this assertion. For it is also clear that participants in unjust institutions have a *prima facie* right to interfere with the normal functioning of those institutions (at least where these functionings can be reasonably expected to produce unjust outcomes). Indeed, where the injustice is great enough they have a *prima facie* duty to interfere. And in some cases, the strength of this *prima facie* obligation will exceed the strength of any promise-keeping obligation generated by tacit consent. Thus we may say, other things equal, that the commandant of a concentration camp ought to act in a manner that frustrates the genocidal purpose of that institution. And, assuming that that institution is "rationally" designed to serve its purpose, there will be a strong moral presumption in favor of the violation of his positional duty.

What, then, of the morality of accepting bribes in such cases? If an official has no *prima facie* duty to satisfy her positional duties — or if the presumption in favor of satisfying them is outweighed by the presumption against so doing — then, other things being equal, it is difficult to see why it is *prima facie* wrong to accept payment for violating them. After all, there may be serious risks involved. This at least is so where the case against carrying out the purposes of one's organization is strong enough to permit one to violate one's positional duty but is not so strong that one has a *prima facie* obligation to do this. For it does seem *prima facie* wrong to make compliance with a *prima facie* duty contingent on payment (it ought rather to be contingent on an assessment

of what one ought to do, all things considered). And it certainly seems wrong to demand payment for doing what is one's duty, all things considered.

Still, this may be too quick. Consider a concentration camp guard who lacks the courage to help inmates escape but who would be courageous enough to undertake the risks involved were he assured of sufficient funds to transport his family to another country and comfortably to begin a new life. If he is in fact reasonably certain that he would be brave enough to do what is required of him were he paid, it seems not improper of him to demand payment. In general, if the wrong of demanding payment for doing one's duty is outweighed by the importance of doing it and if demanding payment for doing it is causally necessary for doing it, then, all things considered, it is not wrong to demand payment.

If it is not wrong for an official to accept a bribe, one does not induce him to do something wrong by offering him one. Thus, we cannot say in all contexts that it is *prima facie* wrong to offer someone a bribe *because* this is an attempt to induce him to do something wrong or to corrupt him.[7] On the other hand, there may be cases in which it is *prima facie* wrong to offer a bribe despite the fact that it is perfectly acceptable for the bribed party to accept one. Recall the case of the boxer slave. Despite the fact that the slave has no obligation to try to win, a wagering master may have a *prima facie* obligation not to pay him to lose. For by so doing the master may gain an unfair advantage over his fellow wagerers. It might be objected that the master's obligation in this case is misleadingly described as an obligation not to bribe. He is obligated, rather, not to fix fights; or, more generally, not to take unfair advantage of his fellow wagerers. This objection raises issues we need not consider here. It is enough to point out that the purpose of offering a bribe is very often to seek some unfair or undeserved benefit or advantage and that this is one reason we are rightly suspicious of the morality of bribe offers.

We are now in a position to state a fifth interesting feature of bribery. Even if it is not *prima facie* wrong to offer and to accept bribes in all contexts, it is *prima facie* wrong to do so in morally uncorrupted contexts. Accordingly, a bribe offerer or a bribe taker must defend the morality of his act either by showing that there are countervailing moral considerations in its favor or alternatively by showing that the moral context is so corrupt that the factors that generate *prima facie* duties in uncorrupted contexts do not apply here. This strategy of moral justifications, of course, is not unique to bribery. It may hold in relation to a wide range of what are ordinarily taken to be *prima facie* duties. In the case of bribery, however, arguments to the effect that the moral context is corrupted will have a certain characteristic form. Thus, in the most important case — the case of officials — they will be arguments that challenge the legitimacy of an institution.

II

I now turn to the first of three problem areas I shall address in this paper, namely, the problem of distinguishing between bribery and extortion. Compare the following cases:

(a) Executive P hopes to sell an airplane to the national airline of country C. The deal requires the approval of minister R. P knows that R can make a better deal elsewhere and that R knows this as well. P's researchers have discovered that R has a reputation for honesty but that R is in serious financial difficulties. Accordingly P offers R a large sum of money to buy from him. R accepts and abides by the agreement.

(b) The same as *a* except that P knows that he is offering the best deal R can get, and R knows this too. Nonetheless, P is informed by reliable sources that R will not deal with P unless P offers to pay him a considerable sum of money. P complies, and R completes the deal.

According to my analysis *a* is bribery; *b* is not.

The difference between *a* and *b* is clear enough. In *a* P pays R to violate R's duty (in this case, to make the best deal that R can). In *b* P does no such thing. Instead, he pays R to do what is required of R by his institutional commitments in any case. Moreover,

he does so in response to R's threat to violate those commitments in a manner that jeopardizes P's interests. Accordingly, *b* resembles extortion more than it does bribery. For, roughly speaking, R extorts P if R threatens P with a penalty in case P fails to give R something to which R has no rightful claim.

If this is true it may be that American corporate executives accused of bribing foreign officials are sometimes more like victims of extortion than offerers of bribes. For in at least some cases they are required to make payments to assure that an official does what he is supposed to do in any case. This is especially true in the case of inspectors of various kinds and in relation to government officials who must approve transactions between American and local companies. An inspector who refuses to approve a shipment that is up to standards unless he is paid off is like a bandit who demands tribute on all goods passing through his territory.

It does not follow that it is morally correct for American companies to pay off such corrupt officials. There are cases in which it is morally wrong to surrender to the demands of bandits and other extortionists. But it is clear that the moral questions that arise here are different sorts of questions than those that arise in relation to bribery. The moral relations between the relevant parties differ. The bribery agreement is not by its nature an agreement between victims and victimizers. The extortion agreement is. Moral justifications and excuses for complying with the demands of an extortionist are easier to come by than moral justifications and excuses for offering bribes.

Of course, the distinction in question is often easier to draw in theory than in practice. An inspector who demands a payoff to authorize a shipment is likely to fortify his demand by insisting that the product does not meet standards. In some cases it may be difficult to know whether or not he is lying (e.g., whether the shipment has been contaminated in transit). And given the high cost of delays, a company may decide that it is too expensive to take the time to find out. In this case, a company may decide to pay off without knowing whether it is agreeing to pay a bribe or surrendering to extortion. Since the morality of its decisions may well turn on what it is in fact doing in such cases, a company that does not take the time to find out acts in a morally irresponsible manner (unless, of course, it is in a position to defend both courses of action).

What sorts of justifications can a company present for offering bribes? It is beyond the scope of this paper to provide a detailed discussion of this question. However, I have already mentioned a number of considerations that count as moral reasons against bribery in a variety of contexts. To begin with, in reasonably just contexts, officials ordinarily are obligated to discharge the duties of their offices. In these cases bribe offers are normally attempts to induce officials to violate duties. Moreover, if accepted, a bribe offer may make it more likely that that official will violate future duties. Accordingly, it may contribute to the corruption of an official. In addition, the intent of a bribe offer is often to secure an unfair advantage or an undeserved privilege. Where this is the case, it too counts as a reason against bribery. To determine whether a bribe offer is wrong in any particular case, then, we must decide: (1) whether these reasons obtain in that case; (2) if they obtain, how much weight we ought to attach to them; and (3) how much weight we ought to attach to countervailing considerations. (Suppose, e.g., that it is necessary to bribe an official in order to meet an important contractual obligation.) It is worth remarking in this regard that, where officials routinely take bribes, the presumption against corrupting officials normally will not apply. Similarly, to the extent that bribery is an accepted weapon in the arsenal of all competitors, bribe offers cannot be construed as attempts to achieve an unfair advantage over one's competitors.

III

It is sometimes suggested that an environment may be so corrupt that no payments count as bribes. These are circumstances in which the level of official compliance to duty is very low, and payoffs are so widespread that they are virtually institutionalized. Suppose, for example, that the laws of country N impose very high duties on a variety of products but that it is common practice in N for importers and exporters to pay customs officials to overlook certain goods and/or to underestimate their number or value. Suppose, moreover, that the existence of this practice is common knowledge but that no effort is made to stop it by law enforcement officials at any level;[8] indeed, that any attempts to stop it would be met with widespread social disapproval. One might even imagine that customs officials receive no salary in N but earn their entire livelihood in this way. One might further imagine that customs officials are expected to return a certain amount of money to the government every month and are fired from their jobs for failure to do so. Finally, one might suppose that the cumulative advantages and disadvantages of this way of doing things is such that the economy of N is about as strong as it would be under a more rule-bound alternative. Are these officials bribed?

In my analysis, the answer to this question depends on how we understand the duties of the customs officer. If the official job description for the customs officer in N (and the written laws of N) is like those of most countries, the customs officer violates his official duties according to these codes by allowing goods to leave the country without collecting the full duty. The question, however, is how seriously we are to take these written codes. Where social and political practice routinely violates them, nothing is done about it, and few members of the legal and nonlegal community believe that anything ought to be done about it, it is arguable that these codes are dead letters. If we find this to be true of the codes governing the duties of the customs officials in country N, we have good reason for saying that the real obligations of these officials do not require that they impose the duties described in those written codes (but only that they return a certain sum of the money they collect to the central government each month). Anything collected in excess of that amount they are entitled to keep as salary (recall that they are officially unpaid). In reality we might say that duties on exports in country N are not fixed but negotiable.

Of course if we decide that the written law of N is the law of N, we must describe the situation otherwise. In that case, the official obligations of the customs officials are as they are described, and the system in N must be characterized as one of rampant bribery condoned both by government and by popular opinion. It seems to me that the philosophy of law on which this account rests is implausible. However, there is no need to argue this to defend my analysis of this case. My position is simply that whether or not we describe what goes on here as bribery depends on what we take the real legal responsibilities of the customs official to be. To the extent that we are inclined to identify his duties with the written law we will be inclined to speak of bribery here. To the extent that we are unwilling so to identify his duties we will not.[9]

IV

Let us now consider the problem of distinguishing bribes from rewards and gifts. The problem arises because gifts are often used in business and government to facilitate transactions. And to the degree to which a business person, professional person, or government official is influenced in her decision by gifts, it is tempting to conclude that she is violating her duties. In such cases we are tempted to speak of these gifts as bribes.

If I am correct, however, this temptation should be resisted. A bribe, after all, presupposes an agreement. A gift may be made with the intention of inducing an official to show favoritism to the giver, but unless acceptance of what is transferred can be construed as an agreement to show favoritism, what is transferred is not a bribe.

In some cases, of course, the acceptance of what is offered can be so construed. Again, if I offer fifty dollars to a policeman who has stopped me for speeding, he has a right to construe my act as one of offering a bribe, and I have a right to construe his acceptance in the corresponding manner. If I regularly treat the neighbourhood policeman to a free lunch at my diner and he regularly neglects to ticket my illegally parked car, we have reason to say the same. Agreements need not be explicit. My point is just that to the degree that it is inappropriate to speak of agreements, it is also inappropriate to speak of bribes.

It follows from this that, if I present an official with an expensive item to induce him to show favoritism on my behalf, in violation of his duty, I have not necessarily bribed him. It does not follow from this, however, that I have done nothing wrong. So long as you are morally obligated to perform your official duty, normally it will be wrong of me to induce you to do otherwise by presenting you with some expensive item. Moreover, if you have any reason to believe that accepting what I offer will induce you not to do your duty, you have done something wrong by accepting my gift. To prevent such wrongs we have laws prohibiting persons whose interests are closely tied to the decisions of public officials from offering gifts to these officials. And we have laws for forbidding officials to accept such gifts.

It might be objected that this account is too lenient. Specifically, it might be argued that wherever P presents Q with something of value to induce Q to violate Q's official duties P has offered a bribe.

But this is surely a mistake. It suggests, among other things, that an official is bribed so long as she accepts what is offered with this intent. Yet an official may accept such a gift innocently, believing that it is what it purports to be, namely, a token of friendship or goodwill. And she may do so with justifiable confidence that doing so will not in any way affect the discharge of her duty.

It may be replied that officials are bribed by such inducements only when they are in fact induced to do what is desired of them. But again, it may be the case that an official accepts what is offered innocently, believing it to be a gift, and that she believes falsely that it will not affect her conduct. In this case she has exercised bad judgment, but she has not been bribed. Indeed, it seems to me that it is improper to say that she accepts a bribe even when she recognizes the intent of the inducement and believes that accepting it is likely to influence her. There is a distinction between accepting a drink with the understanding that one is agreeing to be seduced and accepting a drink with the knowledge that so doing will make one's seduction more likely. To be bribed is to be bought, not merely to be influenced to do something.

From a moral point of view, whenever failure to

perform one's official duties is wrong it may be as bad to accept a gift that one knows will influence one in the conduct of one's duty as it is to accept a bribe. And clearly we are entitled morally to criticize those who offer and accept such inducements. Moreover, we are right to attempt to prevent this sort of thing by legally restricting the conditions under which persons may offer gifts to officials and the conditions under which officials may accept such gifts. Nonetheless, such gifts ought not to be confused with bribes. If P accepts a gift from R and does not show the desired favoritism, R may complain of P's ingratitude but not of P's dishonesty (unless, of course, P led him on in some way). If P accepts a bribe from R and does not show the desired favoritism, P has been dishonest (perhaps twice).

This point is not without practical importance. People who work in the same organization or in the same profession often form friendships despite the fact that some of them are in a position to make decisions that affect the interests of others. Here, as everywhere, friendships are developed and maintained in part by exchanges of favors, gifts, meals, and so forth. Were we to take seriously the inducement theory of bribery, however, this dimension of collegial and organizational existence would be threatened. In that case, if P's position is such that he must make decisions affecting R, any gifts, favors, et cetera from R to P should be regarded with at least some suspicion. To guard against the accusation that he has been bribed by R, P must be in a position to offer reasons for believing that R's intent in inviting him to dinner was not to induce him to show favoritism. And for R to be certain that he is not offering P a bribe in this case, R must be certain that his intentions are pure. All of this would require such vigilance in relation to one's own motives and the motives of others that friendships in collegial and organizational settings would be more difficult to sustain than they are at present.

Since decision makers are required to show impartiality they must in any case be careful not to accept gifts and favors that will influence them to show favoritism. Moreover, if they are required by their position to assess the moral character of those affected by their decisions, they may be required to

assess the intent with which such gifts or favors are offered. Most officials, however, are not required to assess character in this way. In order to avoid doing wrong by accepting gifts and favors they need only be justly confident of their own continued impartiality. Thus, they are ordinarily entitled to ignore questions of intent unless there is some special reason to do otherwise. If the intent to influence were sufficient for a bribe, however, they would not be at liberty to bestow the benefit of the doubt in this way.

Again, there are cases in which impartiality is so important that decision makers should be prohibited both from accepting gifts or favors from any persons likely to be directly affected by their decisions and from forming friendships with such persons. And they should disqualify themselves when they are asked to make a decision that affects either a friend or someone from whom they have accepted gifts or favors in the reasonably recent past. Judges are a case in point. In other cases, however, institutions and professions should be willing to risk some loss in impartiality in order to enjoy the benefits of friendship and mutual aid. For these are essential to the functioning of some organizations and to the well-being of the people within them. Consider, for example, universities. The practical disadvantage of the inducement account is that it may require us to be unnecessarily suspicious of certain exchanges constitutive of mutual aid and friendship (at least if we take it seriously).

V

An interesting related problem arises in cultures in which a more formal exchange of gifts may be partly constitutive of a special relationship between persons, namely, something like friendship. In such cultures, so long as certain other conditions are satisfied, to make such exchanges is to enter into a system of reciprocal rights and duties. Among these duties may be the duty to show favoritism toward "friends," even when one acts in an official capacity. Moreover, the giver may be expected to show gratitude for each occasion of favoritism by further gift giving. On the face of it, this certainly looks like bribery. Is that description warranted?

To begin with, we need to distinguish between cases in which the special relationships in question are genuine and cases in which they are not. In the latter case certain ritual or ceremonial forms may be used to dress up what each party regards as a business transaction of the standard Western variety in a manner that provides an excuse for bribery. I shall say more about this presently. But let me begin with the first case.

Where the relationships in question are genuine and the laws of the relevant society are such that the official duties of the relevant official do not prohibit favoritism, this practice of gift giving cannot be called bribery. For in this case there is no question of the violation of duty. All that can be said here is that such societies condone different ways of doing business than we do. Specifically, they do not mark off a sphere of business and/or bureaucratic activity in which persons are supposed to meet as "abstract individuals," that is, in which they are required to ignore their social and familial ties. Their obligations, rather, are importantly determined by such ties even in the conduct of business and governmental affairs. Favoritism is shown, then, not in order to carry out one's part of a bargain but, rather, to discharge an obligation of kinship or loyalty. Failure to show favoritism would entitle one's kinsman or friend to complain not that one reneged on an agreement but, rather, that one had wronged him as an ally or a kinsman.

This is not to say that one cannot bribe an official in such a society. One does this here, as elsewhere, by entering into an agreement with him such that he violates his official duties for payment. The point is just that favoritism shown to friends and kinsmen is not necessarily a violation of duty in such societies. Indeed, one might be bribed not to show favoritism.

The official duties of an official, of course, may not be clear. Thus, the written law may prohibit favoritism to kin and ally, though this is widely practiced and condoned and infrequently prosecuted. This may occur when a society is in a transitional state from feudalism or tribalism to a Western-style industrial society, but it may also occur in an industrial society with different traditions than our own.

To the extent that it is unclear what the official duties of officials are in such cases it will also be difficult to say what count as bribes. Indeed, even if we decide that an official does violate his duty by showing favoritism to kin and allies who reciprocate with gifts, we may not be justified in speaking of bribery here. For the official may not be acting as he does in order to fulfill his part of an agreement. Rather, he may be acting to fulfill some obligation of kinship or loyalty. Again, his failure so to act may not entitle his kinsmen or allies to complain that he had welched on a deal; rather, it would entitle them to complain that he wronged them as kinsmen or allies.

Of course, all this is so only when the relationships in question are genuine. In some cases, however, the rhetoric and ceremonial forms of a traditional culture may be used to camouflage what are in fact business relations of the standard Western variety. To the extent that this is so, the favoritism in question may in fact be bribery in ethnic dress. The relationships in question are not genuine when they are not entered into in good faith. It is clear, moreover, that when American executives present expensive gifts to foreign businessmen or foreign government officials they do so for business reasons. That is, they have no intention of entering into a system of reciprocal rights and duties that may obligate them in the future to act contrary to their long-term interest. Rather, they perform the required ceremonies knowing that they will continue to base their decisions on business reasons. Their intention is to buy favoritism. And the foreign officials and companies with whom they do business are typically aware of this. This being the case, invitations of the form "First we become friends, then we do business" cannot plausibly be construed as invitations to participate in some traditional way of life. Typically, both parties recognize that what is requested here is a bribe made in an appropriate ceremonial way.

VI

On the basis of this analysis it seems clear that American officials are not always guilty of bribery when they pay off foreign officials. In some cases they are victims of extortion; in other cases, the context may be such that the action purchased from the relevant official does not count as a violation of his duty. The fact that American executives engaged in international commerce are innocent of some of the charges that have been made against them, however, does not imply that those who have made them are mistaken in their assessment of the character of these executives. One's character, after all, is a matter of what one is disposed to do. If these executives are willing to engage in bribery whenever this is necessary to promote their perceived long-term business interests, whatever the morality of the situation, it follows (at very least) that they are amoral.

ENDNOTES

1. At the time this paper was written there were no references to bribes or bribery in the *Philosopher's Index*. Since that time one paper has been indexed — Arnold Berleant's "Multinationals, Local Practice, and the Problems of Ethical Consistency" (*Journal of Business Ethics* 1 [August 1982]: 185–93) — but, as the title of this short paper suggests, Berleant is not primarily concerned with providing an analysis of the concept of bribery. However, three presentations on the topic of bribery were made at the 1983 "Conference for Business Ethics" (organized by the Society for Business Ethics at DePaul University, July 25–26) and have subsequently been accepted for publication. These are: Kendall D'Andrade's "Bribery" (forthcoming in a special issue of the *Journal of Business Ethics*, devoted to the DePaul conference, 1984); John Danley's "Toward a Theory of Bribery" (forthcoming in the *Journal of Business and Professional Ethics*, 1984); and Tom Carson's "Bribery, Extortion and the Foreign Corrupt Practices Act" (forthcoming in *Philosophy and Public Affairs*, Summer 1984). Where my position on substantive questions differs significantly from D'Andrade's, Carson's, or Danley's, I shall discuss this in the notes.

2. Danley defines "bribing" as "offering or giving something of value with a corrupt intent to induce or influence an action of someone in a public or official capacity." Carson defines a bribe as a payment to someone "in exchange for special consideration that is incompatible with the duties of his position." Both go on to discuss bribery as if it were restricted to officials of organizations. Since these are the most typical and important cases of bribery, their focus is understandable. But it does have at least one unfortunate consequence. For it leads both Danley and Carson to think that the question of whether it is *prima facie* wrong to offer or accept bribes reduces to the question of whether officials have obligations to satisfy their positional duties. Danley argues that they do not if the institutions they serve are illegitimate. Carson argues that they do on the ground that they have made a tacit agreement with their institution to discharge those duties (accepting a bribe, for Carson, is an instance of promise breaking). Whatever the merits of their arguments concerning the responsibilities of officials, both approach the question of the *prima facie* morality of bribery too narrowly. For different issues seem to arise when we consider bribery outside the realm of officialdom. Clearly it is more difficult for Carson to make his tacit consent argument in relation to the bribed athlete. For it is not clear that a runner who enters a race tacitly agrees to win it (if so, he would be breaking a promise by running to prepare for future races or by entering to set the pace for someone else). Nor is it clear that a boxer who accepts payment not to knock out his opponent in the early rounds violates a tacit agreement to attempt a knockout at his earliest convenience. Danley must expand his account to accommodate such cases as well. For it is not clear what it means to say that a practice such as running or boxing is legitimate.

3. Such cases present a problem for the accounts of both Danley and Carson. At the very least they must expand their accounts of positional duties such that we can distinguish between a bribe, on the one hand, and a salary paid to a spy recruited from within an organization, on the other.

4. Thus D'Andrade defines bribery as "alienation of agency." In his account bribery occurs when someone is seduced into abandoning his role as an agent of one person or organization and, for a price, becomes the agent of another. This highlights an important feature of bribery that is ignored by Carson and Danley and that was neglected in my own earlier thinking on this

subject, namely, that a bribe taker acts on behalf of someone. But D'Andrade's claim that agency is alienated when one accepts a bribe implies that the bribe taker necessarily is committed to act on behalf of some person or organization before he is in a position to accept a bribe. And is is difficult to see what helpful truth this might express in relation to the scientist, runner, or boxer of my examples. Surely it is not helpful to say that a bribe taker begins as his own agent in these cases and, for pay, alienates that agency to another. This applies to anyone who takes a job. Nor is it helpful to say — as D'Andrade did say at one point — that he may begin as an agent of some abstraction (e.g., truth). Surely the point behind this obscure claim is better made by speaking of what is expected of someone as a participant in a practice. It is also worth noting that D'Andrade's alienation of agency account offers no basis for distinguishing between bribed officials, on the one hand, and undercover agents and spies, on the other. For these too alienate agency.

5. Carson fails to recognize the significance of this feature of bribery. This view of bribery, moreover, is inconsistent with Danley's account. Danley understands a bribe as an attempt to induce or influence someone. In this matter he appears to have most dictionaries on his side (including the OED). However, as I argue in more detail in Sec. IV he is mistaken.

6. This is Carson's argument.

7. Nor can we say that it is *prima facie* wrong because it is an attempt to get someone to do something that is *prima facie* wrong. This argument is flawed in two ways. To begin with, as we have seen, the premise expresses what is at best a dangerous half-truth. Were we to reason from the whole truth we must conclude that there are some contexts in which the presumption in favor of violating one's official duties is stronger than the presumption against it. In the second place, moreover, the inference is invalid: it is not necessarily *prima facie* wrong to induce someone to do something that is *prima facie* wrong. Rather, it is *prima facie* wrong to induce

someone to do something that is wrong, all things considered. Thus, if it is *prima facie* wrong for P to do A, but P ought to do A, all things considered, there is no presumption against my inducing P to do A; I do not need to justify this by appealing to countervailing moral considerations. I require such justification only when it is wrong for P to do so. Cases of this sort are interesting but typically neglected by philosophers. (The following are examples: [a] P is a soldier in a war in which each side has equal claim to justice; R is a guard on the opposite side. Though it might be wrong for R to accept a bribe from P, it is not wrong for P to offer R a bribe. [b] P's father is certain to be convicted of a crime he did not commit because the evidence is overwhelmingly against him. It is permissible for P to offer a bribe to R, an assistant district attorney, to "lose" some evidence; but it is wrong for R to accept the bribe.) In any case, the upshot of this is that even if there were a general moral presumption against accepting bribes it would not follow that there is a comparable presumption against offering bribes.

8. In D'Andrade's account bribes are necessarily secret, so these could not count as bribes.

9. A corresponding point holds in relation to bribery outside the realm of officialdom. Consider the case of professional wrestling. Most of us believe that the outcome of professional wrestling matches is determined in advance. Are the losers bribed? (To simplify matters let us assume that they are paid a bit of extra money for losing.) The answer here depends on how we understand their practice. If we take them to be participating in a wrestling competition, we must say that they are bribed. In that case, by failing to compete they violate an understanding constitutive of their practice. It is reasonably clear, however, that professional wrestlers are not engaged in an athletic competition. Rather, they are engaged in a dramatic performance. This being the case the losers are not bribed. They are merely doing what professional wrestlers are ordinarily paid to do, namely, to play out their part in an informal script.

38

To Stay or to Leave:
The Moral Dilemma
of Divestment
# of South African Assets

KENNETH M. BOND

Introduction

This paper addresses the question "Are U.S. corporations which do business in South Africa morally obligated to divest?" The analysis will be divided into two major arguments. The first argument discusses general corporate behavior and obligations for social responsibility (macro issues). Once that discussion is concluded, an analysis of the type and nature of specific products will be developed (micro issues).

PART I

Concerning the general issue of U.S. corporate involvement in South Africa, arguments for and against divestment can be separated into four sub-issues: (1) Is apartheid immoral? (2) Do corporations have social responsibilities? (3) Do the rights of South African blacks to freedom and dignity outweigh the right of the corporations to do business freely? (4) Is the benefit to South African blacks greater with divestment than without?

The relationship of these questions to the main issue is illustrated in the decision network shown in Exhibit I. Only affirmative answers to all four questions will indicate that U.S. corporations are morally obligated to divest.

Is apartheid immoral?

This first question almost does not require discussion. A search of the literature reveals no legitimate argument for apartheid as a moral system. The author was able to only find one white South African woman, an Afrikaner, who argued for the morality of apartheid. Her argument was:[1]

1. It is God's plan that Afrikaners are in Africa. They were put there for a certain task and have to stay.

From *Journal of Business Ethics* **7** (1988) 9–18. © 1988 by D. Reidel Publishing Company. Reprinted by permission.

EXHIBIT I

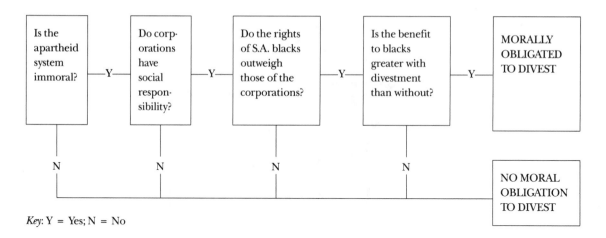

Key: Y = Yes; N = No

2. The division of people into groups is God's way.
3. Blacks do not want to own property, nor have more responsibility than to hold a clerical position.
4. The black homelands are being developed to their full potential.
5. The blacks want to be with their own people.
6. Riots and protests are started only by outside agitators.

My own casual reading of scripture would not support her several contentions that the apartheid system is "God's plan." All other writers, whether for or against divestment, accept as fact that apartheid is immoral, and that it is so clearly immoral, that no supportive argument is needed. This consensus is a strong indicator that apartheid is an immoral system. The theories of Rawls' (Liberty and Difference Principles): Kant; and the Fundamental Principle of Distributive Justice are only a few of the main line models of ethical thought which would condemn the system. The answer to the question in the first box of Exhibit I is clearly yes. We must proceed horizontally in our model.

Do corporations have a social responsibility?

Concepts of corporate responsibility have been evolving for decades, but there is still a lack of consensus regarding the meaning of the term. Most definitions fall into three distinct areas:

1. A basic definition (i.e., does our responsibility go beyond economic and legal concerns?)
2. A listing of the issues for which social responsibility exists (i.e., environment, discrimination, privacy, etc.)
3. The philosophy of response.

The three-dimensional model of Archie B. Carroll is among the more popular models of trying to integrate the three areas. His model is shown in Exhibit II.

The point of showing Dr. Carroll's model is not to specifically use this particular construct, but to illustrate that there are numerous methodological models available which attempt to prescribe a series of relationships between business and society. Any definition of social responsibility must include economic, legal, ethical, and discretionary categories. The four categories are not mutually exclusive, nor do they portray a continuum. "Social Issues" are the topical areas to which the responsibilities are tied, again not necessarily mutually exclusive. The philosophy of responsiveness describes management's way of dealing with the issues. This is a continuum.

The model in Exhibit II can be used to assist understanding the relationships or differences among various views on social responsibility. This

EXHIBIT II Three-dimensional model of corporate social responsibility

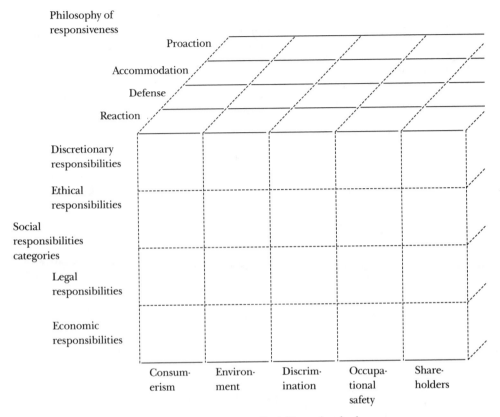

may help one to evaluate the views and choose the one that best suits his/her perspective.[2]

The question, "Do corporations have social responsibility?" has been hotly debated for many years. Leading the argument against corporations having social responsibility beyond legal requirements and profit seeking are Milton Friedman and Butler D. Shaffer. The other side of the question is argued by, among others, James J. Brummer, and Brown and Haas.[3]

Both Friedman and Shaffer state that a business manager is responsible to maximize profits for the shareholders while conforming to the letter of the law. Friedman adds that they must conform to the basic rules of society regarding ethical custom. Friedman offers as supporting arguments:[4]

1. A corporate manager is an agent of shareholders responsible to them. His only social responsibilities are personal.

2. Any social responsibilities that the shareholders have, they can fulfill personally.

3. If the manager acts to the social good at the expense of profit maximization, someone must pay. The payer can be the shareholders through lower earnings, the employees through lower wages, or the consumer through higher prices. This constitutes taxation which is a government function. Such a tax would represent taxation without proper representation. Also, taxing authority cannot be given to business, because business leaders are chosen by each other.

Shaffer also believes that corporations have no social responsibilities. He offers as supporting arguments:[5]

1. The whole concept of social responsibility is vague.

2. If a businessman is not in an effective position to change a problem area, he has no duty to act.

3. Where there is no duty to act, the duty to maximize profit takes precedence over an individual's concern for social welfare.

4. When corporations try to implement social change, they make society worse off than it would otherwise be if they maximized profit. . . . [W]hen they are no longer measured by financial performance they have no incentive to reduce costs. Thus, inefficiency is the social cost of corporate social responsibility.

5. Because there is no private market for social services one cannot conclude that the service has significance.

6. Social good is a valuational concept rather than economic, and value judgments cannot be supported.

James Brummer, in arguing for corporate social responsibility, states that:[6]

1. Every party is obligated to avoid harm to others in his or her actions. If corporations are the exceptions, the proponents of that view must prove it. (Brummer then attempts to refute all opposing arguments.)

2. There are many definitions of social responsibility which do not agree with each other. If looked at individually, some are quite clear.

3. The ability to solve a problem is not necessary in order to have a duty to act. If a corporation can impact the problem in any way, there is duty. All businesses can have an impact in moral issues.

4. Society is not necessarily worse off when a corporation tries to implement social change. First, if inefficiency is the cost of corporate social responsibility, it is a value judgment to say it costs too much. Secondly, a businessman may feel that it is a social responsibility to keep costs down.

5. Shaffer's argument contains value judgments. Value judgments are one thing for which he condemns the proponents of corporate social responsibility.

Brown and Haas argued that there is no private market for many services that are clearly of value. Police protection, fire protection, and military defense are examples of such services. Shaffer's argument would lead to these services being provided by private enterprise. It is not acceptable to be protected by soldiers who are there only for the money, or by an army run by a corporation whose only responsibility is to further its own interests. Thus, some social services have value over economic efficiency.[7]

Friedman's arguments appear to be stronger than Shaffer's. However, his arguments do not support his definition. By his own definition of managers' responsibility Friedman states that they must conform to ethical customs, while his arguments indicate no ethical responsibility. If Friedman's arguments are true, ethics need not be included in the definition of corporate social responsibility. His real disagreement with those who state that corporations have social responsibility appears to be one of degree rather than fact.

There is another school of thought which says that a corporation cannot have social responsibility because it is not a person and therefore cannot have intent.[8] Along with those authors just cited, Velasquez elaborates this argument as follows:[9]

> Let me summarize my main criticisms. Those, who like French, want to attribute moral responsibility to corporations must distinguish two entities, the corporation and the corporation's members, for they want to hold that the corporation, as distinct from its members, can be morally responsible for its acts. However, moral responsibility for an act attaches to the entity that originates the act — i.e., the entity that formed the intention to bring about the act and that carried out that intention by its direct bodily movements. Since the acts of a corporation are brought about not by the direct bodily movements of the corporation (as an entity distinct from its members) but by those of its members, and since the intentions of the corporation (if there are such things) are not the intentions with which those members acted, it follows that the corporation is not the entity that is morally responsible for those acts.

Velasquez goes on to point out that he is not arguing from a view of reducing organizations to merely the sum of its members. He fully appreciates the tradition, history, and environmental synergy which encompass all corporate entities. Velasquez does maintain that all corporate acts originate in its members and that the fundamental *moral* responsibility remains resident in those members.

The arguments for business social responsibility are the more convincing. Ross has numerous propositions in his *Prima Facie* Duties Theory.[10] Among his duties which would be of most interest to a discussion of corporate social responsibility are:

Duties of fidelity (to stockholders)
Duties of self-improvement
Duties of justice (distributing goods according to merit)
Duties of non-injury

Within the context of the present discussion, several other of his duties seem to have special significance. Those are . . . :

Duties of beneficence (to help others)
Duties of non-injury

Some brief comments about this second set of duties will be made in the second section of this paper dealing with the nature of products produced. For the present discussion, it is apparent that managers have several of these duties towards other groups. Ross says that when there are conflicting duties that actual duty is the one with the greatest amount of *prima facie* rightness over wrongness.[11] Clearly, there can be cases where the duty to society does have the greatest *prima facie* rightness. The conclusion is that corporations do have social responsibilities. With a yes answer to our second question, we must continue to move horizontally across Exhibit I.

Do the rights of South African blacks to freedom and dignity outweigh those of the corporations to do business freely?

Those who argue that the corporation's rights take precedence claim that the corporations are inno-

cent of any wrong doing and that it is not "just" to penalize the innocent. They argue that the blacks have been wronged, but they say that the guilty parties should be penalized rather than the innocent corporations. The opposing side argues that the corporations can afford divestment better than the blacks can afford apartheid. They also claim that U.S. corporations share guilt by failing to divest.

Rawls' Maximin Principles of Justice offer a workable method of analyzing numerous problems of morality.[12] The principles seem to fit this issue because they deal with maximization of the status of those minimally advantaged.[13] The South African blacks are minimally advantaged. The blacks do not have equal liberty with the corporations. The inequality is not to their advantage and they did not have an equal opportunity to be the party to receive more than equal liberty. Innocence or guilt is not a factor in this model. According to Rawls, the rights of the blacks would outweigh those of the U.S. corporation due to their relative degree of being disadvantaged.

A second model is called the Social Goals model by Velasquez.[14] This model does *not* direct its attention to who has been wronged and who wronged them (as do theories such as compensatory justice), but rather analyzes the present environment and tries to determine if a different environment would be *more just*. The basic question would be: "Is world 'A' (with apartheid) a better place than world 'B' (without apartheid)?" If the answer to this question is "yes", that world 'B' would be a better place, then the question becomes, "Are there morally justifiable reasons for moving from world 'A' to world 'B'?" While using a compensatory justice argument that blacks are owed compensation is ineffective in this argument, the model of Social Goals does provide a legitimate argument. Under a Social Goals argument,[15]

. . . a more just society (which is a morally acceptable end), could be achieved in a society in which an individual's opportunities are not limited by his or her race. This goal is morally legitimate insofar as it is morally legitimate to strive for a society with greater equality of opportunity.

In the logic of both Rawls' Maximin Principles of Justice and the Social Goals model, the black South African's rights outweigh the rights of the U.S. corporation. A "yes" answer to question #3 requires us to move horizontally in Exhibit I.

Is the benefit to South African blacks greater with divestment than without?

For the purpose of this paper, it is assumed that a corporation will behave morally if it stays in South Africa. Within the confines of the present discussion, it is obvious that to stay and behave immorally is not worth considering. (This is not to say that some companies do not fall into this group.) Socially responsive companies in South Africa adhere to the philosophy of points #2 and #3 of Exhibit I. This philosophy is implemented in guidelines such as the Sullivan Principles or other similar sets of standards.[16] In looking at the benefits of staying versus pulling out, it will be assumed that the corporations will adhere to the Sullivan Principles if they decide to stay.

Reverend Leon H. Sullivan, a black member of the board of directors of General Motors, authored the Sullivan Principles in 1977. They are a set of fair employment practice guidelines for American companies doing business in South Africa. The principles are:[17]

1. Nonsegregation of races in all eating, comfort, and work facilities.
2. Equal and fair employment practices.
3. Equal pay for comparable work.
4. Training programs to prepare non-whites for supervisory, administrative, clerical, and technical jobs in substantial numbers.
5. More non-whites in management and supervisory positions.
6. Improving employees' lives outside the work environment in such areas as housing, transportation, schooling, recreation, and health.

The argument at this point then comes down to the following. If a firm is practicing the Sullivan Principles (principles basically encompassed in questions #2 and #3 of Exhibit I), should such a firm continue to operate in South Africa or to divest? Clearly, those firms *not* conforming would already be behaving in an immoral manner and, in a sense, beyond the scope of this model. Such immoral behavior should dictate the ceasing of business operations in any organization in any cultural environment, not just South Africa.

To develop a mechanism to evaluate the term "benefit," a distinction will be made between macro and micro issues. Exhibit III illustrates the types of phenomenon discussed in both the macro and micro areas.

EXHIBIT III

Probable areas of impact for macro and micro issues to blacks for U.S. involvement in South Africa

MACRO ISSUES
Gross National Product (G.N.P.), Unemployment, Educational, Inflation, etc.

MICRO ISSUES
Nature of product produced
Who does the product directly benefit

Returning to the firms which are in spirit and practice following the Sullivan Principles, the arguments to divest are made by many U.S. political liberals. They include ex-senator Dick Clark of Iowa and Randall Robinson, director of TransAfrica. Their arguments include:[18]

1. American companies have poor civil rights records in South Africa.
2. Whatever helps South Africa's economy helps apartheid.
3. The South African government is immune to persuasion.
4. Divestment would cripple the South African economy.
5. South Africa has a trade deficit financed by U.S. investment.
6. There is no impetus for social change in South Africa.
7. U.S. business in South Africa offers legitimacy to apartheid.

The arguments against divestment are made by many, including, Gatsha Buthelezi, elected chief minister of the Zulu homeland and founder of the National Cultural Liberation Movement, a South African black rights movement; ex-U.S. ambassador Andrew Young; and Percy Qoboza, South Africa's foremost journalist. Their arguments (and numerous others') include:[19]

1. American companies can be a vital link in bringing about peaceful change.
2. American companies are leading the way in racial integration.
3. A strong South African economy is good for South African blacks, insures positive social change, and undermines apartheid.
4. Divestment cannot cripple the South African economy although it can slow growth and cause black unemployment.
5. South Africa does not have a trade deficit and does not need foreign capital.
6. Progress toward racial integration is being made.

Using a brief statistical history and analysis, the above points will be discussed. In 1978, all U.S. firms in South Africa paid starting wages above the Household Subsistence Level set by economists at the University of Port Elizabeth in South Africa, with most averaging 50% higher. Most U.S. companies support industrial training centers or have their own programs. They also offer integrated lavatories and cafeterias.[20]

A strong South African economy helps the black cause. White unemployment in South Africa has historically and consistently been under one percent (recently rising a bit). Black unemployment is normally 12 percent. If South Africa continues at its normal 6% growth rate, 3.8 million more jobs will be available within two years. Most of these jobs will go to blacks. From 1970 to 1978, black wages rose 118%, while white wages rose 58%. Historically, all racial progress worldwide has been in good economic times, and all good economic times have been good for minorities.[21]

The South African government has been criticized for years and no persuasion has been able to end apartheid, but South African business leaders are responding to persuasion at this time. Since 1975, South African business leaders have begun to shift toward capitalist growth and political freedom for all.[22]

As to crippling the South African economy by divestment, that is not possible. South Africa has the most self sufficient economy in the world. The large South African gold mining companies have enough cash reserves to buy all U.S. business in South Africa.[23] There is no South African trade deficit. For most countries, trade deficits are financed by foreign investment, cash, or gold reserves. South Africa exports gold, but many who claim that they have a trade deficit forget to count gold sales as part of the trade totals. The last reason that divestment cannot cripple South Africa's economy is that South Africa is self sufficient in raw materials, but the U.S. needs South Africa's strategic metals.

The only argument for divestment that cannot be adequately refuted is that U.S. business in South Africa gives legitimacy to apartheid. However, for those businesses which refuse to operate by the apartheid rules, this argument may not be true. These companies promote blacks to supervisory positions, pay equal wages, train blacks, force white workers to accept an integrated work place, and openly oppose the apartheid system. The certain advantages of having U.S. corporations in South Africa seem to outweigh the disadvantages of giving legitimacy to apartheid. Based upon this analysis, the answer to question #4 is "no."

PART II

In Section I of this analysis, an attempt was made to illustrate the necessary set of conditions which should be met for a corporation to operate ethically in South Africa. When one considers the macro relationships, the assumptions and restrictions of the analysis indicate that a limited number of organizations would probably meet these requirements. However, for those few organizations which *effectively meet the requirements of positive social responsibility*, the issue of legitimacy of their South African operations is not yet established.

A second area of analysis now becomes the nature or use of the product (micro issues). Though this analysis will be a bit more abbreviated than the analysis in Part I, some initial observations and conclusions can be drawn. Some of the products produced by U.S. corporations in South Africa are of direct benefit to the black population. Other products directly benefit and support the white government. Finally, there are a group of products which benefit both the black community and the government. An expanded development of the lower right corner of Exhibit I is shown in the decision tree of Exhibit IV.

The top and bottom decision tree branches in Exhibit IV are relatively easy to deal with. Manufactures of clothing, text books for the black schools, etc. could be placed in the upper branch of the exhibit. Assuming that a U.S. corporation was meeting all the criteria of Part I of this analysis, and the nature of their product fell in the upper branch of Exhibit IV, the conclusion would be for the morality of that organization staying in South Africa. From a utilitarian point of view, the benefits would simply outweigh the costs.

The bottom branch of the decision tree in Exhibit IV appears to lead to a decision to divest. However, there are arguments against such an action as well. One might argue that a specific product (i.e., surveillance equipment or police equipment) is available on the world market and the South African government can purchase the needed equipment through other sources. The reality of our international economy is such that, in all probability, the *same* corporations' product can be purchased in England, France, or the U.S. and then shipped to the appropriate South African agency. Divestment may do nothing more than disrupt the marketing channel but would clearly *not* block the acquisition of the equipment. Against such a consequentialist argument, the divestment position would stand on the reality that the product's *direct impact* on the black population is negative. Also such a U.S. corporation would be among those which seem to add the most legitimacy to the apartheid system. Those philosophical arguments which would address this issue from a non-consequentialist position would clearly argue for divestment.

The most interesting area of the decision tree in Exhibit IV is the middle branch. The group of products in this area would include numerous items from construction activity (roads and bridges), to consumer products such as telephones and Polaroid's instant camera. Government troops use bridges and roads, telephones, etc. and benefit directly from such products. Also, the black population uses and benefits from such products as well.

Polaroid is a particularly interesting and much publicized case in this area. Their instant camera technology was (and still is) used in the pass book system. The pass books are an integral part of the apartheid mechanism. The product is also used in traditional picture taking activities of both black

EXHIBIT IV **Impact of the nature of the product of the legitimacy of South African operations**

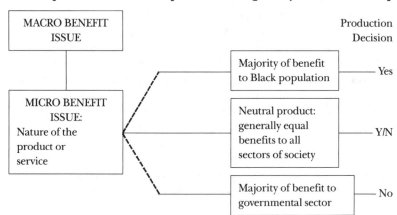

and white families. By the analysis of this author, Polaroid clearly meets the criteria of Exhibit I via operations such as the "Polaroid Experiment." Further, the necessary equipment for the pass book operation could be purchased almost anywhere in the world on the open market. Finally, Polaroid specifically forbade direct sales to the South African government. The question then is, "should they divest?"

Brummer [cited earlier] argues that corporations have *both* economic and social responsibilities that are not mutually exclusive. Brummer notes that ". . . firms are socially responsible to the extent that their executives sincerely seek to promote the common good in their business decision making."[24] He adds, "The basic requirement and responsibility of morality . . . is to minimize or eliminate those conditions of human life that cause avoidable or unnecessary suffering, hardship, and pain."[25]

Under Carroll's model (Exhibit II), or under Brummer's model, Polaroid's position is a difficult one. To Brummer, the most basic obligation is ". . . the obligation to avoid bringing more suffering and hardship into the world by their actions than would have existed had they acted differently or . . . done nothing at all."[26] Ross' *Prima Facie* Duty Theory, especially the duties of non-injury and the duty of beneficence (mentioned earlier), would add additional support to such an argument.[27]

The original Exhibit I now needs to be expanded into the final decision tree which takes into account the uncertainty involved in those products which have noticeable benefit to both groups. Exhibit V presents the completed analysis. The lower right portion of the Exhibit has been expanded to include a secondary decision branch for "both benefit" issues.

As is apparent, the best answer of the author to

EXHIBIT V

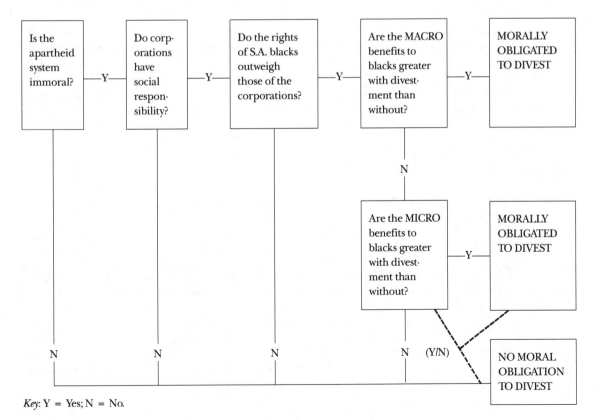

Key: Y = Yes; N = No.

those product groups which have benefits to both sectors of the South African economy is . . . *"I don't know."* It would seem that a case by case analysis is required and even then, the conclusion is not apparent. Polaroid, as an illustration, chose to divest. They were doing a lot of good for the blacks they employed but felt they did not have adequate control of the end use of their product and their weighing of the costs and benefits led them to divest.

PART III

A final, and very abbreviated, discussion centers around the issue of obligation for positive action against the apartheid system. Assuming proper moral behavior (i.e., Sullivan Principles or equivalent actions) and an acceptable product decision, the question then becomes, "are there moral obligations to *actively* oppose apartheid both inside the economic sphere and outside the economic sphere in areas such as political activity?"

As an illustration of an economic activity, Polaroid's "experiment" involved the promotion of blacks into positions of supervision. The South African apartheid system legally forbids a black to supervise a white worker. Are their moral obligations to *actively seek* confrontations such as these?

In the political sphere one could evaluate the moral obligation of supporting individuals and political parties opposed to the apartheid system. Brummer's analysis of the "basic requirement and responsibility . . . to minimize or eliminate those conditions of human life that cause avoidable or unnecessary suffering" would clearly argue the legitimacy of such actions. However, a philosophy of doing nothing to make the system worse would allow for economic actors but would not call for direct positive steps beyond the direct economic sphere.

Conclusion

The immorality of the apartheid system is clear and almost universally agreed upon. However, for a U.S. corporation to operate in South Africa does not necessarily mean support for apartheid. Assuming that a U.S. corporation is acting with a high level of corporate social responsibility (Part I) and has a product which also meets an appropriate evaluation (Part II), then there would be no moral obligation to divest. The mechanisms for evaluation of products which have positive benefits for both the government and the black population are far from clear. Finally, the issue of obligation for positive intervention to end the apartheid system (both political and economic activity) is a unique and total issue unto itself.

ENDNOTES

1. June Goodwin, "2 Views of Apartheid," *St. Peterburg Times*, p. D1.

2. Archie B. Carroll, "A Three Dimensional Conceptual Model of Corporate Performance," *Academy of Management Review*, Vol. 4, 1979, pp. 497–505. (Dr. Carroll's original model included one additional factor.)

3. James J. Brummer, "In Defense of Social Responsibility," *Journal of Business Ethics*, Vol. 2, 1983, p. 111.

4. Milton Friedman, "The Social Responsibility of Business Is to Increase Its Profits," *The New York Times Magazine*, September 13, 1970, pp. 32–33. (See this text p. 41 ff.)

5. Brummer, pp. 111–114.

6. *Ibid.*, pp. 111–122.

7. *Ibid.*, p. 120.

8. Numerous authors including: Thomas A. Klein, "Corporate Moral Responsibility: A Matter of Degree," *Business and Professional Ethics Journal*, Vol. 3, No. 2 p. 70; Part II of Donaldson and Werhane, eds., *Ethical Theory and Business*, 2nd ed., Prentice-Hall; Donaldson, *Corporations and Morality*, Ch. 2: and Werhane, *Persons, Rights, and Corporations*, Ch. 1.

9. Manuel G. Velasquez, "Why Corporations Are Not Morally Responsible for Anything They Do," *Business & Professional Ethics Journal*, Vol. 2, No. 3, Spring 1983, p. 9.

10. William D. Ross, *The Right and the Good* (Oxford, England: Clarendon Press, 1930, pp. 19–22).

11. Tom L. Beauchamp, *Philosophical Ethics: An Introduction to Moral Philosophy* (New York, NY: McGraw-Hill, 1982), p. 125.

12. Rawls, John, *A Theory of Justice* (Cambridge, Mass.: Harvard University Press, 1971).

13. *Ibid.*, pp. 298–303.

14. Manuel G. Velasquez, *Business Ethics: Concepts and Cases* (Englewood Cliffs, NJ: Prentice-Hall, 1982), pp. 283–287.

15. *Ibid.*, p. 285.

16. John Train, "South Africa: U.S. Don't Go Home," *Forbes Magazine*, November 27, 1978, pp. 33–35.

17. *Ibid.*, p. 35.

18. *Ibid.*, pp. 33–34.

19. *Ibid.*, pp. 34–35.

20. Alfred O. Hero, Jr. and John Barrett, *The American People and South Africa* (Toronto: Lexington Books, 1981), p. 181.

21. Herman Nickel, "The Case for Doing Business in South Africa," *Fortune*, June 19, 1978, p. 64.

22. Hero and Barrett, p. 187.

23. *Ibid.*, p. 55.

24. Brummer, p. 113.

25. *Ibid.*, p. 116.

26. *Ibid.*, p. 116.

27. Ross, *The Right and the Good*, pp. 19–22.

39

Comments on Kenneth M. Bond, "To Stay or to Leave: The Moral Dilemma of Divestment of South African Assets"*

PETER MADSEN

We owe Professor Kenneth Bond a good deal of gratitude for having addressed the issue of South African corporate divestment in the highly original way that he does. By asking four central questions, Professor Bond is able to raise discussions of the concept of corporate social responsibility, contemporary theories of justice and morality, and principles of normative ethics, while on the way to answering the general question of whether corporations have any duty to divest their assets from involvement with the apartheid government of the Republic of South Africa. We are indebted to Professor Bond not only for bringing these philosophical issues to bear on the South African divestment debate, but also for having done so in such a concise and precise way.

However, I will take the opportunity of these comments to argue that while Professor Bond's paper raises some of the right questions about corporate divestment, he hasn't raised all of them and in so doing he arrives at the wrong general answer

and thereby offers an erroneous conclusion about the question of the morality of corporate involvement in South Africa. Since Part I of the paper contains the crux of Professor Bond's analysis of the morality of corporate involvement, I will concentrate on it. In particular I will want to focus on the way in which the last of the four central questions of this part is both formulated and answered, since it is here where Professor Bond puts his own emphasis and it is here where, I think, his paper pivots to either succeed or to fail in proving the general thesis of the work. Before I turn to these matters, though, I would like to make some brief preliminary remarks about some of the other sections of the paper.

First, the fact that this work attempts to integrate the now perennial question of business ethics as to whether or not corporations have specific social responsibilities with special respect to the issue of South African apartheid is indeed admirable and long overdue. I agree with Professor Bond that apartheid is immoral and that there is no *bona fide*

From *Journal of Business Ethics* **7** (1988) 19-21. © 1988 by
D. Reidel Publishing Company. Reprinted by permission.

argument available which could prove otherwise. I further agree that businesses have social responsibilities, albeit for different reasons than those held in his analysis. Because business is inherently a social activity and its basic purpose is to fulfill various social needs, corporations engaged in business must be taken as full-fledged members of the moral community which is made up of a diverse number of members. Moreover, the members of a corporation are themselves likewise members of this moral community and as such they too have social responsiblities. Moral rules which determine moral responsibilities are never diluted by professional roles. We can never escape the primacy of our moral agency as individual members of a moral community. Likewise, corporations can never evade the primacy of their own moral agency as actual members of the same community. Thus, I have no quarrel with the outcomes of the first two central questions in Professor Bond's analysis even though my analysis differs.

Also, the answer to question number three is unproblematic. While Professor Bond utilizes John Rawls' account of justice and the social goals model of Manuel Velasquez to prove that the rights of South African blacks to freedom and dignity outweigh the rights of corporations in South Africa to do business freely, one could itemize other reasons as well which would support this claim. To mention but one such additional justification, I would merely point to the Kantian principle of respect for persons which holds that it is morally wrong to treat people as a means toward an end. In short, one need not even raise the question of whether a South African black's rights to freedom and dignity outweigh some corporate right to practice business freely. By merely being a person, the South African black is entitled to the exercise of freedom and is worthy of dignity befitting personhood. Of course, as a philosophy of racism, this is exactly what the system of apartheid has denied. Conversely, it is the respect of the South African black as a person which is affirmed by divestment proponents. Thus, any corporate right to practice business must take a place behind the rights of personhood which should be automatically ascribed to South African blacks.

The final question of Professor Bond's four central questions is the crucial one. His formulation of it is: "Is the benefit to South African blacks greater with divestment than without?" Now immediately after raising this question, Professor Bond states: "For the purpose of this paper, it is presumed that a corporation will behave morally, if it stays in South Africa." By this what is meant is that those corporations which choose to stay in South Africa will act in a "socially responsive" way. They will, e.g., be signators of the Sullivan Principles and otherwise be good corporate citizens. The question now is formulated as whether these corporations so designated should pull out of South Africa. Professor Bond then goes on to survey and summarize some often-repeated arguments on both sides of the divestment issue and then offers his own position which can be characterized as a stilted species of the constructive engagement stance of the Reagan administration. He gives a purely consequentionalist view of this stance and holds that [1] a strong South African economy will have good consequences for blacks there, and [2] divestment will not have the consequences of crippling the South African economy. Given these consequences, Professor Bond concludes that there is no moral obligation for U.S. corporations to divest themselves of their South African holdings.

Although I think these two consequences in Professor Bond's analysis can be debated on an empirical basis — e.g., alternative statistics can be and have been cited other than those from *Forbes* and *Fortune* magazines which Professor Bond chooses to cite and which demonstrate that blacks have not fared very well in good economic times in South Africa. Not to include these statistics amounts to a suppression of the evidence. Likewise, there is no telling or predicting the impact upon the South African economy, if there were to be a total economic isolation of South Africa by the free world of which the U.S. divestment movement is but one segment. But rather than debate on this empirical level, I would like to keep my critique on a plane where logical and ethical analysis is central.

The major thrust of such a critique is that purely consequentionalist analysis of divestment issues never does complete justice to the deeper issues of morality. Given the formulation of the last central question in his work, given its teleological bias, there is little doubt as to where it will land its author. Of course divestment will not be beneficial to the economic life of black South Africans, but this does not automatically discount divestment from the realm of moral obligation. Rather, one can argue as follows: Since apartheid is immoral (Professor Bond's first answer), and since corporations do have positive moral responsibilities (Professor Bond's second answer), and since South African blacks have a right to freedom and dignity (Professor Bond's third answer), and since divestment will not benefit blacks economically (Professor Bond's fourth answer), then it can be concluded that U.S. corporate divestment is a moral obligation (given answers 1, 2, 3) which will carry with it some burdens (given 4). In other words, Professor Bond's first three answers do establish, and establish well, a moral obligation on the part of U.S. corporations to divest. The consequentionalist's analysis of the fourth point does not contradict what has been established, but only qualifies this moral obligation as one which is not free from hardship like so many other moral obligations. Professor Bond's work does prove, I think, that divestment is a moral obligation which will provide future benefits to South African blacks while requiring present burdens.

Another approach to the claim of this paper that the consequences of divestment will harm blacks and that therefore U.S. firms are not morally obligated to practice divestment is to point out that such a teleological stance ignores real deontological import.

It can be held with good reason that *any* involvement with the government of the Republic of South Africa is tacitly an approval of apartheid and an explicit support of it with a monetary tell-tale trail. Professor Bond essentially admits this point and in my eyes also puts his just made conclusions in doubt when he writes: "The only argument for divestment that cannot be adequately rebuted is that U.S. business in South Africa gives legitimacy to apartheid." To put the issue quite straightforwardly, U.S. firms have a moral obligation to divest themselves of their South African assets regardless of the consequences of this divestment simply because it is the right thing to do. Deontologically speaking, this non-consequentionalist argument is acceptable because to maintain business in South Africa is to maintain apartheid, continue it and legitimize it. Sometimes some actions are necessary, good, and obligatory regardless of the consequences of those actions because these actions are inherently right. Divesting from South Africa is one of these inherently right actions.

To conclude, we give Professor Bond much thanks for his point of departure in bringing many important and significant philosophico-ethical positions to bear on an analysis of the divestment debate. However, we can and must go beyond his starting point and not only include a consequentionalist flavor to our work but bring in a bit of deontological reasoning, if we are to get clear on the whole picture. While Professor Bond certainly asks some of the right questions in his paper, he does err when he overemphasizes the teleological and when he leaves the deontological questioning of apartheid out of the question. By raising the deontological we thereby conclude that divestment is not only a good, but that it is a *bona fide* moral duty which should be practiced regardless of its consequences.

ENDNOTE

*See pp. 423-433, this text.

40

Business Ethics: Economic Sanctions and Political Change in South Africa

GARY WARNER

Apartheid is a *constitutional* system of racial segregation designed to guarantee white control of the economy and an unlimited supply of cheap black labour, and to preserve "white Western civilization" as the dominant force in South African society. Blacks constitute approximately 74% of the population of South Africa, are restricted to 13% of the land, much of it barren, have no vote, and are the principal victims of the apartheid laws. A black child is eight times more likely to die before the age of one than a white child. The average wages for a black mineworker are six times less than for a white. In no other country for which records are available is the discrepancy between rich and poor (that is, between white and black in this context) greater than in South Africa. The 11% of Indians and Coloureds have token representation in a segregated powerless parliament designed for them. Absolute power rests in the hands of the 15% minority white population who control 87% of the land and 90% of the wealth of the country. The government of the country is elected by the 3% of the population who constitute the adult white voters.

It is important to begin by underlining the fact that apartheid is not a historical anomaly but rather the dying stages of the colonial order which witnessed over a period of three centuries or so the subjugation of Africa by European peoples. Colonialism was based on the premise of racial inequality, which was given philosophical respectability by books such as the Arthur de Gobineau's *De l'inégalité des races humaines*, published in the mid-nineteenth century. Colonialism essentially involved the subjugation of supposedly "backward" indigenous peoples and the economic exploitation of their resources, often in the name of a civilizing mission. For example, as late as 1931, Albert Sarraut, French Minister of the Colonies, presented the case for colonialism in *Grandeur et Servitude coloniales*[1] in these terms:

> If we colonize, if we establish our authority outside of France, it is first and foremost to serve our own interests. Europe has more and more need of raw materials and these raw materials, source of well-being for all, are unequally distributed over the earth. They are some-

This essay was written especially for this volume.

times to be found in abundance in regions where backward, primitive peoples are incapable of putting them to good use. Should we supposedly out of respect for the rights of the first occupier, abandon resources which, in other hands, would spread prosperity and riches? Should we, out of obedience to the dictates of an ideal and absolute law, allow primitive peoples to lead a miserable life alongside unexploited resources which could guarantee their happiness and ours? The reply is not in doubt, and that is the reason for colonization.

But if we colonize, it is not just for selfish reasons and for our advantage only. The benefit accrues to both the protector and the protégé. The native gets rich from trading with the European; he has his share in the profits from the increased value of the land and of the local products. His material conditions improve, the mortality rate is lowered, famines disappear, epidemics are throttled. . . . The converse of the act of authority which installs us abroad is the moral responsibility to lead forward the primitive populations and to bring them up to our level, to help them catch up their evolutionary backwardness.

By the mid-1950s, independent states began to spring up in Commonwealth Africa, soon to be followed by the former French colonies, which for the most part became independent countries in 1960. Another wave of independence began in the mid-1970s as a result of liberation wars, first in the Portuguese colonies, then in Zimbabwe, and most recently in Namibia. South Africa stands as the last bastion of colonialism in Africa.

In spite of the lessening of overt repression that has followed the accession to power of the De Klerk government in September 1989, the essential structures of the apartheid system remain firmly in place. Racial classification is still in force, as is the Bantustan policy by which the government has decreed that all black Africans belong to one of ten tribal homelands, located in economically unviable regions and constituting only 13% of the area of South Africa. The original goal of the Afrikaners was to force all Blacks to live in a homeland, and then cut them off from South African citizenship by

granting nominal political independence to these homelands. More than two million people have been uprooted and shipped to homelands since 1948. Variations on the Bantustan model are being considered by white South African planners.[2] One such option would involve a modification of the constitution to create a federal state with some powers devolved to a dozen or so local governments, some black-dominated, some white-dominated. The black-dominated areas would correspond more or less to the present homelands. The key portfolios of defence, foreign affairs, and finance would remain under white control, so that even if the policy of one person one vote was instituted, the substance of power would remain effectively under white control. Clearly, however, such clever devices, designed to modernize apartheid by concealing its reality behind the mask of constitutional change, will not satisfy the black majority. The system of apartheid cannot simply be reformed. It must be radically eliminated so that all traces of racial inequality and discrimination also are expunged. This change entails the replacement of present government structures by a non-racial democracy within a unitary state and the reorientation of the economy and social services to serve the interests of the whole population. International sanctions form part of the strategy to bring about such fundamental change as peacefully as possible. The basic issue, therefore, is not sanctions *per se* but rather the eradication of apartheid, a struggle which is waged on many fronts and primarily by the victims of apartheid themselves. This is the context within which the debate over sanctions in South Africa must be viewed. Sanctions can take many forms, including economic, social, sports, cultural, diplomatic. This essay's main focus will be economic sanctions.

The Friedmanite argument against sanctions is that the essence of business is to maximize profit. Milton Friedman wrote in *Capitalism and Freedom* that "Few trends could so thoroughly undermine the very foundations of our free society as the acceptance by corporate officials of a social responsibility other than to make as much money for their shareholders as possible." According to this view, profit and financial self-interest constitute the supreme values of commercial activity. The premise of this line of thinking is that the market functions according to its own natural laws and operates outside of the realm of social morality. Investment in South Africa would be appropriate as long as it was profitable. Friedman's formula attempts to establish a dichotomy between ethics and business practice, as if business were conducted in a vacuum, and did not involve social relations. And indeed, fortunes have been made and are still being made today by individuals, companies, and supposedly civilized governments in such areas as arms sales precisely on the basis that ethical considerations have no place in business decisions. The international companies that continue to invest and do business in South Africa do so primarily because it is profitable: "For one thing, the return on direct investment since 1970 has been in the 14% to 16% (of assets) range, with occasional bonanza years (like 1980) in which after-tax profits soar as high as 30%. For another, companies are convinced that South Africa's economy is, by any measure, the strongest of the 40-plus African countries, with tremendous market prospects for the future."[3] The victims of apartheid and of other forms of oppression can expect no sympathy from these quarters.

The geopolitical/strategic argument against sanctions is that South Africa is key to Western economic and security interests. South Africa is seen to serve as a bulwark against communism and a vital supplier of strategic minerals needed for the defence industries of the West. Dr. Peter Duignan, Director of African and Middle East Studies at Stanford University's Hoover Institute, and a Reagan advisor, articulated this argument in the *Baltimore Sun* (c. 1980):

> The U.S. needs to re-think its policies in Africa. Africa is important to the U.S. for its strategic regions, for its markets, for its supply of raw materials. Hence the U.S. should denounce the Soviet and Cuban expansion in Africa. We should respond to African requests for security assistance when such aid benefits our purposes. Instead of criticizing the South Africans and the French for their efforts to maintain a modicum of regional security, we should lend them our cautious assistance.[4]

On the specific issue of strategic minerals, the Congressional report, *Imports of Minerals from South Africa by the USA and other OECD Countries*, commissioned by the Senate Foreign Relations Committee (1980) pointed out that "contrary to conventional wisdom, South African minerals are of significant but not critical importance to the west." Taken as a whole, the essence of the geopolitical/strategic argument is that the oppression of the black majority by the white minority is subordinated to the pursuit of Western economic and security interests. Its proponents share the same basic perspective as the Friedmanites insofar as they both seek to maintain and extend the power of the dominant economic and political forces. Questions of social equity and of decolonization lie beyond their horizons.

Another group acknowledges that apartheid constitutes an institutionalized and violent form of racism, and that state-sponsored repression of the black majority by the white minority is abhorrent — but does not elect to sever ties with the apartheid state. It is useful to recall, as Mahatma Gandhi pointed out, that non-cooperation with evil is an essential aspect of ethics. One of the arguments advanced by this group is that of "*constructive engagement*" (or the carrot versus the stick). Constructive engagement is supposed to lead to a change of heart among members of the ruling white elite, enlightened by the fair practices of international corporations. This approach reflects the obsession with white politics in South Africa. An operational strategy for businesses to effect change within this framework has been expressed in the following way:

> First, they should continue to move aggressively on their own turf through affirmative action toward genuine equal opportunity employment. Second, they should, through their personal relationships with South African leaders, black and white, and through their basic business decisions, give clear support to the four fundamental goals of the black population and farsighted whites: recognition of national citizenship in the Republic of South Africa for everyone regardless of race; an equitable share in political power without discrimination; equal access to everything necessary for economic well-being; and an immediate end to all

arbitrary relocation of black people along with a guarantee of the right of families to live near their place of livelihood. The government has refused or blocked all real progress toward these four basic goals. But their eventual acceptance is necessary if the country is to survive the stark reality that, by the year 2000, whites will comprise only 12% of the population, and that the willing participation of skilled black workers will be necessary on every level of public and private operations for growing economic strength.[5]

The assumption is that this strategy would lead to gradual internal reform — the alternative being violence and revolution (= disorder, "communism," and a bad investment climate) led by black liberation movements. The main interlocutors under this strategy are whites (who control the economic, political, and military levers) and compliant Blacks (who have a stake in preserving their own real or perceived privilege). This argument is based on the premise that apartheid can be reformed while maintaining a business-as-usual situation. Its proponents also try to stake out some of the moral high ground by claiming to view apartheid with as much abhorrence as those who promote sanctions. They point to the fact that they provide jobs, training, and more equitable benefits for the black employees in their South African businesses.

The argument that foreign investment is a liberalizing influence in South Africa through the activities of international companies which respect the Sullivan principles or other voluntary codes of conduct and thereby set an example of fair treatment for Blacks in South Africa is fundamentally flawed. The simple fact is that apartheid is the legally entrenched framework within which these companies operate. The apartheid system permeates all aspects of South African life, and determines the educational levels of Blacks, their living standards and place of residence, job opportunities, social services available to them, etc. It is a constitutional system designed to maintain white privilege. No amount of compliance with the Sullivan principles or other codes of conduct can alter this overwhelming national fact. The wave of massive arrests, including countless children held awaiting trial in police cells, the brutal repression of Blacks and widespread use of torture, state-sponsored assassinations of ANC representatives abroad, and military aggression against neighbouring African states, belie the rosy view of liberalization heralded by the prophets of reform through foreign investment.

After 10 years of operation, the Sullivan Code and other codes of conduct clearly made no dent on apartheid. The author of the Sullivan Code, Rev. Leon Sullivan, a black clergyman, announced on June 1987 in the *New York Times* that corporations should pull out of South Africa and that the U.S. should sever all trade and diplomatic links with South Africa until apartheid was ended. "In spite of our efforts, the main pillars and apartheid remain and Blacks are still denied basic civil rights. Repression against Blacks grows. People are brutalized. The government's intransigence to fundamental change continues."

As far as the significance of foreign investment for South Africa is concerned, the words of former President Vorster are clear enough: "Each trade agreement, each bank loan, each new investment is another brick in the wall of our continued existence." Bishop Tutu makes the same point from the black perspective: "Those who invest in South Africa should please do so with their eyes open. They must not delude themselves that they are doing anything for the benefit of Blacks. Please let us at least get rid of this humbug. They must understand that they are buttressing one of the most vicious systems since Nazism. At least they should know that this is what they are doing. This is what *Blacks* feel."

The "constructive engagement" argument is often accompanied by two other propositions that are used to reinforce it. The first is that sanctions will hurt the Blacks they are intended to help. It is mindboggling to hear this argument propounded by the likes of Margaret Thatcher as a justification for promoting continuing investments in South Africa. Not surprisingly, the South African government along with whites with business interests in South Africa vigorously expound this line of argument in public fora. The second proposition is that divestment is ineffective because companies that leave South Africa can lose money in the process and are replaced in any case by other investors. For example, Adrian Cadbury argues that

> In deciding what weight to give to the arguments for and against divestment, we must consider who has what at stake in the outcome of the decision. The employees of a South African subsidiary have the most direct stake, as the decision affects their future; they are also the group whose voice is least likely to be heard outside South Africa. The shareholders have at stake any loss on divestment, against which must be balanced any gain in the value of their shares through severing the South African connection.[6]

Cadbury's stakes are fashioned to fit the needs of the accountant's tally sheet and of the conscience of the paternalistic manager. They do not address the structural question of the eradication of the system of apartheid, the enfranchisement of the disenfranchised majority, and equitable participation in the economy for the millions of dispossessed, not just the employees of international firms. Robert Chambers in *Rural Development: Putting the last first* (p. 74) defines the development perspective in these terms: "The search is for approaches which are . . . able to see into, and out from, the predicament of the rural poor themselves." What the proponents of the Friedmanite, geopolitical/security, and constructive engagement arguments have in common, however diverse their motivations, is the inability to see into, and out from, the predicament of the victims of apartheid.

On the positive side, sanctions constitute a *moral statement* — they are a clear message to South Africa of international revulsion for its policy of apartheid. Sanctions are an internationally recognized form of exerting pressure and isolating nations which grossly offend international norms. The Charter of the United Nations makes provision for the use of sanctions by the international community against states which are deemed to be acting outside the accepted norms of international behaviour. Since 1962, the General Assembly of the United Nations has repeatedly called for sanctions against South Africa. The August 1989 Harare Declaration

by the O.A.U. ad-hoc Committee on Southern Africa, while calling for negotiated change in South Africa, renewed the call for mandatory and comprehensive sanctions against apartheid South Africa, and for the total isolation of the apartheid state.

More than moral pressure, sanctions do work over time as an *economic lever*, especially if they are widely applied. The U.S. has made effective use of sanctions, for example, to provoke the overthrow of the Allende regime in Chile in 1973. In spite of all the sanction-busting schemes deployed by the Smith regime, sanctions eventually played a role, along with the war of liberation waged by the forces of Mugabe and Nkomo, in forcing Ian Smith of Rhodesia to the negotiating table. Sanctions in this case are intended both to pressure the South African regime to negotiate a peaceful transition to democratic rule and to weaken its capacity to wage war on its citizens and to destabilize the neighbouring front-line states.

The impact of sanctions on the South African economy has been documented. The impact would be greater if South Africa's main trading partners, the U.S., Britain, West Germany, and Japan, tightened sanctions against South Africa. Nonetheless, there has been a significant flight of capital from South Africa, as many companies have withdrawn their investments. The trade embargo, although limited, has made it more difficult for South Africa to sell its manufactured goods abroad. The country's foreign reserves are very low. South Africa is vulnerable to sanctions because of its dependence on imports of sophisticated technology. The imposition of selective sanctions by the U.S. Congress sent the South African government into a frenzy — Pik Botha phoned several congressmen and threatened to cut off imports of American grain. The South African government considers this issue important enough to have created special diplomatic sections devoted exclusively to countering sanctions.

Although it is a crime punishable by five years' imprisonment, *Blacks have overwhelmingly called for sanctions* as part of the broader strategy to eliminate apartheid.[7] In response to the argument that the Blacks will suffer most from sanctions, we should ask: who speaks for the oppressed majority in South

Africa? Is it the Boards of corporations and financial planners who have no concrete experience of oppression? One should listen instead to what the reputable black leadership says:

> "The economic boycott of South Africa will entail undoubted hardship for Africans. But we do not doubt that it is a method which shortens the bloodshed. The suffering to us will be a price we will be willing to pay." (Chief Albert Luthuli, Nobel Peace Prize Winner)

> "The number of people who are without jobs because of sanctions is negligible compared to the number caused by the apartheid system itself. So the question of employment and unemployment is not the issue. The real issue is how you get rid of apartheid." (Rev. Frank Chikane, General Secretary of the South African Council of Churches)

One of the few prominent Blacks opposing sanctions is Chief Gatcha Buthelezi — a proponent of tribalist politics as head of the Zulus; a pawn in Pretoria's game of disenfranchising black South Africans by making them citizens of Bantustans, one of which, Kwazulu, is presided over by Buthelezi himself (even if Buthelezi has resisted actual independence for Kwazulu); objectively a tool used by the South African government to ease the consciences of Western liberals and business interests about continuing investments, insofar as Buthelezi articulates the official South African government line that sanctions will hurt the Blacks. By engaging in violent conflict with rival groupings such as the U.D.F., Buthelezi is also playing the South African government's card of "Black on Black violence."

Bishop Tutu has put this question of sanctions and the alleged concern for Blacks in sharp perspective:

> And if sanctions are wrong in principle and must always fail, then why is it that even up to today the U.S. applies trade sanctions against Cuba? And why was it that President Reagan was prepared to risk the friendship of his NATO allies when he insisted on the embargo of scientific knowhow to Russia because of her behaviour in Poland and Afghanistan? . . . We are not unreasonable in asking for consistency — is it that the West thinks things are serious only when whites

[e.g., Poles] are involved and that the freedom and suffering of Blacks does not count? . . . We are told that sanctions will mean suffering especially for those they intend to help. First, when did whites suddenly become so altruistic? Have they not benefitted from massive black suffering in the form of migatory labour and cheap labour for many years? Why should they suddenly worry whether Blacks suffer or not? Have not two million been uprooted and dumped as rubbish in unviable poverty-stricken and drought stricken Bantustan resettlement camps?

Furthermore, from the purely economic viewpoint, a growing body of evidence suggests that, although some black workers would suffer[8] (e.g., mineworkers), "the larger proportion of waged black workers and the estimated 10 million Bantustan population (who are largely unemployed or live in a subsistence economy) would not be hurt by international sanctions." The fact is that Blacks already suffer under apartheid. It is the white minority which benefits from apartheid, and which therefore is more vulnerable to a loss in standard of living as a result of international sanctions. We should therefore not be fooled by the official South African government propaganda that Blacks will suffer as a result of sanctions, and should listen instead to the voices of the authentic leaders of the oppressed majority of South Africa.

Slavery and child labour were once considered essential for the economic growth of the businesses which exploited these human resources. Yet both would today be considered contrary to the international norms of minimum human rights. Similarly, less than half a century ago the conventional wisdom in the metropolitan countries that governed colonies and territorial dependencies was that this pattern of patron-client relationship would endure into the twenty-first century. One of the most significant political events of our age has been the breaking of this pattern — at least at the formal level, as most colonies have achieved political independence. Global economic relationships continue to reflect historical inequalities in favour of the affluent industrialized North. But the process of liberation of the former colonies has been set in motion.

South Africa stands on the verge of liberation from its particular brand of settler colonialism. The advent of a non-racial, genuinely representative government is as inevitable as the demise of slavery and child labour. The highest ethical stance for international business is to cease economic cooperation with the apartheid state and the institutions that sustain it, recognizing that they are the modern equivalent of the slave-owners and exploiters of child labour. Or to draw a more contemporary analogy, the apartheid state and its institutions are the Nazis of our age, in dealing with whom it would not be ethical to plead neutrality. As the South African theologian Albert Nolan put it, "If we do not take sides with the oppressed, then we are, albeit unintentionally, taking sides with the oppressor." In the context of the decolonization of South Africa, businesses by their decisions to invest or divest (including the manner in which they divest) objectively choose to side either with the victims of apartheid or the oppressors.

ENDNOTES

1. Reviewed in the January-March 1933 issue of *L'Education Africaine*, Bulletin de l'Enseignement en A.O.F., p. 51. My translation.

2. See *Africa Confidential*, Vol. 28, no. 25, 16 December 1987.

3. See Howard Schomer, "South Africa: Beyond Fair Employment," *Harvard Business Review*, May–June 1983.

4. Quoted in Richard Deutsch, "Reagan's African Perspectives," *Africa Report*, July–August 1980, pp. 4–7.

5. Howard Schomer, *op. cit.*

6. See Adrian Cadbury, "Ethical Managers Make Their Own Rules," *Harvard Business Review*, September–October 1987, reprinted in this text, p. 72 ff.

7. The South African Chamber of Mines undertook a tactic of corporate disinformation by hiring Gallup to poll black workers on divestment. The Gallup poll, released in May 1989, revealed 80% opposition to sanctions and divestment. The methodology of the survey and the results have been widely discredited by social scientists. The tactic does reveal, however, the lengths to which the corporate sector will go to counter sanctions.

8. Black trade unions are concentrating on negotiating terms for the withdrawal of foreign companies which ensure maximum pressure on the economy at minimum cost to the workers.

41

Equal Pay for Equal Work in the Third World

HUGH LEHMAN

I

Transnational corporations have found it profitable to establish manufacturing operations in third-world nations in part because labor costs are considerably reduced. The practice of paying workers in a third-world nation at a lower rate apparently conflicts with a principle which has gained widespread support in other contexts, the principle of equal pay for work of equal value. For example, it has been claimed that certain jobs traditionally performed by women are of equal value to employers as other jobs traditionally performed by men but that since the women are paid at a lower rate they are being unjustly treated. The argument is that since the jobs are of equal value and since jobs of equal value should be remunerated at the same rate, the salaries for the traditional women's jobs should be equal to the salaries for the comparable men's jobs.

If the principle of equal pay for work of equal value is valid as a principle of justice, then it appears that the practice of paying workers in third-world countries at a lower rate than workers doing the same jobs in industrialized nations is unjust.

Recently however, Henry Shue has argued that the principle of equal pay for equal work is unacceptable because it has unacceptable implications.[1] His argument is open to several criticisms. In order to express these criticisms I shall first state his argument as I understand it. After criticizing his argument I shall suggest alternative criticisms of the equal pay for work of equal value principle. I shall argue that Shue is correct in thinking that this principle is valid only with a restriction in scope. Outside such restrictions, violations of the equal pay for equal work principle may be in accord with more basic moral principles such as either the difference principle or utilitarian principles concerning the satisfaction of interests.

II

Shue suggested three possible interpretations of the equal pay for equal work principle. The alternative interpretations arise in light of different ways of construing "equal pay." The claim that workers should receive equal pay could mean either that

From *Journal of Business Ethics* **4** (1985) 487-491. © 1985 by D. Reidel Publishing Company · Reprinted by permission.

they should receive the same number of dollars per hour (or per week or per item, etc.) or it could mean that workers in third-world nations should be paid enough so that their standard of living in the third-world country was the same as that of workers at comparable jobs in industrialized nations or it could mean that workers in third-world nations should be paid enough so that their standard of living relative to other people in the same country was the same as the standard of living of the workers in the industrialized nation relative to other people in the industrialized nation.

Shue argued that on any of the three interpretations the equal pay for equal work principle is unacceptable. Given the third interpretations of the principle, the salary paid to workers in third-world nations might be so low that it would not provide for the physical needs of the workers or other people dependent upon them. I have no criticism to make of Shue's objection to the principle interpreted in this third way. According to Shue, if the principle is interpreted in either the first or the second way, then the pay that a corporation is required to pay to workers in third-world nations is too high. Applying the equal pay for equal work principle, under either of the first two interpretations, according to Shue, is unrealistic. Further, he maintained, paying workers in third-world nations at such a high rate would give them salaries sufficient to give them a standard of living equivalent to the *elite* of those nations. To pay workers in third-world countries at such a high rate would mean that such workers would earn more in a week than most workers in such countries earn in a year. Shue objects that, intuitively, such salaries are too high. He concludes that the equal pay for equal work principle ought not to be understood as applying regardless of social context.

While I have a certain amount of sympathy with Shue's remarks, these objections are poorly formulated. The claim that applying some moral principle yields "unrealistic" consequences is not, so far as I can see, a sound objection to the principle. On many occasions people opposed to the implications of a moral principle have claimed that the principle is unrealistic. I suspect that all that they mean is that

people will not voluntarily conform to the principle. However, to say that people or corporations will not voluntarily conform to the principle of equal pay for equal work is not necessarily a good reason for saying that the principle is mistaken or that it ought not to be applied.

Shue's other objection, namely that to pay the workers in third-world countries at a rate that would give them a standard of living equivalent to the *elite* of those countries is poorly formulated also. Surely, we ought to ask, why would it be wrong for these people to be paid at such a relatively high rate? To suggest, as Shue does, that such a high rate of pay is counter-intuitive does not explain why it would be wrong that workers in such countries be paid at such a high rate.

III

Is there a serious objection then to the principle of equal pay for work of equal value, if that principle is interpreted in either of the first two ways that Shue suggests? I am inclined to agree with Shue that the principle, interpreted in either of these ways, is open to serious criticism. In arguing against the principle, I shall on the one hand appeal to utilitarian considerations and on the other hand argue that justice does not require that workers in third-world nations be paid such high salaries. Henceforth when I refer to the principle, I shall understand it as interpreted in either the first or the second way.

I shall assume that under proper restrictions if a transnational corporation moves a manufacturing, mining, or argricultural operation to a third-world nation, that can lead to increases in the quality of life of a significant number of the poor people of that nation. Such increases in the quality of life will be reflected in an increase in total utility. Improving the quality of life of the poorest people in such a manner need not reduce the quality of life of the wealthy people of the nation. Thus, the increase in the quality of life of these poor people will increase utility overall, at least within the third-world nation. However, in some cases, if a corporation opens a commercial operation in a third-world nation, there will be some loss of employment by workers in first-world nations. Thus, it is possible that the increase in total utility within the third-world nation would be negatively balanced by a loss of utility elsewhere. Indeed, not only is this possible, it has, of course, occurred repeatedly. However, in many cases there is good reason for believing that the increase in utility which may occur in the third-world nation is not counter-balanced by the increased unemployment and consequent loss of utility in the first-world nations. The workers in the first-world nations, even while unemployed, do not become as badly off as the people in the third-world nation.

Of course, if a corporation begins a business operation in the third-world, it does not automatically lead to significant increases to the quality of life of poor people there. The poor people may remain essentially as poor as they were while any benefits that accrue in that world accrue to the wealthiest people. In light of this, what can be argued is that if there are restrictions on the operation of a corporation so that if it were to set up operations in a third world nation it would lead to significant improvements in the quality of life of people in the third world, then it is morally right or desirable that corporations set up such operations in the third world. Now, we may ask, should the corporations who are considering setting up such operations be required to pay workers in the third world at a rate equal to that which they pay comparable workers in the industrialized parts of the world? The answer, I believe, is probably negative. The requirement that workers in third-world nations be paid at such a high rate would, in many cases, have the consequence that there would be no economic incentive for the corporation to transfer operations to the third world. The decision not to make such a transfer would produce less overall utility than would be produced by making a transfer and paying workers at the lower rate. Thus, on utilitarian grounds, we can argue that subject to the conditions indicated, the adoption of the equal pay for equal work rule would be morally wrong. Indeed, it appears that on utilitarian grounds, corporations should be encouraged to transfer operations to third-world nations subject to the condition indicated, namely, that there be significant improvements to the quality of life of the poorest people of those nations.

If we think about the conditions in some third-world nations that make life miserable there we find that major contributing factors to the poor quality of life are such things as the level of health care, the level of nutrition, the level of education, and the like. If one were a benevolent dictator in such a country, one would presumably maximize utility in that country by bringing about significant improvements in some of these areas. Thus, rather than requiring corporations to provide equal pay for equal work, one would choose to require corporations to make significant improvements to the native water supply, sewage, hospitals, etc. Such improvements would improve quality of life far more than the greater salaries required by the equal pay for equal work principle since, even with those greater salaries a worker in a third-world nation could not buy decent hospitals, sewage treatment, water, etc. Thus, again, we see that the principle of equal pay for equal work is unacceptable on utilitarian grounds. Total utility would be maximized by paying lower salaries.

Now, it may be objected that while it is true that acting in accord with the principle of equal pay for equal work would not maximize utility, that that is irrelevant. Those who appeal to the principle in arguments concerning women's rights apparently believe that accepting the principle would improve the quality of life of women relative to that of men. They appear to argue, for the most part, that the basic reason for adopting the equal pay for equal work principle is that the lower quality of life of women as compared to men's is unjust. Such injustice, they may argue, should be eradicated regardless of whether this leads to an increase in total utility. We may wonder then whether the utilitarian arguments offered above for rejecting the principle of equal pay for equal work would be undercut by similar appeals to justice in this case. In my view, such is not the case. Arguments in favor of Shue's intuitions may be grounded on several distinct fundamental moral principles.

Shue suggests that the principle of equal pay for equal work may be valid only in social contexts within which the difference between the highest and lowest standards of living is restricted to certain limits. Where one is comparing conditions within a modern welfare state with those in a Central American country in which, among other things, people drink untreated water which they and their animals use for bathing and other purposes, the principle does not apply. We suggest that the reason why the principle does not apply is that it is indeed a derivative moral principle which is limited in scope. The precise character of the limitations of the principle is a controversial matter. How one formulates such limitations depends on his more basic moral principles. I shall argue however that on the basis of either of two moral principles one can provide explanations which tend to justify Shue's intuitions.

One may argue, in accord with John Rawls's difference principle, along the following lines: Unequal treatment is justified, according to the difference principle, providing that the inequality benefits the poorest peoples in the community and providing there is equality of opportunity. In countries with a large middle class, as in the industrialized democracies, unequal pay for equal work does not benefit the poorest workers. Unequal pay for equal work may benefit, for example, male workers who receive the higher pay than women doing comparable jobs, or it may benefit white workers who receive higher pay than black workers who do comparable jobs. It would be arguable that it benefitted the poorest workers only if the alternative for them was a significantly lower living standard. In industrialized democracies this is not normally the case. If people are unemployed, their essential needs are satisfied through various forms of social welfare. This is true, for the most part, even in the United States and Canada, although some people do slip through the social welfare net.

When we consider the question at issue concerning the salary for workers in third-world countries, the case is clearly not the same. Living conditions for many people in many of such countries are deplorable. Industrialization can provide a significant alternative. The inequality in pay for workers in these countries as compared to workers in Europe or North America is justifiable, in accord with the difference principle, on the grounds that it yields a significant benefit for the workers in the third-world countries.

We can argue for a similar conclusion in a second way — in accord with utilitarian principles concerning the satisfaction of interests to which many philosophers subscribe. It is assumed that people's interests differ in weight. One's interest in sufficient nourishing food has greater weight than one's interest in casual entertainment. Given a choice, one ought to try to satisfy weightier interests prior to attending to less weighty interests. If we assume that in general people's interest in their own survival and in the survival of their close relatives is weightier than their interest in equal treatment, we can argue that we ought to accept wage scales in the third-world countries which are are lower than those in industrialized countries. The argument, of course, depends on the assumption that the alternative to working and being paid at the lower rate for the worker in the third-world country is that the corporation won't set up operations in that country and that, in consequence, it is far more likely that his life or the lives of his family and friends will be nasty, brutish and short.

We should consider two objections to the above argument. We have been considering the issue of whether salary scales for workers in third-world countries which are lower for workers at comparable jobs in the industrialized countries are unjust to the workers in the third-world countries. We have argued that it is not unjust to those workers. However, it may be objected that by allowing corporations to pay workers in third-world countries at a lower rate we are permitting injustice to workers in the industrialized democracies who, in consequence of corporations moving to third-world nations, become unemployed and suffer in significant ways as a result of that.

In replying to this objection, I would argue along the following lines: the policy of permitting lower wage scales for workers in Bangladesh and comparable places need not be unjust. We have argued that it is in accord with the difference principle. It is also in accord with the principle of equal consideration of interests. Since the interests of workers in third-world countries in survival are weightier than the interests of workers in first-world countries in having a job, we ought to take steps to satisfy the interests in survival where this can be done prior to satisfying interests in employment. However, we have not yet considered the possibility that workers have a right to their job. A worker may claim that he has a right to his job and thus that when this job has been taken from him and given to someone else, he is being treated unjustly. This objection raises many issues and is too complex to fully answer here. However, if the objection is valid, it means at most that an employer ought not to shut down a manufacturing operation which is profitable and re-open in another location and hire new workers at lower salaries. In other words, it may be that a worker who has had a job has a right to that job. He ought not to be replaced by another worker if he is doing the job well. However, for new jobs, it is not at all clear that workers in one country have a right to those jobs — unless of course the new jobs were treated with the benefit of tax or other incentives on the part of the government of that country.

Our reply to this objection does not, of course, imply that the interests of workers in first-world countries in having jobs are not weighty. They are indeed weighty. They ought to be satisfied prior to other less weighty interests. This may require that within first-world countries social policies be adopted which contribute to elimination of unemployment. The unemployment of workers in first-world countries cannot be traced to one cause only. While we have spoken above in ways that suggest that the unequal wage scales are the cause of unemployment of workers in first-world countries, this is an oversimplification. The unequal wage scales are not a sufficient condition for people in first-world countries being unemployed. At most, the unequal wage scales are a part of a set of conditions which is sufficient for that effect. Other factors are also part of the same set of conditions. Modification of these

other factors would reduce or eliminate any unemployment which is associated with corporations transferring operations to third-world countries.

Another objection to the position we have supported is that the considerations we have cited as allowing corporations to pay third-world workers less for work of equal value appear also to permit exploitation of people who are extremely poor. Thus, it might be argued that reasoning such as I have defended would provide a justification for a corporation doing business in South Africa to pay black or colored workers at a lower rate than white workers in that country. It might be argued that the colored or black workers will be significantly better off if they are employed regardless of the fact that their salary is less than that of white workers doing the same or closely similar work.

In reply I would say that the question of investment in South Africa is a complex issue and the principle of equal pay for equal work is a middle-level moral principle. Presumably other moral principles would have a bearing on the question of investment in South Africa. The South African political system is fundamentally unjust. I would argue that corporations ought not to set up shop at all in South Africa unless their doing so contributes in a significant way towards eliminating the injustices practiced in that country. It is not at all clear that a multinational corporation, that set up shop in South Africa but paid black or colored workers at the low salaries paid such workers by South African business, would make any contribution toward eliminating that unjust system. However, were it reasonable to believe that a foreign corporation could contribute toward the reduction or elimination of injustice in South Africa while paying black or colored workers in that country less than workers in industrialized countries are paid for doing the same job then I believe such investment should be encouraged. Thus, this second objection is not really an objection to the thesis that I have defended.

REFERENCE

Shue, Henry, 1984. "Transnational Transgressions,"
New Introductory Essays in Business Ethics, ed. Tom
Regan. Random House, New York. p. 274 ff.

SUGGESTED FURTHER READINGS

ARNOVE, R.F. [ed] *Philanthropy and Cultural Imperialism: The Foundations at Home and Abroad.* Bloomington: Indiana Press University Press, 1982.

BEEMAN, DONALD AND SHERMAN TIMMINS. "Who Are the Villians in International Business?" *Business Horizons*, Vol. 25, No. 5, Sept./Oct. 1982.

BERLEANT, A. "Multinationals, Local Practice, and the Problem of Ethical Consistency." *Journal of Business Ethics*, Vol. 1, No. 3, 1982.

BRUMMER, J.J. "The Foreign Corrupt Practices Act and the Imposition of Values." *International Journal of Applied Philosphy*, Vol. 2, No. 2, 1985.

_____. "Business Ethics: Micro and Macro." *Journal of Business Ethics*, Vol. 4, No. 4, 1985.

D'ANDRADE, K., JR. "Bribery." *Journal of Business Ethics*, Vol. 4, No. 4, August 1985.

DI NORCIA, V. "The Leverage of Foreigners: Multinationals in South Africa." *Journal of Business Ethics*, Vol. 8, No. 11, 1989.

DONALDSON, T. "Multinational Decision-Making: Reconciling International Norms." *Journal of Business Ethics*, Vol. 4, No. 4, 1985.

JOHNSON, H. "Bribery in International Markets: Diagnosis, Clarification and Remedy." *Journal of Business Ethics*, Vol. 4, No. 6, 1985.

LANSING, PAUL AND SAROSH KURUVILLA. "Business Divestment in South Africa: In Whose Best Interest?" *Journal of Business Ethics*, Vol. 7, No. 8, 1988.

LONGNECKER, J., JOSEPH McKINNEY AND CARLOS MOORE. "The Ethical Issue of International Bribery: A Study of Attitudes Among U.S. Business Professionals." *Journal of Business Ethics*, Vol. 7, No. 5, May 1988.

RUDD, A. "Divestment of South Africa Equities: How Risky?" *California Management Review*, Vol. XXIII, No. 4, 1981.

UDOIDEM, INIOBONG. "Tips in Business Transaction: A Moral Issue." *Journal of Business Ethics*, Vol. 6, No. 8, Nov. 1987.

PART NINE
Advertising Ethics

INTRODUCTION

What constitutes the good life? From the time of Plato and Aristotle to the current day, philosphers have posed and continue to pose this question. The relevance of this question to Part Nine of this text may not at first be obvious. Yet when you think about advertising for a moment, you will realize that, for the most part, advertising introduces products to consumers which they either need or want. There are philosophical debates and a considerable literature about the difference between needs and wants. Presumably in the case of both needs and wants, the assumption is that their satisfaction will improve the quality of life and, hence, make for a better life.

But what is a better life? Is it the same as a good life? Would a good life mean not caring about material goods as much as we do in Western industrialized countries, and caring more about humanity? And what if we are deluded into believing falsehoods about products? What if I believe that product X will make my face look younger when it is just a common moisturizer? Does it matter that I am deluded, living in a fool's paradise, if I am happy? Or is it better to know the truth and be miserable than be fooled but content? Does false advertising matter if the consumer is satisfied with the product, be it moisturizer or floor cleaner or laundry detergent which promises to get your clothes "cleaner than clean" and "whiter than white"?

And what if we all actually shared the same vision of the minimal requirements for the "good life" but denied those who could not afford to meet those requirements access to them?

Many of the authors in this section of the text pose questions which raise these larger issues about the quality of life and what kind of a life is worth living. Advertisers, on the other hand, often find such a portrayal of advertising and marketing distorted and exaggerated. Their position is that, on the face of it, the ethics of advertising is clear and simple. Advertisers should, and generally do, supply us with information about desirable characteristics of the products they or their clients propose to sell. On the basis of this information, we, the consumers, are then rationally able to determine whether or not to purchase a product. We are able to determine whether the product with its advertised characteristics satisfies to an acceptable degree and at an acceptable cost certain of our wants, desires, or needs. Of course, sometimes this process misfires. The advertiser may provide us with false information; and in those cases where he does this knowingly and intentionally, his conduct is immoral, and possibly illegal. He has quite simply lied to us.

But matters are not always as clear-cut as this simple picture suggests. The deliberate utterance of a falsehood with the clear intention to deceive is only one, relatively infrequent, way in which morally questionable advertising can occur. As James Gaa and Charles Smith pointed out in another context in Part Three, the selective withholding or underplaying of relevant information can be just as deceptive, given certain expectations, as the explicit utterance of a falsehood. In "Advertising: Its Logic, Ethics and Economics," Alex Michalos outlines just such a case involving the federal government and its Loto Canada advertisements. According to Michalos, the government had unconscionably underplayed the rather meagre chances of actually holding a winning ticket. This, he claims, was unfair advertising, even though no falsehoods were uttered.

There are, of course, many other ways in which advertisements can be deceptive. Sometimes claims can be made which, though true, are uttered with the expectation that consumers will invalidly infer false conclusions from them. As Reese Miller suggests in "Persuasion and the Dependance Effect," they may unwittingly infer from the claim that no toothpaste has been proven more effective than Crest at removing plaque, that Crest *has* been proven to be *more* effective at removing plaque than *all* other toothpastes. The intention here is quite possibly to deceive and mislead, but once again no falsehoods have been uttered. Other examples leap readily to mind. We are all familiar with "Sale" signs declaring that everything in the store is "Up to 20% Off." The consumer mistakenly infers that items may be purchased for 20% below the going rate. But of course this may be false. The sign neglects to mention 20% *off what*. Perhaps it's 20% off the artificially inflated prices charged last week! And in any case, the sign does not say that things can be purchased *at* 20% off; what it says is that they may be purchased at *up to* 20% off. The shopper could discover upon entering the store that almost everything is being sold at only 5% below the norm. Once again there has been deception — and once again no falsehood has been uttered. Are the advertisers' actions morally wrong in these cases? Or must we invoke the doctrine of *caveat emptor* (let the buyer beware) to absolve the advertiser of moral responsibility? Must the advertiser be responsible for what the consumer, perhaps foolishly, does with the information he provides? Is it the advertiser's fault if, on the basis of her claim that "It's better in the Bahamas!", I foolishly infer that a quick trip to Freeport will do wonders for my sex life? These are questions which admit of no easy resolution.

So the ways in which immoral deception can occur in advertising are both numerous and complex, and this complicates our simple picture. Another complication lies in the assumption that advertisements are purely informational. According to Alex Michalos, to be effective, advertisements *must*, at least normally, be more than simply informational. "If ad sponsors only distributed information, then, unless their products really were superior to others *and* people could be counted upon to prefer superior products more often than inferior products, there would be no reason to suppose that information would motivate people to buy their products." However, he suggests, many products are practically indistinguishable from others in the same line. Advertisers are therefore "left with the logically and morally outrageous task of designing ads to persuade people to differentiate indistinguishables and to prefer one to another!"

Yet another difficulty arises from the assumption that advertisers simply cater to our antecedently existing desires and needs. This assumption was questioned some time ago by the economist John Kenneth Galbraith. Galbraith argued that the central function of advertising is not to provide information about how antecedently existing needs and desires might be satisfied, but to *create* desires and needs which it then offers to satisfy. Many of our desires and needs, on this view, are *dependent* on the processes by which they are designed to be satisfied.

This theory of "the dependence effect" has sparked considerable controversy among economists, philosophers, and advertisers. Of particular interest to the philosopher is the question whether, in manufacturing desires and needs, as well as the products to satisfy them, advertisers are manipulating and controlling us in ways which violate our dignity and autonomy. In the words of Robert Arrington, "Puffery, indirect information transfer, subliminal advertising — are these techniques of manipulation and control whose success shows that many of us have forfeited our autonomy and become a community, or herd, of packaged souls?" Arrington's answer is a qualified "No." The creation of desires through advertising may, but does not always or even frequently, control behaviour or create wants which are not rational or are not truly ours. More often than not, he submits, advertising creates and is intended to create the desire "for a particular object *given* that the purchaser has other desires." Given our antecedently existing "basic desire" for a youthful appearance, the advertiser influences but does not control us by creating the desire for Grecian Formula 16. She leads us to desire this particular object as a means of fulfilling the more basic desire. It is perhaps worth noting that on this view a beer company violates our autonomy only if, in addition to creating a desire to drink a particular brand of beer, it also helps create the desire to drink beer (or alcohol). And this is just what the typical beer ad is designed to do according to some of its critics. In their defence against this charge, many beer companies assert that their aim is merely to capture a larger share of existing markets, not to create new ones. Their aim, they say, is not to encourage drinking *per se*, only the drinking of their particular brand.

So, according to Arrington, the creation of desires through advertising is not in and of itself morally wrong. It is wrong only when it creates within the consumer desires which are foreign to her nature. Reese Miller agrees with the first point, but not the second. In his view, the deliberate creation of a desire by way of an advertisement is morally questionable when (but not necessarily only when) (a) the desire is based on a false or groundless belief concerning the product's inherent capacity to satisfy; and (b) this belief has been fostered, encouraged, or reinforced by the advertiser for the express purpose of creating desires she can then satisfy. In the course of his analysis, Miller distinguishes between "first-order" and "second-order" satisfaction. The former does, while the latter does not, result from any feature or effect of the product itself. The satisfaction of owning and wearing a *warm* overcoat on a cold winter's day is first order. The satisfaction of owning and wearing a *fashionable* overcoat through which the wind cuts mercilessly is entirely second order. It rests not on the inherent properties of the coat but on our belief about what sort of clothing is "in" — beliefs which, curiously enough, are true if and only if they are believed to be true. It is the encouragement through advertising of such groundless (and expensive) beliefs, and of the desires they produce, that interests Miller. In his view, there is something highly questionable in persuading a consumer to purchase a product if his having and retaining a belief that is either false or groundless is essential to any satisfaction which might result from that purchase.

In the final selection, John Waide argues that his main concern with advertising is with the quality of values created by advertising. Waide believes that what he calls "associative advertising" desensitizes those qualities in advertisers which we believe to be virtuous (e.g., compassion, concern, and sympathy for others), and also influences consumers to neglect the non-market-oriented values of humanity. Thus, argues Waide, associative advertising diminishes the quality of human virtue and what is most praiseworthy and good in human life.

42

Advertising: Its Logic, Ethics and Economics

ALEX C. MICHALOS

I. Introduction

The aim of this paper is to disclose some of the logical, ethical and economic features of contemporary advertising in North America. For reasons that are explained later, there appeared to be no satisfactory way to avoid ethics and economics, although the primary focus of this [paper] is logic.

After adopting a working definition of "advertising" in Section II, I show how the theory of public goods plus a few plausible assumptions would lead one to expect some deceptive advertising (Section III). Loto Canada advertising is considered as a case of deceptive advertising with a public sponsor (IV), and subliminal advertising is considered as a particular species of deceptive advertising (V). Finally, (VI) several criticisms of advertising and responses by two contemporary apologists are examined.

II. A working definition

According to the authors of a popular contemporary textbook on advertising, "Advertising is *mass communication* of *information* intended to *persuade* buyers so as to *maximize dollar profits*."[1] This definition has a number of implications that may not be immediately apparent or acceptable for all purposes. Although it is suitable for my purposes, some of its limitations should be mentioned before proceeding.

First, according to this definition advertisers are interested in communicating messages on a large scale. While we don't know how big "large" is, it may be assumed, for example, that at least not every display of products for sale will count as advertisement. Second, the immediate aim of the messages according to this definition is to get people to buy things. Thus, so-called social marketing or

From *Informal Logic*, J.A. Blair and R.H. Johnson (eds.). Pt. Reyes, CA: Edgepress, 1980. Reprinted by permission.

public service advertising is ignored. For example, Health and Welfare Canada's ads intended to get people to stop smoking and drinking are not covered by this definition. Third, the realisation of the immediate aim of advertising is supposed to contribute directly to the final aim which is the maximization of dollar profits. This apparently presupposes that the individuals or firms sponsoring advertising have as their primary aim the maximization of dollar profits. I suppose many of them have that aim, but there is some evidence that neither maximization generally nor dollar profit maximization in particular are universally accepted goals.

By accepting the Littlefield and Kirkpatrick definition of advertising, I have limited my discussion in some ways and expanded it in others. The limitations have already been indicated. The expansion comes as a result of thinking about advertising in its North American setting as a socioeconomic institution. From this point of view, it is virtually impossible to untangle logical, ethical and economic issues in a logically tidy fashion. We just have to put up with some fudge.

III. From information to persuasion and deception

Insofar as ads provide information more or less indiscriminately to great numbers of people, ads may be regarded as public goods. (To simplify things I usually use the single term "goods" as short for "goods and services." Strictly speaking, ads seem to be typically more like services (e.g. information) than material goods.) There is a substantial body of literature on the theory of public goods. Such goods are supposed to be distinguishable from private goods on the basis of *either* of two characteristics, namely, jointness and non-exclusiveness.[2] To say that a good is characterized by jointness is roughly to say that using it does not imply using it up. To say that a good is characterized by non-exclusiveness is roughly to say that non-purchasers cannot be excluded. Information is a perfect example of a public good displaying the character of jointness, and clean air or national defense are

examples of public goods displaying non-exclusiveness.

The fundamental problem concerning the provision of public goods is often referred to as the free-rider problem.[3] Since, without taking special measures, no one in a society can be excluded from public goods displaying non-exclusiveness, there is a temptation for (hypothetically self-serving) citizens to try to pass the costs of such goods on to everyone else. So, for example, Jones will leave his thermostat up because he will be able to enjoy the benefits of a national effort to conserve energy no matter what he does (one person's action has a negligible effect on the total picture,) and he won't have to bear the increased costs in chilly discomfort. Similarly, Smith will continue to throw his beer cans out the car window, to stay home on election day, and so on. If the environment is ever cleaned up or good politicians are ever elected, Smith will enjoy the benefits anyhow. Meanwhile, he lets the other people pay the tab. Smith and Jones, then, are free-riders.

If free-riders are regarded as the fundamental problem for the provision of public goods, coercion is usually regarded as the fundamental solution. People must finally be forced to pay taxes for public safety and fines for public pollution. For failing to be informed about the activities of their political leaders, they pay the price of polluted political processes. Of course in the best of all possible worlds, people would be aware of the nature of public goods, there would be no free-riders and no coercion. Part of the task of moralists is to help us get from this world to that other one — without, I would hope, leaving our corporeal bodies behind.

From the theory of public goods and the assumption that advertising involves the distribution of information, one may infer with some plausibility the reason for trying to make ads persuasive. If ad sponsors only distributed information, then, unless their products really were superior to others *and* people could be counted upon to prefer superior products more often than inferior products, there would be no reason to suppose that the information would motivate people to buy their products. In fact, many products really are practically indistinguishable from others in their line, e.g. cigarettes, beer, bicycles, soap, and so on. (Neither producers nor consumers have unlimited discriminatory powers.) So, if ads were only informative, they would probably produce random purchasing of such products. People would be informed that, say, one soap is as good as any other. So there would be no incentive to shop carefully. What's more, there would be no incentive in the form of private profit for producers to advertise. Information about such products would be a clear public good and producers would all tend to take a free ride.

Apparently, then, from the point of view of producers reaping private profits, many ads must be persuasive. However, insofar as products are practically indistinguishable from others in their line, advertisers are left with the logically and morally outrageous task of designing ads to persuade people to differentiate indistinguishables and to prefer one to another! As Rosser Reeves put it:

> Our problem is — a client comes into my office and throws two newly-minted half-dollars on my desk and says, 'Mine is the one on the left. You prove it's better.'[4]

To avoid misunderstanding, let me emphasize that I am *not* claiming that it is good or smart to accept private enterprise, profit maximization, self-serving behaviour or even advertising itself.[5] What I have tried to do is show that certain assumptions about these things and the theory of public goods lead fairly directly to the conclusion that sometimes (not necessarily always) advertisers are committed to logically and morally bad practices. I have no doubt at all that this fact is probably more or less clear and more or less tolerable to different advertisers. As a class of human beings, I imagine they are no better or worse than the rest of us.

IV. Misleading Ads: A Case Study

The last section may give one the impression that deceptive advertising is only a product of private enterprise. So I would like to review a particular case of such advertising that involves the Canadian government. Although the advertising is sponsored by the government through a Crown Corporation, it is not public service advertising or social marketing.

The amendments to the Combines Investigation Act which became law in December 1975 included several clauses concerning misleading advertising. The new clauses are supposed to "apply to all kinds of serious misrepresentation concerning products or services made to public, rather than merely to published advertisements. Not only the literal meaning of a representation, but also the general impression it conveys is to be taken into account."[6]

When I read the new provisions of the Act, I was impressed by the amount of protection the government was willing to give me. After failing to get the federal government to prosecute itself for patently misleading Loto Canada ads, I was impressed by the amount of deception the government was willing to practise. I can't go into all the details, but the following correspondence will demonstrate some of the logical and moral problems involved with misleading advertising.

The first letter was sent to "Box 99", which is the official complaint address in the Department of Consumer and Corporate Affairs.

July 19, 1977

Box 99
Dept. of Consumer &
Corporate Affairs
Ottawa, Ontario

Sir:

I am writing to appeal to you to put a stop to the seriously misleading advertising of Loto Canada on television. The ads continue to be very attractive and undoubtedly persuasive, but they are clearly giving a distorted picture of reality.

The ads make it seem as if the national lottery presented a good opportunity or chance to increase one's income with a windfall winning ticket. But since it is about 150 times more probable that one will die in an auto accident than that one will hold a winning ticket, the chances of the latter should not be described as good. If they are good, then the others are so much better that it is foolish to buy a ticket. It would seem unlikely that one will be alive long enough to collect it. That of course is false. We are much more secure in our autos than this scenario would suggest. The truth is that it's highly unlikely that any given individual will hold a winning ticket. So it is immoral and should be illegal for our government to create a quite different impression day after day on national television.

The credibility of government information releases is always under some strain in virtually all societies. But with blatantly misleading advertising the tension is needlessly increased. The government cannot expect to be able to con us with phoney ads at one moment and mobilize our support for national unity, belt tightening or other serious problems the next.

At the very least I urge you to see that the odds of winning are always in plain sight wherever lotteries are advertised. Honesty in advertising must be taken seriously.

Sincerely,

Alex C. Michalos

ACM/sdm

cc: Pierre Trudeau
     A. Alan Borovoy

I was notified that my letter had been forwarded to another office, and I sent the next letter to that office.

August 30, 1977

Chief of Operations
Marketing Practices Branch
Place du Portage, Phase I
68 Victoria Street
Hull, Quebec

Sir:

Concerning my complaint about Loto Canada TV ads which was forwarded to your office (File No. TP 100.402), I call your attention to the paragraph below from the Combines Investigation Act. I believe the most frequently broadcasted TV ads for Loto Canada violate this section of the Act by not explicitly stating the chances of winning.

Surely the intention of Parliament in this section is to preclude misleading advertising that stimulates people to act in the absence of full knowledge of the likely consequences of their action. The point of the TV ads is precisely to get people to do what Parliament was trying to prevent them from doing, namely, buy on impulse rather than on the basis of a rational calculation of the likely benefits of the purchase. Accordingly, I urge you to do your duty and see that these illegal and immoral ads are stopped.

Combines Investigation Act

Section 37.2(1): No person shall, for the purpose of promoting, directly or indirectly, the sale of a product, or for the purpose of promoting, directly or indirectly, any business interest, conduct any contest, lottery, game of chance or skill, or mixed chance and skill, or otherwise dispose of any product or other benefit by any mode of chance, skill or mixed chance and skill whatever unless

(a) there is adequate and fair disclosure of the number and value of the prizes and the chances of winning in any area to which prizes have been allocated.

Sincerely yours,

Alex C. Michalos.

ACM/sdm

I received the following response.

Director of Investigation & Research
Combines Investigation Act
Ottawa-Hull
K1A OC9

October 24, 1977

Dear Mr. Michalos:

Thank you for your letter of October 19, 1977 concerning your earlier complaint against Loto Canada Television advertising.

Section 37.2(1) (a), of the Combines Investigation Act states that in any contest promoting directly or indirectly the sale of a product there must be the following:

"adequate and fair disclosure of the number and approximate value of the prizes and of the area or areas to which they relate and of any fact within the knowledge of the advertiser that affects materially the chances of winning."

With respect to this section of the Act, we have reviewed past and present Loto Canada advertising and we believe that all the requirements of the section have been met. The facts which would materially affect one's chances of winning, i.e. the number of tickets available to be sold and the number and value of the prizes were disclosed. It was also the Director's opinion that adequate and fair disclosure occurred when the above information was made freely available to the public in newspapers and point of purchase display material during the run of the contest.

Should you have any additional questions on this matter please do not hesitate to contact this office.

Yours very truly,

Douglas G. Fraser,
Marketing Practices
Branch

DGF/kc

To that I replied:

77 10 31

Douglas G. Fraser
Marketing Practices Branch
Consumer and Corporate Affairs
Ottawa, Ontario

Dear Mr. Fraser:

I am very disappointed by your conclusion regarding Loto Canada advertisements. You apparently believe that if 99 percent of an advertising campaign is misleading but one percent is not, then the campaign is fair. This is outrageous.

Not once has Loto Canada advertised the odds of winning to a national TV audience. Occasionally a TV news reporter will mention the problem. You don't even perceive it as a problem. Posters can be found on most government buildings urging people to buy, but the posters never give the odds. So in most display areas, the odds are not "freely available" as you say. People have to go out of their way to find the odds of winning, but they are bombarded with advertising material urging them to "buy a ticket on their dream."

The advertising is not fact, and you ought to be ashamed of yourself if you are not able to perceive its serious bias and unfairness. We are being systematically misled and encouraged to buy on impulse by Loto Canada and Wintario ads, and it is your responsibility to prevent such things. But you won't. What a sad state of affairs. What a pathetic way to carry out an oath of office or run a government.

Sincerely yours,

Alex C. Michalos.

There was no reply to this last letter. I have since written to some MPs and received some sympathetic replies, but there has been no action by the government. If we assume that, for example, Mr. Fraser and others in the Marketing Practices Branch are just ordinary honest civil servants, then it must be granted that they see nothing in Loto Canada advertising that violates the Combines Investigation Act, Sec. 37.2(1) (a). At a minimum that tells us that the determination of misleading advertising is by no means a straightforward issue. I have already suggested what it tells us at a maximum in my last letter.

Since the above letters were written, a battle has raged between provincial and federal governments over the right or wisdom of federal versus provincial lotteries. Both levels of government see the lotteries as good sources of revenue, and both are apparently going to fight to keep the money coming in. There is no noticeable difference in the advertising for the two levels of government.

Given the wide variety of ways to win various sums of money, I now doubt that it will help much to give the odds of winning each sum. What is required is a clearly visible report of the *expected value* of every ticket purchased. If, for example, buyers knew that any ticket had an expected value of 50 cents or whatever and cost a dollar, then they could make an informed choice. Maybe most buyers would be willing to pay for the fun of the gamble. I certainly have no objection to people spending their own money in that way. But at present it's practically impossible to make an informed choice about a lottery ticket's value, and that is intolerable.

V. Subliminal Advertising

In the third section it was claimed that people pursuing private profit would often be engaged in deceptive advertising, and in the previous section it was claimed that government agencies also engage in such practices, wittingly or not. In this section I want to address the problem of subliminal advertising. This is the sort of advertising that Key claimed involved "intuitive or insight logic."[7] It is also the sort Johnson and Blair seem to have been thinking of when they wrote that

> . . . although advertising is an attempt to persuade, the type of persuasion generally used is not *rational*. Instead, advertising attempts to persuade us by appealing to our emotions (our hopes, fears, dreams), to the vulnerable spots in our egos (our desire for status and recognition), by applying pressure to the tender areas of our psyches. . . . In sum, *advertising has a logic of its own.* Thus, learning how to evaluate ads from the standard logical point of view becomes a gratuitous exercise."[8]

Key's *Subliminal Seduction*, like Vance Packard's *The Hidden Persuaders*[9] fifteen years earlier, stimulated a lot of discussion about advertising tactics. Key refers to subliminal perception as any "sensory inputs into the human nervous system that circumvent or are repressed from conscious awareness."[10] The most famous experimental proof of such perception involves the flashing of brief messages on a screen with a tachistoscope.[11] Although subjects typically have no recollection of seeing the messages, certain features of their behaviour, attitudes or beliefs indicate that the messages were received. For example, Key reported that in one experiment

. . . test groups were shown a sketch of an expressionless face. One group was subliminally exposed to the word *angry* subliminally tachistoscoped (at 1/3000th of a second) over the expressionless face. Another group received the word *happy* over the same face at the subliminal level. Both groups overwhelmingly interpreted the emotional content of the blank face consistent with the subliminal stimuli.[12]

When the Canadian Radio-Television Commission (CRTC) held hearings on subliminal ads in March 1975, no one seemed to have any use for them. The report of the Research Branch of CRTC concluded that

> There is no evidence currently available which indicates that advertisers can effectively use subliminal techniques to sell products because it is not clear what behavioural effects, if any, result from subliminal stimulation.[13]

Mr. K.B. Wong, a Research Assistant in the School of Business at Queen's University, told the CRTC that "the inability of a researcher to be able to predict how subliminal [stimuli] will be responded to, makes [them], for all practical purposes, very inadequate as a marketing tool."[14] The Counsel for the Association of Canadian Advertisers informed the CRTC that his client affirmed "that subliminal advertising techniques are not socially or morally justifiable in any media."[15] And the President of the Canadian Advertising Advisory Board claimed that

> We are unaware of any evidence that the use of such techniques has commercial value in the marketplace. Our objections to the process are based on ethical grounds. We in the business of advertising agree that advertising as such should be clearly identified and clearly identifiable and heartily support a ban on any explicit representations made in such a way as to escape conscious detection.[16]

Notwithstanding all these disclaimers, I have the distinct impression that the unwashed orphan that is uniformly turned away from everyone's front door is routinely welcomed at some other entrance. Some of the evidence leading to this impression can only be revealed by examining ads themselves. But remarks like the following from a spokesman for the Association of Canadian Advertisers can hardly be discounted.

> Once we accept my basic premise and that is that advertisers are entitled to do more than simply deliver a factual description of their product and service and price; once one acknowledges that *an advertiser is entitled* to appeal for the viewer's demand, *to create demand* for a class of goods and for his goods in particular, once we acknowledge that as being a principle — then *we have got to allow the advertiser to appeal to the conscious and sub-conscious appetites of the viewer.*[17] (Emphasis added.)

Insofar as the logic of advertising is the logic of subliminal perception and "subconscious appetites," I'm inclined to regard the subject as more suitable to empirical investigation than to conceptual analysis. Unfortunately, I just don't know how far the logic of advertising is a matter of such perception and appetites.

It has been suggested that subliminal advertising involves a unique sort of inference or implication relation. Maybe so. But I think what's involved is more a matter of interpretation than inference. Once a particular interpretation has been made of a feature of an ad, the move from that interpretation to the conclusion (practical or cognitive) planned by the advertiser may be a move that's indistinguishable from ordinary inference. The history of attempts to clarify concepts of implication, inference, entailment and so on is such that I am reluctant to wade into that sea of troubles unless absolutely forced.

At this point I want to set out in a slightly different direction, and to consider in detail a set of alleged criticisms of advertising and responses offered to the critics by Littlefield and Kirkpatrick (hereafter LK).

VI. Criticism, replies and comments

Before I begin the series of arguments in this section,

it may be worthwhile to expand a point that was just barely suggested in the second section. People have traditionally defended free speech or expression on two grounds. For some it has been a matter of moral principle that people ought to be allowed to express their views without fear of reprisals. While it may be a defeasible moral right, it is nevertheless a fundamental moral right, like the right to life, for example. For others, free expression has been defended as a matter of epistemological good sense. These people are more interested in the pursuit of truth and the avoidance of falsehood than they are in moral principles, and they see the free expression of ideas as a necessary condition of their epistemic aims.[18]

Of course, no one has to choose between these two different grounds for defending free expression, but historically I think people have tended to lean toward one or the other as especially weighty. (If one is primarily interested in the free expression of fictional or visual material (stories, films, paintings, sculptures) then one's defence might run more smoothly from moral grounds, while if one is primarily interested in the free expression of non-fictional or descriptively accurate material, then one's defence might run more smoothly from epistemic grounds.) The point I want to emphasize here, however, is that the two grounds often coalesce. In particular, objections to advertising practices may involve epistemological (or narrowly logical) and moral principles at the same time. Indeed, I suspect that this is typically the case. Hopefully, this will become clearer as the discussion proceeds. Let us turn immediately to a consideration of LK's critique.

1. LK begin by answering the charge that advertising is often "false, deceptive, and misleading, and that it conceals information which should be revealed and omits limitations and comparative disadvantages of the item advertised." In their view, "There is no justification for false, deceptive, or misleading advertising."[19] They don't deny the charge at all, and they claim that self-regulation and enlightened self-interest (buyers must want to return) tend to minimize such practices. In a very revealing passage they tell us that

To tell advertisers to limit themselves to non-emo-
tional, non-persuasive advertising would be to take
a step in a direction repugnant to most of us. 'It is
not the primary function of advertising to educate
or to develop reasoning powers.'[20]

Comment. We have already seen how an advertiser might be led down the garden path to deception. The question is: Are there any good reasons
for thinking that there is anything "repugnant"
about insisting on "non-persuasive advertising?"
Why should LK think that is demanding too
much? Presumably they have given their answer to
these questions a few pages later. "Persuasion and
influence here" they write, "are just as ethical as in
politics, religion, or education."[21] That is, they
believe that there is nothing in principle morally
wrong with trying to be persuasive as well as informative.

One would like, I suppose, to respond that there
is something better about trying to persuade people
to vote, worship God or get an education. But by
the time the words are uttered or written, I begin
to have second thoughts. *A priori* I doubt that any
old persuasive case made in behalf of any old political, religious or educational cause must be somehow morally superior to any old case made for any
old product or service. There are too many worthless and even dangerous political, religious and
educational causes and too many worthwhile
marketed products and services to permit full-scale
whitewashes. So I think we have to agree that there
is nothing in principle wrong with persuasive
advertising, and objectionable cases will have to be
tracked down and eliminated one at a time.

2. In response to the charge that "advertising
confuses and bewilders more than it helps," LK
claim that "differences of opinion are a basic element in our mores and in our norms." Besides, they
don't believe anyone can be "objective about his
brand any more than can . . . a bridegroom about
his bride . . ."[22]

Comment. The latter claim would be self-defeating if it were true, because the claim itself would
lack objective persuasiveness. But it's plainly false.
Everyone has all sorts of "objective" information

about his or her most cherished persons or things.
For example, I know the colour of my wife's hair
and eyes, her height and weight, how she prefers
her tea, and so on. Loving someone or something is
not the same as being struck dumb. Even the most
ardent fans are often prepared to admit that their
team doesn't have a hope in hell of winning, and
there would be no sense at all in anyone's favouring
the underdog unless there were a more or less objective assessment of just who *is* the underdog.

Some years ago David Braybrooke leveled the
charge of confusion against corporations in an
excellent article called "Skepticism of Wants, and
Certain Subversive Effects of Corporations on
American Values."[23] He mentioned in particular
"the systematic abuse of sexual interests, so that
people have their wants for automobiles and all
sorts of other things seriously mixed up with their
sexual desires."[24] On top of that he claimed that

> . . . corporations not only assist in confusing the
> public about what it might want, they also obstruct
> institutional remedies for the lack of information
> that leads . . . consumers into misjudgments about
> wants. . . . How shameful to find, besides the auto-
> mobile companies dragging their feet about safety
> standards, the tire companies doing the same
> thing; the grocers and packagers objecting to truth-
> in-packaging; the credit firms protesting against
> truth-in-lending."[25]

Braybrooke's primary concern was as much
epistemological as moral. Allegedly incorrigible
first-person reports about wants, he argued, could
be muddled and in need of revision given the heavy
hand of corporate advertising. What's more, it
seemed to him (as it does to me) to be morally
wrong for corporations to "obstruct institutional
remedies" in the ways he mentioned. It is one thing
to have differences of opinion, but something else to
prevent the unbiased assessment of claims and
counter-claims.

3. In response to the charge that advertising is
often "vulgar, and in poor taste," LK claim that
"advertising has no responsibility to raise
consumers' tastes, to preach, to try to elevate." In
fact, they insist that a wise advertiser "should deter-

mine what your tastes are" and "he should then cater to those tastes . . ."[26]

Comment. I wonder first, just whose responsibility LK suppose it is "to raise consumers' tastes" and "to try to elevate." I suppose they would want to claim that it is the business of teachers, professors, theologians and moralists "to try to elevate." Advertisers are in a different business, the business of selling products for profit. Therefore, they should have nothing to do with elevating people — unless it's a matter of elevated shoes, airplanes, and so on.

This is a familiar piece of buck-passing that must be met head-on. It is a mistake to think that things like values, norms and morality must exist in some proper ontological pigeon hole of the universe which one can dip into or avoid pretty much as one pleases. There is no good or evil in the abstract. Good and evil, values if you like, must be attached to things, actions, people and so on if they are to have any existence at all. Thus, for example, if there is any moral behaviour then it will be found by looking at ordinary behaviour from a moral point of view. If an advertiser produces ads in which false claims are intentionally made then the advertiser is a liar. All and only people who intentionally make false claims *can* be liars. They will be lying advertisers, lawyers, philosophers, plumbers, housewives or whatever, but they will be liars all the same. Therefore, and this is the main point, in order to have a world in which there are no liars, advertisers must stop lying when they are practicing their trade, lawyers must stop lying in their work, housewives must stop lying, and so on. There is no other way to make a world without liars.

The mistake involved here seems to be in regarding moral behaviour as a special kind of sociological role playing. However, being a morally decent person is not analogous to being a butcher, dentist or school teacher. It is not another role or alternative hat one slips on now and then. Insofar as analogies help, one may say that being a morally decent person is like being clean in the literal sense of well-scrubbed. There is no once-of-a-life-time bath one can take that will keep one clean forever. Every day brings new dirt. However, when one is clean or dirty, one is clean or dirty at dinner, selling shoes or buying hamburger. Being clean or dirty is not a sociological role in addition to the consumer's role, the farmer's role and so on. It is an aspect or feature of anyone operating in any of those roles. Just so, being a morally decent person or a person of high moral character is an aspect or feature of a person no matter what his or her sociological role. And it is an aspect that must be forever cultivated.

Insofar as one believes, for instance, that a world without liars is preferable to a world with liars, one ought to recognize one's responsibility for bringing about such a world. People who perform morally good actions are performing public services *par excellence* (which is not to say that agents receive no private benefits from such actions). Whenever one resists the temptation to lie, for example, one is engaged (in a limited way to be sure) in building a better world. It is the business of advertisers, bakers and all people in any role whatever "to try to elevate" the world by adopting a moral point of view *in that role.* To say that they might adopt a moral point of view when they are in some other role, like children in Sunday school, is to say that they don't know what it means to adopt a moral point of view or to try to be a morally decent person.

LK's second claim, namely, that advertisers should cater to consumer's tastes, must be understood conditionally in order to avoid contradicting their first commitment to persuade people to buy products so they can make a profit. Their aim must be to use people's tastes as instruments for manipulating people's consumption habits. Nothing in their position suggests that they would not mould people's tastes to suit their own purposes if they thought they could get away with it. Indeed, just the opposite is true. They are committed to persuading people to buy their products. In LK's own words: "In a sense, demand must be stimulated continuously." "The advertiser's hope is to make prospects dissatisfied with the present status and to keep current customers satisfied."[27] Insofar as anyone has a taste for something that is incompatible with an advertiser's product, the latter must try to alter the taste, the product or the appearance of the product. Since his primary objective is profit max-imization, any of these three alternatives would seem to be live options.

4. Advertisers have been charged with getting "consumers to buy what they (a) do not need, (b) should not have, and (c) cannot afford."[28] But LK reply that nothing is ever bought that is "not in response to an admission of *need*." Besides,

> . . . who knows what Mrs. Homemaker needs and can afford better than Mrs. H. herself? No one, of course. Just try to get her to buy something that will not (a) protect or (b) enhance her self concept.[29]

Comment. This is an incredible passage, but a fair reflection of LK's position. Roughly speaking, they have only substituted "need" for "want" in the old cliché "We only give the public what it wants."[30] The latter claim was thoroughly discredited by Braybrooke in the article cited earlier. But what can we make of the suggestion that sellers only give buyers what they need? Does anyone need Hostess Twinkies, Pringles, fat ties, thin ties, short skirts, long skirts, and so on? People have a need for food in order to live; but for Pringles? For grapefruits with skins that belong on footballs? That can't be true.

LK's claim about the role of the protection and enhancement of one's self concept in marketing is probably not as outrageous as it may appear. Basi-cally their view seems to be only that people will not pay money to be assaulted in any serious or threatening way. That's weaker than what seems to be claimed in the quotation above, namely, that people will only pay money for things that protect or enhance their self concept. I doubt that they imagine that, for example, everyone buying bananas, bandaids and buttons is somehow build-ing up his or her self concept.

5. In response to the charge that advertising helps create a society of "greedy, self-centered indi-viduals who worship materialism," LK reply that "The great majority of U.S. consumers believes that each person should expand his needs and then gratify them." What's more, however, they insist that "the purpose and responsibility of advertising

are to make ultimate consumers want to consume more."[31]

Comment. The sentence about "the great major-ity of U.S. consumers" leads me to suspect that LK have a peculiar notion of "needs." They seem to be claiming that one, anyone and everyone, ought to have more needs. For example, I suppose, they would want to say that I ought to need a Cadillac, hair dryer and over-the-calf socks. (In the latter case I would also need bigger calves — or garters.) On the contrary, I can't think of any good reason for having an obligation to need such things. I even suspect that the idea of obligations to need things is incoherent. So, *a fortiori* I think the claim that a majority of Americans believes I have such obliga-tions is completely unfounded and farfetched.

The second quotation from LK seems to grant the charge to which they are replying. The respon-sibility of advertisers, as LK see it, is to make people "want to consume more." It is not claimed, you may notice, that advertisers should try to make us want to consume more *if* that suits our tastes, *if* that's what we want or *if* that's what we need. The obligation is categorical. The name of their game is "Make people want to consume more." They explicitly claim that "Materialism should not be an end — it should be a means to even better ends."[32] But it's not clear what "better ends" LK might have in mind. Whatever we have, their aim is to make us want more. For advertisers with this view, the best of all possible worlds is one in which all human problems and solutions are manufactured and sold in the marketplace. It is a world in which everyone believes that he or she has some problem that can be solved by buying something that some-one else wants to sell. It is a merchandiser's para-dise. Indeed, LK suggest that the dream is not too far away.

> Every individual who wants to can be just as indi-vidualistic as he or she prefers. And there are enough dollars and enough different goods and services in our affluent society to afford wide ranges of choice. . . . Where else, indeed, in the world can the consumer find the assortment of merchandise and services with which to express his individ-uality?[33]

How easily they neglect the poor slobs who might want to "express their individuality" without buying something. The very idea of such individuals seems to have escaped these authors completely.

6. It has been charged that advertising constitutes a severe constraint on the content of media which rely on its revenue to stay in business. For example, because advertisers use TV programs as means of getting people to sit still for their ads, controversial programs or programs revealing views about the world that are incompatible with ads are systematically eliminated. LK reply that "commercial media can be 'free' of government subsidies, 'free' of political control because of dollars from advertisers. . . . Prices of media would have to be higher if there were no advertising."[34]

Comment. Apparently LK grant the charge but believe that constraints by advertisers are less objectionable than constraints by government, and there must be some constraints. Since some Canadian media are not free of government subsidies *or* advertisers, we may have the worst of both worlds. The mind boggles at the prospect of having all media run on the model of Pravda, but one can hardly be sanguine about the continuous parade of reminders of yellow teeth, bad breath, smelly armpits, flakey hair, irregular bowel movements, and so on. It seems to me, however, that this is a false dichotomy. CBC radio has no ads but is not constrained by the Canadian government any more than, say, CBS is constrained by the American government. The Trudeau administration has threatened the CBC through the CRTC and otherwise, but the Nixon administration was at least as difficult for CBS. It is also possible to sustain media outlets with private subscriptions, as we do with some journals, radio and TV stations. Finally, one can always withhold one's support (e.g. change the channel, avoid the product) or take action against offensive outlets (e.g. join citizen action groups opposed to misleading advertising, obscene displays, and so on). Granted that there must be constraints, one doesn't have to be on the receiving end all the time.

7. In response to the charge that ads stress "*insignificant* product details, *minor* product differences,

unimportant product changes," in a word, trivia, LK claim that what's minor today may be major tomorrow, that what's minor to you may be major to someone else and that what's perceived as major *becomes* major with increased consumption.[35]

Comment. Since ads are often intended to perform the logically impossible task that I earlier described as differentiating indistinguishables, the present charge would seem to be practically a truism. When products are essentially the same, only trivial differences will be discoverable. The point of LK's reply seems to be that if, for example, people are willing to pay two or three times as much for Bayer aspirin as they are for aspirin *simpliciter*, then it is at least misleading to regard the brand name as a trivial feature of the product. But that seems to be irrelevant to the critic's point. The latter seems to be that from the point of view of the effectiveness of the product or that for the sake of which the product is purchased, the brand name is an unimportant feature. (To simplify matters I am ignoring the fact that many drugs are purported to have a 30 percent placebo effect and that for some people the effectiveness of Bayer aspirin may be greater than the effectiveness of other brands.) Hence, by emphasizing the brand name, advertisers are guilty of trying to make something (significant) out of nothing (significant). Again, that is objectionable on epistemological and moral grounds.

8. It has been charged that advertising wastefully increases the cost of products. But LK claim that advertising represents "the shortest way to the market," to a mass market at least. It would be far more expensive to try to reach the same number of people with personal selling, house by house, person by person. They also insist that in theory effective advertising leads to increased sales volume which leads to lower per unit costs and the possibility of lower prices.[36] They grant, however, that "there is waste in advertising just as there is waste in competition," and then they wax poetic.

If advertising were outlawed, something would take its place, and that something would most probably be more wasteful and more expensive. Actually, attacks on *advertising* are really attacks on our system and structure of *business*. Advertising is a part of and in harmony with our free enterprise system. Our free enterprise or competitive system is the cause of advertising, not the result. . . . Abolish advertising because it is wasteful and competitive? Then abolish competition.[37]

Comment. As a former Fuller Brush man, I'm prepared to accept the claim that almost anything is more efficient than door to door selling. But personal problems aside, I would accept LK's first claim. Their theoretical defence of advertising is theoretically unexceptional, but not very useful in fact. What we would like to know, but don't, is the relative frequency with which the option of lowering prices is adopted over the option of reinvesting the new profits, distributing them to stockholders, employees, and so on. It would also be useful to know how wasteful advertising practices are, not necessarily in relation to nonadvertising activities but in relation to some hypothetical optimum. (Presumably there is a vast literature on the return-on-the-dollar of various sorts of advertising, although I'm unfamiliar with most of it.)

The most interesting part of LK's remarks in response to the charge of wastefulness is their claim, hardly necessary in this context, that our "competitive system is the cause of advertising." Does competition for market shares entail advertising? Could there be a competitive marketing system without ads? From a logical point of view, of course the two ideas are separable. We have already contrasted door to door marketing with marketing through advertising. In fact many producers simply produce their products and make them available to purchasers without advertising as that term has been defined here, e.g. farmers in community markets or roadside stands. Unless one loosens up the definition of advertising to include any sort of display of products for sale, it should be possible to easily multiply such examples of non-advertising marketing.

It is illegal to advertise some services in some areas, although the services themselves are quite legal, e.g. legal and medical services. While competition is probably far from the minds of many professionals, a spokesman for the Canadian Medical Association once said in a radio interview that one must remember that doctors are small businessmen. (Some of them are relatively big businessmen.)

Granted that competitive marketing does not logically imply advertising, the former seems to be a major contributing factor toward the existence of the latter. After all, it doesn't require much imagination to realise that, for example, if farmer Brown can sell his corn by merely putting it on display in a roadside stand, then he can increase the chances of a sale by increasing the visibility of his stand with big signs, by placing some signs far enough away so people can prepare to stop and finally by putting "signs" (ads) in news media to get people to make a special trip out to the stand. If they like his corn, maybe they will go for his chickens too. Maybe people that won't go for the corn will go for the chickens. Given the aim of selling something for profit in a world of scarce resources, it's difficult to imagine anything arising more naturally than advertising. That may be what led LK to see advertising and competition inexorably connected.

It is perhaps worthwhile to add here that I suspect a better case can be made for allowing advertising on the basis of a Principle of Liberty than on the basis of competition. By a "Principle of Liberty" I mean something like the maxim that people ought to be allowed to do whatever they wish as long as it doesn't harm anyone else. Not many people are likely to object to that idea. It follows immediately, then, that insofar as advertising is harmless, it is allowable, and much of it probably is harmless. Perhaps this is the sort of argument LK had in mind when they mentioned "free enterprise" in conjunction with competition. Nevertheless, neither "free enterprise" nor a Principle of Liberty implies advertising.

9. Several charges have been leveled against advertising as a monopolistic force in the marketplace. For example, advertising has been charged with creating barriers to entry for new products or firms, discouraging price competition and contributing to large-scale economic concentration.[38] LK's general position with respect to such criticisms is that monopolies came before advertising.

While they don't and shouldn't deny that advertising represents some sort of a barrier to entry, they mention several others that may be at least as significant, e.g. "inadequate capital; lack of a full line of products; lack of competence, either manufacturing *or* marketing; channel difficulties, such as unavailability of essential distributors, or the magnitude of the job of building a dealer organization; patents."[39]

Comment. LK's response is perilously close to claiming that advertising is *not* objectionable because other things *are* objectionable. Whether or not that is their argument, it is obviously unsound. *A priori* I suppose that anything that gives one a marketing advantage over competitors might contribute toward monopoly, perfect competition or something in between, depending on the total distribution of advantages and disadvantages. So it's misleading to claim that any particular marketing advantage, as for example a good advertising scheme, is *on its own* a monopolistic force. In principle such schemes could bring about perfect competition if all other competitors were lucky enough to create equally advantageous schemes. Of course in fact some producers, for one reason or another, can mount more successful advertising campaigns than other producers, and the latter have nothing to compensate for their weakness. Some people are

economically wiped out in such cases, even though the losers may be more efficient operators than the winners on a dollar for dollar or product for product basis. That's the sort of thing most small businesspeople, which means most businesspeople, want to see prevented; but it happens. Legislation like the Combines Investigation Act provides some protection against big or unscrupulous operators, but, as suggested earlier in the case of Loto Canada ads, the legislation is not self-implementing.

VII. Conclusion

The aim of this investigation was to disclose some of the logical, ethical and economic features of contemporary advertising in North America. Given such a diffuse goal, it was fairly easy to hit the mark. After adopting a working definition of "advertising", I showed how the theory of public goods plus a few plausible factual assumptions would lead one to expect some deceptive advertising. Loto Canada advertising was reviewed as a case of deceptive advertising with a public sponsor. Subliminal advertising was briefly reviewed as a particular sort of deceptive advertising. Finally, several criticisms of advertising and responses by Littlefield and Kirkpatrick were examined.[40]

ENDNOTES

1. J.E. Littlefield and C.A. Kirkpatrick, *Advertising: Mass Communication in Marketing*, Boston: Houghton Mifflin Co., 1970, p. 100.

2. M. Olson, "The Plan and Purpose of a Social Report," *The Public Interest*, 1969, p. 94. See also M. Olson, *The Logic of Collective Action*, Cambridge: Harvard University Press, 1965.

3. R.N. McKean, "Collective Choice," *Social Responsibility and the Business Predicament*, ed. J.W. McKie, Washington: The Brookings Institution, 1974, pp. 109-134.

4. Quoted from R.H. Johnson and J.A. Blair, *Logical Self-Defense*, Toronto: McGraw-Hill Ryerson, 1977, p. 222.

5. I have argued against maximization policies and self-serving in *Foundations of Decision-Making*, Ottawa: Association for Publishing in Philosophy, 1978.

6. Canada, Consumer and Corporate Affairs, *Proposals for a New Competition Policy for Canada: First Stage*, Ottawa, 1973, p. 5. Excellent discussions of misleading advertising and the Combines Investigation Act may be found in D.N. Thompson, "The Canadian

Approach to Misleading Advertising." *Problems in Canadian Marketing*, ed. D.N. Thompson, Chicago: American Marketing Association, 1977, pp. 157-184, and W.T. Stanbury, *Business Interests and the Reform of Canadian Competition Policy, 1971-1975*, Toronto: Methuen, 1977.

7. W.B. Key, *Subliminal Seduction*, New York: The New American Library, 1973, p. 11.

8. Johnson and Blair, *op. cit.*, p. 218.

9. V. Packard, *The Hidden Persuaders*, New York: David McKay Co., 1957.

10. Key, *op. cit.*, p. 18.

11. Key, *op. cit.*, p. 21, and S.J. Arnold, J.G. Barnes and K.B. Wong, *Brief to the Canadian Radio-Television Commission on Subliminal Perception: Implications for Regulation*, mimeographed, March 11, 1975, p. 11.

12. Key, *op. cit.*, pp. 33-34.

13. Canadian Radio-Television Commission, Research Branch, *Subliminal Perception and Subliminal Advertising: An Overview*, mimeographed, March 1975, p. 29.

14. Canadian Radio-Television Commission, *Hearings on Proposed Amendments to the Television Broadcasting Regulations (Advertising "Subliminal Technique")*, mimeographed, March 11, 1975, pp. 446-447.

15. From a letter of the ACA Counsel, C.R. Thomson, to the CRTC, February 17, 1975, p. 1.

16. From a letter of the President of CAAB, R.E. Oliver, to the CRTC, February 24, 1975, p. 2.

17. C.R. Thomson in the CRTC *Hearings*, pp. 458-459.

18. For an epistemic approach see J.S. Mill, *On Liberty*, London: Parker, 1859, and for a strictly moral approach see the United Nations Universal Declaration of Human Rights or the Canadian Bill of Rights in P.E. Trudeau, *A Canadian Charter of Human Rights*, Ottawa: Information Canada, 1968.

19. Littlefield and Kirkpatrick, *op. cit.*, p. 115.

20. *Ibid.* The quotation is from S.V. Smith, "Advertising in Perspective" in J.W. Towle, ed., *Ethics and Standards in American Business*, Boston: Houghton Mifflin

Co., 1964, p. 174. For a good analysis of self-regulation in Canada see M.S. Moyer and J.C. Banks, "Industry Self-Regulation: Some Lessons from the Canadian Advertising Industry," *Problems in Canadian Marketing*, ed., D.N. Thompson, Chicago: American Marketing Association, 1977, pp. 185-202.

21. Littlefield and Kirkpatrick, *op. cit.*, p. 115.

22. *Ibid.*

23. D. Braybrooke, "Skepticism of Wants, and Certain Subversive Effects of Corporations on American Values," *Human Values and Economic Policy*, ed. S. Hook, New York: New York University Press, 1967, pp. 224-239.

24. *Ibid.*, p. 230.

25. *Ibid.*, pp. 230-231.

26. Littlefield and Kirkpatrick, *op. cit.*, pp. 116-117.

27. *Ibid.*, p. 124 and p. 102.

28. *Ibid.*, p. 117.

29. *Ibid.*

30. On the differences between needs and wants see Michalos, *op. cit.*

31. Littlefield and Kirkpatrick, *op. cit.*, p. 117.

32. *Ibid.*

33. *Ibid.*, p. 118.

34. *Ibid.*

35. *Ibid.*, pp. 118-119.

36. *Ibid.*, p. 119.

37. *Ibid.*, pp. 123-124.

38. *Ibid.*, pp. 121-123.

39. *Ibid.*, p. 122.

40. I would like to thank Rodrique Chiasson, Acting Director-General of the Research Branch of the CRTC for providing a copy of the Examination File on "Regulation and Policies Proposed Amendment to the Television Broadcasting Regulations," Ottawa Hearing, March 11, 1975.

43

Advertising
and Behavior Control

ROBERT L. ARRINGTON

Consider the following advertisements:

(1) "A woman in *Distinction Foundations* is so beautiful that all other women want to kill her."

(2) Pongo Peach color from Revlon comes "from east of the sun . . . west of the moon where each tomorrow dawns." It is "succulent on your lips" and "sizzling on your finger tips (And on your toes, goodness knows)." Let it be your "adventure in paradise."

(3) "Musk by English Leather — The Civilized Way to Roar."

(4) "Increase the value of your holdings. Old Charter Bourbon Whiskey — The Final Step Up."

(5) Last Call Smirnoff Style: "They'd never really miss us, and it's kind of late already, and its quite a long way, and I could build a fire, and you're looking very beautiful, and we could have another martini, and its awfully nice just being home . . . you think?"

(6) A Christmas Prayer. "Let us pray that the blessings of peace be ours — the peace to build and grow, to live in harmony and sympathy with others, and to plan for the future with confidence." New York Life Insurance Company.

These are instances of what is called puffery — the practice by a seller of making exaggerated, highly fanciful or suggestive claims about a product or service. Puffery, within ill-defined limits, is legal. It is considered a legitimate, necessary, and very successful tool of the advertising industry. Puffery is not just bragging; it is bragging carefully designed to achieve a very definite effect. Using the techniques of so-called motivational research, advertising firms first identify our often hidden needs (for security, conformity, oral stimulation) and our desires (for power, sexual dominance and dalliance, adventure) and then they design ads which respond to these needs and desires. By associating a product, for which we may have little or no direct need or desire, with symbols reflecting the fulfillment of these other, often subterranean interests, the advertisement can quickly generate large numbers of consumers eager to purchase the product advertised. What woman in the sexual race of life could resist a foundation which would turn other women envious to the point of homicide? Who can turn down an adventure in paradise, east of the sun where tomorrow dawns? Who doesn't want to be civilized and thoroughly libidinous at the same time? Be at the pinnacle of success — drink Old Charter. Or stay at home and dally a bit — with Smirnoff. And let us pray for a secure and predictable future, provided for by New York Life, God willing. It doesn't take very much motivational research to see the point of these sales pitches. Others are perhaps a little less obvious. The need to feel secure in one's home at night can be used to sell window air conditioners, which drown out small noises and provide a friendly, dependable companion. The fact that baking a cake is symbolic of giving birth to a baby used to prompt advertisements for cake mixes which glamorized the 'creative' housewife. And other strategies, for example involving cigar symbolism, are a bit too crude to mention, but are nevertheless very effective.

Don't such uses of puffery amount to manipulation, exploitation, or downright control? In his very popular book *The Hidden Persuaders*, Vance Packard points out that a number of people in the advertising world have frankly admitted as much:

> As early as 1941 Dr. Dichter (an influential advertising consultant) was exhorting ad agencies to recognize themselves for what they actually were — "one of the most advanced laboratories in psychology." He said the successful ad agency "manipulates human motivations and desires and develops a need for goods with which the public has at one time been unfamiliar — perhaps even undesirous of purchasing." The following year *Advertising Agency* carried an ad man's statement that psychology not only holds promise for understanding people but "ultimately for controlling their behavior."[1]

Such statements led Packard to remark: "With all this interest in manipulating the customer's sub-conscious, the old slogan 'let the buyer beware' began taking on a new and more profound meaning."[2]

B.F. Skinner, the high priest of behaviorism, has expressed a similar assessment of advertising and related marketing techniques. Why, he asks, do we buy a certain kind of car?

> Perhaps our favorite TV program is sponsored by the manufacturer of that car. Perhaps we have seen pictures of many beautiful or prestig[ious] persons driving it — in pleasant or glamorous places. Perhaps the car has been designed with respect to our motivational patterns: the device on the hood is a phallic symbol; or the horsepower has been stepped up to please our competitive spirit in enabling us to pass other cars swiftly (or, as the advertisements say, 'safely'). The concept of freedom that has emerged as part of the cultural practice of our group makes little or no provision for recognizing or dealing with these kinds of control.[3]

In purchasing a car we may think we are free, Skinner is claiming, when in fact our act is completely controlled by factors in our environment and in our history of reinforcement. Advertising is one such factor.

A look at some other advertising techniques may reinforce the suspicion that Madison Avenue controls us like so many puppets. T.V. watchers surely have noticed that some of the more repugnant ads are shown over and over gain, *ad nauseam*. My favorite, or most hated, is the one about A-1 Steak Sauce which goes something like this: Now, ladies and gentlemen, what *is* hamburger? It has succeeded in destroying my taste for hamburger, but it has surely drilled the name of A-1 Sauce into my head. And that is the point of it. Its very repetitiousness has generated what ad theorists call *information*. In this case it is indirect information, information derived not from the content of what is said but from the fact that it is said so often and so vividly that it sticks in one's mind — i.e., the information yield has increased. And not only do I always remember A-1 Sauce when I go to the grocers, I tend to assume that any product advertised so often has to be good — and so I usually buy a bottle of the stuff.

Still another technique: On a recent show of the television program 'Hard Choices' it was demonstrated how subliminal suggestion can be used to control customers. In a New Orleans department store, messages to the effect that shoplifting is wrong, illegal, and subject to punishment were blended into the Muzak background music and masked so as not to be consciously audible. The store reported a dramatic drop in shoplifting. The program host conjectured whether a logical extension of this technique would be to broadcast subliminal advertising messages to the effect that the store's $15.99 sweater special is the "bargain of a lifetime." Actually, this application of subliminal suggestion to advertising has already taken place. Years ago in New Jersey a cinema was reported to have flashed subthreshold ice cream ads onto the screen during regular showings of the film — and, yes, the concession stand did a landslide business.[4]

Puffery, indirect information transfer, subliminal advertising — are these techniques of manipulation and control whose success shows that many of us have forfeited our autonomy and become a community, or herd, of packaged souls?[5] The business world and the advertising industry certainly reject this interpretation of their efforts. *Business Week*, for example, dismissed the charge that the science of behavior, as utilized by advertising, is engaged in human engineering and manipulation. It editorialized to the effect that "it is hard to find anything very sinister about a science whose principal conclusion is that you get along with people by giving them what they want."[6] The theme is familiar: businesses just give the consumer what he/she wants; if they didn't they wouldn't stay in business very long. Proof that the consumer wants the products advertised is given by the fact that he buys them, and indeed often returns to buy them again and again.

The techniques of advertising we are discussing have had their more intellectual defenders as well. For example, Theodore Levitt, Professor of Business Administration at the Harvard Business School, has defended the practice of puffery and the use of techniques depending on motivational research.[7] What would be the consequences, he asks us, of deleting all exaggerated claims and fanciful associations from advertisements? We would be left with literal descriptions of the empirical characteristics of products and their functions. Cosmetics would be presented as facial and bodily lotions and powders which produce certain odor and color changes; they would no longer offer hope or adventure. In addition to the fact that these products would not then sell as well, they would not, according to Levitt, please us as much either. For it is hope and adventure we want when we buy them. We want automobiles not just for transportation, but for the feelings of power and status they give us. Quoting T.S. Eliot to the effect that "Human kind cannot bear very much reality," Levitt argues that advertising is an effort to "transcend nature in the raw," to "augment what nature has so crudely fashioned." He maintains that "everybody everywhere wants to modify, transform, embellish, enrich and reconstruct the world around him." Commerce takes the same liberty with reality as the artist and the priest — in all three instances the purpose is "to influence the audience by creating illusions, symbols, and implications that promise more than pure functionality." For example, "to amplify the temple in men's eyes, (men of cloth) have, very realistically, systematically sanctioned the embellishment of the houses of the gods with the same kind of luxurious design and expensive decoration that Detroit puts into a Cadillac." A poem, a temple, a Cadillac — they all elevate our spirits, offering imaginative promises and symbolic interpretations of our mundane activities. Seen in this light, Levitt claims, "Embellishment and distortion are among advertising's legitimate and socially desirable purposes." To reject these techniques of advertising would be "to deny man's honest needs and values."

Philip Nelson, a Professor of Economics at SUNY-Binghamton, has developed an interesting defence of indirect information advertising.[8] He argues that even when the message (the direct information) is not credible, the fact that the brand is advertised, and advertised frequently, is valuable indirect information for the consumer. The reason for this is that the brands advertised most are more likely to be better buys — losers won't be advertised a lot, for it simply wouldn't pay to do so. Thus even if the advertising claims made for a widely advertised product are empty, the consumer reaps the benefit of the indirect information which shows the product to be a good buy. Nelson goes so far as to say that advertising, seen as information, does not require an intelligent human response. If the indirect information has been received and has had its impact, the consumer will purchase the better buy even if his explicit reason for doing so is silly, e.g., he naively believes an endorsement of the product by a celebrity. Even though his behavior is overtly irrational, by acting on the indirect information he is nevertheless doing what he ought to do, i.e., getting his money's worth. "'Irrationality' is rational," Nelson writes, "if it is cost-free."

I don't know of any attempt to defend the use of subliminal suggestion in advertising, but I can imagine one form such an attempt might take. Advertising information, even if perceived below the level of conscious awareness, must appeal to some desire on the part of the audience if it is to trigger a purchasing response. Just as the admonition not to shoplift speaks directly to the superego, the sexual virtues of TR-7's, Pongo Beach, and Betty Crocker cake mix present themselves directly to the id, by bypassing the pesky reality principle of the ego. With a little help from our advertising friends, we may remove a few of the discontents of civilization and perhaps even enter into the paradise of polymorphous perversity.[9]

The defense of advertising which suggests that advertising simply is information which allows us to purchase what we want, has in turn been challenged. Does business, largely through its advertising efforts, really make available to the consumer what he/she desires and demands? John Kenneth Galbraith has denied that the matter is as straightforward as this.[10] In his opinion the desires to which business is supposed to respond, far from being original to the consumer, are often themselves created by business. The producers make both the product and the desire for it, and the "central function" of advertising is "to create desires." Galbraith coins the term 'The Dependence Effect' to designate the way wants depend on the same process by which they are satisfied.

David Braybrooke has argued in similar and related ways.[11] Even though the consumer is, in a sense, the final authority concerning what he wants, he may come to see, according to Braybrooke, that he was mistaken in wanting what he did. The statement 'I want x', he tells us, is not incorrigible but is "ripe for revision." If the consumer had more objective information than he is provided by product puffing, if his values had not been mixed up by motivational research strategies (e.g., the confusion of sexual and automotive values), and if he had an expanded set of choices instead of the limited set offered by profit-hungry corporations, then he might want something quite different from what he presently wants. This shows, Braybrooke thinks, the extent to which the consumer's wants are a function of advertising and not necessarily representative of his real or true wants.

The central issue which emerges between the above critics and defenders of advertising is this: do the advertising techniques we have discussed involve a violation of human autonomy and a manipulation and control of consumer behavior, *or* do they simply provide an efficient and cost-effective means of giving the consumer information on the basis of which he or she makes a free choice. Is advertising information, or creation of desire?

To answer this question we need a better conceptual grasp of what is involved in the notion of autonomy. This is a complex, multifaceted concept, and we need to approach it through the more determinate notions of (a) autonomous desire, (b) rational desire and choice, (c) free choice, and (d) control or manipulation. In what follows I shall offer some tentative and very incomplete analyses of these concepts and apply the results to the case of advertising.

(a) **Autonomous Desire.** Imagine that I am watching T.V. and see an ad for Grecian Formula 16. The thought occurs to me that if I purchase some and apply it to my beard, I will soon look younger — in fact I might even be myself again. Suddenly I want to be myself! I want to be young again! So I rush out and buy a bottle. This is our question: was the desire to be younger manufactured by the commercial, or was it 'original to me' and truly mine? Was it autonomous or not?

F.A. von Hayek has argued plausibly that we should not equate nonautonomous desires, desires which are not original to me or truly mine, with those which are culturally induced.[12] If we did equate the two, he points out, then the desires for music, art, and knowledge could not properly be attributed to a person as original to him, for these are surely induced culturally. The only desires a person would really have as his own in this case would be the purely physical ones for food, shelter, sex, etc. But if we reject the equation of the nonautonomous and the culturally induced, as von Hayek would have us do, then the mere fact that my desire to be young again is caused by the T.V. commercial — surely an instrument of popular culture transmission — does not in and of itself show that this is not my own, autonomous desire. Moreover, even if I never before felt the need to look young, it doesn't follow that this new desire is any less mine. I haven't always liked 1969 Aloxe Corton Burgundy or the music of Satie, but when the desires for these things first hit me, they were truly mine.

This shows that there is something wrong in setting up the issue over advertising and behavior control as a question whether our desires are truly ours *or* are created in us by advertisements. Induced and autonomous desires do not separate into two mutually exclusive classes. To obtain a better understanding of autonomous and nonautonomous desires, let us consider some cases of a desire which a person does not *acknowledge* to be his own even though he *feels* it. The kleptomaniac has a desire to steal which in many instances he repudiates, seeking by treatment to rid himself of it. And if I were suddenly overtaken by a desire to attend an REO* concert, I would immediately disown this desire,

claiming possession or momentary madness. These are examples of desires which one might have but with which one would not identify. They are experienced as foreign to one's character or personality. Often a person will have what Harry Frankfurt calls a second-order desire.[13] In such cases, the first-order desire is thought of as being nonautonomous, imposed on one. When on the contrary a person has a second-order desire to maintain and fulfill a first-order desire, then the first-order desire is truly his own, autonomous, original to him. So there is in fact a distinction between desires which are the agent's own and those which are not, but this is not the same as the distinction between desires which are innate to the agent and those which are externally induced.

If we apply the autonomous/nonautonomous distinction derived from Frankfurt to the desires brought about by advertising, does this show that advertising is responsible for creating desires which are not truly the agent's own? Not necessarily, and indeed not often. There may be some desires I feel which I have picked up from advertising and which I disown — for instance, my desire for A-1 Steak Sauce. If I act on these desires it can be said that I have been led by advertising to act in a way foreign to my nature. In these cases my autonomy has been violated. But most of the desires induced by advertising I fully accept, and hence most of these desires are autonomous. The most vivid demonstration of this is that I often return to purchase the same product over and over again, without regret or remorse. And when I don't, it is more likely that the desire has just faded than that I have repudiated it. Hence, while advertising may violate my autonomy by leading me to act on desires which are not truly mine, this seems to be the exceptional case.

Note that this conclusion applies equally well to the case of subliminal advertising. This may generate subconscious desires which lead to purchases, and the act of purchasing these goods may be inconsistent with other conscious desires I have, in which case I might repudiate my behavior and by implication the subconscious cause of it. But my subconscious desires may not be inconsistent in this way with my conscious ones; my id may be cooper-

---

*A "heavy metal" rock band—ED.

ative and benign rather than hostile and malign.[14] Here again, then, advertising may or may not produce desires which are 'not truly mine.'

What are we to say in response to Braybrooke's argument that insofar as we might choose differently if advertisers gave us better information and more options, it follows that the desires we have are to be attributed more to advertising than to our own real inclinations? This claim seems empty. It amounts to saying that if the world we lived in, and we ourselves, were different, then we would want different things. This is surely true, but it is equally true of our desire for shelter as of our desire for Grecian Formula 16. If we lived in a tropical paradise we would not need or desire shelter. If we were immortal, we would not desire youth. What is true of all desires can hardly be used as a basis for criticizing some desires by claiming that they are nonautonomous.

(b) Rational Desire and Choice. Braybrooke might be interpreted as claiming that the desires induced by advertising are often irrational ones in the sense that they are not expressed by an agent who is in full possession of the facts about the products advertised or about the alternative products which might be offered him. Following this line of thought, a possible criticism of advertising is that it leads us to act on irrational desires or to make irrational choices. It might be said that our autonomy has been violated by the fact that we are prevented from following our rational wills or that we have been denied the 'positive freedom' to develop our true, rational selves. It might be claimed that the desires induced in us by advertising are false desires in that they do not reflect our essential, i.e., rational, essence.

The problem faced by this line of criticism is that of determining what is to count as rational desire or rational choice. If we require that the desire or choice be the product of an awareness of *all* the facts about the product, then surely every one of us is always moved by irrational desires and makes nothing but irrational choices. How could we know all the facts about a product? If it be required only that we possess all of the *available* knowledge about

the product advertised, then we still have to face the problem that not all available knowledge is *relevant* to a rational choice. If I am purchasing a car, certain engineering features will be, and others won't be, relevant, *given what I want in a car*. My prior desires determine the relevance of information. Normally a rational desire or choice is thought to be one based upon relevant information, and information is relevant if it shows how other, prior desires may be satisfied. It can plausibly be claimed that it is such prior desires that advertising agencies acknowledge, and that the agencies often provide the type of information that is relevant in light of these desires. To the extent that this is true, advertising does not inhibit our rational wills or our autonomy as rational creatures.

It may be urged that much of the puffery engaged in by advertising does not provide relevant information at all but rather makes claims which are not factually true. If someone buys Pongo Peach in anticipation of an adventure in paradise, or Old Charter in expectation of increasing the value of his holdings, then he/she is expecting purely imaginary benefits. In no literal sense will the one product provide adventure and the other increased capital. A purchasing decision based on anticipation of imaginary benefits is not, it might be said, a rational decision, and a desire for imaginary benefits is not a rational desire.

In rejoinder it needs to be pointed out that we often wish to purchase subjective effects which in being subjective are nevertheless real enough. The feeling of adventure or of enhanced social prestige and value are examples of subjective effects promised by advertising. Surely many (most?) advertisements directly promise subjective effects which their patrons actually desire (and obtain when they purchase the product), and thus the ads provide relevant information for rational choice. Moreover, advertisements often provide accurate indirect information on the basis of which a person who wants a certain subjective effect rationally chooses a product. The mechanism involved here is as follows.

To the extent that a consumer takes an advertised product to offer a subjective effect and the

product does not, it is unlikely that it will be purchased again. If this happens in a number of cases,
the product will be taken off the market. So here the
market regulates itself, providing the mechanism
whereby misleading advertisements are withdrawn
and misled customers are no longer misled. At the
same time, a successful bit of puffery, being one
which leads to large and repeated sales, produces
satisfied customers and more advertising of the product. The indirect information provided by such
large-scale advertising efforts provides a measure of
verification to the consumer who is looking for
certain kinds of subjective effect. For example, if I
want to feel well dressed and in fashion, and I
consider buying an Izod Alligator shirt which is
advertised in all of the magazines and newspapers,
then the fact that other people buy it and that this
leads to repeated advertisements shows me that the
desired subjective effect is real enough and that I
indeed will be well dressed and in fashion if I purchase the shirt. The indirect information may lead
to a rational decision to purchase a product because
the information testifies to the subjective effect that
the product brings about.[15]

Some philosophers will be unhappy with the
conclusion of this section, largely because they have
a concept of true, rational, or ideal desire which is
not the same as the one used here. A Marxist, for
instance, may urge that any desire felt by alienated
man in a capitalistic society is foreign to his true
nature. Or an existentialist may claim that the
desires of inauthentic men are themselves inauthentic. Such concepts are based upon general theories
of human nature which are unsubstantiated and
perhaps incapable of substantiation. Moreover,
each of these theories is committed to a concept of
an ideal desire which is normatively debatable and
which is distinct from the ordinary concept of a
rational desire as one based upon relevant information. But it is in the terms of the ordinary concept
that we express our concern that advertising may
limit our autonomy in the sense of leading us to act
on irrational desires, and if we operate with this
concept we are driven again to the conclusion that
advertising may lead, but probably most often does
not lead, to an infringement of autonomy.

(c) Free Choice. It might be said that some
desires are so strong or so covert that a person
cannot resist them, and that when he acts on such
desires he is not acting freely or voluntarily but is
rather the victim of irresistible impulse or an
unconscious drive. Perhaps those who condemn
advertising feel that it produces this kind of desire
in us and consequently reduces our autonomy.

This raises a very difficult issue. How do we
distinguish between an impulse we *do* not resist and
one we *could* not resist, between freely giving in to
a desire and succumbing to one? I have argued
elsewhere that the way to get at this issue is in terms
of the notion of acting for a reason.[16] A person acts
or chooses freely if he does so for a reason, that is,
if he can adduce considerations which justify in his
mind the act in question. Many of our actions are
in fact free because this condition frequently holds.
Often, however, a person will act from habit, or
whim, or impulse, and on these occasions he does
not have a reason in mind. Nevertheless he often
acts voluntarily in these instances, i.e., he could
have acted otherwise. And this is because if there
had been a reason for acting otherwise of which he
was aware, he would in fact have done so. Thus
acting from habit or impulse is not necessarily to act
in an involuntary manner. If, however, a person is
aware of a good reason to do x and still follows his
impulse to do y, then he can be said to be impelled
by irresistible impulse and hence to act involuntar-
ily. Many kleptomaniacs can be said to act involun-
tarily, for in spite of their knowledge that they likely
will be caught and their awareness that the goods
they steal have little utilitarian value to them, they
nevertheless steal. Here their 'out of character'
desires have the upper hand, and we have a case of
compulsive behavior.

Applying these notions of voluntary and compulsive behavior to the case of behavior prompted
by advertising, can we say that consumers influenced by advertising act compulsively? The unex-
citing answer is: sometimes they do, sometimes not.
I may have an overwhelming, T.V. induced urge
to own a Mazda Rx-7 and all the while realize that
I can't afford one without severely reducing my
family's caloric intake to a dangerous level. If,

aware of this good reason not to purchase the car, I nevertheless do so, this shows that I have been the victim of T.V. compulsion. But if I have the urge, as I assure you I do, and don't act on it, or if in some other possible world I could afford an Rx-7, then I have not been the subject of undue influence by Mazda advertising. Some Mazda Rx-7 purchasers act compulsively; others do not. The Mazda advertising effort *in general* cannot be condemned, then, for impairing its customers' autonomy in the sense of limiting free or voluntary choice. Of course, the question remains what should be done about the fact that advertising may and does *occasionally* limit free choice. We shall return to this question later.

In the case of subliminal advertising we may find an individual whose subconscious desires are activated by advertising into doing something his calculating, reasoning ego does not approve. This would be a case of compulsion. But most of us have a benevolent subconsciousness which does not overwhelm our ego and its reasons for action. And therefore most of us can respond to subliminal advertising without thereby risking our autonomy. To be sure, if some advertising firm developed a subliminal technique which drove all of us to purchase Lear jets, thereby reducing our caloric intake to the zero point, then we would have a case of advertising which could properly be censured for infringing our right to autonomy. We should acknowledge that this is possible, but at the same time we should recognize that it is not an inherent result of subliminal advertising.

(d) Control or Manipulation. Briefly let us consider the matter of control and manipulation. Under what conditions do these activities occur? In a recent paper on 'Forms and Limits of Control' I suggested the following criteria:[17]

A person C controls the behavior of another person P if

(1) C intends P to act in a certain way A;
(2) C's intention is causally effective in bringing about A; and
(3) C intends to ensure that all of the necessary conditions of A are satisfied.

These criteria may be elaborated as follows. To control another person it is not enough that one's actions produce certain behavior on the part of that person; additionally one must intend that this happen. Hence control is the intentional production of behavior. Moreover, it is not enough just to have the intention; the intention must give rise to the conditions which bring about the intended effect. Finally, the controller must intend to establish by his actions any otherwise unsatisfied necessary conditions for the production of the intended effect. The controller is not just influencing the outcome, not just having input; he is as it were guaranteeing that the sufficient conditions for the intended effect are satisfied.

Let us apply these criteria of control to the case of advertising and see what happens. Conditions (1) and (3) are crucial. Does the Mazda manufacturing company or its advertising agency intend that I buy an Rx-7? Do they intend that a certain number of people buy the car? *Prima facie* it seems more appropriate to say that they *hope* a certain number of people will buy it, and hoping and intending are not the same. But the difficult term here is 'intend'. Some philosophers have argued that to intend A it is necessary only to desire that A happen and to believe that it will. If this is correct, and if marketing analysis gives the Mazda agency a reasonable belief that a certain segment of the population will buy its product, then, assuming on its part the desire that this happen, we have the conditions necessary for saying that the agency intends that a certain segment purchase the car. If I am a member of this segment of the population, would it then follow that the agency intends that I purchase an Rx-7? Or is control referentially opaque? Obviously we have some questions here which need further exploration.

Let us turn to the third condition of control, the requirement that the controller intend to activate or bring about any otherwise unsatisfied necessary conditions for the production of the intended effect. It is in terms of this condition that we are able to distinguish brainwashing from liberal education. The brainwasher arranges all of the necessary conditions for belief. On the other hand, teachers (at least those of liberal persuasion) seek only to influence their students — to provide them with information and enlightenment which they may absorb *if they wish*. We do not normally think of teachers as controlling their students, for the students' performances depend as well on their own interests and inclinations.

Now the advertiser — does he control, or merely influence, his audience? Does he intend to ensure that all of the necessary conditions for purchasing behavior are met, or does he offer information and symbols which are intended to have an effect only *if* the potential purchaser has certain desires? Undeniably advertising induces some desires, and it does this intentionally, but more often than not it intends to induce a desire for a particular object, *given* that the purchaser already has other desires. Given a desire for youth, or power, or adventure, or ravishing beauty, we are led to desire Grecian Formula 16, Mazda Rx-7's, Pongo Peach, and Distinctive Foundations. In this light, the advertiser is influencing us by appealing to independent desires we already have. He is not creating those basic desires. Hence it seems appropriate to deny that he intends to produce all of the necessary conditions for our purchases, and appropriate to deny that he controls us.[18]

Let me summarize my argument. The critics of advertising see it as having a pernicious effect on the autonomy of consumers, as controlling their lives and manufacturing their very souls. The defense claims that advertising only offers information and in effect allows industry to provide consumers with what they want. After developing some of the philosophical dimensions of this dispute, I have come down tentatively in favor of the advertisers. Advertising may, but certainly does not always or even frequently, control behavior, produce compulsive behavior, or create wants which are not rational or are not truly those of the consumer. Admittedly, it may in individual cases do all of these things, but it is innocent of the charge of intrinsically or necessarily doing them or even, I think, of often doing so. This limited potentiality, to be sure, leads to the question whether advertising should be abolished or severely curtailed or regulated because of its potential to harm a few poor souls in the above ways. This is a very difficult question, and I do not pretend to have the answer. I only hope that the above discussion, in showing some of the kinds of harm that can be done by advertising and by indicating the likely limits of this harm, will put us in a better position to grapple with the question.

ENDNOTES

1. Vance Packard, *The Hidden Persuaders* (Pocket Books, New York, 1958), pp. 20-21.

2. *Ibid.*, p. 21.

3. B.F. Skinner, 'Some Issues Concerning the Control of Human Behavior: A Symposium,' in Karlins and Andrews (eds.), *Man Controlled* (The Free Press, New York, 1972).

4. For provocative discussions of subliminal advertising, see W.B. Key, *Subliminal Seduction* (The New American Library, New York, 1973), and W.B. Key, *Media Sexploitation* (Prentice-Hall, Inc., Englewood Cliffs, N.J., 1976).

5. I would like to emphasize that in what follows I am discussing these techniques of advertising from the standpoint of the issue of control and not from that of deception. For a good and recent discussion of the many dimensions of possible deception in advertising, see Alex C. Michalos, 'Advertising: Its Logic, Ethics, and Economics' reprinted above, pp. 357-370.

6. Quoted by Packard, *op. cit.*, p. 220.

7. Theodore Levitt, 'The Morality (?) of Advertising', *Harvard Business Review* 48 (1970), 84-92.

8. Phillip Nelson, 'Advertising and Ethics', in Richard T. De George and Joseph A. Pichler (eds.), *Ethics, Free Enterprise, and Public Policy* (Oxford University Press, New York, 1978), pp. 187-198.

9. For a discussion of polymorphous perversity, see Norman O. Brown, *Life Against Death* (Random House, New York, 1969), Chapter III.

10. John Kenneth Galbraith, *The Affluent Society*; reprinted in Tom L. Beauchamp and Norman E. Bowie (eds.), *Ethical Theory and Business* (Prentice-Hall, Englewood Cliffs, 1979), pp. 496-501.

11. David Braybrooke, 'Skepticism of Wants, and Certain Subversive Effects of Corporations on American Values', in Sidney Hook (ed.), *Human Values and Economic Policy* (New York University Press, New York, 1967); reprinted in Beauchamp and Bowie (eds.), *op. cit.*, pp. 502-508.

12. F.A. von Hayek, 'The *Non Sequitur* of the "Dependence Effect"', *Southern Economic Journal* (1961); reprinted in Beauchamp and Bowie (eds.), *op. cit.*, pp. 508-512.

13. Harry Frankfurt, 'Freedom of the Will and the Concept of a Person', *Journal of Philosophy* LXVIII (1971), 5-20.

14. For a discussion of the difference between a malign and a benign subconscious mind, see P.H. Nowell-Smith, 'Psycho-analysis and Moral Language', *The Rationalist Annual* (1954); reprinted in P. Edwards and A. Pap (eds.), *A Modern Introduction to Philosophy*, Revised Edition (The Free Press, New York, 1965), pp. 86-93.

15. Michalos argues that in emphasizing a brand name — such as Bayer Aspirin — advertisers are illogically attempting to distinguish the indistinguishable by casting a trivial feature of a product as a significant one which separates it from other brands of the same product. The brand name is said to be trivial or unimportant "from the point of view of the effectiveness of the product or that for the sake of which the product is purchased". This claim ignores the role of indirect information in advertising. For example, consumers want an aspirin *they can trust* (trustworthiness being part of "that for the sake of which the product is purchased"), and the indirect information conveyed by the widespread advertising effort for Bayer aspirin shows that this product is judged trustworthy by many other purchasers. Hence the emphasis on the name is not at all irrelevant but rather is a significant feature of the product from the consumer's standpoint, and attending to the name is not at all an illogical or irrational response on the part of the consumer.

16. Robert L. Arrington, 'Practical Reason, Responsibility and the Psychopath', *Journal for the Theory of Social Behavior* 9 (1979), 71-89.

17. Robert L. Arrington, 'Forms and Limits of Control', delivered at the annual meeting of the Southern Society for Philosophy and Psychology, Birmingham, Alabama, 1980.

18. Michalos distinguishes between appealing to people's tastes and molding those tastes (*op. cit.*, p. 104), and he seems to agree with my claim that it is morally permissible for advertisers to persuade us to consume some article *if* it suits our tastes (p. 105). However, he also implies that advertisers mold tastes as well as appeal to them. It is unclear what evidence is given for this claim, and it is unclear what is meant by *tastes*. If the latter are thought of as basic desires and wants, then I would agree that advertisers are controlling their customers to the extent that they intentionally mold tastes. But if by molding tastes is meant generating a desire for the particular object they promote, advertisers in doing so may well be appealing to more basic desires, in which case they should not be thought of as controlling the consumer.

44

Persuasion and the Dependence Effect

REESE P. MILLER

I

Traditionally, discussions concerning the ethical status of advertising have tended to concentrate on one of two aspects of the subject. One obvious feature of advertising is that it may be deceptive and hence unethical. The other, and usually quite separate, area of concern has involved the fact that advertising is intended to persuade us to desire things that we might not otherwise desire by means of a process Galbraith has called the dependence effect.[1] This is a phenomenon whereby "wants," to use Galbraith's term, "... are increasingly created by the process by which they are satisfied. This may operate ... by suggestion or emulation ... [or] through advertising and salesmanship."[2] Galbraith considers the effect important for two reasons. First, traditional economic models regard wants or desires as being antecedently given and relatively fixed. Thus, such models are simply not equipped to deal with a situation in which wants are brought into existence by the very people whose business it is to satisfy those wants, and economists have tended to ignore the phenomenon, thereby producing quite inadequate theories of consumer demand.[3]

By itself, this would be of interest only to an economist, but Galbraith's major point is that the phenomenon can, and does, operate in such a way as to decrease social benefit. The standard justification for increased production, which might be called "the Adam Smith justification," assumes that production increases in order to satisfy pre-existing (or "independent") wants, and thus that an increase in production will lead to an increase in, and indeed to the maximization of, social benefit. But if wants are not independent, the argument may not apply, and Galbraith's point is that social benefit would be increased if more money were spent on independent public needs and less on such dependent private ones.[4]

Other critics have focused on the ethical status of the process itself rather than on its social effects. It has been felt that there is something inherently objectionable about a process that persuades us to desire things if it is in the persuader's interest, though not necessarily in ours, for us to have such desires. Of course, Galbraith *et al.* have their critics as well, who, it seems to me, have had the better of the argument so far. My intention here is to attempt

This essay was written especially for this volume.

to clarify at least some of the main issues involved in the controversy and to argue that, while a distinction can be made between acceptable and unacceptable forms of persuasion, the critics of persuasive advertising have overstated their case to such an extent as to invalidate it.

In an article entitled "The *Non Sequitur* of 'The Dependence Effect',"[5] F.A. von Hayek has pointed out that the fact that some wants depend for their existence on the process that satisfies those wants does not entail that the wants are not worth satisfying. To show this, he offers the following *reductio*:

> If the fact that people would not feel the need for something if it were not produced did prove that such products are of small value, all the highest products of human endeavor would be of small value. Professor Galbraith's argument could easily be employed, without any change in the essential terms, to demonstrate the worthlessness of literature or any other form of art. Surely an individual's want for literature is not original with himself in the sense that he would experience it if literature were not produced.[6]

This is, of course, a perfectly good reply, but it is made possible only because Galbraith has described the dependence effect in terms so sweeping as to obscure the point he is trying to make. In order to show this, it will be useful to distinguish between demands, desires, and needs.[7] For my purposes, a demand will be regarded as being more or less specific; that is, it will always be a demand for a specific product or type of product. Needs, in my usage, will be states that could be altered to one's benefit and that result from some sort of interaction between our selves and our physical or social circumstances. A recognized or acknowledged need will result in some sort of corresponding desire, although needs of which one is not aware will not.

Consider the following cases; one quite real, and the other, at present, imaginary. A homesteader on the North American prairies in 1838 would doubtless have discovered that prairie sod was, advantageously, an adequate building material. He would also have discovered that sod had the disadvantage of being virtually impossible to plough. Thus, he has an urgent need and a corresponding desire for something that will enable him to plant his crops and feed his family. Of course, in 1838, no demand for a John Deere plough existed, nor could it. Neither could there be a demand for something like a John Deere plough, since nothing like it had ever existed prior to 1838. But this clearly does not show that there was no need for such an implement nor that there was no desire for one (unless one insists that "desire" be specific in the way I have stipulated for my use of "demand"). Thus, at least part of von Hayek's point is trivially true, since there can be no demand for something prior to its existence. But there clearly can be a need and desire for something that does not exist, e.g., a cure for AIDS. Further, although there can be no demand, and perhaps even no desire, for novels, say, prior to their existence, von Hayek's general claim about the desire for literature is problematic at best. The desire for some sort of story-telling appears to be as universal as the desire for food and seems to arise spontaneously with the learning of language. Thus, the possibility of a society that produced no literature is remote, to say the least, and the most that the existence of such a society would show is either that its members were simply unaware that story-telling was possible (and hence could not articulate their need for it), or that they lacked a very basic human characteristic.

Compare the homesteader's situation with that of the homemaker whose television set rather nosily asks whether her[8] mattress pad spray is really furnishing the protection that she and her family have a right to expect from such a product. Previously, she had been under the (correct) impression that washing mattress pads once a week was entirely adequate and had not even known that such a product existed (quite possibly because it hadn't). Guilt-stricken, she rushes out and purchases a can of the appropriate brand of spray. The homemaker's need for cleanliness and hygiene is as real as the homesteader's need for an effective plough, though perhaps less urgent. There is, however, an obvious difference between the two situations. Whereas a John Deere plough will satisfy the homesteader's need, mattress pad spray will not in fact satisfy the homemaker's need for greater cleanliness. She is no better off in that respect than she was before.

Indeed, assuming that the instructions call for a daily spraying and a weekly washing of the pad, she is worse off because she now has an extra task.

There is more to von Hayek's point than the triviality that a demand cannot exist unless there are products that can satisfy it, however. There is surely something badly wrong with making the distinction between acceptable and unacceptable desires depend on the question of whether the desires are innate, "original",[9] or "absolute in the sense that we feel them whatever the situation of our fellow human beings may be."[10] As Mill, discussing the feeling of obligation, remarks:

> On the other hand, if, as is my own belief, the moral feelings are not innate, but acquired, they are not for that reason the less natural. It is natural for man to speak, to reason, to build cities, to cultivate the ground, though these are acquired faculties.[11]

Or, as R.L. Arrington puts it in discussing the distinction between autonomous and nonautonomous desires, "I haven't always like 1969 Aloxe Corton Burgundy or the music of Satie, but when the desires for these things first hit me, they were truly mine."[12] It is perfectly true that one must learn to enjoy many of the things and experiences that make life worthwhile, and that much of the progress of civilization involves the emergence or recognition of genuine needs which did not, or were not thought to, exist previously. At one time, almost no one, even in the most advanced societies, had any real need to be able to read, but that need is now almost universal and quite urgent, since without that ability it is, to say the least, difficult to have a satisfactory life. The need for cleanliness has presumably always been present, although it was recognized as a need only as a result of our coming to understand the nature of disease and contagion. But this only shows that one cannot determine whether a particular desire is a worthy one by considering its origin, and that desires must be evaluated on the basis of their individual merits. Desires and needs may be learned, acquired, or even manufactured in all sorts of ways, and still be worth satisfying. What makes them worthwhile is the fact that people discover that they possess the capacity to

find certain experiences or things inherently enjoyable, or they discover that satisfying such needs is a means to other enjoyable or beneficial experiences or things. This is, of course, simply not the case with mattress pad spray. Using it is vastly more likely to be bothersome than inherently satisfying, and it is not, in fact, a means to hygiene or health. It may make being in one's bedroom resemble being inside a lemon, or a turpentine factory, but it is difficult to imagine most people finding such an experience satisfying unless they have previously been persuaded that such odours are a sign of cleanliness.

At this stage of the argument, those who equate consumption with social benefit tend to point out, quite correctly, that "[w]hen man has satisfied his physical needs, then psychologically grounded desires take over"[13] and that many psychological needs are entirely worthy ones that deserve to be satisfied. As Littlefield and Kirkpatrick, replying to the charge that advertising influences consumers to purchase unneeded goods, rather patronizingly put it:

> As for need, can you point to a single purchase made voluntarily by a consumer (by *you* for example) which was not in response to an admission of *need*? You simply cannot. And who knows what Mrs. Homemaker needs and can afford better than Mrs. H. herself? No one, of course. Just try to get her to buy something that will not (a) protect or (b) enhance her self concept! She does not replace a product which can still supply utility unless such a move, to her, is the smart course of action.[14]

Of course, the qualification "to her" makes the final claim trivial, and the supplied answers to the questions are outrageously false (people buy all sorts of things that they discover they do not need or even like, and advertisers certainly behave as if at least *they* know better than we what we need and can afford). But that should not obscure the fact that people do buy things for all sorts of reasons that do not primarily involve the physical properties of the product. As Arrington puts it:

> . . . it needs to be pointed out that we often wish to purchase subjective effects which in being subjective are nevertheless real enough. The feeling of adventure

or of enhanced social prestige and value are examples of subjective effects promised by advertising. Surely many (most?) advertisements directly promise subjective effects which their patrons actually desire (and obtain when they purchase the product), and thus the ads provide relevant information for rational choice. Moreover, advertisements often provide accurate indirect information on the basis of which a person who wants a certain subjective effect rationally chooses a product.... To the extent that a consumer takes an advertised product to offer a subjective effect and the product does not, it is unlikely that it will be purchased again.[15]

Granting this claim, however, should not obscure two further possible features of such situations. First, as Arrington points out,[16] and as advertisers know very well, one of the important effects of advertising is to create a situation in which such subjective effects, which might otherwise not result from a purchase, do result. Constant advertising provides constant reassurance to the purchaser concerning the correctness and wisdom of his choice. Of course, it might be the case that the most heavily advertised product of a certain kind is superior to, or at least as good as, any other. But this is clearly not necessarily true. In fact, when the second possible feature of such situations is present, the claim that one's choice was a wise one is obviously false. Purchasing mattress pad spray certainly may result in psychological effects that are highly desirable, since they involve the satisfaction of very real psychological needs concerning one's performance as a homemaker. In this case, however, the satisfaction involved is of a kind that might be described as "entirely second-order." Though perfectly genuine, the satisfaction is "second-order" because obtaining it involves presupposing that a different and prior need has in fact been satisfied. If "Mrs. H." felt no need for cleanliness, using mattress pad spray could not possibly "enhance her self concept." The satisfaction is *entirely* second-order in the sense that the presupposed first-order need has not in fact been satisfied. Thus, exactly the same satisfaction might have resulted from the purchase of a similarly advertised but quite different sort of product, or, most importantly, *from no purchase whatever*.[17] The purchase of a liquid floor cleaner that leaves a shiny but unclean film on the floor (as many of them do) could have provided exactly the same subjective effect and would at least have made a visible, though illusory, difference. Further, if some public agency (or detergent manufacturer, for that matter) were to institute a campaign to persuade people that mattress pads should be washed at least every two weeks, "Mrs. H." would obtain the same feeling of pride in her abilities as a homemaker with the added benefit of being able to feel superior to and scornful of all those slovenly homemakers who made the campaign necessary in the first place. Of course, there is no possibility of entirely second-order satisfaction in the case of the homesteader who purchases a new plough, since in such a case second-order satisfaction will occur only if the plough actually satisfies the more basic need of feeding one's family.

The contrast between the two cases is by now painfully obvious. However real the physical and psychological needs involved and however great the satisfaction obtained from the use of mattress pad spray, the satisfaction depends entirely on "Mrs. H.'s" mistaken belief about the product. She has been deceived into doing something which she ought, economically speaking, not to have done and which, in reality, she did not need to do. Nor is it plausible in this case to argue that the benefits "Mrs. H." and her family will receive as a result of her enhanced self-image may well outweigh the costs, in time and money, of using the product, since the same benefits might have been obtained at no cost. Further, those same benefits could have been obtained at equal or lower cost by a product that also produced the additional benefit of satisfying the first-order need involved.

If this example seems too far-fetched to be believable, consider the recent introduction of Tartar Control Crest. Accompanying literature describes the product as an "Important Major Improvement" and states that it "Helps protect your teeth against *tartar*...". It emphasizes the importance of "preventing unsightly tartar" and claims that "... now, new Tartar Control Crest gives you a clinically *proven* way to help prevent tartar buildup." It then, somewhat incoherently, states that tartar and plaque are totally different and that "No toothpaste has been proven more effective than Crest at removing plaque." (The apparent incoherence arises because it is never explained that plaque becomes tartar if not removed.) It does not, of course, point out that no toothpaste has been shown to be *less* effective, either. Only at the very end does the literature note that "dental visits" are necessary for the removal of tartar that is underneath the gumline; it makes no mention of the fact that that is the only kind of tartar that is actually harmful. The entire thrust of the message is to persuade people to believe (incorrectly) that the product will make a significant contribution to one's dental health, which might well persuade some people that visits to the dentist will become less necessary or unnecessary. The similarity to the previous case is especially striking in view of the fact that plaque can be removed by brushing with any other toothpaste or by brushing with no toothpaste at all; the removal is entirely mechanical and does not in any way require the use of a dentifrice. Admittedly, such products have *some* effect in that they slow the rate at which *unremoved* plaque builds up and hence the rate of tartar formation. But it is obviously questionable whether this qualifies as a major improvement and whether such an effect can honestly be described as "helping" to prevent tartar, since the only way to actually prevent it is to completely remove the plaque.

While the analysis being offered here might appear to be confusing the two areas that were distinguished in the beginning paragraph, the suggestion being made is simply that the presence of deception, actual or implied, provides at least one way of discriminating between morally acceptable and morally unacceptable persuasion. This is so because, in the case of advertising at least, being deceived is almost invariably not in one's best interest. In fact, deception, or at least something very like it, may offer the only way of making the distinction in a hard and fast manner. After all, the persuasive techniques used by advertisers are also used by all sorts of people who have no direct economic interest in the result and who quite sincerely believe that it is in the best interest of others to be so persuaded;

occasionally, such people are even correct in their belief. Further, it is difficult to see how one might defend the general claim that there is something immoral about persuading someone to buy something. The fact that the purchase is in the persuader's own interest would seem to be relevant only if the purchase or the means of persuasion were already morally questionable, e.g., if being so persuaded was against the purchaser's interest. In such cases, one might wish to contrast the persuader's motive in knowingly advancing his own interests at the expense of the interests of others with that of a distinterested persuader who sincerely (though incorrectly) believed that it was in a person's interest to purchase a particular product. Compare the efforts of cigarette manufacturers to persuade people that smoking is an adult, sophisticated, and desirable activity with the efforts of a sincere though misguided person to persuade a friend who is suffering from cancer that Laetrile offers a cure.

The fact is that people are persuaded in all sorts of ways to do all sorts of things, some of which are worthy and beneficial, and some of which are not. One who is persuaded, by whatever means, to purchase a product that effectively satisfies a genuine need at a reasonable cost[18] has not been harmed in the moral sense unless the product is harmful in some other way, e.g., physically. Similarly, persuading people to contribute to famine relief by using the sorts of appeals to the emotions that characterize many current advertisements is not wrong if that is the only or best way of doing so. Of course, rational persuasion is to be preferred to non-rational, but it is by no means clear that it is *morally* preferable, much less that non-rational persuasion is morally wrong. Even deceptive persuasion may be acceptable in some cases. Persuading a homesteader to purchase a plough that he in fact needs by deceiving him about its advantages may be justifiable if he cannot be persuaded in any other way.

In fact, I suspect that many who have argued that persuasive advertising is inherently undesirable have been influenced, at least to some extent, by the knowledge that many products simply do not live up to the promises, express or implied, made by the advertisements that promote the products. All sorts of things that are advertised as being valuable and desirable are virtually, and sometimes totally, worthless. Galbraith's objection to products that are not intended to satisfy basic needs might have been better directed against products that do not adequately satisfy the needs, basic or not, that they claim to satisfy. Thus, in cases in which the satisfaction involved is entirely second-order and is based on deception (and it is difficult to imagine how else such satisfaction might be produced), there is, at the very least, a clear *prima facia* reason for claiming that the persuasion involved is morally unacceptable.

II

I wish next to consider a rather broad and somewhat vague range of cases having to do with the creation or promulgation of what might be described as social or cultural norms. While such cases are importantly different from, and much more complex than, the relatively straightforward types of deception just discussed, there are also some important and revealing similarities. In cases of entirely second-order satisfaction, the satisfaction obtained was the result of a "second-order" belief about oneself (e.g., that one was a better home-maker) which depended on that person's having a particular "first-order" belief about the product (that it was an aid to hygiene). Certain cases involving social norms are structured in a similar way in the sense that the satisfactions involved result from a certain second-order belief about oneself which depends for its validity entirely on the fact that many people, including the person in question, subscribe to certain norms or values, and therefore have certain first-order beliefs about the effects of the product or type of product involved.

Consider a person who always buys the latest fashions in order to be well-dressed and in style, or a person who expects a diamond ring in order to be able to proclaim her engagement in a manner acceptable to her friends and rivals. Wearing the latest fashion does make one well-dressed and elicits the admiration and envy of others, and, with rare

exceptions, an engagement that did not involve a piece of crystalline carbon would be regarded as being in some way flawed. Thus, the satisfactions involved arise from and depend on the actual effects of the product, or rather on the effects of owning the product, and do have a genuine basis in reality. No one has been deceived in any direct way about the desirability or effects of the product or about the second-order satisfactions that will be produced. Arrington implicitly relies on this fact in his discussion of the claim that advertisers immorally control consumers. He argues that one person's action is controlled by another if and only if the controller intends the person to act in that way and the intention is causally effective in bringing about the action. Third, the controller must also intend ". . . to ensure that all of the necessary conditions of [the action] A are satisfied."[19]

Replying to Michalos' claim that advertisers mould tastes, Arrington says:

> It is unclear what evidence is given for this claim, and it is unclear what is meant by *tastes*. If the latter are thought of as basic desires and wants, then I agree that advertisers are controlling their customers to the extent that they intentionally mould tastes. But if by moulding tastes is meant generating a desire for a particular object they promote, advertising in doing so may well be appealing to more basic desires, in which case they should not be thought of as controlling the consumer.[20]

Previously, he says:

> Undeniably advertising induces some desires, and it does this intentionally, but more often than not it intends to induce a desire for a particular object, *given* that the purchaser already has other desires. . . . In this light, the advertiser is influencing us by appealing to independent desires we already have. He is not creating those basic desires. Hence it seems appropriate to deny that he controls us.[21]

One problem with an argument of this kind (and Arrington uses such arguments repeatedly) is that it will not enable one to distinguish between advertising and brainwashing (to use Arrington's own example of a case in which a person *is* being controlled) even though that is exactly what the argument is intended to do. If one takes the third criterion literally, as one must if his arguments are to be conclusive, then no one could possibly control another person's actions, because no one could possibly intend that *all* the necessary conditions of the action were satisfied. An advertiser cannot intend that I can afford to buy a new automobile every year, since there is absolutely no way that his efforts could bring that about. (He can, of course, intend to make me believe that I can afford it, even if I cannot, but that would simply be a deception of the kind already discussed.) Similarly, a brainwasher cannot intend that the sun not explode nor that he will not suffer an unpredictable heart attack before he has persuaded his victim. In elaborating on his analysis of the concept of control, Arrington offers a weaker version of his third condition, requiring only that "the controller must intend to establish by his actions any otherwise unsatisfied necessary conditions,"[22] but this version will not enable one to make the distinction, either. Indeed, it would seem to describe exactly what an advertiser clearly *does* intend to do; if that is not the intention, it is difficult to understand how advertising could possibly be intended to influence one's actions. Similarly, a brainwasher intends to bring about certain effects *given that* his victim already has certain very basic desires (primarily the desire to avoid mental and physical distress.) Thus, the fact that a person had certain desires and beliefs before experiencing a desire to purchase a particular product will not enable one to distinguish between cases in which a person is immorally controlled and cases of control by means that may be perfectly acceptable.[23]

More importantly, in order for the argument to apply to the kinds of cases Arrington usually considers, "basic" or "independent" desires cannot be independent in Galbraith's sense of the term. The desires in question will be "independent" *only* in the sense of not having been created by the *particular* advertisement in question. Thus, the most that Arrington's argument can show is that our purchases are usually not completely controlled by the specific advertisement to which we respond. But that does not show that the purchaser was not

immorally controlled by advertising, since the essential prior beliefs may themselves be the result of having been previously controlled by advertising and might have been produced by morally questionable means similar to those involved in cases of outright deception. Indeed, if the social norms involved have been created wholly or primarily by means of prior advertising, such norms are like false first-order beliefs in several ways.

First, as with mattress pad spray, the second-order satisfactions that result from complying with such norms may not depend in any way on the inherent properties or direct effects of the item concerned. Rather, they result solely from the fact that most people (or at least the people who matter) have been persuaded that the possession of such a product is a necessary condition of a satisfactory or happy life. An engagement or marriage will not be made better by anything that a diamond itself actually does, since a counterfeit stone would produce exactly the same satisfactions provided that the deception remained undetected by all concerned. Such a first-order belief is arbitrary in the sense that, like false beliefs, it could be replaced by any number of other beliefs without in any way reducing the second-order satisfactions that result from acting in accordance with such beliefs. If garnets were somehow to come to be considered the most suitable stones for engagement rings, exactly the same second-order satisfactions could be obtained at less cost. Further, if there were any number of equally acceptable methods of proclaiming an engagement, one could obtain all the satisfaction that only a diamond can now provide and also obtain the added satisfaction of choosing the method that one found most pleasing or congenial. Similarly, if people were to believe that being well-dressed required dressing in whatever styles happened to be the most flattering to oneself, people could obtain the same satisfaction that wearing the latest (perhaps quite unflattering) fashion produces and be more attractive as well. Thus, if the relevant first-order beliefs were different, the same or greater satisfaction might be obtained from the purchase of a different product or from no purchase whatever. (Suppose that an engagement was considered acceptable and "official" if and only if it had been announced in the local newspaper and that newspapers, realizing the importance of such announcements, ran them without charge as a public service.)

At this point, it is tempting to suggest that such arbitrary first-order beliefs are simply false and are the result of the sustained and long-term efforts of De Beers or the fashion industry to deceive people. Unfortunately, the situation is not that simple. Of course, if people were to believe that diamonds had some sort of physical or magical properties that increased the chances of a happy marriage or that the latest fashion was more attractive than the previous ones simply because it *was* the latest, those beliefs would simply be false. But the beliefs in question are not beliefs about the properties of such things but about the status that possessing them conveys. And these beliefs have the unusual property that if enough people, or the right people, believe them, they become true. However, if one were to ask *why* a diamond is an essential ingredient for an engagement, the only possible reason that could be given in defence of the claim would be to point out that that is what people believe. Now, the fact that people believe something may be a perfectly good reason for believing it oneself. But it is a good reason only if at least some of the people who hold the belief have grounds for believing it. We believe the claims of scientists because we know that they have grounds for their beliefs. We do not in general think that the mere fact people believe something is grounds for thinking that it is true, but that is the only possible reason that could be offered in defence of certain beliefs of this kind. So the beliefs in question are not merely arbitrary, in the sense explained, they are objectively groundless. Such beliefs have the curious property of being made true if they are popularly accepted and made false if they are not, and are thus quite distinctively different from most of our other beliefs.

None of this should be taken to imply that all social norms or values involve only first-order beliefs of this peculiar kind. The belief that cleanliness is desirable surely reflects an important social norm, but there are quite obvious reasons why such a norm should be preferred to the alternatives, and

it is quite obvious that some ethical norms are preferable to certain of their alternatives. Many, perhaps most, social norms will involve some element of truth but will be arbitrary to some extent. The possession of a new and expensive automobile, for example, conveys prestige and status and elicits envy at least in part because such vehicles offer features and advantages that cheaper models do not provide. So there are reasons for believing that expensive cars are, simply because of their merits, more desirable than inexpensive ones. But this is clearly not the only reason that such possessions convey as much prestige as they do; an important part of the phenomenon depends on the widely-held belief that the more expensive possessions one has, the better and more successful one is, and that belief is surely in large part the result of the massive and sustained efforts of those who are in the business of manufacturing and selling luxuries of all sorts.[24] As a result, a person who owned a new expensive car would not only acquire high status, but might very well obtain a great deal of second-order satisfaction even if she had neither a need nor any desire for the particular features and advantages such vehicles offer. If she shares the first-order belief that such possessions are essential for a successful and happy life, then she will, at least in her own terms, be successful and happy, even though in this case the satisfaction involved is entirely second-order since she gets no direct satisfaction from the fact that her automobile is better than many others. Thus, even in the individual case, believing in such norms seems to make them true. A person who felt that a diamond was an essential ingredient of a happy marriage might feel cheated and resentful if one was not, or could not be, provided, and that could make the marriage less happy than it might otherwise have been. Further, a person who does not accept such norms, i.e., one who does not share the first-order beliefs involved, will receive no second-order satisfaction from complying with such norms.[25]

The fact that first-order beliefs of this kind seem to be self-validating if and only if one believes them can, I think, be explained by pointing out that the ordinary concept of validation simply does not apply in such cases. If such beliefs are to be said to be true in some sense, they can be true only in the sense that there is this very curious and circular sort of evidence in their favour. It has already been pointed out that the fact that many people accept such arbitrary values, and thus have the corresponding belief, does not *in itself* count as evidence in favour of the belief. But in such cases, that seems to be the only thing one can say about the belief that even might be relevant to its truth. That one happens to hold such a belief oneself is, to say the least, no better a reason, since to claim that something is true *simply* because one believes it is to admit that one really has no reason. And this is true despite the fact that the second-order effects of one's holding the belief are those that one would expect if the belief were true in the usual sense. Thus, such beliefs are similar to false beliefs in yet another way. As with false beliefs, they cannot be *known* to be true. False beliefs cannot be known to be true simply because they are not true, even though there may be some grounds for believing them. Beliefs of the kind being considered cannot be known to be true because any attempt to show that they are true will result in their being called into question as objectively groundless whenever one tries to defend them.

Imagine an advertisement for mattress pad spray that stated, quite truthfully, that although the product has absolutely no physical benefits, those who have used it report that they are more satisfied about their role as a homemaker as a result. Not only would such an advertisement be unsuccessful,

it would be self-disconfirming. A person who had been a satisfied user will not feel reassured and even more satisfied; she will feel like a fool. Similarly, imagine an advertisement that stated, again quite truthfully, that a particular product had no real advantage over less expensive ones, but that, because of its high price, users of the product feel better about themselves than do users of virtually identical but less expensive products; i.e., imagine an advertisement that stated that any additional satisfactions produced by the product would be entirely second-order. While it is difficult to imagine what the response to such an advertisement might be, it seems clear that someone who responded positively would be acting irrationally and against his own interests. And this strongly suggests that such a person has been victimized by having his values manipulated and reinforced in such a complex and covert manner and to such an extent that they are now immune to his rational control.

In short, it seems implausible to contend that persuasive advertising is somehow inherently immoral. Nor is it necessarily the case that deception is an infallible guide to immoral persuasion, although it is a remarkably good indicator in the case of advertising. But there is something morally questionable, to say the least, in persuading someone to purchase a product if that person's having and retaining a belief that is either false or groundless, in the sense explained, is essential to any satisfaction that might result from that purchase.

ENDNOTES

1. J.K. Galbraith, *The Affluent Society* (London: Houghton Mifflin Co., 1958), Ch. 11. and *passim*.

2. Galbraith, *op. cit.*, p. 124.

3. Galbraith's charge that economists simply ignore the phenomenon is no longer true. The dependence effect has been studied, at least in the area of medical services. See, for example, Anderson, House, and Ormiston, "A Theory of Physician Behaviour with Supplier Induced Demand," *Southern Economic Journal* 48, (1981), pp. 124–133: or, V. Fuchs, "The Supply of Surgeons and the Demand for Operations," *Journal of Human Resources* 13 (1978), Supplement, pp. 35–56.

4. Galbraith, *op. cit.* See especially Chs. 9 and 10.

5. F.A. von Hayek, "The *Non Sequitur* of the 'Dependence Effect'," *Southern Economic Journal*, April 1961. Reprinted in Beauchamp and Bowie, eds., *Ethical Theory and Business* (Englewood Cliffs, NJ: Prentice-Hall, 1979), pp. 363–366.

6. von Hayek, *op. cit.* The quoted material appears on p. 364 of Beauchamp and Bowie, *op. cit.*

7. I do not wish to claim that my use of these terms is entirely correct, much less that it constitutes an adequate analysis of the concepts involved. I rely here on Lewis Carroll's view that one may use terms however one likes provided that one is consistent and gives fair warning. See Lewis Carroll, *Symbolic Logic* (New York: Dover Publications, 1958), p. 166.

8. Or "his," if you prefer.

9. Galbraith, *op. cit.*, p. 119.

10. Galbraith (quoting Keynes), *op. cit.*, p. 118.

11. J.S. Mill, *Utilitarianism* (New York: Library of Liberal Arts, 1957), p. 39.

12. R.L. Arrington, "Advertising and Behavior Control," *Journal of Business Ethics*, 1 (1982), p. 7, reprinted in this text, p. 469 ff.

13. Galbraith, *op. cit.*, p. 143.

14. Littlefield and Kirkpatrick, *Advertising: Mass Communication in Marketing* (Boston: Houghton Mifflin Co., 1970), p. 117.

15. Arrington, *op. cit.*, p. 8.

16. Arrington, *op. cit.*, pp. 8–9.

17. I am indebted for this point to Stanley Benn's article "Freedom and Persuasion," *Australasian Journal of Philosophy*, Vol. 45 (1967), p. 273. His use of the point is different from mine in that he applies it only to cases in which there is no actual need involved.

18. It should be remembered that, in my terms, the satisfaction of a genuine need produces a direct or "first-order" benefit, although it is quite possible to have mistaken or groundless beliefs as to what one's genuine needs are. The qualification concerning cost is necessary because charging a considerably higher price than is charged for similar products of comparable worth is to inflict an economic harm. Further-

more, it is not implausible to suggest that such practices may well involve a kind of deception. Many people believe that "you get what you pay for," which is frequently false, and that a comparatively higher price is an indication of higher quality, which is surely sometimes true. Thus, to place a comparatively high price on a product is to represent that product as being proportionately superior. For an actual example and analysis of the way in which a higher price can operate in exactly this way, see R.B. Cialdini, *Influence: the new psychology of modern persuasion* (New York: Quill, 1984), pp. 15–33.

19. Arrington, *op. cit.*, p. 10.

20. Arrington, *op. cit.*, p. 12.

21. Arrington, *op. cit.*, p. 11.

22. *Ibid.*

23. Although Arrington seems to believe that control is inherently immoral, such a distinction is obviously necessary if the concept of control is to have any practical application. One fairly simple way of distinguishing might be to point out that the actions and intentions of a brainwasher are in themselves immoral, whereas this is clearly not true in all cases. Teaching children to read, which might well involve controlling them, surely does not require one to do anything immoral.

24. There are, of course, countless advertisements that make no claims whatever about the merits of the product, allowing that to be inferred from the advertisement's emphasis on the expensive nature of the product or on the prestige that possessing it conveys.

25. Naturally, complying with such norms may have all sorts of direct social benefits, but these will be the result of the fact that other people *do* accept the relevant norms and hence believe certain things about the people who comply with such norms.

45

The Making of Self and World in Advertising*

JOHN WAIDE

In this paper I will criticize a common practice I call associative advertising. The fault in associative advertising is not that it is deceptive or that it violates the autonomy of its audience — on this point I find Arrington's arguments persuasive.[1] Instead, I will argue against associative advertising by examining the virtues and vices at stake. In so doing, I will offer an alternative to Arrington's exclusive concern with autonomy and behavior control.

Associative advertising is a technique that involves all of the following:

1. The advertiser wants people[2] to buy (or buy more of) a product. This objective is largely independent of any sincere desire to improve or enrich the lives of the people in the target market.

2. In order to increase sales, the advertiser identifies some (usually) deep-seated non-market good for which the people in the target market feel a strong desire. By "non-market good" I mean something which cannot, strictly speaking, be bought or sold in a marketplace. Typical non-market goods are friendship, acceptance and esteem of others. In a more extended sense we may regard excitement (usually sexual) and power as non-market goods since advertising in the U.S.A. usually uses versions of these that cannot be bought and sold. For example, "sex appeal" as the theme of an advertising campaign is not the market-good of prostitution, but the non-market good of sexual attractiveness and acceptability.

3. In most cases, the marketed product bears only the most tenuous (if any) relation to the non-market good with which it is associated in the advertising campaign. For example, soft drinks cannot give one friends, sex, or excitement.

4. Through advertising, the marketed product is associated with the non-market desire it cannot possibly satisfy. If possible, the desire for the non-market good is intensified by calling into question one's acceptability. For example, mouthwash, toothpaste, deodorant, and feminine hygiene ads are concocted to make us worry that we stink.

From *Journal of Business Ethics* **6** (1987) 73–79. © 1987 by D. Reidel Publishing Company. Reprinted by permission.

5. Most of us have enough insight to see both (a) that no particular toothpaste can make us sexy and (b) that wanting to be considered sexy is at least part of our motive for buying that toothpaste. Since we can (though, admittedly, we often do not bother to) see clearly what the appeal of the ad is, we are usually not lacking in relevant information or deceived in any usual sense.

6. In some cases, the product actually gives at least partial satisfaction to the non-market desire — but only because of advertising.[3] For example, mouthwash has little prolonged effect on stinking breath, but it helps to reduce the intense anxieties reinforced by mouthwash commercials on television because we at least feel that we are doing the proper thing. In the most effective cases of associative advertising, people begin to talk like ad copy. We begin to sneer at those who own the wrong things. We all become enforcers for the advertisers. In general, if the advertising images are effective enough and reach enough people, even preposterous marketing claims can become at least partially self-fulfilling.

Most of us are easily able to recognize associative advertising as morally problematic when the consequences are clear, extreme, and our own desires and purchasing habits are not at stake. For example, the marketing methods Nestlé used in Africa involved associative advertising. Briefly, Nestlé identified a large market for its infant formula — without concern for the well-being of the prospective consumers. In order to induce poor women to buy formula rather than breastfeed, Nestlé selected non-market goods on which to base its campaigns — love for one's child and a desire to be acceptable by being modern. These appeals were effective (much as they are in advertising for children's clothing, toys, and computers in the U.S.A.). Through billboards and radio advertising, Nestlé identified parental love with formula feeding and suggested that formula is the modern way to feed a baby. Reports indicate that in some cases mothers of dead babies placed cans of formula on their graves to show that the parents cared enough to do the very best they could for their children, even though we know the formula may have been a contributing cause of death.[4]

One might be tempted to believe that associative advertising is an objectionable technique only when used on the very poorest, most powerless and ignorant people and that it is the poverty, powerlessness, and ignorance which are at fault. An extreme example like the Nestlé case, one might protest, surely doesn't tell us much about more ordinary associative advertising in the industrialized western nations. The issues will become clearer if we look at the conceptions of virtue and vice at stake.

Dewey says "the thing actually at stake in any serious deliberation is not a difference of quantity [as utilitarianism would have us believe], but what kind of person one is to become, what sort of self is in the making, what kind of a world is making."[5] Similarly, I would like to ask who we become as we use or are used by associative advertising. This will not be a decisive argument. I have not found clear, compelling, objective principles — only considerations I find persuasive and which I expect many others to find similarly persuasive. I will briefly examine how associative advertising affects (a) the people who plan and execute marketing strategies and (b) the people who are exposed to the campaign.

(a) Many advertisers[6] come to think clearly and skillfully about how to sell a marketable item by associating it with a non-market good which people in the target market desire. An important ingredient in this process is lack of concern for the well-being of the people who will be influenced by the campaign. Lloyd Slater, a consultant who discussed the infant formula controversy with people in both the research and development and marketing divisions of Nestlé, says that the R&D people had made sure that the formula was nutritionally sound but were troubled or even disgusted by what the marketing department was doing. In contrast, Slater reports that the marketing people simply did not care and that "those guys aren't even human" in their reactions.[7] This evidence is only anecdotal and it concerns an admittedly extreme case. Still, I believe that the effects of associative advertising[8] would most likely be the same but less pronounced in more ordinary cases. Furthermore, it is quite common for advertisers in the U.S.A. to concentrate their attention on selling something that is harmful to many people, e.g., candy that rots our teeth, and cigarettes. In general, influencing people without concern for their well-being is likely to reduce one's sensitivity to the moral motive of concern for the well-being of others. Compassion, concern, and sympathy for others, it seems to me, are clearly central to moral virtue.[9] Associative advertising must surely undermine this sensitivity in much of the advertising industry. It is, therefore, *prima facie* morally objectionable.

(b) Targets of associative advertising (which include people in the advertising industry) are also made worse by exposure to effective advertising of this kind. The harm done is of two kinds:

(1) We often find that we are buying more but enjoying it less. It isn't only that products fail to live up to specific claims about service-life or effectiveness. More often, the motives ('reasons' would perhaps not be the right word here) for our purchases consistently lead to disappointment. We buy all the right stuff and yet have no more friends, lovers, excitement or respect than before. Instead, we have full closets and empty pocket books. Associative advertising, though not the sole cause, contributes to these results.

(2) Associative advertising may be less effective as an advertising technique to sell particular products than it is as an ideology[10] in our culture. Within the advertising which washes over us daily we can see a number of common themes, but the most important may be "You are what you own."[11] The quibbles over which beer, soft drink, or auto to buy are less important than the over-all message. Each product contributes its few minutes each day, but we are bombarded for hours with the message that friends, lovers, acceptance, excitement, and power are to be gained by purchases in the market, not by developing personal relationships, virtues, and skills. Our energy is channeled into careers so that we will have enough money to *be* someone by buying the right stuff in a market. The not very surprising result is that we neglect non-market methods of satisfying our non-market desires. Those non-market methods call for wisdom, compassion, skill, and a variety of virtues which cannot be bought. It seems, therefore, that insofar as associative advertising encourages us to neglect the non-market cultivation of our

virtues and to substitute market goods instead, we become worse and, quite likely, less happy persons.

To sum up the argument so far, associative advertising tends to desensitize its practitioners to the compassion, concern, and sympathy for others that are central to moral virtue and it encourages its audience to neglect the cultivation of non-market virtues. There are at least five important objections that might be offered against my thesis that associative advertising is morally objectionable.

First, one could argue that since each of us is (or can easily be if we want to be) aware of what is going on in associative advertising, we must want to participate and find it unobjectionable. Accordingly, the argument goes, associative advertising is not a violation of individual autonomy. In order to reply to this objection I must separate issues.

(a) Autonomy is not the main, and certainly not the only, issue here. It may be that I can, through diligent self-examination neutralize much of the power of associative advertising. Since I can resist, one might argue that I am responsible for the results — *caveat emptor* with a new twist.[12] If one's methodology in ethics is concerned about people and not merely their autonomy, then the fact that most people are theoretically capable of resistance will be less important than the fact that most are presently unable to resist.

(b) What is more, the ideology of acquisitiveness which is cultivated by associative advertising probably undermines the intellectual and emotional virtues of reflectiveness and self-awareness which would better enable us to neutralize the harmful effects of associative advertising. I do not know of specific evidence to cite in support of this claim, but it seems to me to be confirmed in the ordinary experience of those who, despite associative advertising, manage to reflect on what they are exposed to.

(c) Finally, sneer group pressure often makes other people into enforcers so that there are penalties for not going along with the popular currents induced by advertising. We are often compelled even by our associates to be enthusiastic participants in the consumer culture. Arrington omits consideration of sneer group pressure as a form of compulsion which can be (though it is not always) induced by associative advertising.

So far my answer to the first objection is incomplete. I still owe some account of why more people do not complain about associative advertising. This will become clearer as I consider a second objection.

Second, one could insist that even if the non-market desires are not satisfied completely, they must be satisfied for the most part or we would stop falling for associative advertising. This objection seems to me to make three main errors:

(a) Although we have a kind of immediate access to our own motives and are generally able to see what motives an advertising campaign uses, most of us lack even the simple framework provided by my analysis of associative advertising. Even one who sees that a particular ad campaign is aimed at a particular non-market desire may not see how all the ads put together constitute a cultural bombardment with an ideology of acquisitiveness — you are what you own. Without some framework such as this, one has nothing to blame. It is not easy to gain self-reflective insight, much less cultural insight.

(b) Our attempts to gain insight are opposed by associative advertising which always has an answer for our dissatisfactions — buy more or newer or different things. If I find myself feeling let down after a purchase, many voices will tell me that the solution is to buy other things too (or that I have just bought the wrong thing). With all of this advertising proposing one kind of answer for our dissatisfactions, it is scarcely surprising that we do not usually become aware of alternatives.

(c) Finally, constant exposure to associative advertising changes[13] us so that we come to feel acceptable as persons when and only when we own the acceptable, fashionable things. By this point, our characters and conceptions of virtue already largely reflect the result of advertising and we are unlikely to complain or rebel.

Third, and perhaps most pungent of the objections, one might claim that by associating mundane marketable items with deeply rooted non-market desires, our everyday lives are invested with new and greater meaning. Charles Revson of Revlon once said that "In the factory we make cosmetics; in the store we sell hope."[14] Theodore Levitt, in his passionate defense of associative advertising, contends that[15]

> Everyone in the world is trying in his [or her] special personal fashion to solve a primal problem of life — the problem of rising above his [or her] own negligibility, of escaping from nature's confining, hostile, and unpredictable reality, of finding significance, security, and comfort in the things he [or she] must do to survive.

Levitt adds: "Without distortion, embellishment, and elaboration, life would be drab, dull, anguished, and at its existential worst."[16] This objection is based on two assumptions so shocking that his conclusion almost seems sensible.

(a) Without associative advertising would our lives lack significance? Would we be miserable in our drab, dull, anguished lives? Of course not. People have always had ideals, fantasies, heroes, and dreams. We have always told stories that captured our aspirations and fears. The very suggestion that we require advertising to bring a magical aura to our shabby, humdrum lives is not only insulting but false.

(b) Associative advertising is crafted not in order to enrich our daily lives but in order to enrich the clients and does not have the interests of its audience at heart. Still, this issue of intent, though troubling, is only part of the problem. Neither is the main problem that associative advertising images somehow distort reality. Any work of art also is, in an important sense, a dissembling or distortion. The central question instead is whether the specific appeals and images, techniques and products, enhance people's lives.[17]

A theory of what enhances a life must be at least implicit in any discussion of the morality of associative advertising. Levitt appears to assume that in a satisfying life one has many satisfied desires — *which* desires is not important.[18] To propose and defend an alternative to his view is beyond the scope of this paper. My claim is more modest — that it is not enough to ask whether desires are satisfied. We should also ask what kinds of lives are sustained, made possible, or fostered by having the newly synthesized desires. What kind of self and world are in the making, Dewey would have us ask. This self and world are always in the making. I am not arguing that there is some natural, good self which advertising changes and contaminates. It may be that not only advertising, but also art, religion, and education in general, always synthesize new desires.[19] In each case, we should look at the lives. How to judge the value of these lives and the various conceptions of virtue they will embody is another question. It will be enough for now to see that it is an important question.

Now it may be possible to see why I began by saying that I would suggest an alternative to the usual focus on autonomy and behavior control.[20] Arrington's defense of advertising (including, as near as I can tell, what I call associative advertising) seems to assume that we have no standard to which we can appeal to judge whether a desire enhances a life and, consequently, that our only legitimate concerns are whether an advertisement violates the autonomy of its audience by deceiving them or controlling their behavior. I want to suggest that there is another legitimate concern — whether the advertising will tend to influence us to become worse persons.[21]

Fourth, even one who is sympathetic with much of the above might object that associative advertising is necessary to an industrial society such as ours. Economists since Galbraith[22] have argued about whether, without modern advertising of the sort I have described, there would be enough demand to sustain our present levels of production. I have no answer to this question. It seems unlikely that associative advertising will end suddenly, so I am confident that we will have the time and the imagination to adapt our economy to do without it.

Fifth, and last, one might ask what I am proposing. Here I am afraid I must draw up short of my

mark. I have no practical political proposal. It seems obvious to me that no broad legislative prohibition would improve matters. Still, it may be possible to make small improvements like some that we have already seen. In the international arena, Nestlé was censured and boycotted, the World Health Organization drafted infant formula marketing guidelines, and finally Nestlé agreed to change its practices. In the U.S.A., legislation prohibits cigarette advertising on television.[23] These are tiny steps, but an important journey may begin with them.

Even my personal solution is rather modest. *First*, if one accepts my thesis that associative advertising is harmful to its audience, then one ought to avoid doing it to others, especially if doing so would require that one dull one's compassion, concern, and sympathy for others. Such initiatives are not entirely without precedent. Soon after the surgeon general's report on cigarettes and cancer in 1964, David Ogilvy and William Bernbach announced that their agencies would no longer accept cigarette accounts and *New Yorker* magazine banned cigarette ads.[24] *Second*, if I am even partly right about the effect of associative advertising on our desires, then one ought to expose oneself as little as possible. The most practical and effective way to do this is probably to banish commercial television and radio from one's life. This measure, though rewarding,[25] is only moderately effective. Beyond these, I do not yet have any answers.

In conclusion, I have argued against the advertising practice I call associative advertising. My main criticism is two-fold: (a) Advertisers must surely desensitize themselves to the compassion, concern, and sympathy for others that are central emotions in a virtuous person, and (b) associative advertising influences its audience to neglect the non-market cultivation of our virtues and to substitute market goods instead, with the result that we become worse and, quite likely, less happy persons.

ENDNOTES

* An earlier draft of this paper was presented to the Tennessee Philosophical Association, 10 November 1984. I am indebted to that group for many helpful comments.

1. Robert L. Arrington, "Advertising and Behavior Control," *Journal of Business Ethics* 1, pp. 3–12.

2. I prefer not to use the term "consumers" since it identifies us with our role in a market, already conceding part of what I want to deny.

3. Arrington, p. 8.

4. James B. McGinnis, *Bread and Justice* (New York: Paulist Press, 1979), p. 224. McGinnis cites as his source INFACT Newsletter, September 1977, p. 3. Formula is often harmful because poor families do not have the sanitary facilities to prepare the formula using clean water and utensils, do not have the money to be able to keep up formula feeding without diluting the formula to the point of starving the child, and formula does not contain the antibodies which a nursing mother can pass to her child to help immunize the child against common local bacteria. Good accounts of this problem are widely available.

5. John Dewey, *Human Nature and Conduct* (New York: Random House, 1930), p. 202.

6. This can be a diverse group including (depending upon the product) marketing specialists, sales representatives, or people in advertising agencies. Not everyone in one of these positions, however, is necessarily guilty of engaging in associative advertising.

7. This story was told by Lloyd E. Slater at a National Science Foundation Chatauqua entitled "Meeting World Food Needs" in 1980-81. It should not be taken as a condemnation of marketing professionals in other firms.

8. One could argue that the deficiency in compassion, concern, and sympathy on the part of advertisers might be a result of self-selection rather than of associative advertising. Perhaps people in whom these moral sentiments are strong do not commonly go into positions using associative advertising. I doubt, however, that such self-selection can account for all the disregard of the audience's best interests.

9. See Lawrence A. Blum, *Friendship, Altruism and Morality* (Boston: Routledge and Kegan Paul, 1980) for a defense of moral emotions against Kantian claims that emotions are unsuitable as a basis for moral

judgement and that only a purely rational good will offers an adequate foundation for morality.

10. I use "ideology" here in a descriptive rather than a pejorative sense. To be more specific, associative advertising commonly advocates only a part of a more comprehensive ideology. See Raymond Geuss, *The Idea of a Critical Theory* (Cambridge: Cambridge University Press, 1981), pp. 5–6.

11. For an interesting discussion, see John Lachs, "To Have and To Be," *Personalist* **45** (Winter, 1964), pp. 5–14; reprinted in John Lachs and Charles Scott, *The Human Search* (New York: Oxford University Press, 1981), pp. 247–255.

12. This is, in fact, the thrust of Arrington's arguments in "Advertising and Behavior Control."

13. I do not mean to suggest that only associative advertising can have such ill effects. Neither am I assuming the existence of some natural, pristine self which is perverted by advertising.

14. Quoted without source in Theodore Levit, "The Morality (?) of Advertising," *Harvard Business Review*, July–August 1970; reprinted in Vincent Barry, *Moral Issues in Business* (Belmont, CA: Wadsworth Publishing Company, 1979), p. 256.

15. Levitt (in Barry), p. 252.

16. Levitt (in Barry), p. 256.

17. "Satisfying a desire would be valuable then if it sustained or made possible a valuable kind of life. To say this is to reject the argument that in creating the wants he [or she] can satisfy, the advertiser (or the manipulator of mass emotion in politics or religion) is necessarily acting in the best interests of his [or her] public." Stanley Benn, "Freedom and Persuasion," *Australasian Journal of Philosophy* **45** (1969); reprinted in Beauchamp and Bowie, *Ethical Theory and Business*, 2nd ed. (Englewood Cliffs, NJ: Prentice-Hall, 1983), p. 374.

18. Levitt's view is not new. "Continual success in obtaining those things which a man from time to time desires — that is to say, continual prospering — is what men call felicity." Hobbes, *Leviathan* (Indianapolis: Bobbs-Merrill, 1958), p. 61.

19. This, in fact, is the principal criticism von Hayek offered of Galbraith's argument against the "dependence effect". F.A. von Hayek, "The *Non Sequitur* of the 'Dependence Effect'," *Southern Economic Journal*, April 1961; reprinted in Tom L. Beauchamp and Norman E.

Bowie, *Ethical Theory and Business*, 2nd ed. (Englewood Cliffs, NJ: Prentice-Hall, 1983), pp. 363–366.

20. Taylor R. Durham, "Information, Persuasion, and Control in Moral Appraisal of Advertising," *The Journal of Business Ethics* **3**, p. 179. Durham also argues that an exclusive concern with issues of deception and control leads us into errors.

21. One might object that this requires a normative theory of human nature, but it seems to me that we can go fairly far by reflecting on our experience. If my approach is to be vindicated, however, I must eventually provide an account of how, in general, we are to make judgments about what is and is not good (or life-enhancing) for a human being. Clearly, there is a large theoretical gulf between me and Arrington, but I hope that my analysis of associative advertising shows that my approach is plausible enough to deserve further investigation.

22. The central text for this problem is *The Affluent Society* (London: Houghton Mifflin, 1958). The crucial passages are reprinted in many anthologies, e.g., John Kenneth Galbraith, "The Dependence Effect," in W. Michael Hoffman and Jennifer Mills Moore, *Business Ethics: Reading and Cases in Corporate Morality* (New York: McGraw-Hill, 1984), pp. 328–333.

23. "In March 1970 Congress removed cigarette ads from TV and radio as of the following January. (The cigarette companies transferred their billings to print and outdoor advertising. Cigarette sales reached new records.)" Stephen Fox, *The Mirror Makers: A History of American Advertising and Its Creators* (New York: William Morrow and Co., 1984), p. 305.

24. Stephen Fox, pp. 303–4.

25. See, for example, Jerry Mander, *Four Arguments for the Elimination of Television* (New York: Morrow Quill Paperbacks, 1977).

SUGGESTED FURTHER READINGS

AAKER, DAVID, DOUGLAS STAYMAN, AND MICHAEL HAGERTY. "Warmth in Advertising: Measurement, Impact and Sequence Effects." *Journal of Consumer Research*, Vol. 12, 1986.

BEAUCHAMP, TOM. "Manipulative Advertising." *Business and Professional Ethics Journal*, Vol. 3, Nos. 3 and 4 (Spring/Summer 1984), pp. 1–23.

BENNETT, J.R. "*Saturday Review's* Annual Advertising Awards." *Journal of Business Ethics*, Vol. 2, No. 2 (May 1983), pp. 73–79.

BOK, SISSELA. *Lying: Moral Choice in Public and Private Life*. New York: Pantheon Books, 1978.

CLASEN, EARL. "Marketing Ethics and the Consumer." *Harvard Business Review*, January-February 1967.

CONSUMER AND CORPORATE AFFAIRS CANADA. *The Misleading Advertising Bulletin*. Ottawa.

EDELL, JULIE AND MARIAN CHAPMAN BURKE. "The Power of Feelings in Understanding Advertising Effects." *Journal of Consumer Research*, Vol. 14, 1987.

GOLDMAN, A. "Ethical Issues in Advertising." In Tom Regan (ed.) *Just Business*. New York: Random House, 1984.

GOWANS, CHRISTOPHER. "Integrity in the Corporation: the Plight of Corporate Product Advocates." *Journal of Business Ethics*, Vol. 3, No. 1 (February 1984), pp. 21–29.

GRATZ, J.E. "The Ethics of Subliminal Communication." *Journal of Business Ethics*, Vol. 3, No. 3 (August 1984), pp. 181–185.

HELD, VIRGINIA. "Advertising and Program Content." *Business and Professional Ethics Journal*, Vol. 3, Nos. 3 and 4 (Spring/Summer 1984), pp. 61–77.

HYMAN, M. AND RICHARD TANSEY. "The Ethics of Psychoactive Ads." *Journal of Business Ethics*, Vol. 9, No. 2, Feb. 1990.

LATOUR, MICHAEL AND SHAKER ZAHRA. "Fear Appeals as Advertising Strategy: Should They Be Used?" *Journal of Consumer Marketing*, Vol. 6, 1989.

LEISER, BURTON. "Professional Advertising." *Business and Professional Ethics Journal*, Vol. 3, Nos. 3 and 4 (Spring/Summer 1984), pp. 93–109.

LEVITT, THEODORE. "The Morality (?) of Advertising." *Harvard Business Review*, 48, 1970, pp. 84–92.

MILLUM, TREVOR. *Images of Woman: Advertising in Women's Magazines*. Totowa, NJ: Rowman and Littlefield, 1975.

NELSON, PHILIP. "Advertising and Ethics." In Richard deGeorge and Joseph Pichler (eds.) *Ethics, Free Enterprise, and Public Policy*, Oxford: Oxford University Press, 1978, pp. 187–198.

PAINE, LYNDA. "Children as Consumers." *Business and Professional Ethics Journal*, Vol. 3., Nos. 3 and 4 (Spring/Summer 1984).

SEXTY, ROBERT. *Issues in Canadian Business*. Scarborough, Ontario: Prentice-Hall Canada Ltd., 1979.

STUART, FREDERICK (ed.) *Consumer Protection From Deceptive Advertising*. Hampstead, NY: Hofstra, 1975.

TORONTO SCHOOL OF THEOLOGY. *Truth in Advertising*. Toronto: Fitzhenry and Whiteside Ltd., 1972.

WYCKHAM, R., P. BANTING and A. WENSLEY. "The Language of Advertising: Who Controls Quality?" *Journal of Business Ethics*, Vol. 3, No. 1 (February 1984), pp. 45–55.

PART TEN

Deception in Business

INTRODUCTION

Generally speaking, most of us agree that lying is morally wrong. Of course, we can always think of exceptions where we believe that it may be good to tell a lie (e.g., we might tell a suicidal friend that we don't own a gun when she or he asks to borrow one), but such cases confirm our general belief by illustrating their unique features. However, despite our general consensus with respect to lying and truth-telling, many people are unclear as to what constitutes lying in business and what its moral import is in that context. Also, there is some debate about the nature of misrepresentation which doesn't fall under the category of lying but does involve not telling all that you know, with the intent to deceive. Further, there is the issue of who is responsible for lies or deceptions done for the good of the corporation or the union. Many of these issues have already been addressed in preceding sections. Here they are considered in the specific context of commercial negotiation.

Before proceeding with a discussion of how all of this relates to business negotiations, it is useful to define our terms. In the first article in Part Ten, Carson, Wokutch, and Murrmann provide various candidates as definitions of lying. The definition which they believe most plausibly and completely captures what is meant by a lie is that a lie "is a deliberate false statement which is either intended to deceive others or foreseen to be likely to deceive others." This definition presupposes intent and purpose, knowledge of the truth, and freedom from constraint. Thus, the individual who lies is one who knowingly and freely tells someone a false statement which they wish the listener to believe. If we morally condemn most lies, it would seem that we would morally condemn anyone who in business negotiations knowingly and freely states a falsehood which they wished to be believed. However, the case may be more complex than it appears.

In 1968, A.Z. Carr argued in "Is Business Bluffing Ethical?" that making false statements in negotiation is all part of the "game" in business. The difference here, according to Carr, is that, like in any game and unlike life generally, everyone is playing by the same rules. Hence, if a consultant told a company that she or he would not work for less than $1000 per day even though that were false, this would be considered morally acceptable because the company would assume that the consultant was not going to be truthful. Similarly, the company's stated position might be that $500 per day was the upper acceptable salary they were prepared to pay even though they knew that their final offer could go as high as $750 per day. Consequently, Carr distinguishes between lying and bluffing on the grounds that the presuppositions are different. Lying presupposes that, other things being equal, people are going to be truthful. Bluffing suggests that the partners in negotiation both implicitly accept that false statements will be offered as truths.

Carson, Wokutch, and Murrmann do not agree. There may be justifications for some instances of bluffing, but that does not mean that bluffing is not lying. It also means that people can and often should be morally blamed for lying in business negotiations. Carson *et al.* argue that "competitive arrangements do not *cause* people to become dishonest, treacherous, etc." Consequently, to bluff or not to bluff is ultimately a personal decision for which one must take personal responsibility.

Part of the discussion by Carson *et al.* is about the nature of lying and deception. The general purpose of this discussion is to illustrate their claims that 1) bluffing involves lying; 2) other types of deception may be equally reprehensible; and finally, 3) bluffing and other forms of deception may be justifiable "in the absence of any special reasons for thinking that one's negotiating partners are not bluffing (e.g., when one is dealing with an unusually naive or scrupulous person)."

In a response to this article, Jones raises three objections to the treatment of lying by Carson *et al.* Jones' main contention is that Carson *et al.* are incorrect in assuming that the intention to deceive is not a component of lying. The consequence of this, according to Jones, is a misdescription of, for example, "the range of cases of advertising that are deceptive in the sense that they contain lies," a range that is "more restricted than Carson *et al.* have concluded."

James Michelman takes a slightly different perspective on this question. Although Michelman doesn't disagree with the definition proposed by Carson *et al.*, his emphasis is different. While Carson *et al.* argue that bluffing can be justified if everyone is operating by the same rules, they also suggest that bluffing is not necessary for successful negotiation. Michelman, on the other hand, believes that "under certain conditions, given the constraints of economic competition, one must negotiate by means of deception." The disagreement may be moot, however, for Michelman concludes that to participate in such practices is morally wrong, and in fact "diminishes" the humanity of the players in such deceit.

Michelman defines commercial negotiation as "that interchange between buyer and seller in which they attempt to reach price agreement within implicit boundaries on the grounds of their common desire to consummate a deal and in the face of their diametrically opposed price goals." Since the goal of the seller is to sell for the highest price she or he can get and the goal of the buyer to buy for the lowest price she or he can offer, the negotiators are in a stalemate position if they truthfully state what is the optimal price for each, respectively. Since both want to "win," any compromise means failure. However, "deception offers a way out of this dilemma." If the negotiating buyer and seller lie about what the actual optimal price is, then both parties can appear to concede and still win. The result is "a peculiar kind of deception in which both parties are aware that each is trying to deceive the other, and . . . [making] . . . a sad mockery of protestations of truth and fidelity."

What can we make of these various discussions? Carr wishes to argue that business is like a game, and since everyone plays by the same rules, bluffing is fair practice. Carson *et al.* claim that bluffing involves lying and that business practice does not require lying. Jones argues that Carson *et al.* give a faulty account of lying which muddies the waters of moral assessment. Finally, Michelman argues that bluffing is necessary for profitability, although dehumanizing. Further, if deception is intrinsic to business negotiation, what should we do about it? Is capitalism innately immoral or are some of the participants just choosing to operate in unethical ways? Would being completely truthful, as we (usually) are in personal life, work in labour and business negotiations? If unions and corporations, or their agents acting as such, can deceive each other, how can we draw the line between that and individuals, as private persons, lying to corporations for private profit?

46

Bluffing in Labor Negotiations: Legal and Ethical Issues

THOMAS L. CARSON
RICHARD E. WOKUTCH
KENT F. MURRMANN

More than a decade ago a *Harvard Business Review* article entitled 'Is Business Bluffing Ethical' (Carr, 1968) created a storm of controversy when the author defended bluffing and other questionable business practices on the grounds that they are just part of the game of business. The controversy over the ethics of bluffing and alleged deception in business negotiations erupted again recently with the publication of the *Wall Street Journal* article, 'To Some at Harvard, Telling Lies Becomes a Matter of Course' (Bulkeley, 1979). This [article] detailed a negotiations course taught at Harvard Business School in which students were allowed to bluff and deceive each other in various simulated negotiation situations. Students' grades were partially determined by the settlements they negotiated with each other, and hence some alleged that this course encouraged and taught students to bluff, lie to, and deceive negotiating partners. These controversies raised issues concerning the morality, necessity, and even the legality of bluffing in business negotiations which were never adequately resolved. It is the aim of this paper to shed some light on these issues.

In the first section of the paper we will describe briefly the nature of the collective bargaining process and then examine the role of bluffing in that process. The second section of the paper is a discussion of labor-law as it relates to bluffing. Then, in the third and fourth sections of the paper we will argue that bluffing and other deceptive practices in labor negotiations typically do constitute lying. Nevertheless, we will argue that bluffing is typically morally permissible but for different reasons than those put forth by Carr. In our conclusion we consider whether it is an indictment of our present negotiating practices and our economic system as a whole that, given the harsh realities of the marketplace, bluffing *is* usually morally acceptable.

From the *Journal of Business Ethics*, Vol. 1, No. 1, February 1982, pp. 13-22. © 1982, D. Reidel Publishing Company, Dordrecht, Holland. Reprinted by permission.

THE NATURE OF COLLECTIVE BARGAINING

Collective bargaining is fundamentally a competitive process in which labor and management dispute and eventually decide the terms of employment. Through bargaining each party attempts to reach an agreement which each perceives to be at least minimally acceptable if not highly favorable, in light of its vital interests.

Typically there is a range of possible settlement points on wages (and other bargained issues) that each party would accept rather than fail to reach an agreement. This range exists with respect to wages, for instance, because the minimum wage that an employer could pay and still attract the needed employees is typically lower at any point in time than the maximum wage the employer could pay and still manage to operate a competitive business. Neither party knows the exact location of these extreme points. And ordinarily there is no one economically optimal wage level within the range that can be established through reference to objective criteria that are acceptable to both parties.[1] Each party attempts to move the wage agreement toward its preferred end of the range. Also, each attempts to define a point on the range beyond which it would rather endure a work stoppage than accept a settlement. Thus, in practice, the top end of the range becomes the highest wage that management would pay rather than endure a work stoppage. The bottom end of the range becomes the minimum wage that labor would accept rather than endure a work stoppage. These extreme positions are the parties' respective 'sticking points'.

Factors affecting bargaining success

Two factors are instrumental to the ability of either party to negotiate a favorable agreement, i.e., an agreement that both perceive to be more than minimally acceptable. The first factor is the ability to impose significant costs on the other party, or to credibly threaten the imposition of such costs, in order to pressure the other party to make concessions. Thus, in order to bargain successfully, labor must be able to instill in management the belief that labor would initiate a work stoppage, or other form of costly noncooperation, in order to secure what it considers to be reasonable terms of employment. Likewise, in order for management to bargain successfully, it must convey to labor the perception that it would endure a work stoppage rather than accept what it believes to be unreasonable conditions.

The other key factor that affects one's bargaining success is the ability to accurately discern the other party's minimum acceptable conditions while vigilantly concealing one's own minimum terms. Such knowledge enables one to confidently drive the bargain to more favorable terms without risking an unwanted and costly work stoppage.

Bluffing and bargaining success

Bluffing typically plays a very important part concerning both of these factors. Bluffing is an act in which one attempts to misrepresent one's intentions or overstate the strength of one's position in the bargaining process. This is possible because neither party knows for sure the other party's true intentions or 'sticking point'. Bluffing often involves making deceptive statements. For instance, the union bargaining representative may boldly state, "There is no way that our people will accept such a small wage increase", when he/she knows full well that they would gladly accept management's offer rather than go out on strike. However, bluffing can be entirely nonverbal. Nodding confidently as one raises the bet while holding a poor hand in a game of poker is a paradigm case of bluffing. Getting up from the bargaining table in a huff and going out the door is another example of nonverbal bluffing. Through these and similar types of statements and behavior either party can convey to the other an exaggerated portrayal of its ability to impose or endure costs, and thereby can increase its actual ability to gain concessions in the bargaining process.

In addition, aggressive bluffing can be used to test the other party's resolve or otherwise prod the other party to concede certain points. This use of bluffing on different bargaining issues over a period of time, say spanning several bargaining sessions, can significantly increase one's understanding of the other party's true strength, and thus can enhance one's ability to accurately estimate the other party's sticking points on various issues.

There can be no doubt that bluffing is an important bargaining tool. It can be employed to create impressions of enhanced strength as well as to probe the other party to find out the level of its critical sticking points. Through these methods either party can attempt to gain a more favorable settlement than the other party would otherwise be willing to allow. Labor and management alike are more apt to fully abide by those terms of employment that they know were established through a free and vigorous use of their best bargaining skills.

The alleged necessity of bluffing

While bluffing can obviously be advantageous in labor negotiations, one might ask whether it is 'economically necessary'. This does not appear to be the case. Where one of the parties has an extremely strong negotiating position (e.g. an employer in a one company town with a high unemployment rate, a slavemaster, or a surgeon who is the only one capable of performing a new surgical procedure necessary to save one's life) wages and working conditions can simply be dictated by the stronger party.

What about the claim that bluffing is a necessary part of the negotiation of any *voluntary* labor agreement between parties of relatively equal power? This also seems false. Suppose that two very scrupulous parties are attempting to reach a wage settlement and neither wants to engage in bluffing. Assuming that they trust each other and honestly reveal their 'sticking points', they could agree to some formula such as splitting the difference between the sticking points. This is of course unlikely to occur in real life, but only because few individuals are honest or trusting enough for our assumptions to hold.

THE LEGAL STATUS OF BLUFFING

The National Labor Relations Act (U.S.), as amended (1970), provides the legal framework within which the collective bargaining process in the private sector of our economy is carried out. Sections 8(a)(5) and 8(b)(3) of the National Labor Relations Act provide that it shall be an unfair labor practice for a union or an employer in a properly constituted bargaining relationship to fail to bargain in good faith. The statute left it to the National Labor Relations Board and the courts to establish criteria for determining whether a party is bargaining in good faith. Over the years numerous such criteria have been established by the Board and the courts.

The honest claims doctrine

Of particular interest with respect to the legal status of bluffing is the 'honest claims' doctrine, established by the U.S. Supreme Court in its Truitt Mfg. Co. decision (NLRB v. Truitt Mfg. Co., 1956). This states that "good faith necessarily requires that claims made by either party should be honest claims". The central issue in the Truitt Case was whether the employer would be required to substantiate its claim that it could not afford to pay a certain wage increase. In addition to enunciating its 'honest claims' doctrine, the court declared that if an "inability to pay argument is important enough to present in the give and take of bargaining it is important enough to require some sort of proof of its accuracy" (NLRB v. Truitt Mfg. Co., 1956, p. 152). This 'honest claims' policy has been consistently upheld and applied in numerous court decisions to this day. Thus, it is clear that the law requires honesty in collective bargaining. However, the 'honest claims' requirement applies only to those types of claims that pertain directly to issues subject to bargaining and the employer's ability to provide certain conditions of employment. Thus, the 'honest claims' policy requires a union to refrain from presenting false information to management concerning the level of wages and fringe benefits provided by employers under other union contracts. Likewise, the employer must refrain from falsely claiming an inability to provide a certain benefit.

Bluffing and the honest claims doctrine

How does the 'honest claims' doctrine apply to the practice of bluffing? It is clear that bluffing that involves the presentation of false information about issues subject to bargaining (i.e., wages, hours, and condition of employment) is a violation. However, bluffing about objective issues not subject to negotiation such as one's ability to withstand a strike (e.g. the size of the union strike fund, or the union membership's vote on the question of whether or not to go out on strike) is allowable. Also, bluffing that is limited to representations of one's bargaining intentions or one's willingness to impose or endure costs in order to win a more favorable contract does not constitute a violation. Of course, this type of bluffing is more effective and more prevalent because it can not be as easily discredited through reference to objective information as can false statements about working conditions. In sum, though the Truitt decision requires honesty with regard to the making of claims concerning bargaining topics, it does not proscribe the more effective and important forms of bluffing commonly used in bargaining today.

BLUFFING AND THE CONCEPT OF LYING

Suppose (example 1) that I am a management negotiator trying to reach a strike settlement with union negotiators. I need to settle the strike soon and have been instructed to settle for as much as a 12% increase in wages and benefits if that is the best agreement I can obtain. I say that the company's final offer is a 10% increase. Am I lying? Consider also whether any of the following examples constitute lying:

(2) Management negotiators misstating the profitability of a subsidiary to convince the union negotiating with it that the subsidiary would go out of business if management acceded to union wage demands.

(3) Union officials misreporting the size of the union strike fund to portray a greater ability to strike than is actually the case.

(4) Management negotiators saying, "We can't afford this agreement," when it would not put the firm out of business but only reduce profits from somewhat above to somewhat below the industry average.

(5) Union negotiators saying, "The union membership is adamant on this issue," when they know that while one half of the membership is adamant, the other half couldn't care less.

(6) Union negotiators saying, "If you include this provision, we'll get membership approval of the contract," when they know they'll have an uphill battle for approval even with the provision.

Defining lying

What is lying? A lie must be a false statement[2], but not all false statements are lies. If I am a salesman and say that my product is the best on the market and *sincerely believe this to be the case*, my statement is not a lie, even if it is untrue. A false statement is not a lie unless it is somehow deliberate or intentional. Suppose that we define a lie as an intentional false statement. According to this definition, I am telling a lie when I say, "This aftershave will make you feel like a million bucks." This definition implies that we lie when we exaggerate, e.g., a negotiator representing union workers making $10/hour but seeking a substantial raise says, "These are slave wages you're paying us." When I greatly exaggerate or say something in jest, I know that it is very improbable that the other person(s) will believe what I say. The reason that these examples do not appear to be lies is that they do not involve the intent to deceive. This suggests the following definition of lying:

> D1 A lie is a deliberate[3] false statement intended to deceive another person.

This definition is inadequate in cases in which a person is compelled to make false statements. For example, I may lie as a witness to a jury for fear of being killed by the accused. But it doesn't follow that I hope or intend to deceive them.[4] I may hope that my statements don't deceive anyone. We might say that what makes my statements lies is that I realize or foresee that they are likely to deceive others. This then suggests the following definition of lying:

> D2 A lie is a deliberate false statement which is thought to be likely to deceive others by the person who makes it.

This definition is also lacking because a person can lie even if he or she has almost no hope of being believed. A criminal protesting his or her innocence in court is lying no matter how unlikely it is that he/she thinks the argument will be convincing to the judge or jury. The following definition is more plausible than either D1 or 2:

> D3 A lie is a deliberate false statement which is either intended to deceive others or foreseen to be likely to deceive others.

Implications for bluffing. It appears that this definition implies that the statements in our first three examples constitute lies. In examples (1) and (2) one is making deliberate false statements with the intent of deceiving others about matters relevant to the negotiations. In the first case I am making a deliberate false statement with the intent to deceive the other party into thinking that I am unwilling to offer more than 10%. One might object that this needn't be my intent in example (1). No one familiar with standard negotiating practices is likely to take at face value statements which a person makes about a 'final offer'. One might argue that in the two cases in question I intend and expect my statement that 10% is my best offer to be taken to mean my highest possible offer is something around 12%.

If this is my intention and expectation, then my bluffing does not constitute a lie. To this we might add the observation that such intentions are quite uncommon in business negotiations. Even if I don't *expect* you to believe that 10% is my final position, I probably still *hope* or intend to deceive you into thinking that I am unwilling to offer as much as 12%. Examples (2) and (3) are clear instances of lying — they involve deliberate false statements intended to deceive others. It's not so clear, however, that examples (4), (5) and (6) constitute instances of lying. These cases do seem to involve the intent to deceive, but the statements involved are sufficiently ambiguous that it is not clear that they are untrue. We can still say that these are cases in which one affirms (or represents as true) statements which one knows to be dubious with the intent to deceive others. Morally speaking this may be just as bad or wrong as straightforward instances of lying.

An alternative definition of lying. Our proposed definition of lying implies that bluffing in standard negotiation settings constitutes lying. There is at least one other approach to defining the concept of lying which does not have this consequence and it would be well for us to consider it here. In his *Lecture on Ethics*, Immanuel Kant (1775–1780) holds that a deliberate false statement does not constitute a lie unless the speaker has "expressly given" the other(s) to believe that he/she intends to speak the truth.[5] According to Kant's original view, when I make a false statement to a thief about the location of my valuables, I am not lying because "the thief knows full well that I will not, if I can help it, tell him the truth and that he has no right to demand it of me" (1775–1780, p. 227). According to this view, false statements uttered in the course of business negotiations do not constitute lies except in the very unusual circumstances that one promises to tell the truth during the negotiations. Kant's definition is open to serious objections. It seems to rule out many common cases of lying. For example, suppose that a child standing in line to see an X-rated movie claims to be 18 when he or she is only 15. This is a lie in spite of the fact that no explicit promise to tell the truth was made to the ticket seller. There does seem to be one relevant difference between the two cases in question. The ticket taker has a right to be told the truth and a right to the information in question, the thief has no right to the information on one's valuables. This suggests the following revision of Kant's definition:

> D4 A lie is a deliberate false statement which is (i) either intended to deceive others or foreseen to be likely to deceive others, and (ii) either the person who makes the statement has promised to be truthful or those to whom it is directed have a right to know the truth.

Many would take it to be a virtue of D4 that it implies that deliberate false statements made during the course of certain kinds of competitive activities do not constitute lies. Carr quoted the British statesman Henry Taylor who argued that "falsehood ceases to be falsehood when it is understood on all sides that the truth is not expected to be spoken" (1968, p. 143). Carr argued that in poker, diplomacy, and business, individuals (through mutually implied consent) forfeit their rights to be told the truth. It seems at least plausible to say this with respect to standard cases of negotiation. However, it is surely not the case in situations in which one of the parties is unfamiliar with standard negotiating procedures (e.g. children, immigrant laborers, naive individuals or the mentally impaired), and enters into the discussion assuming that all of the parties will be perfectly candid.

If D4 is a correct definition of lying, then it does seem plausible to say that bluffing typically does not amount to lying. So, in order to defend our earlier claim, that bluffing usually involves lying we need to give reasons for thinking that D3 is preferable to D4. We are inclined to think that deliberate falsehoods uttered in the course of games and diplomacy as well as business do constitute lies, and are thus inclined to prefer D3 to D4. This is a case about which people have conflicting intuitions; it cannot be a decisive reason for preferring D3 to D4 or vice versa. A more decisive consideration in favor of D3 is the following case. Suppose that a management negotiator asks a union negotiator the size of the union strike fund. The union negotiator responds by saying it is three times its actual amount. Definition (4) implies that this statement is not a lie since the management negotiator didn't have a right to know the information in question and the union didn't explicitly promise to tell the truth about this. But surely this is a lie. The fact that management has no right to know the truth is just cause for withholding the information, but responding falsely is a lie nonetheless.

There is, to the best of our knowledge, no plausible definition of lying which allows us to say that typical instances of bluffing in labor and other sorts of business negotiations do not involve lying. We should stress that it is only bluffing which involves making false statements which constitutes lying. One is not lying if one bluffs another by making the true statement "We want a 30% pay increase". Similarly, it is not a lie if one bluffs without making any statements as in a game of poker or overpricing (on a price tag) a product where bargaining is expected (e.g. a used car lot or antique store).

The concept of deception

At this point it would be useful to consider the relationship between lying and the broader concept of deception. Deception may be defined as intentionally causing another person to have false beliefs. (It is not clear whether preventing someone from having true beliefs should count as deception). As we have seen, lying always involves the intent to deceive others, or the expectation that they will be deceived as a result of what one says, or both. But one can lie without actually deceiving anyone. If you don't believe me when I lie and tell you that 10% is our final offer, then I haven't succeeded in deceiving you about anything. It is also possible to deceive another person without telling a lie. For example, I am not lying when I deceive a thief into thinking that I am at home by installing an automatic timer to have my lights turned on in the evening. Only deception which involves making false statements can be considered lying.

It seems that one can often avoid lying in the course of a business negotiation simply by phrasing one's statements very carefully. In negotiations, instead of lying and saying that 10% is the highest wage increase we will give, I could avoid lying by making the following true, but equally deceptive statement: "Our position is that 10% is our final offer" (without saying that this position is subject to change). It is questionable whether this is any less morally objectionable than lying. Most people prefer to deceive others by means of cleverly contrived true statements, rather than lies. Some who have strong scruples against lying see nothing wrong with such ruses. It is doubtful, however, whether lying is any worse than mere deception. Consider the following example. I want to deceive a potential thief into thinking that I will be at home in the late afternoon. I have the choice between (i) leaving my lights on, and (ii) leaving a note on my door which says "I will be home at 5 p.m.". Surely this choice is morally indifferent. The fact that (ii) is an act of lying and (i) isn't, is not, itself, a reason for thinking that (i) is morally preferable to (ii).[6]

MORAL ISSUES IN LYING

Common sense holds that lying is a matter of moral significance and that lying is *prima facie* wrong, or wrong everything else being equal. This can also be put by saying that there is a presumption against lying, and that lying requires some special justification in order to be considered permissible. Common sense also holds that lying is not always wrong, it can sometimes be justified (Ross, 1930). Almost no one would agree with Kant's (1797) later view in 'On the Supposed Right to Tell Lies from Benevolent Motives', that it is wrong to lie even if doing so is necessary to protect the lives of innocent people. According to this view it would be wrong to lie to a potential murderer concerning the whereabouts of an intended victim. Common sense also seems to hold that there is a presumption against simple deception.

Assuming the correctness of this view about the morality of lying and deception, and assuming that we are correct in saying that bluffing involves lying, it follows that bluffing and other deceptive business

practices require some sort of special justification in order to be considered permissible.

We will now attempt to determine whether there is any special justification for the kind of lying and deception which typically occurs in labor and other sorts of business negotiations.

Bluffing and other sorts of deceptive strategies are standard practice in these negotiations and they are generally thought to be acceptable. Does the fact that these things are standard practice or 'part of the game' show that they are justified? We think not. The mere fact that something is standard practice, legal, or generally accepted is not enough to justify it. Standard practice and popular opinion can be in error. Such things as slavery were once standard practice, legal and generally accepted. But they are and *were* morally wrong. Bluffing constitutes an attempt to deceive others about the nature of one's intentions in a bargaining situation. The *prima facie* wrongness of bluffing is considerably *diminished* on account of the fact that the lying and deception involved typically concern matters about which the other parties have no particular right to know. The others have no particular right to know one's bargaining position — one's intentions. However, there is still some presumption against lying or deceiving other people, even when they have no right to the information in question. A stranger has no right to know how old I am. I have no obligation to provide him/her with this information. Other things being equal, however, it would still be wrong for me to lie to this stranger about my age.

In our view the main justification for bluffing consists in the fact that the moral presumption against lying to or deceiving someone holds only when the person or persons with whom you are dealing is/are not attempting to lie to or deceive you. Given this, there is no presumption against bluffing or deceiving someone who is attempting to bluff or deceive you on that occasion. The prevalence of bluffing in negotiations means that one is safe in presuming that one is justified in bluffing in the absence of any special reasons for thinking that one's negotiating partners are not bluffing (e.g., when one is dealing with an unusually naive or scrupulous person).

CONCLUSIONS

Granted that bluffing and deception can be permissible given the exigencies and harsh realities of economic bargaining in our society, isn't it an indictment of our entire economic system that such activities are necessary in so many typical circumstances? Even those who defend the practice of bluffing (Carr, 1968) concede that a great deal of lying and deception occurs in connection with the economic activities of our society. Much of this (particularly in the area of bargaining or negotiating) is openly condoned or encouraged by both business and labor. While lying and deception are not generally condoned in other contexts, they often occur as the result of pressures generated by the highly competitive nature of our society. For example, few would condone the behavior of a salesperson who deliberately misrepresents the cost and effectiveness of a product. However, a salesperson under pressure to sell an inferior product may feel that he/she must either deceive prospective customers or else find a new job.

Many people would argue that our economic system is flawed in that it allegedly encourages dishonesty and thus corrupts our moral character and makes us worse persons than we would have been otherwise. Such criticisms are frequently found in Marxist literature. This kind of criticism can be extended into other areas as well. The competitive arrangements of our economic system are not only blamed for encouraging dishonesty, but other kinds of allegedly unethical conduct as well. The so-called competitive business 'rat race' has been cited as a cause of personal treachery, backbiting, and sycophantic behavior. This, it seems to us is a very serious criticism which warrants careful consideration. We suggest the following three lines of response.

(1) One could concede that the economic arrangements of our society are such as to elicit a great deal of unethical conduct, but argue that this is the case in any viable economic system — including various forms of socialism and communism. If this is so, then the existence of immoral conduct which is associated with economic activities in our own society cannot be a reason to prefer some other sort of economic system. The record of the major socialist and communist countries would tend to support this view. There is deception in the bargaining involved in such things as the allocation of labor and raw materials for industry and setting production quotas for industry. There is also the same kind of gamesmanship involved in competing for desirable positions in society and (by all accounts) much greater opportunity and need for bribery. However, there have been viable feudalistic and caste societies which were much less competitive than our own which functioned with much less deception or occasion for deception. If one's place in society is determined by birth, then one will simply not have occasion to get ahead by deception.

(2) While it must be conceded that there are other types of economic systems which involve less dishonesty than our own, these systems have other undesirable features which outweigh this virtue. In a feudal society or a centrally planned 'command' economy there might well be less occasion for bargaining about wages and prices and thus also less occasion for deceiving other people about such things. But such a society is surely less free than our own and also very likely to be less prosperous. There are strong reasons to desire that wages be determined by voluntary agreements, even if that allows for the possibility of dishonesty in negotiations.

(3) It can be argued that the present objections to competitive economic systems such as our own rest on a mistaken view about the nature of moral goodness and the moral virtues. One's moral goodness and honesty are not a direct function of how frequently one tells lies. Thor Hyerdahl did not tell any lies during the many months in which he was alone on the Kon-Tiki. But we would not conclude from this that he was an exceptionally honest man during that period of time. Similarly, the fact that a businessperson who has a monopoly on a vital good or service does not misrepresent the price or quality of his/her goods or services does not necessarily mean that he/she is honest. There is simply no occasion or temptation to be dishonest. The

extent to which a person possesses the different moral virtues is a function of how that person is *disposed* to act in various actual and possible situations. My courage or cowardice is a function of my ability to master fear in dangerous situations. Suppose that I am drafted into the Army and sent to serve in the front lines. If I desert my post at the first sign of the enemy we would not say that being drafted into the army has made me a more cowardly person. Rather, we could say that it has uncovered and actualized cowardly dispositions which I had all along. Similarly, competitive economic arrangements do not usually *cause* people to become dishonest or treacherous, etc. However

these arrangements often actualize dispositions to act dishonestly or treacherously which people had all along. This is not to deny that the economic institutions of our society can in some cases alter a person's basic behavioral dispositions and thereby also his/her character for the worse. For example, the activities of a negotiator may cause him/her to be less truthful and trusting in his/her personal relationships. Our claim is only that most of the 'undesirable moral effects' attributed to our economic institutions involve actualizing pre-existing dispositions, rather than causing any fundamental changes in character.

ENDNOTES

1. It could, however, be argued on utilitarian grounds that, given a decreasing marginal utility for money, there is a presumption to settle as favorably as possible for the employees since they are *generally* poorer than the stockholders.

2. Arnold Isenberg, however, disputes this in 'Conditions for Lying', in *Ethical Theory and Business*, Tom Beauchamp and Norman Bowie (eds.) (Prentice Hall, Englewood Cliffs, N.J., 1979), pp. 466-468. He holds that a true statement can be a lie provided that one does not believe it. He defines a lie as follows: "A lie is a statement made by one who does not believe it with the intention that someone else be led to believe it. This definition leaves open the possibility that a person could be lying even though he says what is true" (p. 466). We feel that this is most implausible. For if what one says is true, this is always sufficient to defeat the claim that it is a lie.

3. There is however some question here as to what it means to make a *deliberate* false statement. Must one believe that what one says is false or is it enough that one not believe it? Roderick Chisholm and Thomas Feehan hold that the latter is all that is necessary in 'The Intent to Deceive', *Journal of Philosophy* 74 (1977), 143-159. This makes the concept of lying broader than it would otherwise be.

4. Frederick Siegler considers this kind of example in 'Lying', *American Philosophical Quarterly* 3 (1966), 128-

136. But he argues that it does not count against the view that a necessary condition of a statement's being a lie is that it is intended to deceive someone. The example only shows that it is not necessary that the liar, him/herself, intend to deceive the others. But it does not count against the view that the lie must be intended *by someone* to deceive others. For, in our present example, *the criminal intends* that the witness' statements deceive others. However, a slight modification of the present example generates a counter-example to his claim that a lie must be intended by someone or other to deceive. Suppose that a witness makes a deliberate false statement, *x* for fear of being killed by the friends of the accused. He/she is lying even if the accused's friends believe that *x* is true, in which case neither they nor anyone else intend that the witness' statements deceive the jury.

5. Kant's analysis of lying offered here differs from the one presented in Kant's later and more well known work, 'On the Supposed Right to Tell Lies from Benevolent Motives' (1797) in Barauch Brody (ed.), *Moral Rules and Particular Circumstances* (Prentice Hall, 1970), pp. 31-36. There he says that any intentional false statement is a lie (p. 32). Kant also gives a different account of the morality of lying in these two works. His well-known absolute prohibition against lying is set forth only in the latter work.

6. We owe this example to Bernard Gert.

47

Lying and Intentions

GARY E. JONES

Isenberg has proferred[1] the following definition of a lie: (1) a statement that is made by the speaker who (2) disbelieves the statement, accompanied by (3) a certain intention by the speaker.[2] Isenberg allows (1) and (2) to be obvious, and concentrates his analysis on the third component. He states that the common sense idea that a liar intends to deceive the listener is erroneous. One can, that is, lie without wishing to deceive. To prove his point, Isenberg considers the following example: Suppose a man tells a creditor that he has no money on his person. He wants the creditor to believe what he says, not to be mistaken in what he is led to believe; it might suit the creditor, in fact, if he *had* no money just then and could say so truthfully.[3]

It is not clear, however, that Isenberg's example proves what he wishes. There are two possibilities — that the debtor has money when he says he does not, and that he has none. If he has money when he says he has none, it seems reasonable to claim that the debtor is lying. Moreover, it seems that he has an intent to deceive the creditor into believing the falsehood. On the other hand, if the debtor actually

had no money when he told the creditor he had none, the debtor is simply telling the truth. Therefore, in the first instance we seem to have a lie with the intention to deceive, and in the second, we have no lie at all. What we do not have is what Isenberg needs to prove his point — an instance of a lie without an intention to deceive.

Isenberg again misses the mark when he states why a wish to deceive *cannot* be a component of a lie. He states that a "wish to deceive" implies that deception is the end and suggests, therefore, that a person would look about at random for a false story to perpetrate upon others in April Fool's Day fashion.[4] Apart from simply stating that the wish to deceive has such an untoward consequence, Isenberg offers no proof for the existence of such an implication. Moreover, there are strong grounds for doubting its existence. A wish to deceive is simply a component, a necessary condition, of a lie. Nothing follows from this regarding the overall *reason* for telling a lie. Indeed, in most cases the deception is a means to an end. German citizens during World War II, for example, lied to Nazi troops regarding the where-

From *Journal of Business Ethics* **5** (1986) 347–349. © 1986 by D. Reidel Publishing Company. Reprinted by permission.

abouts of Jewish refugees not for the mere sake of accomplishing a deception, but for the purpose of saving the refugees. It can thus be said that usually the intended deception is the means to achieving a certain end, which is the motive for the lie.

Another attempt to show that an intention to deceive is not a component of a lie comes from Carson, Wokutch, and Murrmann.[5] They claim that the definition: (1) "A lie is a deliberate false statement intended to deceive another person" is inadequate in cases in which a person is compelled to make false statements. For instance, someone may lie as a witness to a jury for fear of being killed by the accused. It does not follow, however, that she hopes or intends to deceive the jury. She may hope that her statements don't deceive *anyone*.[6] It may be thought that all that has been shown so far is that it is not necessary that the liar *himself* intend to deceive the others. It could still be maintained that the lie must be intended by *someone* to deceive others. After all, in the above example the criminal intends that the witness's statements deceive others. Even this weaker claim is, however, mistaken according to Carson *et al.* Suppose that a witness makes a deliberate false statement, X, for fear of being killed by the friends of the accused. (S)he is lying even if the accused's friends believe that X is true, in which case neither they nor anyone else intend that the witness's statements deceive the jury.[7]

Having concluded that the intent to deceive is not a necessary condition of lying, Carson *et al.* consider the possibility that lying only necessarily involves realizing that one's statements are likely to deceive others. Hence the following definition is suggested: (2) "A lie is a deliberate false statement which is thought to be likely to deceive others by the person who makes it."[8] The authors point out, however, that this definition is also inadequate because a person can lie even if (s)he has almost no hope of being believed. For instance, a criminal protesting his innocence in court is lying even though he does not believe that the jury will believe him.[9] Therefore, in light of the difficulties associated with the first two attempts, Carson *et al.* adopt the following definition: (3) "A lie is a deliberate false statement which is either intended to deceive others or foreseen to

be likely to deceive others." The authors are satisfied with this definition as it is apparently not subject to counterexamples and it supports their claim that typical instances of bluffing in business negotiations involve lying.[10]

There are, however, at least three difficulties with the above analysis. First, the examples that are supposed to prove that one can lie without intending to deceive may be questioned. It will be recalled that the examples relied on the fact that a witness made a deliberately false statement but did not "really" intend to deceive anyone. It is not clear, however, that one who perjures himself can maintain that he did not intend to deceive anyone. It could be claimed that the witness manifested an intention to deceive by the mere fact that he testified falsely, his inner feelings notwithstanding. This situation brings to mind a famous case in Contracts, *Lucy* v. *Zehmer*,[11] wherein two parties seemed to strike a deal for the sale of land. Both men had been drinking, but seemed to know what they were doing; in fact, though the contract was written on a bar napkin, they composed it twice. The defendant in the case contended that though he in some sense went through the motions of entering into a contract, his inner intention was simply to play out a joke. The court ruled, however, that the secret inner intentions of an actor cannot take precedence over the manifested intentions if they conflict. Indeed, it would be difficult if not impossible to reasonably conduct transactions and to hold people responsible for their actions unless it is assumed that their actions demonstrate their intentions. It would be ludicrous and yet a consequence of the view being criticized if a witness could defeat the charge of perjury by claiming that despite deliberately making false statements he really did not intend to deceive anyone. The deliberate making of false statements on the witness stand manifests an intention to deceive and constitutes perjury. In Carson *et al.*'s examples, the proper conclusion is not that the witnesses did not through their actions manifest an intention to deceive, but rather that it may be excused as being the result of duress.

The second problem with their analysis is that the law generally regards as "intended" those consequences of an action that are foreseen with "substantial certainty."[12] The law subsumes highly foreseeable consequences under intended ones for the purposes of assessing liability; i.e., if a defendant knew that certain consequences of his actions were highly probable, he is as responsible for them as if he intended them. To the extent that the law merges foreseeable and intended consequences, the definition Carson *et al.* adopted is frustrated. An actor will be held to be liable for his deception whether he intended or merely foresaw the results. If foreseeable results are "intended," and one can lie without intending to deceive, either one can lie without even foreseeing the resulting deception or Carson *et al.*'s endeavour to make the distinction is pointless.

Finally it seems that the authors have almost furnished their own counterexample to the definition they adopted. They claim that the thesis that a deceptive intent is necessary for a lie is false, and that the mere foreseeability of deception is also unnecessary. So, after disposing of definitions (1) and (2) which respectively assert the necessity of

these conditions, the authors believe they have a solution in a third definition that takes the two failed conditions as alternatives. The assumption *appears* to be that every instance of a lie will satisfy one or the other condition. This assumption is however not argued for, and moreover appears to be false. Consider their *last* example in which a witness deliberately makes a false statement and allegedly no one intends anyone to be deceived. If it is also stipulated that no one *foresees* that anyone will be deceived, the example constitutes a counterexample to the definition the authors finally adopt. Thus the authors' definition is liable to rather facile counterexamples, and was only conjectured as a result of difficulties that allegedly plagued the first definition considered. I submit that the counter-examples to the first definition are themselves dubious and that it is therefore clearly preferable to the faulty definition the authors finally adopt. If so, then the range of cases of advertising that are deceptive in the sense that they contain lies is more restricted than Carson *et al.* have concluded.

ENDNOTES

1. Isenberg's essay, "Conditions for Lying," appears in Beauchamp and Bowie (eds.), *Ethical Theory and Business* (Englewood Cliffs, NJ: Prentice-Hall, 1983), pp. 316–18.

2. *Ibid.*, p. 316.

3. *Ibid.*, p. 317.

4. *Loc. cit.*

5. Their essay, "Bluffing in Labor Negotiations: Legal and Ethical Issues," first appeared in the *Journal of Business Ethics* 1 (1982), pp. 13–22. It is reprinted in

Beauchamp and Bowie, *op. cit.*, pp. 324–34. References are to the latter volume.

6. *Ibid.*, p. 328–9.

7. *Ibid.*, p. 334 note.

8. *Ibid.*, p. 329.

9. *Loc. cit.*

10. *Ibid.*, p. 330–1.

11. 84 S. E. 2d 516.

12. Cf. Restatement of Torts, 2d.

48

Deception in
Commercial Negotiation

JAMES H. MICHELMAN

"... I hate, detest, and can't bear a lie, not because I am straighter than the rest of us, but simply because it appalls me. There is a taint of death, a flavor of mortality in lies..."

—JOSEPH CONRAD, *Heart of Darkness*

I observe that deception seems to be a recurring concomitant of commercial negotiation. My observation leads me to wonder if these deceptions are merely aberrations, reflecting only the moral frailty of the performers; or whether they stem from a different — or additional — cause, one that has to do with the nature of commercial negotiation itself. If the latter is true, then we might find that the logic of commercial negotiation forces those who engage in it to become liars.[1]

In the investigation that follows I attempt to analyze in some depth the notion of a negotiating range. There is nothing novel in the concept itself. In their article, 'Bluffing in Labor Negotiations: Legal and Ethical Issues',... Professors Carson, Wokutch, and Murrmann... also explore the negotiating range.[2] Their conclusions as to its nature agree with mine.[3] We do not agree, however, on an equally fundamental matter. Professor Carson *et al.* state that "competitive arrangements do not usually *cause* [emphasis theirs] people to become dishonest, treacherous, etc." My contrary conclusion is that, under certain conditions, given the constraints of economic competition, one *must* negotiate by means of deception. At the end of this paper I briefly sketch some consequences.

I

The term 'commercial negotiation' carries a firm implication that price is involved; and indeed price may be the only factor being negotiated. The environment in which commercial negotiation takes place is one of freedom with respect to price. If the price were fixed there would be no need for — and

From the *Journal of Business Ethics*, Vol. 2, No. 4, November 1983, pp. 255-262. © 1983 D. Reidel Publishing Company, Dordrecht, Holland. Reprinted by permission.

could not be — any price negotiation. And although quantities, qualities, and dates of delivery may also be the subjects of commercial negotiation, these most often, in the last analysis, involve price. Quality always does; and since quantities and delivery dates affect both seller's costs and purchaser's 'buying power', these factors may be looked on generally as other ways of expressing price. Thus buyer and seller come to the bargaining table not knowing at what price the deal finally will be made.

Consider the respective viewpoints of the negotiators. Without immediately examining the reason why this should be so, it seems clear that the buyer's goal is to buy as cheaply as he can, and the seller's to sell as dearly. Since technically there is no top limit (or at best it is undefined) to the seller's price if he wishes to sell as dearly as possible, and since the buyer's desire to purchase as cheaply as possible is limited only by no cost at all, it is obvious that there is a wide differential between the seller's desired price and the buyer's desired cost. If there is to be a transaction this differential must be narrowed, and finally eliminated, by commercial negotiation. Thus, *commercial negotiation* may be thought of as *that interchange between buyer and seller in which the parties attempt to reach price agreement on the grounds of their common desire to consummate a deal and in the face of their diametrically opposed price goals.* Let this definition stand for the moment. Before modifying it, it will be helpful to identify those situations which are excluded from this analysis. I wish to emphasize, for example, that what we are investigating are those interchanges that take place when the price is not set. For example, we are not concerned with the following scenario: Small supplier, atomistic or nearly so, confronts large powerful buyer — say major retail chain operation. Large powerful buyer tells small, weak supplier — and means it — that the price which he is offering is 'not subject to negotiation', a common enough phrase. The supplier can take the proffered deal or leave it. There is no coercion because the supplier is not being threatened. He may infer a threat but the inference would be incorrect. Nor, since this particular deal is spread out on the table unconcealed, is there

deception. It is true that there may be deception in a more subtle sense. Perhaps the buyer is not sure of how cheap he can buy what he wants and is using his power in order to test the market, to explore how low his costs might be. In this case the seller becomes sort of a guinea pig in an experiment. Nevertheless, there has been no negotiation offered, and in the immediate sense, no concealment or deception. This is not the situation with which we are concerned. By contrast, the subject of my analysis lies only in those circumstances in which the parties expect and agree, for the most part tacitly, to truly negotiate.

II

In order to determine those markets that might be candidates for deceptive practice it will be helpful to scan briefly an array of markets. Consider this array as a spectrum starting with perfect competition at one end, shading by degrees into bilateral monopoly at the other. Save for bilateral monopoly (or bilateral oligopoly), microeconomists view all these markets, even those served by a monopolist, or defined as monopsony, as impersonal. That is, the seller (or in the case of monopsony, the buyer) calculates that at a given price, the market — rather than a buyer — will purchase (or provide) a determinable quantity of his product. This calculation may be very complex indeed since, except for conditions of perfect competition on the one hand or pure monopoly on the other, it must take into account the manner in which other suppliers will respond to the seller's actions. Nevertheless it is a *market* that the seller views; and the concept of markets, in this sense, excludes negotiation. A market, in this sense, is a public, impersonal collection of individual buyers that *in the aggregate*, given a certain price, over a certain period of time will buy a certain quantity of the offered product.

Now, for the most part, this is not the way the commercial world works. What we actually find are nominated buyers dealing with nominated sellers over prices that are not fixed, but negotiable. It is these negotiations and negotiators with which we are finally concerned. But even if these transactions all share in elements of a bilateral market, they do so in different degrees. To make this point clearer, we now eliminate from the spectrum all those (conceptual or real) situations which are truly impersonal, leaving for examination those in which an actual buyer confronts an actual seller. This truncated spectrum remains, as before, fixed at one end described by bilateral monopoly. But the opposite end, the new starting point, no longer is the impersonal, general construct known as perfect competition. Instead, it is that market comprised of real individuals which retains more elements of generality than any other. I will define one such polar example as being made up of a large, but countable and namable, set of suppliers providing a similar set of users with more or less fungible material.

This market with large numbers of suppliers and users, although it cannot be described as (economically) perfect, does have — imperfectly — some of the characteristics of perfect competition. Information is widespread and mostly, but not entirely, complete and accurate. Traders can never be sure that they possess all pertinent facts, nor can they be sure that what they do know is wholly correct. Nevertheless, since there are many buyers and sellers there are many trades, and approximate market levels are commonly known. Under these conditions there is not much negotiating room and outright deception is not only difficult but probably counterproductive. Yet since the market is not general, trading skills must be employed in order to conclude transactions. The negotiators exploit the incompleteness and uncertainty of information. Accompanying their price designations, they marshall and present facts. They are engaged in a process of persuasion in which each tries to make his case compelling to the other. Pertinent data usually includes recent trades — not necessarily known to both; the level of present and projected supply; an assessment of present and projected demand; general economic considerations. Each uses those pieces of information which advances his argument and ignores those which do not. If the buyer is aware of a recent trade close to the price he is bidding, he will certainly inform the seller. If he also knows of a trade significantly higher, he will,

of course, not convey this information. Now a command of the facts and their shrewd selection are not the only skills traders use. There also, for example, can be open or implied threats of loss of continuity or custom; but in active, publicized markets these tactics can be employed only occasionally: otherwise they lose force. The traders are concerned to maintain credibility and this concern constrains their actions.

But if we now skip over all the intervening shades of the market spectrum and examine purely bilateral markets, we find a very different set of considerations. By definition these markets have just a few participants, perhaps only two. There are not very many transactions; thus common information is limited or non-existent. And the traders have no escape. They must deal with each other for they have nowhere else to go. In fact, either might try to deceive the other with respect to his own abilities to deal elsewhere. Negotiating room is probably very extensive since it is determined only by the price limits below which it is not rational for the supplier to sell and above which for the user to buy. Since this information only can be surmised of his opposite by each trader, considerations of credibility become much less of a constraint.

In what follows, it is important to keep in mind that what I am attempting to analyze are those transactions that occur in markets that lie on the bilateral, or less general, side of our truncated spectrum. They need not, of course, conform to the limiting case I have just described. How important they are as compared to more general markets is a separate question.

III

We have already excluded from our analysis take-it-or-leave-it offers; and, even limiting our inquiry to less general markets, there seems to be no reason to relax this exclusion. But there may be circumstances which fall between take-it-or-leave-it and clear negotiation. We can try to exemplify this 'in-between' case: Buyer and seller meet to discuss a deal. There exists a reasonable range — perhaps sharply, but more likely fuzzily, defined — in which there is tacit agreement that a transaction will take place. Buyer makes the initial move. He offers the seller a price at or near the bottom of this range. Seller responds by naming a price closer to the top of the range. Buyer accepts. Now either this has been a 'ritual' negotiation performed out of custom, but with no real conviction, or the range has been so narrow that any further negotiation would have served no purpose, perhaps would not have been worth the time of the negotiators. My observation is that this is a situation more common to more general markets; but even in those less general it occurs often enough to be of more than trifling importance. In it the range, not the single-mindedness or skill of the negotiators, is the overriding consideration, and within it no concealment will occur — merely an offer, counter-offer, and acceptance. But we must take a closer look at this idea of a range.

We will think of it as that price differential in which a transaction can take place. The top of the range is not so high as to make it unacceptable to the buyer, nor is the bottom so low as to make it unacceptable to the seller. In fact we might say that the range is defined by these limits of acceptability. That there really must be limits on the lowest price at which the buyer can hope to buy and the highest price a seller can hope to sell becomes apparent when we consider them both as bidders in the immense economic auction. If the buyer will not pay that price which otherwise could conveniently be commanded by the seller, the seller is free to sell his wares elsewhere.[4] If the seller will not set his price at that level which the buyer could find elsewhere, the buyer is free to part with his dollars at another place.[5] So in the end, both buyer and seller are constrained to be reasonable and the deal will fall within a range somehow defined.

It will be helpful at this point to return to our consideration of the respective viewpoints of the buyer and the seller. These clearly are shaped by participation of buyer and seller in the market scheme. (And they hold true regardless of where the actors fall on the market spectrum.) Now any (free) market scheme needs to be fueled by incentives. These incentives, I believe, are resolvable into eight

categories, not all confined to free market economics. They are:

(1) the material rewards stemming from doing the job well one is paid to do;

(2) the avoidance of loss of material well-being stemming from doing the job poorly one is paid to do. The consequence of poor performance might even be discharge;

(3) the material rewards stemming from contributing to, and association with, a successful enterprise;

(4) the avoidance of loss of material well-being which comes from being associated with an unsuccessful enterprise;

(5) the psychic satisfaction of contributing to the success of a team (the firm) and reaping the recognition therefrom;

(6) the avoidance of pain of an awareness of having let the team down by performing poorly;

(7) the satisfaction, similar to that experienced by a craftsman, of a job well-done; and

(8) the avoidance of discomfort common to those who do a job badly or sloppily.

Although incentives (5) through (8) could apply to non-market economies, they definitely do apply to market economies; and all eight powerfully influence both buyer and seller to do their jobs well — to buy low and sell high. It is true, of course, that after a point buying low and selling high are not the only factors which contribute to the success of a firm. Volume is an important factor and so is monopoly power. It is interesting to note, however, that rationality — the necessity that under competition the participants act so as to maximize profits — demands that given a determined quantity, the parties buy as cheaply as possible and sell as dearly as possible.

There are other influences on the negotiators which act in the opposite manner to those which I enumerated. For example, the bonds of friendship between two negotiators. Or simply feelings of beneficience between two fellow humans. Or, not impossibly feelings of pity toward the weaker (for whatever reason) from the stronger. But to the degree that the negotiators allow these other influences to affect their performance in negotiation they are failing in that capacity. Moreover, if all other negotiators in the economic scheme do their jobs as best they can, those who do not are doomed to certain failure. Further, if they negotiate at less than their best, the negotiators are failing their fellow firm members who, whether they realize it consciously or not, depend upon them to do that best job. So, we may take it that the negotiators, because it is the essence of their responsibilities and because they benefit from doing so both materially and psychically, will do their best, in the one case to sell as dearly as possible, and in the other to buy as cheaply. In commercial negotiation there is no mutual search for value. No one discussed marginal costs and optimum quantities. It should be understood that we are not examining negotiation from the standpoint of ascertaining whether an efficient transaction takes place, nor are we concerned with the contract curve. What I am concerned with is *what takes place between the negotiators, not what results from the transaction.*

If we accept this outline of the motivation and purpose of the negotiators, recall that in the markets we are examining credibility is not easily ascertainable, and now turn again to a consideration of the range in which the negotiation will take place, we find that its limits must be implicit rather than explicit. There are two arguments:

(1) Suppose that the necessary information was supplied by each negotiator to his opposite and thus the limits were made explicit. The buyer would then know — and the seller would know that he knew — the lowest selling price acceptable to the seller; and this would be the best possible price from the standpoint of the buyer, his lowest possible cost. Similarly the seller would know — and the buyer would know that he knew — the highest purchasing cost acceptable to the buyer; and this would be the best possible price from the standpoint of the seller.

Under these conditions the buyer and seller, each (by hypothesis) of equal bargaining 'power' and so neither constrained to cede an advantage to the other, would split the difference. Perhaps an economically efficient purchase, expeditiously concluded, would result. But, *given the aims of the negotia-*

tors, each would have lost. For once either budged from the (opposite) limits of the range he would no longer have the best deal, but only an acceptable deal. His job as a negotiator, however, is precisely to get the best deal, not less.

(2) Even if one of the parties gave accurate information to the other, he could never be sure he was getting accurate information in return. His personal predilection for trusting or not trusting would be of no account. His responsibility remains to look out for his firm's interests and he must assume the same of his trading partner. I do not believe this to be a circular argument — one that states that because the parties engage in deception, commercial negotiation must be deceptive. My claim is different. It is that, given the duties and aims of the negotiators and the difficulty of verifiability, it would be illogical of one to *assume* the veracity of the other and so illogical of himself to be truthful. But in any case the first argument seems to be sufficient.

Now since negotiators work within a range, set out to conclude, and do successfully conclude negotiations, it must be that the range has described an implicit, rather than explicit, set of boundaries. We now qualify our provisional definition of commercial negotiation to be more precisely a definition of *commercial negotiation in less general markets* and to read as *that interchange between buyer and seller in which they attempt to reach price agreement within implicit boundaries on the grounds of their common desire to consummate a deal and in the face of their diametrically opposed price goals.* The adding of the words 'within implicit boundaries' (or similar phraseology) brings the definition into the realm of common experience; but this addition also carries with it its own implication with respect to my original question of whether commercial negotiation necessarily entails deception.

A summary will help. I have eliminated nonnegotiable situations from consideration. These could either be fixed-price arrangements, or they could stem from one party simply announcing that he will not negotiate — by virtue of size conferring power, for example. I have also eliminated offer-counter offer-acceptance deals which can be thought of as a kind of ritual negotiation. Thus we are left with what we might call 'true negotiation' in which the interests of the parties are in opposition, and in which both intend to make the deal at the best possible level — different, of course, for each. Further, we have determined that the parties are negotiating within a range that is tacitly assumed by both and that it is wide enough to allow meaningful negotiation. Bids and offers outside this range would be considered to be frivolous, not to be taken seriously. The buyer takes pretty much for granted that:

(a) the seller's opening offer defines the top of the range, that

(b) this is the seller's idea of the highest cost which would be acceptable to the buyer though not best for the buyer, but

(c) best for the seller.

Analogously the seller takes pretty much for granted that:

(a) the buyer's opening bid defines the bottom of the range, which

(b) is the buyer's idea of the lowest price which would be acceptable to the seller though not best for the seller, but

(c) best for the buyer.

Now if this description of the negotiating stage is accurate, it is hard to see how there could be any negotiation. Each party would feel that his opening bid (offer) was acceptable to the other. And each party has entered the negotiation with the intention of making the best deal and knows that the best deal for him is an acceptable deal for the other. That is, the other will accept the deal if he can not improve on it. Thus if we rule out coercion or bribery we are left with a set of constraints which prevent any movement at all. For once either party moves from his original position he has lost: he can no longer get the best deal. What he has done is redefine the range to the benefit of his adversary.

The fact that the range limits are implicit rather than explicit informs us at once — as a tautology — that concealment and negotiation are inseparable. It makes sense, for example, for the buyer to tell the seller that although he would like to conclude the deal at P which is the lowest cost that he can

reasonably hope to attain, he will pay as much as $P + 3$, which though not best is still acceptable. In that case he surely will pay $P + 3$ and will have failed as a negotiator. He will have failed, for by concealing his top price he might have avoided paying it. And that is an integral part of his job. However, it does not necessarily follow that because concealment is inseparable from negotiation, deception also is.

Once again, a summary will help. Although concealment is inseparable from negotiation, concealment does not assure negotiation. In fact, given even implicit acceptance of the upper and lower limits of the negotiating range by the participants, it remains impossible to understand how any negotiating can proceed. The participants will merely sit on their initial offers each waiting for the other to move off his. But deception offers a way out of this dilemma. Suppose the buyer to have opened the proceedings by making a bid (which turns out to be not lower than the seller's minimum acceptable price). He is then making explicit his idea of the lowest reasonable price, the lowest price at which he thinks the seller will do business.[6] The seller, in effect, either must accept the bid (and fail in his job), or must reply by doing his best to mislead the buyer by making him believe that the price is *not* acceptable, that it is below the bottom of the range; that the seller, if the buyer will not improve his bid, can and will offer and sell his wares elsewhere at a higher level. But this is not the truth; it is deception. What the seller has to do is to mislead the buyer into believing that the lowest selling price is higher than it really is. Even if the buyer's initial bid was, due to misreckoning, *higher* than the seller's minimum acceptable price, the seller's responsibility nevertheless remains the same — to get the highest possible price, to reach, if possible, the top of the range. Thus his reply — deception — also remains the same. Similar remarks, of course, obtain for the buyer. Note also that simple silence as a response to a bid (concealment) will not accomplish the purpose. If the seller only rejects the buyer's offer, and at the same time does not convey to the buyer the idea that this rejection was made because his offer was out of the acceptance range, he has simply retreated to a position of non-negotiation, of take-it-or-leave-it. And we have excluded this case. But if he conveys to the buyer the idea that silence is his response because the buyer's offer was unreasonable, he has conveyed something that is untrue — he has made use of deception. In the end what the negotiators finally do is to narrow the range down to that point where negotiation becomes trivial, where one or both can concede without losing anything important. This narrowing process is accomplished by deception. It is a peculiar kind of deception in which both parties are aware that each is trying to deceive the other; and of course it makes a sad mockery of protestations of trust and fidelity. It seems also that the two deceptions do not cancel each other in some sort of cheerful acceptance of the rules of the game. Instead they sum. For if I, the buyer, intending to deceive you, the seller, think that you are aware of my intent, then I must be that much more subtle, disguising my intentions that much more carefully. And I must reason that you too are following the same logic; and so I must be that much more aware of what subtleties *you* might be employing. In the end, perhaps, our *skills* cancel each other; but our mutual *intent* has never wavered — to gain an advantage over the other by means of deception.[7]

IV

We now take a closer look at the limiting case of bilateral monopoly in order to ascertain how well it fits (or contradicts) our examination just concluded of negotiation in less general markets.

Bilateral monopoly, in which a single seller (monopolist) faces a single buyer (monopsonist) is indeterminate. Quantity will not set price; price will not set quantity. The economist assumes:

(1) The buyer knows the monopolist's costs and so also knows his marginal cost curve, and

(2) The seller knows the monopsonist's demand curve — that unit cost, which for any given quantity of input purchased, will not exceed the market value of that input's last (marginal) product.

These two curves define a range since, for any given quantity, a price out of it would be irrational for either the buyer or seller. If the price were lower than the monopolist's rising (or horizontal) marginal cost curve, it would be irrational for him to make as much as (or any of) the requested quantity. If it were higher than the monopsonist's (downward sloping) demand curve, it would not be rational for him to buy as much. The difficulty is that for any given quantity, the boundary marking rationality (not necessarily profit maximization) is different for each. Given this conclusion, the economist throws up his hands, so to speak, and declares that to find a mutual price and quantity will require bargaining "and the better bargainer will obtain the more favorable terms"[8] or "bargaining power and negotiating skill and public opinion are among the factors determining the final outcome".[9]

There are a number of similarities to our prior conclusions in this analysis. Not only is there a range, its upper and lower boundaries are both known to both parties. (This knowledge of the other's limits also allows each to establish his own profit maximizing point which is any firm's goal.[10]) There is a difference since the range is defined explicitly rather than implicitly. But there remains the identical difficulty in understanding how any trade could be concluded. And deception still provides the same possible solution. Let the seller misrepresent his costs and the buyer the worth to himself of the seller's product, and negotiation has commenced. The very act of misrepresenting would be a negotiating step.

Now in less general markets, insofar as they are dealing with each other, almost any buyer and seller in negotiation will be acting in part as bilateral monopolists. Each is a single actor dealing with another single actor. And there is no escape into a more general market once they have begun negotiation. For their, and our, assumption is that they have decided (possibly incorrectly) that it is not worthwhile to seek a trading partner elsewhere, that the (implicit) range is reasonable, and so trading skills must determine the outcome.

Thus, both in theory and by observation, we have seen markets that demand or admit true negotiation. And if theory does not altogether fit, neither does it contradict observation. In brief, when we cannot have recourse to general markets, when there is no appeal from two traders with proper names dealing with each other, there is also no solution but bargaining.

V

We have seen that more general markets tend to preclude deception; but firms continually seek less general markets which tend to demand it. To see why, consider that the profit motive is the engine of economic competition. If profits were not the hoped-for reward of business activity, other incentives would have to supply the motives to produce, to distribute, or to provide other services. Now in perfect competition, which is the most general of markets and in which negotiation is meaningless and unknown, there are no economic profits. Therefore a firm will flee those situations that approach the conditions of perfect competition if it can find other markets that will afford it greater returns on its investment. In fact, it will strive for monopoly, that best of economic schemes for the firm and the worst for society. And even within monopoly, if it can do so, the firm will engage in price discrimination. That is, it will fragment its market in order to maximize its profit.

Most firms cannot attain monopoly. But many can differentiate their products to some degree and so dissociate themselves from the profit-stifling conditions of perfect competition — and if they can, they must. By doing so they not only reduce each single market they serve, but also tend to increase the variety of inputs they require. It is clear that the quest for profits is the irresistible force which draws firms to the less general side of the market spectrum.

These are grave matters. For they indicate that the world in which we get and spend is partially, but ineluctably, built on a structure of lies. And if we do agree that at least it is not *prima facie* implausible that our commercial world is in part so structured, it will do no good, I believe to hunt for excuses or justifications. Even if my trading partner may be clearly lying and so in sheer self-defense I must lie too, my lie remains a lie. Although by lying to me he has diminished me as a human being by making me mere means to his ends; in treating him in the same way I have diminished him also. And worse, I have diminished myself. For by the very act of treating him as less than human, I have become less human.[11] Given the logic of commercial negotiation, perhaps this is an inevitable consequence. But given its human implications it is also one of great horror. It does not seem altogether bearable, that for the sake of solving the vast problems of allocation and distribution in a manner at least free of central command, men must have recourse to a self-imposed moral catastrophe.

ENDNOTES

1. There seems to be widespread acceptance of the fact that negotiation and deception go hand-in-hand. See for example Thomas L. Carson, Richard E. Wokutch, and Kent F. Murrmann, 'Bluffing in Labor Negotiations: Legal and Ethical Issues', in this book; A.Z. Carr, 'Is Business Bluffing Ethical?', *Harvard Business Review* 46 (1968), 143–153; W.M. Bulkeley, 'To Some at Harvard, Telling Lies Becomes a Matter of Course', *The Wall Street Journal*, 15 Jan. 1979, pp. 1, 37; Sissela Bok, *Lying: Moral Choice in Public and Private Life* (Pantheon Books, New York, 1978). But it is interesting how little attention Bok pays to commerce in her book.

2. Carson *et al.*, *Bluffing in Labor Negotiations: Legal and Ethical Issues*.

3. Though we arrived at our ideas independently, they are in very close agreement. This is not surprising for upon reflection they seem almost self-evident.

4. Even if his market is monopsonistic he eventually can

shift his resources into serving others which are more remunerative.

5. Excluding, monopoly, of course. But even the monopolist must keep his customers in business. If he sets his prices too high he will drive them into other ventures.

6. This explicit offer does not violate the conditions of implicit boundaries. Any offer must be explicit. But the buyer and seller still have not conveyed to their opposites what the limits of the range really are. The buyer's offer is an attempt to define what only the seller has the right to define — the bottom of the range.

7. Those, like Carr, who justify commercial deception by analogies with games like poker — because both in commerce and poker everyone knows the rules —

forget that in poker no one *claims* honesty, trustworthiness, and the rights of friendship. This is a vital difference.

8. See Richard A. Bilas, *Microeconomics: Theory*, 2nd ed. (McGraw-Hill, New York, 1971), p. 301.

9. See Edwin Mansfield, *Microeconomics: Theory and applications*, (Norton, New York, 1970), p. 272. 'Public opinion' refers to labor negotiation.

10. For accessible accounts of bilateral monopoly see Bilas, *op. cit.*, p. 301, and Mansfield, *op. cit.*, p. 272.

11. There is, of course, nothing original in this notion. And it is not confined to philosophers or theologians. For example, see Gene Levine, 'Authenticity', *Bobbin*, Oct. 1982. *Bobbin* is a trade magazine serving the apparel industry.

SUGGESTED FURTHER READINGS

BEACH, JOHN. "Bluffing: Its Demise as a Subject unto Itself." *Journal of Business Ethics*, Volume 4, No. 3 (June 1985), pp. 191–196.

BLODGETT, TIMOTHY B. "Showdown on 'Business Bluffing.'" *Harvard Business Review* (May–June, 1968), pp. 162–170.

BOK, SISSELA. *Lying: Moral Choice in Public and Private Life*. New York: Pantheon Books, 1978.

BOWIE, NORMAN E. "Should Collective Bargaining and Labor Relations Be Less Adversarial?" *Journal of Business Ethics*, Vol. 4, No. 4 (August 1985) pp. 283–293.

BROWN, L. "Ethics in Negotiation." *Female Executive*, Vol. 7 (January/February 1984), pp. 34–37.

BULKELEY, W.M. "To Some at Harvard, Telling Lies Becomes a Matter of Course." *Wall Street Journal*, January 15, 1979, p. 1, 37.

CARR, A.Z. "Is Business Bluffing Ethical?" *Harvard Business Review*. 46 (Jan.–Feb. 1968), pp. 143–153.

CHISHOLM, R. and FEEHAN, T. "The Intent to Deceive." *Journal of Philosophy*, 74, 1977, pp. 143–159.

ISENBERG, A. "Conditions for Lying." in T. Beauchamp and N. Bowie (eds.). *Ethical Theory and Business*. Englewood Cliffs, N.J.: Prentice-Hall, 1979, pp. 466–468.

KANT, I.: (1775–1780), *Lectures on Ethics*. (Louis Infield, trans.) New York: Harper and Row, 1963.

KANT, I.: (1797), "On a Supposed Right to Tell Lies from Benevolent Motives," in B. Brody (ed.), *Moral Rules and Particular Circumstances*. Englewood Cliffs, N.J.: Prentice-Hall, 1970, pp. 31–36.

ROSS, D *The Right and the Good*. Oxford: Oxford University Press, 1930.

SIEGLER, F. "Lying." *American Philosophical Quarterly*, 3, 1966, pp. 128–136.

49

Honesty and Deception in Business: Fudging the Travel Claim

DEBORAH C. POFF

Donna Potts and Janice Pearson frequently travel for their company but they have different ideas about what constitutes legitimate use of travel expense funds. Both women belong to a frequent flyer plan and use the points they accumulate on business trips to subsidize vacations and pleasure trips. Neither one has ever informed the company of this but since the company seems to have no policy about travel points, they both think it is perfectly acceptable.

Donna and Janice are both on the same *per diem* rate when they travel. However, they have very different attitudes about how such monies can honestly be expended. Donna often slightly underspends her travel allowance and returns the balance. Janice always spends very little and keeps it all. Donna will treat herself to an expensive meal which is over her daily limit but will make up the difference by spending less on subsequent days. Janice always eats in inexpensive restaurants and sees business trips as a way of supplementing her income. Recently, both women were required to make a three-week overseas

trip together. They had a number of disagreements because of their different perceptions of what was morally right or wrong. Both had money left over after the trip. Donna wanted to return her money. Janice said that would mean she would have to return her money as well. They had also fought over where to eat and how to travel. Donna accused Janice of being cheap. Janice accused Donna of being wasteful. Here is a synopsis of each account of what went on.

Donna

I think that Janice's behaviour is unacceptable. My general practice is to stay within the company guidelines. These guidelines are more than adequate if one is being reasonable. In fact, if I am cautious, I can even splurge — have a nice meal in an expensive restaurant after I have closed a deal or had a productive day. That seems perfectly legitimate to me. However, the company is giving me expenses when I travel, not a bonus to my salary. If the trip only costs me $1000 and the company allots $1500 for that amount of time, I feel morally obliged to return the difference. Nobody checks that closely. We're on a flat daily rate but I think it's cheating. In fact, I'd put it more strongly. It's definitely stealing.

Janice

Donna is a hypocrite. She's happy to take the free trips from the frequent flyer plan through company dollars but not keep the *per diem* set aside for company travel. She will rent a car instead of taking public transportation but then criticize me for keeping the difference in cost between the two. If I'm smart I can usually pocket $100 per day on trips and I don't suffer while I'm away. If Donna really cares that much about the company, why isn't she more frugal? Then she could return even more after a trip. When I travel I make money for the company. I see nothing wrong with making a little more for myself while I'm at it. Besides, I'm sure the company knows that many people do what I do. It's both expected and accepted. People like Donna just make it hard on the rest of us.

SUGGESTED FURTHER READINGS

BEACH, JOHN. "Bluffing: Its Demise as a Subject unto Itself." *Journal of Business Ethics*, Vol. 4, No. 3, (June 1985), pp. 191–196.

BLODGETT, TIMOTHY B. "Showdown on 'Business Bluffing.'" *Harvard Business Review*, (May-June, 1968), pp. 162–170.

BOK, SISSELA. *Lying: Moral Choice in Public and Private Life*. New York: Pantheon Books, 1978.

BOWIE, NORMAN E. "Should Collective Bargaining and Labor Relations Be Less Adversarial?" *Journal of Business Ethics*, Vol. 4, No. 4 (August 1985), pp. 283–293.

BROWN, L. "Ethics in Negotiation." *Female Executive*, Vol. 7 (January/February 1984), pp. 34–37.

BULKELEY, W.M. "To Some at Harvard, Telling Lies Becomes a Matter of Course." *Wall Street Journal*, January 15, 1979, p. 1, 37.

CARR, A.Z. "Is Business Bluffing Ethical?" *Harvard Business Review*, 46 (Jan.-Feb. 1968), pp. 143–153.

CHISHOLM, R. and T. FEEHAN. "The Intent to Deceive." *Journal of Philosophy* **74**, 1977, p. 143–159.

DONALDSON, T. and P. WERHANE. *Ethical Issues in Business: A Philosophical Approach*. 2nd ed. Englewood Cliffs, NJ: Prentice-Hall, 1983.

ISENBERG, A. "Conditions for Lying." In T. Beauchamp and N. Bowie (eds.) *Ethical Theory and Business*. Englewood Cliffs, NJ: Prentice-Hall, 1979, pp. 466–468.

KANT, I.: (1775–1780), *Lectures on Ethics*. (Louis Infield, trans.) New York: Harper and Row, 1963.

KANT, I.: (1797), "On a Supposed Right to Tell Lies from Benevolent Motives." In B. Brody (ed.) *Moral Rules and Particular Circumstances*. Englewood Cliffs, NJ: Prentice-Hall, 1970, pp. 31–36.

LUTHANS, FRED, RICH HODGETTS and H. THOMPSON. *Social Issues in Business*. New York: MacMillan, 1987.

RICKLEFS, R. "Honesty and Ethical Standards." *The Wall Street Journal*, Oct. 2, 1983.

ROSS, D. *The Right and the Good*. Oxford: Oxford University Press, 1930.

SIEGLER, F. "Lying." *American Philosophical Quarterly*, 3, 1966, p. 128–136.

CONTRIBUTORS

ROSALIE ABELLA is Chair of the Ontario Labor Relations Board and a Judge in the Ontario Family Court. From 1975–80 she served on the Ontario Human Rights Commission. Justice Abella has received many honors for her work including honorary doctorates from Dalhousie University and Mount Saint Vincent University. She is the author of *Access to Legal Services By the Disabled*, *Equality in Employment* and numerous articles in legal journals. Justice Abella is also co-editor of *Family Law: Dimensions of Justice*.

ROBERT L. ARRINGTON is the Associate Dean, College of Arts and Sciences, and Professor of Philosophy, Georgia State University. He was American Council of Learned Societies Fellow 1974–75. He is the author of *Rationalism, Realism, and Relativism: Perspectives in Contemporary Epistemology* as well as numerous articles on the philosophy of Wittgenstein, environmental ethics, criminal responsibility, and other topics in applied ethics.

RUSSELL P. BOISJOLY is the Associate Dean of the School of Business at Fairfield University. His research focuses on applications of finance to regulated firms – especially in trucking and electric utility industries. Dr. Boisjoly has published a number of articles on capital structure, mergers, bankruptcy prediction, and ethics.

KENNETH M. BOND is a Professor of Business Administration at Humbolt State University. His interests are in business ethics and corporate social responsibility. His book *Bibliography of Business Ethics and Business Moral Values* is presently in its 4th edition. He also has published in the areas of white collar crime, international bribery, and the measurement of moral values in organization.

CONRAD G. BRUNK is an Associate Professor of Philosophy at Conrad Grebel College, University of Waterloo. He has contributed articles to *Philosophical Issues in the Nuclear Arms Race*, *Ethical Issues in Social Work*, *Dialogue* and the *Law and Society Review* on topics in moral, political and legal philosophy.

ADRIAN CADBURY

ARCHIE B. CARROLL is a Professor of Management and holder of the Robert W. Scherer Chair of Corporate Public Affairs and Management at the Univer-

524

sity of Georgia. Dr. Carroll has published nine books and over sixty articles. His latest book is *Business and Society: Ethics and Stakeholder Management*. His articles have appeared in such publications as the *Academy of Management Journal, Sloan Management Review, Academy of Management Review, California Management Review*, the *Journal of Business Strategy, Public Affairs Review* and *Business Horizons*. He is also a contributor to the *Handbook for Professional Managers* and the *Strategic Planning and Management Handbook*.

THOMAS L. CARSON is an Associate Professor of Philosophy at Loyola University. He was awarded the NEH Fellowship 1980–81. He is the author of *The Status of Morality* and numerous papers and reviews in ethical theory and applied ethics.

ELLEN FOSTER CURTIS is an Associate Professor of Management at the University of Lowell where she specializes in business policy, corporate social responsibility, and transportation. Her research focuses on labor relations, impacts of transportation, deregulation, and ethical issues in business. She has published a number of articles on topics such as labor relations in the transportation industries and ethics.

FRANCES H. EARLY is an Associate Professor of History and Women's Studies at Mount Saint Vincent University. Dr. Early has published articles in many journals such as *Labour/Le Travailleur, Histoire sociale/Social History, Journal of Family History, Urban History Review, Contemporary Sociology*, and *Canadian Review of American Studies*.

FREDERICK A. ELLISTON was a Professor with the College of Education at the University of Hawaii before his untimely death. He published numerous articles and was editor and co-editor of several texts in ethics and applied ethics including two recent works on "whistleblowing."

PETER A. FRENCH is Lennox Distinguished Professor of the Humanities and Professor of Philosophy at Trinity University, Texas. He is the author of fourteen books including *The Spectrum of Responsibility, Collective and Corporate Responsibility, The Scope of Morality*, and *Corrigible Corporations and Unruly Laws* (with Brent Fisse). He has published numerous articles in the professional journals and is the senior editor of the *Midwest Studies in Philosophy* and the editor of the *Journal of Social Philosophy*.

MILTON FRIEDMAN is an influential economist at the University of Chicago. His many publications include *Capitalism and Freedom*.

JAMES C. GAA is an Associate Professor of Accounting and an associate member of the Philosophy Department at McMaster University. In addition to work in philosophy of science and ethics, he has published a number of articles and a book on ethical and public policy issues in accounting and auditing.

ALAN GEWIRTH is E.C. Waller Distinguished Service Professor of Philosophy at the University of Chicago. His publications include: *Reason and Morality, Human Rights: Essays on Justification and Applications,* and *Marsilino of Padua and Medieval Political Philosophy.*

HARRY J. GLASBEEK is Professor of Law, Osgoode Hall Law School, York University. He is the author of numerous articles on such topics as labor law, compulsory arbitration, industrial relations, corporate crime, and the law of evidence.

MARY E. HAWKESWORTH is an Associate Professor in the Department of Political Science at the University of Louisville. Dr. Hawkesworth's articles have appeared in *Social Theory and Practice, Politics and Policy,* the *Journal of Applied Philosophy, Kentucky Government and Politics,* and the *International Journal of Women's Studies.*

GARY E. JONES is an Associate Professor of Philosophy at the University of San Diego. Dr. Jones has published in numerous journals, including articles in *Studies in History and Philosophy of Science,* the *Journal of Medicine and Philosophy,* the *Journal of Business Ethics, Philosophy of Science,* the *Canadian Journal of Philosophy,* and *Philosophical Quarterly.*

HENRY W. LANE is Donald F. Hunter Professor in International Business, School of Business Administration, University of Western Ontario. He has conducted international research both in Africa and South America. Dr. Lane has published in numerous journals and anthologies. He is also the co-author of three texts: *International Management Behavior: From Policy to Practice,* (with Joseph J. DiStefano); *Effective Managerial Action: A Casebook in Organizational Behaviour,* (with James C. Rush, Joseph J. DiStefano, and Jeffrey Gandz); *Managing Large Research and Development Programs,* (with R. Beddows and Paul R. Lawrence).

THE LAW REFORM COMMISSION OF CANADA was formed in 1971 by an Act of Parliament to study issues, hold public hearings, and make recommendations directly to Parliament on issues in criminal law, administration law, and "protection of life" legislation. Commission consists of lawyers, jurists, philosophers, teachers of law, and other specialist professionals.

HUGH LEHMAN is a Professor in the Department of Philosphy at the University of Guelph. He is co-editor of the *Journal of Agricultural Ethics.* His articles on topics in philosophy of mathematics, philosophy of science, philosophy of education, and ethics have been published in many philosophy and scientific journals.

PETER MADSEN is Executive Director and Senior Lecturer at the Center for the Advancement of Applied Ethics at Carnegie Mellon University. His work includes training in ethics with private, public, and nonprofit organizations.

RITA C. MANNING is an Associate Professor at San Jose State University. She is the Executive Secretary for the Pacific Division of the Society for Women in Philosophy. Dr. Manning has published in a number of journals including *Southern Journal of Philosophy*, *Informal Logic*, *Environmental Ethics*, *Social Theory and Practice*, and the *Journal of Business Ethics*.

EUGENE MELLICAN is Chairperson of the Philosophy Department at the University of Lowell. He describes himself as "a student of philosophy concentrating on issues in applied ethics."

ALEX C. MICHALOS is a Professor of Philosophy at the University of Guelph. He is the author of ten books and over thirty articles. His five-volume *North American Social Report* received the Secretary of State's Award for Excellence in Interdisciplinary Research in the field of Canadian Studies in 1984. He is the Founder and Editor-in-Chief of the *Journal of Business Ethics*, and also Founder and Editor-in-Chief of *Social Indicators Research*.

JAMES H. MICHELMAN is President of the Mainzer Minton Co. Inc. He has published articles in the *Journal of Business Ethics*.

REESE P. MILLER is Associate Professor of Philosophy at Huron College, University of Western Ontario, where he teaches business ethics. His most recent publication of note is an annotated translation into English of Descartes' *Principles of Philosophy*.

THOMAS M. MULLIGAN is an Assistant Professor of Management in the Faculty of Business, Brock University. His publications include "The Two Cultures in Business Education" in *Academy of Management Review* and "Justifying Moral Initiative by Businesses" in the *Journal of Business Ethics*.

KENT F. MURRMANN is an Associate Professor in the Department of Management at Virginia Polytechnic Institute and State University. Dr. Murrmann is a member of The Academy of Management and The Industrial Relations Research Association. He has published numerous articles on labor relations and employment law.

JAN NARVESON is a Professor of Philosophy at the University of Waterloo. Dr. Narveson has published numerous articles on topics in moral and political philosophy in a wide variety of journals. He is also the author of *Morality and Utility* and the editor of *Moral Issues*. His most recent book, *The Libertarian Idea*, supports free market business practices.

MICHAEL PHILIPS is a Professor of Philosophy at Portland State University and a Visiting Professor of Philosophy at the University of British Columbia. Dr. Philips has published over twenty papers on a wide range of topics in philosophy. He has recently completed a book on moral theory.

DEBORAH C. POFF (*co-editor*) is an Associate Professor and the Executive

Director of the Institute for the Study of Women, Mount Saint Vincent University. Dr. Poff has published in a number of anthologies and journals including *Feminist Ethics, Resources of Feminist Research* and *Social Indicators Research.* She is the editor of the *Journal of Business Ethics* and a co-editor of *Atlantis: A Women's Studies Journal.*

HARRIET G. ROSENBERG is an Associate Professor in the Social Science Division and Director of the Health and Society Program at York University. She has done field work in North America, France and Botswana and is the author of *A Negotiated World: Three Centuries of Change in a French Alpine Village* and co-author of *Through the Kitchen Window: The Politics of Home and Family* and *Surviving in the City: Urbanization in the Third World.*

BETH SAVAN teaches environmental ethics at the University of Toronto. She is the author of *Science Under Siege* which examines the role of vested interests in scientific research in administration. She has written and spoken extensively on that subject. Dr. Savan's current areas of research include: environmental assessment, urban planning, and environmental education.

TED SCHRECKER lectures in the Department of Political Science at the University of Western Ontario, where he is completing a doctoral dissertation on Canadian criminal justice policy. Previously, he taught in the Environmental and Resource Studies Program at Trent University, and served as consultant to a variety of government agencies and non-governmental organizations.

DONALD G. SIMPSON is Vice-President and Director at The Banff Centre for Management. Since 1982, Dr. Simpson has been the President of Kanchun International. He has been founder and/or director of a number of non-profit international aid organizations. Dr. Simpson is a teacher, researcher and entrepreneur. He has worked as a private consultant to Canadian and foreign governments, the World Bank, UN agencies, and numerous other agencies and organizations.

ANASTASIA M. SHKILNYK is currently an associate with the Secretary of State of the Government of Canada. She is the author of a four-hour CBC Radio documentary entitled "Grassy Narrows – Under Attack" which was broadcast on *Ideas* in February, 1983. She is also a recent recipient of the John Harris Award for Community Service, Rotary Clubs International.

BILL SHAW is a Professor of Business Law, Graduate School of Business, The University of Texas. He is currently the President of the American Business Law Association. Dr. Shaw is the co-author of *Structure of the Legal Environment* (with Art Wolfe) and *Environmental Law: People, Pollution, and Land Use.* His recent publications include: "*Wards Cove* v. *Atonio,*" *The Labor Law Journal*; "Shareholder Authorized Inside Trading," the *Journal of Business Ethics*; "Fifth Amendment Failures and RICO Forfeitures," *American Business Law Journal*; and "Employment Appraisals," *Business Horizons.*

CHARLES H. SMITH is Peat Marwick Professor of Accounting and Chair of the Department of Accounting at the Pennsylvania State University. He has published a wide variety of articles on accounting and auditing issues, in both academic and professional journals.

HOWARD R. SMITH is a Professor of Management at the University of Georgia. Dr. Smith has published numerous monographs, articles, and books including *The Capitalistic Imperative, Democracy and Public Interest*, and *Government and Business*.

J.T. STEVENSON is Professor of Philosophy, University College, University of Toronto. His interests are in epistemology, metaphysics, Canadian intellectual history, and applied ethics. He has had many speaking and consulting engagements with professional associations in accounting, social work, and engineering. Among his publications is a book, *Engineering Ethics: Practices and Principles*.

LLOYD TATARYN is an investigative journalist who has been, among other things, a documentary producer with CBC's "As It Happens", a parliamentary assistant and a Director of the Program in Journalism for Native People at the University of Western Ontario. In addition to *Dying For a Living*, he has authored *Formaldehyde On Trial*, which examines the controversy surrounding urea formaldehyde foam insulation, and *The Pundits*, which dissects the work of leading political writers in Britain, the United States and Canada.

JOHN WAIDE is a family therapist at Oasis Center in Nashville, Tennessee. Dr. Waide holds a PhD in Philosophy from Vanderbilt University and a MSSW in Clinical Social Work from the University of Tennessee. He has published in a number of journals and anthologies including *Teaching Philosophy* and *Philosophy and Phenomenological Research*.

WILFRID J. WALUCHOW (*co-editor*) is an Assistant Professor of Philosophy at McMaster University. His articles have appeared in a number of journals including *Philosophical Quarterly, Oxford Journal of Legal Studies, Dialogue* and *Canadian Associations Canadiennes*. He is also a co-author of *Case Studies in Bioethics*.

GARY WARNER teaches Francophone African and Caribbean Literature at McMaster University. He has also lectured frequently to university, professional, and community groups on topics related to international development. Warner was Director of the CUSO program in Sierra Leone for two years and chaired the International Board of Directors of CUSO for three years. He was appointed Director of McMaster International in July 1988.

PATRICIA HOGUE WERHANE is the Henry J. Wirtenberger Professor of Business Ethics at Loyola University. She is the author or editor of seven books including *Ethical Issues in Business* (co-edited with Tom Donaldson), *Persons, Rights, and Corporations, Profits and Responsibility*, and *Philosophical Issues in*

Human Rights (edited with David Ozar and A.R. Gini). She is past president of the Society for Value Inquiry, founding member, past president, and Executive Director of the Society of Business Ethics, and Chairperson of the Ethics Advisory Council of Arther Anderson & Co. She serves on the editorial boards of the *Journal of Business Ethics*, the *Journal of Value-Based Management, Public Affairs Quarterly,* and *Employee Responsibilities and Rights Journal,* and is editor-in-chief of *Business Ethics Quarterly.* Her book, *Adam Smith and his Legacy for Modern Capitalism* is forthcoming with Oxford University Press.

RICHARD WOKUTCH is a Professor of Management, The R.B. Pamplin College of Business, Virginia Polytechnic Institute and State University. He was a Fulbright Research Scholar at the Science Center, Berlin, West Germany and a Fulbright Research Scholar at the Hiroshima Institute of Technology, Japan. Dr. Wokutch's publications include *Cooperation and Conflict in Occupational Safety and Health: A Multinational Study of the Automotive Industry* and articles in such journals as *Academy of Management Executive,* the *Journal of Business Ethics,* and *California Management Review.*